RESURGENT ANTISEMITISM

STUDIES IN ANTISEMITISM

Alvin H. Rosenfeld, *editor*

RESURGENT ANTISEMITISM

GLOBAL PERSPECTIVES

EDITED BY
Alvin H. Rosenfeld

INDIANA UNIVERSITY PRESS
Bloomington and Indianapolis

This book is a publication of

Indiana University Press
Office of Scholarly Publishing
Herman B Wells Library 350
1320 E. 10 10th St.
Bloomington, IN 47405

iupress.indiana.edu

Telephone orders   800-842-6796
Fax orders   812-855-7931

Library of Congress Cataloging-in-Publication Data

Resurgent antisemitism : global perspectives / edited by Alvin H. Rosenfeld.
     pages cm. — (Studies in antisemitism)
   "The scholarly papers collected in this book originated in the inaugural
conference of Indiana University's newly established Institute for the Study
of Contemporary Antisemitism held in Bloomington in April 2011"—
Introduction.
   Includes bibliographical references and index.
   ISBN 978-0-253-00878-7 (cl : alk. paper) — ISBN 978-0-253-00890-9 (eb)
1. Antisemitism—History—21st century—Congresses. I. Rosenfeld, Alvin
H. (Alvin Hirsch), 1938- editor of compilation. II. Rosenfeld, Alvin H.
(Alvin Hirsch), 1938- End of the Holocaust and the Beginnings of a New
Antisemitism.
   DS145.R47 2013
   305.892́4—dc23
                                                        2012050898

1 2 3 4 5 18 17 16 15 14 13

This book is dedicated to
  Louis and Sybil Mervis
  and to
  the memory of Sara I. and Albert G. Reuben
  with immense gratitude

Contents

Acknowledgments

I<small>N AN EXCEPTIONAL</small> display of collegiality, all of the authors who contributed to this book did so in a friendly and timely manner. I thank them, therefore, not only for their important critical insights into the challenging subject matter before us but for their cooperation with an editor who insisted on their producing scholarly work of the highest caliber and on meeting strict publication deadlines.

My editorial assistants, Defne Jones and M. Alison Hunt, proved to be invaluable in more ways than one in helping to prepare the manuscript for publication. I thank them for being such congenial and efficient co-workers.

The scholarly papers collected in this book originated in the inaugural conference of Indiana University's newly established Institute for the Study of Contemporary Antisemitism. This conference, which was held in Bloomington in April 2011, brought together some thirty-five scholars from a dozen different countries. Special thanks go to Sarah Wasserman, Melissa Deckard, and Janice Hurtuk for their steadfast assistance in helping to organize the conference.

I am also deeply grateful to various benefactors whose generosity, in addition to being of direct practical help, is the best vote of confidence in our work that I could possibly hope for. I am especially grateful to Jay and Marsha Glazer, who endowed the Irving M. Glazer Chair in Jewish Studies, which was a major source of financial support for the conference, as well as to Alice and Theodore Cohn, Michael and Sue-ann Finkelstein, Michael Leffell, and Jacob and Dafna Levanon.

Major gifts from Louis and Sybil Mervis and from Lawrence M. Reuben, in memory of his parents, Sara I. and Albert G. Reuben, not only enabled us to convene the April 2011 conference but have made possible the publication of this book. My deepest thanks go to these devoted and magnanimous friends.

A number of my colleagues in the Borns Jewish Studies Program at Indiana University chaired conference sessions and in other respects as well have shown interest in the work of the Institute for the Study of Contemporary Antisemitism. I thank them all and, in particular, wish to express appreciation to Jeffrey Veidlinger, the Director of the Borns Jewish Studies Program, for his support.

Few undertakings are more dispiriting for scholars than the study of antisemitism. For lightening the hearts and strengthening the resolve of conference participants, it is a pleasure to acknowledge the special contribution of Marija Krupoves-Berg, whose gift of Yiddish songs helped us through some difficult, but meaningful, days.

Finally, I am most grateful to President Michael McRobbie, former provost Karen Hanson, and dean of the College of Arts and Sciences Larry Singell for their support of the work of the Institute for the Study of Contemporary Antisemitism. Indiana University is one of only two institutes of higher learning in the United States that houses a research institute of this kind. It is both a privilege and a pleasure to work at a university whose administrative leadership is as understanding, cooperative, and supportive of such new initiatives as these distinguished colleagues are.

Alvin H. Rosenfeld

RESURGENT ANTISEMITISM

Introduction

Alvin H. Rosenfeld

Nazism was defeated in Europe almost seventy years ago. Antisemitism was not. Resurgent over the past decade, it is once again a disturbing presence on the European continent, in many Arab and Muslim countries, and elsewhere. According to the *Year in Review 2008/09* report of the Stephen Roth Institute for the Study of Contemporary Antisemitism and Racism at Tel Aviv University, the year 2009 began with "a wave of antisemitic manifestations [that] swept the world," with close to one thousand attacks reported in January alone. Such incidents have become virulent over the past decade. Denis MacShane, a British Labour Party MP and author of *Globalizing Hatred: The New Antisemitism* (2008), notes that "hatred of Jews has reached new heights in Europe and many points south and east of the old continent." He continues: "Synagogues attacked. Jewish schoolboys jostled on public transportation. Rabbis punched and knifed. British Jews feeling compelled to raise millions to provide private security for their weddings and community events. On campuses, militant anti-Jewish students fueled by Islamist or far-left hate seeking to prevent Jewish students from expressing their opinions."[1]

In response to this upsurge in violence, Prime Minister Tony Blair commissioned MacShane and others to investigate new outbreaks of antisemitism in the United Kingdom. Their report, issued in 2006, is sobering. In a parallel move, the U.S. Congress passed the Global Anti-Semitism Review Act of 2004, which requires the Department of State to document acts of antisemitism globally. The annual reports issued by the State Department to date confirm the rise of antisemitic hostility throughout much of the world. Similar reports issued by monitoring agencies in Europe confirm these same troublesome findings.

To cite MacShane again: "The antisemitism of old has morphed into something new. . . . Neo-antisemitism is a twenty-first century global ideology, with its own thinkers, organizers, spokespersons, state sponsors and millions of adherents."[2] He concludes, "We are at the beginning of a long intellectual and ideological struggle. It is not [only] about Jews or Israel. It is about everything democrats have long fought for: the truth without fear, no matter one's religion or political beliefs. The new antisemitism threatens all of humanity."[3]

A phenomenon of this scope and consequence demands scrutiny at the highest scholarly levels. This book undertakes to provide such scrutiny by presenting fresh research on contemporary antisemitism by many of the world's leading scholars of the subject. The nineteen authors whose work is represented in these pages come from a dozen different countries and demonstrate how anti-Jewish hostility is now resurgent on a global scale. Focusing especially on the social, intellectual, and ideological roots of the "new" antisemitism, their work elucidates many of the forces that nurture such hostility and bring it prominently into the public sphere.

There are intense debates today about the nature and causes of antisemitism and whether today's antagonism to Jews and, especially, the Jewish state is continuous with past manifestations of Jew-hatred or a departure from them. These debates frequently turn on conceptual differences—with sharply contrasting views on what antisemitism is and is not—and, consequently, also on definitional differences. The contributors to this volume understand antisemitism and engage it in their work in ways that are generally in accord with the main emphases of the European Union's "Working Definition of Antisemitism."[4] Some invoke this document by name and quote some of its key passages. Others share the document's basic assumptions even if they do not refer to it explicitly. All recognize that, in contrast to past antisemitisms, which drew largely on religious and racial biases against Judaism and the Jews, much of today's anti-Jewish animus is driven by ideological and political biases. The older forms of Jew-hatred are not altogether gone, but among most enlightened people in the West they no longer are considered respectable or persuasive. In the aftermath of the Holocaust, which made shockingly clear the genocidal thrust of race-based antisemitism, racial hatred of Jews has largely been discredited. As for religious arguments against Judaism and the Jews, they, too, have lost much of their former power, in part owing to reforms instituted in Christian teachings and liturgical practices in the post-Holocaust period and in part owing to the fact that many Western countries seem to have entered a post-Christian phase, their populations no longer falling under the once-powerful sway of negative church teachings regarding the Jews. Despite these changes, though, anti-Jewish passions and ideas remain tenacious, and recent years have witnessed the emergence of a third phase of antisemitism. As Bernard Lewis describes it, this "political-cum-ideological Judeophobia. . . . provides a socially and intellectually acceptable modern disguise for sentiments that go back some 2,000 years."[5] Typically expressing itself in objections to Jewish particularism and, especially, in efforts to demonize and delegitimize Jewish national existence in the State of Israel, this new version of Judeophobia is at the core of much of today's anti-Jewish hostility. It is a prominent focus of many of the essays that follow.

The geographical reach of today's antisemitism is broad, as the chapters of this book reveal. As readers will see, it is fed by multiple sources and is apt to take on the specific coloration of local circumstances and national settings. One can recognize commonalities in anti-Jewish actions and utterances wherever they appear, but these unfold differently in Oslo and Paris than in Istanbul and Tehran. Blaming the Jews, accusing the Jews, excoriating and demonizing the Jews, holding the Jews to a different standard of behavior—these are constants that will be familiar to observers of antisemitism. So, too, will be the textual basis for such forms of hatred—prominent among them *The Protocols of the Elders of Zion, Mein Kampf,* and certain oft-cited religious writings. Joining these older, now canonized works, newly produced and widely circulated antisemitic books, pamphlets, films, videos, songs, jokes, television programs, and websites add still more to this toxic brew and further stimulate the antisemitic imagination. The aggressive fantasies that flow from it are now in wide circulation and, when unrestrained, can cause serious problems. These problems are now a fact of contemporary life and have the potential to become still more threatening. The reasons why are evident to anyone alert to recent developments around the world.

Within European countries and other parts of the West, the taboos that kept antisemitism in check in the post-Holocaust years have been loosened and no longer seem to exercise the full protective power they once had. The familiar German phrase, "Die Schonzeit ist vorbei"—which can be translated, within this context, as "Jews are now fair game"—is indicative of this change. Some who embrace it experience a newly felt freedom to strike an adversarial posture toward Israel and its supporters.

After a long period of what some regard as an unfair form of social and linguistic suppression, attacking the Jews has become acceptable. Along with anti-Americanism, anticapitalism, antiglobalization, antimilitarism, and the like, what is euphemistically called "anti-Zionism" is now an ideological given in certain intellectual and political circles. As it appears in the media, in politics, and on university campuses, anti-Zionist opinion runs the gamut from outright vilification and denunciation of the Jewish state to an overdetermined interrogation of the country's origins and even of its right to continued existence.

On the street level, these rhetorical turns toward anti-Israeli and anti-Jewish expression sometimes find parallels in violence directed against Jews and Jewish institutions. The social climate has deteriorated in many European cities, unsettling the Jews who live there and stirring more than a few to leave the continent or to seriously consider doing so. In a heretofore unthinkable development, certain public figures are encouraging them to do just that. In December 2010, for example, Fritz Bolkenstein, a former European Union commissioner from the Netherlands, declared that religiously identified Dutch Jews have no future in his country and recommended that they would do well to leave. He stated his reasons clearly: an increase in antisemitism among Muslims living in Amsterdam and other Dutch cities threaten to put Jewish lives and property at risk. Already subjected to such threats, some Swedish Jews have left Malmö, encouraged in part by statements voiced by the city's mayor equating the alleged sins of Zionism with antisemitism. Similar attitudes of warning and reproval have been expressed by other prominent European personalities, including the late Justin Keating, a former Irish cabinet minister, who in 2005 denounced Zionism as a "blind alley," declared that "the Zionists have absolutely no right in what they call Israel," and pronounced himself "an anti-Zionist because I am pro-Jewish."[6] Daniel Bernard, a former French ambassador to the United Kingdom, dismissed Israel as "that shitty little country," which, he allegedly said, was responsible for "all the current troubles in the world" and seemed bent on bringing on World War III.[7] Jennifer Tonge, a former Liberal Democrat member of the British Parliament who later became a member of the House of Lords, subscribed to similarly derisive and conspiratorial notions. Tonge, who more than once spoke out in defense of Palestinian suicide bombers, voiced an increasingly common sentiment when, in 2006, she declared, "The pro-

Israel lobby has got its grips on the Western world, its financial grips. I think they have probably got a certain grip on our party."[8] Also expressing such conspiratorial thinking, in 2003 Tam Dalyell, a former Labour Party MP, had accused Prime Minister Tony Blair of "being unduly influenced by a cabal of Jewish advisers" and further claimed that U.S. President George W. Bush was being similarly influenced by well-placed Jews in Washington, D.C. Such views, not too long ago considered beyond the pale, are widely shared in some circles today and frequently appear in the media. They represent a disturbing drift of antisemitic sentiment from the margins into the mainstream of Western societies.

As disturbing as these developments are, they are surpassed by a far more militant rhetoric of antisemitic denunciation, vilification, and incitement emanating from many Muslim-majority countries. As several of the contributors to this book demonstrate, aggressive anti-Jewish sentiments are pervasive today in the Arab world, Iran, and Turkey. They are also to be found within Europe's growing Muslim communities. Scholars of Islam and historians of the Middle East debate the sources and aims of Muslim antisemitism, but almost all would agree that deeply embedded in the religio-political agenda of radical political Islam is a call to bring an end to the State of Israel. Radical Islamists regard a sovereign Jewish state in what is considered to be sacred Muslim land as an unacceptable anomaly and an intolerable affront that is not to be sanctioned. Hence the calls for jihad. One hears this eliminationist goal voiced constantly in the preaching of religious leaders, in the speeches of political figures, in television and radio programs, in the state-controlled press, on popular websites, and in such foundational documents as the Hamas Charter and the writings of Muslim Brotherhood ideologues. In virtually all of these media, the lexicon of anti-Jewish diatribe typically intermingles "Israeli" and "Jew," as if the two were always one and the same. At other times, the elision is dropped and Jews are attacked outright, as in the Hizbullah leader Hassan Nasrallah's often quoted statement of October 2002: "If we searched the entire world for a person more cowardly, despicable, weak, and feeble in psyche, mind, ideology and religion, we would not find anyone like the Jew. Notice I do not say the Israeli."[9]

These views, heaping scorn on both Jews and Israelis, are advanced by prominent Sunni and Shiʿite religious and political leaders alike. Broadcast to wide publics across the Middle East, they often go hand in hand with denigration and denial of the Holocaust and sometimes also with expressions of Holocaust approval, or bloody fantasies to emulate the mass murder of the Jews, this time by Muslims. Witness the words of Sheikh Yusuf al Qaradawi, one of this generation's most prolific, respected, and influential Sunni theologians: "Oh Allah, take this oppressive, Jewish, Zionist band of people. Oh Allah, do not spare a single one of them. Oh Allah, count their numbers and kill them, down to the very last one."[10]

Al-Qaradawi's pronouncements carry considerable weight among the Sunni faithful, vast numbers of whom are apt to take his incendiary words to heart as sanctioning a new genocide of the Jews. They find their counterpart in the words of the most influential Shiʿite theologian of the past half-century, Iran's Ayatollah Ruhollah Khomeini, who likewise never tired of calling for the wrath of Allah to descend upon the hated Jews. Here, from one of his many hostile declarations, is a sample of Khomeini's rejectionist appeals to his followers: "To have any relationship with Israel and its agents, commercially or politically, is forbidden by Islam. . . . We must all rise up and destroy Israel and replace it with the proud Palestinian nation."[11] Khomeini's successors follow his lead in calling for the destruction of Israel. In October 2011, the Supreme Leader of the Islamic Revolution, Ayatollah Seyed Ali Khamenei, spoke forcefully against a two-state solution to the Palestinian–Israeli conflict, claiming it was merely a cover "to legitimize the existence of the Zionist regime, and asked for the full liberation of all Palestinian territories." He denounced Israel as a "cancerous tumor and a permanent threat to the Islamic Ummah" and fervently advocated its removal.[12] It is not possible to accurately gauge the numbers of people who embrace such views, but such statements are endlessly repeated in one form or another across Muslim lands and by now can be taken as a central part of a widespread and popular antisemitic creed. If supported one day by what its adherents covet as an "Islamic bomb," this form of antisemitism carried to its ultimate endpoint is genocidal in its goals.

Defeating these destructive forces, according to Denis MacShane, will require a rigorously pursued politics of *anti*-antisemitism. Such a politics is not much in evidence today. What has been emerging instead are the forms of anti-Jewish hostility described above and analyzed with clarifying insight in the chapters of this book. Because it dates back millennia, antisemitism has been called the "longest hatred." The passions that fuel it—among them fear, envy, jealousy, resentment, suspicion, anger, xeno-phobic wariness, and distrust—remain constant, but the forms this hatred takes change over time. Through careful examination of these forms in their most ubiquitous contemporary expressions, the chapters that follow elucidate what is new and what has been inherited from the antisemitic traditions of the past. Given its longevity and tenacity, antisemitism probably cannot be eliminated once and for all, but if its sources, goals, and consequences are properly understood, perhaps it may be possible to diminish its appeal and mitigate some of its more harmful effects. This book aims to contribute to such understanding by helping readers recognize antisemitism for what it is: a social pathology with a long and destructive lineage that should be granted no place whatsoever in the contemporary world.

NOTES

1. Denis MacShane, "The New Antisemitism," *The Washington Post* (September 4, 2007).

2. Denis MacShane, *Globalizing Hatred: The New Antisemitism* (London: Weidenfeld and Nicolson, 2008), p. viii.

3. MacShane, "The New Antisemitism."

4. See page 473 for the text of the EU "Working Definition of Antisemitism."

5. Bernard Lewis, "The New Anti-Semitism," *The American Scholar*, 75, no. 1 (Winter 2006), pp. 25–36.

6. For the source of these statements and more on Prime Minister Keating, see the essay by Emanuele Ottolenghi in this volume.

7. See *"Anti-Semitic" French envoy under fire*, BBC, December 20, 2001.

8. For a full catalogue of such statements and a detailed analysis of them within the long history of British antisemitism, see Anthony Julius's authoritative study, *Trials of the Diaspora: A History of Anti-Semitism in England* (New York: Oxford, 2010). For Jenny Tonge's words, see pp. 462–63.

9. Cited in Robert Wistrich, *A Lethal Obsession: Anti-Semitism from Antiquity to the Global Jihad* (New York: Random House, 2010), p. 764.

10. Al-Quradawi's words are cited in Paul Berman, *The Flight of the Intellectuals* (Brooklyn, N.Y.: Melville House, 2010), p. 92.

11. Cited in Eirik Eiglad's chapter in this book.

12. "Supreme Leader Reiterates Full Liberation of Palestinian Territories," http://english.farsnews.com/newstext.php?nn=9007090033.

1 Anti-Zionism, Antisemitism, and the Rhetorical Manipulation of Reality

Bernard Harrison

Mal nommer les choses, volontairement ou pas, c'est ajouter au malheur du monde.

—ALBERT CAMUS

I

OVER THE PAST decade or so, in the Western world, it has become customary, on university campuses, in certain sections of the media, and among a diverse collection of "public intellectuals," to argue, in the name of something called "anti-Zionism," that Israel is an "illegitimate" state: a state that should never have been allowed to come into existence in the first place and whose continued existence is to be condemned as morally and politically intolerable.

It has become equally commonplace for those holding such views to be accused of propounding a "New" antisemitism, or at the very least of creating a climate of opinion favorable to the marked rise in antisemitic attacks in Western countries since the end of the 1990s.

Those charges have provoked a number of standard rebuttals, which characteristically include one or more of the following:

1. If there has been a resurgence in antisemitism in the West, and in the Islamic world, it is entirely occasioned by justifiable indignation at the conduct and policies of Israel.
2. The "Israel Lobby" and its tools allege antisemitism on the part of anti-Zionists for purely political reasons, as part of a campaign to discredit and silence progressive voices by branding "all criticism of Israel" antisemitic.

3. Anti-Zionism, by its nature, cannot be antisemitic, since it consists in opposition to Zionism, not in opposition to Jews or to Judaism per se.

The resulting exchanges tend to have the character of dialogues of the deaf: both sides burn with moral indignation, but neither side moves an inch beyond its original stance of accusation or rebuttal.

Can any light be shed on the rights and wrongs of this acrimonious debate? One obvious and immediate thought is that criticism of Israel, if by that is meant one or another rationally and empirically well-grounded objection to the conduct of this or that government of the State of Israel, cannot, in the nature of things, be antisemitic. Antisemitism is, by definition, a form of prejudice. Prejudice is hostility based upon falsehoods or faulty reasoning. It is not, as Catherine Chatterley, director of the Canadian Institute for the Study of Antisemitism, has recently put it,[1] "a form of normal human hostility or even a function of normal human outrage, both of which are inevitable human reactions to war and conflict."

At first sight, that thought appears to give game, set, and match to the "anti-Zionists." Critics of Israel cannot, to the extent that their criticisms are factually well founded and soundly reasoned, be antisemites.

On the other hand, the same thought is fatal not just to one but to two of the standard rebuttals I mentioned a moment ago.

Take the second, for example. This alleges that accusations of antisemitism represent merely an attempt to silence critics of Israel by smearing "all criticism of Israel" as antisemitic. Given the deafening daily chorus of opposition to Israel to be encountered every day in the media and on the blogosphere, one thing to be said is that if that were the goal intended by these accusations, they have proved remarkably ineffectual in advancing it. But does it even make sense to allege that that *is* the intended goal? Criticism of Israel cannot, all agree, be antisemitic to the extent that it is factually well founded and soundly reasoned. Hence, who but a complete fool would wish to contend that "all" or "any" criticism of Israel is, by the mere fact of being critical of Israel, antisemitic? It follows that, unless those advancing such accusations are one and all complete fools—and manifestly, I would have thought, they are not—the attempted rebuttal fails.

Or take the first. This alleges that *if* there has been a resurgence in antisemitism in the West, and in the Islamic world, it is entirely occasioned by justifiable indignation at the conduct and policies of Israel.

The difficulty for this line of rebuttal enters with the word "justifiable." By definition, *justifiable* indignation is indignation aroused by factually well-based and soundly reasoned criticism of its object. It follows that, if factually well-grounded and soundly reasoned criticism of Israel cannot by definition be antisemitic, then neither is any indignation it may arouse. Hence it follows, that if a rise in antisemitism can be shown to have occurred, the proposed explanation is intrinsically incapable of explaining it.

So how *are* we to explain the widespread conviction, among many not unintelligent people, that current anti-Zionist polemic has more than an edge of antisemitism to it?

That question might be supposed to be still further darkened by the fact that virtually all those in the "anti-Zionist" camp at present regard themselves, and wish to be regarded, as principled "antiracists." But light begins to dawn, it seems to me, at precisely this point.

Anti-Zionists are evidently justified in presenting themselves as antiracists if Zionism itself is a form of racism. According to a notorious UN resolution of 1975, it is, and the equation of Zionism with racism continues to figure, explicitly or tacitly, in much anti-Zionist writing. The 1975 resolution was repealed in 1991, being by then widely recognized as pernicious. It is certainly absurd. Zionism is a form of nationalism. Only if all nationalism is racist per se can one argue that Zionism, as a form of nationalism, is intrinsically racist. But, manifestly, not all nationalism is racist. Any demand by a nation to exercise sovereign control over its own affairs is nationalist. That demand has been enforced by successful war in the case of Irish nationalism, and remains unsatisfied in the cases, for instance, of Kurdish or Basque nationalism. It remains quite unclear, however, why Irish or Kurdish or Basque nationalism should be regarded as "racist"; and if the Kurds, the Basques, and the Irish escape having this fashionable albatross hung around their necks, why not the Jews?

In any event, and whether or not Zionism is a form of racism, most anti-Zionists are opposed to racism as the notion of racism is normally understood. Does it follow that they are, therefore, necessarily opposed to, and therefore incapable of disseminating, antisemitism?

Plainly, that conclusion could follow only if the totality of phenomena ordinarily taken to constitute racism embraces the totality of phenomena ordinarily taken to constitute antisemitism—or to put it less pedantically, if antisemitism is no more than a special case, a mere variant, of racism as that is conventionally understood. And that requirement, it seems to me, is not met. That is to say, antisemitism is not *just* a form of racism, at least in the sense usually attached to the latter notion. Some of its manifestations are indeed manifestations of "racism" in the sense usually given to the word. But others are not. Antisemitism, though it does at times overlap with racism as that is usually defined, manifests a number of aspects that fall outside it, and cannot be understood in the same terms: aspects deeply bizarre and entirely sui generis.

If someone is insensitive to the aspects of antisemitism that distinguish it from racism as generally comprehended, that, in fact, render it sui generis as a form of prejudice, then of course, it will be entirely possible in principle for that person to be resolutely opposed to *racism,* but nevertheless lax, or entirely ineffectual, in his or her opposition to *antisemitism.* And that seems to me to be the case, sadly, with many current promoters of "anti-Zionism."

Let us look more closely both at the areas of overlap between the notions of racism and antisemitism and at the areas where they part company: where the facts of antisemitism overflow the limits of the notion of racism as ordinarily understood.

II

At some point during the six decades that separate us from the end of the Second World War (my own memory locates that point somewhere in the 1960s), people stopped talking about "racial prejudice" and started talking about "racism." The latter form came to be preferred mainly because it gave voice to a growing sense that prejudice, whatever its ostensible object, is *always the same thing:* the same in its nature and the same in its causes. The "ism" locution appeals because it gives one a way of writing that presumption into the very structure of the language one uses to describe this supposedly homogeneous phenomenon: "racism," "sexism," "ageism," "elitism," and so on.

The underlying thought motivating this particular linguistic shift is that the essence of prejudice is *exclusion, operating always to maintain the power of a certain favored group.* "Racism" works to sustain white power structures by excluding brown and black people, "sexism" sustains male power structures by excluding women, "ageism" favors the power of the middle-aged by excluding the elderly, "elitism" excludes those who fail to meet the putatively arbitrary "standards" that define cultural elites, and so on. This simple thought gives us both an explanation of why prejudice should exist at all and an explanation of why it is right to oppose it. Prejudice exists because there exists a rational motive for people to be prejudiced: namely, the maintenance of "power structures." Prejudice should be opposed, not, or not primarily, because it promotes *injustice,* but rather because it promotes *exclusion:* the hiving off from "society," as second-class citizens, of members of devalued social groups, whether so constituted by race, sex, age, class, or perceived educational inferiority.

The "ism" locution, in short, works to enshrine, at the heart of the very language we nowadays use in describing prejudice, a certain analysis, specific and, as we shall see, contestable, both of the nature and causes of prejudice and of the nature of the moral objections to it. It is an analysis that derives its moral credentials from the Enlightenment—specifically Rousseauian—ideal of a society without class distinctions of any kind. A just society, according to Rousseau, is one in which each citizen can look every other in the eye and say, truthfully, that he desires nothing that will disadvantage that Other. This cannot be the case in a society that is not homogenous; in a society divided into interest groups, "partial societies" (Rousseau's term is *société partielle*), loyalty to which can easily divert the citizen from what should be his primary, and indeed sole, loyalty: loyalty to the General Will. Hence it cannot be the case in a society from which any group of citizens is excluded on account of the rest despising them as unworthy or inadequate. What is wrong with prejudice, then, according to the analysis we are considering, goes deeper, is more political in character, than any injustice it might inflict upon this or that individual. It is that, by promoting group exclusion, prejudice of any kind stands in the way of the achievement of a perfectly classless, and hence perfectly just, society.

The result of this shift in our speaking and thinking is that many, perhaps most, educated people tend to see antisemitism as just one more form of "racism." They consider it morally akin to other forms of racism (and indeed to sexism, ageism, and elitism) in that, by stigmatizing Jews as Other and inferior, it endeavors to exclude them from full, and fully participatory, membership in society. This assimilation of antisemitism to "racism" has several consequences. First of all, it fosters the comfortable conclusion that, if that is what antisemitism is, there isn't much of it around these days, at least in Europe and America. Nobody, nowadays, gets away with excluding Jews from hotels or social clubs. Nobody gets away, at least if they are discovered doing it, with operating a *numerus clausus* in education or the professions. That in turn fosters the rather widespread belief that antisemitism "belongs to the past," is "no longer a problem," and that, therefore, Jews who continue to complain and raise the alarm about it can only be doing so for more or less sinister political reasons.

Secondly, the belief that "racism"—and thus antisemitism construed as a variety of "racism"—is all about, and only about, *exclusion,* tends to drive a wedge between Jews and other victims of prejudice, in a way that is felt to give them less of a claim than others on the sympathies of "antiracists." For is not Judaism itself marked, in the perception of many non-Jews, not by the putatively generous universalism of both Christianity and the Enlightenment, but by an *exclusiveness entirely of its own creation,* deriving from the self-understanding of an observant Jew as a member of a "chosen people"? Have not Jews, precisely in consequence of the crabbed particularism of their religion, always gone to considerable lengths to refuse the choice of assimilation, of their disappearance, both as a separate "race" and as a species of *société partielle* exercising special claims on the loyalty of its members, into the general body of society: a choice held out to them as an enlightened alternative, ever since the French Revolution, by a long succession of progressive voices beginning with those of Voltaire and Clermont-Tonnerre? So do we not have to admit, in all honesty, as "sincere antiracists," opposed to all forms of exclusion, that the Jews have been very much the architects of their own exclusion? And must not that admission force us to grant, equally, if antisemitism is indeed merely one more form of "racism," that the Jews have themselves, to a great extent, been the architects of antisemitism?

The third consequence of the general presumption that antisemitism is just one more variety of "racism," racism being understood as, essentially, hostility to the idea of an inclusive society, is one whose possibility we have already considered: namely, that it makes it very difficult, if not impossible, for a "sincere antiracist" to entertain the possibility that he or she might, somehow, be speaking or acting in antisemitic ways. After all, the sincere antiracist in no way wishes to exclude or stigmatize the

Jews, but rather to welcome them into the ranks of progressive, forward-looking people, of all creeds and colors. From his—or her—point of view it is the Jews themselves, or rather the more conservative among them, who not only refuse any such offer, but do so out of considerations, be they Judaic or Zionist, which seem to him, precisely because they manifest an obstinate preference for separateness and self-determination over "inclusion," to be themselves quasi-"racist" in the sense that most people nowadays give to the term. From his (or her) point of view, therefore, any accusation of antisemitism must appear merely factitious, or politically motivated, or both.

These consequences can be avoided in one's thinking only when one begins to grasp that antisemitism, while in some of its forms equivalent to "racism," in others vastly oversteps the conceptual boundaries of that category, as usually understood.

III

Most of what we call "racism," "ageism," "sexism," and so on, I would prefer to call "social prejudice." Social prejudice does indeed seek the exclusion from society (or "decent society") of members of groups it despises, and seeks to achieve that aim through the dissemination of contemptuous stereotypes. According to such stereotypes, for example, Scots are sanctimonious and incorrigibly mean, women (as Virginia Woolf makes the uneasily male chauvinist young Cambridge don Charles Tansley insist in *To the Lighthouse*) "can't write," money has a way of sticking to Jewish fingers, West Indians are stupid and lead noisy, disorganized lives. The first thing to notice about social prejudice is that there is always a grain of truth in such stereotypes, because there has to be. One cannot despise a person for qualities that he or she manifestly does not possess. Contempt, to feed itself, to give itself something to brood resentfully on, has to fasten on something with at least some tenuous connection with reality. So there have to be at least *some* West Indians around who make noisy, raucous neighbors. There have to be at least *some* incorrigibly vulgar Jews with a mysterious talent for making money. There have to be *some* ludicrously bad women writers, *some* self-righteous, penny-pinching Scots, and so on. What is wrong with such stereotypes is merely, on the one hand, that there are always plenty of West Indians, Jews, women writers, and Scots who fail to conform in any respect to the usual stereotype, and on the other, that there are always, equally, plenty of people around who conform exactly to it, but who happen, unfortunately, not to be Jews, West Indians, Scots, or women, as the case may be. The second thing to notice about social prejudice is that it operates, as the logicians say, *distributively*. That is to say, the person who despises Scots, or West Indians, or women, takes out his contempt on *individual* Scots, or West Indians, or women. He despises them for being members of a despicable class, but he despises them, as it were, *taken one by one*. To put it another way, while he may feel contempt for the collectivity of Scots, or women, or West Indians, he does so because it is a collectivity made up of despicable individuals, not because it is a despicable *collectivity*. The third thing to notice about social prejudice is that fear, except very occasionally when it involves special concerns over matters such as employment opportunities or property values, plays very little part in it. Contempt drives out fear. We kick into the gutter with confidence those whom we despise on social grounds, because our very contempt for them persuades us that these miserable persons are far from possessing either the means or the temerity to fight back.

Most people, I think, are of the opinion that social prejudice, of this general kind, is the worst form of discrimination that we have to face: the worst, that is, that those discriminated against have to face in others, and the worst we ourselves have to face in our very occasional and limited examinations of the darkness in our own hearts. That, I fear, is an over-complacent view. There is an even more dangerous form of prejudice, not only of immense historic importance, but widely operative today, one that has been in the past, and is today, almost exclusively directed against Jews. For reasons which will appear, I shall call it "the prejudice of panic," to distinguish it from mere social prejudice, the prejudice of contempt.

The prejudice of panic, as directed against Jews, springs from belief in the following three propositions:

1. The Jews are a mysteriously but absolutely depraved people, whose aim is world domination, and who pursue that aim by incessant destructive activity aimed at the control of non-Jewish societies and at the destabilization of the world order.

2. Membership of the Jewish people differs from membership in any other human society, in that it is essentially membership in a conspiracy to dominate and exploit non-Jews.
3. Jews, because of the inimical and conspiratorial nature of Jewish culture, and its power to extend sinister tentacles of Jewish influence throughout the institutional fabric of non-Jewish society, constitute a permanent threat both to the well-being and to the autonomy of any society that harbors them.

I have argued elsewhere—though it should not be necessary to argue the point at all—that there is not a shred of truth in any of these propositions. In this, they are quite unlike the kinds of accusations that fuel social prejudice. People do sometimes match the stereotypes put about by the socially prejudiced. Nobody matches the stereotypes advanced by the prejudice of panic. The "Jewish Conspiracy" has no members. The idea that a widely scattered nation of approximately eleven million people could conceivably, by elaborate and secret machinations, "control" vast and powerful alien nations, let alone destabilize a world order perfectly capable, in any case, of bloodily destabilizing itself at frequent intervals without the slightest help from "the Jews," is an absurd and paranoid fantasy. The actual content of the prejudice of fear belongs in the same box as belief in UFOs, or ley-lines, or the real existence of the Aesir gods. But the fear it can create in susceptible minds is real enough. One can get a good sense of the inner landscape of such a mind by reading the works of the French writer and antisemite Louis-Ferdinand Céline. Sartre, who admired Céline while dissenting from his antisemitism, wrote of him,

> Anti-semitism is thus seen to be at bottom a form of Manichaeism. It explains the course of the world by the struggle of the principle of Good and the principle of Evil. Between these two principles no reconciliation is conceivable; one of them must triumph and the other be annihilated. Look at Céline: his vision of the universe is catastrophic. The Jew is everywhere, the earth is lost, it is up to the Aryan not to compromise . . . the anti-Semite does not have recourse to Manichaeism as a secondary principle of explanation. It is the original choice he makes of Manichaeism which explains his anti-Semitism.[2]

Sartre's account of Céline reminds us that the object of the prejudice of panic, as distinct from the prejudice of contempt, is not the individual but the collective. Céline's terror, his sense that "the Jew is everywhere," is prompted not by this or that individual Jew but by "the Jews": by the Jewish collectivity. It is because of this that, for the antisemite swayed by the prejudice of panic, there is not *a problem with this or that individual Jew* (such an antisemite, quaking in terror at the threat posed by the Jews taken *collectively,* may even, as we well know, regard this or that *individual* Jew as "one of his best friends"), but rather *a Jewish Problem.* And it is also why the Jewish Problem, so perceived, cannot be solved by the gradual assimilation, or the conversion of the Jews, but only by what the Nazis called an *Endlösung:* a final solution to the Jewish Problem: extermination. One does not, after all, prosecute a campaign of genocide against a group because one considers its members, *taken one by one,* to be inferior, or despicable, or even a nuisance to others. One embarks on genocide not to get rid of individuals but to destroy a collectivity: to delete altogether a nation from the tally of nations. For that to become a project in which many people can be expected to cooperate, many people must be brought to believe that the nation in question is a source of otherwise unheard of, unparalleled, apocalyptic evil: evil that can be brought to an end only if the nation in question ceases to exist. As we know, this is what the Nazis believed concerning the Jews, and what they sedulously sought, with some success, to persuade others to believe.

IV

The central, guiding claims of antisemitism, then, are one and all delusional, and evidently so. They are not, that is to say, claims capable of being backed up by securely based evidence and sound reasoning. They can, at best, be insinuated by time-honored rhetorical means, which include outright defamation, moral hyperbole, double standards, and bad logic.

Rhetorical excess of all these varieties, however, is seldom absent from political polemic of any kind. As we shall see, anti-Zionist polemic is no exception. And that, I think, may offer a clue to explaining why it is that critics of anti-Zionism are so obstinate in finding antisemitic content in documents whose authors see them merely as articulating an unexceptionably antiracist critique of Israel.

The problem is not that such documents are critical of Israel, as least so far as the criticisms are factually well grounded and soundly argued.

The problem is, rather, that the radically pro-Palestinian stance of many anti-Zionist intellectuals and journalists requires more than that Israel should be shown to be vulnerable, like any other nation-state, to well-grounded criticism of one sort or another. It requires that it be shown, in the words of one recent anti-Zionist polemicist,

> that Israel is, generally speaking, in the wrong in its conflict with Palestin-
> ians . . . [and] the . . . Palestinians . . . generally speaking in the right. There
> are grey areas in this black-and-white landscape: no doubt the Zionists at
> times did something right, and the Palestinians something wrong. But it
> is definitely the Palestinians, not Israel, who deserve the world's support.[3]

There are no doubt some human conflicts as unrelievedly black-and-white as this. The conflict between the Nazi regime in Germany and its enemies is no doubt a case in point. But it requires considerable rhetorical ingenuity to transform any collection of empirically soundly based, reasonably arguable criticisms of Israel into the radically black-and-white condemnation sought by many "anti-Zionist" writers at present: a condemnation so absolute as to call into question the very existence of the State of Israel as morally intolerable.

When one looks in detail at the objections leveled at much current anti-Zionist writing on grounds of antisemitism, it is impossible to resist the conclusion that what is objected to is not to writing *critical of Israel per se*. What arouses the objector's wrath is, rather, in virtually every case, that the *rhetoric* employed in such writing, to make plausible the transformation of piecemeal criticism into global, radical, absolute condemnation, is such as to revive, to equip with new content, all or most of the traditional founding delusions of antisemitism, including the four I listed earlier.

To this line of objection it is by no means sufficient to reply that the writings in question cannot be antisemitic, because their intention is not to attack Jews per se but rather to attack Israel, or "Zionists." That won't work, because the objection is not to the intentions animating the writings in question but rather to the means chosen of articulating those intentions. Similarly, for reasons I have already explored, it won't do to argue that because most Western anti-Zionists are principled antiracists they cannot in the nature of things be guilty of disseminating antisemitic tracts. If antisemitism is a form of prejudice not only radically distinct in nature from the bulk of what we ordinarily call "racism," but sui generis in essence, then it becomes, logically speaking, perfectly conceivable, not only that an antiracist tract may deploy inherently antisemitic rhetoric, but that the author may be rendered, by his or her naïve belief that a sincere commitment to "antiracism" is enough to make one a fortiori incapable of antisemitism, incapable of recognizing the fact.

V

The ways in which inflated political rhetoric and bad reasoning can combine to give an objectionably antisemitic flavor to anti-Zionist writing are multifarious, but they fall into a few broad categories, of which I will now try to offer some examples. For a start, there is the intellectually overconfident leap from innocuous premises to putatively exciting conclusions. One example, provided by the late professor Tony Judt, concerns the notion of legitimacy deployed in arguing for the illegitimacy, or "delegitimation," of the State of Israel.

In a much-cited 2003 article in the *New York Review of Books*,[4] Judt suggests that Israel

> is an oddity among modern nations not—as its more paranoid supporters assert—because it is a *Jewish* state and no one wants the Jews to have a state; but because it is a Jewish *state* in which one community—Jews—is set above others, in an age when that sort of state has no place.

Other things being equal—as, I shall suggest later, they fundamentally are—not to want "the Jews to have a state," while granting a right of national self-determination, and hence of statehood, to virtually every other group contesting such a right, including the Palestinians, is prima facie antisemitic. It suggests, not to put too fine a point on it, that the Jews constitute not just one more human community, but a group outside, and at odds with, the human community as a whole. This is, clearly, a suggestion from which Judt, if he is to avoid the imputation of antisemitism, must distance himself. The necessary distance is supposed to be inserted by the shift from "*Jewish* state" to "Jewish *state*." The supporting argument is that, in a Jewish *state* "one community—Jews—is set above others." But that argument fails entirely to create the required distance, for the evident reason that *any* national state, any state, that is, which serves to realize and implement the right to political self-determination of a coherent community, must, *in some sense,* set that community "above others." The foundation of the Republic of Ireland, initially as the Irish Free State, in December 1922, for example, effectively brought to an end what had been known as the Protestant Ascendancy in Southern Ireland, replacing it, in effect, with what might be termed a Roman Catholic Ascendancy. From that point onward, that is to say, the Catholic community in the Republic found itself "set above" the residual Protestant community, in the obvious sense that it acquired overwhelming power to determine the character and direction of national life in its broadest, and also in many of its more detailed, aspects. But that kind of "setting above" is, after all, what the nation state is about. There is no point in a community's seeking political autonomy by means of the foundation of a state, unless it is to be reasonably anticipated that once the state is achieved, the community in question will find itself in a position to largely direct its affairs.

If that is so, then, trivially, Judt's attempt to avoid the vaguely antisemitic implications of opposing a "*Jewish* state" by shifting the focus of criticism, instead, to the idea of a "Jewish *state,*" collapses, leaving those implications still clinging to his overall position on the "legitimacy" or otherwise of Israel. It is acceptable, it seems, for Irish Catholics, or for that matter Palestinians, to be "set above" other communities in the manner inseparable for the existence of national states per se, but not for a Jewish community to occupy that role. Why not? Judt is silent on that point; but of course, in the wings of any such argument conducted within the ambit of Western culture, stands the antisemite, ready to step on stage with a whole list of reasons, whose plausibility to many Western minds is in no way diminished by their essentially delusive character.

VI

A central theme of antisemitism has been the unmitigated depravity of the Jewish people, displayed in their supposed determination to dominate, at all costs, and at whatever expense to others not of the "chosen" people. These ideas cannot but be evoked once more, and to many susceptible minds given new substance, by the persistent tendency of much current anti-Zionist writing to represent Israel not only as open to criticism but as guilty of *utterly exceptional* crimes. Jacqueline Rose, Professor of English at Queen Mary College, University of London, catches the general tone of this line of anti-Zionist rhetoric: "How did one of the most persecuted people of the world come to embody some of the worst cruelties of the modern nation-state?"[5]

The late Edward Said similarly describes Israel's occupation of the West Bank and (at that time) of Gaza, as " . . . in severity and outright cruelty, more than rivaling all other military occupations in modern history."[6]

The logic of this stance is easily discerned. If one wishes to argue that a state or regime should never have been allowed to come into existence in the first place, and that its continued existence should be regarded as morally intolerable, the iniquities committed by that state must indeed be of such a kind as to place it in a category all its own.

The problem encountered by anti-Zionists in making this sort of case, both against the original grant, and against the continued toleration, of political autonomy to the Jewish population of Israel, is that other, non-Jewish nations have long since set the bar of iniquity over which Israel must be deemed to vault, and set it very high indeed. One need only mention the twenty-year war in Sudan, between the Muslim Arab north and the Christian/Animist south, hardly reported in the West, and only now within sight of final resolution through the secession of the south, which is estimated to have killed more than three million people; or the Hutu genocide against the Tutsi in Rwanda, or the Serbian massacre of Bosnian Muslims at Srebrenica, or the use of nerve gas by Saddam Hussein's regime to kill up to five thousand Kurdish villagers at Halabja—the list is, unfortunately, endless—to encounter recent atrocities that dwarf anything of which Israel can be accused on sound evidence.

Anti-Zionist writers frequently show themselves well aware of the difficulty these appalling cases create for the attempt to depict Israel as, if not worse than any of them, then at least among the worst of them; and they deploy various arguments, all of them bad, in an attempt to minimize or evade the difficulty.

Thus, for instance, Jacqueline Rose plaintively enquires, "Why is criticism of everyone else a *precondition* of criticizing Israel?"[7] If the issue were some specific and well-grounded criticism of Israel, then that would be an entirely sane and proper remark. But if what is at issue is rather—as it is in the body of Rose's book—some generalized, hectoring claim to the effect that Israel is simply *off the scale* of human wickedness, then it is a crazy remark, or rather a remark egregious in its boneheaded stupidity, because in that case, of course, the fact that other nations behave infinitely worse is highly relevant.

Two further, commonly employed evasive moves, both equally ineffectual, are deployed in the following passage from another recent anti-Zionist essayist, Michael Kuper: "But let's be honest. Isn't Israel singled out above all possible justification? Doesn't this encourage antisemitism? Isn't Israel demonized? The answer is, sometimes, yes. Yes, there is demonization and it should be condemned. It is not uncommon for causes people support to be idealized and their enemies cast into outer darkness."[8]

Kuper sees, evidently, the entire force of the point I have just made. But it failed to worry him nearly as much as it should. He wants, like so many of us, both to have his cake and eat it too. He deploys two devices that he thinks open the way to that pleasant option. The first: "Yes, there is demonization *and it should be condemned*" [my italics], relies upon the belief that one can wash one's hands of responsibility for the behavior of those who take one at one's word, and act accordingly, by issuing a "condemnation" of those who rashly take one to mean what one says. The second: "It is not uncommon for causes people support to be idealized and their enemies cast into outer darkness" relies on the equally common belief that political "idealism" excuses just about anything, including what otherwise one might be inclined to call rabid, and latently antisemitic, political hysteria. Because these "arguments" leave the charge of demonization unanswered, they also fail to address the connection, which Kuper admits, between the demonization of Israel and the revival of antisemitism through the reanimation of the traditional antisemitic stereotype of the Jews as a people whose depravity exceeds that of all other nations.

That stereotype also finds expression in the incessant repetition of the claim that the Israelis are "the new Nazis," as well as in the equation between the Star of David and the swastika that often figures prominently in anti-Zionist literature and demonstration. In this connection it is perhaps worth remembering that, historically, one of the main political uses of antisemitism has been to whitewash the iniquities of the non-Jew. "We may be bad, but our wickedness is as nothing compared to the wickedness of the Jew, that poisoner of wells, that polluter of the meal destined for the Passover matzo with the blood of Christian children." That pattern of selective relative exoneration is no less in evidence today. It is seldom pointed out that if it were really true that the Jews of Israel, and all those Jews, not to mention the many non-Jews like myself, who defend Israel, are "the new Nazis," or "worse than the Nazis," it would follow rigorously that the Nazis were, in effect, right about the Jews, who thus resume their traditional role as perpetrators of a degree of wickedness so extreme as virtually to exonerate everyone else, while the Germans under Hitler, while no doubt extreme in their dealings with those incorrigible Jews, for their part regain a certain moral respectability as having foreseen, and possibly even fore-suffered, the Jewish atrocities, allegedly equal at the very least to theirs, being played out in Palestine.

Demonization, and the fanciful invocation of National Socialism apart, what do the "crimes" of Israel, which Rose takes to be "among the worst cruelties of the nation state," actually amount to? The consensus in "anti-Zionist" circles appears to be that they primarily concern, or grow out of, "the Occupation": that is to say, the occupation of the West Bank and (formerly) Gaza. Judt's lexicon of iniquity will do duty here for most others in the genre.

> We can see, in retrospect, that Israel's victory in June 1967 and its continuing occupation of the territories it conquered then have been the Jewish state's very own *nakhbar [sic]*: a moral and political catastrophe. Israel's actions in the West Bank and Gaza have magnified and publicized the country's short-comings and put them on display to a watching world. Curfews, checkpoints, bulldozers, public humiliation, home destructions, land seizures, shootings, "targeted assassinations," the Wall. . . . What is the universal shorthand symbol for Israel, reproduced worldwide in thousands of newspaper editorials and political cartoons? The Star of David emblazoned upon a tank.[9]

One's feeling, reading this, and many other such tirades of accusation, is not only that, bad as they may be, the crimes of Israel, even when they are indeed crimes, are very small beer indeed in comparison to the major political crimes and disasters of the past century, but that the indictment itself is curiously schematic: devoid of relevant detail. The aim of Judt's rhetoric, and of most committed "anti-Zionists" is, as they would doubtless be happy to put it, to *put Israel on trial* (before the Court of World Opinion, or some such nebulous judiciary). But what kind of trial? In a real court, under the rule of law, witnesses for, as well as against, the plaintiff are heard. But that is not the sort of trial Israel receives at the hands of what Elhanan Yakira, in a powerful recent book, calls "the

Community of Opprobrium."[10] Their idea of a trial seems to have more in common with the show trials inseparable, as Hannah Arendt and others have argued, from totalitarian regimes: the indictment is read out by a politically committed prosecutor, who then immediately puts on a different hat and becomes, without further ado, the judge. Howard Jacobson, in his recent prizewinning *roman à cléf The Finkler Question,* has his hero Sam Finkler say of Tamara Krausz, a character in the book who strangely resembles Jacqueline Rose in real life, "her methodology . . . was to quote whoever said something that supported her, and then to ignore them when they said something different."[11] That is very much the style of the current literature of "anti-Zionism."

The suppression of mitigating circumstance endemic in the literature of "anti-Zionism" is not a simple thing. It is not a matter of one or two counterarguments, or one type of counterargument, being passed over in silence. The counterarguments airbrushed from the discussion in this arbitrary way are not merely multiple but layered, one whole class of objection behind another.

For a start, the indictment is invariably so framed as to marginalize, since it can hardly be altogether evaded, the evident fact that the "Occupation" and all its consequences arise from the past and continuing state of war, open or undeclared, in which Israel has been embroiled since 1948. The attempt to popularize the term "Apartheid Wall" for the West Bank barrier is a case in point. Besides insinuating a baseless analogy, which I shall consider in more detail in a moment, between what even Judt conceded to be the richly multicultural State of Israel[12] and the Apartheid regime in South Africa, the expression serves to obscure the fact that the point of the barrier is not to keep two "races" apart, but to reduce the frequency of suicide bombings, which it has done very effectively.

Insofar as the basic fact that various Palestinian and other agencies consider themselves at war with Israel, and act accordingly, is allowed to appear in the "anti-Zionist" charge sheet, it is passed off as a consequence of Israel's alleged "unwillingness to make peace with the Palestinians." This ignores a number of further facts, each undeniable in itself. The most obvious is that, at the Camp David summit talks in 2000, an Israeli offer to relinquish 100 percent of the Gaza strip and (ultimately) 90 percent of the West Bank, withdrawing from sixty-four settlements and retaining only a few near the Green Line, was rejected by the Palestinians, against advice from some of their main Arab supporters. It also ignores Israel's demonstrated willingness to make peace, involving exchange of conquered territory with other former enemies, notably Jordan and Egypt.

It further ignores the difficulties for peace negotiations created by the fact that the Palestinians are not only politically disunited, but beset by something approaching civil war between Fatah and Hamas, not to mention many other smaller factions, whose actions are frequently only loosely controllable by either of the main Palestinian political groupings.

The chosen strategy of all these groups is, as is incontestably evident, terror directed against civilians. A main goal of anti-Zionist apologetics must therefore be, and is, to represent armed resistance to terrorism as itself a form of terrorism. An egregious example is provided by Michael Neumann's attempt to establish the moral equivalence of terrorism, particularly in the form of suicide bombing, with conventional warfare. His argument is as follows.[13] Those planning almost any campaign in modern warfare know perfectly well, Neumann argues, that it will, inevitably, claim some civilian lives. To accept the predictability of those deaths is to accept responsibility for them. In the same way, the terrorist or suicide bomber both predicts, and accepts responsibility for, the civilian deaths his action will cause. Hence there is no morally significant difference between the Israeli or American commander and the suicide bomber.

That is it. That is Neumann's argument. And I can imagine it seeming persuasive to many a politically committed adolescent, and even to some older folk of strong passions and weak intellect. But, of course, it is utterly specious. It is specious because it leaves—I am tempted to say *smuggles*—out of account the one consideration that in fact makes the difference between terrorism and any morally decent form of warfare, namely, that while the military commander is trying to kill or maim as few civilians as he can, the aim of the terrorist is to kill as many as possible. From that point of view, the evidence given by Col. Richard Kemp, former commander of British forces in Afghanistan, to the UN Human Rights Council, is surely relevant: "Mr. President, based on my knowledge and experience, I can say this: during Operation Cast Lead, the Israeli Defense Forces did more to safeguard the rights of civilians in a combat zone than any other army in the history of warfare."

A second layer of strategic silences and evasions is encountered when one considers the extraordinary sparseness and simplicity of the picture of the "Middle East conflict" promoted by the bulk of intellectuals, academics, and journalists in the "anti-Zionist" camp. According to that picture, there are two parties, and two parties only, to the conflict: on the one hand Israel, on the other "the Palestinians." This ignores, among other things, the fact that Israel currently faces permanent low-level hostilities not merely from armed Palestinian factions, but from two major regional powers as well, Iran and Syria, the first generally admitted to be on the point of acquiring nuclear weapons, operating through front organizations, notably Hizbullah and Hamas, armed and financed from abroad.

That, of course, makes nonsense of the claim, constantly repeated in "anti-Zionist" articles and political tracts (and essential to the argument that blame for the continued existence of the Middle East conflict falls wholly on Israel's shoulders), that Israel wields such overwhelming "power" in the region as to make it wholly and solely responsible for the absence of peace. As Judt put it, "It [Israel] *is* in control of its fate; but the victims are someone else. It *is* strong (*very* strong) but its behavior is making everyone else vulnerable."[14] Only a theoretically inclined academic with a taste for denunciation and a total lack of grasp of political reality, it seems to me, could imagine that any state (however "strong," in ways which, since they are never specified, may be entirely irrelevant) is ever so wholly "in control of its fate" as to have no need to take prudential decisions that address, precisely, the limits of "power" per se: the limits, that is, of any power to determine events, the actions of enemy powers, and the solidity of alliances, that any state can reasonably hope to wield. If it were true that the Middle East conflict were solely a conflict between an otherwise unthreatened Israel and the Palestinian population in the Occupied Territories, the argument that Israel is strong enough to make peace on any terms it pleases would have some force. Once one takes a view wide enough to include the other, far more formidable players in the complex political geometry of the conflict, of course, that argument collapses.

What does lie, of course, entirely in Israel's power is the capacity to withdraw unilaterally from occupied territory without either treaty-based or international guarantees. This is the course recently pursued in Gaza, with the voluntary or forcible repatriation of the entire Jewish population. It has resulted neither in peace nor in any amelioration of the conditions of life of the Palestinian population, but merely in the setting up of a hostile armed enclave, run by Hamas and various smaller Islamist groups, with Iranian support, from which swarms of rockets have been directed against towns in Israel. So much for the fabled "power" of Israel to manipulate events in its favor.

One encounters a third layer of strategic silences in connection with the picture offered, or presumed, by much "anti-Zionist" writing, of the social, ethnic, religious, and political composition of Israeli and Palestinian society. An incautious reader of this literature might reasonably conclude, for instance, that, if the inhabitants of Israel are not uniformly Jewish, the personnel of the Israeli Defense Force certainly are; that all Palestinians, including the very large numbers holding Israeli citizenship and resident in Israel proper are, to a man, on the one hand Muslims, and on the other, uniformly and staunchly opposed to Israel; and that between these two intensely homogeneous groups there subsists only violent and implacable hostility.

In real life, the situation is more complex and ambiguous. In fact, Israeli society is about 75 percent Jewish; of the remainder, the 20 percent of Arab descent are divided between Muslims (close to 80 percent), Christians (around 20 percent), Druze, Circassians, Bedouin, and others. The last four groups have integrated more deeply into Israeli society than Israeli Muslim Arabs. Druze, Circassians, and Bedu serve in large numbers in the Israeli army. With few exceptions, Israeli Druze do not consider themselves Palestinians, but rather Israelis. Both Druze and Arab Christians have faced, and still face, religious persecution in the Muslim world (one particularly bad recent case was the bombing, with many deaths, of the cathedral in Baghdad), which they are largely spared in Israel proper. Non-Jewish Israelis of course have the vote. Of the 120 members of the Knesset, 14 are currently Arabs. The first Arab cabinet minister, Raleb Majadele, with responsibility for science and technology, was appointed in 2007. The Jewish majority is also politically divided, with eighteen parties represented in the Knesset, including the United Arab List, their politics ranging from the far right to a far left and including a number of leading figures in Yakira's Community of Opprobrium.

As might be expected, given this degree of ethical, religious, and political diversity on all sides, the degree of day-to-day hostility between Jews and Palestinians is extremely variable. From an anecdotal point of view, little in the writings of the supporters of delegitimation would lead one to predict the existence of numbers of areas of economic and social cooperation between Jewish and Arab Israelis such as Neve Shalom/Wahat al Sallam,[15] a community founded to demonstrate "the possibility of coexistence between Jews and Palestinians based on mutual acceptance, respect and cooperation," or for that matter, that of the website Arabs for Israel,[16] subtitled "Arabs and Muslims who support the State of Israel and the Cause of Peace in the Middle East," or its recently organized British analogue, "British Muslims for Israel."[17] Or that Palestinian Arab voices might include that of Khaled Abu Toameh, the Israeli Palestinian journalist and filmmaker, among other things West Bank and Gaza correspondent for the *Jerusalem Post* and *US News and World Report*. Toameh is one of many Muslim liberals who hate and fear the many varieties of repressive authoritarianism, Islamist and otherwise, that dominate the landscape of Arab politics, and who have little patience with the readiness of sections of the Western left-wing intelligentsia to both court and whitewash such movements. His writings[18] compose an extensive, articulate, and well-reasoned response to the kind of "anti-Zionism" that has been occupying us. He writes as follows of the treatment he received from "activists who imagine themselves to be 'pro-Palestinian,'" during a tour of American campuses in 2009:

> The majority of these activists openly admit that they have never visited Israel or the Palestinian territories. They don't know—and don't want to know— that Jews and Arabs here are still doing business together and studying together and meeting with each other on a daily basis because they are destined to live together in this part of the world. They don't want to hear that despite all the problems life continues and that ordinary Arab and Jewish parents who wake up in the morning just want to send their children to school and go to work before returning home safely and happily.[19]

Finally, a fourth level of strategic silence in most "anti-Zionist" writing by Western intellectuals concerns the issue of what consequences are envisaged, sought, or likely to flow from the success of campaigns to "delegitimize" Israel, to equip it with "pariah status in the eyes of the world," and so forth.

The goal sought by such campaigns is, manifestly, the ending of Jewish political autonomy in Israel. It is therefore entirely legitimate to inquire what the consequences of that might be, and what sort of regime might be likely to succeed it. What is envisaged by most supporters of the project is what is known as the One-State Solution. What seems to be most usually envisaged under this heading is a unified Palestine, including the Occupied Territories, still with its present population, still democratic, still committed to the maintenance within its borders of "universal human rights," including presumably, religious and political tolerance and the right of all citizens, of whatever religion or ethnicity, to pursue their lives in peace: only, of course, no longer a *Jewish* state. The Jewish inhabitants of Israel would, by definition, have lost political control, and thus control over their own fate. What would that fate be? Much, of course, would depend on the nature of the successor regime. Would it, in fact, be at all likely to be one committed to either democracy or human rights? The briefest acquaintance either with Israel's main political opponents, Fatah, Hamas, and Hizbullah, or for that matter with the regional powers that stand behind them must suggest that such an outcome would be extremely unlikely. And in that case, what would be the actual nature of a post-Zionist Israel? Evident historical and political considerations make it difficult to see how it could be anything but a Muslim state of radical, perhaps Islamist tendency dominated by the drive to get rid of the Jewish presence in any shape or form. This has led to charges, by the British journalist Melanie Phillips and others, that those on the Left who wish to end Jewish political autonomy in Israel are in danger of promoting a second Holocaust. No doubt there is much in this. But what also needs to be considered is the likely fate of the substantial numbers of non-Jewish groups—Druze, Circassians, Bedu, moderate Muslims—who have served in the IDF or in innumerable other ways collaborated with the Jewish majority. Neither the fate of collaborationist elements in Algeria, nor the scale and prevalence of civil war and religious persecution, including intra-Muslim persecution, throughout the Muslim world at present, gives one any reason to hope that the fate of many in these groups would be very much better than that of the Jews.

This creates a problem for "anti-Zionists." For the most part, they present themselves as admirers of multicultural societies and enemies of ethnic or religious "cleansing." But what if the preservation of multiculturalism in Israel and the freedoms and relative respect for human rights that go with it should, as the above argument suggests, be in practice inseparable from the maintenance of Jewish political autonomy?

Once one fills in the strategic areas of silence in "anti-Zionist" writing, what becomes of the claim that Israel is virtually unique among the nations of the world, and for that matter in modern history, as an agency of human suffering? Pretty evidently, it collapses. What we have to deal with, in modern Israel, is a multicultural society governed by democracy and the rule of law, with a Jewish majority moving, intermittently and with much intercommunal friction, it is true, but also with considerable success and long-term promise, toward accommodation with the large non-Jewish minorities who share its territory; a state beset at the same time, since its foundation, with low-level hostilities, occasionally erupting into war, both from a range of Palestinian factions at war among themselves and from certain hostile regional powers including Iran and Syria. It has to be admitted, I believe, that the Jewish majority in Israel deals with this extraordinary ongoing situation, though with occasional inhumanity, more humanely than most societies would, and that, compared with, say, the treatment meted out by Saddam's Iraq to the Kurds, the actions of the Serbs under Milošević in Bosnia-Herzegovina, of Russia in Chechnya and South Ossetia, of the Khartoum government in the Sudan, of the Hutu militias in Rwanda, the actions of Israel, while occasionally deserving of severe criticism, are very far from being such as to warrant treating Israel as a "pariah" or "illegitimate" state.

VII

The "Nazi analogy" finds its natural partner in the proposition, promoted, among others, by ex-President Jimmy Carter and Archbishop Emeritus Desmond Tutu, that Israel practices "Apartheid" against Arabs, a rhetorical charge usually accompanied by the designation of the security barrier built to deter suicide bombers and other terrorists from entering Israel proper from the West Bank, an aim in which it has achieved considerable success, as the "Apartheid Wall."

In much the same way as the rhetoric of Off-the-Scale Evil, the rhetoric of Apartheid recycles familiar antisemitic motifs, specifically the claim that Jews are incapable of forming or maintaining equal relationships with other groups or peoples because they have only their own interests at heart. This particular line of antisemitic chatter in effect excludes Jews from the human race by postulating a radical conflict of interest between Jews and every other human group. It is a line of talk that receives considerable, if tacit, support from the frequent repetition, in putatively respectable sections of the press and other media, of the charge that, on acquiring political autonomy in Israel, the first use Jews have made of it has been to establish an Apartheid state.

None of this would matter, of course, if it were true that Israel *were* an Apartheid state, for then talk of Apartheid in connection with Israel would not *be* "rhetoric" but simply political plain speaking. The picture presented by the actual demographic structure of Israeli society, briefly summarized earlier, however, is deeply inhospitable to that suggestion. Apartheid in South Africa was a system designed to prevent the intermarriage and secure the "separate development" of two (actually several) distinct races. Blacks and whites were not allowed to live in proximity to one another, attend the same schools or universities, use the same hospitals or the same sections of trains and buses. No such system operates in Israel, and indeed it is impossible to see how such a system could operate in such an ethnically and religiously kaleidoscopic community. The different ethnic and religious groups are simply too jumbled together. Arabs and Jews attend the same universities, are treated in the same hospitals, ride the same buses and trains. There is in Jewish Jerusalem a splendid Islamic Museum, usually crowded: one searches in vain in the Arab world for equivalent signs of interest in Jewish culture. Added to which, Israel is the only country in the world to have brought, entirely on its own initiative, tens of thousands of black Africans to its shores to be citizens and not slaves.[20]

These facts might still be considered irrelevant to the issue, and the antisemitic picture of the Jews as a haughty, self-absorbed people, self-isolated from the rest of the human race might still go through, if it were the case that the Jewish and non-Jewish communities of Israel merely lived and worked in physical proximity to one another, without any trace of what one might call human proximity: no friendships, no common or intercommunal projects, no intercommunal helping hands; merely a morally featureless landscape of uniform intercommunal hatred and animosity. The late Edward Said was a staunch supporter of this view of things. "There are no divisions in the Palestinian population of four million. We all support the PLO."[21] ". . . every Palestinian, without significant exception, is up in arms against the Jewish . . . state."[22]

Once again, these are extreme, not to say apocalyptic claims, of a type that the twentieth century has accustomed us to expect from authoritarian regimes and movements of both Left and Right. While they appeal to political romantics of all colors, they fly in the face of the vast weight of everyday experience, which teaches us that radical political uniformity of the sort of which Rousseau dreamed in *Du contrat social* is a political fantasy, and that common nationality, ethnicity, or religion opposes only the feeblest of barriers to the naturally schismatic tendencies of humankind. That these operate with undiminished force among non-Jewish as among Jewish Israelis, and for that matter among Palestinians, Muslims, or Christians, in general, is evident from the many instances of which, in Section VI, I cited a small selection; all of them, if we are to believe Said, are "insignificant." Political and moral disagreement is endemic to the human condition, which is why the totalitarian regimes so copiously bequeathed to the world since 1789 by the Rationalist political philosophies of the Enlightenment must invariably resort to liquidation and internal terror in the desperate, but always in the end unavailing, effort to contain it.

The final redoubt for those who support the rhetoric of "Apartheid" is, of course, the Security Barrier, or, as they would have it, the "Apartheid Wall," usually coupled with the "Blockade" of Gaza. Both these actions are defended by Israel as a necessary defense against terrorism. As far as the blockade of Gaza goes, media reports usually fail to mention that a similar blockade is imposed by Egypt on its short common frontier with Gaza, and for the same reason; that Gaza is effectively ruled by Hamas, a front organization for Syrian and Iranian interests in the region, which present as much of a threat to Egypt as to Israel. Secondly, of course, as is also rarely admitted, the blockade has proved, to some extent at any rate, temporary, and limited in its effects. A report of Monday, July 10, 2010, in the London *Independent,* a newspaper known for its settled hostility toward Israel, covers the opening of a brand-new shopping mall in Gaza, "filled with goods imported from Israel, not smuggled in through tunnels from Egypt,"[23] the blockade having weakened and become more limited in recent months.

Israel has always insisted that both the Wall and the blockade could be dismantled in short order, given reasonable guarantees of an end to terrorism, including rocket attacks and suicide bombing. Terrorism, it should hardly need pointing out, is inherently hostile to reconciliation between two communities, because its express aim is to kill civilians. It sends a message to the effect that the community sponsoring terrorism regards not merely the armed forces of the opposed community, but every member of that community, as a potential target. Plainly, therefore, the community attacked cannot, rationally, drop its guard, or dismantle whatever even moderately successful means it has found of limiting terrorism, without some guarantee that terror operations against it will, in that event, cease.

Two essential points of analogy with the situation of Apartheid in South Africa are thus missing. The complex of restrictions on the black and colored population that constituted Apartheid, for the vast bulk of which, in any case, as I have already argued, no parallel exists or could exist in Israel, was imposed by the white minority not under the threat of terror, but as an entirely voluntary set of measures designed to maintain the "purity" of the white race in South Africa. Neither the motives, nor the freedom of the South African authorities to act as they pleased, are matched in Israel. On the other hand, they are matched in other Middle Eastern countries from which Jews have been systematically purged. The whole hectoring of Israel about Jewish settlements in the occupied territories is predicated, after all, on Arab insistence that a Palestinian state would not allow any Jews whatsoever within its borders.

VIII

It is no doubt because of the cumulative empirical force of the considerations I have been presenting that very large numbers of ordinary people in both Britain and America see Israel as a small, vulnerable beacon of Western values surrounded by enemies who, if it were to fall, would show very little mercy either to its Jewish population or to the very large numbers of its non-Jewish citizens who would find themselves tagged as "collaborators," that is, as the sort of people whom no less a political, as well as an intellectual authority than Edward Said once defended the right of the "revolutionary" Palestinian movement to liquidate at will.[24] The popularity of the cause of Israel, and the relative unpopularity of "anti-Zionism," not only among Jews but among non-Jews outside the charmed circles of the campus, certain media and arts organizations, certain political parties, and certain sections of the governmental and bureaucratic elites, present a further difficulty for anti-Zionists. It is distressing, but in no way surprising to those at all well-read in the history of antisemitism, that the explanation they choose to offer, for the most part, is that anyone, Jew or non-Jew, who happens to disagree with them is a dupe of the Jewish Conspiracy. The most famous recent deployment of this argument is, of course, the essay, and subsequent book, *The Israel Lobby,* by the Chicago political scientist John Mearsheimer and his Harvard colleague Stephen Walt. Both book and essay argue that the support afforded Israel by the United States is, and always has been, so grossly contrary to American national interest that some special circumstance, over and above the ordinary workings of politics and opinion-forming in America, must be sought to explain it. That special circumstance, according to the authors, is to be found in the machinations of "the Israel Lobby," a collection of political organizations of which AIPAC, the American-Israel Public Affairs Committee, is a leading member.

In the second half of this thesis—the part dealing with the role of AIPAC—we are confronted here with a fairly standard variant of the myth of Jewish Conspiracy. The Israel Lobby is said to work secretly, by bringing pressure to bear on legislators, either through Jewish control of finance or through the threat of being "smeared" as antisemites. The effect of these machinations is to pervert the powers and resources of an overwhelmingly non-Jewish society away from the service of its real and proper interests, to the service of purely Jewish interests, in this case those of the State of Israel. And, as usual, the powers of the conspiracy—in his case, the Israel Lobby—are made out to be as immense as they are shadowy; even to the extent of accounting for the decision to open the second Iraq War.

Clearly, however, this second part of the argument can only begin to get off the ground if its first part—the bit, that is to say, that endeavors to show that the gap between the interests of Israel and those of the United States is so wide that it is simply inconceivable that successive U.S. administrations, both Republican and Democrat, would have continued to support Israel *had it not been for the activities of the Israel Lobby*. As many commentators have pointed out, this claim is very hard to accept. And it has to be said, and indeed has been said, both by me and by many other more qualified commentators, that Mearsheimer and Walt make very little attempt to place this part of their argument on a sound footing. What they have to say in its support, indeed, amounts to little more than repetition of the standard anti-Zionist rhetoric that we have had under consideration here. Israel has "perpetrated crimes" against the Palestinians, whose recourse to terrorism in response is "wrong but . . . [not] surprising," and so on. Beyond that, the claim that support for Israel is so massively contrary to American national interest as to require a special conspiracy theory to explain it is simply taken for granted. And it is, of course, precisely because this essential component of their argument smacks more of rhetoric than of reason, as does, when closely examined, the conspiracy theory it supports, that their work has been widely accused—and by no means only by Jewish commentators—of antisemitism.

IX

To what extent are we to regard the more extreme kinds of putatively "anti-Zionist" rhetoric as complicit in the encouragement of hostility to and attacks upon Jews in general?

Sometimes the pretence that Zionists, not Jews, are the target, wears very thin indeed, as in the case of the left-wing British playwright Caryl Churchill in her one-act play "Seven Jewish Children," put on at the at the Royal Court Theatre in February 2009 in the face of a storm of controversy. The play concerns the problems supposedly faced by Jewish adults endeavoring to conceal from a child the "truth" concerning various events singled out by the playwright as turning points in the history of Israel, concluding with the action by the IDF in Gaza then in progress. The phrases "tell her," "don't tell her" recur as a leitmotiv throughout the action. At one point a character is made to say, "Tell her we killed the babies by mistake," with the clear implication, as the novelist Howard Jacobson pointed out in a blistering piece on British antisemitism in the *Independent* newspaper, that in fact they were killed on purpose, and possibly singled out precisely with that end in view. Hardly surprisingly, many Jewish and non-Jewish critics concurred in seeing in the play, in the words of Jonathan Hoffman, vice chairman of the Zionist Federation of Great Britain and Ireland, "A modern blood libel, drawing on old antisemitic myths."[25]

Jacobson's novel *The Finkler Question,* mentioned earlier, which satirizes, among other things, the minority of British Jews whose politics, where Israel is concerned, chime with those of Churchill's wing of the British intellectual Left, was to win the Man Booker Prize in 2010. The plot of the novel turns on an antisemitic attack of the kind becoming all too common in the streets of European cities in which the twenty-two-year-old grandson of a character in the book is "stabbed in the face and blinded by an Algerian man who had shouted 'God is great' in Arabic and 'Death to Jews.'" The previous year, Jacobsen had accused Churchill's play of encouraging such attacks. Churchill's reply, in her *Independent* letter replying to Jacobson's criticisms, is worth citing:

> When people attack English Jews in the street saying "This is for Gaza" they are making a terrible mistake, confusing the people who bombed Gaza with Jews in general. When Howard Jacobson confuses those who criticise Israel with anti-Semites he is making the same mistake.

There is a certain pathos in this reply. But the reply is also deeply shocking for what it reveals about the political, moral, and psychological assumptions of its author. Churchill seems incapable of grasping that to put on a play like hers constitutes a political act, that political acts carry consequences in the public arena, and that once such an act has been embarked upon, there is no way in which its author can avoid responsibility for its consequences.

Churchill plainly feels that the main thing she has to establish, if she is to evade Jacobson's attack, is her own moral purity: the moral purity, that is to say, of her intentions as a dramatist. It is *other people,* people "making a terrible mistake," who attack English Jews in the street in revenge for the bombing of Gaza. She is in no way to be held responsible. *She* is not an antisemite. Her play criticizes *Israel,* not "Jews in general."

But the title of her ten-minute playlet is not *Seven Israeli Children,* but *Seven Jewish Children.* Nor does it in any way concern, let alone impugn, those actually responsible for the conduct of the Israeli action in Gaza: that is to say, presumably, the government and military establishment of Israel. Its action, brief as it is, presents, in a way altogether free of political or historical context, the more or less inadequate attempts of a group of Jewish parents to explain to their children the awkward "fact"—*that Jews kill children.*

The play gains whatever power it possesses, in short, from tapping into one of the deepest motifs of Manichaean antisemitism: the motif of the Blood Libel. It is beyond belief that those who clapped and cheered the play at the Royal Court Theatre were not cheering it for transgressing, once again, and with all the saving window dressing associated with left-wing humanitarianism, a postwar veto that anyone who cares to chat to people in the bar of a British public house will discover to be widely felt and resented in England: not at all a veto on criticizing Israel, but a veto on criticizing "the Jews."

So where is the "terrible mistake"? What, in fact, distinguishes the ethos of the play from, let us say, the ethos of the *Protocols*? There exists an English folk saying: "those who sup with the Devil should take a long spoon." Those who, like Churchill, imagine that they can make the vile, antihuman rhetoric of Manichaean antisemitism serve humanitarian ends are, whether they know it or not, supping at the black table with a very short spoon indeed. They must not be surprised if later, when they protest the moral purity of their motives, the lips of their amiable, vulpine host curve into the ghost of a smile.

Some recent "anti-Zionist" rhetoricians, of course, are less tender-minded than Churchill. There are those among them who admit cheerfully that much current left-wing propaganda is antisemitic both in intent and in its practical effect of helping to create a climate of hostility toward Jews, but that that is of no consequence if it is serves the purpose of "isolating" Israel and turning it, in the eyes of the world, into a "pariah state." Thus the "distinguished British film director Ken Loach" (I quote from a recent *New Republic* piece, "Pox Britannica," again by Howard Jacobson)[26] "dismissed a report on the rise of antisemitism across Europe as designed merely to "distract attention" from Israel's military crimes. "An increase in antisemitism is perfectly understandable," Loach said, "because Israel feeds feelings of antisemitism." We saw earlier why this is defective as an argument: factually well-grounded and soundly argued criticism of Israel could not, *by its nature,* "feed antisemitism." But equally disturbing are the two mute but evident subtexts that this fallacious argument supports here: (1) that if Israel in any way "feeds feelings of antisemitism" on a massive scale, the rest of us need not be very much worried about feeding them; and (2) that if "feelings of antisemitism" really amount to no more than moral indignation at the behavior of Israel, then maybe people on the Left shouldn't be too worried, anyway, about feeling them!

A still more interesting case is that of the philosopher Michael Neumann, of Trent University in Canada. In an e-mail debate with the webmaster of the *Jewish Tribal Review* website, later published, he is reported as saying, "If an effective strategy [in support of the Palestinians] means encouraging reasonable antisemitism, or reasonable hostility to Jews, I . . . don't care. If it means encouraging vicious, racist antisemitism, or the destruction of the state of Israel, I still don't care."[27] What is interesting about this response is that Neumann clearly believes that it is possible to use "encouragement" of antisemitism as a purely instrumental tactic in the service of an "effective strategy" for serving the basic humanitarian goals of combating oppression and discrimination.

That is a tall order. The power of "vicious, racist antisemitism" (or for that matter "reasonable antisemitism," whatever that may be) to give rise to murder and associated savagery on a vast scale is abundantly documented—and I am thinking here, not just of the last, and most destructive, Shoah, but of the pogroms of the 1880s, and all the innumerable train of episodes of large- and small-scale atrocities that preceded them at intervals throughout the history of the Common Era. If, therefore, you think, as Neumann plainly does, that the encouragement of antisemitism of all kinds is a small price to pay for the goal of isolating and demonizing Israel, you must believe that the "crimes" of Israel are so heinous, morally speaking, as to outweigh any atrocity that your "encouragement" of "vicious, racist" antisemitism might help to bring to pass. But if you think *that, and think it, as you must, in defiance of the evident facts of the case,* you are yourself buying into the central, quasi-paranoid, thesis of Manichaean antisemitism, the antisemitism of Céline or Hitler: that the Jews and their state are so transcendentally evil that, on balance, it would be no loss to humanity were they to be expunged, *at whatever cost,* from the face of the earth. In short, the cheerful insouciance with which Neumann embraces the proposition that any evils that might conceivably result from the "encouragement" of antisemitism pale into insignificance beside the good to be achieved by the destruction of Israel, fatally subverts his claim not to be, himself, an antisemite of a profoundly traditional type.

To see this central flaw in Neumann's position is to see, also, the nature of the abyss, on the precipitous edge of which much supposedly "left-wing" or "left-liberal" political rodomontade concerning Israel is perilously teetering. What, in the end, is supposed to distinguish such a "Left" from the extreme nationalist "Right"? Representatives of the far Right have not, after all, been slow to claim the "New" antisemites as their own. David Duke, the founder of the Alabama Ku Klux Klan, and of a youth group affiliated with the American National Socialist White People's Party, was quick to welcome Mearsheimer's and Walt's paper on the "Israel Lobby" and to hail them as converts to his views. Messages of congratulation from people of similar political affiliation appeared on the website of the British left-wing weekly *The New Statesman* after it published an overtly antisemitic cover in 2002, and were hastily removed by the self-described "sincere antiracists" running the magazine. When these things are pointed out, the usual reply is to allege "smear tactics." However it is not a "smear," but simply the case, that people like Duke perceive the "new" antisemites as brothers; as people who have finally, if belatedly, come to their senses on the "Jewish Question." And the problem for the kind of "Left" liable to suffer the unwanted embrace of Duke and his ilk is to explain precisely how, in consistency, that embrace can be evaded.

X

That brings me back to the main thesis of this essay. I have argued that what exposes much current "anti-Zionist" writing to the charge of antisemitism is not that it is critical of Israel per se, but, rather, (1) that its rhetoric bestows new content and new respectability on some of the core delusions of historic antisemitism; and (2) that the reason it must avail itself of such rhetoric is that in no other way can it weld together the piecemeal and limited criticisms of Israel which are all that well-grounded empirical enquiry and sound moral reasoning will support, into a radical, not to say apocalyptic, condemnation of Israel as an "illegitimate" or "pariah" state.

We have in the process, it seems to me, uncovered a fairly crushing reply to the third of the rebuttals I mentioned earlier: that anti-Zionism can't be antisemitic, because it opposes Zionists, not Jews per se. The retort which that suggestion invites is that, while there are indeed plenty of ways of criticizing Israel without falling into antisemitism, they are left behind the moment one reaches out to themes and structures of rhetoric characteristic of traditional antisemitism, for the sake of making the case against Israel seem, at least to a gullible and uncritical reader, stronger and more radical than can be managed by observing the ordinary constraints of truth and logical consequence.

The collapse of this third rebuttal also carries away with it in its ruin any remaining plausibility attaching to the first: to the suggestion, that is to say, that any resurgence of antisemitism in the West can be explained as the result of just indignation at the conduct of Israel. As I noted earlier, *just* indignation cannot in the nature of things be antisemitic. The reverse is true, however, of indignation stirred up by empirically and rationally unsustainable rhetoric. What antisemitism *is,* and always has been, indeed, is a system of rhetorically sustained delusion having no basis in fact and sound reasoning. Present-day anti-Zionists thus stand, it seems to me, in greater need of examining both their chosen political rhetoric and their consciences as well as the internal coherence of their alleged commitment to "antiracism," more rigorously than any of them seem at present disposed to recognize.

Notes

The epigraph is from Albert Camus, "Sur une philosophie de l'expression," "Poésie 44" (1944) discussing the work on language of his friend the philosopher Brice Parain. The idea expressed by this much-quoted remark, universally attributed to Camus, is actually Parain's, though the wording, and the way of putting it, are indeed Camus's (I owe a debt of gratitude to my friend Edward Alexander for this information).

1. Catherine Chatterley and Michael Keefer, "Right of Reply: Michael Keefer Responds to Catherine Chatterley" (November 23/25, 2010), www.winnipegjewishreview.com.

2. Sartre, *Anti-Semite and Jew* (New York: Grove Press, 1962), pp. 41–42.

3. Michael Neumann, *The Case Against Israel* (Petrolia, Calif.: Counterpunch, 2005), p. 3.

4. Tony Judt, "Israel: The Alternative," *New York Review of Books* (October 23, 2003).

5. Jacqueline Rose, *The Question of Zion* (Princeton, N.J.: Princeton University Press, 2005), pp. 115–16.

6. "An Exchange on Edward Said and Difference," *Critical Inquiry* 15 (Spring 1989), p. 641.

7. Rose, p. xix.

8. Richard Kuper, "The New Antisemitism," in Anne Karpf, Brian Klug, Jacqueline Rose, and Barbara Rosenfeld, eds., *A Time to Speak Out: Independent Jewish Voices on Israel, Zionism and Jewish Identity* (London and New York: Verso, 2008), p. 101.

9. Tony Judt, *Reappraisals: Reflections on the Forgotten Twentieth Century* (London: Heinemann, 2008), p. 288.

10. Elhanan Yakira, *Post-Zionism, Post-Holocaust: Three Essays on Denial, Forgetting and the Delegitimation of Israel* (Cambridge and New York: Cambridge University Press, 2010), p. 220.

11. Howard Jacobson, *The Finkler Question* (London: Bloomsbury, 2010), p. 231.

12. Tony Judt, "Israel: The Alternative," *New York Review of Books* (October 23, 2003), "Israel itself is a multicultural society in all but name. . . ."

13. Neumann, pp. 155–70.

14. Judt, *Reappraisals*, p. 290

15. http://nswas.org/.

16. http://arabsforisrael.blogspot.com.

17. http://www.britishmuslimsforisrael.com/.

18. Available at the website of the Hudson Institute, http://www.hudson-ny.org /author/Khaled+Abu+Toameh.

19. Khaled Abu Toameh, "On Campus: The Pro-Palestinians' Real Agenda," at the website of the Hudson Institute, http://www.hudson-ny.org/424/on-campus-the-pro -palestinians-real-agenda.

20. I owe both these last points to Edward Alexander.

21. Edward Said, *New Leader* (August 11, 1980). I owe this reference, and subsequent references to Said, to Edward Alexander.

22. Interview (Tunis), December 1988.

23. http://www.independent.co.uk/news/world/middle-east/as-the-israeli-blockade -eases-gaza-goes-shopping-2035432.html?origin=internalSearch.

24. "An Exchange on Edward Said and Difference," *Critical Inquiry* 15 (Spring 1989), pp. 645–46.

25. Leon Symons, "Outrage over 'Demonising' Play for Gaza," *The Jewish Chronicle* (February 13, 2009), p. 3.

26. *The New Republic* (April 15, 2009), http://www.tnr.com/article/pox-britannica.

27. Cited in Jonathan Kay, "Trent University's Problem Professor," *National Post* (April 22, 2009).

2 Antisemitism and Anti-Zionism as a Moral Question

Elhanan Yakira

I

THE PAST FEW years have witnessed concerted efforts to bring about what is called Israel's delegitimation.[1] What explains these anti-Israeli and so-called anti-Zionist campaigns, such as the BDS (or the Boycott, Divestment, Sanctions campaign), the Free-Gaza flotillas, the aftermath of the bloody struggle on the *Mavi Marmara,* the Israel Apartheid weeks, the legal warfare against Israel and Israeli officials, the Durban conferences, the anti-Israeli discourse held by human-rights organizations and other nongovernmental organizations (NGOs)? Do these activities and the language that accompanies them belong to the old traditions of antisemitism (or Judeophobia), or do they represent something else?

Whether anti-Zionism is or is not a form of antisemitism is an interesting theoretical question, but it may also have significant practical implications. For Israelis, anti-Zionism has become a real problem, and understanding its nature, scope, origins, and the stakes involved in it goes well beyond theoretical concerns. The same holds true for Jews living outside of Israel, who often find themselves the targets of Israel's detractors. The immediate and almost automatic association of Israel with Jews proves that anti-Israeli feelings and acts are very closely linked to anti-Jewish feelings and acts. The fact is that non-Israeli Jews are today vulnerable to anti-Israeli rhetoric and activities (the late Tony Judt was not alone in thinking that Israel had become a liability to Diaspora Jews). In Arab anti-Israel discourse, the terms *Jews* and *Israelis* are very often synonymous. It comes as no surprise, then, that many Jews now dissociate themselves from Israel, refuse to see it as representing them as Jews (or otherwise), or claim that their own anti-Israeli positions are nothing but an expression of legitimate criticism of Israeli policies judged to be objectionable. Jewish protests against being associated with Israel may well be just one more expression of a classical aspect of antisemitism that has come to be known as "Jewish self-hatred." One famous attempt to understand what is referred to with this unhappy term depicts it as a complex psychological transfer mechanism: Jews apply to other Jews the images they believe the stereotyped non-Jew has of "bad Jews."[2]

However, just claiming that anti-Zionism and antisemitism belong to the same family of phenomena, or even pointing to such sociopolitical phenomena as those just mentioned, does not suffice. Moreover, experience shows that from a practical point of view equating anti-Zionism and antisemitism is more often than not counterproductive and may cause more harm than good. Self-proclaimed "critics" of Israel often charge the counter-critics with being guilty of McCarthyism, of seeking to enforce an inquisitorial denial of their freedom of speech, or of being otherwise totalitarian.

Many scholars and others insist, however, that there is a close affinity between antisemitism and anti-Zionism and that they in fact constitute one phenomenon. This claim deserves serious consideration, more from a theoretical than from a practical or strategic point of view. Because antisemitism is a historical phenomenon of great longevity, the issue of its relation to anti-Zionism presents itself as a question of diachronic continuity. There are also factors that are arguably common to both in a so-called "synchronic" manner. One obvious way to show the connection between antisemitism and anti-Zionism is to point to significant *thematic* continuities between traditional expressions of Judeophobia and the current criticism of Israel—the recurrence of familiar hostile images, of stereotyped metaphors, of language used, and so on. A scholar who has recently done impressive work in this area is the French political theorist Pierre-Andre Taguieff.[3] There are also a number of excellent histories of antisemitism, many of which consider anti-Zionism as part of its long history.[4] Others are more reserved and try to draw distinctions between manifestations of anti-Zionism that are antisemitic and others that are not; the latter are, hence, allegedly legitimate forms of criticism of Israel or of opposition to Zionism. Lately there have been a number of attempts to find comprehensive definitions of antisemitism,[5] some of which consider radical anti-Zionist discourse to be antisemitic.

But there is more to it. If we insist on regarding anti-Zionism as a form of antisemitism, we do so precisely for the reasons that cause the deep indignation of anti-Zionists when they are said to be (potentially or manifestly) antisemites. The reason for this indignation is not so much an allegedly *factual* inaccuracy, or even hermeneutical inadequacy, in describing anti-Zionism as antisemitism. The real reason behind the sometimes violent opposition to identifying these two attitudes or positions as such is essentially *moral*. What is really, albeit often implicitly, at stake is a question involving the fundamental decency or moral acceptability of anti-Zionism. The real significance of the allegation that anti-Zionism is a form of antisemitism is that in its two main forms it consists of the same moral substance of which antisemitism is made—in the denial of the legitimacy of the fundamental Zionist claim to establish and maintain a sovereign Jewish state in (part of) the land of Israel, and in its systematic vilification and criminalization of what is commonly called "the politics of Israel," anti-Zionism is just as morally unacceptable as antisemitism has always been. More than pointing to diachronic and synchronic continuities, to say that anti-Zionism is a form of antisemitism is to draw an extremely severe moral judgment on anti-Zionism: just as antisemitism is an outrage, as is nowadays more or less universally admitted, so is anti-Zionism: both are morally unacceptable.

II

To deal seriously with the *moral* question, to inquire whether anti-Zionism is or is not made of the same moral substance as antisemitism, to go beyond the moralizing, recriminatory, and accusatory discourses so common in this context—another question, a seemingly banal question perhaps, should be addressed first: Is antisemitism really a bad thing? And if it is, why? No one would have much doubt about the answer to the first part of the question. For most people, it goes without saying: antisemitism is evil. But the second part is seldom, if at all, asked: What is the source of the moral quality of antisemitism? Why, indeed, is it evil? This question is rarely asked, for presumably everyone knows what antisemitism is and why it is bad: the killings, the pogroms, the persecution, the discrimination, the indifference—aren't all these sufficient to prove and explain antisemitism's evil? They should be sufficient, and yet more needs to be said.

In keeping with the major questions before us, our fundamental concern also has to do with the moral value of anti-Zionism. If anti-Zionism is indeed a form of antisemitism, it would be so mainly because both belong to the same moral family, because both would be morally objectionable, and with the same severity and intensity. To demonstrate as much, it is necessary to look first at antisemitism, at this strange phenomenon that makes Jews, no matter how they choose to live their Jewishness,[6] despised, a perpetual object of hatred and rejection, of sporadic violence, the target of what is probably the most systematic—and successful—genocide that has ever taken place. However, I shall look at this phenomenon neither as a historian nor as a social or political scientist but from the point of view of a moral philosopher. I shall not look for more historical, social, economic, or psychological facts, or offer any new definitions or redefinitions of antisemitism. Instead, I shall ask the simplest question of all: Why is antisemitism bad?

III

In order to propose a moral judgment of antisemitism (eventually of anti-Zionism as well), one has to take this form of hostility seriously. To just dismiss it as a primitive, vulgar, or irrational attitude will not do; it has to be proven to be morally wrong. That does not require developing or offering apologetics in support of Judaism, Zionism, or Israel. Nor does it require opposition (if one may call it so) to both antisemitism and anti-Zionism based on the falsity of their claims and arguments. I would concede, at least for the sake of argument, that both antisemites and anti-Zionists sometimes advance truthful claims and make valid charges against Jews in general or against Israel in particular. In fact, one element of the diachronic continuity that links different forms of antisemitism over time is that, just as in the past, so is it in the present: contemporary anti-Zionists and anti-Israelis labor to support their positions with arguments. These arguments should not be dismissed offhandedly, not so much with regard to their content but because of the very fact that they are brought forward as *arguments*.

But arguments, even if we are ready to admit that some are plausible, cannot, and have never really been able to, justify or even explain negative perceptions of the Jews *as such*—perceptions we refer to as *anti-semitic*. It remains the same today: the allegedly valid arguments brought against Israel and against Zionism do not necessarily explain, let alone justify, their delegitimation. In fact, more than being actual arguments these are excuses and rationalizations. Truth is used, or abused, and not looked at for its own sake. The point of this remark is not that there is a need to draw a line between "legitimate" and "illegitimate" criticisms of Israel, just as the point has never been to define how to draw a line between antisemitism—admittedly unacceptable—and "legitimate" criticism of some form or other of Jewish existence. My point is different, and more radical: sound and often truthful arguments constitute *an integral and essential* component of a phenomenon that is neither sound nor truthful, which is indeed a form of "radical evil." As such, these arguments are part of the problem, a symptom of a disease rather than a justification of a position, "critical" or otherwise. The fact that one can find in the writings of the antisemites—even in the writings of Nazi ideologues—some truthful claims about the Jews is immaterial: antisemitism is nevertheless an abomination and even a crime. Our judgment of antisemitic discourses has to be based on a reversal of the order of reasons: not from the argument to the conclusion, but *vice versa*: if the conclusion is antisemitic, it is necessarily morally wrong. Consequently, the arguments that are supposed to sustain it are also morally wrong. Even if they are both good and valid, if such arguments support an antisemitic conclusion, they are morally wrong.

That antisemites and anti-Zionists rely so heavily on arguments, however, is not a trivial matter. In fact, it is one of the most important distinctive traits of both. This mixture of the sound and the valid with the outrageous is part of the conundrum of antisemitism. There are numerous attempts to unravel it, and two main, inevitable questions are usually asked: *why* and *how*: how can we explain that Jews have been treated the way they have been? Why does Israel attract so much hostility? How has this hostility in both the past and now been so important an element of Western high culture? Why does the BBC, for one, permit itself to cover the Israeli–Palestinian conflict in the demonstrably biased way it does? The distortions in the Goldstone report (and the recent public repentance of its chief author),[7] the Durban conferences, or the malice exhibited in the BDS campaigns on American or British campuses: where does it all come from?

These are all legitimate questions. I want, however, to follow another path and ask another question: not so much to *explain* as to *describe;* not so much to inquire into the *why* and *how* of antisemitism and anti-Zionism, but to reflect on their *what.* Put differently, what is the conceptual core of the cluster of phenomena we call "antisemitism" and "anti-Zionism?" Such an approach does not necessarily imply an "essentialist" or unhistorical approach. An adequate descriptive concept can be the outcome of a "dialectical" analysis, and thus can avoid the pitfall of ascribing an eternally and a priori given "essence."

IV

Phenomenologically speaking, then, what kind of evil is antisemitism/anti-Zionism? One important aspect of it reveals a mixture of the sound and the outrageous, alluded to above. Although, as Robert Wistrich has said, antisemitism is the oldest hatred, it is not necessarily the *hatred* itself that is its most significant feature. Consider the term itself: *antisemitism* is the name of a historically well-situated phenomenon, a name given to a well-defined political-ideological movement by its own ideologues (by Wilhelm Marr in the second half of the nineteenth century, to be more precise). It is ironic that this term has become a universally accepted name for Jew-hatred at all times and in all forms and, in particular, an emblem of depravity and despicability. So much so, that, as we have seen, people are profoundly offended when they are said to be antisemites; Marr, for one, referred proudly to himself as an antisemite. One way or another, the movement that called itself *antisemitism* was a thoroughly modern movement that purported to give a scientific basis to what it presented as opposition to some Jewish—or, precisely, "Semitic"—cultural-historical essence, allegedly rooted in biology. Of course, the "scientific" basis of antisemitism was a completely absurd, distorted, and nonsensical one; what matters most is the very fact that such a scientific justification was thought to be important.

It has been suggested lately, notably by Pierre-André Taguieff, that *Judeophobia* is a term more appropriate than *antisemitism*. Here, I would like to emphasize its less *affective* sides. *Phobia* means some nonrational affect: fear, hatred, or some mixture of these and similar feelings like dread, horror, terror, loathing, detestation, aversion, antipathy, revulsion, and so on. All these affects have always been constituent features of the attitude toward Jews. More interesting, though, is the *being against,* the *anti,* which the term *antisemitism* implies. Hatred, phobias, and the like are mute, and, as such, not very interesting for a phenomenological study of antisemitism. Many people hate, loathe, despise, and fear; they have always had these feelings, and the objects of their hatred or fear are as varied as the haters themselves. But such hatred is perhaps both trivial and banal. The faces of people shouting at the Israeli ambassador during a public program in 2010 at the University of California-Irvine campus (or at me, for that matter, on the occasion of a public discussion on Zionism at the École normale supérieure in Paris), do not seem to be significantly different from faces of other hateful people on different occasions—for example, at certain soccer games in Israel. Hatred is hatred is hatred, as they say, and insofar as antisemitism is hatred, or a phobia, it is not necessarily different from other hatreds, except perhaps for its longevity. I would even dare say that often enough hatred, insofar as it is an *affect* in the strict, nonrational meaning of the word, is prior to the object hated: first there is hatred, or a need to hate, and then an object is found to be hated. Hatred needs an object, and in our case culture and history present hatred with a ready-made object: the Jew. In this respect, the hatred of Jews is not more interesting than the hatred of blacks or homosexuals. The thugs assailing a homosexual are not interestingly different from their colleagues who desecrate tombstones in a Jewish cemetery or harass an Orthodox Jew in the subway. Both act hatefully without any *reason;* they look for prey, and the Jew, the homosexual, or the black are readily available targets that give satisfaction for their need to hate.

But there is more to it. The longevity of antisemitism is just one indication of its sui generis nature.[8] It is in order to pinpoint the specificity of the hatred of Jews that I prefer to use the term "antisemitism." What makes it interesting—and telling—is the prefix *anti.* Hatred is not an *anti*-attitude. Being *anti* something means being against it or opposing it; but people who hate, say, the winter or eating fish are not *against* the winter or opposed to fish. Similarly, people who hate blacks or gays are not, strictly speaking, *against* blacks or *opposed* to gays. In order to be against gays, some idea has to be joined to the object of hatred—something like gay marriage or openly serving in the army. People may be against having blacks as neighbors or opposed to gay marriage; they would often—but not always—invent one or another kind of justification—ideological, theological, pseudo-scientific, and so on, in support of their feelings. But what it means to be against blacks or gays as such is not altogether clear. Jean-Paul Sartre was probably thinking along these lines when he said that antisemitism was not an opinion or a position but a crime; he had to say this—probably no one would have felt the need to say it of other hatreds—because antisemitism often pretends to be a position or an opinion: to be a position *against* the Jews, or being *antisemitic.*

If hatred, as we have just suggested, is mute, antisemitism—ancient, medieval, modern, and contemporary—is not. It has always had an *ideational* dimension. If hatred expresses itself with fists and guns, antisemitism speaks and writes, using words and concepts. It has always been eloquent. Alongside the more mute forms of Jew-hatred, or Judeophobia, which are typically vulgar, stupid, and primitive, or violent and even murderous, antisemitism is, and always has been, also an *intellectual* phenomenon. More than any other form of hatred, it has been widespread among the intellectual and cultural elites, a criminal penchant[9] of the intelligentsia. One of the most conspicuous traits of contemporary anti-Zionism is that it is emphatically an intellectual phenomenon. In anti-Zionism, antisemitism has perhaps reached its final fulfillment; or maybe it has rejoined its ancient origins, being at first an obsession of the theologians, or church *clerics,* it has become nowadays a matter of the modern cleric—the intellectual.

The *ideational* dimension that has always characterized antisemitism is in fact one of its more important distinctive traits. It has been advocated by those whose occupation is language and ideas, namely intellectuals; and it has been shared by intellectuals on both the Left and the Right. Indeed, antisemitism is and always has been an attitude shared by many people whose hearts are generally assumed to be in the right place, that is, on the "Left" (taken here in a general, hence necessarily anachronistic, typological sense). Some of the best and the brightest—sophisticated, intelligent, refined, and morally accomplished members of Western societies and European nations—some of the most illustrious representatives of European culture (among them, of course, Jews) have been antisemites. They have not necessarily hated Jews (at least not in the simpler, affective way of hating), or advocated (let alone exercised) violence against Jews, or wished to harm them in physical, psychological, or other ways. They have never dreamt of their extermination. Nevertheless, they have been *against* Jews (or Judaism, Jewish culture, Jewish mentality, Jewish modes of life and habits, etc.). They have been literally *anti*-Jewish. St. Paul (in an ambiguous way), numerous church fathers, Shakespeare, Voltaire, Dickens, Dostoyevsky, Pascal, Marx, Kant, the young Hegel, or Wittgenstein (just to mention these few names) were all, sometimes very, eloquently anti-Jewish. Some of them had more reactionary leanings, others more progressive and revolutionary ones, but all shared a strong anti-Jewish animus. The Jew might represent the alien, the unassimilable element in the "nation"; money and the banks; the Bolshevik; the cosmopolite; the nationalist; the colonialist; and so on—but whatever the specific cause, for all of them the Jew incarnated and symbolized what they were theologically, philosophically, politically, morally, against. Such people might be intellectually and often morally irreproachable, but the fact that they said or wrote what they did about Jews shows that antisemitism is *not* just another form of primitive and irrational hatred, that it is irreducible to its more conspicuous manifestations of violence and savagery, that it is part of high culture.

So what could it mean for all these people (and for many others as well) to be *anti*-Jewish? Of what exactly have they been *anti*-? Against precisely what did they set out to write or speak? What exactly does it mean to be *against* the Jews or against Judaism? It means that they—the non-violent, the intellectual, or, so to speak, theoretical antisemites—rejected what they took Judaism to be all about. *Rejection*, it should be emphasized, has to be understood here not as a *psychological* attitude, but as a theoretical, or pseudotheoretical, one. All the same, it is *ideational* and expressible in meaningful language, at least on the surface. Judaism has in fact been rejected in this sense on the basis of theological and religious motives. In a serious way and by serious and often intelligent and honest people, it has been conceived as a wrong and blasphemous or sacrilegious religious belief, as a stubborn refusal to accept the true word of God, to acknowledge the true messiah, or to join the new Covenant; as a stubborn adherence to an outdated, legalistic interpretation of the Divine Law, and so on. Jews have also been rejected on the basis of pseudo-scientific theories as a non-European, carnal, and materialistic culture or as an alien "race," and also because of their allegedly stubborn refusal to give up their particularism and join the march of humanity toward progress and universalism. And today there are new forms of rejection: Jews are rejected because of their real or imaginary support of, or identification with, Israel. Zionism is rejected as an anachronistic nationalism, outmoded in a post-nationalistic, cosmopolitan world. And Israel is rejected for diverse reasons as unfit for membership in the international community of nations, as occupying Palestinian land in defiance of international law, as systematically not respecting human rights.

The question is whether all of this could in the past and can in the present justify the kind of *rejection* antisemitism demands. There are many forms of *rejection*: an organism may reject a substance or a transplanted organ; someone may reject a job offer; or a group may reject a newcomer. To reject, as the *Concise Oxford Dictionary* says, is to "dismiss as inadequate or faulty; refuse to consider or agree to." What is typically dismissed in this way, as being inadequate, faulty, or flawed, are opinions, propositions, theories, arguments, claims, or possible solutions to a problem. In short, what is dismissed or rejected is whatever belongs to the realm of *the ideational,* or whatever appears in the form of *ideas,* of what has *meaning.*

At particular times in history, Jews have been rejected as aliens, as *others,* and in various ways that invite using the biological/medical metaphor of *rejection.* Many antisemites have taken recourse to just these metaphors. Jewishness or Judaism has been rejected, however, or been purported to be rejected, as some unacceptable kind of *idea* or as an *essence.* Ideas and essences belong to the realm of the ideational. Essentialism has become a questionable position in recent times, and rightly so; but even if we allow that there is an *essence* of the Jewish phenomenon, and that it is possible to capture it in a concept, the notion that it can be *rejected* as an opinion is rejected, that one can argue for and against it, as if it were a discussible theoretical possibility, is an aberration and also a moral scandal. If there is an essence of Judaism that is representable by a concept, that concept is one of a comprehensive mode of human existence. To consider rejecting such a thing is a *category mistake* (to employ a philosophical notion in use until not very long ago). One does not "reject" a concrete mode of life, a historical reality, a collective existence; what presents itself as "rejection" cannot be, in such a case, anything but a wish to annihilate. And annihilation is a moral evil.

There is a basic and paradigmatic equivocation here, an equivocation that can perhaps be used to advance our search for a phenomenological understanding of antisemitism. Most forms of antisemitism thrive on this equivocation, in which hatred assumes a form which it cannot have, that of an opinion, a theory, an argument (recall the allusion to Sartre made before); and opinion, theory, or argument become something which they should never be, namely hatred. Thus, an obscene dialectic is born, an unnatural coupling between thinking and feeling, between reason and the irrational. Instead, however, of controlling each other (as rationalist philosophers since Plato and the Stoics have always thought about the relationship that should hold between the "upper" and "lower" faculties of the human mind or soul), they enflame and strengthen each other. Hatred usually is not a metaphysical negation of the right to exist; even killing is not a negation of this kind—unless, that is, metaphysics licenses and justifies it or purports to make sense of it. Hatred makes reason a passion; reason confers respectability upon hate. By casting thought into affectivity, antisemitism has too often been just that—a respectable abomination.

V

To conclude this first step toward a phenomenology of antisemitism, I shall come back to the delegitimation of Israel and to the question of whether anti-Zionism and anti-Israelism are or are not forms of antisemitism. During its long life, the particular kind of affective *cum* intellectual rejection which, according to my argument, constitutes an important and distinctive feature of antisemitism has assumed different forms and has been variously articulated. Anti-Judaism changes as the *Zeitgeist* changes: Judaism has been rejected by some on theological grounds, by others on nationalist and cultural grounds, at certain times even on scientific grounds. The current intellectual *Zeitgeist* is heavily marked by concepts, forms of thought, norms of argumentation, and rhetoric taken from legal and legal-moral discourses. Although not exclusively on one side of the ideological divides, these forms of discourse are especially apparent in schools or traditions of thought that are commonly referred to as "liberal." In the post-Second World War period, the Western intelligentsia in particular has become deeply suspicious of the nation-state and of the idea of the State in general. Ethical and legal concepts have often replaced or intermingled with more political and historical concepts as the basic theoretical and ideological tools for understanding and judging social reality. It is here that the concept of *legitimacy* acquires special importance, and it is also here where there appears the idea that "entities" like the State of Israel can be said to be *illegitimate*. The notion of *delegitimation* seems to be directly derivable from the fundamental concepts of the legal-moral theory of the State. This, however, is not altogether the case. As noted, the notion of *delegitimation* has only lately become omnipresent. Not an issue, at least on the Israeli public scene, until just a few years ago, it is now widely acknowledged as a major concern—a strategic one, as is often said nowadays—and even a threat. But the notion of *delegitimation* is rather ambiguous, similar in its ambiguity to the ambiguity and equivocation that accompanies the notion of *rejection*. It is in fact doubly ambiguous, and it is precisely this ambiguity that makes it so useful and effective in the ideological struggle against Zionism and Israel and also links it to older forms of antisemitism.

It is, in fact, not always clear if delegitimizing Israel means that Israel is already an *illegitimate* state (or "entity," as it is sometimes called precisely with the intent of delegitimizing it) or if delegitimizing it is the attempt to render it illegitimate in the eyes of, say, world public opinion. What remains even vaguer is what might be the consequences—theoretical, moral, and political—of denying the legitimacy of either Zionism or the State of Israel or both. One way or another, it is quite often explicitly said that Israel, as a Jewish state, is illegitimate both as an idea and as a reality. Although it is not always easy to decipher the exact intention of the so-called "critics" of Israel, it is clear that on many occasions what is implied in the critical discourse is that Israel either never has been "legitimate" or that it has lost its legitimacy by its allegedly criminal behavior.

It is important to note that the conceptual cluster comprised of *legitimate, illegitimate, legitimacy, illegitimacy,* and, in particular, *legitimating, legitimation,* and *delegitimation,* is very ambiguous from a strictly theoretical point of view. One element of the ambiguity of the concept of *delegitimation* is well known. Max Weber famously saw the legitimacy of dominion or authority as a special kind of motivating power that drives members of an organized group to willingly obey the commands of its leader or leaders.[10] What distinguishes legitimacy-based obedience from other kinds of obedience is that it is based on a *belief* in some non-naturalistic reasons for obedience (e.g., legal or altruistic), while the latter kinds are more calculative (self-interest, coercion, etc.).

Weber distinguished between three main kinds of legitimation or legitimacy-conferring attitudes, but for the sake of brevity and simplicity I shall focus on just two: *non-normative* and *normative*. The first comprises legitimating authority on the basis of tradition and history, on the one hand, and, on the other, on the special property of certain kinds of rulers and governors, which Weber famously called *charisma*. Normative, or objective, legitimacy is a property believed to be possessed by a regime insofar as it rules and is established according to certain objectively binding norms, either legal or political (freely elected, representing the electing citizens, etc.).

A first element of ambiguity is already apparent here: Being essentially a matter of *belief*, how can legitimacy also be *objective* and, hence, *universally binding*?[11] In the context of the debates about Israel it often seems, indeed, that what is at stake is mainly the subjective willingness, in some rather vague sense—of public opinion, of the intelligentsia, of the so-called international community—to consider Israel as such, or the conduct of its successive governments, as "acceptable." This vagueness is implicitly supposed to be dissipated by the even vaguer feeling that there is some "objective" set of norms that are the ground of the acceptability or unacceptability of Israel, but this normativity is rarely spelled out.

The truth is that when attempts are made to spell out the norms or principles on which Israel is accorded or denied legitimacy, things become even hazier. As is clear from Weber's theory, and in fact from all the classical philosophers and political theorists who have developed the modern theory of sovereignty and legitimacy of political authority (Bodin, Hobbes, Rousseau, Locke, and others), this property of leadership that we call *its legitimacy* is a relational property and, more importantly, it necessarily exists in the space delineated by the agents of (political) power and its subjects. Legitimacy is accorded (or denied) by those who are subjects to authority, regime, ruler or rulers, institutions, and the like. Whether subjective or objective, legitimacy concerns the ruling prerogative of the ruler and the grounds of obedience by which the ruled, or the subjects of the exercise of power, accept an obligation to obey.

The question of the sources of legitimacy of regimes is more or less equivalent to the question of the sources of the obligation to obey commands given by a ruler, a government, a regime, or the State as such. It is, in other words, the fundamental question of the justification of the State, which, especially in modern times, is answered through the idea of the social pact: the legitimacy of political power is said to depend on a mutual agreement and a kind of legal engagement to respect the initial agreement entered into by all members of the political commonwealth. But what is justified in this way is a general idea of the State, or of the fundamental, unavoidable, and, hence, justifiable need to give common human existence the form of a *polity*. In no simple way can this be turned into a principle on which the legitimacy of particular states is affirmed or denied as states.

To the extent that the concept of the social contract informs the idea of legitimacy as a political-legal theory, it is applicable to the theoretical space existing between the state as an institutionalized use of power (political power—what the classical theory of the state called *potestas*) and the citizen as a subject. In this sense the idea that one can as much as question, on legal terms, or in terms of the theory of political legitimacy, the legitimacy of a state as a State, is highly problematic. It is as problematic as the idea that it is possible to imagine a commonwealth of states concluding a "social pact" in a similar way and on the same grounds that we imagine a group of individual men and women agreeing to form a binding contract. It simply does not work on the interstate level. It does not work because the "social pact" theories were born in a state in which the concept of *sovereignty* could be reasonably both conceived and applied, which is not the case—has never been the case in the past and still is not the case today—in the international arena. Despite the great progress in institutionalizing international cooperation and jurisprudence, the "international community" is a "community" only in metaphorical sense and certainly does not constitute a *polity*.

We witness in recent times the appearance of what is sometimes called the "theory of Humanitarian Intervention." The idea behind this theoretical discussion is that sometimes the "international community," the

UN, coalitions of democratic nations, the United States, and so on, have the right, or perhaps the obligation, to transgress the sovereignty of certain states and use military power in order, for example, to protect threatened populations. As these lines are being written, the United Kingdom and France, with the active backing of the United States, were waging military operations in order to secure the safety of the Libyan civilian population. The ruler of this country, the infamous Colonel Muammar Qaddafi, it was said, has lost legitimacy.[12] It is unclear if and how he had possessed this legitimacy before, how or when he lost it later, what were the criteria according to which one could judge it, who could bestow it or take it away, or even what this legitimacy exactly means. What is quite clear is that the legitimacy of the Libyan state itself has not been questioned, even if its regime was.

One can question the legitimacy of a regime—in this instance the Qaddafi rule in Libya and previously the Apartheid regime in South Africa—precisely on the ground that it is has lost its legitimacy by not expressing anything that can be said to be "a general will." But this lost legitimacy is conditioned on the will and interests of the citizens or subjects and by their perception of the regime. Many people inside and outside South Africa aspired, or actively worked toward, the demise of the Apartheid regime; at no point, though, even during the darkest days of Apartheid, was there a question of the illegitimacy of the *state* of South Africa. The frequently heard comparison between Israel and South Africa on the basis of an alleged similarity between the latter's Apartheid regime and what is called "the Occupation" is questionable. It is so not only because there is not much similarity between the situation that had prevailed in South Africa and the situation in Israel, including Israel's possession of parts of the West Bank or the Golan Heights, but because the notion of legitimacy is used in Israel's case to negate something that the theory of legitimacy and legitimation cannot possibly negate or deny: the legitimacy of Israel as a state.

When the state whose legitimacy is being questioned is a democratic state, or a state that presumably is seen as legitimate by the majority of its citizens—as is Israel—its alleged illegitimacy is nonsensical. In such cases not only can the state as such not be said to be illegitimate, but also its regime cannot meaningfully be said to be illegitimate. Delegitimation of such states, as is apparently the case in the attempt to delegitimize Israel, targets neither a regime nor an abstract "state" but the whole body politic. In effect, what is at stake here is the legitimacy of the existence of the whole Jewish population living in the State of Israel. Even if this is not said explicitly, at least not by Western intellectuals, this is precisely the meaning of denying legitimacy to the Jewish State of Israel. The reason for this is as simple as it is true: this state is the expression of the innermost political wishes of the absolute majority—much above 90 percent—of the Jewish population living in Israel.

Since the Second World War and especially after the demise of the Soviet Union and the end of the Cold War, the theory of political legitimacy and of a few related matters have gone through important developments. Among these, the subject of international law is now at the center of innumerable debates, controversies, and discussions. One important outcome is the establishment of international tribunals charged with the task of judging war criminals of all kinds. The following point is important: it is mainly in the pursuit of individuals, or, at the most, of institutions or regimes that have allegedly committed or instigated crimes as defined by international law that a legal action is taken. It is never aimed directly at states as such. This is why legal action attempted against individual Israeli leaders—what has become known as "lawfare"—is mostly of a symbolic nature. This can be easily seen from the absolute lack of discrimination in these legal pursuits. It is enough that someone has occupied some kind of public office during, say, the Gaza military operation, that he or she cannot travel to the United Kingdom nowadays. Israeli parliamentarians Tzipi Livni or Dan Meridor are two notable examples. But it is not really either one of these two who is the target here; rather, they are made to symbolize the State of Israel as a criminal entity.

In line, however, with the current generalized suspicion of statehood as such, diverse attempts have been made to offer theoretical grounds that may allegedly allow for moral-legal judgment of states as such. One attempt to develop moral criteria that might enable distinctions to be drawn between states is that by John Rawls, one of the most important and influential American philosophers of the second half of the twentieth century. He addressed this question in two relatively late works, and although perhaps less convincing than the rest of his work, his reflections on the moral norms that have to hold in international relations attracted and still attract a great amount of academic attention.[13] Leaving aside his theory of law, or justice, among what he calls "peoples"—analogous to his "Theory of Justice" in the interhuman realm—he arrives at the end of his discussion at formulating a concept of "outlaw regimes." For Rawls, though, these states are "outlaw" mainly because they do not respect basic human rights, by which he means that the question of the moral character of states is to be judged primarily by what happens between the holder(s) of political power and the subjects.

Also notable are the appearance and use of the term *rogue state.* This term was coined during the 1990s by the American administration to characterize states that act in ways that jeopardize peace, are hostile to the United States, do not respect norms of international law, try to acquire weapons of mass destruction, and sponsor terrorism. The term was used in the context of conceiving appropriate national security strategies such as the deployment of ballistic missile defense systems or using other means to deter such states. According to *Wikipedia,* current states considered by the State Department to be rogue states include Cuba, North Korea, Iran, Sudan, Syria, and Libya. Although Israel does not figure on this list—which may need updating—it has become a permanent candidate for the title of rogue state. The Debate Club of Cambridge seriously considered the possibility that Israel is in fact a rogue state, and other respectable academics have no doubt that Israel should be seen in this light.[14]

Interestingly enough, some people—mostly from the entourage of Noam Chomsky, I believe—think that the United States is itself a rogue state. However, even these "critics" of America do not really envisage the country's demise. Nor do they call for "changing the foundations of its legitimacy," to quote a memorable phrase Judith Butler, the famous American philosopher, used in one of her writings on Israel. The logic of the use of terms such as *rogue* is the logic of dealing with criminal behavior. Usually this logic is not the logic of delegitimation. Since, according to social pact theories, the *individual* is the only source and condition of the legitimacy of a government, but also of the original emergence of a space—the political community—where the concept of *legitimacy* makes sense to begin with, the criminal or the delinquent, qua individual, is never *illegitimate* as such. He or she can breach the original pact and become an outlaw or even a public enemy; sometimes it is licit to kill him or her. But we shall never say that his or her existence is *illegitimate,* that there are grounds on which we can reasonably *reject* the entity of the criminal itself. Paradoxically as it may seem—and this is not the place to dwell on this—in a certain sense, even when a criminal is executed (which no longer happens in most Western societies) his basic or original right to exist is usually not questioned. The whole logic, for example, of legal execution is precisely this: the criminal has rights, which means that he is not an *illegitimate* entity. Neither the law, nor the judge, *hate* the convicted whom they send to the gallows. The antisemite, even when he or she hides by using theoretical language, as has been suggested above, *does* hate the Jew or the Zionist.

Rogue states may have to be restrained, called to order, or acted against in a variety of ways, even militarily. Their governments may be toppled. But no one thinks they should be dismantled, unless the citizens themselves want it. After the Second World War, Germany was divided—temporarily as it turned out—but even then no one questioned the "legitimacy" of the notion or principle of a German state.[15] What can be *illegitimate* in any coherent sense of the word is never the state as such, only its behavior or conduct. Many people oppose, for example, the occupation and annexation of Tibet by China. But no one is *against* China as such or calls for its demise, not only because China is too big and too powerful, but also because it does not make any sense to think about it, or any other existing state, in these terms. There is no *Chinaism* to add to the prefix *anti*. Being anti-China is simply meaningless, in the simplest and most literal sense of the word. The same should hold true for anti-Zionism or anti-Israelism, as it does for antisemitism as well.

One can imagine, say, a band of pirates who take over a piece of land somewhere, subjugate the local population by force and terror, and use their territory to sow fear on the seas. Even if we would take action against such a group, we would be acting against a band of common criminals and not against an illegitimate "state."[16] Just to take one example from the philosophical tradition: Hobbes thought that a legitimate government could emerge even if its leader or leaders initially acquired power criminally. Arguably, most states—most obviously those established in ex-colonial territories—have their historical roots in some criminal act. It does not mean that they have not later become fully legitimate states. The anti-Israeli discourse too often gives the impression that Israel is such a colony of pirates: it is declared guilty of dispossessing the Palestinians, robbing them of their land, houses, goods, identity, and culture, acting criminally—didn't we say "pirates"?—against ships bringing humanitarian aid to Gaza, and committing other such outrages.

But in Israel's case—arguably *only* in Israel's case—charges of criminalization often lead to the denial of the country's basic legitimacy in the sense of denying it its right to exist. To take Judith Butler again as an example, her proposal for a "change of the foundations of legitimacy"—and here Butler is echoing a broader, ongoing campaign of "criticism" of Israel—would, if executed, destabilize or destroy the very foundations on which the State of Israel exists, namely its being a Jewish state. What is denied here, without explicitly acknowledging it, is nothing less than the existence of the State of Israel as such, not its occupation of the West Bank or other allegedly unacceptable elements of its conduct.

The main problem here is the use—the displaced and misplaced, the explicit and implicit use—of the legal-political category of *legitimacy* in a context where it cannot make any real legal, political, or legal-political sense. Conceptually speaking, in itself what is called the *delegitimation* of Israel *does* not have and *cannot* have any positive content. The argument is incoherent if not simply self-contradictory, and anti-Zionism is nothing but an attempt to give sense to nonsense. This has always been the case with antisemitic arguments.

VI

If the kind of discourse that claims Israel to be "illegitimate" or, more vaguely, that aims at "delegitimizing" Israel, does not and cannot have the meaning it pretends to have, then it must have another meaning beneath the surface. And since, as I maintain, anti-Zionism, like antisemitism, is not less an intellectual phenomenon—and perhaps is more of one—than "mute hatred" and violence, we are indeed entitled to look at what hides behind the jargon, pseudo-theoretic language, *mauvaise foi,* hypocrisy, and, sometimes, just naiveté and ignorance. The intellectual, by definition, thinks, and if his or her discourse is not what it seems to be *prima facie,* it is bound to contain some thought all the same. If the delegitimation of Israel is nonsense on the surface, it does, of course, have a sense underneath it: not the legalo-political sense it pretends to possess, but what it implies semi-implicitly (when it is not said explicitly). And what it implies in this way is the old antisemitic potential license to kill.

Above, I formulated two main questions and one hypothesis: I asked first what is it that makes antisemitism the moral outrage it is. I then raised the question about whether anti-Zionism and anti-Israelism are or are not forms of antisemitism; and I advanced the hypotheses that if the answer to the second question is "yes," as I believe it is, then what unites these three "anti's" as one phenomenon, multifaceted as it is, is not so much the thematic elements, or narratives, they contain, but the moral substance of which they are made. I shall now add another hypothesis, which I am able only to formulate here, without further elaborating on it: Judeophobias have always been enterprises of delegitimation. Theologically, culturally, politically, biologically, and now legally, the Jew has always been seen as an incarnation of the "illegitimate." In the last analysis, this is of what the moral substance of the rejection of the Jew, and now of the Zionist, consists.

Outside the legal-political context to which it rightly belongs, the meaning of denying legitimacy to something is denying its right to exist. In the case of the self-contradictory denial of the "legitimacy" of the political incarnation of the Jew or of Jewishness—the "Jewish State" or Israel— such denial is, as I have just said, and as antisemitism has always been, a license to kill. It joins "killing" to "license" in two ways, according to the two senses of "license": the purportedly legal killing; the potential unleashing of violence and of barbarous criminality. I tried to show that the concept of *legitimacy* and its derivatives do not and cannot have any intelligible meaning in the context of discourses such as the anti-Zionist and anti-Israeli discourse. Saying of something that it is *illegitimate,* if meant seriously and with all the weight of the words, implies that the law would not have allowed its original coming into existence and now commends its demise. If there is any truth in these suggestions, then the only possible meaning the so-called delegitimation of Israel can have is that the law (or some fanciful idea of law or of legality) not only forbids the existence of the "Jewish State" but also actually and positively commands its annihilation. In its long history, Judeophobia has more than once meant just that: it is not forbidden, and it is even required, to kill the Jews. It is more than probable that a dejudaization of Israel will not be possible without a serious bloodbath and may very well require the killing of many Jews and Israelis.[17] Hopelessly mixing, in the traditional antisemitic way—which, as I have suggested above, is what is particular about it—the affective and the ideational, the delegitimizing discourse does nothing but give false intellectual respect to what is wholly disreputable and shameful.

NOTES

1. I wish to thank Bernard Harrison, Ido Landau, Yoash Meisler, Alvin Rosenfeld, Sidney Rosenfeld, Daniella Yakira, and Alex Yakobson for reading earlier versions of this article and generously offering comments and suggestions on how to improve it.

2. *Antisemitism, anti-Zionism, anti-Israel,* and *post-Zionism* are notoriously ambiguous and hard-to-define terms. In what follows, I call anti-Zionism or anti-Israelism such attitudes or positions that either proclaim Zionism, or the idea and practice of establishing a Jewish polity in the Land of Israel, as immoral or illegitimate; or depict Israel's policies as essentially and profoundly immoral or criminal; or both.

3. See his *La nouvelle judeophobie* (Paris: Mille et une Nuits, 2002) (*Rising from the Muck: The New Anti-Semitism in Europe,* translated by P. Camiller [Chicago: Ivan R. Dee, 2004]); *La nouvelle propagande anti-juive* (Paris: Presses Universitaires de France, 2010).

4. A particularly important example is Robert Wistrich's *A Lethal Obsession: Anti-Semitism from Antiquity to the Global Jihad* (New York: Random House, 2010).

5. Wikipedia, for example, says that "Antisemitism . . . is prejudice against or hostility towards Jews, often rooted in hatred of their ethnic background, culture, and/or religion. In its extreme form, it 'attributes to the Jews an exceptional position among all other civilizations, defames them as an inferior group and denies their being part of the nation[s]' in which they reside." The commonly accepted definition of antisemitism is nowadays the one proposed in 2005 by the European Monitoring Centre on Racism and Xenophobia (now the Fundamental Rights Agency), then an agency of the European Union. According to this definition, "antisemitism is a certain perception of Jews, which may be expressed as hatred toward Jews. Rhetorical and physical manifestations of antisemitism are directed toward Jewish or non-Jewish individuals and/or their property, toward Jewish community institutions and religious facilities. In addition, such manifestations could also target the state of Israel, conceived as a Jewish collectivity. Antisemitism frequently charges Jews with conspiring to harm humanity, and it is often used to blame Jews for 'why things go wrong'. . . . contemporary examples of antisemitism in public life, the media, schools, the workplace, and in the religious sphere [include] making mendacious, dehumanizing, demonizing, or stereotypical allegations about Jews; accusing Jews as a people of being responsible for real or imagined wrongdoing committed by a single Jewish person or group; denying the Holocaust; and accusing Jewish citizens of being more loyal to Israel, or to the alleged priorities of Jews worldwide, than to the interests of their own nations. . . . Denying the Jewish people the right to self-determination, e.g. by claiming that the existence of a state of Israel is a racist endeavor; applying double standards by requiring of Israel a

behavior not expected or demanded of any other democratic nation; using the symbols and images associated with classic anti-Semitism (e.g., claims of Jews killing Jesus or blood libel) to characterize Israel or Israelis; drawing comparisons of contemporary Israeli policy to that of the Nazis; holding Jews collectively responsible for actions of the State of Israel" are also defined here as antisemitic.

6. Or even, sometimes, when they choose to forsake their Jewishness and not to live it in whatever form. I thank Ido Landau for this remark.

7. South African judge Richard Goldstone headed the United Nations Fact Finding Mission on the Gaza Conflict of the UN Human Rights Council, which accused Israel of committing war crimes and potentially crimes against humanity during the December 2008 Gaza operation. In an article in the *Washington Post* (April 2011), Judge Goldstone claimed that had he known before what he knew now, his report's conclusion would have been different.

8. That antisemitism is not just another form of racism is forcefully argued by Bernard Harrison in his chapter in this book. I had the privilege of reading it while working on my own chapter. He makes a very important point, and I permit myself to repeat it here. There are good reasons to argue that antisemitism is not simply one form among others of xenophobia, racism, or the like of them but—in many ways—is a sui generis phenomenon.

9. I borrow this idiom from Jean-Claude Milner, *Les penchants criminels de l'Europe démocratique*(Paris: Verdier, 2003).

10. See, in particular, Max Weber, *Economy and Society: An Outline of Interpretive Sociology* (Berkeley and Los Angeles: University of California Press, 1978), Ch. 3, "The Types of Legitimate Domination."

11. A typical example of this ambiguity, if not confusion, is taken from the preface of a recent book: "In the success of stability operations [conducted by the Western states in the post-Cold War world], legitimacy is the key. In order to achieve success, the intervening forces *must create a sense of legitimacy* of the mission among the various constituencies concerned . . . ," italics added; Chiyuki Aoi, *Legitimacy and the Use of Armed Forces: Stability in the Post-Cold War Era* (London and New York: Routledge, 2011), p. 1.

12. A joint communiqué by the leaders of the G-8 countries, issued in May 2011, states that Qaddafi and his government "have failed to fulfill their responsibility to protect the Libyan population and have lost all legitimacy." Cited in Christopher Ford, "Law, Legitimacy and Libya: Tyranny and Customary Law," at http://www.newparadigmsforum .com. Ford also cites here from the Montevideo Convention on the Rights and Duties of States, signed in 1933, and which he describes as the "classic formulation of international standards for the existence of states. . . . Article 1 of that treaty provides that a state, as an object of international law, should possess four qualifications: '(a) a permanent population; (b) a defined territory; (c) government; and (d) capacity to enter into relations with the other states.'"

13. See J. Rawls, "The Law of Peoples," in Stephen Shute and Susan Hurley, eds., *On Human Rights* (New York: Basic Books, 1993), pp. 41–82; J. Rawls, *The Law of Peoples* (Cambridge, Mass.: Harvard University Press, 1999).

14. The debate at Cambridge, not a particularly important event, gained some notoriety after one of the debaters in the "for" team presented a quite amusing caricature of the attempt to picture Israel as a rogue state. If I am not mistaken, he was forbidden by the club to participate in future debates, maybe as he was considered to be rogue, too. One can read his text online in http://www.jpost.com/Opinion/Op-EdContributors/Article.aspx?id=195602. A different opinion can be found in a blog of Stephen Law, a British philosopher. On January 7, 2009, he wrote: ". . . I have to say I have a great deal of sympathy with [an article published in the *Guardian* by] Avi Shlaim—a Professor of International Relations at Oxford—and a former member of the Israeli military, [who] concludes: 'This brief review of Israel's record over the past four decades makes it difficult to resist the conclusion that it has become a rogue state with an utterly unscrupulous set of leaders.' A rogue state habitually violates international law, possesses weapons of mass destruction and practices terrorism—the use of violence against civilians for political purposes. Israel fulfils all of these three criteria; the cap fits and it must wear it. Israel's real aim is not peaceful coexistence with its Palestinian neighbors but military domination."

15. A remark made by Alex Yakobson, a connoisseur of the Soviet Union: "as Stalin famously said, 'Hitlers come and go, but the German people, the German state remains'; what comrade Stalin conceded to Germany during the Great Patriotic War, the anti-Zionists don't concede to Israel. So while they compare Israel to Nazi Germany, the truth is they treat it worse than Nazi Germany."

16. The distinction between *legality* and *legitimacy* is the subject of a well-known book by Carl Schmitt, *Legalität und Legitimität,* originally published in 1932 (*Legality and Legitimacy,* translated by Jeffrey Seitzer (Durham, N.C.: Duke University Press, 2004). Despite the very questionable nature of both the man and his work, in this book, too, the question of *legitimacy,* discussed in relation to the constitution of the Weimar Republic, is conceived solely as a matter of the relations between political power and institutions and citizens.

17. I think here of works such as Norman Cohn's *Warrant for Genocide: The Myth of the Jewish World Conspiracy* and *The Protocols of the Elders of Zion* (London: Eyre & Spottiswoode, 1967). The Hebrew translation bears as title הכשר לרצח עם, which means literally license to murder (a people). More comprehensive history from a similar perspective can be found in the older works of Jules Isaac, notably his *Jésus et Israël.* Hannah Arendt said something similar to this in her book on the Eichmann trial. But she meant it to be one more argument on behalf of her theory of "the banality of Evil." My very deep reservations about her treatment of Eichmann, of his trial and of antisemitism in general as well as—from a philosophical point of view—about her "banality of Evil," are spelled out in my *Post-Zionism, Post-Holocaust* (New York and Cambridge: Cambridge University Press, 2009); I shall not get into it here.

3 Manifestations of Antisemitism in British Intellectual and Cultural Life

Paul Bogdanor

BRITISH ANTISEMITISM has a long and depressing history. The first re-corded blood libel occurred in England in 1144. A Christian document testified thus: "The Jews of Norwich brought a child before Easter, and tortured him with all the tortures wherewith our Lord was tortured, and on Long Friday hanged him on a rod in hatred of our Lord, and after-wards buried him."[1] It was an English poet, Geoffrey Chaucer, who pre-served the calumny for all time in his *Canterbury Tales*.[2] One of the first pogroms took place in York in 1190. A century later came the first total expulsion of a Jewish population from a European country; Jews were not readmitted to England until 1656, after a nearly four-hundred-year ab-sence. In England the tradition of literary antisemitism was inaugurated, and it includes some of the greatest classics of English literature: from the usurious Shylock in *The Merchant of Venice* to the villainous Fagin in *Oliver Twist*, stereotypes of Jewish power and cruelty (Shylock's "pound of flesh") have merged seamlessly with contempt for Jewish claims of vic-timhood ("If you prick me, do I not bleed?") and a scarcely hidden de-sire for the Jew's humiliation (Shylock forfeits his wealth and converts to Christianity).[3]

In spite of hopes and expectations that such prejudices would disap-pear over time, it is clear that they have deep cultural and psychological roots and that British Jews are now experiencing another outbreak.[4] This is not to suggest that there is an unbroken line of continuity from the first blood libel in medieval England to the latest blood libel on the London stage. Just as the composition of the country's population has changed over the centuries, so too has the prevalence and nature of anti-Jewish prejudice. Whereas antisemitism was as likely to be found among the general public as among the ruling elite as recently as a few generations ago,[5] today it is expressed primarily by members of the intellectual and cultural establishment (whether or not they see themselves as such). Whereas anti-Jewish prejudice used to be far more common among the denizens of the traditionalist right (although it was never exclusive to them),[6] today it is more likely to be espoused by the proponents of politically correct leftism (although, again, it is by no means exclusive to them). And it is a commonplace that whereas British antisemites once cried "send the Jews back to Palestine," the pretext for their outbursts nowadays is often the fact that the Jews *have* returned to Palestine.

One straightforward measure of the prevalence of antisemitism is the level of hate crimes against British Jews, diligently monitored by the Community Security Trust. Its reports show that, since records began in 1984, antisemitic incidents reached their highest levels in 2009 (926) and 2010 (639).[7] A second relevant test is the opinion polls. From these we learn that in 2004, nearly one in seven Britons considered the Holocaust exaggerated, and nearly one in five thought that a Jew would be less acceptable than a non-Jew as prime minister.[8] Five years later, more than one in seven held Jews in the financial sector somewhat culpable for the global financial crisis, and almost one in five blamed Jews for the death of Jesus.[9] The results in other European countries were even more disturbing, but what such quantitative measures do not reveal is the role of British antisemites in initiating antisemitic or potentially antisemitic campaigns that later spread overseas. Furthermore, quantitative measures cannot tell us to what extent antisemitism is *tolerated* by the wider society. It is the conjunction of antisemitic episodes and the ever-increasing tolerance for them that will be investigated in what follows.

We can enumerate several stages in the relationship between antisemitism and the wider democratic society. In the best-case scenario, antisemitic outbursts are rare, and each episode is instantly and forcefully rejected by the government and the media. In the second stage, antisemitism begins to spread, but is still widely condemned. In the third stage, antisemitism spreads and is widely tolerated, despite pious denunciations. Finally, antisemitism continues to escalate; it is generally tolerated; and there is no longer any serious pretence of condemnation. This paper contends that over the past decade, British society has moved from the second to the third stage. It considers four qualitative measures of this tendency:

1. "Israel Derangement Syndrome"
2. Stereotypes of Jewish power
3. Tolerance of, and excuses for, alleged antisemites
4. Distortion of the Holocaust.

"Israel Derangement Syndrome"

The first issue that must be examined is not in itself a form of antisemitism, but it tends to create a hospitable *climate* for antisemitism in Britain, at least in intellectual and media circles. This is the phenomenon that has been labeled "Israel Derangement Syndrome":[10] a visceral hatred of the Jewish state, wholly disproportionate to its actions (right or wrong) and to its role in world affairs (large or small). The symptoms of this condition are hysterical reactions whenever the Jewish state is in the news headlines; receptivity to the most obvious and grotesque falsehoods about its conduct; boycotts of Jewish academics and institutions in Israel; and tolerance, even support, for antisemitic demagogues and terrorists whose targets are Jews in Israel.

Although difficult to quantify, it is an easily observable fact that whenever any event involving Israel is in the news headlines, a sort of hysteria tends to erupt in the intellectual and media elite. When other nations are strongly criticized, hysteria tends to focus on individuals (e.g., George W. Bush); when Israel's actions are in question, it is the whole *nation* that seems to be on trial. It is well known that the attention lavished on Israel far exceeds the publicity accorded to the world's worst tyrannies (such as North Korea and Syria). The intense emotional commitment involved— and how easily it shades into bigotry—is illustrated by three images that appeared in British newspapers at times of particular controversy. (1) The day before the 2003 Israeli general election, which Ariel Sharon was expected to win, *The Independent* published a cartoon depicting Sharon not kissing an Israeli baby but *eating* a Palestinian baby, as a megaphone from an overhead helicopter gunship blared "Vote Sharon, Vote Sharon."[11] Inspired by Goya's painting of *Saturn Devouring His Children,* the image inspired protests—rejected by the Press Complaints Commission—that it was redolent of the blood libel. In spite of these protests (or because of them?) the cartoonist Dave Brown won the country's Political Cartoon of the Year award.[12] (2) Another such cartoon appeared on the op-ed pages of *The Guardian* during the 2006 Israel–Hizbullah war. At the center of the image is a gloved fist with an arm covered in hideous boils. The fist is brutally striking the face of a child. Blood pours from the child's face, which is being mutilated by six metallic Stars of David on the fist.[13] This certainly reflects the frenzied reaction that Israel's conduct in that war provoked in sections of the British media. But the theme of the Jew mutilating and drawing blood from a child is, again, uncannily reminiscent of the blood libel. And why is the State of Israel represented by *six* Stars of David (not five, not seven), if not to make a point about the Holocaust? (3) A third image appeared in *The Guardian* during the controversy over the so-called "Palestine Papers" (leaked documents recording alleged Palestinian concessions to Israel) at the beginning of 2011. Mahmoud Abbas, the Palestinian leader, is portrayed as a stereotypical Orthodox West Bank settler, with *kippah, peyot* and *tzitzit,* and carrying a machine-gun; to drive the point home, the Israeli flag, with Star of David, is emblazoned on his clothing.[14] Of special interest is the fact that the image was drawn by Carlos Latuff, a Brazilian cartoonist notorious for his antisemitic drawings, and a prize-winning entrant in Iran's state competition for cartoons denigrating the Holocaust. Why did Britain's premier left-wing newspaper see fit to publish this—or any—material by such a notorious antisemite and panderer to Holocaust denial?

No less disturbing than these repeated lapses in standards of decency—and here the question of (unconscious?) prejudice arises again—is that not only Israeli Jews, but Diaspora Jews, are held accountable for Israel's conduct. The most egregious example of this tendency—apart from the antisemitic assaults and synagogue vandalism that often coincide with British media hate campaigns against Israel—was an article by veteran British journalist Max Hastings, former editor of the *Daily Telegraph* and the London *Evening Standard,* which appeared in *The Guardian.* After the ritual denunciations of the revival of antisemitism in Europe, Hastings turned to instructing British Jews on how best to combat it. He lamented that several newspaper proprietors were "fervent Zionists" and disdained the "ferocity" of Israel's Jewish supporters. These Jews, he added, want to allow their state "a special quota of excesses, in compensation for past sufferings." Hastings referred to the "ruthless exploitation of the Holocaust card" and "moral blackmail." And he concluded with this observation:

> If Israel persists with its current policies, and Jewish lobbies around the world continue to express solidarity with repression of the Palestinians, then genuine anti-semitism is bound to increase. . . . No one can ever criticise the Jewish diaspora for asserting Israel's right to exist. But the most important service the world's Jews can render to Israel today is to persuade its people that the only plausible result of their government's behaviour is a terrible loneliness in the world.[15]

As Stephen Byers MP, chairman of the Parliamentary Committee Against Antisemitism, replied in the same newspaper, asking Jews to take a "morality oath" as a precondition for non-Jewish solidarity in the fight against prejudice "undermines the very foundations of freedom on which our society stands. Yet present-day anti-semites demand precisely that of Jews."[16] Hastings had been given space to demand something quite similar of Britain's Jews on the opinion page of a major British newspaper.

More ambiguous than the examples above are the repeated instances of British public figures (politicians as well as journalists) retailing the most bizarre and delusional allegations against Israelis—allegations that they would surely hesitate to level against any other target. Was it prejudice or mere paranoia that led Clare Short, a former Labour government minister, to allege that Israel "undermines the international community's reaction to global warming," which may well "end the human race"?[17] Was it prejudice or mere paranoia that led Baroness Jenny Tonge, a former Liberal Democrat MP now elevated to the House of Lords, to call for an investigation of charges that the Israeli rescue team was harvesting organs from victims of the earthquake in Haiti—provoking one colleague to comment that on such a basis, there should be calls for an investigation to clear the Jews of guilt for their imagined adherence to *The Protocols of the Elders of Zion*?[18] Was it prejudice or mere paranoia that prompted author and newspaper columnist A. N. Wilson to accuse Israel of "poisoning of water supplies" in West Bank (i.e., Jews poisoning wells) or to cite, in another column, the neo-Nazi Holocaust denier Michael A. Hoffman II as a credible source on Israel's wickedness?[19] And what are we to make of the former BBC journalist Alan Hart, a biographer of Yasser Arafat, who has taken the trouble to pen a three-volume work entitled *Zionism: The*

Real Enemy of the Jews, and who argued, in a public meeting I attended, that Zionism is driving the whole world to "Armageddon" and that Jews should beware of provoking "Holocaust II"?[20]

Illustrative of this hysterical and fantasy-laden attitude to the Jewish state, and its implications for British attitudes toward Israeli and British Jews, are the repeated campaigns to isolate, demonize, and humiliate collectives of Jews for their real or alleged associations with Israel. During the 1970s and 1980s this took the form of an effort—sometimes successful—to ban Jewish student groups on the basis that they were Zionist, and therefore racist and fascist.[21] More recently, the international campaign to boycott Israeli academics commenced in Britain, where it was initiated by Marxist activists on campus. Another British creation is the Boycott/Divestment/Sanctions (BDS) movement, which has achieved its greatest victories among British trade unionists.[22] The academic boycott campaign, waged under the aegis of the University and College Union (UCU), continues to resurface in spite of legal advice that it breaches anti-discrimination laws.[23] It has featured a speech by a union presidential candidate in front of a projected reading list that included material by a French Holocaust denier;[24] the distribution of material by the American neo-Nazi David Duke;[25] the circulation of a head count of Jewish MPs;[26] the claim that boycott opponents are financed by people with "bank balances from Lehman Brothers";[27] and a formal invitation to a South African accused of hate speech against Jews.[28] It is telling that the UCU has debated a motion opposing the European Union Monitoring Centre's working definition of antisemitism;[29] that a government minister has called for the UCU itself to be investigated for tolerating antisemitism;[30] and that the union is currently facing legal action for creating a climate of institutionalized bigotry—a climate that has driven some of its Jewish members to resign.[31] Such incidents are not confined to the universities; a local government council in Scotland recently announced a boycott of books by Israeli authors, even as its libraries continued to stock literature such as *Mein Kampf* and *The Protocols of the Elders of Zion.*[32]

One final aspect of the climate of tolerance for antisemitism created by Israel Derangement Syndrome should be considered. This is the willingness of its exponents, typically on the British Left and Far Left, to excuse antisemitic demagogues and terrorists. Occasional statements of sympathy for Palestinian suicide bombers—for instance by the politician

Jenny Tonge—have been attributed to an excess of anti-Israel zeal. The same might even be said of certain left-wing outfits—such as former Labour MP George Galloway's organization Viva Palestina—that systematically support the genocidal antisemites of Hamas; or the antiwar activists who have marched in London to the slogan "We are all Hezbollah."[33] But what is to be made of the orgy of apologetics that greeted the arrival in Britain and subsequent arrest of Raed Salah, an Islamist leader from Israel accused of repeating the blood libel? *The Guardian* in particular devoted article after editorial after article to defending Salah and discrediting his critics.[34] Such apologetics betray a cold indifference to the anti-Jewish fanaticism of Islamic extremists and to its dangers for Jews in Britain and elsewhere.

The inevitable conclusion is that anti-Israel hysteria, whatever its real motives, creates fertile ground for antisemitic incidents in the media, in the universities, and elsewhere; and that its ubiquity is creating a tolerance for antisemitic demagoguery that would have been unthinkable at the turn of the century.

The Fixation on Jewish Power

By the middle of the past decade, elite opinion in Britain had solidified around a new consensus on the subject of Israel and the Jews. Integral to this consensus was the proposition that almost all Islamist and Middle Eastern terrorism was provoked by Israeli policies; that American support was the main reason for the continuation of those policies; that this support was attributable to the power of "the Jewish lobby"; and that if not resolved, the Israel–Palestine conflict and the terrorism it inspired would threaten the peace and security of the world. From the conjunction of these propositions it is but a short step to the conclusion that the power of the American Jewish community threatens the peace and security of the world. From the casual assumption that American political life is controlled by Jews, to baseless allegations that British politicians and newspapers (but not, of course, the politicians and journalists making the allegations) are under Jewish or Zionist influence, the fixation on stereotypes of Jewish power has become a core element in British antisemitism and British tolerance for antisemitism.

Perhaps the most important point in the upward trajectory of this trend was the January 14, 2002 issue of the *New Statesman*, the country's main left-wing weekly magazine.[35] Although it has a long and check-ered history—ranging from apologetics for Stalin in the 1930s to support for Tony Blair's modernization of the Labour Party in the 1990s—and was even supportive of Israel in its early years, the periodical has always prided itself on its "anti-racist" principles. Readers glancing at the January 14th issue were therefore in for a shock. The illustration on that issue's front cover may be summarized in five points. (1) It is dominated by the image of a huge Star of David in gold, signifying Jewish money. (2) Beneath this is a British flag, implying British submission to Jewish power. (3) The base point of the Star of David seems to pierce the red center of the flag, hinting that Jews are stabbing the heart of the nation. (4) The Star of David casts a shadow, recalling the conspiracist stereotype of Jews as people who lurk in the shadows. (5) The headline below the image asks outright: "Is There a Kosher Conspiracy?"[36]

The cover story introduced by this image, written by Dennis Sewell, was entitled "A Kosher Conspiracy?" Purporting to be an investigation of the influence of the "Zionist lobby," it contains numerous antisemitic references. These are as follows: (1) The author begins by describing an Auschwitz survivor as being in his "plutocratic prime," invoking the stereotype of the rich and powerful Jew. (2) He then recounts the survivor's career as an arms manufacturer with customers as far afield as America and Malaysia, thus hinting at Jewish world-domination. (3) Subsequently, the reader is told, this same survivor diversified his business interests "if not into ploughshares exactly, then at least into saucepans"—an obvious reference to the elevated Christian message that the Jews rejected, so it appears, because they preferred their mundane business dealings. (4) It is then explained that the Auschwitz survivor and his son are "wired into the US national-security apparatus" and that they once employed neoconservative official Richard Perle. They are, in short, Jews pulling the wires of the world's most powerful nation. (5) The son is then described as "the Mr. Moneybags behind Bicom . . . the semi-public face of Britain's Zionist lobby." (6) The article next offers a summary of what it calls the "Left" position: "That there is a Zionist lobby and that it is rich, potent and effective goes largely unquestioned on the left. Big Jewry, like big tobacco, is seen as one of life's givens." The evidence for this thesis is then reviewed. For example, (7) Lord Weidenfeld, the respected publisher, "was and remains a serious operator at the level of government, editors and media proprietors . . . but his media interventions have always been discreet." Here is an appeal to the image of the Jewish conspirator operating in the shadows. (8) Consistent with this stereotype, the author notes that Britain's pro-Israel lobbyists prefer to hire non-Jews to put their case directly to the media. (9) When the author concludes, after careful consideration, that the Left's "unquestioned" belief in the power and unity of Big Jewry is exaggerated, he does so in these terms: "The only Jewish stereotype [that pro-Israel groups] reinforce is the one portrayed in Woody Allen films, where a dozen members of a family sit around the dinner table, all shouting different things at the same time." Even so, (10) Sewell cannot resist one last jibe, alluding to the Israeli embassy spokesman who is a "close textual analyst" of Hamas pronouncements, which conjures up in the reader's mind the image of a Talmud scholar.

In the space of a three-page cover story, Britain's major weekly magazine of "progressive" left-of-center opinion published no fewer than ten explicitly or implicitly antisemitic remarks. But this was just one article. The same issue carried the Far-Left journalist John Pilger's column excoriating the British Labour government for its supposed pro-Israel policies. The column was mostly standard radical leftist material, but Pilger also managed to insert a condemnation of one of Tony Blair's advisers: "Michael Levy, a wealthy Jewish businessman who had fundraised for new Labour."[37] Readers of that week's issue might have been forgiven for wondering: Has the *New Statesman* heard of even a single Jew in the country who is *not* a rich businessman and/or political lobbyist secretly manipulating Western governments on behalf of foreign Zionists?

That issue of the *New Statesman* provoked an immediate and indignant reaction. The letters pages of the following issue were almost wholly devoted to the matter, and in most of the correspondence the magazine was accused, explicitly or implicitly, of purveying antisemitism. Among the critics was the general secretary of the Labour Party, who did not mince words:

> Your front cover . . . showing a gold Star of David impaling a Union Jack and titled "A kosher conspiracy?" must be one of the most offensive images I have seen. It gathers together a symbol of Jewishness (not of Israel), conspiracy and wealth in ways candidly redolent of the extreme right. . . .

> The articles introduced by the cover (by Dennis Sewell and John Pilger)
> make matters worse. . . .
>   I have read—agreed and disagreed with—the *New Statesman* for 40 years.
> I never thought I would come to regard it as anti-Semitic. But I do today.

Other reactions were similar. One Cambridge academic thought that the cover illustration "was in the best traditions of *Der Stürmer,* as were the generalisations made about wealthy and powerful Jews."[38]

Two weeks later came another development: a partial apology by the magazine's editor, Peter Wilby. Explaining that he had been besieged with complaints by friends and colleagues, and that the magazine's offices had even been occupied by four disgruntled activists, he admitted that he had made a mistake and that "a few anti-Semites . . . took aid and comfort when it appeared that their prejudices were shared by a magazine of authority and standing." But this only related to the cover image. The "kosher conspiracy" lead article was, thought Wilby, "fair and balanced." As for Pilger's column, "it was not anti-Semitic," and its argument had to be taken seriously. Wilby did not miss the opportunity to point out that he had provoked far more protest by offending Jews than he had by publishing previous material insulting to Muslims. Jews, he explained, "have an advantage in making their case to me and to other newspaper editors." ("I am not suggesting that their influence in the media is disproportionate," he hastened to add.)[39]

The significance of the *New Statesman* incident is three-fold: first, the magazine published an issue that was riddled with antisemitic stereotyping and paranoia on its front cover, in its lead article, and in its most popular column; second, the fact occasioned considerable protest from its readers, including a highly placed figure in the governing party; and third, the editor quickly realized that a line had been crossed and published a partial retraction. This was in early 2002.

Fast forward to 2006. Two American foreign policy academics, Stephen Walt and John Mearsheimer, had been unable to find an outlet at home for their new essay blaming the "Israel Lobby" for their country's war in Iraq. They examined foreign media and alighted on the *London Review of Books,* a fashionable left-wing journal that models itself on the *New York Review of Books,* and whose contributors are known for their intense dislike of the Jewish state. Of all the foreign outlets Walt and Mearsheimer could have chosen, they opted for a British one. (Britain has a reputation for "libel tourism"—in which foreigners take advantage of the country's sympathetic courts to pursue their libel cases—and thanks to Walt and Mearsheimer and their imitators—to be discussed below—it deserves a reputation for what may be called "antisemitic-libel tourism.") Writing in the *London Review,* the pair expressed the certainty that they would be accused of antisemitism[40] (an accusation that is justified, as it now seems, certainly in the case of Mearsheimer).[41]

How did British society react to their long essay (subsequently expanded into a bestselling book)? Walt and Mearsheimer were acclaimed as courageous dissidents who had exposed the dirty secret of American (and global) politics: the control of the world's superpower by the Jewish lobby. Congratulatory press articles promptly followed, as did speaking invitations. And within two weeks of the original essay, *The Independent* printed a lengthy interview with the pair by its star Middle East correspondent, Robert Fisk. Accompanying the interview was a front-page photograph of the American flag, with the five-pointed stars replaced by six-pointed Stars of David, and a headline: "The United States of Israel?"[42] The image is a familiar one from Nazi propaganda.

In the space of four years, British public discourse had deteriorated from a situation in which the country's main left-wing weekly published a *Der Stürmer*-type image and felt compelled to apologize within weeks, to the point where the country's major liberal daily newspaper could publish a *Der Stürmer*-type image and evoke no response outside the Jewish community. Other incidents illustrate the same trend. Tam Dalyell, a senior Labour MP, was widely condemned in 2003—and threatened with disciplinary action by his own party—after alleging that the Iraq war had been promoted by "cabal of Jewish advisers" inside the British government.[43] In 2006, then-MP Jenny Tonge received similar treatment from *her* party after she told her fellow Liberal Democrats that "the pro-Israel lobby has got its grips on the Western world, its financial grips; I think they have probably got a certain grip on our party."[44] But just over a year later, a political donations scandal involving two Jewish businessmen occasioned this comment from another columnist at *The Independent*: "I have no wish to bring the wrath of Moses upon me and I can already hear the accusations of anti-Semitism. . . ." The same article characterized one of the two businessmen as "the strange shape-shifter at the heart of the fund-raising furore," evoking the image of the sinister and not-altogether-human Jewish manipulator.[45] There was no penalty. In 2009, a report in that newspaper on the resignation of an American diplomat began with the inauspicious words: "Fears over the Jewish lobby's excess influence on US foreign policy flared anew yesterday. . . ."[46] Again, there was no penalty. Later that year, a former British ambassador to Libya took to the pages of the same liberal newspaper to object to the presence of two Jewish academics on the panel appointed to investigate the decisions that led to the Iraq war; such an inquiry, according to Sir Oliver Miles, a veteran British diplomat, "should not only be balanced; it should be seen to be balanced," the implication being that no Jew could serve on such a panel without arousing suspicion.[47] During the 2010 election campaign, Martin Linton MP, chairman of Labour Friends of Palestine, announced before a meeting in the Houses of Parliament: "There are long tentacles of Israel in this country who are funding election campaigns and putting money into the British political system for their own ends."[48] And in 2011, left-wing firebrand Arthur Scargill's Socialist Labour Party observed on its website: "[I]t sounds like the Zionist leadership of the Labour Party are busily scratching each others' backs whilst ignoring the needs of the ordinary people of Britain."[49] There was almost no discernible reaction in the mainstream media to any of these remarks.

For the *ne plus ultra* of *Protocols*-type conspiracy theorizing in Britain, one must turn to a quasi-academic journal published by Routledge. The *Journal of Contemporary Asia* is a long-standing Marxist periodical. During the 1970s, its founder and editor, Malcolm Caldwell, a lecturer at the School of Oriental and African Studies in London, was one of the world's most notorious champions of the Pol Pot regime.[50] Today the journal still adheres to the Caldwell tradition of Marxism. Not atypical of its current output is an essay by James Petras, a North American radical veteran who evidently sought out this British journal, in another instance of the antisemitic-libel tourism mentioned above. Petras articulates his theory of the organized American Jewish community as a "Zionist Power Configuration" (ZPC)—an acronym that he apparently developed as a substitute for the neo-Nazi term "Zionist Occupation Government" (ZOG). He inveighs against the "the 52 organizations that make up the Presidents of the Major Jewish Organizations of America, or the thousands of PACs, local federations, professional associations and weekly publications which *speak with one voice as unconditional supporters* of every twist and turn in the policy of the Zionist State" (emphasis in original). He refers to "Zionist policy makers in the Executive branch and US Congress" and the success of American Jewish groups in "in authoring legislation, providing (falsified) intelligence, engaging in espionage (AIPAC) and turning documents over to Israeli intelligence (now dubbed 'free speech' by liberal Zionists)." He accuses the "Zionist Power Configuration" of playing "a major role in the major wars of our time, wars capable of igniting new armed conflicts," and cautions against "the role of the Zionist/Jewish Lobby in promoting future US wars."[51] None of this material is readily distinguishable from contemporary neo-Nazi propaganda.

Worse still—if that is imaginable—is a review of the Petras book appearing in 2011 in the very same journal. The author, Frederic Clairmont, is a former UN official who has held academic posts at numerous universities. He, too, lives overseas and has sought out a British forum for his views. His review is littered with references to "the ongoing crimes of what I have called the Zio-fascist state," "acts of colonial bestiality among the most atrocious in humankind's tortured history," "blood and torture, imprisonment and mass murder," the "genocidal" nature of Israel, and so on. But there is more to Clairmont's output in this British journal than mere abuse. He continues:

> The mobilisation of [Israeli] power in the USA is by elected and appointed Zionist officialdom . . . it is a mass grassroots organisation buttressed by the financial support of scores of millionaires, dozens of billionaires and a mass media that is its handmaiden. In many ways it has paralyzed the US Congress and the Executive. It influences Treasury, State, the Pentagon and all leading Congressional committees that relate to Israeli expansionism. . . . The career profiles of its professionals that are the quintessence of the "Fifth Column" are to be found in every nook and cranny of Wall Street, the globe-girdling corporate law firms, the insurance industry, the big three stock market-rating agencies, the big three accounting firms and the media . . . the ramifications of the Zionist behemoth is [sic] by no means solely confined to the US political oligarchy. Indeed its tentacles are globalised. . . . [52]

In the above passages alone, there are (at least) five antisemitic themes: (1) Jewish cruelty (e.g., "blood and torture"); (2) Jewish wealth (the Zionist lobby has "the financial support of scores of millionaires, dozens of billionaires"); (3) Jewish control of the media ("its handmaiden"); (4) Jewish disloyalty (the Zionist "Fifth Column"); and (5) Jewish world-domination ("its tentacles are globalised"). Clairmont does not actually cite *The Protocols of the Elders of Zion,* but this may have been an oversight on his part. In any case, the journal's editors saw nothing amiss in publishing another tirade that would not have been out of place in *Pravda* during the 1970s or on any neo-Nazi website today. Indeed, these contributions from Petras and Clairmont are nearly identical to David Duke's outpourings on "the Zionist media, political and financial matrix."[53]

What is remarkable about these episodes is not only that two foreign antisemites consciously decided to expose their views to the light of day in a British academic forum, but that Routledge, which allowed these writings to appear under its imprint, issued no public response when the scandal was uncovered—confirming that the authors were correct in their expectations of British tolerance for the dissemination of such material.

Tolerance and Excuses

A distinctive feature of British antisemitism and tolerance for antisemitism is the reversal of the burden of proof. Normally, when members of a vulnerable minority raise accusations of bigotry, it is (quite rightly) the bigots who find themselves in the dock. But when Jews charge antisemitism, it is not the alleged antisemites but the Jews in question who are expected to justify themselves. In striking contrast to their displays of heightened sensitivity to all other forms of bigotry (notably Islamophobia), British opinion-formers bend over backwards to excuse the purveyors of anti-Jewish prejudice. The consensus view in Britain is that antisemitism is a serious subject that is cynically abused by the Jews to evade legitimate condemnation of the conduct of their coreligionists.

It is de rigueur for practitioners of antisemitism-denial to caution Jews against confusing antisemitism with mere "criticism of Israeli policy." The argument—or tactic—has two aspects. On the one hand, any outburst, no matter how prejudiced, can be written off as mere criticism of the Israeli government; after all, isn't every antisemite opposed to whatever the Jewish state happens to be doing at any particular time? Conversely, protest against such outbursts is labeled as a clever (but easily exposed) ploy to silence the poor critic, who courageously refuses to be intimidated by the threat of verbal crucifixion. The argument is suffused with assumptions about Jewish deviousness and dishonesty, Jewish domination of public debate, and Christian martyrdom at the hands of the Jews.

Examples of this tactic are legion. There is Tam Dalyell, a senior Labour MP at the time, who defended his jibe about a Jewish "cabal" in the British government thus: "The trouble is that anyone who dares criticise the Zionist operation is immediately labelled anti-Semitic."[54] There is former Labour MP Ken Livingstone, who, as mayor of London, knowingly insulted a Jewish newspaper reporter by calling him a German war criminal and concentration camp guard: "For far too long," protested Livingstone, "the accusation of anti-semitism has been used against anyone who is critical of the policies of the Israeli government, as I have been."[55] There is former newspaper editor Max Hastings, who proclaimed: "Many of the remarks that Jewish critics denounce as anti-semitic are, in reality, criticisms of Israel or its government."[56] There is the foreign affairs editor of *The Observer* newspaper, who discerned "an attempt to deflect criticism from the actions of an Israeli government by declaring criticism of Israel out of bounds and invoking Europe's last great taboo—the fear of being declared an anti-Semite."[57] There is the *New Statesman*'s "kosher conspiracy" author, who complained that "A tendency to equate anti-Zionism—indeed any criticism of Israel—with anti-Semitism is a persistent vice of Zionist campaigners."[58] There is the senior journalist at *The Guardian*, who referred to "the—clearly orchestrated—pressure to equate any criticism of Israeli government action with antisemitism" and lamented the "blackmail of making one feel ashamed to criticise Israeli actions."[59] There is the *Financial Times*, which referred, in an editorial hailing the publication of the Walt–Mearsheimer volume, to "the fear that any criticism of Israeli policy and US support for it will lead to charges of antisemitism."[60] There is the editor of an arts newspaper that falsely accused Israeli Jews of vandalizing mosques and churches: "Israel is now to be treated as being always in the right, beyond reproach. And if you dare question this, you are called an anti-Semite, which automatically invalidates anything you say."[61] And so on, ad infinitum.

When the pretence that Britain is quaking in fear of Jewish intimidation falls flat, there are other methods of deflecting condemnation. The late Paul Foot, a veteran investigative journalist, Trotskyist activist, and *Guardian* columnist, offered this riposte: "Especially pathetic on the part of our apologists for Israeli oppression is their bleating about anti-semitism. For the sort of oppression they favour is the seed from which all racialism, including anti-semitism, grows."[62] Another well-known columnist, Richard Ingrams, was still more contemptuous of Jewish concerns: "I have developed a habit when confronted by letters to the editor in support of the Israeli government to look at the signature to see if the writer has a Jewish name. If so, I tend not to read it."[63] It is indeed difficult for such writers to take worries about antisemitism seriously when they have trained themselves to dismiss anyone raising such concerns as a racist and/or a Jew.

Another familiar method of defusing any allegation of antisemitism is to cite the tiny but vocal minority of anti-Zionist Jews who—out of conviction, conformism, or prejudices of their own—hasten to denounce and demonize their fellow Jews in Israel and the Diaspora.[64] Typical of this minority are organizations such as J-BIG (Jews for the Boycott of Israeli Goods) and individuals such as Sir Gerald Kaufman, a veteran Labour MP and castigator of Israel who maintains that "right-wing Jewish millionaires" own much of the Conservative Party.[65] The function of these Jews as an alibi for antisemitism and its apologists does not differ substantially from that of Jewish converts to Christianity who were used as witnesses against their former coreligionists during the Middle Ages. And the Good Jew/Bad Jew distinction—the "good Jews" being those who excoriate the "bad Jews" for the entertainment of non-Jews—is often made quite explicitly. When Tam Dalyell was under attack for his comments about a Jewish "cabal" in the government, Paul Foot volunteered these observations in his defense:

> [O]bviously he is wrong to complain about Jewish pressure on Blair and Bush when he means Zionist pressure. But that's a mistake that is constantly encouraged by the Zionists. The most honourable and principled Jews, here, in Israel and everywhere else, are those who oppose the imperialist and racist policies of successive Israeli governments.[66]

The more extreme the positions of the Jewish anti-Zionist, the more latitude he or she affords the non-Jewish antisemite. Left-wing publishers, for instance, are able to avoid criminal prosecution under Britain's stringent laws against racist incitement when they issue books alleging that Orthodox Jews worship Satan, or that "the Holocaust religion is probably as old as the Jews themselves"—provided that the authors of those books have names like Israel Shahak or Gilad Atzmon.[67] It is difficult to say whether these Jewish converts to anti-Zionism have made many non-Jewish converts to antisemitism, but British antisemites and apologists for antisemitism are certainly grateful for the alibi they supply.

As an example of the mentality of British antisemites and the tolerance they are accorded in academe and the media, there is the case of Tom Paulin: Oxford academic, poet, and BBC arts critic. Paulin's first contribution to the genre of anti-Jewish prejudice came in the aftermath of the Muhammad al-Dura affair, when the death of a Palestinian child in Israeli–Palestinian crossfire, broadcast on world television, was misattributed to the IDF. Paulin reacted by composing a poem on the subject entitled "Killed in Crossfire." It announced that another child

> is gunned down by the Zionist SS
> whose initials we should
> —but we don't—dumb goys—
> clock in the weasel word *crossfire*.[68]

It should be unnecessary to parse the antisemitic content of these lines. What is notable is that they were judged worthy of publication in *The Observer*, Britain's major Left-Liberal Sunday newspaper.

Not content with versifying about the "Zionist SS" and the "dumb goys," Paulin decided to put his prejudices into practice. He identified one of his Oxford colleagues, Fritz Zimmerman, as an Israeli racist and encouraged one of the colleague's students to complain of his "racism." In some two hundred phone calls to university officials and the media, he charged, inter alia, that Zimmerman had been "bunged off to Israel to get him out of the way." Only when the case came to court in April 2002 was this campaign brought to an end, as the judge determined that "Dr. Zimmermann was not in any way motivated by race," that "neither [the complainant] nor Mr. Paulin honestly thought there was any racial element in the complaint," and that Paulin "may have had his own axe to grind regarding Dr Zimmermann," who—as the judge pointed out—was in fact neither Jewish nor Israeli (as Paulin had alleged in his campaign of harassment).[69]

Meanwhile, Paulin had enmeshed himself in another scandal. In an interview with the Egyptian newspaper *Al-Ahram*, he announced that he "never believed that Israel had the right to exist at all," that suicide bombings against Israelis were understandable, and that Brooklyn-born Jews living in the West Bank "should be shot dead. I think they are Nazis, racists, I feel nothing but hatred for them." While inciting the extermination of this group of Jews, he mocked concerns about antisemitism: those expressing the concerns were "Hampstead liberal Zionists," he explained. "I have utter contempt for them. They use this card of anti-Semitism. They fill newspapers with hate letters. They are useless people." He also denounced Britain's ruling Labour Party as a "Zionist government."[70]

Although Paulin's words were in clear violation of British antiterrorism laws, there was no thought of bringing him to justice. Nor was there any attempt to remove him from his academic post—or even his teaching duties—at Oxford. He did not even lose his sideline as a regular arts critic on the BBC. Nevertheless, in light of the criticism he had received from the Jewish Board of Deputies, he now felt entitled to proclaim his martyrdom. In January 2003, the *London Review of Books* published his new poem, "On Being Dealt the Anti-Semitic Card" (the title alone implies that Jews hand out charges of antisemitism with the cynicism of dealers in a casino). Paulin's verse included thoughts such as this:

> the program though
> of saying Israel's critics
> are *tout court* anti-Semitic
> is designed daily by some schmuck
> to make you shut the fuck up.[71]

Not even this outburst resulted in any penalties—legal, academic, or social—for Paulin. Instead the 133-line poem was reprinted, in full, on the website of *The Guardian*.[72]

The Paulin case is telling because it reveals that in twenty-first-century Britain, an individual of the appropriate social standing and of fashionable (left-wing) political views can be forgiven—even celebrated—for the crudest—even murderous—antisemitic utterances.[73] An even more shocking illustration of this fact is the output of the dramatist Caryl Churchill. A member of the board of the Palestine Solidarity Campaign (which agitates for the destruction of Israel), Churchill (no relation to the World War II leader) reacted to the 2009 conflict in Gaza by composing a short work entitled "Seven Jewish Children." The theme of the play is that Jewish parents are manipulative sadists who lie to their children in order to justify the theft of Arab land and the slaughter of Arab children. At the climax of her script, Churchill has the fictitious parents reciting these lines:

Tell her [i.e., a Jewish child] I wouldn't care if we wiped them out, the world would hate us is the only thing, tell her I don't care if the world hates us, tell her we're better haters, tell her we're chosen people, tell her I look at one of their children covered in blood and what do I feel? Tell her all I feel is happy it's not her.[74]

Is the portrayal of Jewish parents as latter-day versions of King Herod accidental? Is the allegation that Jews hate non-Jews more than antisemites ever hated Jews accidental? Is the mocking reference to Jews as "chosen people" accidental? And were critics wrong to interpret the line about non-Jewish children "covered in blood" as a conscious reversion to the blood libel?

"Seven Jewish Children" has been performed at the Royal Court Theatre in London. Both a video and the script of the play have been posted in *The Guardian*'s website, where they remain at the time of writing, despite protests by Jewish groups.[75] The play has been exported to theaters in Europe and the United States. And in response to charges that an antisemitic production is being staged, the Royal Court Theatre has resorted to the now-standard line of defense: "While *Seven Jewish Children* is undoubtedly critical of the policies of the state of Israel, there is no suggestion that this should be read as a criticism of Jewish people. It is possible to criticise the actions of Israel without being antisemitic."[76] The criticism-of-Israeli-policies mantra did not persuade *The Guardian*'s theater critic, who blogged enthusiastically that Churchill's play "shows us how *Jewish children are bred* to believe in the 'otherness' of Palestinians" (emphases added).[77] The play is, after all, entitled "Seven Jewish Children" and not "Seven Israeli Children."

If the example of Tom Paulin shows that it is possible to incite the extermination of a group of Jews without incurring any kind of penalty, the treatment of Caryl Churchill demonstrates that in today's Britain, it is possible to resuscitate the blood libel and to be acclaimed by the cultural establishment for doing so.

Holocaust Distortion

As Conor Cruise O'Brien once observed, "People who disliked the Jews before the Holocaust generally didn't dislike them any the less because of the Holocaust."[78] This certainly applies to a not-insignificant strand of British opinion. The strangely obtuse British attitude to the destruction of the Jews has several aspects.[79] First, there is official distortion of the Holocaust, which is commemorated as a product of generic "racism" (not antisemitism) and is treated as an argument for "diversity" (not Jewish rights). Second, while exploiting its memory to propagate their own ideology of multiculturalism, British opinion-formers are wary of the danger that the Holocaust might be "exploited" for the benefit of Jews. And third, they remain receptive—as they were before, during, and after the war—to the equation of Jews (especially Israeli Jews) with Nazis. Let us review some expressions of this mindset.

The official understanding of the crime committed against the six million was in evidence when a Labour government announced the introduction of a national Holocaust Memorial Day in January 2001. The measure was, of course, welcomed by the British Jewish community and by Holocaust survivors. But the government's rationale was less encouraging. The press release issued by the then-Home Secretary, Jack Straw, is worth quoting at length:

> Holocaust Memorial Day is intended as an inclusive commemoration of all the individuals and communities who suffered as a result of the Holocaust—not only Jews, but also gypsies, Slavs, homosexuals, political prisoners and dozens of ethnic and other minorities.
>
> The Day will put a particular emphasis on educating people of all ages about the lessons to be learnt from genocide. The aim is to reach as many people as possible throughout the country, by addressing local and community issues which are relevant to the aims of the commemoration.
>
> The universal lessons of the Holocaust make this commemoration day relevant to everyone in our society. We all have a shared responsibility to fight against discrimination and to help foster a truly multicultural Britain.[80]

The alert reader will have noticed that in these three paragraphs introducing a national Holocaust Memorial Day, the fate of the Jews was mentioned exactly once—and then submerged in a list of other groups decimated by the Nazis. In the context of a Genocide Memorial Day, or a Victims of Nazism Memorial Day, this might not have been so astonishing. But why did the government minimize the importance of the destruction of *the Jews* in its announcement of a *Holocaust* Memorial Day? Not, of course, because its motives were antisemitic. There was, rather, a reluctance to single out the Jews lest the "universal lessons" of the Holocaust be diluted. These lessons were not about the need to combat *anti-*

semitism, but about the duty to fight *discrimination* (a problem that affects other minorities far more than Jews); they were not about the destruction of European Jewry, but about the need for a "multicultural Britain." The Holocaust had to be made "inclusive" and "relevant"—the implication being that a focus on the fate of the Jews would have been neither inclusive nor relevant. Thus was the most terrible atrocity in the history of antisemitism converted into a weapon in the ideological arsenal of Left-Liberal political correctness.

No less intriguing as an expression of mainstream opinion were the comments of Will Hutton, editor of the Sunday newspaper *The Observer* and a bellwether of the Left-Liberal commentariat. Hutton had two recommendations. First,

> we should recast this universal catastrophe as where sustained and unchecked religious and cultural hate can lead. . . .
> The second proper role is as a remembrance of genocide. . . . For to suggest that twentieth-century suffering has only been suffered by Jews is a calumny.

Hutton did not say who had advanced this "calumny"—certainly not the government in the press release just quoted. But having outlined the right ways to commemorate the Holocaust, he turned to the wrong ways: "Euro-scepticism receives another boost. And, of course, the Israeli lobby will be quietly happy—remembrance cast like this is a powerful relegitimisation of the case for a Jewish state, notwithstanding its own endemic racism."

But it appears that not all instrumentalizations of the Holocaust were off-limits. While anxious about imagined benefits to Euro-sceptics and the "Israeli lobby" (not the *pro*-Israel lobby—note the insinuation of foreign control), Hutton also mentioned his fears of domestic "xenophobia" and "racism," which "express themselves in different ways—in our approach to asylum-seekers, for example, or the dark way European integration is interpreted."[81] In summary: abusing the Holocaust as an argument for Euro-scepticism—unacceptable; abusing the Holocaust as a bludgeon against critics of the European Union—unobjectionable. Using the Holocaust to grant legitimacy to a Jewish state—unacceptable; using the Holocaust to denounce the "racism" exemplified by the Jewish state—unobjectionable. Here was a perfect portrait of the British Left-Liberal mentality, with its own endemic double standards on the Final Solution.

If these signs of mainstream insensitivity toward the memory of the six million were troubling, it can come as no surprise to learn of the reaction of the extremists. The hard-line Muslim Council of Britain—at that time (wrongly) treated by the government and parts of the media as representative of Britain's Muslim community—proclaimed a boycott of Holocaust Memorial Day, on the peculiar pretext that the government's plans were *not inclusive enough*. True inclusivity, it explained, mandated a focus on other acts of "genocide," notably the one taking place in "Palestine."[82] Another response came from the Trotskyist Socialist Workers Party—a pioneer in the anti-Israel boycott campaign—which issued its own statement on "the holocaust": "thousands of LGBT people, trade unionists, and disabled people were slaughtered"—but apparently no Jews.[83] For such extremists (as for certain Left-Liberals) Holocaust memory becomes a problem if, and only if, it recalls the suffering of the Jews. It is not so much Holocaust memory as the memory of Jews in the Holocaust that irritates the pseudo-universalists.

A second manifestation of the British attitude to the Holocaust is the Jewish–Nazi equation. This theme—for decades a staple of Marxist and other antisemitic incitement—is largely a creation of the British establishment of the 1930s and 1940s, which found the "aggressive nationalism" of the Zionists "unpleasantly reminiscent of Hitler Youth" and felt that partitioning Palestine would "bring into existence a Jewish-Nazi state."[84] The idea (if it can be called that) resurfaces whenever some controversial action by Israel is in the news, and the motives are obvious:

1. Whether directed at all Jews or at Israeli Jews, it is meant to cancel out any sympathy that Jewish people might expect in light of the Holocaust.
2. It transforms that sympathy into an ideological weapon *against* (some or all) Jews.
3. It serves the antisemitic objective of demonizing (some or all) Jews as the ultimate in evil.
4. It implies that (some or all) Jews deserve the fate of the Nazis, i.e., destruction.[85]

The appearance of this comparison in respectable discourse is therefore no small matter.

Although invented by British officials, the Jewish–Nazi slur entered mainstream discourse in Britain during the hysteria surrounding the 1982 Lebanon war. At that time it became so common that Conor Cruise O'Brien suggested a new term to describe it: "Anti-Jewism—it's an ugly word, so it fits nicely. . . . If your interlocutor can't keep Hitler out of the conversation . . . feverishly turning Jews into Nazis and Arabs into Jews—why then, I think, you may well be talking to an anti-Jewist."[86] The problem worsened in 1987, when a Trotskyist dramatist, Jim Allen, persuaded the Royal Court Theatre to stage his play *Perdition,* which accused Zionists and Jewish capitalists of conspiring with the Nazis to destroy the Jews of Europe. Allen's text was riddled with antisemitic statements and clichés, including a reference to "all-powerful American Jewry" and a description of the Holocaust as the Zionists' "purchase price" for Jewish statehood.[87] The Royal Court ultimately canceled the play before its first performance, causing months of controversy. But it is surely no accident that *Perdition* has since been revived by the Scottish Palestine Solidarity Campaign, which announced that it would stage a production for Holocaust Memorial Day 2007. It is a pattern for Scottish PSC: on Holocaust Memorial Day 2009, the group hosted Hamas loyalist Azzam Tamimi, who spoke on "Resistance to genocide and ethnic cleansing: from Europe in the 1940s to the Middle East today." On Holocaust Memorial Day 2010—in a move labeled "offensive" by the government—it organized an event on the topic of "Israeli mass killings in Palestine."[88]

Nowadays, the Jewish–Nazi equation reappears whenever Israel undertakes any large-scale military operation. So poisonous was the atmosphere during the 2006 war in Lebanon that even the *Daily Telegraph*—a right-wing newspaper—published an editorial cartoon juxtaposing near-identical drawings of a ruined Warsaw Ghetto in 1943 (with a flag bearing the Star of David) and a ruined city of Tyre in 2006 (with a flag bearing the Star of David).[89] During the 2009 war in Gaza these comparisons became quite common, notably on the Far Left. Thus George Galloway, former Labour MP and then a member of the Far-Left/Islamist Respect coalition, told anti-Israel demonstrators in Trafalgar Square:

> In April and May of 1943 the Jews of the Warsaw Ghetto were surrounded by barbed-wire fences, by the occupiers of Poland, and they faced a choice, in the words of the song of the partisans: they could die on their knees or they

could live forever. And they chose to rise up against their occupiers, to use their bodies as weapons. . . . Today, the Palestinian people in Gaza are the new Warsaw Ghetto, and those who are murdering them are the equivalent of those who murdered the Jews in Warsaw in 1943.[90]

The Far-Left journalist and documentarian John Pilger was still more extreme. As printed in the *New Statesman,* the title of his column on the war in Gaza was innocuous. But on his own website it was headlined "Holocaust Denied: The Lying Silence of Those Who Know."[91] Not only was it thus alleged that Israel was the reincarnation of Nazi Germany, but it was also suggested that Jews who support the Jewish state are on a par with Holocaust deniers. For Pilger, Gaza was a "death camp by the sea," Israel's operation recalled "the Nazis' establishment of Jewish ghettos in Poland," and the situation was a "holocaust-in-the-making," now "in its final stages."[92] A journalist of Pilger's experience knows very well the significance of the words he uses, as well as the lessons his readers can be expected to draw from them.

Even these examples, shocking as they may seem, pale into insignificance when compared to Frederic Clairmont's contribution in the *Journal of Contemporary Asia,* quoted earlier. For Clairmont,

> The creation of Greater Israel, which is one of the quintessential pivots of Zionist ideology, owes its provenance to the Nazi-inspired racialist doctrine of the *Herrenvolk,* or the master race, among whose paramount practitioners were Heydrich and Himmler. In this perspective, the Zio-fascist state that labels itself Israel and considers all Arabs as the *Untermensch,* whose lands and people are legitimate plunder, stands forth as the *legatus apostolicus* of Nazidom.[93]

In this passage, the author not only compares the Jewish state to Nazi Germany no less than five times, but adds a Christian antisemitic allusion. It is a chilling sign of the nature of left-wing opinion in Britain today that he not only sought out a British socialist journal as a forum for his opinions, but succeeded in persuading that journal to publish them intact—incurring no visible displeasure from the journal's owners at Routledge, one of the premier academic publishers in the country.

In light of such incidents, it would be reasonable to suggest that comparing groups of Jews to Nazis is no longer considered a barrier to polite company in Britain.

Conclusion

A disturbing picture emerges from this study of antisemitic manifestations in modern Britain. There are boycott campaigns against Israeli Jews in which respectable academics distribute material by neo-Nazis; there are cover stories in the Left-Liberal press that feature antisemitic images worthy of fascist propaganda in the 1930s; the call for the extermination of a group of Jews provokes no legal, academic, or social penalties; a play that revives the blood libel is staged at London's main theater; and official statements on the Holocaust are virtually bereft of Jewish content, but public figures do not hesitate to equate the Jews with the Nazis. These developments are facilitated by the culture of apologetics that has taken root among the British media and intelligentsia. Nowadays almost any statement of anti-Jewish bigotry is rationalized as a mere criticism of Israeli government policy; almost every antisemite is excused as, at worst, an overzealous critic of Israel. As long as such apologetics continue unchallenged, there is little hope of resisting the spread of antisemitic sentiment effectively.

The explanation for the growth of antisemitism and the normalization of *tolerance* for antisemitism (a tolerance now ubiquitous among educated people in Britain) can probably be found in several factors: a general loss of confidence in British national identity, and the consequent suspicion of the Jews for preserving their own nation-state; a (repressed) fear of Islamic extremism, and the (vain) hope of defusing it by victimizing a Jewish scapegoat; the search for an ideological rallying point by left-wing activists (some of whom have formed alliances with Islamists); and the perception of the Jewish community as an undefended target that can easily be intimidated, since—unlike other British minorities—it does not respond aggressively to provocations (Jewish public demonstrations, for example, are few and far between).

The direction of this antisemitic wave depends largely on the response of its adversaries in Britain and abroad. If each new outburst provokes forceful condemnation and protest from at least some quarters—especially the government—many calumniators of the Jews will probably decide that discretion is the better part of valor. But if the present trend of open tolerance for antisemitism persists, outbreaks of prejudice against Jews are certain to escalate.

NOTES

1. On this incident, see Joshua Trachtenerg, *The Devil and the Jews: The Medieval Conception of the Jew and Its Relation to Modern Antisemitism* (New Haven, Conn.: Yale University Press, 1943), p. 130.

2. From "The Prioress's Tale" in Geoffrey Chaucer, *The Canterbury Tales* (London: Penguin, 1977), pp. 172–73.

3. The literature on British antisemitism is now of a very high quality. For a dazzling display of historical erudition and analytical virtuosity, see Anthony Julius, *Trials of the Diaspora: A History of Anti-Semitism in England* (Oxford: Oxford University Press, 2010). The history of British antisemitism is also a frequent topic in Robert Wistrich's equally outstanding work, *A Lethal Obsession: Anti-Semitism from Antiquity to the Global Jihad* (New York: Random House, 2010).

4. The major studies of recent British antisemitism are Julius, *Trials of the Diaspora*; Paul Iganski and Barry A. Kosmin, *A New Antisemitism? Debating Judeophobia in 21st Century Britain* (London: Profile Books, 2003); and Bernard Harrison, *The Resurgence of Anti-Semitism: Jews, Israel and Liberal Opinion* (Lanham, Md: Rowman and Littlefield, 2006). For a selection of other studies particularly relevant to the themes of this paper, see Ben Cohen, "The Persistence of Anti-Semitism on the British Left," *Jewish Political Studies Review* 16, nos. 3–4 (Fall 2004), pp. 157–69; Robert Wistrich, "Cruel Britannia," *Azure* (Summer 2005), pp. 100–124; Melanie Phillips, *Londonistan: How Britain Is Creating a Terror State Within* (London: Gibson Square, 2006), pp. 163–83; Mark Gardner, "'The Zionists Are Our Misfortune': On the (Not So) New Anti-semitism," *Democratiya* (Autumn 2007), pp. 72–86, at http://www.dissentmagazine.org/democratiya/article_pdfs/d10Gardner.pdf; and the five online issues of the *Engage Journal* at http://www.engageonline.org.uk/journal/.

5. For a condemnation of widespread and increasing British popular antisemitism during the Second World War (i.e., during the Holocaust), see George Orwell, "Anti-semitism in Britain," *Contemporary Jewish Record* (April 1945), pp. 332–41.

6. See, e.g., Michael Billig, "Anti-Jewish Themes and the British Far Left—I," *Patters of Prejudice* 18, no. 1 (1984), pp. 3–15, and "Anti-Jewish Themes and the British Far Left—II," *Patters of Prejudice* 18, no. 2 (1984), pp. 28–34.

7. Community Security Trust, *Antisemitic Incidents Report 2010*, http://www.thecst.org.uk/docs/Incidents%20Report%202010.pdf.

8. http://www.guardian.co.uk/uk/2004/jan/23/religion.immigrationpolicy.

9. Anti-Defamation League, *Attitudes towards Jews in Seven European Countries* (February 2009), http://www.adl.org/Public%20ADL%20Anti-Semitism%20Presentation%20February%202009%20_3_.pdf.

10. E.g., http://www.mideastoutpost.com/archives/israel-derangement-syndrome-melanie-phillips.html; http://cifwatch.com/2010/06/15/an-antidote-to-israel-derangement-syndrome/.

11. Editorial cartoon, *The Independent* (January 27, 2003).

12. "*Independent*" Cartoonist Wins Award," *The Independent* (November 27, 2003).

13. Editorial cartoon, *The Guardian* (July 19, 2006).

14. Editorial cartoon, *The Guardian* (January 26, 2011).

15. Max Hastings, "A Grotesque Choice," *The Guardian* (March 11, 2004).

16. Stephen Byers, "Anti-Semitism Is a Virus and It Mutates," *The Guardian* (March 15, 2004).

17. Daniel Schwammenthal, "The Israel-Bashing Club," *Wall Street Journal* (September 3, 2007).

18. Simon Rocker and Martin Bright, "Tonge: Investigate IDF Stealing Organs in Haiti," *Jewish Chronicle* (February 11, 2010).

19. A. N. Wilson, "A Demo We Can't Afford to Ignore," *Evening Standard* (April 15, 2002); idem, "Israel's Record Speaks for Itself," *Evening Standard* (February 10, 2003). The paper published a half-hearted apology for the latter column on February 12, 2003. See Jenni Frazer, "The Unsavoury Tales of Hoffman," *Jewish Chronicle* (February 14, 2003).

20. See Alan Hart, *Zionism: The Real Enemy of the Jews,* vol. 1 (Ashford, UK: World Focus Publishing, 2005), vol. 2 (Ashford, UK: World Focus Publishing, 2007), vol. 3 (Atlanta: Clarity Press, 2010). For statements similar to those I witnessed, see Hart's interview with Iran's Press TV (October 8, 2007): http://edition.presstv.ir/detail/26308.html.

21. See, e.g., Alan Elsner, "Race, Tolerance and the NUS," *New Statesman* (May 13, 1977); Anon., "Anti-Zionism at British Universities," *Patterns of Prejudice* 11, no. 4 (July–August 1977), pp. 1–3; Anon., "Students' War on 'Zionism,'" *Patterns of Prejudice* 11, no. 6 (November–December 1977), pp. 23–24; and David Rose, "Jewish Students Charge Left Groups with Antisemitism," *The Guardian* (June 3, 1986).

22. At the time of writing, the following trade unions boycott all Israeli products: the Fire Brigades Union, the National Union of Teachers, the Public and Commercial Services Union, and the Rail, Maritime and Transport Workers Union. The Trades Union Congress (TUC), which is the umbrella group of British trade unionists, officially boycotts all Israeli settlement products but not products from pre-1967 Israel.

23. http://www.stoptheboycott.org/files/ucu%20opinion_%20Final.PDF.

24. http://www.engageonline.org.uk/blog/article.php?id=832.

25. http://www.engageonline.org.uk/blog/article.php?id=2058.

26. http://engageonline.wordpress.com/2009/02/20/mike-cushmans-protocols-moment/.

27. http://engageonline.wordpress.com/2009/06/05/ucl-ucu-can-see-nothing-antisemitic-in-connecting-anti-boycott-lawyers-with-lehman-brothers/.

28. http://engageonline.wordpress.com/2009/12/04/hate-speech-ruling-against-bongani-masuku/ and http://engageonline.wordpress.com/2010/06/01/ucu-congress-backs-antisemitic-speaker/.

29. http://engageonline.wordpress.com/2011/05/20/ and http://blog.thecst.org.uk/?p=2575.

30. http://www.thejc.com/comment-and-debate/comment/51002/ucus-chilling-vote.

31. http://normblog.typepad.com/normblog/2011/07/ucu-facing-possible-legal-action.html.

32. http://www.thejc.com/news/uk-news/49805/boycott-council-new-protocols-row.

33. Andrew Higgins, "Anti-Americans on the March," *Wall Street Journal* (December 9, 2006).

34. Editorial, *The Guardian* (June 30, 2011); the reports by Alan Travis and Ian Black; and the pro-Salah op-ed by Palestinian Knesset member Haneen Zoabi on the same date.

35. For an excellent, comprehensive analysis of the whole incident, see Bernard Harrison, *The Resurgence of Anti-Semitism: Jews, Israel and Liberal Opinion* (Lanham, Md.: Rowman and Littlefield, 2006), pp. 27–51.

36. *New Statesman* (January 14, 2002).

37. John Pilger, "Blair Meets with Arafat but Supports Sharon," *New Statesman* (January 14, 2002).

38. Letters, *New Statesman* (January 21, 2002).

39. Peter Wilby, "The *New Statesman* and Anti-Semitism," *New Statesman* (February 11, 2002).

40. John Mearsheimer and Stephen Walt, "The Israel Lobby," *London Review of Books* (March 23, 2006).

41. http://www.theatlantic.com/national/archive/2011/09/john-mearsheimer-endorses-a-hitler-apologist-and-holocaust-revisionist/245518/.

42. Robert Fisk, "The United States of Israel?" *The Independent* (April 27, 2006).

43. Colin Brown and Chris Hastings, "Fury as Dalyell Attacks Blair's 'Jewish Cabal,'" *Daily Telegraph* (May 4, 2003).

44. Remarks to a Liberal Democrat Party conference fringe meeting, September 19, 2006, broadcast on the *Today Programme,* BBC Radio 4 (September 20, 2006). See Jonny Paul, "Liberals to Sanction Tonge for Anti-Semitic Comments," *Jerusalem Post* (October 14, 2006).

45. Yasmin Alibhai-Brown, "The Shadowy Role of Labour Friends of Israel," *The Independent* (December 3, 2007).

46. Rupert Cornwell, "'Israel Lobby' Blamed as Obama's Choice for Intelligence Chief Quits," *The Independent* (March 13, 2009).

47. Oliver Miles, "The Key Question—Is Blair a War Criminal?" *The Independent* (November 22, 2009).

48. Martin Bright and Robyn Rosen, "MP: Israel's Tentacles Will Steal the Election," *Jewish Chronicle* (March 29, 2010), http://www.thejc.com/news/uk-news/30000/mp-israels-tentacles-will-steal-election.

49. "May 2011—The New Blue Rinse Brigade," http://www.socialist-labour-party.org.uk/furthernews.html.

50. See Michael N. Ezra, "Malcolm Caldwell: Pol Pot's Apologist," *Democratiya* (Spring–Summer 2009), pp. 155–78, http://www.dissentmagazine.org/democratiya/article_pdfs/d16Ezra.pdf.

51. James Petras, "Why Condemning Israel and the Zionist Lobby Is So Important," *Journal of Contemporary Asia* 37, no. 3 (August 2007), pp. 380–85.

52. Frederic F. Clairmont, "Review of James Petras, *War Crimes in Gaza and the Zionist Fifth Column in America,*" *Journal of Contemporary Asia* 41, no. 2 (May 2011), pp. 346–48.

53. Quoted in Mark Gardner's analysis of the above: http://www.dissentmagazine .org/atw.php?id=443.

54. Catherine Macleod, "Labour Gives Warning to Dalyell," *The Herald* (May 5, 2003).

55. Ken Livingstone, "An Attack on Voters' Rights," *The Guardian* (March 1, 2006).

56. Max Hastings, "A Grotesque Choice," *The Guardian* (March 11, 2004).

57. Peter Beaumont, "The New Anti-Semitism?" *The Observer* (February 17, 2002).

58. Dennis Sewell, "A Kosher Conspiracy?" *New Statesman* (January 14, 2002).

59. Quoted in Ian Mayes, "Balancing Act," *The Guardian* (May 25, 2002).

60. Editorial, *Financial Times* (April 1, 2006).

61. Anna Somers Cocks, "Fascisme Doux," *New Statesman* (July 15, 2002).

62. Paul Foot, "In Defence of Oppression," *The Guardian* (March 5, 2002). Foot was a prominent activist in the Socialist Workers Party, a Trotskyist sect that advocates the destruction of Israel.

63. Richard Ingrams, "Amiel's Animus," *The Observer* (July 13, 2003).

64. On this phenomenon, see Edward Alexander and Paul Bogdanor, eds., *The Jewish Divide over Israel: Accusers and Defenders* (New Brunswick, N.J.: Transaction Publishers, 2006).

65. http://www.thejc.com/news/uk-news/30211/labour-asked-withdraw-anti-zionist -mps.

66. Paul Foot, "Worse Than Thatcher," *The Guardian* (May 14, 2003).

67. See Israel Shahak, *Jewish History, Jewish Religion: The Weight of Three Thousand Years* (1994; rev. ed., London: Pluto Press, 1997), p. 34; Gilad Atzmon, *The Wandering Who? A Study of Jewish Identity Politics* (Alresford, UK: Zero Books, 2011), p. 153. On Shahak, see Paul Bogdanor, "Chomsky's Ayatollahs," in Alexander and Bogdanor, *The Jewish Divide over Israel*, pp. 115–24. On Atzmon, see http://blog.thecst.org.uk/?p=3056.

68. Tom Paulin, "Killed in Crossfire," *The Observer* (February 18, 2001).

69. Joshua Rozenberg, "Lecturer in Race Case is Criticised by Judge," *Daily Telegraph* (April 23, 2002); David Lister and Robert Verkaik, "He's a Poet, Though You Might Not Know It," *The Independent* (April 23, 2002).

70. Tom Paulin interviewed by Omayma Abdel-Latif, "That Weasel Word," *Al-Ahram Weekly Online* (April 4–10, 2002), http://weekly.ahram.org.eg/2002/580/cu2.htm.

71. Tom Paulin, "On Being Dealt the Anti-Semitic Card," *London Review of Books* (January 2, 2003).

72. http://www.guardian.co.uk/education/2003/jan/08/internationaleducationnews .highereducation.

73. On the Paulin affair, see http://www.acpr.org.il/ENGLISH-NATIV/03-issue /alexander-3.htm.

74. http://www.guardian.co.uk/stage/2009/feb/26/caryl-churchill-seven-jewish-children -play-gaza.

75. Ibid., and http://www.guardian.co.uk/stage/video/2009/apr/25/seven-jewish-children -caryl-churchill.

76. http://www.thejc.com/news/uk-news/outrage-over-demonising-play-gaza.

77. http://www.guardian.co.uk/stage/theatreblog/2009/feb/11/royal-court-theatre -gaza.

78. Conor Cruise O'Brien, *The Siege: The Saga of Israel and Zionism* (London: Weidenfeld & Nicholson, 1986), p. 266.

79. The British Far Right's views on the Holocaust need little elaboration. See, e.g., *The Irving Judgment* (London: Penguin, 2000); Richard J. Evans, *Telling Lies about Hitler: History, Holocaust and the David Irving Trial* (New York: Basic Books, 2001). For left-wing attitudes, see, e.g., David Cesarani, "*The Perdition Affair*," in Robert S. Wistrich, ed., *Anti-Zionism and Antisemitism in the Contemporary World* (London: Institute of Jewish Affairs, 1990), pp. 53–60; and Dave Rich, "The Left and the Holocaust," *Engage Journal*, no. 4 (February 2007): http://www.engageonline.org.uk/journal/index.php?journal_id=14&article_id=55.

80. "Plans For the National Holocaust Memorial Day Ceremony," British Government press release, January 22, 2001: http://www.gov-news.org/gov/uk/news/plans_for_the_national_holocaust_memorial/27035.html.

81. Will Hutton, "We All Have Blood on Our Hands," *The Observer* (January 21, 2001).

82. http://www.telegraph.co.uk/news/uknews/1481867/Holocaust-Day-boycott-by-Muslim-Council.html.

83. For a copy of the statement, and a condemnation by a rival Trotskyist sect that has campaigned against antisemitism on the radical left, see http://www.workersliberty.org/story/2008/08/18/jew-free-holocaust.

84. Bernard Wasserstein, *Britain and the Jews of Europe 1939–1945* (Oxford: Oxford University Press, 1979), p. 333; O'Brien, *The Siege*, p. 258.

85. I am grateful to Edward Alexander for his insight on this point.

86. *Jerusalem Post* (July 6, 1982).

87. For the revised text of the play and a selection of press comment, plus analyses by David Cesarani and others of its bigotry, see Jim Allen, *Perdition* (London: Ithaca Press, 1987). For historian Martin Gilbert's list of some of the play's most egregious historical errors, see Christine Toomey, "A Curtain Call for Courting Perdition," *Sunday Times* (January 25, 1987), http://www.paulbogdanor.com/holocaust/perdition/times.pdf.

88. http://www.jpost.com/International/Article.aspx?id=189594.

89. Editorial cartoon, *Daily Telegraph* (July 29, 2006).

90. See Sigrid Rausing, "The Code For Conspiracy," *New Statesman* (April 23, 2009).

91. http://johnpilger.com/articles/holocaust-denied-the-lying-silence-of-those-who-know.

92. John Pilger, "Gaza under Fire," *New Statesman* (January 8, 2009).

93. Frederic F. Clairmont, "Review of James Petras, *War Crimes in Gaza and the Zionist Fifth Column in America*," *Journal of Contemporary Asia* 41, no. 2 (2011), p. 346.

4 Between Old and New Antisemitism: The Image of Jews in Present-day Spain

Alejandro Baer

Sнouтing "We are sick of the Jews" and "Jews out!" a group of students in spring 2009 greeted the president of the Spanish Jewish Community and other speakers about to participate in a conference on racism and antisemitism at Madrid's Complutense University, the second-largest university in Spain. The central topic of the conference, whether antisemitism was still alive in Spain and how it was manifested, was answered right away, empirically, even before the lectures began. One of the scheduled speakers, historian Gonzalo Álvarez Chillida, wrote a few days later in the university's weekly paper that "the main characters of this story were not Spanish fascist, neofascists, nor Catholic fundamentalists, eager to bring up to date the decree of expulsion of the 'saint' Queen Isabel. Even as it may seem strange," wrote Álvarez, "it was a group that considers itself antifascist."[1] In pamphlets posted on the billboards in the hallways of the hosting institute, the conference was defined as part of a campaign orchestrated by the Jewish lobby—"a financial elite specialized in victimization and manipulation"—to silence criticism of the genocide it supposedly was perpetrating against the Palestinians. The Jewish guest was described as an obscure businessman devoted to "usurious practices." As a faculty member at Complutense University at the time, and a participating speaker at the conference, I tried along with two other colleagues to bring about a public reprobation of the incident by the university authorities (the dean and the rector). We were not successful. The incident was interpreted by large sectors of the academic community as a (more or less comprehensible) outcome of the tensions in the Middle East, particularly against Israel's policies toward the Palestinians. Hence, these events not only provided insight through firsthand experience into the intellectual authorship, the ideological composition, and specific semantics of the so-called "new antisemitism" within a particular sector of Spanish society. What this event proved beyond doubt is an even more somber reality: the denial of present-day antisemitism and, at the same time, its "normalization" in a country where the vast majority of researchers, politicians, social figures, and government institutions believe that in today's Spain anti-Jewish sentiment does not in fact exist.

In the following pages I address specific details and the particular nature of the problem of antisemitism in contemporary Spain, as well as what it has in common with other European countries in the context of a global resurgence of antisemitism. Through a close look at Spain, this chapter attempts to contribute to the still somewhat indeterminate field of new antisemitism theory.

A Specter Haunts Spain

A popular Spanish proverb says *"de aquellos barros, estos lodos."* This literally means "those morasses bring this mud," but metaphorically it refers to a past that rears its ugly head. In an analysis of contemporary antisemitism, it is necessary to look back at the rich tradition of Spanish Jew-hatred, which endured from the Inquisition to Franco's dictatorship. Equally important is a critical reflection on the last thirty years of democracy, as the bitter traces of those earlier hatreds did not automatically fade away. As the incident above clearly shows, deeply rooted antisemitic prejudices and stereotypes still form part of the present reality.

In 1492, the Jews were expelled from Castilla and Aragon. From that point forward Spain became a homogeneous Catholic society with no religious minorities. Most historians who have addressed the topic of antisemitism in Spain agree that what remained in the Iberian peninsula after the expulsion is an image of the Jew, detached from actual Jewish individuals, and a "Jewish question" strongly linked to Spanish national identity (above all, to the role of the Catholic religion in the forging of a national unity).[2] Antisemitic motifs of a religious nature—Jews as Christ-killers, accusations of ritual crimes, and profanation of Christian symbols—did not disappear after the expulsion of the Jews but rather remained firmly anchored in the cultural memory, through language, literature, and popular traditions.[3] Anti-Jewish rhetoric underwent a rebirth in conservative circles at the end of the nineteenth century. "Ironically," writes Hazel Gold, at this time "the figure of 'the Jew' inhabits the principal discourses of Spanish society—theology, philosophy, philology, politics, art, literature, journalism—even though Jews are nowhere to be found within the borders of the nation."[4] During the Second Republic (1931–36) antisemitism became a unifying tool that served the conservative forces in attacks on their real and imaginary enemies: the Republicans, the French, and the Soviets. In Spain, the myth of the international Jewish conspiracy adopted the form of a Jewish–Freemason–Communist conspiracy and served as an all-encompassing theory to explain Spain's problems. During the Civil War of 1936–39, antisemitism was a frequent ingredient in nationalist propaganda and iconography.

In her study *The Spanish Right and the Jews, 1898–1945*, Isabel Rohr has traced the discursive forms in which antisemitism crystallized in Spain as an integral component of reactionary discourse. Modern antisemitism in Spain was influenced by French anti-republican literature and, later, by Nazi propaganda (through the Spanish Fascist party, Falange, which was very receptive to Nazi literature), but it took its main inspiration from prejudices deeply rooted in Christian tradition.[5] Besides elucidating the notion that Jewish conspiracies disrupted Spanish society and describing the belief that impurity penetrated the national body through the offspring of the *conversos,* Rohr emphasizes the myth of the *Reconquista,* based on the idea of an eternal Catholic–Spanish essence—*Hispanidad*—born in the Visigoth time and resurrected during the centuries-long fight to capture Spain back from the Moors.[6] *Reconquista* was the cultural prism through which world events were interpreted. This is apparent in the way Nazi anti-Jewish policies were decoded in Franco's Spain. The press liked to remind its readers that Spain had been at the vanguard of the struggle against Jews through a "wise decision" of Isabella and Fernando to expel them from the country in the fifteenth century. Nazis and fascists were only giving continuity to an anti-Jewish policy initiated by the Catholic kings.[7] At the same time, *Der Stürmer*-like Nazi anti-Jewish rhetoric was adopted or directly reproduced from German sources. This was shown, for instance, in the treatment given to the news of *Kristallnacht* in 1938, when Spain was still divided into two belligerent camps. While there were firm condemnations of the Nazi actions, as well as solidarity expressed with the German Jews by Spain's legitimate government, the Francoist side received the news with approval and, indeed, glee.[8] "This is the great enemy of Franco's Spain: International Jewry," wrote *El ideal de Granada* on November 25, 1938, "which has seen in our homeland an easy prey for the policy of turbulence and castrating concessions that began with the 14th of April" (day of the proclamation of the Second Republic in 1931).

"An Incomprehensible Attitude": Francoist vs. Nazi Antisemitism

A brief comparison of Spanish and Nazi antisemitism at the time of the Holocaust helps us grasp the particular nature of its form in Spain. Spanish antisemitism derives mainly from cultural prejudices stemming from Christian tradition and the amalgam of religious and modern (mainly political) anti-Jewish motives rather than from an ideology based on biological racism. This distinction marks the important differences between Spanish and German antisemitic actions: in Spain these did not stem from the radical antisemitic policy that was the central axis of Nazi ideology. Even if the Francoists celebrated German and Italian antisemitic policies, the country passed no racist laws. When, after the fall of France in the summer of 1940, numerous refugees fled to the Pyrenean border, hoping to travel through Spain toward Portugal and America,[9] no formal discrimination between Jewish and non-Jewish refugees was applied. In *Spain, Franco, and the Jews* historian Haim Avni quotes the German ambassador to Spain, who, in November 1941, reported on what he perceived as an ideologically incoherent Spanish policy on the matter: "Since the historical persecution of Jews no new law has been passed against them. For the large majority of the local population and even for the official State ideology there is no Jewish problem."[10] While this statement is not entirely accurate, it highlights significant differences between the two regimes. A few years later, when the deportations of Jews from Saloniki and Paris started, Spain was faced with a dilemma that shows how an antisemitic-driven policy can have very different content and consequences. In January 1943, the Nazis advised the Spanish government that Jews with Spanish nationality who remained in territories under German occupation or influence (these included a considerable number of Sephardic Jews who had obtained Spanish nationality thanks to a decree of 1924) after a certain date would be subjected to the so-called "general anti-Jewish measures"; in other words, they would be deported to concentration and extermination camps. The Spanish reaction to the German ultimatum was at all times hesitant and restrictive. Spain's delaying tactics were in obedience to a clear policy of allowing as few Jews as possible to enter *and settle* in the country (this distinguished this case from the other aforementioned refugees), even if they were entitled to do so as Spanish nationals. But, interestingly, at the same time that the Spanish government requested extensions to the time limit set by Germany, many Spanish consuls and ambassadors tried to protect the persecuted on site, interceding on the victims' behalf with German and local authorities. The insistence of some Spanish consuls that such Jews were Spanish citizens, coupled with Berlin's diplomatic respect, helped to prevent the immediate enforcement of deportation to the death camps. Eberhard von Thadden, head of the German Foreign Office's Jewish Desk, referred to the paradoxical Spanish attitude to the "Jewish question" in these terms: "I find the reason why the government of Spain contends, on the one hand, that this involves Spaniards and yet states, on the other, that these Spaniards must nevertheless not enter Spain, incomprehensible."[11]

This statement by the Nazi bureaucrat draws attention to the significant sociological differences between the National-Catholic antisemitism of the Francoists and the German racial and exterminatory antisemitism. If the Jew is excluded from the national community, the *Volksgemeinschaft*, as is correctly understood by von Thadden in compliance with Nazi ideology and regulations, then even ambivalent support for these Jews would collide fundamentally with his worldview. For the Spanish, things looked very different. Repatriation of Spanish Sephardim was rejected by Franco's antisemitic government. They were, after all, Jews. But the killing of these people, as intended by the Nazis, was met with incomprehension and, on some occasions, consternation and urgent calls to action, particularly by those diplomats who saw the human drama in situ. What follows are the words of a diplomat who alerted the Spanish government about the gravity of the situation:

> If Spain, for reasons that cannot fail to escape anyone, refuses to receive this part of its overseas community, despite the fact that its members enjoy Spanish nationality and have strictly complied with every formality required of

> them by our laws, then it automatically sentences them to death: We will be harshly criticised for the fact that, knowing what was about to happen . . . abandoning to their sad fate these—when all said and done—compatriots, without even raising the slightest protest or doing anything to save them.[12]

Here we see the inner dilemma faced by a diplomat struggling with his own prejudices ("for reasons that cannot fail to escape anyone"), with his thought about compliance with the restrictive policy of his government, and his awareness of the fatal consequences of passivity. How did this drama end? In fact, the decision taken by Franco is again proof of the antisemitic positioning of the regime (which saw bringing Jews to Spain as a threat) coupled with political opportunism. The evacuation of Spanish Jews was finally approved, subject to restrictive conditions. They could come to Spain in reduced groups but had to leave the country as soon as possible. The provision of visas from third countries and the costs of their stay in Spain were to be defrayed by international aid organizations. Hence, the process was not repatriation as such, but rather a transit operation (like that of most of the other Jewish refugees) of individuals who had Spanish nationality. And this was probably achieved only as a consequence of the war balance tilting increasingly in favor of an Allied victory.

To summarize, while Spain's actions cannot be compared to those of the Nazis, the negative image of Jews inherited and cultivated by the Francoists played a role in the decisions taken by the Spanish government during the Holocaust. But the case shows also that cultural antisemitism was more passive than active and that it reached its limits in the face of the German extermination machinery.

From 1945 on, in order to bolster its international position, the Franco regime went to great pains to present a more benign external face so that it could distance itself from its links with Nazi Germany. This included mitigating Nazi-like public antisemitic incitement. Jews ceased to have a prominent influential role in political propaganda, and the triad of mortal enemies was reduced to just the Freemasons and communists. However, the more traditional and religious dimensions of Jew-hatred remained. The stereotypes of the hook-nosed Jewish usurer and of the God-killing people persisted, as did widespread tales of profanation of Christian symbols and legends of Jewish ritual crimes; schools and churches still taught these.[13] An example from this period was the acclaimed release in 1952 of the film *Amaya,* inspired by the novel *Amaya y los vascos* "Amaya and the Basques," written in the nineteenth century by Francisco Navarro Villoslada. In this plot, staged in medieval times, Jews are portrayed as people with perfidious and treacherous ambitions, and the film ends with an ecstatic and joyful hunt for Jews in the streets of eighth-century Pamplona (the capital during the reign of Navarra). "Only seven years after the discovery of Auschwitz," wrote Hispanist Jon Juaristi, "nobody had gone so far in exalting the medieval pogroms as if they were the legitimate predecessors of the Festival of *San Fermín.*[14] Beyond the Pyrenees there were many antisemites on the loose. But nobody dared to make movies." According to Juaristi, this schizophrenia is characteristic of Spanish culture in respect to antisemitism in general and to the Holocaust in particular. "Under Franco's regime it was possible to maintain this *castizo* [traditionalist] version of antisemitism, ignore the destruction of European Jewry. and at the same time boast about having saved thousands or even millions of Jews during the Holocaust."[15] Moreover, Jews came back to Spain in the 1950s and 1960s, mostly Sephardim arriving from newly independent Morocco. As the Franco regime evolved, synagogues were opened and the communities could hold discreet activities.

Israel in the Spanish Mindset

Israeli diplomats often state that there are two countries with which the Jewish State has "special relations." One is Germany, and the reasons are obvious. The other is Spain, in which the reasons are grounded mainly in the very shallow conception of Israel in the Spanish mainstream media and politics, where one often finds a lack of distinction between legitimate critique and unambiguously antisemitic language and imagery. While the occasional antisemitic drift in criticism of Israeli policies is today common in many European countries, Spain's case has distinct characteristics, whose roots also lie in history. Spain was the last European country to recognize Israel, and it waited until 1986 to do so. The anomaly carries over into the present. Needless to say, the young Jewish State and postwar Catholic Franco's Spain were very different types of societies, and Israel was portrayed from the very beginning in a bad light. The new Jewish State was presented in the Spanish press in alternate ways that reflected traditional clerical antisemitism, conspiracy theories, and pervasive anti-communism.[16] In the wake of the Israeli War of Independence, the Spanish press often referred to the "Hebrew–Bolshevik friendship" and reported on "barbaric acts" perpetrated by Jews against Arabs and against Christian sites in the Holy Land.[17]

On the diplomatic level, Israel first ignored Spain's call for recognition, and voted against removing the boycott against Spain in the United Nations. Franco criticized harshly "the ungrateful attitude of this race," in a direct allusion to Spain's questionable efforts to protect Sephardic Jews during the Holocaust.[18] Franco found support among the Arab states, and from then on Spain became a staunch ally of Arab policies. Nonetheless, Israel's position also received positive attention, and was hailed by Republican exiles amid numerous demonstrations of solidarity and sympathy for the new state. The socialism of the Jewish pioneers, the miracle of resurgence after the Nazi genocide, the kibbutzim, and the rebirth of the Hebrew language all had positive resonance among the vanquished of the Civil War. "Israel, the springtime of new nations . . . praising Israel with a full throat: resonant with soul, with true language . . ." wrote communist poet Rafael Alberti in a poem that has been excised from today's anthologies.[19] As in other countries, after the Six Day War in 1967, just as the Arab–Israeli conflict was becoming one of the main stages of the Cold War, the sympathy of the anti-Franco left for Israel gradually shifted to a critical and specifically pro-Palestinian position. Anti-Zionism became part of the larger ideological package consisting of anticolonialism, anticapitalism, and a deep suspicion of U.S. policies.[20] In this respect, opposition to the regime did not alter an a priori hostile view about Jewish matters. Moreover, in the 1960s and 1970s new opposition arose from within, from Francoist national-Catholic society, and it was not immune to prejudicial stereotypes and attitudes about Jews. These old ideas were rekindled and brought into currency again during the dictatorship. A noteworthy exception was Catalan nationalism, as large numbers of adherents developed a particular affinity toward Jews and the State of Israel.[21]

As a consequence of this evolution and alignment, two unfavorable opinions of Israel have coalesced, although they derive from contrary political camps: the pro-Arab conservatives and the anti-Imperialist/anti-Zionist liberals. Both reflect the foundation of a specifically Spanish character, which informs both published and public opinion about Israel in Spain. The establishment of diplomatic relations with Israel signed in The Hague in 1986 has not been a real harbinger of change. In the words of the Hague understanding: "Spain wishes to emphasize its traditional policy of friendship and solidarity with the Arab world." This relationship of friendship—and strategic interest—has been a constant in Spanish foreign relations and explains the greater distance it marks in its relationship to the Jewish state in contrast to other European countries. Such a relationship, with the heavy cultural and political baggage of Spanish antisemitism, has severely conditioned the actual role Israel plays in the Spanish mindset.

A series of academic studies and journalistic essays written over the last decade have analyzed Israel's image in the Spanish media.[22] We can infer a specifically Spanish pattern in these writings, based on the combination of a number of characteristics, which, taken on their own, may not be exclusive to the Spanish media. These include (1) a tendency to pro-Arab Manichean thinking when discussing the parties to the conflict; (2) the overlap of anti-Zionist and anti-American rhetoric,[23] which is especially prevalent in the liberal press but is not absent in the conservative media; and, (3) the use of stereotypes rooted in religious and modern antisemitism, present especially in opinion columns and editorial cartoons. What constitutes a specifically Spanish characteristic is the sheer level of intensity of these discourses as well as their widespread adoption across a broad swathe of the political spectrum. "On Israel, there is no debate," wrote journalist Pilar Rahola, recipient of the Senador Ángel Pulido and the ADL Daniel Pearl awards. "A single way of thinking prevails, the clichés are repeated, and there is a Manichaeism of goodies and baddies which does not help anyone. It is the defeat of objective journalism in Spain." Rahola regards the Spanish media as the most antisemitic in Europe; one can find genuinely antisemitic expressions in the Spanish press.[24]

To summarize, the ready-made slanted view against Israel has not changed with democracy. We may indeed argue that the critical position against the State of Israel within the Left political spectrum has precluded reflection on the mantle of ignorance and prejudice that had covered everything related to Jews and had endured through decades of dictatorship.[25] Antisemitism was considered part of the past and was cast to oblivion, even if criticism of Israel was an explosive cocktail that demanded the delegitimizing of the State, demonization through Nazi comparisons, and, above all, the use of classic antisemitic expressions and motifs. A more recent example of this sort of denial was provided by former Prime

Minister Zapatero, who in his brief visit to Israel, in October 2009, alleged in an interview with the newspaper *Maariv* that antisemitism did exist in Spain under Franco, but that there was no antisemitism in today's Spain whatsoever.[26]

The Crucified Palestinian: A Semiotics of Spanish Cartoons

Israel and the Israeli–Palestinian conflict are frequent topics for political cartoons and caricatures in the Spanish press. During the summer of 2006 alone, when the conflict in Gaza and the second Lebanon war took place, more than 170 cartoons and vignettes were published in Spanish newspapers. Such cartoons draw most of their specific meanings from the sociopolitical context of everyday news events and work with a variety of intertextual elements such as visual, historical, and literary analogies and intracultural winks. Thus, the analysis of these representations allows for an approach to the different discursive frameworks in which these satirical graphic commentaries make sense for their audiences. They permit us to identify the particular "Spanish" schemata of interpretation of events and actors in the Middle East conflict.[27] During the years of the Second Intifada, throughout the Lebanon war in 2006, a military operation in Gaza in 2009, and the Flotilla events in 2010, newspapers and magazines published a great many cartoons in which Israelis, Israel as a whole, or Jewish symbols were linked to the killing of children and to themes of vengeance and cruelty. The depictions echoed ancient anti-Jewish imagery in the Iberian Peninsula. We also note stereotypes of modern antisemitism such as charges of sowing disorder, the subjugation of others, and the recurrent evocations and analogies between Israelis and Nazis. Unabashed antisemitic caricatures are published with a certain regularity by the caricaturist Romeu in *El País,* Spain's most influential and respected newspaper. In the edition of June 30, 2009, for example, we see a cartoon in which a character in red wonders: "But how is Israel able to violate with total impunity all human and international laws?" The other character, a Jew in ultra-Orthodox religious attire, answers: "It costs us a good amount of money." This cartoon exemplifies how critique of Israel embraces, without any inhibition or intellectual contradiction, the stereotypes that once were the exclusive components of classic antisemitism: Jews are rich, manipulative, mean-spirited, vindictive, greedy, and, in the end, inhuman and diabolic.

In Spanish newspapers' cartoons on the Arab–Israel conflict we can identify clear connections to traditional religious imagery and references to historic hostility toward Jews. The newspaper audience might consciously be unaware of the content of medieval child murder legends, but readers may find its recycled continuity in visual representations of Palestinian (or Lebanese) suffering, which are subtexts underlying many of these representations. In the fall of 2000, for instance, in the wake of the death—allegedly at the hands of the Israeli army—of a young Palestinian boy (Muhammed al-Dura) that was met with shock around the world, *El Periódico de Cataluña* published a cartoon showing a Palestinian child crucified on the Star of David of the flag of Israel.[28] Another example of such use of religious and historical content is the cartoon published by the Basque daily *Deia* during the Lebanon War in 2006, which shows King Fernando and Queen Isabella reading a paper with the headline "30 Dead Children after a New Israeli Bombing." Fernando says: "We did right, Isabella, expelling these Jews from the Reign of Castilla," to which Isabella responds: "I am afraid of Zapatero, with his weak character and silly smile. Any day they can embolden and reinitiate the Reconquista." Many different anti-Jewish motifs converge in this representation of the Israeli/Jew (such as the accusation of the killing of children). The allusion to the *Reconquista*, which here confuses Jews with Muslims (the "others" in the construction of Catholic-Spanish national identity) is also revealing. A recent example from the liberal newspaper *El País* supplies further evidence of this theological-political prism through which Israel and its actions are viewed. The cartoon of December 24, 2010 shows an Arab woman (with a Palestinian scarf and covered head) carrying a baby before the background of the separation wall. The inscription reads: "Young Mariam gives birth at a cradle in Bethlehem because she cannot get to a hospital due to Israeli checkpoints." The cartoonist goes to the very core of Christian tradition—the birth of Jesus in the manger in Bethlehem—precisely on the day that the Christian world celebrates his coming into the world. In this sense, the message operates on two levels: one at the level of reason (political criticism: a critique of the State of Israel for its security policies and its separation from the Palestinian population in the territories administered by the Palestinian National Authority) and the other, latent one, at the level of emotion. The latter ventures into the confines of anti-Judaism, as the association with Christian iconography is explicitly sought by the artist. The Palestinian mother is named Mariam and is represented as a modern *Pieta*. Jesus, who was born two thousand years ago, is born again today in the form of a suffering, harassed, and oppressed Palestinian child.

From Published to Public Opinion: A Look at Survey Data and Discourses

After finding some of these representations in the mainstream media, it will come as no surprise that sociological studies of the image and opinion of Jews in Spain yield quite negative results. In recent years several international surveys, such as those of Pew and the Anti-Defamation League (ADL), have put Spain in the spotlight of attention on the matter of antisemitism. Even with legitimate objections to the aptness of such quantitative approaches to the phenomenon of antisemitism, the statistics do highlight several salient points.[29] The 2009 released survey by the Pew Research Center's Pew Global Attitudes Project noted that 46 percent of the Spanish population rated Jews unfavorably. The institute analyzed attitudes in Poland, Russia, Germany, France, Britain, and the United States, and determined that Spain is the Western country with the most negative views of Jews. Moreover, it is the country that holds the highest percentage of such views among all non-Muslim countries. These results echo a trend shown in earlier Pew data, as well as that noted by the ADL in 2005 and 2007 in its study titled "Attitudes toward Jews and the Middle East in Five European Countries" (Spain, France, Germany, Poland, Italy). The ADL survey indicates that 47 percent of Spanish respondents answered "probably true" to at least three of the four antisemitic stereotypes tested. In comparison to the other countries, Spain has higher percentages of accordance with the tested stereotypes, such as "Jews have too much power in international financial markets" (74 percent) or "Jews have too much power in the business world" (56 percent). A recent Spanish study shows similar results: 58 percent of Spaniards believe "Jews are very powerful because they control the economy and the media." The statement that "Jews use the memory of the Holocaust to their benefit" is viewed positively by 54.9 percent.[30] Only one-third of Spaniards disagree with these two unequivocally antisemitic statements. While there is some degree of variance in left-center-right positioning in relation to the Israeli–Palestinian conflict, survey data show no significant variation in attitude toward Jews and antisemitic statements among individuals with liberal, center, or conservative political opinions. This is confirmed by qualitative studies, cited below.

The 2009 ADL survey questionnaire includes questions that are especially revealing for the analysis of the Spanish case. One question asks, "Is your opinion of Jews influenced by actions taken by the State of Israel?" Among the seven countries included in the sample, Spain ranks as the country with the highest percentage of "yes" responses to this question (36 percent). The question is followed by "Is your opinion of Jews better or worse?" Here again, Spain stands out clearly in the first position, with 74 percent of respondents saying: "worse." Finally, the ADL survey asks whether the violence directed against Jews in the respective countries is "a result of anti-Jewish feelings or a result of anti-Israel sentiment." While the public in all the other countries understands more generally that violence against Jews is antisemitism, in Spain this is not the case. Only 26 percent responded "Anti-Jewish feelings." In Spain we find the highest percentage (38 percent) of respondents agreeing with the phrase "anti-Israel sentiment."

What conclusions can we draw from this data? First, that a stable, mainstream character of anti-Jewish prejudice exists in the popular Spanish mentality. Indeed, the comparative statistics show that while Spaniards do not necessarily have more profound antisemitic feelings and opinions in comparison to other European countries, Spain lacks a taboo on expressing openly antisemitic opinions (and they may not even be considered as such). Furthermore, the data shows that Israel and the Middle Eastern conflict have disproportionate impacts on perceptions and attitudes toward Jews. While this appears to be the case in many European countries, in Spain this phenomenon is clearly more pointed. And this is the case because Israel and the conflicts in which it is embroiled are the main and most decisive elements associated with "Jews" and "Jewishness" in Spain today, since the Jewish population is still very small and has a rather invisible public presence.[31] The conflation of Israel with Jews helps to explain why violence against Jews is understood by a substantial part of the population as "anti-Israel sentiment." It reveals the specifically Spanish problem of the denial and rationalization of antisemitism. Even Casa-Sefarad Israel, a public institution that was established in 2007 to increase knowledge of Jewish culture and foster closer ties between Spain and Israel as well as other Jewish communities, occasionally becomes vulnerable to this rationalization of antisemitism. A research report on antisemitism it released in 2010 attributes the fact that 34 percent of the population has a negative or very negative opinion of Jews to the "association of the Jewish community with the State of Israel and its policies." This explanation might be correct, especially in a country with such a tiny Jewish population, but for an analysis of antisemitism it is shallow. The study and its report fail to fathom why the perception of "Israel and its policies" is particularly negative in Spain; also not understood is whether local cultural or religious elements are included as factors. The study's approach even enabled greater "normalization" of antisemitism.[32] The daily *El Mundo,* for instance, reported shortly after the study's release the blunt understanding that "one-third of Spaniards are antisemitic because of Israeli policy."[33]

Qualitative studies supplement the picture provided by survey studies and provide an opportunity to deepen the scope of the analysis. A study based in a discussion group in Spain in 2009 tried to identify the specific workings of antisemitism by exploring the presence, intensity, and relevance of antisemitic semantics, topoi, and ideologemes that are employed in different environments and social milieus. A sample of groups was selected according to social strata, age, political identification, and religious practice.[34] The study probed the image of the Jew and how it appears in relation to various portrayals of the "other" (such as Muslims and Protestants) in a cultural system that still revolves around the identity–difference dichotomy. The study shows an ambivalent identification with Muslims, since they seem to reflect an element of the Spanish past. This was expressed in the group dynamics in terms of "we used to be like that too," meaning religious, male chauvinist, backward, poor, and so on. This view involves a paternalist vision not devoid of racist elements (the Muslim as the "good savage" unpolluted by modernity), which exists among both conservative and more progressive groups. By contrast, the groups showed a clear counter-identification with regard to Judaism and the Jews involving group members entering uncharted territory, which led to a feeling of unease.

Among the most interesting results is one that has already been attested: the fact that antisemitism can be directly related to the absence of Jews in the country. Contrary to other minorities (such as Muslims), whose invisibility would seem to match perfectly the requirement and demand imposed by the collective imagination of the Spanish with regard to *integration* and *respect,* for the Jewish minority in Spain (few in number, indistinguishable, and therefore "invisible") nonvisibility or the absence of differentiation is accompanied by fantasies and delirious suspicions. The problem in relation to Jews is that they cannot be identified, thus the inability to identify them becomes part of the stereotype and its concomitant metaphors: *"Behind the scenes, from behind they pull all the strings . . ."* (Group 4). *"Well you see, we never really know. . . . There are Jews everywhere"* (Group 6). *"They plot . . . and you don't even know it."* (Group 3). In some ways, the absence of empirical experiences with actual Jews, with Spanish Jews, leads to a discussion about Jews that is conducted by way of images, most of which are unequivocally antisemitic—the attribution of their secrecy, their hiding under different flags, their concealing actions in order to advance special interests, and so on—which are mostly employed in the conspiratorial reading of global events, from financial crises to wars. For instance: *"The American banks are Jewish, man, you know I mean just look at what the Jews set up . . ."* (Group 2). *"They've managed to dominate political power in the United States. Rockefeller did what he did." "They've got the world by the rope . . ."* (Group 3).[35]

These discourses are expressed by very different types of groups, and contrary to expectations, there is little to distinguish the Left from the Right. What we have identified is a gradual decline, a gradual residualism of explicit religious-based antisemitic expressions (among older people in small or medium scale rural settings, among the lower middle class): *"The Jews are bad. They killed our Lord . . . ;"* and at the same time the repetition and rationalization of an economics- and politics-based antisemitic discourse (among youth and adults, urban, middle- to lower-middle class, conservative and progressive): *"Behind this [grabbing a can of coke] are the Jews"* (Group of liberal professionals).

It is notable that the interpretative framework for perceiving Jews and Muslims can also be applied to the Palestine–Israel conflict, whose centrality, based on its hypervisibility and special place in the Spanish media, is present in the discourses of all groups, with remarkable intensity. Palestine is the object of a paternalistic outlook toward Muslims (the Arab as the "good savage," who represents our past), while conflict is perceived from a Manichean perspective and a cosmology impregnated with Catholic culture. This framework assigns all the available roles in advance. Palestine, as an antagonist to Israel, can only be an innocent victim, and Israel can only be guilty. *"We need to support the weak side. It's not a left-wing thing. It's just human"* was a consensus phrase in an elderly conservative group from a rural area. The Holocaust was also the subject of discussions in group dynamics and always emerged spontaneously. In historical terms, the Jewish specificity of the Holocaust is very often questioned by the participants (*What about the other victims?*), while Holocaust remembrance is usually perceived as specifically "Jewish" and distant. In this sense, the transnationalization of a Holocaust culture with universal moral and political appeal, whose effects are also felt in Spain, does not encourage sensitivity toward the issue of antisemitism. Rather, it works against it due to the force of its being projected in an accusatory manner against Israel. The frequently cited theme of the former victims acting as present perpetrators in Israeli uniform denies the possibility of any sustained memory of the Holocaust, and it is in turn recycled in a number of negative stereotypes: hypersensitivity and manipulation through victimization, political (Zionist) instrumentalization, and mercantile gain (compensations). For instance: *"These people are here doing all this stuff and then they go to the Holocaust Museum and there is all this moaning, and then they go and continue their target practice . . ."* (Group 5).

The qualitative study has shown that in Spain discussion about "the Jews" operates in categories of thought whose only substantiation is the repetition of unreflective and improvable declarations of a negative kind. Such thinking fits into a sort of subclass of teleology that easily defies any attempt at rationalization, be it from the observation of current events or even in more profound ethical terms. Thus, hostility and negative opinions about Jews exist on a plane of normalcy and discursive first principles.

Conclusions: A New Antisemitism of Long Standing

How helpful for the Spanish case are the theories of the so-called "new antisemitism," which since 2000 and in the context of the Arab–Israeli conflict have attempted to explain the resurgence of antisemitism in Europe? The answer is: not very much. Unlike France, antisemitism in Spain can neither be explained by the growth of Muslim antisemitism (a rather minor phenomenon in Spain because of first-generation immigration and its weak political voice), nor is there an externalization, or "de-territorialisation of the Intifada," as Ulrich Beck has identified the problem in Germany and other European countries. Neither can the demonization of Israel be understood as an effect of a particular interpretation of the significance of the memory of the Holocaust, where citizens assume the role, in Alain Finkielkraut's terms, of "penitent judges."[36] It is not plausible to assume that Israel has served the Spanish as a vessel into which to project all that is bad in European history—that is, that the Jewish state and Zionism are the incarnation of negative properties that Europe has overcome (its colonial past, its ethnic divisions, its institutionalized racism, its excesses of violence).[37] The marginal position of Spain in respect to European history, and to most European memory debates, makes such explanations not very suitable to our case.

While current antisemitism in Spain is undeniably connected to the Middle East conflict and to anti-Israel sentiments, its scope, broad swathe along the political spectrum, as well as its cultural and ideological composition speak for its specificity and homegrown character. The central explanatory variable for antisemitism in Spain is still religion, in a broad cultural sense and, in particular, in the aspect of religion that sociologist Charles Glock has identified as the "consequential" dimension of religion. Belief and religious praxis are losing ground due to growing secularization. Still, religious socialization and religious knowledge have consequences in the everyday life of individuals.[38] Seen in a Weberian sense, there are traces of Catholicism in the individual's *habitus,* a system of dispositions that include thoughts, perceptions, expressions, and, as Bourdieu would formulate it, whose limits are set by the historically and socially situated conditions of its production.

Antisemitic hostility in Spain is expressed in three main types of discourse: religious, economic, and political. However, the religious element is exceptional, acting as a matrix or underlying structure for all the others and encompassing Israel-related antisemitism. There is a weakening of the Christian-Catholic religion on the level of praxis, but it has not automatically led to a loss of its symbolic value and function.[39] Despite secularization and modernization, it has not translated into the deactivation of this deep-rooted Catholic substratum (connected to Spanish identity) in Spanish culture. In this respect we may say that with the passing of time, "exculturation," the process by which culture loses its Catholic roots, will have a direct influence on the issue of antisemitism in Spain, weakening inherently antisemitic semantics and worldviews.

Finally, we need to ask how this deeply rooted, ongoing, and often venomous antisemitic rhetoric translates into antisemitic actions. What are its effects? Even if there are occasionally incidents of abusive behavior in the streets and some cases of threatening graffiti on Jewish community buildings, generally in close connection to the events in the Middle East, physical attacks on Jews and violent incidents of antisemitism are rare occurrences in Spain. There is a significant gap between the strong antisemitic rhetoric (mainly in the media) and the rather scarce number of antisemitic acts, which goes beyond the fact that there is a small Jewish community in the country. Most Spanish Jews will confirm this paradox: Jews usually live a fearless and integrated life in Spanish society and, at the same time, are exposed to a certain normalcy of antisemitic discourse. The Spanish Jewish Journal *Raíces* recently published two insightful texts that shed light on this matter. In "A Letter to a Spanish Friend," writer Arnoldo Liberman identifies a painful underlying silence, a subtle mist that marks his relationship to Spanish non-Jewish friends whenever reference to his Jewish identity is made—at the dinner table, for instance, when the question of the Israel–Palestine conflict is brought up.[40] That's the level, no more but no less, at which antisemitism plays itself out on a personal level. Jacob Abecasis, also a Spanish Jewish writer, offers a possible response to Liberman's concern: "What happens in the relation between us—those who feel Jewish and Spanish—and our good Spanish friends, raised and educated in Catholicism? Their roots are not only different. They are opposed. And this barrier becomes insurmountable. The Spaniard has been breast-fed, historically and viscerally, with a sort of collective identitarian monolithism." This would explain that uncomfortable tension and the fact that communication on a deeper level is almost nonexistent. Even more so if we add "a bit of that ancestral Hispanic, more or less subconscious heritage of contempt towards the Jew." "Surely, Arnoldo" writes Abecassis, "we have never noticed on a personal level the slightest discrimination for being Jewish. . . . but as painful as it is, our double identity of Jews and Spaniards, that will accompany us until our very last day and which for us is natural and logical, will never be understood by our Spanish friends."[41]

We end with an account of the experience of a foreigner in Spain. Sociologist Alfred Schütz argued that it is precisely the stranger, who does not take things for granted because he does not share the particular story and the cultural patterns of the members of the in-group, who possesses objectivity and clear-sightedness as a social investigator.[42] The following anecdote, which was conveyed to me by an American Jewish young man, is illustrative of such an intercultural encounter with "thinking as usual," with the self-explanatory normalcy, and mundane quality of antisemitism in Spain.

> On my latest trip to Spain, I was having some fine Rioja and met six young college educated people in Málaga in their late 20's and early 30's. And I spoke to one woman, Marta, who was from Córdoba. She took a liking to my accent, and I too was enjoying the conversation. We spoke for about half an hour and she was amazed at how much the articulate "giri" (non-Spanish tourist) knew the region. I told her that I thought the culture was so rich because of the complex history of the region and the mix of North African Islamic, Catholic, and Jewish pasts. I asked her whether she identifies with either the Moslems or Jews. Her answer was perhaps the most shocking thing I've ever heard in my life and the only time in my life I felt the "A" word (antisemitism). She said that she does identify with the Islamic influence because it's everywhere. But not with the Jewish people. After all "they hoard wealth from generation to generation and steal other people's money and all you have to do was look at the Rockefellers and Morgans." She then told me that "Jewish people are smart but they would sell their own mothers for money" and their "money is used to build tanks which then murder innocent Palestinians." I corrected her several times regarding the backgrounds of the Rockefellers and Morgans as well as the other claims she made. I also told her that I was Jewish; no apology was requested and none was offered. She kept on drinking the wine and laughed. Her friends were very pleasant and changed the topic. One guy, Francisco, said that he loves NY and wants to visit me in NY. He also shared that the people of Spain are educated and well-rounded and NY is the same way, but deep America was full of ignorant people who don't know where Spain is on the map. I then asked the 6 of them whether they knew who Maimonides was. Francisco said architect, another said a Moslem conqueror, and the rest didn't know. So I said, why do you expect Americans from Kansas to know about Spain when you are from Málaga and Córdoba, Spain, and don't know what happened in your own back yard? We all laughed and the guy took no offense whatsoever and promised to look it up.[43]

NOTES

1. Gonzalo Alvarez Chillida, "¡Fuera los judíos!" *Tribuna Complutense* (May 12, 2009), p. 3. My translation.

2. Enrique Krauze, "Anti-Semitism in the Spanish-Speaking World," in David Kertzer, ed. *Old Demons, New Debates: Antisemitism in the West* (Teaneck, N.J.: Holmes and Meier, 2005), pp. 143–52; Gonzalo Alvarez Chillida, *El Antisemitismo en España. La imagen del judío (1812–2002)* (Madrid: Marcial Pons, 2002).

3. Manuel Pedrosa, "El Antisemitismo en la cultura popular española," in Gonzalo Alvarez Chillida and Ricardo Izquierdo, eds., *El Antisemitismo en España* (Cuenca: Ediciones Universidad Castilla-La Mancha, 2007).

4. Hazel Gold, "Illustrated Histories: The National Subject and 'the Jew' in Nineteenth-Century Spanish Art," *Journal of Spanish Cultural Studies* 10, no. 1 (2009), pp. 89–109, quoted in Daniela Flesler, Tabea Linhard, and Adrian Perez Melgosa, "Introduction: Revisiting Jewish Spain in the Modern Era," *Journal of Spanish Cultural Studies* 12, no. 1 (2011), pp. 1–11.

5. Isabelle Rohr, *The Spanish Right and the Jews, 1898–1945* (Sussex: Sussex Academic Press, 2007), p. 77.

6. Ibid., p. 4.

7. Ibid., p. 66.

8. Alejandro Baer, "Zwischen Aufhetzung und Verurteilung. Die geteilte Rezeption der Novemberpogrome im Spanien des Bürgerkriegs," in Clauda Steur, ed., *Die Novemberpogrome 1938: Versuch einer Bilanz* (Berlin: Stiftung Topographie des Terrors, 2009).

9. The regime's strategy was primarily political: to block the way to enemies of the National Cause (mainly socialists, communists, and Freemasons) and to keep the number of refugees in the country as low as possible. See Bernd Rother, *Spanien und der Holocaust* (Tübingen: Max Niemeyer Verlag, 2001).

10. Haim Avni, *España, Franco y los judíos* (Madrid: Altalena, 1982), p. 68.

11. Rother, p. 225

12. Letter of the Diplomat Federico Oliván to the Spanish Ministry of Foreign Affairs, Berlin (July 23, 1943). Quoted in Alejandro Baer, *Visas for Freedom: Spanish Diplomats and the Holocaust* (Madrid: Ministerio de Exteriores y Cooperación y Casa Sefarad Israel, 2009), pp. 32–33.

13. One of the most well-known and long-lasting Spanish blood libels is that of the Santo Niño de La Guardia (Holy Child of La Guardia). El Santo Niño was an alleged victim of a ritual murder by the Jews in the town of La Guardia in the province of Toledo. This legend greatly assisted the Spanish Inquisition in their campaign against heresy and crypto-Judaism. The cult of the Holy Infant is still celebrated in La Guardia.

14. Jon Juaristi, "Espana ante el Holocausto," *Factual* (April 23, 2010). The festival of San Fermín (or Sanfermines), in Pamplona, is a rooted popular celebration held annually in July. Its most famous event is the *encierro,* or the running of the bulls.

15. In *España y los judíos,* a pamphlet published by the Spanish Diplomatic Information Bureau in 1949, one can read the following self-laudatory statement: "Spain, inspired by its universal Christian spirit of love towards all the races of the Earth, contributed to the rescue of the Jews, motivated more by spiritual interests than by political or merely legal reasons. Our government's aid extended, not only to Sephardim dispersed across every continent, but also to all Jews wherever the occasion arose, without regard to their nationality or whereabouts," p. 15.

16. Alejandro Baer, "Spain's Jewish Problem. From the 'Jewish-Bolchevik Conspiracy' to the 'Nazi-Zionist' State," in Wolfgang Benz, ed., *Jahrbuch für Antisemitismusforschung,* vol. 18 (Berlin: Metropol, 2009), pp. 89–110.

17. José Antonio Lisbona, *España-Israel, historia de unas relaciones secretas* (Madrid: Temas de Hoy, 2002), p. 35.

18. See Bernd Rother, *Franco y el Holocausto* (Madrid, Marcial Pons, 2004). See also Alejandro Baer, *Visas for Freedom.*

19. Rafael Alberti published the poem ¡*Hosanna Israel*! in the Argentine literary magazine *Davar* in 1948. See Jacobo Israel Garzón, *El exilio republicano español y los judíos* (Madrid: Hebraica Ediciones, 2009), p. 72.

20. Shulamit Volkov, "Readjusting Cultural Codes: Reflections on Anti-Semitism and Anti-Zionism," *Journal of Israeli History* 25, no. 1 (2006), pp. 51–62.

21. Edgar Illas, "On Universalist Particularism: The Catalans and the Jews," *Journal of Spanish Cultural Studies* 12, no. 1 (2011), pp. 77–94. See also Joan Culla, "Encuentros y descuentros Hispano-Israelís: una perspectiva periférica," in Raanan Rein, ed., *España e Israel Veinte Años Después* (Madrid: Fundación Tres Culturas, 2004), pp. 99–108.

22. See Gabriel Albiac, "Meditar Jenin," in VVAA, ed., *En Defensa de Israel* (Zaragoza: Certeza, 2004), pp. 21–40; Carmen Lopez Alonso, "La evolución de la prensa española con relación a Israel, el antisemitismo y el conflicto arabe-Israelo-palestino," in Raanan Rein, ed., *España e Israel* (Madrid: Dykinson, 2007), pp. 145–69; Masha Gabriel, "Medios de comunicación, judíos e Israel durante la operación 'Plomo Fundido,'" in VVAA, ed., *Israel en los medios de comunicación espanoles. Entre el estereotipo y la difamación* (Madrid: Hebraica Ediciones); Albert Sabanoglu and Alejandro Baer, "Israel en los medios españoles. Camino a la normalización?" in Jacobo Israel Garzón, ed., *España Israel. 20 años de relaciones* (Madrid, Hebraica Ediciones, 2007).

23. The Transatlantic Trends study of 2004 shows that in Spain hostile sentiments about the United States are the most pronounced in Europe. According to Vinçens Villatoro, modern, grassroots anti-Americanism and antisemitism are, in fact, two branches of the same tree: the rejection of modern Western values, as specifically opposed to Hispanic cultures. This view identifies an older current that takes a hostile position toward the values of the mercantile world, commerce, and industry. In opposition to these values are the mysticism, the heroism, and the so-called chivalrous values of the old regime. The figure of the Jew in general and the State of Israel in particular are perceived and presented as the incarnation of the values of the modern mercantile world, which are rejected; this, then, is the common thread that ties together the confrontation of both the Left and the Right (conservative) with the model of liberal

democracy. See Vicenc Villatoro, "De qué hablamos cuando hablamos de Israel?" in VVAA, ed., *En defensa de Israel* (Zaragoza: Certeza, 2004), pp. 333–50.

24. Pilar Rahola, speech at the Angel Pulido Award ceremony, Madrid, June 5, 2009. See http://fcje.blogspot.com/2009/06/la-comunidad-judia-espanola-premia.html.

25. It is important to point out here the particular nature of the *Transición*. Spain's transition from dictatorship to democracy established a political culture of consensus that advocated forgetting for the benefit of the public good. This collective amnesia meant a tacit ban to publicly confront the legacy of Francoism in all its aspects, including its relation to Nazi Germany and antisemitism. See Alejandro Baer, "The Voids of Sefarad: The Memory of the Holocaust in Spain," *Journal of Spanish Cultural Studies* 12, no. 1 (2011), pp. 95–120.

26. *El Mundo* (October 15, 2009).

27. See Alejandro Baer and Paula López, "El conflicto como caricatura. Israel en el humor gráfico español sobre la guerra del Líbano de 2006," *Cuadernos de Analisis del Movimiento Contra la Intolerancia* 30 (2007), pp. 31–44.

28. *El Periódico de Cataluña* (October 6, 2000).

29. Only questionnaires carried out in a standardized way will produce data that is comparable across different countries. But the question arises about whether one should suppose that the categories used in these survey studies are adequate for measuring antisemitic opinions and attitudes, which in addition to generally being elusive and fuzzy, are marked by their own very homegrown character. See Baer and López, "El conflicto como caricatura."

30. Estudio sobre antisemitismo en España—informe de resultados. Casa Sefarad-Israel, July 2010. The complete report can be accessed at: http://sefarad-israel.es/otros/10550125_inf_rev%207-9.pdf.

31. According to the Federation of Spanish Jewish Communities, there are currently approximately 40,000 Jews living in Spain. Jews comprise less than 1 per 1,000 of the total Spanish population.

32. See Robin Stoller and Alejandro Baer, "A Survey to Deny a Problem," *Jerusalem Post* (October 17, 2010).

33. *El Mundo* (September 8, 2010).

34. Alejandro Baer and Paula López, "The Blind Spots of Secularization: A Qualitative Approach to the Study of Antisemitism in Spain," in *European Societies* 14, no. 2 (2012), pp. 203–221.

35. In some isolated cases, where the participant had actual experience of the subject (that is, knew actual Jews), there is an immediate questioning of the use of these negative stereotypes. In these cases, an important element of reflexivity was introduced into the group dynamic, with phrases such as, "Has anybody actually ever met a Jew?"

36. Alain Finkielkraut, "In the Name of the Other: Reflections on the Coming Anti-Semitism," *Azure* 18 (2004), pp. 21–33.

37. Robert Fine, "Antisemitism and the Politics of Denial," paper presented at the Second International Seminar on Antisemitism, Madrid, November 2009.

38. Rodney Stark and Charles Y. Glock, *American Piety: The Nature of Religious Commitment* (Berkeley: University of California Press, 1970), p. 16.

39. A statement made by a participant in the discussion group made up by progressive professionals makes this point clearly: *"and obviously, most of us are Catholics. As I've said, 'we are' because that's our tradition. In fact, I'm also an atheist."*

40. See Arnoldo Liberman, "Carta a un amigo español," *Raíces* 86 (2011), pp. 65–70.

41. Jacob Abecasis, "Carta (psicoanalítica) a mi amigo Arnoldo," *Raíces*, 87 (2011), pp. 59–60.

42. Alfred Schütz, "The Stranger: An Essay in Social Psychology," *American Journal of Sociology* 49, no. 6 (1944), pp. 499–507.

43. I thank Igor V. for sharing this experience with me.

5 Antisemitism Redux: On Literary and Theoretical Perversions

Bruno Chaouat

Antisemitism can be buried, but it can never be destroyed as long as the Jewish people keeps its ancient position as a clearly defined foreign body in the midst of other peoples' societies.

—JULIUS MARGOLIN

Preamble

I WILL BEGIN WITH a paradoxical and bitter admission: I believe that the transmission of the history and the memory of the Holocaust has triggered a backlash against Jews and Israel, at least in the West if not beyond, and at least throughout the last decade, although the phenomenon is arguably much older. This backlash has been described and analyzed in depth by Elhanan Yakira in his absorbing book, *Post-Holocaust, Post-Zionism*.[1] Yakira argues that in a broad philosophical and journalistic corpus, in the works of a certain, perhaps marginal, Israeli intelligentsia deeply influenced by European and American postmodern and postcolonial theory, Israel is portrayed as owing its legitimacy to the Holocaust, then as exploiting the memory and the history of the Holocaust, and finally as perpetrating a new Holocaust, this time on the Palestinians. The same misrepresentation can be observed in France, and I would argue in Europe in general. Yakira insists that his method is phenomenological and that his purpose is not to provide any explanation. I wish humbly to complement this major contribution to the understanding of theoretical and political perversions with an attempt at tracing the sources of this paradoxical delegitimization of Israel grounded on Holocaust hypermnesia.

The situation is thus clear: a massive increase in Holocaust education, Holocaust awareness, and Holocaust commemoration these last three decades has been concomitant with a resurgence of antisemitism, at least throughout the last decade. Is this resurgence merely the sign of Holocaust indigestion—what philosopher Alain Finkielkraut has called "hypermnesia"[2] or excess of memory, mnemonic bulimia? Are people simply tired of hearing about the Holocaust? Or should we not rather suggest that the Holocaust has been de-Judaized and universalized in a perverse way?

At this juncture, and while I will further focus on the French scene, I wish to evoke a personal anecdote that is truly emblematic of the perverse logic that animates the new antisemitism. A few weeks ago, at a birthday party held by a colleague at the University of Minnesota (I was not invited but received a reliable account of the incident), a professor in the College of Liberal Arts, upon hearing my name mentioned, started to rant about the Holocaust. Alleging that the French department at the University of Minnesota was a "Jewish enclave" that served a "Jewish agenda," the colleague went on about the Jewish "monopoly" on suffering, a monopoly that eclipses, among other atrocities, the "six million Indian deaths" under the British Empire. The phrase "Holocaust envy" or "Holocaust resentment," although somewhat distasteful, seems appropriate to describe this particular outburst. One can also speak of a relativization of the Holocaust that borders on Holocaust denial and that is fueled by structural antisemitism. After all, that colleague continued her rant with allegations of Jewish power in a department with only two Jewish professors out of twelve and in which no one, except for myself, has ever expressed any pro-Israel views. Finally, the intellectual, or rather ideological, niche of the colleague I have mentioned is in the field of postcolonial studies. What we have here is thus a textbook case: postcolonial, anti-Israel ideology directly inspired by Edward Said, coupled with traditional antisemitism (Jews have secret power, they constitute an "enclave," and they help each other), Holocaust minimization or relativization, and Holocaust envy or resentment (Why do the Jews always whine? Indians had it worse, the colonized had it worse, and of course, the Palestinians today have it the worst of all.).

This morbid passion that I call "Holocaust envy" or "Holocaust resentment," while it cannot be justified, can nonetheless be explained by the special place that the Holocaust occupies in public discourse, in schools, in academe, and in the media. It can also be ascribed to the institution-alization of memory, to what in France has been called, since the 1990s, the "*devoir de mémoire*" or "duty to remember."

In France, the Jewish specificity of the Holocaust remained largely unacknowledged for nearly twenty years after the war; Jewish victims were simply lumped into the same category as those of the Resistance and, even as young Frenchmen, forced to work in Germany; Jews were sometimes even treated with contempt because they had not all "earned" their martyrdom by positive acts, the way Resistance heroes had. However, once wartime Jewish victimhood finally was acknowledged, the claim of "uniqueness" rendered it a coveted symbolic commodity. Indeed, who does not want her suffering to be recognized as unique? If the Holocaust is unique, then Jewish suffering is a most enviable moral commodity. Para-doxically, the uniqueness argument, meant to highlight the specificity of Jewish suffering, seems to have fostered the de-Judaization of the Holo-caust mentioned earlier, to the extent that every victimized group wants their suffering to be recognized as unique, indeed, as *a* Holocaust. To reclaim the absolute singularity of the Holocaust risks at the same time universalizing it and stripping it of its historical and moral significance. In the last section of this essay, I will attempt to trace the history of this tragic paradox.

L'antisémitisme est mort. Vive l'antisémitisme . . .

In February 2011, Christian Dior's British creative director John Gal-liano burst into an antisemitic rant in front of dumbfounded tourists in a Parisian café. On March 6, a professor of English at the University of Nebraska published her reaction in the *New York Times* in which she at-tempted to link fashion, antisemitism, and fascism: "there are deep and unsettling parallels between the [fashion] industry, particularly in Eu-rope, and fascism's antidemocratic aesthetic. . . . At the root of the whole system is . . . a cult of physical perfection very much at home in the his-tory of fascism."[3] These solemn pronouncements and bizarre analogies, a typical exercise in what Leo Strauss once called "reductio ad Hitlerum,"[4] fail to mention that fashion partakes of the ephemeral.[5] By contrast, the fantasy that drove fascism was one of eternity. The fashion industry pro-ceeds from liberal, bourgeois individualism rather than from fascist con-formism or Nazi eugenics.

Haute couture is not my area of expertise. Yet, before I turn away from that arguably frivolous topic, I wish to comment on two more reactions to Galliano's antisemitic outburst, which may well encapsulate what is really going on in the resurgence of antisemitism today. The first one is drawn from an op-ed in the Israeli daily *Haʾaretz*.[6] This piece, published a few days after Galliano's rant, contended that antisemitism is alive and kicking. The subtext of the column was that the Israeli right wing should not exploit false threats of Iranian and Palestinian antisemitism while tourists can experience *the real thing* in Parisian cafés. The second reaction is that of philosopher Alain Finkielkraut, on French state television.[7] Interviewed on the Galliano incident, Finkielkraut, renowned for his wit, declared that Nazi antisemitism is quite dead, and "its corpse will certainly not be revived by some pathetic postmodern dandy." While for *Haʾaretz* age-old antisemitism is still a threat, for Finkielkraut, the menace Jews face today lies elsewhere. Rather than turning to the ghosts of the past (Nazism, fascism, Hitler, and the goose-step), Finkielkraut invites us to confront current manifestations of antisemitism. In fact, he has been warning us for a long time now that the ghosts of the past are a smokescreen obfuscating all too real present threats. It is not difficult to imagine that for him, the *Haʾaretz* op-ed would represent just that—a distraction from the actual menace.

What, then, if the real threat against the Jews today, if one exists at all, came from the knee-jerk invocation of Nazism, fascism, Vichy collaboration, and the French resistance, as a way of avoiding genuine engagement with the present? To put it more bluntly: What if the new bigotry wrapped itself in the garment of anti-fascism and *anti*-antisemitism? It is my hypothesis that the memory of occupation by and collaboration with the Nazis has drifted into a perversion of memory and has produced amnesia. This arguably constitutes the Gallic version of what Alvin Rosenfeld has described as "the end of the Holocaust."[8]

A Versatile Form of Prejudice

What remains to be said about the periodic rebirth of one of the oldest forms of hatred? Are we facing a paradigm shift in French and European antisemitism? Distrust of Jews in the Greco-Roman world was motivated by an anxiety with respect to monotheism, superstition, and Jewish exclusivism (expressed in the doctrine of the Chosen People). Throughout the Christian era, Jew-haters denounced Jewish rejection of the universal message of the Church. Recall the famous demand by Paul of Tarsus that the Jews overcome the law and the flesh. In the aftermath of the Pauline objection to Jewish particularism, anti-Jewish medieval Christianity, alloyed with pagan vestiges, expressed itself in superstitious beliefs such as in the blood libel and in the accusation of deicide. Modern antisemitism became political and economic, obsessed with the specter of Jewish conspiracies, and culminated in racial theories put into practice by the Nuremberg Laws that defined the Jew as a "substantial enemy,"[9] and by the Vichy statute on Jews. Jew-hatred, despite all these different motivations, has remained a core passion of European history and culture.[10]

The problem with studying antisemitism, as with researching the corollary phenomenon of Holocaust denial, is that one risks succumbing to boredom at best, despair at worst. An antisemite is an antisemite is an antisemite. The study of antisemitism can be tedious, and one must pay tribute to, and also feel sympathy for, the British lawyer and scholar Anthony Julius, who published a superb eight-hundred-page history of British antisemitism.[11] Likewise, Robert Wistrich deserves similar respect for producing an essential volume on the history of antisemitism from antiquity to global jihad.[12]

And yet, let us recall a witticism by the twentieth-century French Catholic writer Georges Bernanos: "Hitler has discredited antisemitism, once and for all."[13] This cynical statement is not lacking in perspicacity. Antisemitism, though it has not disappeared, has had to morph and adapt to new contexts and ideological environments. Antisemites today must display genuine imagination. I am not suggesting that they have deliberately decided to modify their language lest they be accused of antisemitism. An invariable core of antisemitism has remained while the discourse has transformed into something at times hard to identify as antisemitism.

Indeed, antisemitic rhetoric and acts are still with us. There is no need to cite statistics of physical attacks on Jews and Jewish sites in France and in Europe generally, which reached their peak with the Second Intifada and the beginning of the war in Iraq.[14] However, in order to rise out of the ashes of Auschwitz, antisemitism, this phoenix of European passions, has had to adjust itself to the political, ideological, and moral climate of the postwar period. This climate was put into place by the early acknowledgment of crimes against humanity. The Nuremberg trials were meant to foster awareness of genocide as an effect of war of aggression and racism. In the future, thanks to this new consciousness, a barbaric event such as the Holocaust was supposed never to reoccur. So far, despite a notable rise in French Jewish emigration to Israel since the beginning of the millennium, nothing suggests that an event of the magnitude of the Holocaust is on its way in Europe. Though individual Jews in France are often threatened, they appear to be safe as a group. The laws of the Republic protect them, and legislation on memory and history acknowledges their past suffering and punishes its denial. And yet, this politics of memory has proved insufficient to conjure away antisemitism. The French *Trauerspiel,* the national inability to mourn the past, has bred perverse effects.[15]

After the war, Western Europe wished to establish a sort of Kantian perpetual peace. Europe, falling prey to its nihilistic tendencies, had made two significant suicide attempts in the twentieth century. It is legitimate to attribute these two continent-wide, would-be self-immolations to patriotism and nationalism, to collective narcissism (Freud's "narcissism of small differences"), and to the hatred of the other, the foreigner. Postwar European ideology has thus predictably and perhaps wisely purported to overcome national borders, parochialism and patriotism, and promote a secularized version of Christian *agape.* (I shall elaborate this idea further on.) To be sure, *Realpolitik* continued to function; the Cold War succeeded the Second World War; and colonial wars, Arab and left-wing terrorism started brewing. Yet beginning in the 1960s and with the independence of its colonies, Europe deemed that war, mass violence, and evil had been done away with: nationalism, imperialism, racism, and colonialism, while they had not vanished altogether, became discredited ideologies. France, along with the rest of Western, secular Europe, has renounced Christian anti-Judaism, as well as national narcissism, let alone racial theories. Even the so-called "civilizing mission" of the French Republic, which for a century had justified colonization with the claim that the principles of the French Republic were universal (this was the French equivalent of Kipling's "white man's burden") is no longer defended, except among a small circle of pathologically nostalgic Frenchmen.

What's left, then? If antisemitism is still alive, if one can even argue, with historian Pierre-André Taguieff, that it is "rising from the muck," in what soil does it prosper? French essayists, pundits, and philosophers have contended that antisemitism, a highly adaptable social virus, has been able to feed precisely on a compost of antiracism and postnationalism. Some have even suggested that anti- or postnationalism and antiracism have nurtured an unprecedented avatar of antisemitism, a mutant virus.[16] For at least ten years now, any keen observer of European society has been aware that antisemitism is no longer a matter of racial theory, nationalism, exclusion of the other, or homogenization of society—quite the opposite. Philosophers and historians such as Finkielkraut or Taguieff have convincingly shown that if Europe has a Jewish problem today, it is not because Jews are seen as a heterogeneous element in the nation, a virus, or a disease to be purged, but because they allegedly adhere to a certain idea of identity and roots that contradicts the new strictly universalistic *Weltanschauung*. To wit, Jews as imagined by the new antisemites have morphed into the exclusivist antisemite of yore. If during the period of political and economic antisemitism, Jews were seen as all too modern, "rootless cosmopolitans" (to use Stalin's expression), today's European antisemitism construes them as obsolete *precisely* because they are attached to their roots, their land, their community, and their origin. The alleged anachronism of the Jews is perceived as a reactionary force that hinders the progress of humankind toward multiculturalism, understood as the peaceful, infinitely enriching coexistence of ethnicities, races, religions, and cultures within the same territory. Finally, while the antisemite of yore viewed the Jews as an inferior race, today he views them as racist.

Whence Does Antisemitism Come?

Some could argue that today's antisemites in Europe are of African, Muslim origin, and that therefore we are not dealing here with the old European bigotry. Some even find solace in the belief that the immigrant population alone is responsible for the resurgence of antisemitism. Among those who favor this hypothesis, two different responses prevail. The condescending one has it that these young Muslims, descendants of African immigrants, are antisemitic because they are excluded by the white European majority. (Note that the question is rarely asked as to why the Jews should be a scapegoat for Muslim youth resentful of discrimination by white Europeans.) This culture of excuse is grounded in an explanation provided by "culture," by their right to what is supposedly "their own culture"—another name for multiculturalism. Muslim youth is culturally different; it is up to the French Republic to care for its immigrant youth, to understand it and to adapt to its culture. This is a no less patronizing version of the eighteenth-century fantasy of the noble savage.

Hence the unwillingness to condemn, or perhaps the embarrassment attendant upon condemnation of antisemitic acts; hence the time it took major French newspapers to admit that what was going on during the Second Intifada in the French suburbs and major cities was, indeed, unequivocal antisemitism. To be sure, the French intelligentsia was facing cognitive dissonance: Arab "Semites" cannot be antisemitic; or if antisemitism is racism, the main victims of racism, namely, Muslim Arabs, could not be antisemitic. Not to mention other variations on the same logical and lexical fallacies. . . .

Among the proponents of the hypothesis that the origin of this new antisemitism is solely a Muslim *Lumpenproletariat,* some come up with a radically opposite response: France should never have hosted so many immigrants from Africa who today are responsible for the resurgence of this old bigotry, a bigotry that French people had allegedly been able to eradicate from their midst.[17] While it is true that violence and antisemitic incidents originate massively among disenfranchised Muslim youth, it would be superfluous to add that the most sophisticated rhetoric that fuels this new antisemitism does not emanate from these quarters, but from writers, politicians, essayists, and intellectuals. It is wise, in any attempt to understand the roots of violence and bigotry, to go from deeds to words. There is no acting-out without an ideological climate that unleashes base instincts. There is hardly any doubt that intellectuals bear some responsibility for the malaise in which French Jews have found themselves since the beginning of the millennium.

Denying Antisemitism: A Textbook Case

Among the most egregious cases of denial of this "multicultural" version of antisemitism, one should mention philosophers Alain Badiou's and publisher Eric Hazan's coauthored pamphlet. In *L'antisémitisme partout* (Antisemitism Everywhere),[18] Badiou and Hazan urge us to resist the alleged blackmail that emanates from new "inquisitors" who denounce antisemitism. To be sure, this is a healthy initiative: it is, indeed, urgent to denounce the political exploitation of antisemitism. Such exploitation is doomed to further trivialization of the Holocaust and perversion of the history and memory of Jew-hatred in Europe and beyond. Unfortunately, the authors of this manifesto, part of whose intent may deserve praise, fall into their own trap. Indeed, if one wants to warn against the exploitation of antisemitism, it is better not to resort to it oneself. Let us examine how these anti-inquisitors proceed. First, the authors attempt to identify those who presumably benefit from this campaign against an antisemitism whose empirical reality they deny. They attribute its denunciation to a right-wing ideological conspiracy that can be characterized as "Occidentalist" and "nationalistic." Their response is that this campaign is meant to stifle revolutionary impulses among the socially and geographically peripheral masses perceived as disenfranchised. To accuse these masses, and especially suburban youth of Muslim, African, and Arab immigrant origin, of antisemitism would amount to delegitimizing the violence of these actors whose energy should instead be harnessed to class struggle and to a new proletarian revolution. According to Badiou and Hazan, those who denounce the "new" antisemitism (Alain Finkielkraut, Pierre-André Taguieff, Eric Marty, Nicolas Weill, Jean-Claude Milner, among others) are the true heirs of antisemitism—that of the thirties, of Pétainism and of the antisemitic, pre–World War II movement "Action Française."

At this juncture, the reasoning put forth by Badiou and Hazan sinks into downright theoretical, moral, and political perversion. Here are the main points of their argument: in their view, to focus on the antisemitism of suburban youth would be an ideological weapon distracting the public attention from Israel's alleged crimes. Now, Jews and non-Jews who defend Israel today would be the reincarnation of the petty bourgeoisie of the 1930s who advocated the values of the West against the foreigners, the Jews, the outsider, and so on. Pro-Israel intellectuals, "forgers" of an "imaginary" antisemitism, would thus be real antisemites who collaborate with America (identified with fascist ideology) and with Israel (identified with colonial France).

To accept such reasoning, the reader is asked to take for granted a series of very problematic equivalencies: (1) between liberal democracy and fascism; (2) between Israel (as the vanguard of the West) and the colonial and racist French Empire; (3) between suburban Muslim or African youth and the Jews of the 1930s; and (4) between today's pro-Israel Jews and non-Jews and the collaborationists of yesteryear. (Note that Badiou and Hazan seem to have misread Milner, who critiques, no less severely than they, European liberal democracy and its "criminal tendencies," especially in a book to which I will return later.)[19] One cannot accept Badiou's and Hazan's analogies unless one also takes for granted premises and equivalencies that the authors share with Holocaust deniers on the extreme left.[20] However, while in this particular case it is not a question of "murdering memory" of the Holocaust, to use Pierre Vidal-Naquet's famous phrase, it is a matter of denying the reality of current Jew-hatred. If it is irresponsible to stigmatize poor youth from the outskirts of the cities and to reduce their consciousness to some antisemitic essence or identity, it is no less irresponsible to deny the reality of an antisemitism nourished by class resentment and Islamist propaganda. Badiou and Hazan, by altogether dismissing against all empirical evidence the significance of this antisemitism, legitimize it in the name of their anti-Israel and anticapitalist tropism. By relegating this hatred to the realm of anecdote or paranoid fabrication rather than seeing it for what it is, namely a very well-documented and massive European phenomenon, they become its unwilling (?) accomplices. Thus, the authors exploit two cases, well publicized in France, of psychologically off-kilter individuals who claimed falsely to have been the object of antisemitic attacks. To pretend to prove the nonexistence of this antisemitism by resorting to fabrications by two psychopaths partakes of the same type of reasoning that the authors denounce, namely logical fallacy. Indeed, the fact that two psychopaths claimed to have been attacked by Muslim or black youth[21] for being Jewish is not sufficient to prove that *all* antisemitic aggressions by those of Muslim or African origin are fabricated. Quite the opposite: the fact that France was unanimously moved by these false alarms reveals that, unfortunately, they were all too credible to begin with. Badiou and Hazan succumb to a denial of reality that adds insult to injury by dismissing as unreal or irrelevant a new antisemitism so virulent that it can prove fatal to its victim. Thankfully, as it were, this worst-case scenario has occurred so far only once in France.[22]

French Literature and Holocaust *Trauerspiel*

Antisemitism has been growing in France due to the collapse of borders caused by such factors as the Internet, satellite TV, the influence of Islamic clerics and preachers in certain neighborhoods, and Islamic radicalization. Violent and unabashed, this antisemitism is fueled by the emergence of political Islam as a major force in Europe and in the world. But there exists, next to it, a specifically French strain of neo-antisemitism. The two antisemitisms nurture each other. My focus is on the latter, since the former is not unique to France. I will thus analyze the French specificity of this morbid resurgence and suggest some possible causes. To do so, I turn to two examples of what I see as the ideological perversion of the memory and the history of the Second World War and the Holocaust. These two instances will be taken from the world of letters.

In 2002, the literary critic Maurice Nadeau, who notably discovered and promoted David Rousset's *Univers concentrationnaire* (The Concentration Camp World)[23] some sixty years ago, published Soazig Aaron's first novel, *Le Non de Klara* (Klara's Refusal).[24] Lucille Cairns aptly notes that "[d]espite her Jewish-sounding surname, Aaron is not in fact Jewish, and her attempt to represent Jewishness at what was a nadir in Jewish history (the novel is set in 1945, just at the end of the Shoah) is highly problematic."[25] She adds:

> The pseudonym Aaron has a pronounced Jewish resonance, and the possibility of Jewish filiation is not negated in the book's promotional material: the biographical blurb states that the author had decided "d'écrire sous un nom de plume biblique par fidélité au grand-oncle qui l'a élevée" [to write under a biblical pen-name out of loyalty for the great-uncle who raised her]. However, in a telephone conversation with me in 2007 the author refuted such filiation entirely.[26]

Cairns's analysis highlights the ethical and historical shortcomings of the univeralization of the Holocaust that Aaron's novel effects and to which I will return. However, Cairns's conclusion and judgment on the novel are more mitigated. The critic concludes by praising the author for her literary and moral courage. Cairns ends her essay on the suggestion that fiction and literary artifice are needed to convey trauma, thus nuancing her initial suspicion of a possible exploitation of the Holocaust by a non-Jewish writer. While I recognize the power of literary artifice to convey unsayable experiences, my reading of Aaron's staging of a fictional Jewish survivor and of her universalization of the Holocaust is perhaps less sympathetic than Cairns's.

Aaron's novel bears the stamp, via Nadeau's reputation, of the literature of the French resistance and other militant causes. It tells the story of Klara's return to Paris from Auschwitz in August 1945. It achieves this through the artifice of a diary written by her confidant and sister-in-law, Angelika. *Klara's Refusal,* at times reminiscent of Marguerite Duras's *La Douleur,*[27] retroactively provides survivors with the listeners they were hard-pressed to find on their return from the camps.

Aaron's novel appeared in a period of intense soul-searching among the French, who were torn between sympathy for victims of the anti-semitic past and solidarity with those of the colonial past, between concern for Jews and attentiveness to Arabs or Africans. This moral dilemma is perceptible in the displacement of French anxiety onto the Arab–Israeli conflict and in the encoding of this conflict within the framework of French collective memory. Indeed, *Klara's Refusal* was published during the Second Intifada, when the Israeli military's incursion into the Palestinian city of Jenin triggered international condemnation of the use of military force against a civilian population, and prompted European pundits to accuse Israel at best of massacre, at worst of genocide. Some two months after the publication of *Klara's Refusal,* in March 2002, sociologist Edgar Morin, novelist Danielle Sallenave, and deputy to the European Parliament Sami Nair signed an opinion piece in *Le Monde* accusing Jews of having become the new Nazis and identifying Palestinians as the new Jews.[28]

In this polemical and heated context, Soazig Aaron's fictional survivor, Klara, whose experience of suffering and persecution allegorizes Europe's guilty past, launches her own warning to postwar Jews. In the early years of the third millennium, while France is revisiting its traumatic past, ambiguously legislating history, and arguably undergoing an identity crisis related to globalization and the construction of the new Europe, Aaron suggests that national identity and secured territory are the causes of past and future genocides: "Jews will kill too. One will have to come to terms with this idea. By barking and killing, they will learn how to bark and kill. Jews now have a homeland, a country; this means the war forged one more murderous people."[29] The novel seems to ascribe the occurrence of the Holocaust to national identity and political sovereignty. The very fact of calling a country one's own is, as Aaron's fictional survivor seems to suggest, an inherently murderous stance. For Klara, the establishment of national sovereignty is an ethical threat and virtually genocidal. More, the longing for a land enacts a symbolic self-genocide. As a matter of fact, Jews, within the context of a diasporic idealization, are "Jews" as long as they remain in exile. Zionism, as has been argued by Jewish and non-Jewish anti-Zionists, is the supreme avatar of antisemitism, a tremendous historical irony. Klara is the lost object of an endless mourning introjected, as it were, by the author whose melancholic identification with the fate of European Jewry prompted her to take the pen name of "Aaron." *Klara's Refusal* can thus be read as a French Auschwitz *Trauerspiel.*

Stéphane Hessel: A French Ideological Stew

In 2010, the ninety-three-year-old French diplomat Stéphane Hessel, a privileged witness in the *pax Europaea* I evoked earlier, published a manifesto entitled *Indignez-vous!,*[30] translated into English as *Time for Outrage!* In 1946, after fighting heroically in the resistance and ending up in Nazi concentration camps (Buchenwald and Dora), Hessel pursued a career in diplomacy and claims that he took part in the committee charged with drafting the Universal Declaration of Human Rights, a document ratified by the UN on December 10, 1948. Hessel's claim has been challenged by Pierre-André Taguieff in his new book, *Israël et la question juive* (Israel and the Jewish Question).[31] In this book, Taguieff analyzes Hessel's own contradictory claims and shows rather convincingly that the author of *Time for Outrage!* has inflated his past role in order to gain moral benefit and credibility in his current political and ideological struggle. Taguieff also debunks the myth of a pacifist Hessel who is merely motivated by peace in the Middle East and points to the perverse dialectic between a rhetoric of peace and humanitarianism and the support for terror.

The remarkable success of *Time for Outrage!,* published more than sixty years after these events, should be seen as a *Nachträglichkeit* in the Freudian sense, a belated effect of the Second World War, the Holocaust, and Vichy France. According to the *New York Times* (June 7, 2011), "more than 3 million copies [have been sold] in Europe since its publication in October." An American publication appeared in 2011, with Twelve,[32] an imprint of Hachette Book Group. Granted, neither the price of the book nor its weight is particularly onerous (thirty pages, 3 Euros.) Still, not all slim or inexpensive volumes reach audiences of such astounding magnitude. One wants to understand why this book, or pamphlet, already launched in English, Spanish, German, Chinese, and other languages, has been received with such enthusiasm almost everywhere it has appeared. (For example, even as I write these lines, thousands of self-proclaimed young "indignados," drawing inspiration from Hessel's manifesto, are occupying central plazas in Madrid and Barcelona.)

As a diplomat, Hessel was never in the foreground of the political stage. The success of his booklet can only be explained by the fact that it corresponds to expectations that have little to do with the author, a rather discreet, if self-righteous, man, at least until recently. If he cannot attribute his literary success to name recognition, he owes it even less to the reputation of his publisher, a samizdat-type house named "Indigène," or "indigenous," incidentally an anagram of *indignée,* or "indignant." The publisher Indigène, as the name suggests, dedicates its energies to minority cultures allegedly suffocated by globalization. The ideological colors brandished by this publishing house are thus green-red and "antifascist." It leans toward the so-called Nouveau Parti Anticapitaliste, the "New Anticapitalist Party" founded in 2009.

Back in 1990, historian Henry Rousso had diagnosed a French political pathology for which he coined the now famous phrase "*le syndrome de Vichy,*" or "Vichy syndrome."[33] This metaphor means that France is haunted by its past collaboration with Nazi Germany and periodically acts it out in public manifestations of repentance, shame, guilt, and outrage. One implication of Rousso's thesis is that "Vichy France" has become a metaphor that impedes any lucid analysis of the present. Hardly any expression of outrage can occur in France without an explicit or implicit reference to the dialectic of collaboration and resistance. Hessel's call to outrage is built on an all-too-predictable paradigm that I wish to describe.

A former underground combatant of Nazi occupation, the son of a Jewish father who was Walter Benjamin's friend and the model for the German Jewish Jules in the novel on which François Trauffaut's *Jules et Jim* is based, Hessel seems light years beyond any suspicion of antisemitism. Like sociologist Edgar Morin, he can plead both his Jewish origins and his past in the resistance. Yet if taking up arms against the Nazi occupier was the result of Hessel's initial indignation, the question that comes to the reader's mind is: Who are today's fascists, occupiers, and Nazis? If resistance to Nazi terror was truly heroic, what does Hessel demand from the hero of our time?

In Hessel's monocausal, superficially Marxist interpretation of history, fascist terror was spurred in the 1930s by self-interested bourgeois fear of Bolshevism—a rather reductive explanation for the rise of fascism. Likewise, the so-called "fascist terror" of today would be the global market, embodied in France by President Nicolas Sarkozy (compared to Marshal Pétain by the earlier-mentioned Alain Badiou),[34] and beyond the French borders by an international plutocracy whose wealth allegedly increases in direct proportion to the impoverishment of the socioeconomic underdogs. To achieve good measure and render even more explicit the link between today's economic inequalities and the racism of the 1930s, Hessel draws a parallel between those inequities and the unfair treatment of ethnic minorities (illegal aliens, Roma, and others) in Sarkozy's France. To a French reader, this unfair treatment of ethnic minorities cannot fail to recall the Statute on Jews promulgated by Vichy. Thus, the global marketplace, the growing gap between rich and poor, and the discrimination against foreigners, illegal aliens, or immigrants are mixed together in a typically Gallic ideological stew.

After having devoted a few pages to this global cause of indignation, the manifesto focuses on what Hessel calls his "main reason for outrage." The most scandalous particular situation in the world, in his view, is the fate of the Palestinians in the West Bank and Gaza. If sixty years ago, fascism and Nazism had provoked Hessel to resist, the two main incarnations of fascism today are the global market that increases inequalities and the repressive, colonial Jewish state. Hessel's visit to Gaza and to Hamas leadership reveals that in his mind, the Islamist movement embodies the French resistance of yore, and Israel is the Nazi occupier. Hessel pays lip service to the condemnation of terrorist violence, and in the same breath justifies it by Palestinian "exasperation." While it is hard to argue that Hessel is antisemitic (after all, he claims that the recent French politician he admires most is a Jew: Pierre Mendès-France, prime minister of France in the 1950s), his pamphlet nonetheless deploys a logic that brings it very close to current expressions of antisemitism. Indeed, the former diplomat's selective "indignation" or "outrage" strongly suggests a double standard, as French essayist and novelist Pierre Jourde has noted in an op-ed. Jourde's corrosive irony strongly intimates that Hessel's motivations are at the very least suspicious:

> What triggers Hessel's indignation is neither enslaved women, nor bloody, grotesque, obscene and ludicrous dictatorships overflowing the planet. And yet, 300,000 dead in Darfur, disemboweled pregnant women . . . No! Hessel has made his choice, and he is certainly entitled to it. He has picked his own indignation. But why that one in particular? Because. . . . Oh well. . . . [35]

More than a prophet of his time, Hessel emerges as a mere mouthpiece of the French and European *Zeitgeist*. His epoch has, predictably enough, responded to his manifesto with utmost enthusiasm. Global capitalism, the physical eradication of minorities, fascism, and Nazism are all equated with the Jewish state. These equivalencies, which operate at the structural, unconscious level, cannot be considered antisemitic "in intent," to use Lawrence Summers's phrase. Nonetheless, Judith Butler's outrage notwithstanding, they are antisemitic "in effect."[36]

Theorizing "Outrage": Equivalencies and Inversions

If arguably the stunning success of this pamphlet reflects the widespread currency of its arguments, Hessel, and a significant portion of the French public opinion, are *indignés*, "outraged." A few years ago, political scientist Danny Trom provided a thorough analysis of what he saw as the emergence of a culture of outrage or "indignation." According to Trom, the development of a culture of outrage is conterminous with the aporiae of "radical social critique," especially in France. In *La Promesse et l'obstacle*,[37] Trom suggested that the "promise" of redemption formulated by the intellectual, radical left runs headlong into a Jewish "obstacle."

Before discussing this idea further, I must provide an account of a book alluded to earlier, whose main thrust informs Trom's work: Jean-Claude Milner's *Penchants criminels de l'Europe démocratique*, a sui generis, austere, and at times hermetic book whose central thesis is that modern, democratic Europe is confronted by a structural problem that Milner identifies as the "Jewish name." There is, according to Milner, a structural incompatibility between, on the one hand, European Enlightenment, and, subsequently, postwar European ideology of perpetual peace;

and, on the other hand, the Jews. Here is Jeffrey Mehlman's critical and somewhat tongue-in-cheek rendition of Milner's thesis—a thesis in which Mehlman nonetheless finds merit despite its excessively theoretical rigidity:

> An ever-expanding and war-averse Europe, besotted with whatever it can think of as other than itself, appears to have encountered its own mirror image in an ever-expanding, war-bent Islamic extremism, which is, symmetrically, *infuriated* by anything it can think of as other than itself. Such is the empirical reality that underlies the argument. The internalization of Europe's specular image or reflection . . . occurred at the United Nations congress of Durban and was consolidated around an antipathy to the Jews. It is this "structural" hatred of Europe for the Jews that is Milner's theme, which he encapsulates, rather than argues, in terms of the Jew being what the Lacanians call "the *objet a* of the West." Or the unconscious.[38]

For Milner, European universalism is a "complacent universalism" or "abstract universalism." The Jews, on the other hand, bear witness to and embody a "demanding universalism," based on a profound attachment to concrete history. Jewish "particularism" is based, according to Milner, on both genealogical transmission and sexual difference, a foundation that has allegedly been abandoned by postmodern, postwar Europe. Here is Mehlman again, on Milner, and again with the distance of irony especially with respect to Milner's use of Heideggerian jargon:

> In a postmodern . . . world intent on limitless technological advance, the Jew keeps alive an almost archaic question: "What shall I tell my children?" To that question, articulating the four poles of parents, children, male, and female, Milner gives a Heideggerian name, "quadruplicity," and invites us, since he barely elaborates the matter, to pour whatever Heideggerian profundity we can muster into that rectangular vessel. For it is this profundity that an increasingly superficial and technologized Europe would repress.[39]

European, romantic nationalisms and Nazism were a mere perversion of the "demanding universalism," something that can be called a "perverse imitation" of the doctrine of the chosen people. In a subsequent book, *Le Juif de savoir* (The Jew of Science)[40] Milner deepens his exploration of the distinction between these two universalisms, the "demanding" one and the "complacent" one. He writes, in somewhat apocalyptic tones:

> Not only has the time come to conceive of a "demanding universalism"; the return of the name "Jew" compels us to do so. We must posit a universalism

that would not be reducible to the ordinary [*quelconque*]; a universalism that would not be in the image of the Church; a universalism whose ultimate cost would not be a call for conversion of all mankind. . . .

Milner's book responds to and takes issue with the recent return to Pauline universalism in French radical thought, evident in Alain Badiou's *Saint Paul: The Foundation of Universalism*,[41] and *Portées du mot juif* (Meanings of the Word "Jew"),[42] published one year before the appearance of Milner's *Le Juif de savoir*. In *Meanings of the Word "Jew*," Badiou defines Israel as a racist, colonialist, and genocidal state. He further exhorts the Jews to "forget" the Holocaust, explaining that the word *Jew*, an empty predicate devoid of historical, cultural, and religious significance, finds its ultimate meaning in Hitler's metaphysics. If for Bernanos, "Hitler discredited antisemitism once and for all," for Badiou Hitler discredited the word *Jew* once and for all. Badiou goes on to argue that the memory of the Holocaust pushes Israeli Jews to perpetrate another Holocaust on the Palestinians, who are today's "real Jews."

In his *Quarrel with Alain Badiou*, Eric Marty[43] refutes each of the sophisms that flaw the book in question, which Marty terms a "philosophical and uncanny carnival" in which everything is turned upside down: Jews are the Nazis, Israel is an antisemitic country, Claude Lanzmann's *Shoah* is a Nazi film, the true Jews are those who give up the name *Jew*, and so on. In the end, with extreme theoretical sophistication—or should we say sophistry?—Badiou manages to blame Jewish "exceptionalism" for the Holocaust. Therefore, so goes Badiou's argument, today real Jews are none other than the Palestinians.

It is worth linking Badiou's "complacent universalism" (a more or less secularized version of Catholicism) that leads him to the paradoxical and extreme propositions in *Meanings*, to the inversion between victims and perpetrators and to the pathos of suffering as it has developed these last three or four decades. This inversion is determined by a cultural *Zeitgeist* and by social mutations whereby the claim for recognition and the institutionalization of the figure of the victim have become considerable and indisputable phenomena.[44]

Returning to Trom's work, we learn that, beginning in the 1970s, a certain French reception of Hannah Arendt's thesis on the banality of evil, reinforced by the success of Stanley Milgram's famous experiments on obedience to authority and of Chrisopher Browning's book on "ordinary men" capable of mass murder, has paved the way for a series of inversions that empty the word *Jew* of its empirical substance, and the Holocaust of its Jewish specificity. Trom thus evokes the "triptych Arendt–Milgram–Browning" as a symptom (or cause?) of those inversions. Cause or symptom, Trom shows convincingly the immense influence of this "triptych" on radical social critique in France. All three theoretical endeavors (Arendt's, Milgram's and Browning's) are informed by a tendentious reading of the Holocaust; or, to put it more sympathetically, the way in which these three scholars have been read is indisputably tendentious. Trom's argument is especially compelling when he indicates the perverse effects of the process of "familiarization" that has turned the Holocaust into an event seemingly close to our ordinary experience: "The most extreme Nazi atrocities have been made familiar to us. Furthermore, it is through the most extraordinary (exotic) deeds of Nazism that we are supposed best to understand our most intimate, ordinary condition."[45] Therefore, (1) if "Jew" is merely a synonym for "victim" and (2) if, from the proposition that Eichmann was an ordinary man, one infers that every ordinary man is a potential Eichmann,[46] if the perpetrator himself is the victim of the inhumanity of the "system," then one can safely draw equivalencies between Israel and the Third Reich, Palestinians and Jews, and between Jewish sovereignty and antisemitism. The "system" can have different names. In Hessel's case, the so-called "system" is "neo-liberalism," globalization, the structural economic, and social injustices between "South" and "North." Thus, Trom adds, one can speak of a "Nazification of modernity." Think, for example, of Giorgio Agamben's notorious statement: "The concentration camp is the nomos of modernity."[47] Hence, certain writers and sociologists can anathematize equally the doctrine of the chosen people and Aryan racism.[48]

To conclude, I will quote philosopher Vladimir Jankélévitch's bon mot, published in a 1971 polemical essay dedicated to the Holocaust and forgiveness: "Israelis are wrong to be victorious, but Jews are wrong to have been victimized."[49] This *Witz* points to what psychoanalyst Jacques Lacan would have called a "*vel* of alienation," or a double bind, according to which Jews lose on two grounds. On the one hand, achieving power and sovereignty triggers envy and resentment; on the other, victimization breeds contempt and resentment. This aporia encapsulates the tragic feature of contemporary antisemitism.

NOTES

Special thanks to my friend Alan Astro for his scrupulous editing and fruitful suggestions.

1. On the perversion of history and memory of the Holocaust and the delegitimization of Israel, see Elhanan Yakira, *Post-Zionism, Post-Holocaust: Three Essays on Denial, Forgetting and the Delegitimation of Israel* (Cambridge and New York: Cambridge University Press, 2010).

2. See especially Alain Finkielkraut, *Remembering in Vain: The Klaus Barbie Trial and Crimes against Humanity* (New York: Columbia University Press, 1992).

3. Rhonda Garelick, "High Fascism," *New York Times* (March 6, 2011).

4. See Leo Strauss, *Natural Right and History,* based on the 1949 Walgreen Foundation Lectures (Chicago: University of Chicago Press, 1953).

5. On fashion and modern beauty, see Charles Baudelaire, *The Painter of Modern Life and Other Essays* (London: Phaidon Press, 1995).

6. *Ha'aretz.com* editorial (March 3, 2011).

7. France 2. The interview is found at: http://www.youtube.com/watch?v=4kiOzzKd3a4.

8. Alvin Rosenfeld, *The End of the Holocaust* (Bloomington: Indiana University Press, 2011).

9. On the Nuremberg Laws, see Yves-Charles Zarka, *Un détail nazi dans la pensée de Carl Schmitt: La justification des lois de Nuremberg du 15 septembre 1935* [A Nazi Detail in Carl Schmitt's Thought: The Justification of the Nuremberg Laws of September 15, 1935] (Paris: Presses Universitaires de France, 2005).

10. For an overview of the history of antisemitism, see, among the abundant literature, Philippe Burrin, *From Prejudice to the Holocaust: Nazi Anti-Semitism* (New York: New Press, 2005).

11. Anthony Julius, *Trials of the Diaspora: A History of Anti-Semitism in England* (New York: Oxford University Press, 2010).

12. Robert Wistrich, *A Lethal Obsession: Anti-Semitism from Antiquity to the Global Jihad* (New York: Random House 2010).

13. Georges Bernanos, *Le Chemin de la croix-des-âmes* (Paris: Gallimard, 1948).

14. Dire repercussions of the Middle East conflict on the French Jewish community were documented in several books and official documents. See, for data, the website of the Commission Nationale Consultative des Droits de l'Homme, http://www.cncdh.fr/; see also "Chantier sur la lutte contre le racisme et l'antisémitisme (rapport présenté par Jean-Christophe Rufin, écrivain, médecin et responsable de nombreuses associations d'aide humanitaire, remis à Monsieur le Ministre de l'Intérieur, de la Sécurité Intérieure et des Libertés Locales le 19 octobre 2004 suite à une lettre de mission en date du 29 juin 2004." (This document is available on the website of the French Ministry of the Interior, http://www.ladocumentationfrancaise.fr/var/storage/rapports-publics/044000500/0000.pdf). Likewise, see Pierre-André Taguieff's *Rising from the Muck: The New Anti-Semitism in Europe* (Chicago: Ivan R. Dee, 2004). For a pointed and witty intellectual and cultural history of this allegedly "new antisemitism," see Jeffrey Mehlman, "Sad News: l'antisémitisme nouveau est arrivé," *Contem-*

porary French Civilization 27 (Summer–Fall 2003), pp. 277–96. Finally, see Jonathan Judaken's more recent analysis of the phenomenon, in "So What's New? Rethinking the 'New Antisemitism' in a Global Age," *Patterns of Prejudice* 42, nos. 4–5 (Autumn 2008), pp. 531–60.

15. On French postmodern *Trauerspiel* and its relation to Auschwitz, see Elisabeth J. Bellamy, *Affective Genealogies: Psychoanalysis, Postmodernism, and the "Jewish Question" after Auschwitz* (Lincoln: University of Nebraska Press, 1997). More pointedly, and also on the differences and similarities in thinking about death in Maurice Blanchot and Emmanuel Levinas, see Gillian Rose's intriguing *Mourning Becomes the Law: Philosophy and Representation* (New York: Cambridge University Press, 1996).

16. This is Finkielkraut's and Taguieff's argument.

17. Needless to mention the Machiavellian exploitation of Muslim antisemitism by European extreme right-wing movements. . . .

18. Paris: La Fabrique, 2011.

19. I am referring to Jean-Claude Milner's *Les penchants criminels de l'Europe démocratique* (Paris: Verdier, 2003).

20. On left-wing Holocaust denial, see Pierre Vidal-Naquet's *Assassins of Memory: Essays on the Denial of the Holocaust* (New York: Columbia University Press, 1993), and Alain Finkielkraut's *The Future of a Negation* (Lincoln: University of Nebraska Press, 1998). Most of the analogies that I have listed can be found in the rhetoric of left-wing Holocaust denial.

21. In 2004, two incidents were reported. A young woman named Marie L. claimed to have been assaulted in the Parisian subway by black and Muslim youth, and a Jewish man set fire to a Jewish community center on rue Popincourt (in Paris) and disguised his crime as an antisemitic attack. The Marie L. affair was made into a compelling film by André Téchiné, *La fille du RER [The Girl on the Train.]*

22. The murderous instance of antisemitism is the Ilan Halimi affair, discussed in Adrien Barrot's book *Si c'est un juif: réflexions sur la mort d'Ilan Halimi*(Paris: Michalon, 2007).

23. Paris: Editions de Minuit, 1965.

24. *Le Non de Klara* (Paris: Maurice Nadeau, 2002), translated as *Refusal* (London: Harvill Secker, 2007). Very few essays have been written about this novel. On its reception in France and the United States, and on the ethical problems posed by this fictional account of a Jewish survivor and by the minimization of Jewish identity, see Lucille Cairns, "La mémoire de la Shoah: The Contentious Case of Soazig Aaron's *Le non de Klara*," *French Studies* LXIV, no. 4 (2010), pp. 438 – 50.

25. Cairns, p. 439.

26. Ibid. The reference to a telephone conversation is in the essay by Cairns. The telephone conversation was between Cairns and Aaron.

27. *La douleur* (Paris: P.O.L., 1985).

28. See Sami Nair, Edgar Morin, and Danièle Sallenave, "Israel-Palestine: le cancer" in *Le Monde* (June 3, 2002).

29. *Le Non de Klara*, p. 102.

30. Montpellier: Indigène, 2010.

31. Saint-Victor-de-Morestel: Les Provinciales, 2011.

32. Time for Outrage! (New York: Twelve).

33. Henry Rousso, *The Vichy Syndrome* (Cambridge, Mass.:: Harvard University Press, 1994, for the English translation).

34. See Alain Badiou, *De quoi Sarkozy est-il le nom?* (Paris: Nouvelles Editions Lignes, 2007).

35. Pierre Jourde, quoted in Pierre-André Taguieff, *Rising from the Muck,* p. 75.

36. See the polemic between Lawrence Summers and Judith Butler. An account of the polemic can be found in *Butler's Precarious Life: The Powers of Mourning and Violence* (New York: Verso, 2006).

37. *La Promesse et l'obstacle: La gauche radicale et le problème juif* (Paris: Editions du Cerf, 2007).

38. "A New Judeocentrism?" in Nathalie Debrauwere-Miller, *Israeli–Palestinian Conflict in the Francophone World* (New York: Routledge, 2009).

39. Ibid.

40. Paris: Grasset, 2006.

41. Stanford, Calif.: Stanford University Press, 2003.

42. Paris: Editions Lignes, 2005.

43. *Une querelle avec Alain Badiou, philosophe* (Paris: Gallimard, 2007).

44. Some tendentious conclusions notwithstanding, Jean-Michel Chaumont has analyzed with precision the emergence of the figure of the victim and the competition among victimized groups in the West throughout the last decades. See *La concurrence des victimes* (Paris: La Découverte, 2002.)

45. Trom, p. 137.

46. "While Arendt provoked a scandal when she asserted that Eichmann was in fact ordinary, Milgram impressed everyone by showing that any ordinary man was Eichmann." (Trom, p. 135).

47. *Homo Sacer: le pouvoir souverain et la vie nue* (Paris: Le Seuil, 1998), p. 179.

48. See Nair, Morin, and Sallenave: "In the last days of the reconquest of the West Bank, the IDF has been guilty of looting, gratuitous destruction, homicide, execution, incidents in which the chosen people has behaved like the superior race."

49. See *L'Imprescriptible* (Paris: Le Seuil, 1986), p. 78.

6 Anti-Zionism and the Resurgence of Antisemitism in Norway

Eirik Eiglad

On July 21, 1973, Ahmed Bouchiki was shot dead on the streets of Lillehammer. Although he was a Moroccan citizen, Bouchiki had lived in Norway since 1965 and was expecting a child with his Norwegian wife when agents connected to Mossad, the Israeli intelligence service, killed him. The Norwegian police immediately caught the agents, and five served jail sentences in Norway. Until the recent atrocities at Oslo and Utøya, the Lillehammer affair, as it was to be called, was considered by many to be the worst terrorist act ever to have occurred on Norwegian soil.

In 1973 the impact of the Second World War was already ebbing, and Lilliputian Norway stood on the threshold of an oil adventure that would pump unprecedented wealth into its national infrastructure. Due to its wealth as well as its outsider status, Norway was soon to gain a reputation as a generous donor to Third World development. The country was also considered to be an impartial international observer, and ultimately a peace broker. Today, the small town of Lillehammer is most famous for hosting the Olympic Winter Games in 1994, and one year earlier the Norwegian capital city lent its name to the Oslo Peace Accords. Together with its Scandinavian neighbors, Norway has gained an international reputation in sportsmanship, impartiality, and commitment to peace.

In the early 1970s antisemitism was not a general problem in Norway. After the war and the Nazi extermination program for the European Jews—and the Quisling regime's complicity in the Holocaust—antisemitism was utterly discredited among the general population.[1] The Labor Party, as well as its Conservative counterpart, was clearly sympathetic to the Jewish struggle for a homeland in Palestine, and the country's powerful labor unions had strong ties to the Israeli trade union movement and the kibbutzim. Polls revealed that the overwhelming majority of the Norwegian public was sympathetic to the Israeli State, and that the Israelis fought a just cause in the recurrent military conflicts with its neighboring Arab nations.[2] In sharp contrast to Norway, Denmark had managed to help save its Jewish population during the Holocaust, and the Danes remained highly sensitive to the plights of the Jewish people. Sweden had a different historical legacy from Norway and Denmark because of its neutrality during the war, but there, too, sympathy for the State of Israel was strong, and explicit anti-Jewish prejudices were taboo, whether formulated in racial or anti-Judaic terms.[3] To be sure, antisemitism *did* exist—in all the Scandinavian countries—but it did so mainly within fringe milieus on the far right. There, paranoid delusions of a Zionist world conspiracy, mixed with Holocaust denial and an often rabid anti-Jewish outlook, provided crucial links between veterans from the Eastern front and new generations of neo-Nazis. Explicit anti-Jewish attitudes, however, were never allowed to take center stage in public discourse in any of the Scandinavian countries.[4]

Today, the situation has changed. Alarming reports of anti-Jewish harassment and vandalism have become more common, and many attitudes that can properly be termed antisemitic have become publicly acceptable, as open antisemitic rhetoric has been smuggled back into mainstream political debates—we even have seen explosive outbursts of antisemitic hatred on the streets of the capital.[5]

To understand this monumental shift, and how it was at all possible, we have to look at another trend that emerged back in the 1970s. More specifically, we have to look at how anti-Zionism gradually constituted itself as a political force on the Left.[6]

The Emergence of Anti-Zionism in Norway

The end of the 1960s saw the emergence of a New Left in Europe and America and a radicalization of students and workers. These trends percolated northward, but the full impact of the new social movements and the counterculture hit Norway later, at a time when authoritarian and terrorist sects already had succeeded in elbowing out the more libertarian and populist impulses on the continent and across the Atlantic. At the turn of the decade, Norwegian followers of Mao Zedong had already established solid networks that could monopolize the debate on the Left.

This delay, I believe, was a fateful one for the trajectory of radicalism in Norway and can help explain the strong influence that Maoism came to achieve.

Maoist elements first influenced the Socialist Youth Organization (SUF) in 1966 and then went on to win over the whole organization. In 1969 they broke with their mother party, Sosialistisk Folkeparti. In February 1973, they launched Arbeidernes Kommunistiske Parti (AKP [m-l]). Although the Maoist movement never numbered more than a few thousand members in Norway, its zeal and discipline ensured a disproportional influence. In the 1970s this relative strength even granted their cadres audiences with Pol Pot and Chairman Mao.

Maoism was expressly an attempt to retain a Marxist-Leninist (and Stalinist) approach after the Soviet Union defected to "social imperialism." Ideologically it was, above all, characterized by the significant role it ascribed to the peasantry as well as its emphatic anti-imperialism—an approach that elevated cultural identity and national struggles as a political principle. Norwegian Maoists advocated the "dictatorship of the proletariat" and were greatly influenced by the theories of the "People's War" developed by Mao and the Vietnamese General Giáp. This was a military approach that sought to undermine the technological advantages of imperialist armies—both Western, notably U.S., and Soviet—by extending and protracting armed conflicts, in order for the revolutionary armies to fight successful wars of attrition from broad popular bases in the interior. These Maoists were greatly inspired by the tenacity and the successes of anti-imperialist struggles, notably in Indo-China, and it was through this ideological prism that they would interpret Arab and Palestinian nationalism and its struggle against Israel.[7]

The Maoists introduced anti-Zionism to Norway, first through SUF and then later through AKP (m-l) and its front organizations. Even in 1968, the political platform of SUF integrated demands for "the right of Palestinian Arabs' right to live in the areas that constitute present Israel," and furthermore stated, "The State of Israel in its present form as a bridge-head for imperialism must cease to exist."[8] In 1970, activists formed Palestinakomiteen (The Palestine Committee; Palkom), dedicated to work against "Zionism" and "all forms of imperialist oppression." This front organization was modeled on the experiences in support of the Vietnamese struggle against U.S. imperialism. This factor was crucial, as thousands of activists came to see Vietnam as a victory and expected Palestine to be the next focal point in the global struggle against imperialism. In Norway, as the historian Tarjei Vågstøl points out, this work was focused on "revolutionary anti-imperialism" rather than "humanism and pacifism." The Norwegian political climate interpreted Palestine in light of the Vietnam conflict: "Palestine was the new Vietnam, and the Israeli state was considered a lackey for U.S. imperialism."[9] As with the Vietnam experience, the "radical activists were not focused on peace but on Palestinian or Arab victory."[10]

The Palestine Committee engaged in extensive propaganda work but at first seemed mostly to influence segments on the Left already receptive to their basic anti-imperialist message. In the mid-1970s, the movement was riveted by disagreements over the nature of "Soviet imperialism," whereupon significant segments split off, and in 1976, Palestinafronten (The Palestine Front; Palfront) was formed to compete for activists' allegiance. After the suffocating atmosphere in the Palestine Committee, this organization chose a different strategy. They shared the basic anti-Zionist outlook, to be sure, but downplayed their anti-imperialist message. Acknowledging the need to win broader public support for the Palestinian cause, they laid conscious strategies for winning over parties and trade unions, starting from the Left and moving in toward the center. In the words of its first leader, Nils A. Butenschøn: "The aim was to win whole parties and organizations for Palestine."[11]

Despite early tensions, the split seemed to have created a division of labor that benefited both organizations. While the Palestine Front moved steadfastly to convince Norwegian mass organizations, the Palestine Committee continued its ideological work, sending health teams to the region and gaining credibility for its practical fieldwork. Toward the end of the decade, both organizations were highly active, and the breakthrough in Norwegian public opinion began from 1980 on. The Palestine Front had succeeded in forming a wider coalition consisting of parties, youth organizations, and trade unions in Fellesutvalget for Palestina (The Coalition for Palestine), and the invasion of Lebanon marked the turning point for public perceptions of Israel in Norway. The 1980s may have been a period where mass activism receded, but the organizations became more professional and were able to maintain a strong, visible presence. Most important, however, was the fact that many of the ideas and demands of these organizations now were shared by public opinion and among influential politicians.[12]

Palkom still exists and remains one of the oldest such group in Europe, and the Coalition (Fellesutvalget) still musters broad support. It must be remembered, however, that intransigent refusals to accept Zionism and Israel from the start were at the core of Pro-Palestinian activism in Norway. Let us therefore have a closer look at how these activists presented their anti-Zionist narrative.[13]

The Anti-Zionist Narrative

The eventful year of 1973 also saw the publication of *Palestinerne,* Peder Martin Lysestøl's influential account of Palestinian Arabs' resistance to Israel.[14] Lysestøl was a key activist in AKP (m-l), was instrumental in creating the Norwegian Palestine Committee, and helped form Palestine solidarity groups in Sweden and Denmark.

According to Lysestøl, the summer of 1973 revealed to Norwegians the "ruthlessness and the brutality of the Israeli police system." The Lillehammer affair was "an example of how Israeli terror has spread to Norway," and Lysestøl unveils how the Israeli state arrogantly broke all international jurisdiction and "openly declared that all countries of the world is its terrain of battle." The affair caused great commotion in the media and strained relations between Norway and Israel—justified criticisms were leveled against Israel and the Mossad. Lysestøl, however, gives the narrative a peculiar twist. For him, the event proved that the Israelis are simply "murderers in the service of imperialism."[15]

What is conveniently left out of Lysestøl's account, of course, is the wider historical context. Lysestøl fails to mention how eleven Israeli athletes had been killed the year before by Black September, a Palestinian terrorist group, at the Munich Olympics. It is generally acknowledged that the killing of Bouchiki was a failed reprisal action, and that the Israeli agents made a mistake: they had aimed to kill Ali Hassan Salameh, who was thought to have masterminded the Munich operation. Lysestøl fails to mention how *Palestinian* terrorists *already* had declared all countries of the world their terrain of battle; and how this action by Black September was part of a wave of wanton hijackings and murders in the early 1970s.[16] Several terrorist actions, like the later Dawson's Field Hijackings, were staged by the influential PFLP (which also were Marxist-Leninists) in order to direct "special attention to the Palestinian problem." This, to Lysestøl, was not relevant information.[17] Furthermore, the book consistently downplays the Palestinian role in exacerbating the conflict between Palestinian guerillas and Jordan, which led to the crackdown called Black September, and later the destabilization of Lebanon that led to the fifteen-year-long civil war. As we will see, this one-sided and dubious account marks the whole narrative.

Lysestøl presents the establishment of Israel as an unmitigated disaster and a betrayal of the Palestinian people. The book describes Israelis as imperialists, oppressors, and colonialists, while Palestinians are called freedom fighters and "leaders of the international liberation movement"—except, of course, those that favor Arab–Israeli reconciliation, who are duly denounced as lackeys of the bourgeoisie and Zionist power.

Furthermore, Lysestøl explicitly refuses to acknowledge Jewish nationhood (although he claims that Arabs belong to one nation), and he denies any historical ties between Jews and the land of Israel. Zionism was, we learn, not a legitimate struggle for national liberation and consolidation. Quite the contrary: "Zionism was from the start an imperialist ideology. The aim of the Zionists was to conquer land for 'European culture.'"[18] He portrays the establishment of Israel as a particularly clever move by racist Europeans who did not want to have a Jewish problem within their own national borders but sought to extend their power to geopolitical and strategic control over the Middle East and its rich oil fields. Zionism is presented as a cynical ideological instrument to use Jews to colonize important territories for the imperialist powers.

However, Zionism was not merely an instrument of British imperialism. Lurking in the shadows were cunning rich Jews in Europe who used Palestine to ensure that poor Jews emigrating from the East did not endanger their own positions of privilege and power. In a section titled "Rich Jews Get a Problem," Lysestøl explains how Zionism was conceptualized: Large Jewish capital owners joined forces to make sure the influx of poor Eastern Jews—"the Jewish surplus-proletariat"—did not threaten their position in Europe.[19] In this account, he brings up a series of traditional anti-Jewish stereotypes: "The impetus in the Zionist movement was Lord Rothschild and his class brothers: European monopoly capital, culturally attached to Judaism."[20] Apparently, Zionism was just a means for the rich Jewish bourgeoisie to fend off socialism and channel poor Jews somewhere else—and gain an important bridgehead for imperialism in the process.[21] During the Mandate period, Lysestøl laments, the British imported tens of thousands of "prison guards"—that is to say, they allowed for Jewish immigration in the troubled interwar period. These Jews were "alien elements in the Arab world," but with the help of British imperialists they became "alien elements with power."[22]

With the Second World War and the victory of the Allies over Nazism came a changed political constellation of Europe as well as a new international balance of power. October 1945 saw the birth of United Nations, and precisely when the British relinquished their responsibility for their Palestinian Mandate in May 1948, the State of Israel was proclaimed. In the Anti-Zionist narrative, these events get a peculiar twist.

Indeed, reading Lysestøl, one is led to believe that the Second World War was fortunate for the Zionists, just as earlier migrations of poverty-stricken Jews from persecutions and pogroms in the Pale of Settlement are presented as minor victories in cunning Zionist schemes to gain a foothold in Palestine. Lysestøl does mention the brutal persecutions of Jews in Europe, but only in passing, and only to explain how this "ensured plentiful access to Jews who wished to emigrate." Lysestøl wryly expresses how "Nazism solved the immigration problem for the Zionists" by causing a wave of emigrants from Europe to Palestine.[23] The war also changed the situation in Palestine, he explains: "Even though the country was not pulled directly into the war, the balance of strength between Palestinians and Zionists was significantly tipped in favor of the Zionists."[24] This was particularly so because "Zionist propaganda exploited Jewish suffering during the war to generate sympathy for the establishment of a Jewish state."[25]

While anti-Jewish pogroms, persecutions, and the Holocaust receive but scant attention from Lysestøl, he deplores the plight of the Palestinians and the Arabs having to live with an alien entity in their midst: "With the establishment of the British Mandate over Palestine, the Palestinians were subjected to *harsher repression than almost any other people in history.* Not only were they subject to colonial control, but the land was also opened up for immigration of European Jews. They arrived in the thousands."[26] Later, in describing the martial laws implemented by the British and continued after the establishment of Israel, Lysestøl even has the audacity to claim, "*The brutality of the laws is without parallel.*"[27] In his attempts to demonize Israel, Lysestøl also goes a long way in comparing Israel—from its very inception—to the Nazi regime.

Above all, Israel is chastised for being an imperialist bridgehead in the Middle East: "The historical role for the Jews in Palestina," Lysestøl reveals, became apparent after the First World War, as part of the cunning schemes of the colonial powers.[28] It cannot be emphasized too strongly that these perspectives fit into the coarse, Manichean worldview of the Maoists, formulated in suspense of intensified global conflict between "anti-imperialists" and "imperialists." The late Tron Øgrim, the leading ideologue of the Norwegian Maoists throughout the 1970s, explained the crucial significance of becoming involved in the struggle for Palestine: "Palestine is an intersection for conflicting superpowers' interests," and, he adds, it could well be the place where the third, imperialist world war breaks out. And there, "in Palestine stands one of the world's strongest liberation movements up against imperialism."[29]

As mentioned, the Maoists clearly distanced themselves from the standard bloc policies of the Cold War and came to view the "social imperialism" of the USSR with as much contempt as their Western counterparts. In *Palestinerne*, Lysestøl clearly condemns the activities of the Soviet Union—which in the early 1970s launched openly antisemitic campaigns against the global evils of Zionism—for supporting the Palestinians in words only: "In practice they send *material* support to the worst enemies of the Palestinian people!" What was this material support? The Soviet Union allowed the annual emigration "of tens of thousands of people Israel is using to occupy the land of the Palestinian people and serve as cannon fodder in the Zionist aggression-army."[30] In language that sounds awkward to more cosmopolitan leftists today, Lysestøl rails against immigration, particularly illegal immigration—regardless of all the persecution and hardships Jews had suffered elsewhere, both before and after the Second World War. Indeed, one of his main arguments against "the imperialist powers" of Great Britain, America, and the Soviet Union is that they allowed for Jewish immigration into the Mandate area and later into Israel. From the very start, these sentiments were shared by anti-Israeli activists, as when, in 1968, SUF published its demand for the dissolution of Israel, duly accompanied by a revealing caricature that shows Uncle

Sam steering the ship *Exodus* to shore (while he stretches out to grab oil refineries), pouring out a massive column of uniformed soldiers with Israeli flags, who are bayoneting and trampling Palestinians underfoot.[31]

Most importantly, Lysestøl asserts that the Jewish presence in Palestine was a problem from the beginning; they should under no circumstances have been granted an independent state. Lysestøl vociferously protests against dividing Palestine and allowing any parts to be "handed over to a foreign power, Zionism." It is adamantly clear that he considers not only Gaza and the West Bank as Palestine, but also the territory of Israel.[32] He repeatedly asserts that armed struggle is the only way to liberate Palestine.

The Struggle against the Zionist Enemy

An ideologue who more extensively clarified the theory behind the armed resistance to Israel was Abu Fadi, an influential theorist in Fatah in the 1970s; he was the head of its Marxist-Leninist wing and the unofficial leader of the Maoists in the Middle East.[33] Abu Fadi had close personal and political connections to the Norwegian Maoists, and in the spring of 1970 a lecture tour was organized to inform Norwegian students and anti-imperialists about the conflict with Israel. According to Lysestøl, Fadi was "an excellent thinker and strategist"—"No Palestinian leader exerted greater influence on us in the Palestine Committee in those years."[34] In 1973, the journal *Røde Fane* published his theses about the importance of the Palestinian struggle and the necessity for a "protracted People's War" against "the Zionist enemy."[35]

From the outset, Abu Fadi was adamantly clear that "the contradiction between Palestine's Arab people and the Zionists is antagonistic."[36] He claimed that "the Zionists occupied Palestine and chased the Arab Palestinian people from its soil, and established a colonialist and racist regime that is fascist and expansionist in nature."[37] From the perspective of the anti-imperialist People's War, Fadi specifies, "the main distinct feature of the Palestinian situation is that it is impossible to liberate *the whole of the Palestinian territory* and for Palestinian Arabs *to obliterate Israel's Zionist state* without help from the outside."[38] It was therefore crucial to unite Palestinians within Israel with Palestinians and Arabs in the neighboring regions and to associate this movement with a global anti-imperialist rising against Zionism and imperialism. Still, since "the contradiction is *absolutely antagonistic,* and that it can *only* be solved through armed confrontation," Fadi warns against compromising with the ultimate goal and striving for a final, negotiated peace settlement. "It follows that this contradiction cannot be solved by either pacifist or political means, nor by the intervention of the United Nations or the superpowers with plans to steer a middle course and strike some kind of balance to remove the contradiction."[39] The alternatives Fadi offers to his Palestinian compatriots—and to the Israelis—are, at best, limited. According to Abu Fadi, his conclusions about the exceptional contradictions in the Palestinian situation are elevated to an "objective law" that leaves only two alternatives: "Either the People's War will be victorious," he claims, or "everything will be lost."[40]

A crucial component of this Maoist strategy in Palestine was to remain steadfast and to wear down "the Zionist enemy" through incessant low-scale warfare, in order to demoralize and persuade large sections of the Jewish population living in the Zionist state that there was no use for maintaining Israel and continuing the armed struggle. This protracted People's War, he insisted, had nothing to do with a mere concern for basic rights and mutual recognition; it was a life-and-death struggle, one that required drastic measures. "In Palestine the situation is such that we have to fight a colonial state that is fully established and not merely the outgrowth of an imperialist state," Abu Fadi continued. "This means that it will be possible to gain a final victory solely with armed force, and that it will not be sufficient to be victorious in one major battle only, to persuade the enemy of the futility in continuing the fight, but it will be necessary to cleanse out his positions, settlement for settlement, house for house."[41]

The aim was to crush Israel completely and rid Palestine of the Zionist enemy in order to actualize the aspirations of the greater Arab nation. Apparently, this aim was deemed logical, since, in the words of Fadi, "Palestine is a part of the Arab fatherland, and Zionism and imperialism seek to dominate the Arab fatherland and the Arab nation."[42] From his paranoid perspective, Arab national aspirations are, presumably, barred by the presence of Zionist settlements on Arab land, and it is the prerogative of the Palestinian revolution to play the role of instigating and realizing the greater Arab awakening.

In light of Fadi's and Lysestøl's analyses, we should evaluate the Maoist obsession with Israel and Palkom's "consistent support for the Palestinian people's struggle for national liberation."[43] Arguably, Lysestøl's utter and embarrassing inability to comprehend political antisemitism, German Nazism, and the emergence of Jewish nationalism—as well as the Holocaust and its traumas—and his crude "anti-imperialist" analysis, borrowed from intransigent anti-Zionists like Abu Fadi, all provide good reasons for shelving his book, *Palestinerne*. Yet, Lysestøl's book is well worth perusing, not for its many comments on revolutionary strategy—based on lessons given by Stalin and Mao—but for its consistency in presenting the anti-Zionist narrative. For Lysestøl and the Palestine activists, Israel is an illegitimate, alien entity created by British imperialism in a cunning game to outsmart the Arabs. The Manichean worldview Lysestøl offers has been instrumental in fomenting strong anti-Zionist sentiment in Norway.

When Lysestøl's *Palestinerne* was republished in 2009, contemporary Palkom activists hailed the book as a "classic," and Ebba Wergeland, another long-time leading supporter of Palestine, wrote how it "was formative for a generation of activists for Palestine."[44] The book has apparently had enormous significance for the direction of Palestinian solidarity and for developing its demands; reading it is, Wergeland concludes, "important for understanding how the Palestinians and their Norwegian friends were thinking." Furthermore, the author's prominence should not be underestimated: in 1967 Lysestøl was the leader of SUF, just as the organization made its turn toward Maoism. In Norway, as Vågstøl asserts, "the Palestine movement started as Peder Martin Lysestøl's one-man-project in 1967 and ended up as well integrated with official Norwegian policy twenty years later."[45] Finn Sjue, another key Palkom activist, confirms how Lysestøl was the movement's high-profile figure, crucial to its "first and critical phase."[46] Not only did the pioneering efforts undertaken by a handful of Maoist pioneers make a heavy imprint on Norwegian political culture, but it is widely recognized that the Palestine movement in Norway has been among the strongest in Europe.

Anti-Zionism in Norway Today

Forty years later, we can attest that anti-Zionists have been exceptionally successful in winning over whole parties and organizations to their cause—and public opinion too. In the early 1970s, anti-Zionism was considered a fringe phenomenon associated with the Maoist-influenced left, but in April 2009, when the party Rødt republished Lysestøl's book, the cultural and political attitude to Israel had fundamentally changed. Anti-Zionist attitudes are now respectable; they are held by leading figures in academic life, trade unions, and politics, and have clearly colored Norway's interpretation of the conflicts in the Middle East. As the publishers claim in the preface to the book, "today public opinion to a great degree supports the side of the Palestinians."[47]

Since the early 1970s, Lysestøl and others like him have called for Norway to break diplomatic relations with Israel, to initiate a series of sanctions against the country, to wholeheartedly support Palestinian military efforts and, later, to formally recognize Palestinian authorities. Over these troubled decades important changes have taken place in the international arena and in the Middle East itself. Most striking, of course, are the rapprochements and failures of the peace processes. Also striking is the declining appeal of Pan-Arabic nationalism, as well as the secular and socially progressive focus that guided earlier militant movements and the emergence of Islamism as a major political force. Hamas, the Palestinian branch of the Muslim Brotherhood, entered the arena during the 1987 Intifada.

In 2006, as the world reacted against the electoral victories of Hamas—and its explicit antisemitic charter calling not only for the physical destruction of Israel but also for religiously sanctioned murdering of Jews—Norway was the first Western country to recognize the elections, and in March 2007, Deputy Foreign Minister Raymond Johansen was the first Western government representative to visit the leaders of Hamas. Neutral Norway was put in a very awkward position, as it seemingly legitimatized a party that flatly refused to recognize "the Zionist entity." Lysestøl argued in *Klassekampen* against the stigmatization of Hamas as fundamentalists; he called for the organization to be valued for its social role, and their elected leadership to be respected as representing the will of the Palestinian people.[48] Despite its regressive social policies and its intransigent antisemitism, Lysestøl still brushes these matters off and consistently describes Hamas as an Islamic liberation movement. He claims that he is unable to detect anything directly antisemitic in the Hamas charter,[49] and uses Abu Fadi (Monir Shafiq) as an example of secular, liberal Islamists within Hamas: religion is not so important to them, Lysestøl says—what unites Palestinian activists in Hamas is their legitimate resistance to the occupation. In 1980, Lysestøl's old friend, the influential Maoist ideologue Abu Fadi, converted to Islam, and was later a key figure in developing Hamas's organizational infrastructure.

There are, however, other direct links between the militant pro-Palestinian activism endorsed by the Norwegian Maoists and the anti-Zionist outlook propagated by political Islam. In 1979, the AKP (m-l) welcomed the Iranian Revolution, and their vigorous mobilizations against the Soviet invasion of Afghanistan led to a new anti-imperialist movement, the Afghanistan Committee, which supported the "liberation movement." Many within the AKP (m-l) were attracted to the "anti-imperialistic" tenacity of militant Islamic movements. Some members even converted to Islam in the process and have been outspoken representatives for Muslims in Norway.

One such figure is Trond Ali Linstad, who runs the webpage Koranen .no, upon which he offers interpretations and advice on Muslim thought and behavior and gives exposure to anti-imperialist politics. Linstad has marked himself as a vocal, and controversial, proponent of Islam in Norway, recently proposing a "Muslim Manifesto" in which it is apparent that he had replaced the Maoist scorn for liberal democracy with an Islamic one.[50] In particular, Linstad has publicly defended Hamas and its intransigent refusals to recognize Israel. Against those within Palkom today who are willing to accept peace terms and stability for Israel, he forcefully insists on the mantra that he claims has always guided Norwegian solidarity with Palestine: "Israel is a colonialist phenomenon! Unconditional support for the Palestinian struggle for liberation!" We should note that Linstad was not just a rank-and-file Maoist: quite to the contrary, he was the leader of Palkom for a full decade—from 1976 to 1987.

In the mid-1980s, Linstad and other Maoists advocated active support not only for the Afghan Mujahedeen but also for the expressly reactionary Khomeinist regime in Iran.[51] Linstad's admiration for the Ayatollah has remained: on the anniversary of the death of Ayatollah Khomeini, Linstad sang his praises and urged his audience to learn from the great "Imam Khomeini." In particular, Linstad points out Khomeini's teachings about "Palestine and the so-called Israel," and sums up the lessons with quotations from the Ayatollah: "Israel was created by colonialist regimes in the East and the West to oppress and break the Islamic nation." Furthermore, "To have any relationships with Israel and its agents, commercially or politically, is forbidden and contradicts Islam." In conclusion, he advises: "We must all rise up and destroy Israel and replace it with the proud Palestinian nation."[52]

Like Linstad, Lena Larsen is another outspoken convert with a background in the AKP (m-l). She is married to Basim Ghozlan, a prominent Muslim spokesman and imam in Norway. Ghozlan distanced himself from Linstad's "Manifesto"[53] and is generally considered moderate—except, of course, when it comes to Israel. In a nasty poem called "I am Israel," he vents his rage and states that Israel brags about being founded on terror, torture, and violence—on ethnic cleansing and a deep hatred of Palestinians. In Ghozlan's poem, Israel claims that "all Palestinians are our enemies and must leave our Holy Land before they are executed." In this piece, Ghozlan also refers to Ahmed Bouchiki, stating that he was killed only because Israel mistook him for a Palestinian.[54] His fanciful projection is not very subtle. Ghozlan explicitly insists that Israel has *full* control over the United States and *the whole of* the American administration— the voice in the poem declares, "I practically run the country"—and controls the American media too: "*All* decisions that the United States makes are primarily meant to serve me and my own interests." Indeed, Ghozlan admits that his charges "may seem exaggerated," but he perniciously assures us that "the truth is actually worse than this."[55]

Ghozlan is not merely a poet, however. He is also a leader of the Islamic Union who contributes to the public discourse in Norway. In 2003, he justified suicide bombers against Israeli civilians on the assumption that all Israeli citizens are occupiers. In his view, Israel simply has no innocent civilians. On the sixtieth anniversary of the liberation of the Nazi death camps, Ghozlan even spoke out against Holocaust Remembrance Day, calling it a provocation. "I get offended," he groans, "when so many people are stuck in what happened sixty years ago."[56] The commemoration of the Holocaust, Ghozlan contends, "contributes to create a naïve image of 'the poor Jews,' which in turn is exploited by political and religious groups to legitimize Israel achieving its own state."[57]

With a more refined pen, the international best-selling author of *Sophie's World,* Jostein Gaarder, wrote a startling commentary in *Aftenposten* in 2006 to protest the invasion of Lebanon. Apparently speaking on behalf of an outraged Norwegian public, his call for the dismantling of Israel was shockingly forthright: "Israel is history. We no longer recognize the State of Israel. There is no way back. The State of Israel has raped the world's recognition and will get no peace until it lays down its weapons. The State of Israel in its current form is history."[58] In a rather perverse gesture of "generosity," Gaarder ended his prophetic diatribe with an appeal to treat the forthcoming Jewish refugees well, once Israel is no longer there to protect them. Gaarder's frankness generated an intellectual storm in Norway, and he was accused of blatant antisemitism.

Gaarder was upset when he learned that he had offended so many, particularly since he was, as he professed, a true friend of the Jewish people; he expressed sadness upon hearing that individual Jews were affronted and that he was accused of leveling charges against Judaism as a faith. He offered his apologies to all *individuals* whom he might have unintentionally offended. At face value, we could perhaps excuse Gaarder for his alleged naiveté. Yet it should be noted that Gaarder not only had taught the history of religion in schools for two decades but had published some twenty books over a period of twenty-five years, a third of which are used as curriculum textbooks on major world religions and ethical issues.[59] His infamous text, titled "God's Chosen People," was not only well written; it was bone-chillingly well informed. Allegedly written as a "political protest" of the Lebanon War and its civilian casualties, Gaarder managed the remarkable feat of presenting almost all the central elements of classic anti-Judaic thought in modern anti-Zionist garb. The fact that Gaarder, with his sensitive mind and his wealth of experience, could write such an explicit antisemitic tract and expect to get away with it seems to prove the deep roots that anti-Zionist thinking and rhetoric have struck in Norway.

In an afterthought published in 2011, Gaarder apparently regretted his harsh commentary, and said, "We must never express ourselves in such a way that legitimate criticisms of Israeli policies can be mistaken for an illegitimate and by all means intolerable harassment of Jews or Judaism."[60] However, it should be noted here that Gaarder's apology applied only to the extent that his criticisms had stigmatized Jews and Judaism, particularly Jews living outside of Israel's borders. He evidently is oblivious to the fact that he articulated the logical conclusions of contemporary anti-Zionism. He apparently learned very little during these five years.

Usually, the kind of explicit imagery that Gaarder expressed is reserved for political cartoonists. As is well known, both Nazi antisemitism and Soviet anti-Zionism made extensive use of caricatures to convey their hostile messages.[61] Norwegian newspapers regularly publish caricatures of their own that draw on familiar antisemitic elements, often masterfully blending the age-old "illegitimate" stereotypes with more modern and allegedly more "legitimate" ones. Cartoonists seem to be particularly fond of the inversion myth, as exemplified in the way they portray Israeli leaders as Nazi commanders and KZ (concentration camp) guards and in how they merge Jewish and Nazi symbols. In June 2006, for instance, the award-winning cartoonist Finn Graff had to face charges of antisemitism for his caricature of Ehud Olmert as a grinning Amon Goeth (the historical sadistic SS commandant portrayed in *Schindler's List*), with a rifle firing at will at Palestinians who were drawn in a camp resembling Buchenwald.[62] The caricature of Olmert may be the worst of the lot, but for decades now, Finn Graff has excelled in developing such aggressive images in his art.

Strong anti-Israeli resentments are also thoroughly entrenched in contemporary youth culture. In 2008, the Norwegian hip-hop group Gatas Parlament released a song in which they sarcastically toasted the sixtieth anniversary of "Lebensraum" and "the Holy Land." They scorned the Israeli experience "from its first year" as representing oppression, displacement, racism, and Apartheid. Israel, the song goes, is backed by the United States, "who, too, likes genocide." Most chillingly, perhaps, is a basic theme in the song stating that a "victim of harassment" has turned into "a gang leader."[63] Apparently, centuries of anti-Jewish persecution, pogroms, and—ultimately—the Holocaust, can be jeeringly compared to a "troubled childhood." The neo-punk darlings in the band Honningbarna follow similar themes in a track on their latest album: they also like to point out that they see how the Jews "grew up being harassed," and describe how the victim now has turned into a bully. Their judgment is harsh but simple: "Cage the Zionists!" they suggest. Not only "for 1967" but *"for every time."* Not only "for ethnic cleansing" but *"for the whole invasion."*[64] These are not just the provocative lyrics of fringe bands; the most significant aspects of these lyrics are not their extreme positions but the utter moral ease in which these bands surf on deeply entrenched prejudices and how thoroughly the general anti-Zionist narrative informs them.

Anti-Zionism is by no means limited to youth culture: it is apparently one of the very few political issues today that seem to offer ready-at-hand material for a broad spectrum of artists, with songs, paintings, and installations. The practical influence of anti-Zionism in the major trade unions and parties is also significant. In 2002, Gerd Liv Valla, the former leader of the powerful Norwegian Confederation of Trade Unions (LO), called for boycotts of Israel from the main Labor Day pulpit at Youngstorget, and a series of various syndicates have organized boycotts and sympathy strikes against the "Israeli aggressor." In January 2006, Kristin Halvorsen, then the Norwegian minister of finance, made headlines by publicly supporting consumer boycotts of Israeli goods. She was soon pressured by her cabinet to retract her statements, but the party which she leads, the Socialist Left Party, and particularly the Socialist Youth, are heavily involved in campaigning for sanctions against Israel. The more activist boycott campaigns have worked intensely to hurt distributors and vendors of Israeli products and have also protested against and even attacked commercial stalls.

In March 2011, Lillehammer adopted "Israeli Apartheid Week," a Canadian-born initiative with intransigent demands for a total boycott of Israel. Lysestøl has been a key figure in spreading the calls for boycotts and sanctions in Norway. In fall 2009, he was—with, among others, Ebba Wergeland and the rabid anti-Zionist Trond Andresen—one of the architects behind the employees' challenge to the board of the Norwegian University of Science and Technology (NTNU) in Trondheim, calling for a full academic and cultural boycott of Israel.[65] The issue of anti-Israeli boycotts is also very important for the Rødt Party, and their councilors recently held a major campaign to raise the issue of economic sanctions in all Norwegian municipalities and counties. Back in 2005, the county of Sør-Trøndelag was the first regional government to adopt a boycott resolution.[66]

Furthermore, today, as pro-Palestinian activists have focused on a strong humanitarian image that stresses human rights, international legal issues, opposition to violence, and the need for a new peace process, we *should* be confused—these were precisely the points that anti-Zionists consistently rejected as deviations from their real objective: the liberation of Palestine and the eradication of Zionism and its state from the Middle East. It is paradoxical that pro-Palestinian activism now presents an essentially humanitarian program, even as the more unyielding opposition to Zionism and Israel still underlies every demand. Often, however, anti-

Zionists are deliberately vague about exactly *when* and *how* Israel crossed the line of legitimacy. Convinced anti-Zionists have never been uncertain as to what they believe: *Israel* crossed that line the very moment it came into existence. Simmering just below the surface are more extreme positions; although Palkom now publicly calls on Israel to withdraw from the West Bank and end the siege of Gaza, it still considers Zionism to be fundamentally racist and imperialist and advocates the creation of one Palestinian state in the full territory of the former British Mandate. Although the Coalition for Palestine, perhaps the most moderate of the main organizations, allegedly will accept both a one-state or a two-state solution, its logo still presents one united "Palestine" in which Israel is razed from the map. Recently the youth organization of Rødt distributed a popular green team-shirt: unsurprisingly, their dream team is "Palestine," but who is the player and what is the team's number? *Intifada 48.*

Explosions of Anti-Jewish Hatred

In January 2009 the Intifada came to Norway. The Israeli bombing and ground invasion of Gaza prompted thousands to demonstrate in all of Scandinavia's major cities. There were protests every Saturday in Oslo. The first clashes broke out on January 8th, when pro-Palestinian protestors attacked a pro-Israeli demonstration in front of the Norwegian Parliament with bottles and rocks, and scattered groups attacked individuals they believed to be Jews or Zionists.[67] Later that evening there was a torch-lit "peace march" with thousands of people, but identifiably Jewish participants were told to leave; the march also displayed stark antisemitic messages. The leaders of the Palestine movement in Norway refused to criticize the violent attacks, though they paid lip service to peaceful activism. Olav Svorstøl, the leader of the Coalition for Palestine, certainly made it clear that his organization "does not distinguish between worthy and unworthy demonstrations."[68]

Two days later, the events were repeated on a larger scale. In Oslo, the main demonstration that day brought a huge turnout; the thousands of protesters included prominent politicians, intellectuals, and artists, who had broad support from trade unions, community organizations, and political parties—although the demonstrations conveyed explicit anti-Jewish messages. People carried banners and posters identifying Israel with Nazism and Hitler and denouncing the Israeli "child murderers." "Death to the Jews" was heard repeatedly in Arabic, and walls in Oslo were painted with the unmistakable message: "Kill the Zionists." The main demonstration went from the Norwegian parliament to the Israeli embassy and subsequently disintegrated into smaller groups that attacked and vandalized presumably Jewish targets. Not only did they assault the Israeli embassy, but they also attacked the Masonic lodge, allegedly because it was considered an instrument for Zionist world domination. Five McDonalds' restaurants were smashed when text messages and social media spread a rumor that the McDonalds corporation would send their profits to support the Israeli invasion of Gaza. It was even reported that young children were told by older "activists" to "hunt Jews," and again rampant gangs attacked individuals in the streets because they were presumed to be Jews.[69] Repeated clashes with the police during these several days resulted in 176 arrests.

I was present in Oslo during the demonstrations and the furious riots. I witnessed how easy it was that seemingly legitimate protests against Israel could explode into unmitigated anti-Jewish hatred. Still, to me, the most terrifying experience was yet to come.

In the following days and weeks, politicians, media commentators, and public intellectuals warned against social polarization and the prospects of further estrangement and radicalization of immigrant youth—who were seen to be the main instigators of the riots—in order to avoid "French conditions." Politicians initiated a series of public "dialogue meetings" to gain understanding about the source of this anger and violence and to let the "voiceless" speak out. Norwegian police authorities conducted intensive dialogues with detained youth, communicated extensively with schools, and expressly sought to alleviate tensions between what seemed to be mainly youth of immigrant origin and Norwegian authorities. The authorities and the media condemned the violence and the vandalism, to be sure, but they *consistently* downplayed and ignored the overt antisemitism in the protests and riots. Even worse, perhaps, leading Norwegian intellectuals were remarkably silent. Indeed, quite a few expressed sympathy with the rebellious youth, as did the notable commentator Anders Heger, who warned against taking the violence too seriously. "These 'riots,'" Heger claimed, were hardly any worse than the average "post-Christmas-party disturbances."[70] Strong voices warned against stigmatizing the immigrant youth and insisted that the real problem was Israeli brutality and the dire humanitarian situation in Gaza.

The riots represent a historical watershed. Despite insistent attempts to explain away the radical anti-Israeli messages, the riots were not only the most violent street confrontations Norway had seen for decades, but the country had also *never before* witnessed explicit anti-Jewish riots, *not even in the darkest years of our history.* The most frightening aspects of the riots, as I see it, were not the events themselves, but the complacency of the media, leading intellectuals and politicians, and particularly of influential spokespeople of the Left. During the Gaza War, a number of politicians posed in the Parliament with keffiyehs to express where their sympathies lay.

The event showed how Norwegian politicians, media, and police experts proved to be completely unable to detect the political messages explicitly advanced in the riots, and thus to assess the full gravity of the situation. The protests, vandalism, and violence shared slogans, placards, and banners, and the well-documented attacks on "classical Jewish targets" provided ample proof of the sinister dimension of the events. However, a full year after the events, police authorities stated that they had investigated the matter thoroughly by "listening to the youth" and claimed that "anti-Jewish attitudes did not distinguish themselves as a factor."[71] All 176 detainees were acquitted. Alas, the riots were not seen as a necessary wake-up call. The obvious *lack* of basic analytical tools and reasonable political reactions sent an ambiguous message to the small Jewish community in Norway. Was it really safe here? Would anti-Jewish hate crimes be taken seriously in the future? The situation for Jews in Scandinavia seems increasingly tense, though until now there has been little research devoted to analyzing the present conditions.

Although the Oslo riots were particularly baleful, all major Scandinavian cities displayed various ways to protest "Israeli aggression." Sometimes there was violence similar to that witnessed in Oslo. A few months later, Malmö, the third-largest city in Sweden, hosted the Davis Cup match between Swedish and Israeli teams. As the tennis match was threatened with mass disruption, the organizers shamefully decided to close the event to the public. Then, when the tennis match did take place, fenced off and without an audience, six thousand angry protestors attacked the police barriers in attempts to physically stop the match. Malmö has received much attention lately, not the least for the increasing harassment that has been marginalizing its small but long-standing Jewish community. On Holocaust Memorial Day 2010, when the Social Democrat mayor, Ilmar Reepalu, was asked to comment on the insecurity felt by Jews in his city, he obviously thought Malmö's Jewish community was to be held accountable for Israeli politics and considered the hardships they faced quite understandable in light of the situation in the Middle East. Reepalu challenged Sweden's Jewish citizens to distance themselves more explicitly from Israel, and made it clear that in Malmö, "We accept neither Zionism nor antisemitism."[72]

In February 2010, Norwegian broadcasting reported how Jewish children were being harassed and threatened at schools in Oslo, and this news item immediately prompted the government to look into the matter. It is safe to say that in Norway, open racism or discrimination against Jewish citizens is not tolerated. The problem is, rather, that many observers have a hard time discerning antisemitic attitudes unless they explicitly fit into classical, racist categories. So far, however, the reports presented have not grasped the significance of anti-Zionism's outlook and its basic ideas and their effects on Norwegian Jews.

Another issue that is not tolerated is Holocaust denial. When Anders Mathisen, a Labor Party representative to the Sametinget (The Sami Parliament), denied the Holocaust via social media, he soon found out he had crossed the line and immediately became a political persona non grata: The Labor Party rushed to oust him from their ranks and made it clear that they did not want members like him.[73] Open anti-Jewish racism is quite easy to discern, and expressions of indiscreet Holocaust-denials are too. These transgressions of the moral norm warrant prompt responses. But when the targets are Israelis, Zionists, or Israel, the hostility seems to fall within the range of legitimate protest.[74] One recent report effectively reduced antisemitism to a broad question of racism and then dismissed it into the general issue of discrimination.[75]

Anti-Zionism and Antisemitism

Most contemporary radicals insist on a strict distinction between anti-Zionism and antisemitism. Indeed, like Reepalu, most leftists seem to oppose Zionism *as well as* antisemitism and refuse to acknowledge any implication that their resistance to Israel has antisemitic qualities.[76] Furthermore, the disproportional attention devoted to Israel and the high standards demanded of its every political or military move are not unique for Norway, but are part of broader European tendencies challenging Israel and its legitimacy.[77] Today, we also see that anti-Israel attitudes are accompanied by a wider global resurgence of antisemitism.[78]

What, after all, is at the core of anti-Zionism? How does it fit into general antisemitic patterns? First, we should be clear about our definition of antisemitism. A common mistake is to equate it with xenophobia in general or to see it intrinsically linked to racism. Another mistake is to regard antisemitism just as a convenient *Prügelknabe,* a scapegoat that ruling elites can use to deflect attention away from social problems. A third error is to assume that antisemitism has ever had anything to do with "Semitism" or "Semites." We should also note that, minimally, antisemitism—prejudice against and hatred of Jews—has historically taken a variety of religious, cultural, racist, and political forms and that its specific varieties are part of a broad tradition. In his treatment of racist antisemitism, George L Mosse pointed out how "at times Christian, medieval, and racist ideas were so mixed that any distinction between them cannot be made."[79] As with earlier forms of antisemitism, anti-Zionist arguments take a variety of parallel and intersecting forms, some of which are openly hostile to Jews, but, like, antisemitism, the "Zionism" that anti-Zionists claim to fight acquires larger-than-life proportions.[80] Anti-Zionism, however, is not simply another word for antisemitism, nor is it just a coded word for anti-Jewish hatred. The immense ideological force of anti-Zionism would not have been at all possible without linking protests against Israel to older anti-Jewish prejudices, including stereotypes of Jewish control over the media, politics, the economy, and a Jewish conspiracy to dominate world affairs.

Few in Norway see antisemitism as a genuine problem of our times. The American anthropologist Matti Bunzl speaks for many of them when he suggests that "traditional anti-Semitism has run its course," and that in its place, "Islamophobia is rapidly emerging as the defining new condition for the new Europe."[81] Muslims' "structural position as Other," Bunzl claims, is ultimately analogous to that of Jews.[82] In a remarkably shallow analysis, Bunzl claims that "the traditional, modern form of anti-Semitism was designated to effect the exclusion of Jews from the national body"[83]—and Bunzl can therefore claim that Islamophobia now is "a genuine political issue," while "Anti-Semitism, by contrast, is not."[84] In Sweden, the influential anti-Israeli activists Andreas Malm and Mattias Gardell have written extensively against the rise of Islamophobia and the hatred of Muslims.[85] Both downplay the significance of antisemitism as a political force today.[86]

Not surprisingly, Jostein Gaarder agrees. Immediately after the horrific Utøya massacre, Gaarder presented his analysis in the *New York Times*: while racism generally was receding, he claimed, hostility toward Muslims was on the rise—indeed, today Islamophobia has become the new antisemitism.[87] Gaarder's own peculiar success in embodying the continued significance of contemporary antisemitism seems to make his analysis just a little too convenient.

While we can agree that anti-Muslim prejudice and hatred *are* genuine problems that must be fought, we must also recognize that antisemitism—"new" as well as "old"—has always been directed against Jews. And even if the legacy of open anti-Jewish prejudice and hatred was strongly discredited by the Holocaust, new forms of antisemitism soon gained importance in Norway. These new attitudes first influenced the political left, then the mass media, and, then, ultimately, broader public opinion.[88] The significant change came with the emergence of militant anti-Zionism at the end of the 1960s. Against those who insist on strict distinctions between anti-Zionism and antisemitism, Henrik Bachner notes that "the empirical proof for the links between anti-Zionism and antisemitism is overwhelming."[89]

Furthermore, anti-Zionism, Bachner continues, emerged as an international phenomenon with three main propaganda centers: first, the Soviet Union and the Eastern Bloc countries; second, the Arab world; and third, the revolutionary Marxist movements in the West. While Soviet and Arab propaganda was openly antisemitic, "the Western form of anti-Zionism was generally not openly antisemitic, but expressed nonetheless a range of ideas that constituted the core of their Arab and Soviet parallels."[90] Still, the most dangerous aspect of modern anti-Zionism, I would argue, is not its open, explicit antisemitism, but the moral indifference it fosters regarding the fate of Israel and Jews.

Lest this seems like an exaggeration, the historical lessons are terrifying. Historian Jeffrey Herf makes the point succinct when he reminds us that the Holocaust "was not the inevitable outcome of the continuities of German, or of European history. The long tradition of elite and popular anti-Semitism created a climate of indifference in which the murderers could operate but did not per se inspire a policy of mass murder."[91] Herf's colleague Ian Kershaw attests that the "vast majority of Germans" had "no more than minimal interest" in the fate of Jews. In turn, mass support for genocide was unnecessary: the latent antisemitism and apathy were sufficient to allow the increasingly criminal "dynamic" hatred of the Nazi regime the autonomy it needed to set in motion the Holocaust.[92] In his study of Nazi propaganda, Herf deals not only with the paranoid worldview of Nazi antisemitism but also on how the party media crafted *an antisemitic consensus,* consciously feeding into earlier traditional, religious, and racial forms of antisemitism.[93] Herf concludes that "a fanatical but not meager minority embedded in the Nazi party and in its front organizations" disseminated their genocidal message "to a society in which milder forms of anti-Semitism had become commonplace."[94] The parallels to the formation and dissemination of contemporary anti-Zionist ideas are eerily striking. Herf explains how, in this context, even the *Endlösung* could be explained as "a necessary campaign of retaliation in the context of a broader war of defense waged by Nazi Germany against international Jewry, world Jewry, and less frequently 'the Jews.'"[95] Furthermore, "The core ideological justification for the Holocaust lay in the depiction of the Jewry as constituting a powerful international conspiracy that was the driving force behind the scenes of the world war," and, "In the Nazi imagination there was no such thing as an innocent Jew."[96]

Norwegian Anti-Zionism in Perspective

As we have seen, for the Maoists of the early 1970s, struggles for national liberation were integral to anti-imperialist politics, and their condemnation of Israel was linked directly to their rejection of U.S. foreign policy. The Norwegian Maoist party AKP (m-l) had been in perpetual crisis since 1980—over party appeal, apparatus, and ideology. The historian Håkon Kolmannskog explains the exceptional rise and decline of Norwegian Maoism, with the "Faustian pact" the leaders of AKP (m-l) made with Mao's thought: the exotic recipes of Mao's Chinese experience offered party activists the promise of superhuman powers, which compensated for the actual insignificance of their politics for the Norwegian working class.[97] When, one by one, their bright Eastern lighthouses faded out, the cadres slowly realized that it was not sufficient to remove the (m-l) from their name to rescue their party brand, and they reconstituted themselves as Rødt in 2006. Throughout these years of party decline, however, the activist front organizations were strengthened and dug more deeply into the Norwegian political landscape. Ironically, while its general anti-imperialist politics became more obviously irrelevant, the Palestinian issue became more and more important.

The ever-increasing significance of the Palestine issue *as a symbol* seems directly related to the gradual insignificance of other politically symbolic issues for the anti-imperialist left. Besides the exceptional influence of Maoism and its "anti-imperialist" imperatives, these trends are not in any way unique to Norway or the Scandinavian countries. The immense historical opportunities that opened up with the fall of the Berlin Wall in 1989 and the crumbling of "real existing socialism" were generally not grasped by the Left, which has witnessed a steady ideological decline in the decades that have followed. This decline of the Left has been accompanied by the rise and entrenchment of anti-Zionism.[98]

It is true that anti-Zionism in Norway today is an integral part of the political culture of the Left *as a whole*.[99] This does not necessarily imply that most left-leaning Norwegians are self-declared anti-Zionists, nor do they consciously adhere to the anti-imperialist theories of the Three Worlds. Still, many Norwegians—particularly leftists and peace activists—have accepted the broad outlines of the Palestinian narrative that Maoists like Lysestøl worked so hard to spread in Scandinavia. Lysestøl, as we remember, insisted that the Jewish State "was created by imperialism and it has served imperialism."[100] Even "moderate" anti-Zionists seem to agree that it is about time for Israel to be taught a real lesson, perhaps even suffer a major military defeat—like Nazi Germany in 1945, as the controversial political scientist Norman Finkelstein has proposed. The Socialist Left Party politician and prominent member of the Peace Initiative, Ingrid Fiskaa, has admitted that she sometimes "wishes for the UN to fire precision missiles against select Israeli targets," to stop the "slow genocide of the Palestinian people."[101] The only reason the UN does not consider attacking Israel, she claims, is that it does not serve U.S. interests.

Lysestøl still argues that "Israel is the last colonial power in the world"[102] and still believes in the "Palestinian revolution." He is adamant in considering Gaza, the West Bank, *and Israel* as "Occupied Palestine."[103] The Oslo agreement was "a tragedy and a derailment of the struggle," he contends: "It has barred development for more than 15 years. Palestine became a question of development in the so-called 'self-governed' territories, the West Bank and Gaza."[104]

"Acceptable" forms of anti-Zionism are juxtaposed with the "unacceptable" forms of classical antisemitism and thereby succeed in transmitting fundamental messages of anti-Jewish hostility to new generations of activists. Although the Western variety of anti-Zionism seldom expresses explicit genocidal intentions, others willingly declare their opposition to Israel in such terms. Time and again representatives of Hamas, Hizbullah, Islamic Jihad, and others have repeatedly urged for a jihad against the "Zionist Entity," and the murderous regime in Tehran has repeatedly called for Israel's annihilation. If matters ever come to a terminal showdown, countries like Norway, and particularly its anti-Zionists, will be complicit in fostering a "culture of indifference."

Antisemitism, it must be remembered, was, at least in its genocidal form, not merely racist or xenophobic: it was a *Weltanschauung* that promoted a theory of *power,* hidden and immense, that the Jews—and now the Zionists—allegedly hold. There is, to borrow a term from Saul Friedländer, a strong "redemptive" aspect of contemporary anti-Zionism. To rid the world of oppression, colonialism, and racism, more than *any* other political issue, anti-Zionism is affirmed today as the mark of radical authenticity. The continuation of an antisemitic legacy through the prism of anti-Zionism is obvious when we understand antisemitism as a theory of *conspiratorial power,* always the most lethal component of anti-Judaism and antisemitism. Today, "Zionism is stigmatized as a spectre threatening peace, progress and prosperity throughout the world," Robert S. Wistrich warns us; "it is pictured as a vast, mysterious, dark and omnipotent power manipulating world imperialism behind the scenes through its alleged control of the media, the banks, the multinationals and a multitude of other transnational organizations."[105] It is in light of such a theory of conspiratorial power that we should evaluate contemporary forms of anti-Zionism; its intense immediacy within Norway was revealed in the placards, banner, slogans, and actions of the ominous Oslo riots.

A consequence of the allied victory over the Nazis in the Second World War, Jürgen Habermas concluded, was that "the rug was pulled out from under *all* claims to legitimacy that did not at least rhetorically embrace the universalistic spirit of the political Enlightenment."[106] The liberation of the death camps in 1945 did more than anything else to discredit racism in its blatant ideological forms. It was therefore crucial that anti-Zionism, in particular its Western variety, succeeded in presenting itself as clearly distinct from classical antisemitism—indeed, it seemed in direct opposition to it. With a perverse historical irony, today, though, resistance to Israel and Zionism is presented as a universalist struggle against oppression, colonization, and racism—and against the particularism of Nazi antisemitism.

Norway has been charged with being "the country with the strongest anti-Israeli attitudes in Europe."[107] It is certainly safe to say that there exists an "anti-Zionist consensus" in Norway today. The contemporary Left in Norway gravely underestimates the lethal thrust that drives the anti-Zionist imagination. Here, it is well worth remembering that the history of Nazism is also to a large extent the history of its underestimation. The antisemitic programs of the Nazis were not just propaganda lies, as Hannah Arendt insisted: we should "recall the much more numerous instances when Hitler was completely sincere and brutally unequivocal about the definition of the movement's true aims, but they were simply not acknowledged by a public unprepared for such consistency."[108] For those who care to look, the genocidal intentions of Israel's enemies are amply documented.

Armed and Organized

In the aftermath of the Six Day War in 1967, and the fateful "three No's" at the Arab League's Khartoum summit, the renowned libertarian socialist author Jens Bjørneboe composed a ringing appeal to radical young Norwegians. Having seen Nazi propaganda and antisemitism in action in the 1930s and 1940s, Bjørneboe warned against underestimating the antisemitic rhetoric of the Arab leaders and popular masses. Those who cry out for the destruction of the Jews must be taken seriously, he insisted. Bjørneboe was deeply troubled by increasing tendencies to succumb to anti-Israeli rhetoric among a new generation of students and radicals, and his only consolation was the fact that "this time, what remains of this people [the Jews] will not allow themselves to be slaughtered like lambs at the altar. They are organized, and they have weapons."[109]

Unfortunately, the emerging "New Left" in Norway did not heed Bjørneboe's anguished appeal, and by 1973 there was a stable and significant segment of the radical left that publicly advocated a strong anti-Zionism. During the Yom Kippur War, *Klassekampen* could publish an editorial stating that the aim of the Palestinian liberation struggle was to wipe Israel off the map.[110] Less than thirty years after the Holocaust, basic Jewish demands for collective politics, identity, and security—indeed, survival—could be interpreted by Maoist demagogues as imperialism, racism, and colonialism.

In the early 1970s, these views were still confined to the Maoist-dominated extreme Left. In December 1973, six months after the Lillehammer affair, polls showed that a full 78 percent of the Norwegian public supported Israel, a percentage higher than in any other Western country.[111] Although the murder of Ahmed Bouchiki generated much media attention, and much criticism of Israel, it did not generate deep hostility toward Jews, or strike antisemitic chords. But a good deal has changed since then, and for forty years now, anti-Zionist ideas have poisoned radical socialist politics in Norway and struck solid roots in the general population. This change within public opinion has not only created a sinister "climate of indifference" regarding the fate of Israel, but has even served to shield a broader resurgence of antisemitism in its wake.

In Norway today, explicit calls for the destruction of Israel are accepted as "criticisms of Israeli policies," and anti-Zionist hatred is discreetly tolerated as legitimate frustration over alleged acts of Israeli inhumanity. These extreme views are now so commonplace that one can even call for the final military defeat of Israel, as Jostein Gaarder did, and still expect to be considered a "friend of the Jewish people." Gaarder and his colleagues will not acknowledge it, but anti-Zionism does not primarily have a humanitarian or pacifist agenda; as we have seen in the ideas of Peder Martin Lysestøl and Abu Fadi, it promotes the dissolution or destruction of Israel. Indeed, it is precisely the fact that Jews now have a state and are prepared to defend it that annoys anti-Zionists the most. More than anything else, it is this rejection of the Israeli right of sovereign nationhood, including the right of the Jews to be armed and defend themselves, that carries the age-old legacy of antisemitism into the new century.

NOTES

1. Which is not meant to deny undercurrent antisemitic attitudes among the general public, as was expressed in 1947 when a full quarter of Norwegian voters were unwilling to allow the immigration of Jewish "displaced persons" after the Holocaust; see Bjørn Alstad, ed., *Norske meninger*, vol. 1 (Oslo: Pax, 1969), p. 139. Neither is it meant to deny certain problematic aspects of official policy, particularly regarding the delayed process of restitution for values confiscated from Norwegian Jews shipped off to Nazi death camps, as the journalist Bjørn Westlie brought to light as late as 1995; see Bjørn Westlie, *Oppgjør: I skyggen av Holocaust* (Oslo: Aschehoug, 2002).

2. Karl Egil Johansen, *Jødefolket inntar en særstilling: Norske haldningar til jødane og staten Israel* (Kristiansand: Portal forlag, 2008).

3. Sweden, which was neutral during the Second World War, seemed to have both more continuous antisemitic trends and a more open anti-Zionist rhetoric in the early years. For an account of resurgent antisemitism in Sweden after World War Two, see Henrik Bachner, *Återkomsten: Antisemitism i Sverige efter 1945* (Stockholm: Natur och Kultur, 1999).

4. Changing perspectives in the Norwegian media regarding Jews, Israel, and its military conflicts, are dealt with in Johansen, pp. 74–177.

5. One of the few books dealing with the resurgence of antisemitism in Norway today is Manfred Gerstenfeld, ed., *Behind the Humanitarian Mask: The Nordic Countries, Israel, and the Jews* (Jerusalem: Jerusalem Center for Public Affairs, 2008).

6. There have also been anti-Zionist elements on the political right in the 1990s and the current century, notably Alfred Olsen's Folkets Motstandsbevegelse, Tore Tvedt's Vigrid, and Terje Sjølie's Boot Boys—and today also the violent Slavic Union—but these tendencies are expressly antisemitic in a classic sense, and have no influence whatsoever on public opinion or official policy. They are therefore not the subject of this essay.

7. The Chinese theory of the "Three Worlds" was to become influential to the point of being dogma in the Norwegian Maoist movement, helping to explain the pivotal importance that AKP (m-l) attributed to the conflict with Zionism, Israel, and "imperialism."

8. See Sosialistisk Ungdomsforbund, "Om situasjonen i Midt-Østen," *Den politiske platformen og andre viktige vedtak* (Oslo: SUF, 1968), p. 13.

9. Tarjei Vågstøl, *Den norske solidaritetsrørsla for Palestina, 1967–1986* (Hovedoppgave IAKH, UiO, våren 2007), p. 26. Vågstøl's work provides a partisan yet informative account of the emergence of Palestine solidarity work in Norway: Based on interviews of key personalities in the movement, it reveals much of their underlying motivations and strategies. All translations from Norwegian are mine.

10. Vågstøl, *Solidaritetsrørsla*, p. 21.

11. Nils Butenschøn, interviewed in Vågstøl, *Den norske solidaritetsrørsla*, p. 63.

12. As regards official Norwegian policy, Vågstøl mentions 1987 as the definitive turning point, with the accession of a new Labor government, in which ministers and advisors with pro-Palestinian sympathies gained prominent positions.

13. This problem was explored by Judith Vogt, "Left-Wing 'Anti-Zionism' in Norway," *Patterns of Prejudice* 9, no. 6 (1975), pp. 15–18; and Jan Benjamin Rødner, *Løgnere iblant oss: En analyse av den anti-sionistiske propagandaen* (Oslo: Exodus, 1976).

14. Peder Martin Lysestøl, *Palestinerne: Historie og frigjøringskamp* (1973; Oslo: Rødt, 2009). All translations from Norwegian are mine.

15. Ibid., pp. 192–93.

16. Between 1971 and 1973, Black September carried out dozens of terrorist attacks— sixty in 1973 alone. See Yaacov Lozowick, *Right to Exist: A Moral Defense of Israel's Wars* (New York: Anchor Books, 2003), pp. 149–50.

17. Lysestøl blames the "pro-Israeli Western media" for condemning the terrorism of Palestinian groups. At times, however, he personally discredits the spectacular terrorist actions, as they are not compliant with the idea of the "People's war" Maoists favored. See Lysestøl, *Palestinerne*, pp. 178, 184; and discussion on pp. 200–203.

18. Ibid., p. 193.

19. Ibid., pp. 62–63. The Norwegian term *Storkapitalen* is itself highly problematic in this context: Here, Lysestøl uses the term *Jødisk storkapital* ("Jewish large capital").

20. Ibid., p. 71.

21. Ibid., pp. 58–66.

22. Ibid., p. 89.

23. Ibid., p. 90.

24. Ibid., pp.125–26. Contrary to the anti-Zionist narrative, it should be noted that both before and during the Second World War, the Nazis were heavily involved in cultivating anti-Jewish sentiments in the Middle East. See, for instance, Jeffrey Herf, *Nazi Propaganda for the Arab World* (New Haven: Yale University Press, 2009). In sinister ways, the conflicts in the Palestinian Mandate were also directly connected to the Nazi war effort. Recent studies have discovered that the Nazis harbored concrete plans to extend their Final Solution to Palestine: in the summer of 1942 there was an Einsatzkommando stationed in Athens—with SS veterans from the Eastern theater ready for deployment in Palestine—but war fortunes turned against the Nazis in Africa and the Middle East before the plans could be implemented. See Klaus-Michael Mallmann and Martin Cüppers, *Nazi Palestine: The Plans for the Extermination of the Jews of Palestine*, trans. Krista Smith (New York: Enigma Books, 2010). For a general account of Nazi collaboration with Palestinian leadership in the interwar period, and its influence on contemporary Islamic antisemitism, see Mathias Küntzel, *Jihad and Jew-Hatred: Islamism, Nazism, and the Roots of 9/11*, trans. Colin Meade (New York: Telos Press, 2007).

25. Lysestøl, *Palestinerne*, ch. XII; particularly p. 131.

26. Ibid., p. 78; emphasis added.

27. Ibid., p. 154; emphasis added.

28. Earlier, "the colonial powers had not yet discovered the possibilities of using European Jews." And later, "The Zionist leaders in Israel were chosen for the role of being agents of the United States in Palestine," Lysestøl, *Palestinerne*, pp. 56, 117.

29. Tron Øgrim, "Ei viktig bok," Lysestøl, *Palestinerne*, pp. 20–22.

30. Lysestøl, *Palestinerne*, pp. 194–95; emphasis in original.

31. SUF, *Den politiske platformen*, p. 13.

32. These views are still prevalent in the recently penned postscript to the 2009 edition, "Kampen for et fritt Palestina fortsetter," in *Palestinerne*, pp. 245–66.

33. Lysestøl quoted in Vågstøl, *Solidaritetsrørsla*, pp. 28–29. Abu Fadi is also known as Mounir Shafiq; he wrote most of Yassir Arafat's speech to the UN Assembly in 1974.

34. Lysestøl, *Palestinerne*, p. 265.

35. Abu Fadi, "Den Palestinske revolusjonen vil seire!" *Røde Fane* 6 (1973); the translations from Norwegian are my own. *Røde Fane* was a Maoist theoretical journal, published by the AKP (m-l).

36. Fadi, pp. 63, 60.

37. Ibid., p. 60. Fadi laments that "the Zionist enemy has established an actual state in the greater part of Palestine," and claims that Israelis are "always ready to steal more territories and Zionize them."

38. Ibid., p. 64. Emphasis added.

39. Ibid., pp. 60, 61. Emphasis added.

40. Ibid., p. 68. I should add that the mere use of terms such as *contradictions* and *objective laws* here does not in any sense make Fadi's analysis "Marxist." His perspectives should be duly acknowledged as a crude, and deeply antisemitic, form of Arab nationalism.

41. Ibid., p. 66.

42. Ibid., p. 62.

43. See, for instance, Palkom, "Fra 10. Landsmøte i Palestinakomiteen," *Røde Fane* 3 (1976), p. 79. Last revised in March 2008, the basic principles of Palkom have remained essentially unchanged since the organization was founded in 1970.

44. Ebba Wergeland, "Palestinerne: Boka som formet en generasjon Palestina-aktivister," *Rødt! Marxistisk Tidsskrift*, no. 3 (2009). This book was "of enormous significance," Wergeland claims, "for the political platform that the Palestine Committee without notable changes has kept ever since."

45. Vågstøl, *Solidaritetsrørsla*, p. 95.

46. Finn Sjue, "Forord 2009," *Palestinerne*, p. 18; Vågstøl claims that Lysestøl and Sjue, together, were the "architects" of the Palestine movement in Norway. See Vågstøl, *Solidaritetsrørsla*, pp. 42, 112.

47. Erik Ness, "Forord fra forlaget," *Palestinerne*, p. 12. Despite global public support, Ness continues, "Palestinians are worse off then ever before. Gaza has been bombed to pieces, Palestine is divided into Bantustans, and the people are treated like the blacks were under the Apartheid regime in South Africa."

48. *Klassekampen* (July 5, 2006). He maintains that Hamas is a Palestinian liberation movement that just happens to be Islamic, and that its charter is not really antisemitic.

See also the new epilogue in Lysestøl, *Palestinerne,* pp. 245–66, revealing Lysestøl's position on the Islamization of the Palestinian resistance movement, the Oslo process, and the prospects for peace with Israel. Nowhere does he retract any statements or views he presented in 1973.

49. Lysestøl, *Palestinerne,* p. 255.

50. Trond Ali Linstad, "Muslimsk manifest," *Aftenposten* (January 24, 2010).

51. Only a few months after radical mass movements toppled the Shah, the clerical and antisocialist nature of the victorious Khomeinist regime was revealed. Still, many anti-imperialists argued for its progressive, mass-based nature throughout the 1980s. See, for instance, Trond Ali Linstad and Erik Fosse in *Klassekampen* (November 2, 1985). Linstad and Fosse share the background from AKP (m-l) and medical field work in Palestine and Lebanon, through the Palkom and Norwac.

52. Trond Ali Linstad, *Koranen.no* (June 6, 2011). The translation from Norwegian is my own.

53. *Aftenposten* (February 1, 2010).

54. Basim Ghozlan, "I Am Israel," *Islam.no* (May 6, 2005). The translation from Norwegian is my own.

55. Ghozlan; emphasis added.

56. Morten Harper," Muslimer angriper Holocaust-dagen," *Fri Tanke* 6 (2006), pp. 18–23. The translation from Norwegian is my own.

57. Ibid., p. 18. As is obvious, Ghozlan does not yet recognize Israel.

58. Jostein Gaarder, "Guds utvalgte folk?" *Aftenposten*(August 5, 2006). The translation from Norwegian is my own.

59. It was reported that Gaarder had consulted some ten highly esteemed prominent intellectuals and "experts on the Middle East" before publishing the commentary. According to *Verdens Gang,* one of these was Odd Karsten Tveit, who has been a Middle East correspondent for Norwegian Broadcasting since 1977.

60. Jostein Gaarder, "Ettertanke" (April 20, 2011). The translation from Norwegian is my own.

61. Judith Vogt, *Historien om et image: Antisemitisme og antizionisme i karikaturer* (København: Samlerens forlag, 1978).

62. Finn Graff, *Dagbladet* (July 10, 2006).

63. Gatas Parlament, "Sekstiårslaget," 2008. Indeed, in the line "Startet som mobbeoffer, endte opp som bandeleder" alone, Gatas expresses three central tenets of contemporary antisemitism: the trivialization of the Holocaust; the inversion myth; and the conspiratorial notion that Israel or the Jews are somehow in control of a criminal network.

64. Honningbarna, "Fri Palestina" (2011); emphasis added.

65. "Since 1948 the state of Israel has occupied Palestinian land and denied the Palestinians basic human rights." The call is available in full at Akademiskboikott.no.

66. The decision was deemed illegitimate and was later overturned.

67. The weekend of January 8–11 is fully documented and analyzed in Eirik Eiglad, *The Anti-Jewish Riots in Oslo* (Porsgrunn, Communalism Press, 2010).

68. *Aftenposten* (January 9, 2009).

69. *Dagbladet* (January 11, 2009). See also Eiglad, *Anti-Jewish Riots.*

70. Anders Heger, "Sitrondrops og sensur," *Dagsavisen* (January 10, 2009).

71. Ingjerd Hansen og Runa Bunæs, "Det antijødiske er ikke framtredende," *Aftenposten* (January 29, 2010).

72. Mikael Tossavainen, "The Reepalu Affair as a Paradigm of Swedish Left-wing Antisemitism," Stephen Roth Institute, *Topical Brief* 6 (2010). As Tossavainen shows, Reepalu thought antisemitism was a right-wing phenomenon, and he was unable to detect antisemitism that did not neatly fit into a broader, more general definition of racism.

73. Interestingly, however, Mathisen was soon picked up by virulently anti-Zionist milieus around Mohamed Omar. See Mohamed Omar, "Man måste få säga sanningen: Intervju med Anders Mathisen" (March 18, 2011), alazerius.wordpress.com (website no longer available). Omar represents disquieting trends to consolidate anti-Zionism as a distinct political approach (independent of the traditional left–right axis), and has expressed ambitions to create an anti-Zionist party in Sweden, modeled on Dieudonné's Parisian experience.

74. Symptomatically, the Coalition for Palestine answers charges of antisemitism by attempting to distinguish between Jews and Israelis: as long as one uses the words *Zionism* and *Israelis,* not *Judaism* and *Jews,* one apparently stays within the boundaries of legitimacy. See Elisabeth Palerud og Benjamin Endré Larsen, "For saken—Ikke mot menneskene," *Palestine.no* (June 27, 2011).

75. Kunnskapsdepartementets arbeidsgruppe om antisemittisme og rasisme i skolen, *Det kan skje igjen,* Report, January 12, 2011.

76. For their part, the programs of the Palkom and Rødt show their inability to face antisemitism beyond the simple, crude racist form that was defeated in 1945. See, for instance, Rødt, *Antirasistisk Manifest* (Vedtatt av Rødts landsmøte, March 10–11, 2007), p. 5. Anti-imperialist activists pride themselves on being able to distinguish between Jews and Judaism, on the one hand, and Israel and Zionism, on the other, yet the demarcation lines are not at all obvious. Sometimes, these anti-Zionist attitudes spill over into explicit anti-Jewish prejudices. In 2004—after intense intraparty debates—Rød Valgallianse and AKP deemed it necessary to exclude Hans Olav Brendberg, a longtime party member and religion teacher, after he had made numerous claims about how "Jewish power" was a cornerstone of international politics and that Jews nourished bitter hatred of non-Jews. He even held them collectively responsible for killing Christ—all "classic" elements of antisemitism. See Kjetil B. Simonsen, "Antisemitism in the Socialist Tradition," *Communalism* 11 (August 2007). Yet, unfortunately, the exclusion of Brendberg seems to be an exception that proves how interwoven these concepts actually are.

77. Robin Shepherd, *A State beyond the Pale: Europe's Problem with Israel* (London: Orion, 2009).

78. See, for example, Pierre-André Taguieff, *Rising from the Muck: The New Antisemitism in Europe,* trans. Patrick Camiller (Chicago: Ivan R. Dee, 2004); Walter Laqueur, *The Changing Face of Antisemitism: From Ancient Times to the Present Day*

(Oxford: Oxford University Press, 2006); and Robert S. Wistrich, *A Lethal Obsession: Anti-Semitism from Antiquity to the Global Jihad* (New York: Random House, 2010).

79. George L. Mosse, *Toward the Final Solution: A History of European Racism* (New York: Howard Fertig, 1978), p. 231. Today, this confusion persists, but we may also add Islamist, Arab nationalist, Palestinianist, and anti-Zionist ideas to this antisemitic repertoire.

80. "The history since 1948, in any case, is that of Israel, not of Zionism"; Laqueur, p. 208.

81. Bunzl is convinced of "thorough insignificance at the current time of the modern variant of anti-Semitism," and adds that "the modern form of anti-Semitism has run its historical course"; Matti Bunzl, *Anti-Semitism and Islamophobia: Hatreds Old and New in Europe* (Chicago: Prickly Paradigm, 2007), pp. 4, 14, 24.

82. The analogy, Bunzl claims, is that Islamophobia "functions less in the interest of national purification than as a means of fortifying Europe." Furthermore, "Anti-Semitism was designed to protect the purity of the ethnic nation-state, Islamophobia is marshaled to safeguard the future of European civilization"; Bunzl, pp. 10, 13, 44.

83. Ibid., p. 26.

84. It is interesting to see that Bunzl notes how the possible rise of Islamophobia "would likely lead to a new radicalization, both in Europe and across the Islamic world, where more and more young Muslims would become holy warriors in an endless clash of civilizations. A consequent rise in anti-Semitism would then be the least of our problems." Bunzl, pp. 45, 46.

85. See Andreas Malm, *Hatet mot muslimer* (Stockholm: Atlas, 2009), and Mattias Gardell, *Islamofobi* (Stockholm, Leopard förlag, 2010).

86. Malm expressly thinks that contemporary Islamophobia shares the genocidal intentions of historical antisemitism. Gardell, on the other hand, seems to miss the particular characteristics that drew antisemitism to its "redemptive" conclusions, and he essentially likens antisemitism with antiziganism (p. 20). It is worth noting that, in his other works on political Islam, Gardell consistently downplays the ideological centrality of antisemitism for thinkers like Said Qutb, Yussuf al Quaradawi, and Louis Farrakhan.

87. Jostein Gaarder and Thomas Hylland Eriksen, "A Blogosphere of Bigots," *New York Times* (July 28, 2011).

88. Johansen, p. 176.

89. Bachner, p. 332. The translation from Swedish is my own.

90. Ibid. To be more specific, the "Marxist movements" Bachner refers to were self-consciously "Marxist-Leninist"—Stalinist or Maoist—and distinguished themselves sharply from the broader Marxist parties and Social Democratic movements. These distinctions were important in Norway in the 1970s, separating the journal *Orientering* from *Kontrast* and *Røde Fane*. Only later would anti-Zionist ideas influence broader segments of the "Marxist movements," along with broader segments of public opinion.

91. Jeffrey Herf, *The Jewish Enemy: Nazi Propaganda during World War II and the Holocaust* (Cambridge and London: The Belknap Press, 2006), pp. vii–viii.

92. Ian Kershaw, quoted in Herf, pp. 276–77.

93. Herf, pp. 17–49, 264–78.

94. Ibid., pp. 15–16. For the cultivation of the "antisemitic consensus," see also George L. Mosse, *The Crisis of German Ideology: The Intellectual Origins of the Third Reich* (New York: Grosset and Dunlap, 1964) and *Toward the Final Solution: A History of European Racism* (New York: Howard Fertig, 1978); and Yehuda Bauer, *Rethinking the Holocaust* (New Haven, Conn.: Yale University Press, 2001).

95. Herf, p. 9.

96. Ibid., p. 266.

97. Håkon Kolmannskog, *Ideologisk leierskap i den norske ml-rørsla: Det umogleges kunst 1965–1980* (Hovedoppgave, IAKH, UiO, våren 2006).

98. The ease in which contemporary anarchists, syndicalists, and autonomists un-critically adopt the anti-imperialist dogmas of the Maoist left attests to their failure to develop an independent, libertarian socialist politics.

99. I agree that if leftists "can at times sound relatively moderate in their anti-Zionism, that is just a sign of how far things have gone on the left"; Robert S. Wistrich, "Left-Wing Anti-Zionism in Western Societies," in Robert S. Wistrich, ed., *Anti-Zionism and Antisemitism in the Contemporary World* (New York: New York University Press, 1990), p. 49. Emphasis in original. For a useful Marxist analysis of the ideological degeneration of the Left, see Moishe Postone, "History and Helplessness: Mass Mobilizations and Contemporary Forms of Anticapitalism," in *Public Culture* 18, no. 1 (2006), pp. 93–110.

100. Lysestøl, *Palestinerne*, pp. 63, 110–117, 157.

101. *Klassekampen* (April 19, 2008).

102. Lysestøl, *Palestinerne*, p. 246.

103. Ibid., p. 262. The table is reproduced in Mats Gilbert og Erik Fosse, *Øyne i Gaza* (Oslo: Gyldendal, 2010, 2nd ed.), p. 308; In this eyewitness report from the Shifa hospital, the two Norwegian doctors—and anti-imperialist veterans—claim that the invasion of Gaza was a premeditated massacre of Palestinian children and civilians.

104. Lysestøl, *Palestinerne*, p. 263.

105. Robert S. Wistrich, "Introduction," in *Anti-Zionism and Antisemitism in the Contemporary World*, p. 3.

106. Jürgen Habermas, quoted in George M. Frederickson, *Racism: A Short History* (Princeton, N.J.: Princeton University Press, 2002), p. 128.

107. Jonas Gahr Støre, *Om å gjøre en forskjell: Refleksjoner fra en norsk utenriks-minister* (Oslo: Cappelen Damm, 2008), pp. 135–36. Foreign Minister Støre does not take this charge seriously, but insinuates that it simply is a tool Israel uses to pressure European governments.

108. Hannah Arendt, *The Origins of Totalitarianism* (Cleveland: Meridian, 1958), p. 343.

109. Jens Bjørneboe, "Israel og araberstatene: Et åpent brev til norsk, radikal ung-dom," *Dagbladet* (November 4, 1967). The translation from Norwegian is my own.

110. *Klassekampen*, 37 (1973); quoted in Johansen, pp. 117–18.

111. Johansen, pp. 119–20.

7 Antisemitism Redivivus: The Rising Ghosts of a Calamitous Inheritance in Hungary and Romania

Szilvia Peremiczky

RELIGION, HISTORY, race, ethnicity, nationality, social memory, socialization: these are the explosive ingredients of every form of Jew-hatred, the crazed obsession that forms an all-pervasive psychopathology in Eastern and Central Europe. The virulent grassroots antisemitism rife across the whole region combines traditional Christian Judeophobia with ethnic and nationalist[1] racial hatred of the Jew. Contemporary Hungary and Romania both fit squarely into this regional picture.[2] History in this region is particularly important as the root cause and driver of contemporary manifestations of grassroots antisemitism: it is conspicuously present in contemporary public discourse and obsessively engages the public mind in sterile blame games, which in Hungary, in particular, become an all-pervasive culture of grievance and ressentiment, an overwhelming sense of having been treated badly by the world, and particularly by "the Jews."

The twentieth century was indeed not kind to Hungary—as it certainly had been to Romania—for early in the century Hungary had suffered grievous losses of territory, population, and regional status. As a result of the Treaty of Trianon (1920), Hungary became landlocked. It lost two-thirds of its former territory and one-third of its non-Jewish Hungarian population to the surrounding successor states to the Habsburg Empire. Trianon cost the country much of its agricultural base, its mining industry, its perimeter railway system, the Croatian seaports, as well as its status as a serious player in the Great Game of Europe and as the dominant power in the Carpathian Basin. Above all, the Treaty meant the painful loss of millions of Hungarians to the successor states and the relinquishing of many country towns that were 100 percent Hungarian. Romania, on the other hand, emerged as the clear winner in the post-World War. With one great reordering of the geopolitics of the region, along with the annexation of Transylvania, Romania walked away with the jackpot in the Balkan sweepstakes. It may well be said that Hungary's agony has been Romania's triumph.[3]

In the second half of the nineteenth century, the Kingdom of Hungary became the dominant partner in the Austro-Hungarian Dual Monarchy, and, as a result, was able to carry much more weight in the affairs of nineteenth-century Central and Eastern Europe than would seem to have been warranted solely by its size, population, and economic development. The ramshackle Kingdom was a socially backward, still largely feudal country, badly in need of economic development, where Hungarians constituted only 48 percent of the population among a multitude of increasingly restive ethnic/language groups with independence ambitions of their own. It was in this sociopolitical context that the 5 percent of Jews in the population[4] were granted unconditional political and social emancipation in 1867. A win-win situation was thereby created for both the Hungarian leadership and the Jews of Hungary. With the 5 percent Jewish population of Hungary electorally registered as "Hungarians of the Mosaic Faith," the Kingdom of Hungary was able to claim an instant Hungarian majority at the stroke of a pen. On the other hand, a grateful Hungarian Jewry—or at least its reformist Neolog[5] segment—was more than happy not just to adopt the Hungarian language, to culturally assimilate, and to take front and center in driving national development, but also to participate in the drive to forcibly Magyarize[6] various non-Hungarian ethnic groups.[7]

What followed was half a century of florescence known as the Golden Age of Hungarian Jewry. But even though emancipation led to the emergence of a confident Hungarian Jewish middle class that achieved, within three short decades, comprehensive domination in banking, industry, commerce, science, culture, education, media, and the liberal professions, all was not well in the Hungarian Jewish Camelot. Both religion-based and race-based antisemitism were on the march and popular discontent with the relatively favorable status of Jews was steadily increasing. It was in Hungary that Europe's first antisemitic political party—the National Antisemitic Party—was established in the 1870s, and it was thanks only to massive political and international intervention that a notorious blood libel case was prevented from succeeding in court in the early 1880s. None of this, however, stanched the boundless confidence of Hungarian Jewry in a rosy future ahead, although a handful of Zionist seers, first and foremost among them Theodor Herzl himself, clearly foresaw as early as the turn of the century the horrors that were to come a mere four decades later.[8] There were frequent conversions by assimilationist Jews to one or another of the Christian denominations, intermarriage became common among wealthy upper-class Jews and down-at-heel, impecunious Hungarian gentry, and by the turn of the century, a younger, increasingly secularized, and often antireligious generation of Hungarian Jews became politically hyperactive at the cutting edge of left-wing radicalism.

The loss in the First World War was popularly attributed to Jewish war profiteering and outright Jewish treachery[9] by Hungary's majority Christian nationalists, whose proto-fascist political default position was by then a combination of right-wing nationalist conservatism, antisemitism, ressentiment, and irredentism. It was in these circumstances that young Jewish radicals founded the Hungarian Communist Party in 1918[10] and then promptly instituted four months of Red Terror following a successful *putsch* in 1919 to set up the second Soviet republic in Europe after Russia. Their defeat was followed by White Terror and pogroms that exacted a terrible revenge on completely innocent Jews, which Hungarian antisemites to this day deem to have been an entirely inadequate revenge for the wrongs suffered under the "Jewish Terror" of the Hungarian Soviet.[11]

The 1920 Treaty of Trianon transformed remnant Hungary into a largely monoethnic country, where ethnic Germans remained the only other significant ethnic minority besides Jews.[12] The loss of territories was popularly attributed to dark machinations by international Jewry and Freemasonry, and Transylvania in particular was widely perceived as having been awarded to Romania in return for a promise to emancipate Romanian Jews. International Jewry was accordingly seen as having perfidiously stabbed Hungary in the back, in base ingratitude for the more than generous emancipation volunteered by Hungary for its Jews five decades earlier, and having done so with the active connivance of a treacherous home-grown Hungarian Jewry. Trianon thus wrought a wrenching transformation for Hungarian Jewry; from economic locomotive and demographically indispensable Hungarian ally in a Hungarian-dominated multiethnic Carpathian Basin, to hated competitor of a hopelessly uncompetitive Christian middle class for jobs and opportunities in the much reduced circumstances of remnant Hungary.[13] In stark contrast to its powerful prewar position in the Dual Monarchy, Hungarian Jewry suddenly found itself in a situation of egregious political weakness, in an overwhelmingly antisemitic and strongly proto-fascist country.[14] Yet, a superpatriotic post-Trianon Hungarian Jewish community refused all offers of help and assistance from international Jewish organizations, because, as the Hungarian Neolog-Jewish politician Vilmos Vázsonyi[15] put it at the time: "The sorrow of our nation cannot be the source of our civil rights," and that "we must love our Motherland even if she does not love us back."[16]

The ferocious and virtually universal antisemitism of the interwar years, fanned as it was by an all-pervasive propaganda war against Jews in Hungarian politics and in much of the Hungarian media, was principally fueled by the intense Christian resentment of Jewish economic and cultural dominance, the memories of the 1919 Red Terror, the perceived Hungarian Jewish treachery that was supposed to have cost Hungary victory in the Great War, and the perceived international Jewish treachery that was supposed to have been the principal cause of Hungary losing two-thirds of its land area and one-third of its Hungarian-language population.[17] The incessant antisemitic propaganda of those years was not merely an indispensable precondition for preparing the psychosocial groundwork for the implementation of the Hungarian Holocaust, but survived undiminished through four decades of Communist suppression to powerfully reach across four generations of Hungarians with such strong historical memories that they continue to drive an increasingly ferocious antisemitism in contemporary Hungary.

In neighboring Romania, where ethnic Romanians constituted the overwhelming majority of the population,[18] the two principal traditional drivers of antisemitism were commercial competition between Jews and ethnic Romanians and the all-pervasive Judeophobia of Orthodox Christianity. Mainstream political, cultural, and intellectual leaders of the Romanian nation were for the most part openly vehement antisemites almost without exception, right from the very beginnings of sovereign Romanian statehood in 1881 (as the Regat or Old Kingdom of Romania)[19] and remained so until the communist takeover after the Second World War. Romanians had no need of Jews to boost their demographic numbers against other ethnic groups, and they perceived very real dangers in Jewish emancipation attracting ever-increasing masses of indigent Jews into Romania from the neighboring Pale of Settlement in the Russian Empire to their east. Thus, Jewish emancipation or "naturalization" remained out of the question until after the First World War. It was enacted thereafter, in 1923, only as a price to be paid, albeit most reluctantly, for a guarantee of the postwar borders of Greater Romania by the victorious Entente powers. Indeed, right from the very beginnings of the sovereign Romanian state, the political and cultural elite of Romania had always regarded the insistence of the European Great Powers on the emancipation of Romanian Jews as intolerable interference in the internal affairs of Romania, and in response, had set the cleansing of Romania of its "infestation" by Jews at the top of its national political agenda.

In contrast to Hungary, where Jews had the status of Jewish Hungarians or "Hungarians of the Mosaic Faith" from their 1867 emancipation onward, Jews in neighboring Romania had a simultaneously race- and religion-based ethnic minority status, a situation that continued unchanged after their emancipation under the provisions of the Jewish naturalization law of Romania enacted in 1923. Romanian Jewry thus always remained acutely conscious of the distinctness and overriding importance of its Jewish ethnicity, its Jewish nationality, its Jewish interests, and thus its Jewish politics. In stark contrast to their Hungarian Jewish brethren, they were Jews first, second, and last, without ever having the slightest delusions about being Romanians, which in any case the Romanians were not about to let them have. Taking care of ethnic Jewish national interests had always been the primary political focus of the bulk of Romanian Jewry; they always remained Jews first and Romanians very much a poor second, in sharp contrast to Hungarian Jews, for whom Hungarianness, Hungarian Nationalism, liberalism, internationalism, left-wing radicalism, communism, or cosmopolitanism often came first, with Jewishness barely an afterthought at best. The overwhelmingly Orthodox Romanian Jews were massively and systematically discriminated against in largely mono-ethnic Romania; thus, the Jewish contributions to developing Romania, while quite significant within the Romanian context, had nonetheless always remained rather minuscule in comparison to Jewish achievements in Hungary. Romanian Jews were also largely apolitical and kept away from national politics, from which they were anyway excluded by the Greater Romanian nationalists, and even in communist times they were far less active in politics than their Hungarian brethren.[20] In sharp contrast to Hungarian Jews, the situation they found themselves in had made it rather easy for them to jump at any opportunity to emigrate whenever a chance arose, particularly after the Holocaust. Romania was very far from being any kind of a beloved "Motherland" for most Romanian Jews and there was no memory there of any kind of a lost Jewish Camelot, as in Hungary; it was by and large a miserable place, better left to the Romanians. The best that a Romanian Jew could do with his or her life was to decamp from there as quickly as he could in the direction of greener pastures and friendlier climes.[21]

The catastrophe of Trianon had a particularly brutal impact on the Hungarian-speaking, modernizing, Neolog, and secular Jewry of Transylvania (NSJT). Identifying themselves as Hungarians of the Mosaic Faith, the NSJT constituted about a third of the Hungarian Jewish minority in Transylvania; they were steeped in Hungarian culture and, before the First World War, were in the forefront of forcible Hungarianizing efforts among the majority ethnic Romanian population of the then Hungarian province of Transylvania. Attachment to their treasured Hungarian heritage was so intense that after the Holocaust survivors among them faithfully preserved that heritage even in Israeli or American emigration.[22] The NSJT were in fact designated *evreu-maghaiar* by the Romanian fascist Iron Guard during the Second World War[23]—or "Jew-Hungarians," rather than "Hungarian Jews"—thereby neatly capturing both the primary crime of being Hungarian and the secondary crime of being Jewish. The term is also pointedly illustrative of the linkage between the obsessive anti-Hungarianism and antisemitism of both the psyche and national politics of Romanians, who furthermore generally regarded Hungarians as being intolerably "soft" on their Jews and "in cahoots" with them against the fundamental national interests of Romania. In this connection, it is also worth noting the well-known anti-Hungarian and anti-Hungarian—Jewish biases of Dr. Moses Rosen, the long-serving Orthodox chief rabbi of Romania during the communist era, whose faith-based antagonism toward Hungarian Neolog Judaism was significantly exacerbated by a

Greater Romanian nationalist mindset against Hungary and Hungarians that he shared with non-Jewish Romanians.

Trianon thus resulted in a four-dimensional minority status for the NSJT: (1) as minority Hungarians in a Romania that was violently anti-Hungarian; (2) as minority Jews in a Romania that was violently anti-semitic; (3) as minority Hungarian Jews among significantly antisemitic minority Hungarian non-Jews; and (4) as minority NSJT in a sea of Romanian and ex-Hungarian Orthodox and ultra-Orthodox Jews, who regarded their modernizing NSJT brethren with immense suspicion, antagonism, and distaste, in fact as apostates to Judaism. Later on, during the communist era, the hatreds borne of this four-dimensional minority status were further exacerbated by the addition of a fifth dimension, when many NSJT who survived the Holocaust and chose to remain in Transylvania became communists, like many Hungarians of Jewish descent in neighboring Hungary. In sharp contrast to the NSJT, however, the largely Yiddish-speaking Orthodox and ultra-Orthodox majority of Transylvanian Jews found it immeasurably easier than their NSJT brethren to adapt to their new post-Trianon status as citizens of Romania. Given that Yiddish-speaking Orthodox and ultra-Orthodox Transylvanian Jews were virtually indistinguishable in language, custom, attitudes, and appearance from Romania's own ethnic Jews in Bukovina, Bessarabia, and in rural Romanian Moldavia, they were promptly classed as such by the incoming post-Trianon Romanian administration, which gained thereby the added benefit of instantly and significantly reducing the register of ex-Hungarian Transylvanians by the stroke of a pen.

The Romanian Holocaust had an impact principally on the eastern territories of Bukovina and Bessarabia in Greater Romania and Romanian-occupied Transnistria in Soviet Ukraine, where an estimated 280,000 to 380,000[24] Bukovinian, Bessarabian, and Transnistrian Jews were slaughtered by the Romanian Army between 1941 and 1943, with a ferocious bestiality that astounded even seasoned members of the German *Einsatzgruppen*. The Jews of these East Romanian and Romanian-occupied territories were guilty not just of being Jewish, but of being actual, suspected, or potential communists, thus "self-evidently" enemies of Greater Romania.[25] It needs to be emphasized, though, that the Jewish communities of the old Regat and of Southern Transylvania[26] had largely survived the Holocaust, apart from the one-off mass murder of well over 10,000 Jews in the Iași pogrom in June 1941 at the hands of assorted Romanian Nazis,[27] and some hundreds of other victims of more minor outbreaks of antisemitic violence in Bucharest, Galați, and elsewhere in Romania. That most Jews in the Regat and Southern Transylvania actually survived the Romanian Holocaust was not, however, due to any kind of Romanian solicitude over their well-being, but to Romania adroitly switching sides to the Allies in August 1944 to thereby once again end up among the victors, whereupon the ramshackle fascist administration of Romania simply ran out of time to implement its plan to ship off the Jews of the Regat and Southern Transylvania to Belzec and other German death camps.[28]

In Hungary, the incessant deluge of vile antisemitic propaganda in the interwar years had culminated in the enactment, between 1938 and 1942, by the Hungarian parliament, of three principal "Jew Laws" on the model of the 1935 Nuremberg Laws of Nazi Germany, as well as a number of other supplementary pieces of antisemitic legislation in 1943. Destroying their Jews had by then become a national obsession for Hungarians and was widely considered *the* supreme national objective not just by the leadership, but also by the vast majority of the people at large, who saw only benefit to themselves in the despoliation of the Jews.[29] During the Holocaust, almost 600,000 Hungarian Jews were murdered out of the more than 800,000 that originally lived in wartime Hungary.[30] Hungarians gratified their pathological Jew-hatred by sadistically starving, torturing, and hounding to death tens of thousands of unarmed Jewish men in the slave labor battalions of the Hungarian Army on the Ukrainian front, and then in the final year of the war by brutally rounding up and handing over to the Germans for mass slaughter hundreds of thousands of children, women, men, and elderly people whose only crime was having been born Jewish. In organizing the logistics of the Hungarian Holocaust, the normally lethargic and inefficient Hungarian authorities displayed extraordinary competence, zeal, and efficiency, the like of which was never seen in Hungary before or since. About 100,000 Jews survived the Hungarian slave labor battalions, the death marches, and the German death camps, and approximately another 100,000 principally Neolog, Christian-convert, and secular Jews were also able to survive in Budapest, where the Hungarian Nazis finally ran out of time and failed to fully implement their plan to wipe out Budapest Jewry.

As the last faithful ally of Nazi Germany, Hungary finished the war in utter and complete devastation, the country essentially reduced to heaps of rubble.[31] Defeat in the war if anything just further reinforced the intense Jew-hatred among Hungarians, who to this day flatly disavow any and all responsibility for the Hungarian Holocaust and for the most part remain completely unrepentant in their bitter and unregenerate antisemitism that blames "the Jews" for all personal and national misfortune ever experienced or ever to be experienced by Hungarians. The disastrous defeat in the Second World War, attributed principally to "the Jews," remains a matter of bitter grievance to this day for Hungarian antisemites, as unforgiven as the catastrophic defeat in the First World War, the "Jewish" Red Terror of the Hungarian Soviet, or the oppressive "Jewish" communist dictatorship after the Second World War.

This is the psychological ground upon which forty years of partial suppression of official, government-level antisemitism was then imposed under Red colonialism, initially run by Jews who by and large were 1919-vintage former young Red terrorists, now middle-aged returnees with the Red Army after two decades of political exile and activism in the Comintern. In turn, they were eagerly assisted by groups of young Holocaust survivors in both the leadership and the rank-and-file of the ÁVH—the infamous Hungarian communist security police—in effect, young Jews seeking revenge for the horrors suffered during the war at the hands of a significant majority of non-Jewish Hungarians. But although Hungarian antisemites have a fondness for referring to the ÁVH as "the organ of Jewish revenge," the ÁVH had plenty of Jewish victims too, and not least, many former "professionals" of Hungarian Nazi organizations in its ranks. Be that as it may, the prominence of communists of Jewish descent in establishing and administering the Soviet colonial dictatorship in Hungary and running its machinery of terror for the decade between 1945 and 1955 remains to this day a matter of vehement grievance for Hungarian antisemites, as unforgiven and unforgotten as the prominence of communists of Jewish descent in the 1919 Bolshevik *putsch* or the supposed international Jewish conspiracy against Hungary in two world wars.

The vast majority of Hungarians flatly refused to return stolen Jewish property to its rightful owners after the Holocaust, and there was never any question of government-level compensation for the horrors endured during the Hungarian Holocaust. At the same time, the perception and reality of "Jewish domination" in the first decade of communist dictatorship added further fuel to the fire of grassroots antisemitism among Hungarians, who just a few fleeting years before were confidently looking forward to being rid of their Jews for good. Thus, persons of Jewish or part-Jewish origin continued to be vehemently hated throughout the communist era, regardless of whether they were practicing Jews, saw themselves as secular, nonreligious Hungarians rather than Jews, or had deliberately abandoned their Jewish identity by converting in the tens of thousands to the ideological "religion" of communism, as they previously converted in the tens of thousands to Christianity before and during the war. The colonial regime of the communists had itself a distinctly ambivalent attitude toward antisemitism. On the one hand, it denied its very existence or at most saw it as a minor holdover from "fascism" to be resolved through "the broad anti-fascist class struggle of the masses." On the other hand, in addition to a number of communist-instigated pogroms and even cases of blood libel in the immediate aftermath of the war, many transparently antisemitic campaigns against "speculators" and "Zionists" openly fanned virulent antisemitic passions in the service of totalitarian communist political ends. It was furthermore the remnant Jewish middle class that was disproportionately attacked by the communist terror campagns of nationalization, expropriation, and mass deportation of "class enemies."

Between the end of the war and the aftermath of the failed uprising, well over half the survivors of the Hungarian Holocaust emigrated or escaped from Hungary to make aliya to Israel or settle in overseas countries of immigration. Those who remained were either communists, communist sympathizers, patriotic Hungarian Jewish intellectuals, too old to emigrate, or younger people with elderly dependents who were physically too frail to emigrate. Jews fought on both sides in the brutally suppressed 1956 Hungarian uprising, during which a number of *anticommunist*-instigated pogroms also occurred.[32] A gradual thawing occurred after an initial period of savage communist reprisals, and by 1961 the communist press was even allowed to report on the Eichmann trial. This was followed by a period during the 1960s and 1970s, when antisemitism on a public or institutional level was kept very strictly at bay by the communist government, though virulent grassroots antisemitism continued to rage unabated under the surface, especially in personal relations between those regarded as Jews and most if not all non-Jews. Hungary toed the Soviet line in cutting diplomatic relations with Israel in the wake of the Six Day War in 1967, in keeping a close watch on Jews suspected of "Zionism," and in carefully restricting the quota of comrades of Jewish origin in its ranks. At the same time, however, it allowed the training of Neolog rabbis, was willing to turn a blind eye to visits to Israel, and permitted the publication of books on the Holocaust as long as they could be seen as at least nominally aligning with the party-approved context of universal "anti-fascist struggle."

The Romanian Jewish experience in the communist era was parallel but distinctly different from that of the Hungarian Jews. As in Hungary, the state security services of Romania absorbed into their ranks a large number of assorted former Romanian Nazis, particularly "repentant" former members of the fascist Iron Guard. In the early 1950s, "Zionists" were as venomously prosecuted in Romania as elsewhere in the Soviet Bloc, and, as in Hungary, it was the Jewish middle class that bore the brunt of the nationalization, expropriation, and mass deportation of "class enemies." But unlike Hungary, at no time was any rabbinical training permitted, and there were also mass dismissals of Jews from the Romanian state security services, the police, and the public service after the first few years of communist rule, while the remnant Neolog and secular Hungarian Jews of Transylvania found it almost impossible to get accepted into universities under a de facto *numerus clausus,* despite an apparently higher than average party membership among them. Above all, communism in Romania remained both Stalinist and strongly nationalist throughout the four decades of its history, and its nationalist credentials were put on striking display in 1967, when it refused to follow the rest of the Soviet Bloc in breaking diplomatic relations with Israel—undoubtedly because of its by then highly profitable trade with Israel in Romanian Jews. It is also worth noting that due to the strongly nationalist character of Romanian communism and the apolitical nature of most Romanian Jews, the proportion of active and committed communists among them always remained much smaller than among Jews in Hungary, who took to communism with gusto and in very large numbers.

The overwhelming majority of Romanian Jews regarded themselves first and last as ethnic Jews rather than Romanians, in sharp contrast to Hungarian Jews, who regarded themselves first and last as Hungarians rather than ethnic Jews. Many Romanian Jews were Zionists of one political shade or another, again in sharp contrast to the relatively few Hungarian Jews who embraced Zionism, even after the Holocaust. And unlike a large proportion of surviving Hungarian Jews, Romanian Jews were in a great hurry to get to Israel or America as quickly as possible, rather than remaining behind to build a communist workers' paradise in the land of their birth. Of the more than 400,000 Jews who survived the Holocaust in the territory of post-Second World War Romania,[33] two-thirds had emigrated from Romania by 1959, with the remnant sold to Israel in the 1960s and 1970s for around 3,000 dollars per head.[34] With the successful conclusion of their very own *Judenfrei* policy, the Romanian communist regime had finally accomplished the historic supreme objective of Romanian nationalism to rid their land of "infestation" by the Jews. They did so not just at a handsome profit while simultaneously enhancing their country's reputation with the West, but also made their own Jews happy by allowing them to leave at last, albeit only at a snail's pace, and only after making them jump innumerable humiliating hoops to be at last allowed to leave with barely the shirts on their backs. All in all, the exercise proved to be quite a coup for the Romanian communists, and, as a result, only perhaps 10,000, for the most part helpless, elderly Jews remain today in Bucharest and in some larger provincial towns. There is also[35] a small Lubavitcher Chabad presence and a handful of younger "cultural" Jews intent on perpetuating in one form or another a Jewish community in Romania for as long as possible.

Communist Romania officially denied that there ever was a Romanian Holocaust,[36] and from 1945 on, Romanian authorities would point out that the destruction of North Transylvanian Jewry was after all a Hungarian crime; that the bestial Romanian bloodletting in the East was the fault of the Germans and "a handful of Romanian fascists"; and that the overwhelming majority of Jews in Southern Transylvania and in the area of old Regat actually survived the Holocaust, apart, that is, from the occasional "regrettable excess"—such as the 1941 Iaşi massacre of well over 10,000 Jews—by "out-of-control mobs," which, however, were quickly brought to heel. As the Hungarian scholar Ferenc Horváth points out, "there are few East European countries in which the falsification of history and Holocaust denial had been as widespread and on such a grand scale as in Romania."[37] Government-level Romanian Holocaust-denials continued unabated right until the summer of 2003, when the then Romanian president Ion Iliescu declared that no Jewish Holocaust ever occurred on Romanian territory. As a result of the international outcry that followed this ill-considered statement, Romania agreed to convene an international commission under the chairmanship of Elie Wiesel to thoroughly examine the country's role in the Holocaust. The final report of the international commission incontrovertibly demonstrated Romania's culpability in organizing and implementing the Holocaust of Jewry in Romanian Moldova, Bukovina, Bessarabia, and in Romanian-occupied Transnistria. It was only after the presentation of this report to Iliescu in November 2004 that the Romanian state was finally forced to change its tune and admit to the Romanian share of Holocaust crimes in all their horror. To its credit, in 2005 the Romanian government established a government-funded public institution for the study of the Romanian Holocaust, the Elie Wiesel National Institute, which, according to Horváth,[38] "has since produced a series of significant research papers" that have honestly examined and exposed the role of Romanian society in the perpetration of the Romanian Holocaust.

Notwithstanding the work of the Elie Wiesel National Institute, grassroots popular antisemitism of both the Judeophobic and the racist/nationalist kind remains as much a feature of the Romanian mindset today as it ever has been.[39] The emblematic representative of Romanian antisemitism is Corneliu Vadim Tudor, the Jean-Marie Le Pen of Romania. Tudor is the leader of the Greater Romania Party that gained second place in the 2000 elections with 28 percent of the vote. Currently he is a Romanian representative in the European Parliament. Tudor started out as court poet to the former communist dictator Nicolae Ceauşescu and was a national communist before he turned into a right-wing ultranationalist, in a typical case of Far Left morphing into Far Right. He has since espoused an ideology of irredentism, anti-Hungarianism, crude antisemitism, anti-Israelism, anti-Romaism, and homophobia.

Another of his kind is the brazenly antisemitic Ion Coja, a university professor in Bucharest, who continues to poison the minds of generations of university students with vicious antisemitic diatribe, without any attempt whatever on the part of successive Romanian governments to curb his venomous influence. Similarly, there is little attempt, if any, on the part of Romanian authorities to investigate antisemitic outrages such as mass desecrations of Jewish graves, much less to prosecute for such crimes.[40] At the same time, although open and virulent antisemitism is clearly a prominent feature of the ideology of the political Far Right in Romania—and to some extent and under certain circumstances, may also feature in the rhetoric of the political centre-Right or even of the Left—there is absolutely no ground to suspect the existence of any institutional, policy-level antisemitism on the part of the government of Romania. It is also worth reiterating that however rife and widespread antisemitism may be among ethnic Romanians, and however aggravating that might be for Romanian Jews who have to put up with it, antisemitism in Romania today only affects the lives of a relatively small community of largely elderly Jewish people.

In stark contrast to Romania, many tens of thousands of Jews by descent still live in Hungary—mainly in the capital city, Budapest—where today they form the targets of an aggressive and increasingly menacing grassroots Hungarian antisemitism. There are perhaps 40,000–50,000 Hungarian Jews today where either both parents are Jewish or at least the mother is,[41] another 20,000–30,000 with a Jewish father, and perhaps another 80,000–100,000 with at least one Jewish grandparent. However, none of the statistics proffered in the variety of available sources[42] could be considered as even remotely reliable, since not only has there been no census taken of Hungarian Jews since the Holocaust, but in post-Holocaust Hungary no such census could actually have been taken at all. It needs to be borne in mind that for historical reasons, Jewish self-identification in terms of a separate Jewish ethnicity along the Romanian lines is a totally alien form of self-definition for the Jews of Hungary.[43] A census of Jews is therefore not a realistic possibility in Hungary, for the simple reason that most Hungarians of Jewish origin identify themselves as Hungarian in every respect rather than Jewish, and few even of first-generation Jewish descent would consider themselves Jewish at all in any religious, communal, social, or national sense. Whether they like it or not, though, non-Jewish Hungarians will invariably see them as Jews, thus as aliens to a greater or lesser degree.[44] The overwhelming majority of Hungarians of

Jewish descent are completely secular, nonobservant, assimilationist, and mostly intermarried. And notwithstanding the communist family background in many cases, Hungarian Jews today are overwhelmingly Left-Liberal in their political orientation, very much in the mould of most Jews in the Western world. As such, Hungarians of Jewish origin continue to be prominent in Left-Liberal politics, academia, literature, and media, further stoking the fires of an often strident Hungarian antisemitism. Beside the Hungarian-identifying nonreligious majority, there is also a thriving Neolog community of religiously observant Jews with some thousands of members,[45] who combine a traditionally patriotic Hungarian Conservative Judaism with a by-and-large Left-Liberal political orientation; and there is also an expanding Lubavitcher Chabad presence with some hundreds of members, some small Orthodox and Reform congregations, and not least a devoted band of several hundred purely "cultural" Jews who make up in enthusiasm what they lack in numbers.

The Hungarian Jewish author and theater director László Márton sparked off a fierce public debate in 1989, when in a controversial polemical essay, *The Chosen and the Comminglers*,[46] he remarked that "Jewishness in contemporary Hungary is a racial category . . . in precisely the same terms as those elaborated and later sanctioned by fascist racial theory." Events following the regime change in 1989 fully confirmed this insight, since not only had the Hungarian Far Right immediately reverted to its openly virulent antisemitic traditions, but as a result, the Center Right found itself unable to make it unequivocally clear to its public that it wished to pursue a *non-antisemitic* conservatism, and true to its own worst traditions and worst instincts, immediately commenced making accommodating gestures toward the Far Right. This left the field wide open for the Left side of Hungarian politics to assume the mantle of official torch-bearer in the fight against Hungarian antisemitism—or "antifascist struggle," in the favored anodyne phraseology of the Hungarian Left—despite the undoubtedly many inveterate antisemites in its own ranks. At the same time, formerly faithful communists of non-Jewish extraction began to drift without much further ado toward the Far Right, though among communists of Jewish descent only a few could stomach integrating into a Far Right framework with an ideology openly based on the Nuremberg Laws. A complex picture emerged, which was in sharp contrast to the situation prevailing in Western Europe or the United States, where right-wing, conservative political parties and public intellectuals generally profess a non-antisemitic and strongly pro-Israel stance.

According to longitudinal surveys of trends in Hungarian antisemitism carried out by Professor András Kovács since the early 1990, about 25 percent of non-Jewish Hungarians may be considered antisemitic in one form or another, ranging from "hardcore" to "not quite hardcore":

> . . . 29% of the Hungarian adult population is explicitly non-antisemitic, 25% antisemitic, and 32% accept some of the economic stereotypes formed over the centuries about the Jews without these stereotypes being accompanied by any particular antisemitic feeling. The attitudes of a further 14% cannot be measured owing to the high number of missing responses; given the indifference, this group is also to be classed among the non-antisemites.[47]

The following excerpt from *Virtual Jerusalem* is a concise summary of the current position of Kovács on Hungarian antisemitism today, as given in an interview by JTA:[48]

> A large part of Hungarian society, both Jewish and non-Jewish, is convinced that anti-Semitism has increased in Hungary since the fall of communism, Kovacs writes. "What is said on the street, written in newspapers, and heard on the radio can and does give rise to concern," he writes. "Are the fears legitimate?" The answer, he told JTA in an interview, is a mix of yes, no and maybe. Jobbik [a Far Right political party],[49] with its anti-Semitic rhetoric and virulently anti-Roma, or Gypsy, political platform, won nearly 17 percent of the vote in April elections and entered Parliament as Hungary's third-largest party. But recent evidence shows that it has been losing support amid divisive internal squabbles, and newly imposed legal measures have clamped down hard on its once-feared paramilitary wing, the Hungarian Guard. Still, Jobbik did not emerge from thin air, and Kovacs's book traces the evolution of several anti-Semitic trends against a shifting background of political and social change.
>
> He identifies three main types of anti-Semitism in Hungary. The first is "classic" anti-Jewish prejudice, based on social and religious stereotypes that date back centuries and were kept alive, if suppressed, under communism. The second occurs when anti-Semitism becomes a sort of "language and culture" that fosters a general anti-Semitic worldview. The third is political anti-Semitism, "where political activists discover that they can mobilize certain social groups by using anti-Semitic slogans to achieve their own goals." Kovacs' research shows the recent growth in anti-Semitism to be qualitative rather than quantitative. Surveys show that 10 to 15 percent of Hungarians are

hard-core anti-Semites, while another 25 percent nurtures anti-Jewish prejudices to some degree. Contrary to popular perception, Kovacs said, these figures "have increased to some extent but not dramatically over the past 17 years." What is different and much more alarming, according to Kovacs, is how the type and expression of anti-Semitism is changing within that proportion. For one thing, the percentage of political anti-Semites has grown. These political anti-Semites, he said, are "more urban, better educated and relatively younger" than they tended to be in the past. Jobbik's key leaders, for example, are youthful, clean cut, and media and Internet-savvy—factors that helped enhance their appeal ahead of the April vote. Related to this is the way hate speech among the general public has been emboldened by the open use of anti-Semitic and anti-Roma rhetoric by extreme Right public figures. Kovacs calls this a "dangerous dynamic."

... What follows is unclear. So far, Jobbik's anti-Jewish rhetoric seems aimed at creating a body of like-minded followers rather than serving as a rallying cry for concrete political action against Jews, according to Kovacs. But could the extreme Right eventually elevate political anti-Semitism into a force with significant mainstream influence? Kovacs thinks it's unlikely, but ultimately, he writes in his book, it will depend on how Hungary's mainstream cultural and political leaders react to any attempts to "transform the prejudice that once affected the margins of Hungarian society into a language, culture and ideology."

Thus, even though Kovács finds that there are "only" 10–15 percent "hardcore" and presumably another 10–15 percent "not quite hardcore" antisemites (given the figure of a total of 25 percent antisemites in the 1999 study quoted above), there are also of course the 32 percent who "merely stereotype Jews"—albeit apparently without a smidgen of antisemitic sentiment, according to Kovács—giving a total figure of 57 percent antisemites among Hungarians, which is in turn amply confirmed in the seven-country survey of European antisemitism by the ADL in 2009. In practice, what the statistics produced by Kovács actually mean is that overt and covert antisemitic abuse on the Hungarian street is getting louder, more articulate, more emboldened, and more insolent. At the same time, it is becoming more "respectable" and acceptable to the general public by the day, as it keeps percolating through in ever greater strength from the Far Right fringe to Center Right public discourse in the media and the political arena.[50]

Although there has been no evidence of any institutional or policy-level antisemitism on the part of any government of Hungary in the two decades since the regime change in 1989, it is a matter of some considerable concern that recent statements by A. L. Gál—the undersecretary for public administration, including administrative matters pertaining to Jewish affairs—appear to indicate a determined government-level push by the Center Right populist-nationalist Fidesz Party,[51] currently in power, to somehow exonerate Hungary from legal and moral responsibility for the Hungarian Holocaust. Accordingly, Gál is also pushing for a drastic reorientation of the research and exhibits at the Hungarian Holocaust Memorial Center, a state institution established in 2004 by the previous Left-Liberal alliance government of Hungarian Socialists (MSZP) and Free Democrats (SZDSZ) in a multi-award-winning building complex in Budapest, purpose-built to house both a museum and a documentation center. And although in 2009 the then ruling MSZP government had enacted a bill criminalizing Holocaust denial, in 2010 the incoming Fidesz-dominated Hungarian parliament immediately watered down this law to omit all reference to the Jewishness of the Holocaust and have it instead apply generally to the denial of any and all genocide.[52] At the same time, it does need pointing out that it was a previous Fidesz government in the late 1990s that had actually introduced an official day of Holocaust remembrance in Hungary, as well as mandatory annual Holocaust commemorations in high schools. Unfortunately, however, although since that time there have indeed been government-sponsored educational programs and other initiatives for the dissemination of information about the Holocaust to high school students, there has been a deplorable tendency—whether through incompetent organization or deliberate sabotage—for this material to generally fail to reach its intended target audience. Moreover, the programs of information about the Hungarian Holocaust that do reach high schools fail to show any kind of uniform purpose driven by shared, clear policy objectives. Thus, they tend to be quite incoherent—in palpable and striking demonstration of the complete inability of official Hungary to come to terms with the full horrific facts of Hungarian complicity in the genocide of Hungarian Jews.

Contemporary grassroots antisemitism in Hungary is a composite of religion-driven Judeophobia and racist-nationalist Jew-hatred, in essence driven by the exact same prejudices, resentments, and hatreds that raged across post-Trianon remnant Hungary during the interwar years. Its leading flag-bearers today are a well-educated and technologically savvy younger cohort of Hungarian antisemites, for whom virulent Jew-hatred is a typically Hungarian political default position in face of the disastrous economic and institutional failures of the past two decades of market capitalism and liberal democracy, whether actual or perceived. But does this necessarily entail a broad-based, grassroots anti-Zionism or anti-Israel hatred too, similar to that in Western Europe? In Western Europe, one basic issue is the extent to which mainstream Left-Liberal anti-Zionism is necessarily motivated by traditional antisemitic sentiment. In Hungary or Romania, by contrast, the question is whether traditional antisemitism is in fact necessarily driven by or driving any anti-Zionist popular sentiment at all. The answer to this is quite straightforwardly in the negative. Apart from the extreme Right, traditional antisemitism appears to sit quite well with public sympathy for Israel, and both Center Right and Center Left governments in Romania and Hungary generally show considerable understanding and support for Jewish nationalism in the Middle East. The fact of the matter is that in the broader Central European, East European, and Balkan contexts, animosity toward the State of Israel and Zionism is largely restricted to relatively minor and politically uninfluential fringe groups on the internationalist extreme Left and nationalist extreme Right margins of politics, although in Hungary the latter, in the shape of Jobbik, has of late become so vocal and muscular that unfortunately it can no longer be regarded a mere fringe group on the Far Right margins of politics.

It needs to be noted, however, that the right-wing media in Hungary are much more openly antisemitic than either the party platforms or government policy on the Hungarian Right. Hungarian right-wing newspapers, radio stations, and television channels close to the government often adopt an aggressively anti-Israel stance. In practice, there are no longer any moderate voices on the subject of Israel in Hungarian right-wing media, only the odd exception here and there that merely proves the rule. Most unfortunately, over the past decade or so, the anti-Israel contagion has rapidly spread across from the media outlets of the Far Right into the bulk of Center Right newspapers, journals, radio stations, television channels, and Internet portals, which today can only be regarded as almost uniformly anti-Israel. Hungarian media on the political Right are thus rife with virulent anti-Israel opinion, as well as the usual run of covert and not so covert antisemitic incitement of the most vicious kind.

There is, in fact, no real distinction between moderate and Far Right media concerning these views, and what qualifies as "moderate" in Hungarian right-wing media would be regarded as Far Right in Western Europe, while the "Far Right" in Hungarian media would most certainly be seen as openly Nazi in the West.

In striking contrast to its West European counterparts on the Left side of politics, the "antifascist" and thus supposedly also "anti-anti-Semitic" mainstream Hungarian Center Left[53] is generally sympathetic to Israel and Zionism, and few in its ranks would be willing to embrace the unrestrained anti-Israel rhetoric of "progressive" antisemitism in Western Europe or the United States. One would also be hard put to find Western-style "progressive" antisemites among the otherwise generally left-wing university academics in Hungary, and there are few if any academics or instructors at the universities who would ever give their name in support of antisemitic or anti-Israel initiatives. Also, unlike student groups in Western Europe, no organized groups of students ever participated in any public antisemitic or anti-Israel demonstrations. There are, however, two developments that do give cause for concern. The first is a pronounced right-wing drift among students in a number of university departments and most notably among history students;[54] indeed, it is from among their ranks that the young leadership of the so far highly successful extreme Right Jobbik party has emerged in the past decade. In light of the unfortunate history of vicious antisemitism in Hungarian universities in the interwar years, it is to be hoped that this drift is not an early harbinger of antisemitism gradually gaining ground among students. Another possible indication of the same right-wing drift is at the Institute for Middle East Research at ELTE University in Budapest, which recently has organized not one but two conferences for which they failed to invite any researchers of Israeli history or academics with a pro-Israel orientation. There are also a number of newly arrived Middle East "experts" in the departments of political science and international relations at Corvinus University in Budapest,[55] whose views seem dangerously close to the anti-Israel positions common at universities in the West. The concern is, as Gerstenfeld (2007) points out in respect of Spanish universities, that the international relations departments at Hungarian universities could very easily turn into hotbeds of "progressive" antisemitism.

The mainstream Hungarian Center Right is most emphatically sympathetic to Israel and Zionism; indeed, the ruling Center Right, populist-nationalist Fidesz Party regards the likewise Center Right hard-line nationalist Likud Party in Israel as a natural ideological ally. However, while the populist-nationalist ideology of the Hungarian Center Right may indeed be quite similar in some important respects to that of the Likud in Israel, it is in most respects radically dissimilar from that of the mainstream Center Right parties in Western Europe, or for that matter from the Democratic or Republican center in the United States. And while Fidesz is careful not to blatantly manifest any of the virulent antisemitism that characterized the politics of the Right in the interwar years, it also feels irresistibly drawn to steadily adopt elements of Far Right extremist rhetoric, in order to shore up support among the membership on its own right flank, by taking the wind out of the sails of Jobbik. Hence the generally sly, but increasingly less covert, antisemitic code that has become all-pervasive in all of the media organs of the Center Right, and the blatant antisemitic effrontery of nominally Center Right journalists like the notorious Zsolt Bayer.[56]

Jobbik won 17 percent of the votes in the general election held in 2010, in which Fidesz gained 67 percent—a two-thirds mandate to change the constitution—while the Socialists (MSZP) were reduced to a rump and the Left-liberal Free Democrats (SZDSZ) were eliminated. Jobbik was particularly successful in eastern Hungary, where they espoused a populist law-and-order agenda favored by poverty-stricken Hungarian peasant folk in despair over actual and/or perceived Roma lawlessness of massive proportions. However, although much of the electoral success of Jobbik was clearly attributable to racist rhetoric aimed at the Roma, a vicious antisemitism remains a prominent part of their policy program, since, as far as Jobbik is concerned, antisemitism obviously "sells." In their stance on Israel, Jobbik and the rest of the Hungarian Far Right are ideologically parasitic on the "new" or "progressive" antisemitism of the political Left in the West, and show a marked partiality to gleefully quoting anti-Israel and Holocaust-minimizing diatribes by adversarial, antagonistic Jews, such as Noam Chomsky or Norman Finkelstein from the United States, or Steven and Hilary Rose from Britain. It thus comes as no surprise that the reportage on Middle East affairs in the press and electronic media of the Hungarian Far Right is emphatically and unequivocally pro-Palestinian and anti-Israel without exception.

Over the past two decades, the Hungarian Far Right had, furthermore, invented for itself an entire *Bizarro World* completely detached from any semblance of reality, a panoply of weird conspiracy theories in delusional "explanations" of a world it resents, does not understand, and has no interest in understanding.[57] There is, moreover, a deplorable resurgence in Hungarian cultural life—in both high culture and the popular register—of the kind of coarse, Nazi-style antisemitic propaganda that continues to be rife among many Arabs. As part of this quasi-Nazi literary revival, the Hungarian Far Right and elements of the Center Right have "rediscovered" and are actively popularizing a significant number of prewar and Holocaust-era antisemitic poets and authors. It comes as no surprise, therefore, that the award of the 2002 Nobel Prize for literature to Imre Kertész, the author of seminal works of literature on the Hungarian Holocaust, utterly scandalized not just the Hungarian Far Right, but also many on the Center Right and some even on the Left of the Hungarian political spectrum. What they found most galling was that the first Hungarian-language literary work to win a Nobel Prize was awarded not for what they would regard as a genuinely *Hungarian* work of literature by a "true-born" *Hungarian* author, but for *Fatelessness,* a novel about the *Hungarian Holocaust* by a *Jewish* author.[58]

In sum, the vast majority of non-Jewish Hungarians today have as little stomach to confront the heinous crimes of Hungarian complicity in the implementation of the Hungarian Holocaust as they have for confronting the actual rather than imagined historical causes of the Trianon disaster. There is a dogged refusal to acknowledge that, in reality, Trianon was largely self-inflicted by a thin leadership class of educated Hungarian Christians chronically deluded about geostrategic realities. There is a similar dogged refusal to acknowledge that, in reality, the proximate cause of the sustained, violent flare-up of vicious antisemitism following the implementation of the Treaty of Trianon was the pathetic uncompetitiveness of that Christian educated class with Hungarian Jews. And there is also a just as dogged, even bloody-minded refusal to admit that it was the ceaseless, vile antisemitic agitation by that same Christian educated class in the interwar years that created the psychosocial conditions in which the great majority of non-Jewish Hungarians was brainwashed into believing that it was not merely alright to humiliate, dispossess, or even murder their Jewish compatriots, but a sacred national duty to do so. Any and all historical responsibility for the Hungarian Holocaust is vehemently rejected, and not just by the Far Right and Center Right, but also by many in the ranks of the Left. In fact, to the extent that the magnitude of the Hungarian Holocaust and the depth of Hungarian complicity in its implementation are reluctantly acknowledged at all, the blame is laid entirely at the feet of the "occupying" Nazi Germans, who, incidentally, comprised a grand total of barely two hundred SS henchmen under the command of Eichmann and some German armored groups with troop numbers considerably below those of the Hungarian Army fighting by their side.

Unlike modern Hungarian Jewish history, Romanian Jewish history has never been bedeviled by Jewish illusions and delusions, and is thus in no respects at odds with mainstream Romanian history. In stark contrast, twentieth-century mainstream Hungarian history and Hungarian Jewish history are to this day utterly irreconcilable in most key respects.[59] Thus, the narratives and interpretations of the traumas of the First World War, the Hungarian Soviet, the Treaty of Trianon, the Second World War, the Hungarian Holocaust, the Hungarian communist dictatorship, and those of the traumas of present-day antisemitic outrages and Holocaust-denial remain as wide apart as those of Israel and Palestine. The succession of traumas stretching back to the First World War in fact remain as absolutely frozen in place as long-dead insects suspended in amber. There is little willingness on the non-Jewish Hungarian side of the barricades to engage in any meaningful debate on any of these issues with the Jewish side. It is of course not so much that Trianon or the Holocaust are taboo subjects in social intercourse, but rather that utterly unacceptable and unhistorical interpretations are attributed to them in terms of ideological positions that appear to have been set in concrete back in 1945. In striking contrast to postwar West Germany, there appears to be—on the part of many if not all non-Jewish Hungarians—a desperate fear and horror of attempting in any way to genuinely address and resolve the festering traumas of the past and ultimately to move beyond them, lest "the Jews" gain morally and/or materially by the process of non-Jewish Hungarians honestly coming to terms with their past. The pain, blame, and shame of unprocessed and unresolved historical traumas in turn drive an all-pervasive culture of grievance in Hungary, an outraged sense of having been badly mistreated that is so strikingly prevalent in Hungarian social intercourse on both the Jewish and non-Jewish side of the wall that separates them. In these circumstances, the prospects of an integrated Hungarian and Hungarian Jewish history ever emerging is unlikely,[60] especially in view of the powerful resurgence of strong antisemitic diatribe not just from fringe groups on the Right but increasingly in supposedly respectable public discourse as well.

Let us conclude by observing that however prevalent and vicious it might be, grassroots antisemitism in Romania is becoming irrelevant with the sad passing of the last generation of Romanian Jews. Not so in Hungary, where a growing and virulent popular antisemitism painfully affects tens of thousands of Hungarians of Jewish descent who choose to remain in the land of their birth. The vicious psychopathology of Hungarian antisemitism had remained frozen in suspended animation during four decades of communist suppression, only to burst forth with renewed vigor after the fall of communism.[61] Today, deeply entrenched antisemitic positions reach out from the grave of defeat in the Second World War like so many ideological zombies to dominate the mental space of new generations of non-Jewish Hungarians and suppress any genuine debate on contentious historical issues in post-communist Hungary.[62] What can and must be done about this situation are questions that right now go unanswered.

NOTES

1. The term *nationalist* is intended to denote the national ideology of any language-, ethnicity- and/or religion-based social group dominating or seeking to dominate some given geographical expanse over which historical rights of possession are claimed. The term is used in contradistinction to national sentiments in countries of immigration such as the United States or Australia, which operate as melting pots of ethnicities and religions from all over the world.

2. It needs to be pointed out, however, that notwithstanding the validity of this generalization, honorable exceptions to the all-pervasive grassroots antisemitism in Hungary, Romania, and elsewhere in Eastern Europe do of course exist today, just as they always existed in the past, though most unfortunately these exceptions merely serve to prove the general rule. It also needs pointing out that antisemitic manifestations are not, of course, uniform in kind and intensity, but follow a bell curve of scalarity, with statistically significant concentrations at certain points along that bell curve.

3. It is to be noted that there are a number of issues in bitter contention between nationalist Hungarian and nationalist Romanian historians, such as the Daco-Romanian thesis of the origin of ethnic Romanians, whereby Romanian nationalists lay claim to an illustrious descent from Trajan's Roman legions. Hungarians hotly dispute this, claiming instead that ethnic Romanians are more likely to have been the descendants of nomadic Illyrian tribes from the western Balkans. As these hoary controversies between Romanians and Hungarians have little or no bearing on the topic at hand, there will be no occasion to make further reference to them.

4. The Jewish population in Hungary was almost entirely Ashkenazic and of relatively recent origin. From the late eighteenth century through the nineteenth, often reform-minded German-speaking Jews moved in from the Czech, Moravian, and Austrian provinces in the western half of the Habsburg Empire to settle in western Hungary and larger Hungarian towns in the east, while strictly traditionalist Yiddish-speaking Orthodox and ultra-Orthodox Jews entered Hungary from Habsburg Galicia and Bukovina in the east, settling mostly in the east Hungarian countryside, and particularly in Transylvania and Sub-Carpathian Ruthenia. As a result, the Jewish population of Hungary increased from just over 10,000 ghetto Jews in the middle of the eighteenth century to over 910,000 Hungarians of the Mosaic Faith by the eve of the First World War, or 5 percent of the population numbering 18 million in the exclusively Hungarian part of the then Kingdom of Hungary (i.e., excluding the 4 million people in Croatia in the southwest, who enjoyed a special constitutional status within the Kingdom), and over 20 percent of the population of Budapest.

5. The 1867 emancipation of Hungarian Jewry in fact precipitated an immediate rupture between traditionalist Orthodox Judaism and reformist "Neolog" Judaism, the Hungarian equivalent of what later became Conservative Judaism in the United States. The Orthodox community point blank refused the program of cultural integration and religious reform advocated by an essentially assimilationist Neolog Judaism, and the Hungarian state thereafter recognized three separate strands of Judaism; one Orthodox, one Neolog, and a small Status Quo group that rejected the schism. Judaism was ultimately enacted as a recognized and received religion of state in 1895, whereby in law the three competing affiliations of Hungarians professing the Mosaic Faith simply became Jewish religious denominations on the model of existing Christian ones.

6. Hungarianize.

7. This had won the Jews the lasting enmity of non-Hungarian ethnics in the Kingdom, something that was neither forgotten nor forgiven when Hungarian Jews became subsequently trapped in the ex-Hungarian regions of the successor states after the First World War, where they soon found themselves doubly discriminated against as both Hungarians and Hungarian Jews. Needless to say, the eager prewar Hungarianization efforts of Hungarian Jews were instantly and conveniently forgotten in post-Trianon remnant Hungary as irrelevant historical flotsam from antediluvian times.

8. Cf. Gyurgyák (2001: 239–40).

9. And never mind that tens of thousands of Jewish soldiers and officers served in the Hungarian army during the First World War, many of them with great distinction and bravery, including dozens of Hungarian Jewish generals.

10. After the defeat of the Hungarian Soviet, most of the leadership group escaped to the Soviet Union, where they served in various capacities in the Comintern until their return to Hungary with the victorious Red Army in 1945, to thereafter continue to dominate the leadership of the Hungarian Communist Party until the eve of the Hungarian uprising in 1956.

11. According to a recent mainstream Center Right newspaper article by Zsolt Bayer, the pogroms of 1919–20 were actually far less than what "the Jews" really "deserved." The article appeared in the January 4, 2010 issue of *Magyar Hírlap* (Hungarian Journal). Bayer, a notoriously anti-Semitic journalist, is a member in good standing of the governing Fidesz party and onetime friend and close associate of the current Hungarian prime minister, Viktor Orbán. Back in 2008, Professor Randolph Braham, the renowned researcher of the Hungarian Holocaust, in fact wrote an open letter of protest to Congressman Weiner about a particularly vicious antisemitic article by Bayer, as well as a number of other matters of concern about recent antisemitic manifestations in Hungary.

12. The post-Trianon Hungarian population record shows an 87 percent non-Jewish Hungarian, 5 percent Jewish Hungarian and 5 percent ethnic German population in a total population of 8.7 million.

13. A situation that was further exacerbated by an influx of hundreds of thousands of destitute Hungarian refugees from the lost territories, mostly déclassé gentry and other educated Christians.

14. Hungary enacted Europe's first modern "Jew Law" in 1921, the *numerus clausus,* which aimed at limiting the percentage of Jewish students in institutions of higher education to the percentage of Jews in the population as a whole. Beatings of defenseless Jewish university students soon became a daily occurrence, and remained so right through the interwar years.

15. Vilmos Vázsonyi (1868–1926), Hungarian Jewish politician, publicist, and lawyer whose career focused on the dissemination of democratic ideas in Hungary.

16. Cf. Gyurgyák (2001), pp. 256–57.

17. The competition between the urban-oriented, forward-looking, aggressive, and often cosmopolitan Hungarian Jews and the markedly rural-oriented, backward-looking, passive, and intensely nationalist Christian Hungarians extended even into literature, in which, from around the turn of the century, a fierce *Kulturkampf* began to be waged for the nation's soul between the so-called "urbanists" and "folkists"—code for Jews and non-Jews, respectively, in Hungarian literature—which reached a crescendo in the late 1930s and wartime Hungary, then continued unabated right through the communist era, as indeed it continues with renewed vigor down to present day.

18. Romanian Jewry started out in the eighteenth century with a more or less similar number of Jews to that in neighboring Hungary, albeit mostly made up not of Ashkenazic, but Sephardic Jews who arrived in the ethnic Romanian regions with the Ottoman occupation. However, the inflow of Ashkenazic refugees from the Pale of the Settlement in the neighboring Russian Empire—which at that time also included Romanian speaking Bessarabia (today the Republic of Moldova) ceded to the Russians by the Turks in 1812—soon swamped the Sephardic community. The Ashkenazic Jewish

community grew to over 130,000 by the middle of the nineteenth century, peaking at over 266,000 by the end of the century, then declining through emigration to around 240,000 on the eve of the First World War. The Jews of Romania were disproportionately concentrated in its Eastern provinces, with 40 percent of the population being Jewish in some of the larger towns in Romanian Moldova and Bessarabia. This was far beyond the tolerance limits of the Orthodox Christian majority, hence the frequency of violent persecution of the Jews, which reached crescendos in the Kishinev pogrom of 1905 and the Iași pogrom of 1941.

19. The Romanian state was carved out of the ethnic Romanian-populated northeast Balkan holdings of the Ottoman Empire subsequent to the 1877–78 Russo-Turkish War by the then European Great Powers that were intent upon dismembering the Ottoman Empire, a process that culminated in the recognition of Romania as an independent state under the terms of the 1878 Treaty of Berlin. The first sovereign state of Romania in the form of the Regat or Old Kingdom (comprising historic Wallachia and Moldavia) was thereafter established upon the Hohenzollern-Sigmaringen Prince Karl having been proclaimed King Carol I of Romania on March 26, 1881, subsequent to some further territorial adjustments having been carried out with respect to Russia and Bulgaria that went beyond the terms agreed upon under the Treaty of Berlin.

20. At the same time, it does need pointing out that the majority of the leadership of the Romanian Communist Party was of Jewish descent in the interwar years, in strong parallel with the dominant role of Jewish communists in the Hungarian Communist Party in that same period. This would no doubt have been a significant reason for the fascist mind to indelibly associate Jews with communism in both Romania and Hungary.

21. We might note in passing that Romanian Jewry did not appear to have shown a great deal of interest in mass immigration into the Jewish Camelot in neighboring Hungary during the five decades before the First World War. One might conjecture any number of reasons for this, including Hungarian restrictions on immigration, but one thing is definite: one way or another, Romanian Jews had shown themselves to be far better judges of the prevailing winds of history than their Hungarian brethren, just as the Romanian political leadership had shown itself to be incomparably more adept in playing the Great Game of Europe than their Hungarian opponents.

22. There are uncanny similarities between the unquestioned Hungarian linguistic, cultural, and political loyalties of the NSJT and the touching loyalty of exiled Sephardic Jews to medieval Spain, which, even after centuries, finds eloquent expression in their literature, folk stories, songs and customs.

23. Cf. Erdélyi (2010).

24. Wiesel et al. (2004). In contrast to the verifiably accurate numbers of the victims of the Hungarian Holocaust that are in hand, as in Braham (2007), only minima and maxima estimates are available for victims of the Romanian Holocaust. This is due primarily to the incomplete or otherwise inadequate Romanian and Soviet population registers of the time and the wide divergence in estimates as to how many Jews might have succeeded in making their escape to Soviet-held territory, as against the number that were trapped in territories held by the Romanians and the Germans.

25. Cf. Wiesel et al. (2004) and Carp (1946–48).

26. Which remained with Romania during the war, unlike Northern Transylvania, which was returned to Hungary in 1940 under the terms of the Second Vienna Award (1940).

27. Including members of the subsequently banned fascist Iron Guard, Jew-hating Romanian mobs, and nationalist thugs in the Nazi-sympathizer Romanian gendarmerie, police, army, and government bureaucracy of the *Conducător* or Romanian *Führer*, Ion Antonescu.

28. It needs to be noted, however, that had Antonescu wished to kill the Jews of the Regat during the period of 1941–43, he could have done so. This is not to say that Antonescu would not have pursued this path, had the tides of war not shifted in favor of the Allies, but the point remains that when such an action was possible, he did not take it. Antonescu sincerely believed that the Jews of Bessarabia and Bukovina were communist traitors, and those of Transnistria merely communist traitors-in-waiting. None of this by any stretch of the imagination lessens Antonescu's responsibility for perpetrating genocide, but it is important to note that even within his own antisemitic mania he made a distinction between so-called "native" Jews and those from the territories mentioned above. Antoniescu's attitudes to the Regat Jews were, in fact, quite identical to those of the Hungarian fascist leadership's attitudes towards "their own" Magyarized Jewish middle class, particularly in Budapest, the capital of Hungary, and therein lies the striking parallel between the reasons for survival of the bulk of Regat Jewry and that of the bulk of the Jewry of Budapest.

29. Cf. Kádár and Vági (2005).

30. Post-Trianon remnant Hungary as expanded by the annexation of formerly Hungarian territories extorted under Nazi duress from Romania and Czechoslovakia under the terms of the 1938 First Vienna Award, the 1940 Second Vienna Award, and then by the invasion of Yugoslavia in 1941, all of which reverted to temporary Hungarian sovereignty until they had to be relinquished anew upon the defeat of Hungary in the Second World War.

31. The crazed psychopathology of Hungarian antisemitism is perhaps best illustrated by some examples from the dying days of the Second World War. When the Red Army laid siege to Budapest in the last days of 1944 and in the ensuing six weeks the entire city was reduced to rubble as a result of fanatic resistance by the Germans and their Hungarian cohorts, thousands upon thousands of assorted Hungarian Nazis actually preferred to stay put until the very end and hunt down and kill as many Jews as possible, rather than try to escape the siege and save their skins. The second example is from September 1944, after the Russian front had reached the eastern borders of Hungary. A Hungarian armored division under the command of General József Heszlényi, part of a larger German battle group, successfully counterattacked and recaptured the Romanian township of Arad in Southern Transylvania, which the Germans had previously lost (Ungváry K. 2005: 324). The town was ceded to Romania in 1920 under the Treaty of Trianon, and as such, had a significant non-Jewish Hungarian and Jewish Hungarian population. The temporarily victorious Hungarians soon found that they had a tiger by the tail, as they were immediately put under relentless pressure by over-

whelming Russian and Romanian forces. It appears, however, that despite their dire circumstances, the chief concern of the good general and his armored group was the immediate introduction and enforcement of the Hungarian equivalent of the Nuremberg Laws, and in particular rounding up as many Jews as possible for deportation to Auschwitz, something that the Jews of Arad until then had been able to escape under Romanian fascist rule. That General Heszlényi and his crew had failed in their endeavor to cleanse Arad of its Jewish "infestation" was not at all for lack of trying, but because a few days later their division was smashed to smithereens by Russian and Romanian battle groups.

32. Cf. Kádár and Vági (2008).

33. The census of the Romanian Section of the World Jewish Congress found 428,312 Jews in Romania in 1947, a figure that included about 60,000 Jews who moved into postwar Romania from the lost territories of Northern Bukovina, Bessarabia, and Transnistria (Stark 1999).

34. This is an oversimplification in the interests of brevity. For details of postwar Jewish emigration from Romania and the sale of Romanian Jews to Israel and the West by Communist Romania, cf. Ionid (2005).

35. According to the 2002 Romanian census, just over 6,000 persons identified themselves as ethnic Jewish nationals, and about 8,000 as Jewish by religion, a number confirmed by the actual membership of the Romanian Federation of Jewish Communities (Fedrom). The difference between the two numbers is likely due to some Hungarian Jews in Transylvania registering as Hungarian nationals, and perhaps also because some Romanian Jews, particularly those in or issuing from mixed marriages, might have identified themselves as Jewish by religion, but Romanian by nationality (Salamon 2010). In addition, there may also be some who chose to identify themselves simply as Romanians, i.e., neither Jewish by ethnicity nor Jewish by religion, which might account for another 1,000 or 2,000 people of Jewish descent living in Romania today.

36. It is worth noting in this connection that despite the fact that Romania and Hungary were both members of similar status in the Soviet bloc, appallingly few memoirs of the Shoah had appeared in Romania after 1945 in comparison to Hungary, and only a handful of genuinely valuable works of Holocaust literature, of which the works of Oliver Lustig and Norman Manea are the best known. The North-East Transylvanian-born Elie Wiesel is not considered part of this canon, since his works were written neither in Romanian—and nor, for that matter, in Hungarian—and were published outside Romania.

37. Horváth (2009); literal translation from Hungarian.

38. Ibid.

39. However, it is noteworthy that Aurel Vainer, the president of the Federation of Romanian Jewish Communities (FEDROM), received 23,000 votes when he was elected as an ethnic Jewish representative to the Romanian national parliament in the last general election in Romania, which indicates that a significant number of non-Jewish Romanians also voted for him, since the number of votes he received was clearly far in excess of the membership of FEDROM (Salamon 2010). In contrast to Romania,

there is, of course, no separate parliamentary representation in Hungary for any non-Hungarian ethnic group, nor is there any kind of push for ethnicity-based parliamentary representation by Hungarian Jews, Roma, or the remnant ethnic Germans, Slovaks, Romanians, or Serbs of Hungary.

40. Cf. Salamon (2010).

41. Thus Jewish in the *halakhic* sense, i.e., according to Jewish religious law.

42. WJC, JTA, YIVO/Kovács (2004), Komoróczy (1997), among others.

43. Thus, it is entirely unsurprising that a public political initiative a decade ago that advocated an ethnic self-definition for Hungarian Jews failed to generate any traction at all among Jewish Hungarians.

44. In fact, it is striking how, in so many respects, the story of most people of Jewish descent in present-day Hungary is eerily similar to the story of the Spanish *conversos* five centuries before, as described in the works of, for instance, Netanyahu (1999) or Roth (2002).

45. Cf. Komoróczy (1997).

46. The title in Hungarian is *Kiválasztottak és elvegyülők*.

47. Cf. Kovács (1999)

48. Jewish Telegraphic Agency.

49. Jobbik is an ultranationalist Hungarian political party on the far right of Hungarian politics, with strong Hungarian Nazi coloring. The party's name means "better" or "more right." Jobbik currently holds 47 seats out of a total of 386 in the Hungarian parliament. Whilst virulently antisemitic, its electoral success in the 2010 general election was due primarily to its anti-Roma agenda. The party is led mainly by well-educated history graduates and counts among its informal leadership group the vicious antisemite Krisztina Morvai, an associate professor of law and Hungarian representative in the European Parliament, who is not, however, an actual card-carrying party member. The up-and-coming younger generation of Hungarian antisemites in Jobbik are increasingly replacing an older generation of 'eminent' Far Right antisemites, such as István Csurka, journalist, playwright, and leader of MIÉP, a now largely defunct "old-school" antisemitic political party. Csurka is Hungary's equivalent of Romania's Corneliu Vadim Tudor, and like Tudor, was a former leading light among the literati of the communist era.

50. The social and economic conditions prevailing in Hungary today significantly exacerbate antisemitism. A feeling of disappointment and gloom pervades society about the outcomes of the regime change two decades ago. There is pessimism and a sense of hopelessness among many, a wistful nostalgia for "the good old days" of goulash communism, and a generalized sense of disillusionment with the workings and institutions of liberal democracy and market capitalism. The global financial crisis found the Hungarians unprepared and vulnerable, and the ubiquitous culture of grievance focuses attention on problems, where others might see opportunities. The ground is thus increasingly fertile for antisemitism to flourish.

51. With an over two-thirds majority in the current Hungarian parliament, Fidesz not only dominates the parliament, but has the power to change the Hungarian constitution at will.

52. In contrast, Romania has had a reasonably hard-edged law against Holocaust denial since 2002, although what is on the books and actual prosecutions are, needless to say, as far removed as darkness is from dawn.

53. Decimated in the last general election and for the moment at least no longer a significant player in Hungarian politics.

54. Cf. Ónody-Molnár (2008).

55. A citadel of Marxist history, economy, and political science in Budapest during the communist era, today the institution is more in the nature of a stronghold of neo-liberal economics.

56. Cf. note 11 above.

57. Thus, for instance, while it does not mind in the least massive Austrian, German, and other West European investments in Hungarian real estate, it certainly does resent, and does so profoundly, similar investments by Jews from Israel. Hence the myth of an international Jewish conspiracy to colonize Hungary on the model of Palestine, so Israeli Jews will have a safe place to retreat to in the wake of a soon-to-eventuate glorious Palestinian Arab victory. It does not, of course, seem to occur to those on the Hungarian far-right to ask themselves why in heaven's name any Israeli Jew would wish to settle in miserable little Hungary instead of Long Island, Palm Beach, or Beverly Hills. Then there is also the usual run of outrageous blood libels, a particular favorite of the Hungarian far-right, with ritual killings of Christian children alternating with the brutal murder of innocent Palestinian children by evil Israeli soldiers. And there is also, of course, the hoary old chestnut of the supposed commandments of the Talmud to deceive the gentiles; in fact, there is a whole collection of Judeophobic mythology that is similar in every respect to its former Nazi and current Arab manifestations. The Far Right also deeply resents the reduced circumstances of Hungary in the modern world, and finds consolation in delusional shamanic theories of Hungarian origins involving, among others, a claim that Hungary is the locus of the "heart chakra" of the world, in which the lunatic right in Hungary latches on to a comment made by the Dalai Lama, during a 1996 visit to Hungary, in which His Holiness asserted that "the heart-chakra of Earth is in Hungary, and more exactly in the region called Pilis," a hill-region northwest of Budapest. The Hungarian Far Right also espouses weird, de-Judaized biblical theories, whereby Mary Mother of God is asserted to have really been a Scythian princess, thus Jesus an ancient Hungarian prince, and consequently modern Palestinians the long-lost cousins of modern Hungarians. And all of this is of course supposed to be kept the deepest of deep secrets in a nefarious plot hatched between the Vatican, international Jewry and international Freemasonry. Astounding as the gobsmacking illogic of these unmitigated idiocies might be, the situation can and does become very serious indeed, when literally hundreds of thousands believe in them and act upon them, as is the case not merely on the Hungarian Far Right, but in some cases on the Center Right as well.

58. In their peculiarly deranged ideological universe, the author ceases being "Kertész Imre"—with his name written according to the Hungarian convention of writing family name first and given name second—but becomes "Imre Kertész," whose alienness is underlined by writing his name with given name first, surname second,

according to the conventions of foreigners, and who therefore, thus named, is no longer considered a member of the Hungarian nation. The Nobel Prize awarded to Kertész is moreover perceived on the Far Right as just another example of the nefarious Jewish world conspiracy to culturally discredit and humiliate the Hungarian nation, by making it become a servile puppet of the Jewish narrative, to soften up the ground for the Great Israeli Bailout Project in Hungary. József Hering, for instance, writing in *Hungarian Forum,* the house organ of Csurka's defunct extreme-right MIÉP party, loudly demands to know when and who would be the first Nobel Prize winning *Hungarian* author and takes issue with the Nobel Prize committee for failing to award their prize also to authors writing about what he terms the "Holocausts" of Palestinians and Sudeten Germans. Using a Western-style human rights narrative to draw a parallel between the fate of the Palestinians or Sudeten Germans and the Holocaust—and coming thereby perilously close to skirting Holocaust-denial—Hering cynically misdirects the entire Nobel Prize debate to the Palestinian issue and uses low cunning to assume the mantle of a self-appointed champion of human rights while simultaneously condemning the decision of the Nobel Prize committee and denying the right of Kertész to be Hungarian.

59. There is, of course, one point of unquestioned convergence between the respective modern-day histories of Hungary and of Hungary's Jews, in that both Jewish and non-Jewish Hungarians look back upon the glory days of the Dual Monarchy as the *belle époque* of their nation's history, a golden age that they remember with wistful nostalgia, albeit for quite different reasons. The Jews remember their Camelot on the Danube, whereas non-Jews luxuriate in the five decades of glory as dominant partners in the Habsburg Empire, notwithstanding that it was by then in irremediable decline. Just how powerfully these memories still resonate in Hungary was eloquently demonstrated in the astonishing reception by Hungarian audiences—Jews and non-Jews alike—of the musicals *Elisabeth and Rudolf* portraying the respective lives and times of the nineteenth-century Habsburg Empress and Hungarian Queen Elisabeth of Bavaria and of her son, the Crown Prince Rudolf Habsburg, both of whom lost their lives in tragic circumstances. It goes without saying, of course, that as far as Transylvanian Romanians and modern-day Slovaks are concerned, this so-called *belle époque* of the Hungarians was a dreadful period of heavy-handed ethnic oppression and bitter, though in the end victorious struggle for their national rights.

60. At least as unlikely as, for instance, the prospects of an integrated Hungarian-Romanian or an integrated Hungarian-Slovak history emerging anytime soon.

61. Hence the words chosen for the title of this paper.

62. For an incisive and profoundly insightful analysis of the essentially right-wing, nationalist, and powerfully antisemitic political default position of the Hungarian public, cf. Ungváry (2009).

Bibliography

ADL Anti-Defamation League. 2009.
   Attitudes towards Jews in Seven European Countries. (Internet/pdf file.)

Ágoston: Vilmos. 2007.
A kisajátitott tér: A nemzeti képzelet Doru Monteanu és Wass Albert műveiben [The Expropriated Living Space: The National Imagination in the Works of Doru Monteanu and Albert Wass]. Budapest: EÖKIK. (Internet/pdf file.)

Alexander, Edward. 2004.
"No It's Not Antisemitic": Judith Butler vs. Lawrence Summers. In: Judaism, A Quarterly Journal of Jewish Life and Thought, Winter–Spring 2004. Avraham, Alexander. 2010.
Sephardim. In: YIVO Encyclopedia of Jews in Eastern Europe. (Internet/webpage.)

Barany, George. 1968.
Stephen Széchenyi and the Awakening of Hungarian Nationalism, 1791–1841. Princeton N.J.: Princeton University Press.

Beckerman, Gal. 2010.
Váltságdíj a zsidókért [Ransom for the Jews]. In: Szombat [Sabbath, a Hungarian Jewish cultural and political monthly], September 2010, pp. 10–11.

Benjamin, Lya. 2010.
Moses Rosenről [About Moses Rosen]. In: Szombat [Sabbath, a Hungarian Jewish cultural and political monthly], September 2010, pp. 12–14.

Bibó, István. 2001.
Zsidókérdés Magyarországon 1944 után [The Jewish Question in Hungary after 1944]. In Sándor Szilágyi, ed. Bibó István, pp. 205–299. Budapest: Új Mandátum.

Braham, Randolph L. 1981.
The Politics of Genocide: The Holocaust in Hungary. Vols. 1–2. New York: Columbia University Press.

Braham, Randolph L. 2007.
A magyarországi holokauszt földrajzi enciklopédiája [The Geographical Encyclopedia of the Holocaust in Hungary]. Vols. 1–3. Budapest: Park.

Carp, Matatias. 1946–1948.
Holocaust in Romania: Facts and Documents on the Annihilation of Romanian Jews. Trans. Sean Murphy. Ed. Andrew L. Simon. (Internet/pdf file.)

Chesler, Phyllis. 2003.
The New Anti-Semitism. San Franciso: Jossey-Bass.

Csurka, István. 2001a–c.
Magyar szemmel [With Hungarian Eyes]. In: Magyar Fórum [Hungarian Forum, an antisemitic weekly in Hungary]. July 5, 2002; July 12, 2002; August 2, 2002.

Eörsi, István. 2002.
A túlélés öröksége [The Legacy of Survival]. In: Élet és Irodalom [Life and Literature, Hungary's leading Left-Liberal cultural and political weekly]. Issue 29, 2002.

Eörsi, István. 2004.
Válasz helyett [In Lieu of a Response]. In: Élet és Irodalom [Life and Literature, Hungary's leading left-liberal cultural and political weekly]. Issue 43, 2004.

Erdélyi, Lajos. 2000.
Magyar zsidók Romániában, Erdélyben [Hungarian Jews in Romania, in Transylvania]. In: Múlt és Jövő [Past and Future, a Hungarian Jewish literary and cultural monthly]. Issue 1, 2000.

Erdélyi, Lajos. 2010.
A főrabbi, alulnézet [The Chief Rabbi, Bottom-up View]. In: *Szombat* [*Sabbath*, a Hungarian Jewish cultural and political monthly]. September 2010, pp. 12–14.

Fenyves, Katalin. 2010.
Képzelt asszimiláció [*Imagined Assimilation*]. Budapest: Corvina.

Foundation for the Advancement of Sephardic Studies and Culture. 2004.
Sephardic Jewish Community of Romania. (Internet/webpage.)

Frojimovics, Kinga; Komoróczy, Géza; Pusztai, Viktória; Strbik, Andrea; Török, Gyöngyvér, (ed.). 1995.
A Zsidó Budapest I–II [*Jewish Budapest I–II*]. Budapest: Főpolgármesteri Hivatalos Sajtó Osztály [The Official Publications Department of the Chief Mayor of Budapest].

Gabel, Joseph, 1995.
Jobboldali és baloldali zsidóellenesség [*Right Wing and Left Wing Anti-Jewishness*]. Budapest: MTA Judaisztikai Kutatócsoport [The Jewish Studies Research Group of the Hungarian Academy of Sciences].

Gadó, János; Novák, Attila; Szántó, Gábor T. 2007.
Új antiszemitizmus [*The New Antisemitism*]. Budapest: MAZSIKE.

Gadó, János. 2010.
A holokauszt Romániában [The Holocaust in Romania]. In: *Szombat* [*Sabbath*, a Hungarian Jewish cultural and political monthly], September 2010, pp. 9–10.

Gerő, András; Varga, László; Vince, Mátyás (ed.). 2001.
Antiszemita közbeszéd Magyarországon 2000-ben [Anti-Semitic Discourse in Hungary in 2000]. Budapest: B'nai B'rith Budapest Páholy [B'nai B'rith Budapest Lodge].

Gerő, András; Varga, László; Vince, Mátyás (ed.). 2002.
Antiszemita közbeszéd Magyarországon 2001-ben [*Anti-Semitic Discourse in Hungary in 2001*]. Budapest: B'nai B'rith Budapest Páholy [B'nai B'rith Budapest Lodge].

Gerő, András; Varga, László; Vince, Mátyás (ed.). 2003.
Antiszemita közbeszéd Magyarországon 2002-ben [*Anti-Semitic Discourse in Hungary in 2002*]. Budapest: B'nai B'rith Budapest Páholy [B'nai B'rith Budapest Lodge].

Gerő, András; Déso, János; Szeszlér, Tibor; Varga, László (ed.). 2004.
Antiszemita közbeszéd Magyarországon 2003-ben [*Anti-Semitic Discourse in Hungary in 2003*]. Budapest: B'nai B'rith Budapest Páholy [B'nai B'rith Budapest Lodge].

Gerstenfeld, Manfred (ed.). 2007.
Academics against Israel and the Jews. Jerusalem: The Jerusalem Center for Public Affairs.

Gyáni, Gábor (2004a).
Modernitás, modernizmus és identitásválság: a fin de siècle Budapest [Modernity, Modernism and Crisis of Identity: Fin de Siècle Budapest]. In: *Aetas*, 2004/1, pp. 131–43.

Gyáni, Gábor (2004b).
Image versus identity—Assimilation and Discrimination of Hungary's Jewry. In: *Hungarian Studies* 18, no. 2, pp. 153–62.

Gyurgyák, János. 2001.
A zsidókérdés Magyarországon [The Jewish Question in Hungary]. Budapest: Osiris.
Harrison, Bernard. 2007.
The Resurgence of Antisemitism: Jews, Israel and Liberal Opinion. Lanham, Md.: Rowman & Littlefield, Inc.
Harrison, Bernard. 2008.
Israel, Antisemitism and Free Speech. The American Jewish Committee.
Heller, Ágnes. 1996.
Zsidótlanitás a magyar zsidó irodalomban [De-Judaization in Hungarian Jewish Literature]. In: Szombat [Sabbath, a Hungarian Jewish cultural and political monthly], December 2010.
Heller, Ágnes. 2004.
A "zsidókérdés" megoldhatatlansága [The irresolvability of the "Jewish Question]. Budapest: Múlt és Jövő.
Hering, József. 2002.
Sikeres téma, sikeres iró [A Hit Theme, a Successful Author]. In: Magyar Fórum [Hungarian Forum, an antisemitic weekly in Hungary]. October 17, 2002.
Horváth, Ferenc Sz.
Újabb publikációk a romániai holokausztról [Recent Publications on the Romanian Holocaust]. In: Korunk [Our Era, a bilingual Transylvanian cultural monthly in Hungarian and Romanian], May 2009.
Humoreanu, Daniela. Undated.
His Blood upon Your Children. Interview with Corneliu Vadim Tudor, Romania Team Reporting Project (webpage).
Ioanid, Radu. 2000.
The Holocaust in Romania: The Destruction of Jews and Gypsies under the Antonescu Regime, 1940–1944. Chicago: Ivan R. Dee.
Ioanid, Radu. 2005.
The Ransom of the Jews: The Story of Extraordinary Secret Bargain between Romania and Israel. Chicago: Ivan R. Dee.
Israel, Giorgio. 2002.
La questione ebraica oggi—I nostri conti con il razzismo [The Jewish Question Today—We Call Racism to Account]. Bologna: Il Mulino.
Kádár, Gábor; Vági, Zoltán. 2005.
Hullarablás: A magyar zsidók gazdasági megsemmisitése [Scavenging the Dead: The Economic Destruction of Hungarian Jews]. Budapest: Jaffa.
Kádár, Gábor; Vági, Zoltán. 2008.
Pogromok és rendszerváltások [Pogroms and Regime Changes]. In: Népszabadság [People's Liberty, the largest circulation Hungarian daily, Center Left in political orientation]. November 20, 2008.
Katz, Jakov. 2001.
Az előítélettől a tömeggyilkosságig [From Prejudice to Mass Murder]. Budapest: Osiris.
Kertész, Imre. 2002.
Jeruzsálem, Jeruzsálem [Jerusalem, Jerusalem]. In: Élet és Irodalom [Life and Lit-

erature, Hungary's leading left-liberal cultural and political weekly]. Issue 18, 2002.

Komoróczy, Géza. 1997.
Jewish Hungary Today. Jerusalem Letter/Viewpoints. Jerusalem: Jerusalem Center for Public Affairs. (Internet/webpage.)

Komoróczy, Géza. 2009.
Zsidónegyedek Budapesten: egy kifejezés megtisztítása [Jewish Quarters in Budapest: Cleansing a Term of Expression]. In: *Szombat [Sabbath,* a Hungarian Jewish cultural and political monthly], September 2009.

Konrád, György. 1989.
Zsidó-magyar számvetés. [Jewish-Hungarian Accounting]. In: *Szombat [Sabbath,* a Hungarian Jewish cultural and political monthly], November 1989 and December 1989.

Kovács, András. 1998.
Jewish Assimilation and Jewish Politics in Modern Hungary. (Internet/pdf file.)

Kovács, András. 1999.
Antisemitic Prejudices in Contemporary Hungary. Acta No. 16, Analysis of Current Trends in Antisemitism. The Vidal Sassoon International Center for the Study of Antisemitism. The Hebrew University of Jerusalem. (Internet/webpage.)

Kovács, András. 2000.
Measuring Latent Anti-Semitism. (Internet/webpage.)

Kovács, András. 2003.
Magyar zsidópolitika [Hungarian Policy on Jews]. In: *Múlt és Jövő [Past and Future,* a Hungarian Jewish literary and cultural monthly]. 2003/3.

Kovács, András. 2004.
Hungary. In: *YIVO Encyclopedia of Jews in Eastern Europe.* (Internet/webpage.)

Kovács, András. 2005.
A kéznél lévő idegen [The Alien at Hand]. Budapest: PolgArt.

Kovács, András. 2008.
A másik szeme [The Eye of the Other]. Budapest: Gondolat.

Kovács, András. 2009.
Interjú: A történelmi emlékezet alakitása a politika prédájává vált [Interview: The Shaping of Historical Memory Has Fallen Prey to Politics]. In: *Élet és Irodalom [Life and Literature,* Hungary's leading left-liberal cultural and political weekly]. Issue 33, 2009.

Kovács, András. 2010a.
Hungary's Antisemitism. In: *Virtual Jerusalem.* (Internet/webpage.)

Kovács, András. 2010b.
Jews and Jewishness in Post-War Hungary. In: *Quest. Issues in Contemporary Jewish History,* Issue 1. Milan: CDEC. (Internet/webpage.)

Luzzato-Voghera, Gadi. 1994.
L'antisemitismo—Domande e risposte [Antisemitism—Questions and Answers]. Milan: Feltrinelli.

Luzzato-Voghera, Gadi. 2007.
Antisemitismo a sininstra [*Antisemitism on the Left*]. Torino: Einaudi.
Márai, Sándor. 1990.
Napló 1945–1957 [*Diary 1945–1957*]. Budapest: Akadémiai Kiadó & Helikon.
Marton, Kati. 2006.
The Great Escape: Nine Jews Who Fled Hitler and Changed the World. New York: Simon & Schuster.
Márton, László. 1989.
Kiválasztottak és elvegyülők [*The Chosen and the Comminglers*]. Budapest: Magvető.
Molnár, László. 2010.
Anti-Semitism in Hungary. Jerusalem: Institute for Global Jewish Affairs. (Internet/webpage.)
Netanyahu, Benzion. 1999.
The Marranos of Spain: From the Late 14th to the Early 16th Century, According to Contemporary Hebrew Sources. Third Edition Updated and Expanded. Ithaca N.Y.: Cornell University Press.
Nirenstein, Fiamma. 2002a.
L'abbandono. Come l'Occidente ha tradito gli ebrei [*Abandonment: How the West Betrayed the Jew*]. Milan: Rizzoli.
Nirenstein, Fiamma. 2004.
Gli antisemiti progressisti: La forma nuova di un odio antico [*The Progressive Anti-semites: A New Form of an Old Hatred*]. Milan: Rizzoli.
Novák, Attila. 2003.
A demokrácia vadhajtásai: Antiszemitizmus és viták a zsidóságról Magyarországon (1988–1998) [The Aberrations of Democracy: Anti-Semitism and Debates on Jewry in Hungary (1988–1998)]. In: *Beszélő* [*Speaker,* a Hungarian political and literary bi-monthly], 2004/6.
Ónody-Molnár, Dóra. 2008.
Jobboldali befolyás alatt az egyetemisták és a főiskolások [College and University Students under Right-Wing Influence]. In: *Népszabadság* [*People's Liberty,* the largest circulation Hungarian daily, center-left in political orientation]. March 26, 2008.
Ottolenghi, Emanuele. 2007.
Autodafé. L'Europa, gli ebrei e l'antisemitismo [*Auto-da-fé. Europe, the Jews and the antisemitism*]. Torino: Lindau.
Paksa, Rudolf. 2007.
Szélsőjobboldali pártok és mozgalmak a Horthy-korszakban [Far-Right Parties and Political Movements in the Horthy Era]. *Kommentár* [*Commentary,* a Hungarian political and cultural bi-monthly], 2007/5. pp. 68–75.
Patai, Raphael. 1996.
The Jews of Hungary: History, Culture, Psychology. Detroit: Wayne State University Press.
Peremiczky, Szilvia. 2004a.
A jó zsidó és a rossz izraeli [The Good Jew and the Bad Israeli.]. In: *Szombat* [*Sabbath,* a Hungarian Jewish cultural and political monthly]. 2004/9.

Peremiczky, Szilvia. 2004b.
Árpád and Abraham Were Fellow Countrymen: An Outline of Jewish Literature in Hungary. In: *Hungarian Studies*18, no. 2, pp. 163–78.
Peremiczky, Szilvia. 2004c.
Szirének és hajósok [Syrens and Sailors]. In: *Élet és Irodalom* [*Life and Literature*, Hungary's leading left-liberal cultural and political weekly]. Issue 46, 2004.
Peremiczky, Szilvia. 2006.
Irodalom és antiszemitizmus [Literature and Antisemitism.]. In: M. Szegedy-Maszák and É. Jeney, eds., *A kultúra átváltozásai: Kép, zene, szöveg* [*Transformations of Culture: Image, Music, Text*], pp. 347–98. Budapest: Balassi.
Peremiczky, Szilvia. 2008.
The Hungarian Paradigm: Where Contemporary West European Anti-Zionism Meets Traditional East European Jew-Hatred. Presentation at workshop on antisemitism, USHMM, Washington, July 2008. Unpublished manuscript.
Peremiczky, Szilvia. 2010
A zsidó-keresztény Európa és a multikulturalizmus [Judeo-Christian Europe and Multiculturalism]. In: M. Szegedy-Maszák, ed., *Nemzeti művelődés—egységesülő világ* [*National Culture—Unifying World*], pp. 55–78. Budapest: Napkút.
Poliakov, Léon. 2003.
The History of Anti-Semitism. I–III. Philadelphia: University of Pennsylvania Press.
Rosenfeld, Alvin. H. 2003.
Anti-Americanism and Anti-Smitism: A New Frontier of Bigotry. The American Jewish Committee.
Rosenfeld, Alvin. H. 2004.
Anti-Zionism in Great Britain and Beyond: A "Respectable" Anti-Semitism. The American Jewish Committee
Rosenfeld, Alvin H. 2007a.
Progressive Jewish Thought and the New Antisemitism. The American Jewish Committee. (Internet/pdf file.)
Rosenfeld, Alvin H. 2007b.
Rhetorical Violence and the Jews: Critical Distance. In: *TNR Online*, February 27, 2007.
Roth, Norman. 2002.
Conversos, Inquisition, and the Expulsion of the Jews from Spain. Madison: University of Wisconsin Press.
Salamon, Márton László. 2010.
Az idegen [The Alien]. In: *Szombat* [*Sabbath*, a Hungarian Jewish cultural and political monthly], September 2010, pp. 20–24.
Schoenfeld, Gabriel. 2004.
The Return of Anti-Semitism. San Francisco: Encounter Books.
Shavit, Ari. 2004.
The Jewish Problem, According to Theodorakis. In: *Ha'aretz*, 30 August 2004.
Standeisky, Éva. 2008.
Antiszemitizmusok [*Antisemitisms*]. Budapest: Argumentum.

Stark, Tamás. 1999.
The Migration of Holocaust Survivors from Hungary and Romania. Conference presentation Yad Vashem, Jerusalem. (Internet/pdf file.)

Szalai, Anna (ed.). 2002.
In the Land of Hagar—The Jews of Hungary: History, Society and Culture. Tel Aviv: Beth Hatefutsoth, The Nahum Goldmann Museum of the Jewish Diaspora, Ministry of Defence Publishing House.

Taguieff, Pierre André. 2004.
Rising from the Muck. The New Antisemitism in Europe. Chicago: Ivan R. Dee.

Tamás, Gáspár Miklós. 2001.
Új zsidó nacionalizmus [New Jewish Nationalism]. In: *Népszabadság [People's Freedom,* the largest circulation Hungarian daily, social democratic in orientation]. November 17, 2001.

Tamás, Gáspár Miklós. 2004.
Zur Judenfrage. [On the Jewish Question]. In: *Élet és Irodalom [Life and Literature,* Hungary's leading left-liberal cultural and political weekly]. Issue 43, 2004.

Tatár, György. 2000.
Izrael: Tájkép csata közben [Israel: Landscape Midst Battle]. Budapest: Osiris.

Tatár, György. 2003.
A nagyon távoli város [The Exceedingly Faraway City]. Budapest: Atlantisz.

Toró, Csilla Imola. 2010.
Oliver Lustig és Kertész Imre [Oliver Lustig and Imre Kertész]. Unpublished manuscript. Faculty of Humanities, Eötvös Loránd University of Arts and Sciences, Budapest.

Tolt, Mark. 2010.
Population and Migration. In: *YIVO Encyclopedia of Jews in Eastern Europe.* (Internet/webpage.)

Török, Petra (ed.). 1997.
A határ és a határolt: Töprengések a magyar zsidó irodalom létformáiról [The Confines and the Confined: Meditations on the Ontology of Hungarian Jewish Literature]. Budapest: Az Országos Rabbiképző Intézet Yahalom Zsidó Művelődéstörténeti Kutatócsoportja [The Yahalom Research Group of Jewish Cutural History at the Hungarian National Rabbinical Seminary].

Ungváry, Krisztián. 2005.
A magyar honvédség a második világháborúban [The Hungarian Army in the Second World War]. Budapest: Osiris.

Ungváry, Rudolf. 2009.
A magára találó többség [The Self-Rediscovering Majority]. In: *Élet és Irodalom [Life and Literature,* Hungary's leading left-liberal cultural and political weekly]. Issue 41, 2009.

Ungváry, Rudolf. 2010a.
Magyarország botránya [Hungary's Scandal]. In: *Népszava [People's Word,* a Hungarian social democratic daily], November 6, 2010.

Ungváry, Rudolf. 2010b.
Nem magyar magyarként [As a non-Hungarian Hungarian]. In: *Élet és Irodalom* [*Life and Literature*, Hungary's leading left-liberal cultural and political weekly]. Issue 50, 2010.
Vallasek, Júlia. 2010.
Román zsidó exodus, 1959 [Romanian Jewish exodus, 1959]. In: *Szombat* [*Sabbath*, a Hungarian Jewish cultural and political monthly], September 2010, pp. 15–16.
Varga, László, ed. 2005.
Zsidóság a dualizmus kori Magyarországon [*Jewry in the Era of Dualism in Hungary*]. Pannonica Kiadó: Budapest.
Virtual Jewish Library
Hungary: http://www.jewishvirtuallibrary.org/jsource/vjw/Hungary.html
Hungarian Holocaust: http://www.jewishvirtuallibrary.org/jsource/Holocaust/hungarytoc.html
Romania: http://www.jewishvirtuallibrary.org/jsource/vjw/romania.html
Romanian Holocaust Denial: http://www.jewishvirtuallibrary.org/jsource/Holocaust/Romania_Holo.html
Wiesel, Elie (Chairman).
Friling, Tuvia; Ionescu, Michael E.; Ioanid, Radu (Co-Vice-Chairmen). International Commission on the Holocaust in Romania, 2003–2004. *Final Report to Romanian President Ion Iliescu*. Bucharest, November 11, 2004. (Internet/pdf file.)

8 Comparative and Competitive Victimization in the Post-Communist Sphere

Zvi Gitelman

THE INTERPRETATION of the recent past occupies a prominent place on the agenda of post-communist states and societies. They seek to make sense of the five or seven decades of communist rule and place them in the larger narratives of their national histories, the latter being matters of contention within and between states. History serves as the legitimizer of present states and is therefore highly politicized. As the prominent Soviet historian M. N. Pokrovsky said in the 1930s, "history is politics projected into the past."[1]

One of the most troublesome issues for several of the post-communist states is that significant numbers of their citizens collaborated with the Nazis in the war against the Soviet Union and in the mass murder of Jews. Many assume that this raises questions not only about their behavior in the recent past but also about their political cultures and democratic commitments. If they do not at least address the "dark spots" and "blank spots" in their histories, this would mean, as the Talmud puts it, *shtika ke-hoda'ah damia,* silence is acquiescence. One way to meet this challenge is to equate the evils of fascism and communism and to portray Jews as perpetrators of evil as much as they might have been victims of it. That would, in some people's view, tie the moral score, absolve the present governments and populations of the region of guilt, and put the issue to rest. Of course, this is not the only way the issue is being treated, and there are nuances and complexities that both apologists for their national histories and vocal critics of them choose to ignore. Reinterpreting history is not an academic exercise but a deeply political one, with implications for how Jews are viewed and treated, among many other things.

Some post-communist states struggle to convince the world, and especially their neighbors, of their legitimacy as sovereign states—Macedonia, Slovakia, Ukraine, Belarus, and Moldova come to mind. All try to convince their own populations and the rest of the world of their virtue, high ethical standards, and great cultural achievements. Therefore, it is particularly difficult for insecure states, challenged by their neighbors and by internal forces, to confront "dark spots" in their recent histories.

Countries which were allied with the Axis powers—Slovakia, Croatia, Hungary, Romania—or in which significant numbers of autochthonous people collaborated with the Nazis—Ukraine, the Baltic states—are at particular pains to explain how that came about. Some people simply deny it. Others, however, acknowledge that Jews who had lived among them were victims of genocide and that local people were responsible. Still others aver that Jews were just as much victimizers as victims. If one assumes that communism was as great an evil as fascism—and there is no objective way of measuring the extent or degree of evil—to the extent that one can blame communism on the Jews, as many attempt to do, the latter can be justly accused of being as much perpetrators as victims. The Holocaust need not be denied—it merely has to be equated with crimes perpetrated by "the Jews" against others in order to "cancel the debt" owed by others to the Jews. If Jews were equally murderers, robbers, and evildoers as they were victims of such people, they deserve no special sympathy. Moreover, the only Jewish state in the world, Israel, once a haven for survivors of the Holocaust, in this accusatory view no longer deserves sympathy, for it has turned into a victimizer itself. It has allegedly perpetrated ethnically based crimes against the Palestinians and discriminated against Arabs and other non-Jews who are nominal citizens of Israel. Thus, neither the Jews nor the state that they created are said to deserve special consideration. In the competition for victimization, the Jews have had their day. Europe spent nearly half a century apologizing and making up to the Jews for the evils it had perpetrated against them. But with the Catholic church—though not the Orthodox one—having lifted the burden of guilt of deicide from the Jews, the near universal recognition of the State of Israel, and the enormous, though incomplete, reparation payments made for material destruction and, at least symbolically, for mass annihilation of human beings, the debt has been paid, scores have been settled, and now the Jews and their state must be judged like everyone else without special consideration. Thus runs the argument for a new, more objective, perspective on the Shoah and the reassignment of the roles of perpetrators and victims. Once those who can speak in the name of each group of people apologize, the issue should be considered settled, both evils condemned, and no further investigation—and certainly no pursuit of individuals who might have been guilty of one or another form of collaboration—should be undertaken. Such a national narrative is not an academic exercise alone, because it will profoundly influence present and future generations and perpetuate bad relations between them.

There are several problems with the line of thinking I have described. The first is that there is no factual basis for the accusation of "Jewish collaboration" with communism. There is a different, better case, for collaboration of some East Europeans with fascism, as I shall seek to demonstrate. Second, not everyone would agree that conquest and enslavement are as evil as genocide. Though communism killed many individuals and discriminated unfairly against some social classes and ethnic groups or nations, it did not murder whole peoples, though some groups have used the word *genocide* loosely to describe such horrors as the "Holodomor," the famine of 1932–33 that claimed millions of victims. Third, thus far no collective body of Jews has assumed responsibility for communism, nor should it, whereas some spokesmen of East European nations—presidents of Poland and Lithuania, high-ranking Romanian officials, and others— have apologized to the parliament of Israel or to the general public for the participation of some of their co-nationals in the murder of Jews. However, the Knesset or the State of Israel does not represent world Jewry, and no Jewish collective ever advocated communism, in contrast to East European national groups that cooperated with the Nazis. A Lithuanian president is better able to apologize for actions of Lithuanians, the majority of whom live in Lithuania—though his own parliament condemned him for doing so—than the head of a Jewish organization, who represents no one but his or her organization (at best), or even an Israeli head of government, who cannot speak for more than half of the world's Jews. But the fact that one side, as it were, seems to have assumed some partial responsibility while the other has not, engenders and perpetuates resentments among East Europeans.

Zydokomuna

Let us examine the empirical basis for assertions about collaboration of Jews with communism and some East Europeans with fascism. There is a long-standing myth of the Zydokomuna—the "Kike–Commie conspiracy." Though the myth is not based on fact, that is irrelevant to political and social reality. What matters politically and socially is perception, not fact. To the extent that communism is seen to be as evil as Nazism, and that Jews are viewed as "responsible" for communism, some argue that not only are Jews undeserving of the now prestigious status of victims, but they should be held to account for their own crimes. Certainly, Jews should not be admitted to positions of leadership and prominence in post-communist states, for they will once again exploit the virtuous, suffering masses.

The range of believers in the myth of the Judaeo-communist conspiracies is impressive. In 1936, Cardinal August Hlond, primate of Poland, issued a pastoral letter (to be read in all pulpits) stating that, "There will be a Jewish problem as long as the Jews remain. . . . It is a fact that the Jews fight against the Catholic church, they are free-thinkers, and constitute the vanguard of atheism, bolshevism and revolution."[2] People as different as Winston Churchill and Adolf Hitler believed the Bolshevik Revolution was mounted by Jews and the Soviet regime controlled by them. In 1921, Churchill wrote: "The international Jews. The adherents of this sinister confederacy . . . have gripped the Russian people by the hair . . . and have become practically the undisputed masters of that enormous empire."[3] Hitler asserted, "In Russian Bolshevism we . . . see the attempt undertaken by the Jews . . . to achieve world domination. . . ." He described Russia as a place where "on a Slavic-Tatar body is set a Jewish head."[4] As early as 1920, Hitler "explicitly married the images of Marxism, Bolshevism and the Soviet system in Russia to the brutality of Jewish rule," and routinely used the phrase 'Jewish Bolshevism.'"[5] Thus, we have in agreement that Jews were responsible for communism, a prince of the church, a leader of the Free World at its most heroic, and he who would have enslaved or destroyed much of the world. The facts are otherwise.

In 1922 there were only 958 Jews in the Russian Communist Party who had joined it before 1917.[6] There were far more Jews among Mensheviks and Bundists—and all of them together were outnumbered by Russian Jewish Zionists. The single largest group of Jews were the politically un-affiliated. Yet, the image of Jew-as-Bolshevik became firmly established.[7] That image was made plausible by the presence of Jews in the leadership of communist parties. At the April 1917 conference of Bolsheviks, Jews were 20 percent of the delegates. Of twenty-one members of the Bolshevik Central Committee in August 1917, six were of Jewish origin. In a country where a Jew had not been permitted to hold the lowest civil service job—postman, policeman, clerk—the sight of Jews running the government in 1917–21 was a great shock, as shocking as it would have been to white people in Mississippi in 1950 to have a black woman governor and chief of the state police.

In Hungary, during the failed revolution of 1919, "Some thirty of the forty-eight people's commissars in the Hungarian Soviet Republic . . . were Jewish or of Jewish origin."[8] According to Werner Sombart, "Of 203 higher officials in the [Bela] Kun government, 161 were Jewish."[9] But both in Russia and in Hungary, these Bolsheviks were "non-Jewish Jews," in Isaac Deutscher's term. They were of course not religious, but they were also mostly ignorant of Hebrew or Yiddish and to a remarkable degree had grown up outside Jewish environments. Leon Trotsky (Lev Davidovich Bronshtain) is perhaps paradigmatic.

Born outside the Pale of Settlement on a farm in Ukraine, his father was irreligious and his Jewish education consisted of a few miserable weeks in a *heder* in Odessa where he was mocked by his fellow pupils for his Jew-ish ignorance and inability to speak Yiddish. Trotsky wrote in his auto-biography, "In my mental equipment, nationality never occupied an inde-pendent place, as it was felt but little in everyday life. . . . It never played a leading part—not even a recognized one—in my list of grievances."[10] None of these Bolshevik leaders had a traditional Jewish education or was literate in a Jewish language.

Of course, non-Jews were not interested in the degree of piety or Jew-ish learning of Jewish communists. All that mattered was that they were both Jews and communists. The wildest theories were spun in order to make sense of this *farkerte velt,* this upside-down world in which the lowly Jews had seized the heights of power.

As two aristocratic observers of Hungarian communism asserted,

The People's Commissars, with very few exceptions, were of Jewish extraction, while their staff consisted almost exclusively of Jews, baptised or unbaptised. . . . These Jews commanded, governed, controlled, and supervised everything, and incidentally insulted and sneered at the Christian religion, pulling God and Christ from their thrones just as in Russia, where statues have been raised to Lucifer and Judas Iscariot [sic!]—the latter's statue, as everyone knows [sic!], even bears the inscription: "To the Precursor of the World Revolution."[11]

In Poland, according to Joanna Michlic, "Judeo-Bolshevism (*zydo-bolszewizm*) and Judeo-communism (*zydokomuna*) were the most frequently propagated themes of the Jew as the threatening other in the interwar period. . . . The fear of Communism was widely accompanied by its identification with Jews . . . The Polish ethno-nationalist press frequently described the Soviet political system as a Judeo-Bolshevik political threat endangering the existence of Poland and other European nations."[12]

True, perhaps a quarter or more of the illegal Communist Party in interwar Poland was Jewish. Jews were also overrepresented in relation to their proportion of the population in the Romanian, Lithuanian, and other communist parties. However, as a proportion of the Jewish populations of these countries, communists were a tiny minority. Since communist parties were illegal,[13] it is very difficult to ascertain the size of their memberships, which fluctuated considerably during the interwar period anyway, but the general picture is made clear in the table below.

If there were 9,000 or 10,300 Polish communists[14] and Jews constituted 22–26 percent of the membership,[15] they were at most 2,300–2,700 in a Jewish population of 3,350,000, that is, less than a tenth of one percent.[16] True, in the communist youth movements their proportion was sometimes double their proportion in the party as a whole, but communists were still a very small minority among Polish Jewish youth.[17] Jews in Eastern Europe had little reason to defend the status quo, but the overwhelming majority did not choose to overthrow it by force, as the communists advocated.[18]

In interwar Poland, Jews voted mainly for Jewish parties and only between 2 and 7 percent voted for the Communist Party or its fronts. Looking at the data another way, Kopstein and Wittenberg conclude that about 14 percent of the communist vote came from Jews.[19] Yet, Jews were the single largest group supporting the (anticommunist) government party,

Table 8.1. Jewish Communists, CP Membership and the Jewish Population, Interwar Eastern Europe

	Jews in CP	CP	J%	J Population
Poland	2,700	10,300	26%	3,350,000
Romania	303	1,665	18.2	796,000
Lithuania	346	1,120	31	150,000
Latvia	?	500		96,000

half of them casting ballots for it, while among Catholics (mostly Poles) only 16 percent did so.[20]

Jews were also prominent in the small, illegal communist parties of Romania and Hungary—on the eve of World War Two each party probably had a thousand members or less—and were an even smaller fraction of the Jewish populations in those countries.[21] In Bessarabia, which was part of Romania before 1940, there were at most 375 communists in the year the region was taken over by the USSR.[22] Vladimir Tismaneanu comments that in Romania ". . . it was much easier to resort to the ludicrous but infectious myth of the 'Judeo-Bolshevik conspiracy' than to realize that the issues involved in the communist faith transcended any ethnic or religious affiliation."[23] In 1933, when Jews made up 4 percent of the Romanian population, the 303 Jewish communists made up 18.2 percent of the 1,665 members of the party, the ethnic group third in size after Hungarians (27 percent) and Romanians (23 percent). Of a total Jewish population of some 790,000, there were 300 communists.[24] At the fifth congress of the Romanian Communist Party (1931), one-quarter of the delegates were Jews—that is, six people![25] Nevertheless, the fascist Arrow Cross in Hungary and its Romanian counterpart, the Iron Guard, stressed the supposed alliance between communism and Jewry, both of them inimical to the respective national interests. Communism was seen by the Iron Guard as a new manifestation of the "Jewish danger," though the vast majority of Romanian Jews had no sympathy for communism.[26]

There was a sudden increase in the use of the Judeo-Bolshevism argument after the June 1940 Soviet ultimatum, which resulted in territorial losses and Romania joining the Axis in the war against the Soviet Union. If the representation of the Jews as being disloyal and traitorous . . . was not new . . . the media perception of the Jewish minority, derived from the official one, was simplified even more: the inclination toward communism was considered as defining for the Jews. The journalistic discourse insinuated that there was an irresistible link between the Soviet Union and the Jews from the Romanian state. . . . Many in the press regarded the Soviet Union as a product of Jewish militancy.[27]

In Latvia and Lithuania one can observe parallel developments: tiny communist parties in the interwar period, an overrepresentation of Jews, and a widespread perception that many Jews were communists or communist sympathizers. Thus, in 1938, there were 12 Lithuanians, 4 Jews and 2 Latvians in the Central Committee of the Lithuanian Communist Party.[28] According to the Lithuanian secret police, in 1939 there were 1,120 Communist Party members, of whom 670 were Lithuanians (60 percent), and 346 Jews (31 percent). About 250 communists, half of them Jews and the other half Lithuanians, were in jail,[29] this when the Jewish population of the country was about 150,000.[30] After the annexation of Lithuania by the Soviet Union, in 1941 the number of Jewish communists rose only modestly to 412 (16.6 percent of the total party membership of 2,486), but the number in the Communist Youth League was 1,775 (23.8 percent), reflecting perhaps the greater enthusiasm for communism among some Jewish youth as well as the easier entry to the Komsomol than to the party.[31] As elsewhere, though the number of Jewish communists was tiny, they were overrepresented in the leading organs of the party. In 1940–41, they were 11 percent of Central Committee members (5 of 47) and 19 percent of candidate members (3 of 16), 9 percent (1 of 22) of the Politburo, but 25 percent (1 of 4) of Central Committee secretaries. Still, "At the beginning of 1941 there were about 17 Communists for every 10,000 Jews."[32]

Thus, it is clear that while Jews constituted a disproportionate number of communists, the proportion of communists among Jews was miniscule. "The Jews" did not invent, support, or impose communism, though there were Jews among those who did.

Nazism and Its Supporters

Nazism was a German invention and was supported in 1933 by a plurality of the German voting population. It seems to have gained support among the Germans during the following decade, though that is hard to gauge. It is fair to say that Nazi doctrines had some organized and individual support in other European countries, but that the German attack on the Soviet Union in 1941 had even broader support among people who did not believe in those doctrines. They had other, mainly national or nationalist reasons, for supporting the German war effort. In the territories taken over by the Soviet army in 1939–40, those reasons were mainly that the Germans would liberate them from Soviet political, economic, and social policies and would support their national sovereignty. The first motivation applied also in the territories of the Soviet Union itself, especially in Ukraine, where Bolshevism had not been as popular as in Russia and Belorussia in 1917–30 and where collectivization of agriculture and the famine of 1932–33 had made it even less popular. Thus, the Iron Guard in Romania, the Arrow Cross in Hungary, the Falanga in Poland, and parallel groups in the Baltic States espoused Nazi antisemitism and other doctrines. Antisemites who were not members of those radical movements did the same.

Some people who were not necessarily antisemitic supported the German attack on the USSR not so much because they shared Nazi ideas but because they saw it as liberating them from the ideas, policies, and practices of the Bolsheviks. Thus, the Ukrainian Insurgent Army (UPA), the Lithuanian Patriotic Front, and other Baltic, Belorussian, and Russian armed formations (e.g., General Vlasov's Russian Army of Liberation), as well as the Iron Guard, the Arrow Cross, the Croatian Ustasha, and the Slovak Hlinka Guard collaborated actively with the Nazis largely because they saw them as a means to get rid of their historic or recent enemies. Every one of these movements was content to support the Nazis' policies of exterminating the Jews, and most participated vigorously and happily in doing so. The Ukrainian Nachtigal, SS Halychyna, Latvian SS, and other units fought actively with the Nazis. There were no parallel Jewish organizations or movements supporting communism. Even Hashomer Hatsa'ir, a Marxist-Zionist movement sympathetic to the Soviet experiment, as they saw it, was suppressed by the Soviets.

According to a Russian scholar, overall, about 2.7 percent of the population of the Soviet territories conquered by the Nazis was involved in direct collaboration, while 7 percent were involved in active resistance to the occupation. However, the figure of those who resisted includes those who resisted passively, while the number of those who collaborated includes only active collaborators.[33] Between 4.5 million and 6 million Ukrainians fought in the Soviet military against the Nazis. About 200,000–300,000 residents of Ukraine, mostly but not all ethnic Ukrainians, are estimated to have served the German invaders in several types of official positions: as *polizei* or *Schutzmannschaft,* administrative officials, members of the Waffen-SS, soldiers in German-sponsored units, or in the UPA, the latter playing an ambiguous and perhaps ambivalent role—fighting both the Germans and the Soviets at the outset of the war, but then only the Soviets—and in the Ukrainian National or Liberation Army.[34] Thousands of others took unilateral, often murderous, action against Jews, which the Germans tolerated but did not organize.[35] In West Ukraine, more than 80,000 Ukrainians volunteered for the SS Halychyna Division, a Waffen-SS division, of whom 13,000 ultimately served. Ukrainian police "enforced the ghettoization process, provided cordons during ghetto clearing operations and mass shootings, escorted Jews to local killing sites or to the trains headed for the death camp Belzec, carried out house-to-house searches, and combed forests for hidden Jews."[36] Some 3,000–5,000 Ukrainians were trained as concentration or extermination camp guards at Trawniki. A very rough estimate is that 600,000 Ukrainians worked with the Nazis in some fashion. There were about 4.5 million Ukrainians in Poland before the war and about 24 million in 1939 in the USSR. Thus, the 600,000 represent about 2 percent of the total Ukrainian population, more than ten times the proportion of Jews among the communists. If only Ukrainians in Poland are used as the denominator (including women, children, and the elderly), 13 percent of them would have worked with or for the Germans.[37] Together, these people amounted to about 1 or 2 percent of the Ukrainian population, more than ten times the proportion of Jews among the communists.

Thus, the argument of parallelism and equal responsibility by Jews and non-Jews for atrocities and crimes against humanity finds no support in the historical record.

The Political Uses and Consequences of a False Equation

Nevertheless, some find it politically useful to make that equation. They ask whether communism or Nazism killed more people. With respect to communism, recent historians suggest a likely total of around 20 million from executions, gulags, deportations, and other causes. The number of people killed directly by the Nazis has been estimated at 17 million, with millions of others dying of disease, starvation, and other causes as a result of Nazi persecutions. This should not be taken to mean that communism was "worse" than Nazism. Such judgments, if there is any reason to make them, would have to take into account the way people were killed (more benignly, more cruelly), the amount of time in which the killings were done, the rationales for killing (genuine opponents versus "innocent victims"), the skill of the killers, the survival capacity of the victims, and many other measures. I suggest that such an exercise is misconceived. One can compare orders of magnitude of killings—surely, killing one hundred people is much worse than killing one—but once we deal with orders of magnitude—millions in this case—judging which was worse becomes a useless enterprise. It is parallel to commonly heard discussions about who were the worst tormentors of the Jews during the war: Germans, Ukrainians, Lithuanians, Latvians, Hungarians, Slovaks, Croats, or Romanians? It is understandable that survivors name the people as "worst" with whom they had direct experience, but it is not helpful for developing objective measures of evil. Moreover, as is the case with the Nazi–Soviet comparison, it seems not to be of any particular utility.

But if one could equate Nazism, or to use the term most frequently employed in Eastern Europe, fascism, with communism, the argument about equal responsibility of collaborators with each would hold up. Today in former communist countries there are several tactics being used to downplay historical antisemitism and the Holocaust. One is simply denying or ignoring the Holocaust (there is, of course, a big difference between them; the Soviets never denied the Holocaust but mostly ignored it, as did the Romanians until quite recently). Another is to deny the participation in, and hence partial responsibility for, the Holocaust by native, local peoples. A third is to reinterpret cooperation with the Nazis as a national liberation struggle or a just war on communism. Finally, some have generalized the word *Holocaust* so that it loses its specific focus on the mass murder of Jews and becomes a description of any large scale loss of life—or even a lopsided defeat in a sports match!

An example of the first tactic is that that the first monument commemorating the Shoah was erected in Romania only a few years ago, and then at the prompting of outsiders. Monuments to Soviet soldiers who from the Russian point of view were liberators, have been removed from prominent public display in Latvia and Estonia, evoking protests not only from Slavic residents of those countries but also from the Russian government.[38] The nationalist Hungarian Jobbik Party also called for the removal of a Soviet war memorial from Central Budapest.[39] An example of the third tactic is to say that the Latvian and Estonian SS veterans who have marched in parades celebrating them had fought to liberate their countries from the Soviets.[40]

In January 2010, former president of Ukraine Victor Yushchenko officially "rehabilitated" Stepan Bandera, head of one of the two factions of the Organization of Ukrainian Nationalists and the political sponsor of the Ukrainian Insurgent Army. This act drew condemnation from Russia, Poland, and Jewish groups. Yushchenko bestowed the posthumous rank of Hero of Ukraine on Roman Shukhevich, one of the most important UPA commanders. Yushchenko also declared the Holodomor a genocide, though whether the famine in Ukraine was engineered to kill Ukrainians while sparing Russians and others is still a matter of debate among scholars and politicians.[41] Ukrainian émigrés and some in Ukraine itself have pressed the idea that the Holodomor was a "genocide," the same as the Holocaust, and that the participation of some Jewish communists in the sequestration of grain that led to the famine is proof of Jewish "collaboration" in the genocide of Ukrainians. As one Ukrainian historian has pointed out, "Particularly insulting are the attempts to establish a [causal] relationship between the tragedies of the Famine and the Holocaust, and in some cases even indirect justification of the extermination of Jews at the time of the Second World War."[42]

The idea of a "double genocide," one by communists, the other by Nazis, is widely discussed today in Ukraine and in the Baltic States. It is an argument for moral equivalence of Nazi and Soviet crimes. It stretches the term *genocide* to include Soviet purges and terror, just as some have stretched the term to characterize the experience of Palestinian Arabs in 1948 as a genocide.[43] Horrid as Soviet actions were, they did not amount to genocide. The Soviets never attempted to wipe out an entire nation or even a majority of any nation. Not only does such usage render *genocide* too elastic a term and attempt to deny the specificity of the Holocaust, but all too often the moral equivalence argument is used to absolve collaborators with the Nazis of any guilt, if the acts of collaboration are even acknowledged, which they sometimes are not. For example, in museums and memorials to victims of terror in the Baltic countries and in the so-called "House of Terror" in Budapest, the Holocaust is often unmentioned or played down.[44] The history of the monument at Panierai/Ponary near Vilnius is instructive. The Soviet-era monument had parallel inscriptions in Russian and Lithuanian, neither of which mentioned Lithuanian killers under Nazi direction. During perestroika, the two parts of the monument were pulled apart and a Hebrew–Yiddish part was inserted that mentions the Nazis and "their local assistants." So only the Hebrew or Yiddish reader learns that the Lithuanians participated in the murder of some 100,000 Jews at the site—which they probably know anyway—but the others do not.

Leonidas Donskis, a courageous Lithuanian philosopher, has written, "If you want to downgrade the Holocaust or shove it into the margins of history . . . all you need to do is come up with another genocide that took place in the same country, even it is one that does not quite fit the legal criteria for and definition of genocide."[45] Indeed, in 2008 the Lithuanian prosecutor's office issued a warrant for the arrest of Yitzhak Arad, former head of Yad Vashem, Rachel Margolis, and Fanya Brantsovskaya, all former Soviet partisans, on the grounds of complicity in the murder of Lithuanian civilians during one incident when they were fighting the Nazis. Only an international outcry forced the government to drop the case.

The Prague Declaration

There is good reason to be wary of parallels drawn for political purposes between Nazism and communism. However, the considerable noise in the media about the so-called Prague Declaration is off target, in my view. This Declaration on European Conscience and Communism, made in June 2008 by the senate of the Czech Republic, "recognize[s] communism and Nazism as a common legacy" and calls for spreading consciousness of the crimes against humanity by the communist regimes to the same extent as the Nazi regime's crimes have been made known. It does assert that both regimes engaged in "exterminating and deporting whole nations and groups of population," an inaccurate and misleading formulation. Stalin's regime did deport Crimean Tatars, some peoples of the Caucasus, 187,000 Koreans, and hundreds of thousands of Soviet Germans, but it did not exterminate them, so that "exterminating and deporting" is an inappropriate linkage. The Declaration calls for a Nuremberg-like tribunal to adjudicate the crimes against humanity of communists and for a "day of remembrance of the victims of both Nazi and communist totalitarian regimes in the same way Europe remembers the victims of the Holocaust on January 27." Finally, the Declaration urges the "adjustment and overhaul of European history textbooks so that children would learn and be warned about Communism and its crimes in the same way as they have been taught to assess the Nazi crimes."[46]

Efraim Zuroff of the Wiesenthal Center in Israel, Dovid Katz, formerly a professor in Vilnius, and other Jews condemned the Declaration as "part of a campaign [by people who lived under communism] to be portrayed as the victims also." But the Declaration does not link Jews to communism, nor does it even suggest that victims of communism should be absolved of any guilt for having collaborated with Nazism. A Jewish signatory, Emanuelis Zingeris of Lithuania, defended the Declaration and said, "We are not equating the respective crimes of Nazism and Communism. They should each be studied and judged on their own terrible merits."[47]

The Prague Declaration is clearly not a Europe-wide document. In the version I have seen, there is not a single Slovak, Croat, Romanian, Hungarian, Norwegian, Dane, Belgian, or Dutchman among the signatories, nor is there anyone from the former Yugoslavia, Albania, Bulgaria, or Greece. True, among the twenty-seven "founding signatories" are Václav Havel, four members of the European Parliament, and four members of national parliaments. All the rest are either former officials, or historians, former prisoners, or journalists. Sixteen of the signatories are Czech. To date, it does not appear that anything concrete has come out of the Declaration or that it has had any practical consequences.

Those of us who look at the former communist sphere from the outside should remember that Nazism has passed from memory and experience to history and abstraction for most people in that area. Communism is much more present in the popular memory. Current political actors remember communism and resent it more than they do Nazism. People in the West, including some Jews, may not understand how searing an experience communism was for many. It deprived nations of sovereignty, almost all people of property, many of dignity, and all of freedom. It provided a minimum of material satisfaction, offered opportunities for upward (and downward) social mobility, literacy, free education, and medical care. But many, if not all, choose to remember the evils of communism more than its benefits. One cannot expect people to be more moved by the suffering of Jews seventy years ago than by their own sufferings thirty years ago, even if by any objective measure the Jews' suffering, individually and collectively, was far greater. Those who demand that East Europeans recognize that Jewish suffering was greater *may* be morally right but may also be politically and psychologically obtuse. Traumatic histories and the legacies they leave behind need to be addressed seriously.

Setting the record straight, acknowledging it, and using it to set new courses are important tasks for post-communist states and societies. History matters, and that is why it is contentious. Contrary to the fashionable stance of the "postmodernists," it is important to try to establish "wie es eigentlich war," how things really happened.

NOTES

1. Quoted in "From the editors," *Kritika* 10, no. 4 (Fall 2009), p. 747.

2. Quoted in Brian A. Porter, "Making a Space for Antisemitism: The Catholic Hierarchy and the Jews in the Early 20th Century," *Polin* 16 (2003), pp. 415–29.

3. *Illustrated Sunday Herald* (February 8, 1920).

4. Quoted in Alexander Dallin, *German Rule in Soviet Russia, 1941–1945* (London: Macmillan, 1981, 2nd. ed.), p. 9.

5. Ian Kershaw, *Hitler, 1889–1936: Hubris* (New York: W.W. Norton, 1999), pp. 151 and n.84.

6. We do not know how many Jewish Bolsheviks died during the revolution and civil war, but it can be assumed that there were well over 1,000 who had joined before 1917. It should be remembered that in 1917 the Bund had about 35,000 members; 300,000 Jews in the former Russian Empire had bought the shekel, symbolic of "membership" in the Zionist movement.

7. Zvi Gitelman, *Jewish Nationality and Soviet Politics* (Princeton, N.J.: Princeton University Press, 1972), p. 105. Less than 5 percent of Jewish communists in 1922 had been Bolsheviks before the revolution. In post-Soviet Russia, the extreme nationalist press regularly accused "the Jews" of responsibility for the evils of both communism and capitalism. Even in Australia there were people and publications writing of communism as "a Jewish movement inspired by Satan and hence diabolically clever" and of the "philosophical and religious link between Talmudic Judaism and Marxism-Leninism." Father Patrick Gearson and David Brockschmidt, quoted, respectively, in the pamphlet by Danny Ben-Moshe, "Holocaust Denial in Australia" (Jerusalem: Vidal Sassoon International Center for the Study of Antisemitism, Hebrew University) 25 (2005), pp. 10–11.

8. William McCagg, Jr., "Hungary's Jewish Ministers and Commissars," unpublished discussion paper, March 22, 1969, p. 1.

9. *Der proletarische Sozialismus* (Jena, 1924), II, pp. 299–300, cited in R. V. Burks, *The Dynamics of Communism in Eastern Europe* (Princeton, N.J.: Princeton University Press, 1961), p. 162. Sombart was a controversial figure who ended up—he died in 1941—close to Nazism.

10. Leon Trotsky, *My Life* (New York: C. Scribner's Sons, 1930), pp. 37–38, 86–87.

11. Baron Albert Kaas and Fedor de Lazarovics, *Bolshevism in Hungary: The Bela Kun Period* (London: Grant Richards, 1931), p. 143.

12. Joanna Beata Michlic, *Poland's Threatening Other: The Image of the Jew from 1880 to the Present* (Lincoln and London: University of Nebraska Press, 2006), p. 89. Michlic observes that in recent Polish scholarship on communism in Poland, "the scope of Judeo-Communism seems to be ignored or only partially acknowledged and discussed," pp. 310–311 n. 103.

13. The exception was the Czechoslovak Communist Party. I have been unable to find data on the number of Jews in that party.

14. Estimates for 1933 and 1934, including Communist Parties of West Ukraine and West Belorussia, when party membership was probably at its peak.

15. Andrzej Werblan, "Przyczynek do genezy konfliktu," *Miesiecznik Literacki* (June 6, 1968), p. 66. Werblan comments, "One must say openly that the ethnic composition of the KPP on Polish territory was not correct [*prawidłowy*]." He writes that while Poles who joined the party did so because of their class consciousness as workers, many of the Jews who became communists were not of genuine proletarian origin and joined as an act of protest against ethnic discrimination. Thus they brought in certain "deformations" to Polish communism. R. V. Burks cites *Polityka* (November 29, 1958), as saying that in 1933 "some 26 per cent of party members were Jewish. This figure seems on the low side. Perhaps it covers only those . . . willing to admit that they came from Jewish families. An anti-Communist source estimates the proportion of Jews in the party in 1931 at about half and there are indications that in 1940 the percentage of Jews in the Communist party of neighboring Lithuania was 53.8 [no source cited]. In any case, it is clear that the bulk of the Communist youth organization was Jewish," p. 160.

16. Sh. Zachariasz, perhaps the leading Polish communist active among Yiddish-speaking communists after the war, claims that in March 1933 the party had 17,800 members, as did the communist youth organizations. "Besides them, there were 10,000 communists incarcerated in the jails," Sh. Zachariasz, *Di komunistishe bavegung tsvishn der Yidisher arbetndiker bafelkerung in Poiln* (Warsaw: Idisz Buch, 1954), p. 50. Zachariasz claims that "30,000 organized Jewish workers were under the influence of the party," but he gives no figures on Jewish membership in it. Nor are such data found in H. Goldfinger, M. Mirski, and Sz. Zachariasz, *Unter der fon fun K.P.P.* (Warsaw: Ksiazka i wiedza, 1959). On Jews and communism in Poland, see Michal Bilewicz and Bogna Pawlisz, *Zydzi i komunizm* (Warsaw: Jidele, Wydanie Specjalne, 2000).

The higher estimates for Polish communist membership are from Jaff Schatz, "Jews and the Communist Movement in Interwar Poland," in Jonathan Frankel and Dan Diner, eds., *Dark Times, Dire Decisions: Jews and Communism,* Studies in Contemporary

Jewry, XX (Oxford: Oxford University Press, 2004), p. 18. Schatz gives by far the highest figures of any work I have seen on Communist Party membership. He believes that together with the Communist Parties of West Belorussia and Ukraine, and the youth movements of each party, plus the 6,340 communists in jail in the mid-1930s, in 1933 "the number of committed Polish Communists . . . totaled approximately 40,000 . . ." (pp. 18–19).

17. Of course, Jewish communists were concentrated in the cities, whereas communists of other nationalities were often in rural areas. Tim Snyder observes that in the Communist Party of Western Ukraine, affiliated with the Polish Communist Party, "most members in the countryside were Ukrainians; most members in the towns were Jews. In the provincial capital of Luts'k in 1933, for example, Party records indicate that every member of the Party and its youth organization were Jews." "The Life and Death of West Volhynian Jewry, 1921–1945," in Ray Brandon and Wendy Lower, eds, *The Shoah in Ukraine* (Bloomington: Indiana University Press), p. 82.

18. M. K. Dziewanowski, *The Communist Party of Poland* (Cambridge, Mass.: Harvard University Press, 1959), gives no figures on membership in the Party nor on its ethnic composition. Marek Jan Chodakiewicz, *After the Holocaust* (New York: East European Monographs, Columbia University Press, 2003) says, "The KPP had about 4,000 members at its peak," p. 21, n. 6. Jan de Weydenthal, *The Communists of Poland* (Stanford, Calif.: Hoover Institution Press, 1986, rev. ed.), asserts that in 1924 the communists had 3,346 members but that membership rose to 9,327 in 1933, the peak of its membership (p. 26 and Appendix 1). None of these figures seems to include the tiny Communist Parties of West Ukraine and West Belorussia.

19. Burks estimates that in the 1922 Polish election and in the 1927 Warsaw municipal election Jews were a substantial proportion of communist voters; p. 158.

20. Jeffrey Kopstein and Jason Wittenberg, "Who Voted Communist? Reconsidering the Social Bases of Radicalism in Poland," *Slavic Review* 62, no. 1 (Spring 2003), pp. 87–109.

21. The Romanian Communist Party, before it was banned, "varied between 2,000 and 2,500, but by the time of the Fifth Congress in 1931, it had fallen to 1,200" (Tismaneanu, pp. 57–58). In 1944, "when it emerged from two decades of underground conspiratorial activity, the RCP membership was approximately 1,000" (p. 59). The leading party bodies "were dominated by Jewish, Hungarian and Bulgarian militants" (p. 65).

22. Michael Bruchis, *Nations, Nationalities, People: A Study of the Nationalities Policy of the Communist Party in Soviet Moldavia* (Boulder, Colo: East European Monographs, 1984), p. 197.

23. Ibid., pp. 67, 66. Tismaneanu notes that between 1924 and 1944 "none of the RCP's general secretaries were indigenous Romanians," but rather Bulgarians, Hungarians, Poles, Ukrainians and Jews; p. 73.

24. "Anti-Semitic Propaganda and Official Rhetoric concerning the Judeo-Bolshevik Danger: Romanian Jews and Communism between 1938–1944," in Tuvia Friling, Radu Ioanid, and Mihail Ionescu, eds., *Final Report* (Bucharest: Polirom, 2005), p. 105. I am grateful to Paul Shapiro of the United States Holocaust Memorial Museum for bringing this source to my attention. A historian of the Jews of Bukovina in the interwar

period, then part of Romania and in 1940 annexed to the USSR (Ukrainian republic), notes that Jewish veterans of the underground communist movement "refuse to be interviewed even today" and that there seems to be little information on Jews in the Party even in Romanian police files of the period. When in 1935, seventy-seven Jews were tried as covert communists, "the trial aroused strong echoes in the Romanian newspapers and public opinion but was not mentioned at all by the local Jewish press." David Sha'ari, *Yehuday Bukovina bayn shtay milkhemot ha-olam* (Tel Aviv: Goldstein Goren, Center, Tel Aviv University, 2004), p. 222.

25. William Brustein and Ryan King, "Balkan Anti-Semitism: The Cases of Bulgaria and Romania before the Holocaust," *East European Politics and Societies* 18, no. 3 (2004), p. 449. The others were four Hungarians, three Ukrainians, and two Bulgarians.

26. In South Africa, some Jewish communists had brought radical traditions with them when they immigrated from Lithuania and Latvia in the last decades of the nineteenth and the first half of the twentieth centuries. A second generation of communists emerged from 1930s' street fights with fascists and with the start of the Second World War. Of the twenty-five white delegates to the 1945 communist district conference in Johannesburg, a disproportionate number were Jews, and of sixty active leaders of the Party district, twenty-three were Jews. Militant white organizations and publications were quick to point out the connection between Jews and the Communist Party. On the other hand, just as they did elsewhere, South African Jewish communists denied any connection to the Jewish community or people and proclaimed themselves "internationalists." The Jewish community reciprocated by distancing itself from and even condemning the activities of Jewish communists. Since 1994 and the end of Apartheid, the community has gingerly embraced some of the Jewish communists, portraying them as Jewish contributors to "the struggle" against the previous regime. See Mark Israel and Simon Adams, "'That Spells Trouble': Jews and the Communist Party of South Africa," *Journal of South African Studies* 26, no. 1 (March 2000), pp. 145–62. See also Gideon Shimoni, *Community and Conscience: The Jews in Apartheid South Africa* (Hanover, N.H.: Brandeis University Press, 2003) and Milton Shain and Richard Mendelsohn, eds. *Memories, Realities and Dreams* (Capetown: Jonathan Ball publishers, n.d. [2002]).

In the United States as well, Jewish immigrants from Eastern Europe brought radical traditions with them. When the American socialist movement split in the aftermath of World War One, some Jews cast their lot with those who formed the Communist Party. There were thousands of Jewish communists in the United States, but they were a tiny faction among American Jewry. It has been estimated that at the peak popularity of communism in the United States, there may have been 31,000 members of the Communist Party. Melech Epshtain, *Di geshichte fun arbeter klass in Amerikeh* ((New York: International Workers Order), vol. II, p. 108. In another work, Epstein cites a figure of 54,012 dues-paying members of the Communist Party USA in 1938. Melech Epstein, *The Jew and Communism* (New York: Trade Union Sponsoring Committee, n.d.), p. 277. The source is the House Un-American Activities Committee. In neither work does Epstein give a figure for Jewish membership in the party.

According to Theodore Draper, "In the original [American] Communist party of 1919, the Russians made up the single largest national group with almost 25 per cent of the total, the East-Europeans as a whole represented over 75 per cent, and the English-speaking members only 7 per cent. By the end of 1921, when the Workers party was formed, most of the Slavic membership had either returned to Russia or had drifted out of the organization." *American Communism and Soviet Russia* (New York: Viking, 1960), p. 190. It is likely that many of the "Russians" were Jews, since Jews made up 48 percent of the immigrants to the United States from the Russian Empire. Since "East Europeans" may include Finns—who accounted for 40–50 percent of the total party membership from 1922 to 1925 (Draper, ibid.)—the proportion of Jews in this category was probably much lower. Draper points out that the Yiddish daily newspaper, *Freiheit*, reported a circulation of 22,000 in 1925, when the *Daily Worker*'s circulation was only 17,000. He estimates that "perhaps as much as 15 per cent of the party membership was Jewish, but only a minute percentage of the 4,000,000 Jews in the United States were Communists," (p. 191).

The most extensive treatment I have found on Jews in the American Communist Party is Nathan Glazer, *The Social Basis of American Communism* (New York: Harcourt, Brace and World, 1961), ch. 4, pp. 130–68). Glazer cites a figure of 4,000 Jewish communists in 1938 (p. 222, n.1).

27. *Final Report*, p. 95.

28. Solomonas Atamukas, *Lietuvos zydu kelias* (Vilnius: Alma Littera, 1998), p. 192.

29. Ibid., p. 193. Alfonsas Eidintas, relying on Lithuanian police reports from October 1936, constructs the following table, showing membership by "Jewish nationals" in the Lithuanian Communist Party (LKP), Communist Youth Organization (LKJS) and Society to Aid Political Prisoners (MOPR) [Alfonsas Eidintas, *Jews, Lithuanians and the Holocaust* (Vilnius: Versus Aureus, 2003), p. 125].

Table 8.2

Year	LKP	LKJS	MOPR	Total number	Jewish members	% Jewish members
1932	705	379				53.8
1933	651	214	173	1,038	514	50.1
1934	968	319	267	1,544	754	48,8
1935	1,345	484	680	2,509	1,109	44.2

30. Before the annexation of Lithuania to the USSR and the incorporation of the Vilnius/Wilno region, previously in Poland. There had been 157,000 Jews in Lithuania according to the 1923 census.

31. Atamukas, p. 213. Dov Levin gives a figure for early 1941 of 479 Jews "active in the Communist Party, making up about 15 percent of its 3,130 members," *The Litvaks: A Short History of the Jews in Lithuania* (Jerusalem: Yad Vashem, 2000), p. 193. Michael MacQueen, also estimates the proportion of Jews as "some fifteen per cent of the party

membership versus 7.5 per cent in the population as a whole (which is partly due to the fact that the Komsomol was strongest in urban areas, where Jews were most concentrated). Four hundred and twelve Jews, or 16.5 per cent of total party members, were full members of the Lithuanian Communist party. But the Komsomol was an organization of little power, and the native core of the LCP was very much a junior partner to the imported cadres of the Communist Party." "The Context of Mass Destruction: Agents and Prerequisites of the Holocaust in Lithuania," *Holocaust and Genocide Studies* 12, no. 1 (Spring 1998), p. 33. MacQueen writes "Of the fifteen members of the LSSR Council of Ministers, two were Jews (15 percent)" but of the seventy-nine members of the parliament, only four were Jews (5 percent). "Of the 279 senior employees of the apparatus of repression (NKVD), 148 were Russians, 111 were Lithuanians and twenty 'other,' including Jews and a variety of nationalities drawn from other republics of the USSR" (p. 33). If these figures are accurate, probably no more than 5 percent, at most, of the high NKVD officials were Jews.

32. Mordechai Altshuler, *Soviet Jewry Since the Second World War—Population and Social Structure* (New York: Greenwood Press, 1987), pp. 212–213.

33. I. P. Shcherov, *Kollaboratsionizm v Sovetskom Soyuze* (Smolensk: Universum, 2005), p. 94.

34. Peter Potichnyj, "Ukrainians in World War II Military Formations: An Overview" and Myroslav Yurkevich, "Galician Ukrainians in German Military Formations and in the German Administration," both in Yury Boshyk, ed, *Ukraine during World War II*, (Edmonton: Canadian Institute of Ukrainian Studies, 1982). The Ukrainian Liberation Army, under Mykhailo Omelianovych-Pavlenko, and its successor, the Ukrainian National Army, commanded by Pavlo Shandruk, was formed by the Germans in 1943 and included between 50,000 and 80,000 men. See also Aleksandr Diukov, *Vtoroistepennyi vrag: OUN, UPA i reshenie 'evreiskogo voprosa'* (Moscow: Istoricheskaya pamiat, 2009). Two important works are Wendy Lower, *Nazi Empire-Building and the Holocaust in Ukraine* (Chapel Hill: University of North Carolina Press, 2005); and Brandon and Lower, eds., *The Shoah in Ukraine*.

35. See Taras Hunczak, "Between Two Leviathans: Ukraine during the Second World War," in Bohdan Krawchenko, *Ukrainian Past, Ukrainian Present* (New York: St. Martin's Press, 1993).

36. Frank Golczewski, "Shades of Grey: Reflections on Jewish-Ukrainian and German-Ukrainian Relations in Galicia," in Brandon and Lower, eds., *The Shoah in Ukraine*, p. 139.

37. The population of the Soviet Socialist Republic of Ukraine was given as 30,960,000 in the flawed 1939 census. The number of Ukrainians in the Republic was given as 24 million. In 1939–41, ethnic Ukrainians were incorporated from Eastern Poland and Bessarabia/Bukovina into Ukraine, and about half a million Ukrainians were deported eastward before the German invasion of the USSR on June 22, 1941. See Walter Guinn, "A Footnote to the 1939 Census of the USSR," *Soviet Studies* 14, no. 4 (April 1963), pp. 421–24.

38. See, for example, "Steven Lee Myers, "Friction between Estonia and Russia Ignites Protests in Moscow," *New York Times* (May 3, 2007). When a calendar was published

in Estonia featuring retouched posters in the 1940s that called for Estonians to support the Estonian SS Waffen Grenadier Division of the SS, Russians living in Estonia protested vigorously. Nick Holdsworth, "Russians Protest At [sic] Estonia SS Calendar," *The Telegraph* (London, December 26, 2008).

39. http://politics.hu/20100210/neonazis-plan-rally-with-german-peers-in-budapest.

40. On the other hand, Latvian authorities halted a parade to commemorate the day Nazis troops came in to Riga in 1941.

41. For some citations to the literature in English and Ukrainian, see n. xii in David Saunders, "The Starvation of Ukrainians in 1933: By-Product or Genocide?" in Lubomyr Luciuk, ed., *Holodomor: Reflections on the Great Famine of 1932–1933 in Soviet Ukraine* (Kingston, Ont.: Kashtan Press, 2008), p 103. See also the debate between Michael Ellman in "The Role of Leadership Perceptions and of Intent in the Soviet Famine of 1931–1934," *Europe-Asia Studies* 57, no. 6 (2005), pp. 823–41; and R.W. Davies and Stephen Wheatcroft, "Stalin and the Soviet Famine of 1932–33: A Reply to Ellman," *Europe-Asia Studies* 58, no. 4 (2006), pp. 625–33; James Mace, "Is the Ukrainian Genocide a Myth?" in *Europe-Asia Studies* 58, no. 4 (2006), p. 49; Hiroaki Kuromiya, "The Great Famine: The Issue of Intentionality," in Lubomyr Luciuk, *Holodomor* p. 126; Stanislav Kulchytsky, "Defining the *Holodomor* as Genocide," in Luciuk, ed., *Holodomor*, p. 129; *Wall Street Journal* (November 27, 2007), reprinted in Luciuk, *Holodomor*, p. 193; Andrea Graziosi, "Why and in What Sense was the *Holodomor* a Genocide?" in Luciuk, *Holodomor,*p. 155.

42. Liudmykla Grynevych, "Antisemitic Discourse in Marginal Holodomor Studies in Ukraine," paper prepared for "Ukrainian-Jewish Encounter Initiative," Ditchley Park, England, December 2009, p. 3.

43. Martin Shaw and Omer Bartov, "The Question of Genocide in Palestine, 1948: An Exchange between Martin Shaw and Omer Bartov," *Journal of Genocide Research* 12, nos. 3–4 (September–December 2010), pp. 243–59.

44. See, inter alia, Jonathan Freedland, "I See Why 'Double Genocide' is a Term Lithuanians Want. But it Appals [sic] Me," guardian.co.uk. (September 14, 2010).

45. Leonidas Donskis, "The Inflation of Genocide," *Neopopuliaros izvalgos* [Unpopular Insights] (Vilnius: Versus Aureus, 2009), trans. Darius Ross in *European Voice* (July 24, 2009).

46. http://www.praguedeclaration.org.

47. Ricky Ben-David, Digging up the Future," *The Jewish Herald* (August 3, 2010). Katz accused Zingeris of being "the man who is 'fixing' the Holocaust for the Lithuanians in exchange for political gain. He is betraying the memory of the 200,000 Lithuanian Jews killed during World War Two."

9 The Catholic Church, Radio Maryja, and the Question of Antisemitism in Poland

Anna Sommer Schneider

> As bishop of Rome and successor of the Apostle Peter, I assure the Jewish people that the Catholic Church, motivated by the Gospel law of truth and love, and by no political considerations, is deeply saddened by the hatred, acts of persecution and displays of antisemitism directed against the Jews by Christians at any time and in any place.
> —JOHN PAUL II, MARCH 23, 2000, JERUSALEM

Historical Dimensions of Antisemitism

THE QUESTION of antisemitism has never been thoroughly researched in Poland with regard to ideological, political, and social developments. It is not clear whether antisemitism, in all its forms, is a "by-product" of the growth of antisemitic propaganda in Western Europe or a Polish phenomenon. Apart from some sociological studies, antisemitism has been virtually ignored by Polish scholars. The subject has been considered cumbersome and even taboo.[1] For some, research into this issue is irrelevant since they believe that the problem of antisemitism doesn't exist in Poland. For others who might be inclined to carry out such a study, available survey data is rather fragmentary and inconsistent and does not provide scholars and others with the necessary empirical information.

One of the questions that needs to be asked is whether there is a "unique" type of antisemitism found in Poland, as is argued by many scholars and religious leaders around the world. Or, as others have suggested, perhaps the problem in Poland is really about the denial of the existence of antisemitism. Whether we are discussing the issue of overt antisemitism or the denial of its existence, one thing is certain: over the course of centuries the image of Jews in Christian culture has assumed a strongly symbolic dimension, which has had the effect of increasing the number of negative and stereotypical images of Jews. This illustrative example is widespread in a Catholic country such as Poland, where antisemitic attitudes have been a by-product of Christian society and culture and are not just confined to theological underpinnings. As we examine the Polish church and antisemitism, one of the challenges is to analyze and distinguish between self-identified antisemites and people whose antagonistic feelings toward Jews stem from negative stereotypes.[2] Negative and antisemitic images created by Christian culture have survived and thrived to this day, even without the presence of Jews.

How can one explain the existence of a Polish antisemitism without Jews? Father Romuald Jakub Weksler-Waszkinel said that "the Jews are not needed to perpetuate antisemitism. A sick Christianity is sufficient. And Polish Christianity—and more precisely, what dominates in Polish Catholicism—is sick and infected with anti-Judaism."[3] For centuries, Jews were seen as aliens who never strived to fully assimilate into the local culture. The negative stereotypical images of Jews, derived from the teachings of the Church, cultivated these myths and beliefs especially around such significant events as Easter, as expressed in the Passion of the Christ. Some commentators, like Alina Cała, a distinguished Polish scholar, see this line of debate as more akin to a criminal-murder story than a true theological question. Needless to say, the practice of the Church of accusing Jews of killing Christ has led to a complete distortion of the theological significance and meaning of the death and resurrection of Christ (the basis for the founding of Christianity).[4] It also led the Jews to be held accountable for the death of Jesus and at the same time be viewed as "supernatural" in their powers. The Jew also assumed a symbolic dimension and was often associated with fertility, well-being, and happiness.[5] By contrast, the same belief in the "supernatural power" of Jewish people often turned against the Jews, who were blamed for causing natural disasters, poisoning of wells, and other misfortunes.

For decades, the argument has prevailed in the public discourse in Poland that while a number of European countries tried to banish their Jewish citizens, Poland became a kind of asylum for those refugees, due to privileges granted by Polish rulers that secured Jewish rights and safety. The seventeenth century, which witnessed the high point of the development of Jewish cultural and religious life in Poland, was labeled the *Paradis Judeorum* (Jewish Paradise). It should be recalled, however, that despite the atmosphere of tolerance and the securing of safety, a number of events took place that exerted a stigma and led to the creation of negative stereotypes.

In the sixteenth century, proudly called a Golden Age of Jewish life in Poland, discriminatory laws were introduced called *de non tolerandis judaeis,* which banned Jews from settling in specific towns. The first legal trials in Poland in which Jews were accused of blood libel also took place during this time. The myth that Jews engage in ritual killing for religious purposes is still present among some elements of the Polish population. Although research indicates that this kind of false accusation was prevalent in rural, undeveloped society, Alina Cała heard rumors about ritual killing in the 1980s in Warsaw, the largest urban center in Poland.[6]

It is important to distinguish between strands of religious antisemitism (or anti-Judaism) and ideological antisemitism, which developed after Poland regained independence in 1918 as a direct consequence of political changes throughout Europe. Ideological antisemitism, which has become associated with nationalism, was to some extent driven by centuries-old Christian tradition. Though Christianity does not bear responsibility for the creation of ideological antisemitism, it can be accused of creating a climate in which antisemitism has flourished over the course of centuries. As Ireneusz Krzemiński states: "Ideologies—these great mental creations of the nineteenth and twentieth centuries—have changed traditional images or produced resentment and hostility toward Jews. . . . National ideologies reconstructing historical consciousness and creating a new, distinct type of social identity played a vital role in cementing modern, civil political communities."[7]

National revival in twentieth-century Europe eventually found roots in Poland, especially after more than a century of suppression. As Polish national identity began to reemerge, national groups adopted existing standards, cultures, and traditions as a basis for self-determination and the construction of self-identity. Inevitably, what resulted was an increasing rejection of aspects viewed as alien or foreign. Though religion was not necessarily a determinative factor marking which groups were viewed with suspicion, the Jewish community was increasingly perceived as not part of the majority.

The development of nationalistic movements, conceived in Poland after the First World War by leading ideologues such as Roman Dmowski, gradually led to increased levels of antisemitism.[8] It is worth noting, however, that antisemitism was not a cornerstone of his ideology. In his *Thoughts of a Modern Pole,* written at the beginning of the twentieth century, Dmowski referred with irony to "professional antisemitism, affecting the lower instincts of the masses."[9] Years later, however, antisemitism became a feature of his nationalist agenda. Dmowski belonged to the Polish intelligentsia, and his antisemitism, as Stefan Bratkowski describes it, "was a conscious choice of an intellectual Pole."[10] The process of adopting an antisemitic ideology was gradual and it effectively extended to various strata of society, including the intelligentsia and the Catholic clergy. The latter began to play a key role in spreading the prejudices of this poisonous ideology. Czesław Miłosz, the preeminent Polish writer and Nobel laureate, said the following:

> Points of friction between Jews and Poles were numerous, ranging from the major issue between a Catholic peasant and his rites and small-town followers of Judaism who practiced different customs. Sustained over centuries by the clergy, stereotypes about Jews as Christ killers were connected with the superstitious fear of mysterious Jewish intrigues in trade. . . . Antisemitic propaganda spread by the National Democratic party and a substantial part of the clergy were aimed primarily at the peasant and petty bourgeois. Another stereotype helped to spread the propaganda among workers—the picture of a Jewish factory owner, associated with international capital. Antisemitic riots in Poland were organized by students of law and medicine, who related to the propaganda against Jews in free professions."[11]

The interwar period is particularly important when we try to understand the development of a new form of ideological antisemitism. Prevalence of anti-Jewish sentiments among political and religious leaders had a great impact on the Polish population, and, inevitably, led to callousness and indifference toward Jewish victims during the Holocaust and increased violence directed against Jews after the war. Many stereotypical images of Jews, which emerged in the past centuries, deriving from religious beliefs, as well as political antisemitism of early twentieth-century Poland, were, in a sense, a by-product of changes and antisemitic propaganda prevalent in Western Europe at that time. Even though antisemitism was not a new phenomenon in Poland, the interwar period witnessed many changes in the social and political discourse, affecting the masses in the newly reborn Polish state. This may explain why the new ideological antisemitism gained popularity among a vast number of ethnic Poles. This applies not only to antisemitism, but to different forms of prejudice and xenophobia as well, wildly spread by leading figures in the country, including members of the clergy. These new ideologies made a great impact on society, gradually allowing this new phenomenon to affect people's worldview and increase the aversion toward Jews who were perceived as alien and unwanted in Polish society. Though important, the question of interwar antisemitism and its impact on Polish people has often been ignored by historians who deal with the question of anti-Jewish violence during the Holocaust and its immediate aftermath. Eventually, over time, these events have created scars on Polish–Jewish relations that can be felt to this day.

Antisemitism in Poland Today

Though numerous acts of violence and pogroms against Jews occurred after the end of the Second World War, the 1950s and 1960s witnessed relative tranquility. This short period of peace, however, was brutally interrupted by the antisemitic campaign sponsored by the communist authorities, who carried out such activities in March 1968. As a result of this campaign, more than twelve thousand Jews were expelled from Poland.[12] The 1968 campaign devastated the Jewish community and marked a major turning point in Polish–Jewish relations. For the next three decades, antisemitism by and large faded from public view and did not reemerge until the fall of communism in the late 1980s and early 1990s. At this profound moment in Poland's history, political changes had repercussions both internally and outside the country's borders. Political transformations also gave rise to an increase in nationalistic aspirations for many groups. The heightened political discourse inevitably stimulated discussions about the Jews, who became an easy target, especially when political shifts were soon followed by a devastating economic crisis. Traditional popular antisemitic slogans found fertile ground in a homogenous country dominated by one religion and culture.

Apart from the politics of this era, a series of events opened a new chapter in Polish–Jewish relations and eventually led to increased antisemitism. In the second half of the 1980s, public opinion in Poland was appalled by Claude Lanzmann's film, *Shoah*, which equated Polish with German responsibility for the Holocaust and the murder of Jews. An oft-quoted article was published by Jan Błoński on January 11, 1987 in the Catholic weekly *Tygodnik Powszechny*, entitled "Biedni Polacy patrzą na getto" (Poor Poles Look at the Ghetto). Błoński examined the collective guilt associated with indifference to the extermination of Jews. He raised the question of Polish "responsibility for the crime without having taken part in it" and stated that "eventually, when we lost our home, and when, within that home, the invaders set to murdering Jews, did we show solidarity with them? How many of us decided that it was none of our business? There were also those (and I leave common criminals out of the account) who were secretly pleased that Hitler had solved 'the Jewish problem' for us."

Błoński's article provoked debates among Polish intellectuals rather than within the general public. Many Poles accused him of slandering the Polish nation. As this debate raged on, it became clear that a certain door had opened, and for the first time the nation was forced to confront a dark piece of Polish history.

Soon another controversy emerged that once again forced the nation to reconsider its behavior during the Second World War, and gave rise to a new "old" form of antisemitism. In the second half of the 1980s, a public struggle took place over the issue of the presence of Carmelite nuns in the vicinity of the former Nazi death camp, Auschwitz I, after the nuns had moved into a building adjoining the former camp's fence. The nuns' intention was to pray for the victims of Auschwitz. While Polish Jews didn't find a convent to be a threat to the memory of the Holocaust, overseas, these actions were taken as an insult, especially in Jewish communities. Stanisław Krajewski, a well-known commentator on Polish–Jewish affairs and co-chair of the Polish Council of Christians and Jews, said that the actions of the nuns were perceived as an offence:

> It was accused of being an offence since for centuries the Church had propagated antisemitism and, the argument went, had not offered help during the War; therefore, it should have kept clear of that site. The convent was accused

of being a threat because it would falsify the history and a message of the camp by concealing the Jewish nature of the Holocaust, and contributing to its "Christianization."[13]

On July 22, 1986, church officials as well as representatives of European Jewish communities met in Geneva to resolve the issue of the convent. Negotiations resulted in a resolution on February 22, 1987. The outcome of the meeting was the decision to build a suitable place within two years that would serve as a center for information, education, and prayer and would be located in the vicinity.

The problem was finally solved with help of Pope John Paul II, who sent a letter to the nuns. In 1993, the nuns moved to a newly constructed convent adjoining the Center for Dialogue, across the street from the Auschwitz camp. Even though the Geneva meetings did not bring about the expected results, the declaration adopted at the meetings recognized the exceptional nature of the Jewish tragedy. Officials of the Catholic Church also declared that they would "encourage exchanges between the European churches on the subject of the Shoah,. . . . combat disinformation and trivialization of the Shoah, and . . . combat revisionism."[14] In another chapter of this story, a papal cross was erected in 1988, next to the convent at the site of a former gravel pit—a site where many inmates had died at work and where the Nazis carried out mass executions of Poles. Again, this action was another example of the changing face of memory. For Poles, the cross has more than a religious meaning; it is also a symbol of glory. For many Jews, especially for the families of the victims, this cross, at this location, reminded them of the failure of the church to intercede on their behalf during the war.

Statistical Data

According to leading Polish scholars, there are three types of antisemitism prominent in Poland today. They base this statement on two major surveys that were conducted in 1996 and 2002 among Poles of different ages and religious, educational, and social backgrounds. This major sociological project was conducted by leading Polish scholars, under the supervision of Ireneusz Krzemiński, a distinguished professor of sociology at Warsaw University. The findings of the surveys, presented below, include an analysis by Helena Datner-Śpiewak, who distinguishes between *traditional antisemitism*—historians would describe this as anti-

Judaism—motivated by religion, and *modern antisemitism,* based on political ideology.[15] The research, made public in 2002, revealed the existence of yet a third type of antisemitism, called *secondary antisemitism.*[16]

According to Krzemiński, *modern antisemitism* is defined by three elements: "Jews control the finances, tend implicitly to seize power over the world, and most of all, always stick together, and are characterized by remarkable loyalty to each other. These three elements serve as parallels for ideological convictions that are confirmed by empirical responses to a question about why some people don't like Jews."[17] In interpreting the work of experts such as Krzemiński, one does not get a complete and accurate picture of the societal norms associated with antisemitism. Though surveys conducted both in 1996 and in 2002 indicate a declining proportion of antisemitism in Poland, some social scientists would argue otherwise.

Krzemiński's work is critically important as we strive to better understand the realities in Poland. For instance, if we ignore the survey questions relating to hostility toward Jews, the responses are very different . . . and less positive. Also, interestingly, the degree of hostility toward Jewish people increases among people who have had direct contact with individual Jews. Among respondents who personally knew Jews, far more gave antisemitic responses, such as expressing the belief that Jews have too much influence in the world.

With this in mind, it is virtually impossible to determine the exact degree of antisemitism in Poland. According to Helena Datner-Śpiewak, in 1996, 17 percent of Poles self-identified as antisemitic, but at the same time it was noted that as many as 62 percent of respondents iterated at least one antisemitic response. Surveys conducted in 1992 and 2002 by a team directed by Krzemiński show changes in how Poles perceive Jewish people today. "Above all, the percentage of people representing the *modern antisemitism* stance increased from about 17 percent to 27 percent."[18] This is much less than indicated by surveys conducted by foreign-based research centers and organizations, particularly American Jewish organizations. According to a survey commissioned by the American Jewish Committee in 2005, almost 56 percent of Poles believed that "now, as in the past, Jews have had too much influence on the world's politics" (while 38 percent disagreed with that statement).[19] According to a survey released by Fridrich Ebert Stiftung in 2011, this number had decreased to

49.9 percent. At the same time, using the baseline adopted by Krzemiński, and compared to the 1992 survey, it seems that the number of those who are considered *anti-antisemitic* has nearly doubled. In other words, with a slight increase of antisemitic responses, the percentage of people who completely reject antisemitism has increased.[20]

The way the question was asked about Jewish influence on politics is not clear. First, one cannot tell whether the respondents' answers represent such a worldview. Second, we must ask how many of the respondents accept this view but ignore the majority opinion (in other words, how many only tolerate antisemitism). For example, in the open question "Who do you think, which group has too much influence on Polish politics?," only 1 percent in 2002 and 2 percent in 2010 of respondents cited Jews as their first choice. Interestingly, more people indicated that the Church and Catholic priests as a group were perceived as having too much influence on politics. These questions are critical tools if we are to better understand whether we are dealing with a large number of self-identified antisemites or if there is too much tolerance for antisemitism.[21]

What do we make of these surveys and their results? Certainly, there is some consistency in responses that might be cause for concern. Classical, traditional antisemitism does not seem to be abating. In fact, there appears to be some proof that some segments of the Polish population remain rigid in their views about Jews.[22] More disturbing is the increase in *modern antisemitism*. Are these numbers increasing based on inaccurate or incomplete information on, for instance, what Poles know of Jews and the history of this community? Are the cultural mainstays of the community, such as the church and the media, helping to fuel this problem? Thus, one question that needs to be asked is what do Poles know about Jews, and where does this knowledge come from?

A survey conducted in 1996 looked at how Poles received information about Jews. The research showed that for the vast majority of Poles, the main source was the media (58.5 percent). Another important source of information is from family members in homes (48.3 percent), followed by books, newspapers, and magazines (47.6 percent), occasional conversations with friends (29.9 percent), and personal contact with Jews (22.5 percent). Only 13.9 percent obtained their knowledge about Jewish people from school (13.9 percent) and even fewer from a religion class or church (10.8 percent).[23] According to this survey, the Polish church had less to do with informing people about Jews than the mass media, friends, and the home. Thus, according to this survey, the Church and its teachings have a limited impact on the level of knowledge (both positive and negative) conveyed to the public. These results make it much more difficult to determine to what degree the Church influences antisemitism.

Researchers noted that many of the people questioned in the interviews confessed that what they heard in the house about Jewish people was generally negative and ridiculing. One respondent stated that he had never heard elderly people saying anything positive about Jews. All he heard was that a Jew "worked, cheated, collected money, scrimped and saved, and loaned money," and also that the Jews implemented communism in Poland.[24]

Additionally, the survey of 2002 raised, among other things, the issue of secondary antisemitism and also the ongoing topic of Polish and Jewish victimhood. Krzemiński's research highlights a new and profound aspect regarding the growth of Polish antisemitism (especially from self-identified antisemites). According to him, the level of Polish antisemitism is a direct consequence of how Poles are perceived in the world, particularly by Jews. Related to this is how Holocaust memory has been preserved. Among the findings, the largest number of respondents, approximately 41 percent, agreed with the sentence, "People think of Poles as antisemites, because the Holocaust took place in Poland, and forget that the Germans were behind it." In the same survey, 31 percent of those interviewed stated that this statement is a "direct consequence of anti-Polish propaganda, which has nothing to do with truth." A total of 29 percent stated that "Poles are not any more hostile toward the Jews than other nations; they just honestly say what others wouldn't admit." Finally, 25 percent of respondents agreed with the statement that "Poles know the Jews better than other nations and this is why they don't like them."

These results point to a confluence whereby the horrible fate of Polish Jews during the Second World War collides with the enduring tragic history of Poland. At its core, there is a level of constant competition between Jews and non-Jewish Poles over which group has suffered more in history. For Poles, the country holds a unique and continuing role as the "Christ of Nations." This romantic-messianic ideology was built on Christian values more than two centuries ago and allows Poles to believe that their main mission is to sustain brotherhood and sacrifice for others. The tragic his-

tory of the Poles, who arguably have suffered more than many other nations, has allowed this messianic vision to be built up alongside a "myth
of sacrifice." The Poles unwillingly share their sorrow with others. And,
furthermore, the "myth of victimhood" does not allow Polish people to
regard themselves as victimizers. The question of "antagonism of suffering" was expressed by Archbishop Henryk Muszyński, who in an interview in *Tygodnik Powszechny* referred to Polish and Jewish victimhood
during the war and stated that

> During the period of occupation two basic categories were distinguished:
> perpetrators and victims. And we and Jews were victims. But one must say
> here right away: not in the same way and not to the same degree. The Jew was
> sentenced to death and was supposed to die [while] the Pole could survive as
> *Untermensch*. Nevertheless, when Jews emphasize the exceptional nature, or
> the uniqueness of the Holocaust, Poles are offended. It is difficult for them to
> accept that the Jews suffered more than anyone else or to understand how, for
> example, the murder of an entire Jewish family differs from the murder of a
> Polish family for hiding Jews. . . . Thus is born the antagonism of suffering."[25]

Muszyńki's comment helps us to understand the derivation of the
antagonism over the issue of suffering. For years, Polish people lived in
denial about the historic truth about the Holocaust and death camps like
Auschwitz, due to deliberate distortions of memory by communist authorities. This led to falsification about the Holocaust in the historical
consciousness of Polish society. Apparently, this strand of propaganda
extended to such preeminent figures as Primate Cardinal Józef Glemp,
who at a press conference during his visit to Belgium in the mid-1980s
was asked why he kept referring to the "six million Polish dead" during
the Second World War, since it was known by all that three million of the
six were Jews. As Cardinal Glemp stated at the time, it didn't really matter because the six million died just "because they were Polish citizens."[26]
This is a perfect example of how past events and historical truth can be
twisted, distorted, and abused and additionally strengthened when represented by one of the most important authorities in the country.

In the last decade, a number of events took place in Poland that helped
trigger debates on the Holocaust and the attitude of the Polish people
toward Jews during the Second World War and its aftermath. A major
stimulus for these debates was the publication of two books by Jan T. Gross,

Sąsiedzi (Neighbors) and *Strach. Antysemityzm w Polsce tuż po wojnie. Historia moralnej zapaści (Fear: Antisemitism in Poland after Auschwitz).* Although Gross, a Polish-born scholar who has lived and worked in the United States since 1969, had published books and scholarly articles in the past, none of his previous publications had drawn so much attention. These recent works provoked a national debate and led to accusations that Gross had slandered the Polish nation. As Alvin Rosenfeld rightly stated: "The character of the debate about Jedwabne[27] that took place over many months revealed the country to be in the grip of an intensely painful encounter with its wartime past and an anguished, in some ways disorienting, confrontation with its own national identity. . . ."—particularly in the context of the myth of Poles having suffered incomparably with respect to other nations and the above-mentioned myth of the "Messiah of Nations." Rosenfeld added that "for Poles today to face up to Jedwabne is to acknowledge that, in addition to being victims of Nazi brutality, some of their countrymen were willing accomplices of the Nazi murderers and guilty of murderous actions of their own against Polish Jews."[28]

Coming to terms with the difficult aspects of Polish history made Gross's writing an easy target for some who were quite negative in their reaction to his work. For example, Father Prof. Waldemar Chrostowski said in a 2009 interview that "the Poles [according to Gross] were to kill 'the Jewish half of the town.' This is how the picture of extermination has been falsified. We here, in Poland, see this as absurd, an absurdity so great that we do not even take it under consideration."[29] Interestingly, these words were spoken by Chrostowski several years after the Institute of National Remembrance (IPN) published a 1,600-page, two-volume work presenting research results conducted by prominent Polish historians and supporting Gross's thesis about murder committed by Poles against their Jewish neighbors. Although some Polish historians did not share this view, it was hard or even impossible for many Polish officials and individuals to deal with the harsh reality.[30] This tension was well expressed by the late Father Stanisław Musiał, a great advocate of Polish–Jewish reconciliation, who said:

> One cannot be surprised that after the publication of the truth about Jedwabne, public opinion has split into two camps. One, undoubtedly the more numerous, is situated on the center and the political right thinking nation-

ally. It either negates the participation of Poles at Jedwabne, or tries to play it down. . . . The second, smaller camp sees in the publication of the truth about Jedwabne a chance for cleaning Polish memory of the period of the occupation, and a stimulus toward fighting antisemitism in Poland today."[31]

This "split" in Polish society was apparent before the ceremony marking the sixtieth anniversary of the Jedwabne massacre of July 10, 1941. Primate Cardinal Józef Glemp, for example, had announced that he would not be attending the ceremonies and would not get involved as long investigations into the matter continued. Glemp was also of the opinion that Jews bear great responsibility for the crimes committed by the Jewish community against Polish people.[32] At the same time, he failed to recognize that the same Jews in the communist government had long ago severed their roots to Jewish tradition, community, and identity, and furthermore, that these individuals did not represent the Jewish minority of Poland in the communist regime. This sentiment about Jewish overrepresentation in the communist government has prevailed in public discourse in Poland, particularly among historians representing a nationalistic and conservative right-wing faction. Nonetheless, didn't the same Jewish communists also persecute Jewish people who chose to stay in Poland after the war?

Cardinal Glemp, as well as other church officials, refused to recognize any Christian dimension of this issue and, specifically, of this crime. Similar positions were taken by the majority of government officials, including Prime Minister Jerzy Buzek, who remained silent about the commemorations marking the sixtieth anniversary of the Jedwabne massacre. Only Poland's president, Aleksander Kwaśniewski, decided to attend the ceremonies and publicly apologized for the crime in his "own name and in the name of those Poles whose conscience is shattered by that crime."[33] Archbishop Henryk Muszyński represented a different line than that of the church hierarchy opinion on the subject; he stated that "regardless of whether it will turn out that 1600 Jews, or 160 have been burnt, the crime remains a crime. . . . The responsibility for each crime falls on the immediate perpetrator, yet those who are connected to him by religious or national ties—though they bear no personal guilt—cannot feel themselves to be free of moral responsibility for the victims of this murder."[34]

Many believe that it was Gross's book *Neighbors* that shook Poles to their core. Its publication is viewed as a turning point in Polish–Jewish postwar relations. None of Gross's earlier writings and publications had such a dramatic impact on Polish society.

The latest book by Jan T. Gross and Irena Grudzińska-Gross, *Złote Żniwa* (*The Golden Harvest*), which was published in Poland in March 2011 by the Catholic publishing house Znak (which also published *Fear*), has triggered a similar political, historical, and sociological debate. These debates have become commonplace with Gross's writings and begin even before the books are themselves published and made available to the general public. This latest book was inspired by an article written by Piotr Głuchowski and Marcin Kowalski in the Polish daily newspaper *Gazeta Wyborcza* in 2008. The article dealt with the problem of plundering the site of Treblinka by Poles. The article was of great interest to Gross, as was the accompanying graphic photograph that showed Polish people posing over the remains of Jewish bones, probably taken at the former extermination camp.

As with his previous books, *Neighbors* and *Fear,* Gross delved into some of the darkest corners of Polish history. His analysis of these moments of history have invariably prompted many scholars and others to challenge the way Gross researched and reported on these periods of history. Specifically, they have accused him of the following:

- Lacking comprehensive research and exhibiting a selective attitude toward primary sources;
- Failing to take into consideration the context and nature of the Nazi occupation of Poland;
- Not accounting for specific conditions resulting from the war, including aspects of moral destruction during the war;
- Completely disregarding the actions of Polish Righteous Gentiles;
- Treating as a general rule what Polish commentators view as a minority act of behavior;
- Misrepresenting the numbers of Jews killed by the Poles;
- And, most of all, having a very critical attitude toward the Catholic Church.

The list of accusations against Gross is long. What is interesting, though, are not necessarily the attacks on what he has written, but on what he has omitted. A concern is his alleged one-sidedness. Also, the language he employs is considered aggressive and controversial, often beyond what Poles think of as acceptable in their society today. But *The Golden Harvest* is not a historical monograph but a historical essay, and this type of writing is very rare in Poland. And, most likely, if these books were written by an author who lives and works in Poland, these sorts of writings would probably be overlooked. Polish scholars of late have written extensively about crimes against Jews committed by Poles. However, Gross ignites more controversy in large part because he is identified as a Jewish sociologist, a foreigner who points a finger at the Polish people themselves, despite the fact he was born and educated in Poland. This phenomenon can only be related to the research described by Matthew Hornsey, who finds that the same critical information is more difficult to accept if presented by a stranger than by a member of one's national group.[35]

Other voices have joined in support of Gross. Most notably, the distinguished scholar, literary historian, and Holocaust survivor Michał Głowiński speaks highly of Gross's writings, not primarily because of their historical value but because they prompt an important debate. As Głowiński put it, "Professor Gross challenges our self-esteem. He forces us to minimize thinking about ourselves only in terms of victims."[36]

The vast majority of Polish commentators, however, have a more hostile approach to Gross. Tomasz Nałęcz, an adviser on historical matters to Polish President Bronisław Komorowski, states that Gross "takes only one type of behavior and does not write about other behaviors. He tries to create the impression that this was the mainstream way of acting during the war." Nałęcz adds that Gross failed to write that "the war was demoralizing in an unprecedented manner . . . but as I look at the behavior of Polish society, then I think that in the examination associated with the war Polish people passed with high honors."[37] One might find this level of analysis repugnant, as candid as it is, especially from someone so closely identified with the president of Poland. At the same time, one would expect a more analytic response to Poland's difficult past. As for the Catholic Church, most officials who previously expressed very critical opinions of Gross remained largely silent when his recent book was published. Over time, one would hope that the debates involving Gross might trigger a resolve on the part of Poles for further self-examination. Henryk Woźniakowski, chief editor of Znak (which published Gross's book), said that "we were brought up on the myth of sinlessness. And now we have to make up a history lesson to overcome it."[38]

Is there anything that makes this debate different from what Poles have experienced in the past? Certainly, the fact that people talk about the substance of *Golden Harvest* itself, and not the authenticity of the events described in it, makes a difference, bringing Poles another step forward to finally come to terms with their own history and also the problem of how antisemitism is perceived. Although Muszyński made his position clear, as did many other prominent figures in Polish society (i.e., with the position that Poles do not take responsibility for the Holocaust and the murder of Jews committed on Polish soil), this viewpoint has recently assumed a different dimension. Polish scholars such as Marcin Zaremba said during the debate that "without Jan Tomasz Gross our state of mind would be better, but intellectual life poorer. Also, thanks to him, after years of denial, we are getting aware of our joint responsibility for the Holocaust." This is an extremely brave comment, but it is too early to say whether Zaremba is talking about the moral responsibility for being indifferent for the crime or about joint responsibility for the murder of Jews during the war.[39]

Because of the publication of these books, and the ongoing public debates about their contents, one would imagine that awareness of the Holocaust and the historic suffering of Jews would be higher than in past years. However, recent research indicates the opposite; the number of Poles who believe that Jews suffered more (compared to non-Jewish Poles) during the war decreased from 46 percent in 1992 to about 38 percent in 2002 (roughly a year after *Neighbors* was published).[40]

Despite the widespread and public dialogue about Jewish suffering in the Holocaust, in part prompted by both the media and books written by famous authors like Gross, there remains a continual legacy of "Polish victimhood." This fascination with Polish suffering, though legitimate and very much part of the history of the country, does interfere with a rational understanding of Jewish persecution in Poland and contributes to the perpetuation of antisemitism in the country today. Professor Antoni Sułek says that an "awareness of the exceptional scale and metaphysical dimension of the Holocaust doesn't find an easy way to the minds of Poles. It has been blocked by the long-standing lack of a sense of closeness between Poles and Jews. A vivid awareness of their own suffering (and suffering of their families) and the conviction of his nation's particular martyrdom is accompanied by a defensive conviction that the Jews cannot appreciate the suffering of Poles and do not respect Polish sensitivity."[41]

The Church and Antisemitism

What influence does the Church have on Polish society and its knowledge of key events such as the Holocaust? Does religion, and specifically the Catholic Church, have an impact on the level of antisemitism in Poland today? This is a foundational question that needs to be examined on three specific levels: the Pope and his statements and teachings, other voices in the church, and church-based media.

During his pontificate, Pope John Paul II frequently referred in his encyclicals to the history of the Jews and Jewish martyrdom. One of the major emphases of his teachings was to encourage overcoming the myth of collective responsibility of all Jews for the crucifixion of Christ. This issue became one of the most important missions of his pontificate. In particular, the Second Vatican Council adopted a statement affirming a special "spiritual bond" between the church and Judaism, concluding in the well-known "four points of the *Nostra Aetate*" document. The Pope's repudiation of antisemitism, which he believed was "opposed to the very spirit of Christianity" and which the "dignity of the human person alone would suffice to condemn," was a topic he regularly discussed at audiences with representatives of Jewish organizations. This theme was later repeated many times by Pope John Paul II during his numerous pilgrimages abroad, including visits to Poland.

Despite John Paul II's impassioned plea for closer working relations between the church and the Jewish community and despite his comments repudiating antisemitism, many Polish priests directed critical statements against Jews as a national group. Although not much is known about the content of information transmitted by the Catholic clergy (comprehensive sociological or ethnographical research has never been conducted on this matter), some of the responses of people interviewed in 1996 about the source of their knowledge of the Jews referred to what they heard in church. Some respondents even noted that all they heard in church regarding Jews was reduced to information about their guilt for killing God's son.[42] Connected to the question of antisemitism is the subject of the Holocaust, an issue that the Pope made a central tenant of his outreach to Jewish and non-Jewish communities. This issue has great implications for Catholic–Jewish dialogue and has had an important impact on the level of current feelings toward Jews in and outside of Poland. It is important to recall the teachings of the Pope on this subject. From the very beginning of his pontificate, John Paul II spoke bluntly about what happened at the Auschwitz-Birkenau death camp. His words were even more impressive during the communist era, when the word *Holocaust* was nonexistent and teaching about the extermination of European Jewish populations was taboo. The Pope first made public note of his views during his first pilgrimage back to Poland and his visit to Auschwitz in June 1979. It was there that the Pope said (and it was heard by tens of thousands who attended a holy mass at Birkenau, and also by millions of television viewers),

> I pause with you dear participants in this encounter, before the inscription in Hebrew. This inscription awakens the memory of the people whose sons and daughters were intended for total extermination. . . . The very people who received from God the Commandment, "thou shall not kill," itself experienced in a special measure what is meant by killing. It is not permissible for anyone to pass by this inscription with indifference.[43]

Many can also remember the Pope's blunt condemnation at the twentieth anniversary of the *Nostra aetate* document, when he declared that "antisemitism, in its ugly and sometimes violent manifestations, should be completely eradicated."[44] He repeatedly returned to this subject in his writings. To recall one of them:

> Antisemitism, which is unfortunately still a problem in certain places, has been repeatedly condemned by the Catholic tradition as incompatible with Christ's teaching and with the respect due to the dignity of men and women treated in the image and likeness of God. I once again express the Catholic Church's repudiation of all oppression and persecution, and of all discrimination against people—from whatever side it may come—"in law or in fact, on account of their race, origin, color, culture, sex, of religion" [Octogesima Adveniens, 23, Apostolic Letter of Pope Paul VI, 1971].[45]

Another important action taken by the Pope was his historic visit to the synagogue of Rome in 1986. Like many other actions he took, this visit to the religious and spiritual center of the Roman Jewish community became an occasion for breaking down stereotypes and taboos. Despite this grand gesture, it is debatable how many people in Poland appreciated and understood the meaning of the words expressed by the Pope there when he confessed that "the Church has a very special relation with Judaism" and that Jews are Catholic's "dearly beloved brothers and, in a certain way, it could be said that you are our elder brothers."[46] He also referenced *Nostra aetate,* saying that "the Church of Christ discovers her 'bond' with Judaism by 'searching into her own mystery.'"[47] Despite these words, in 1996 approximately 39 percent of Poles disagreed with the statement that the Jews were "elder brothers" to Christians and Catholics; they were certainly not regarded as "beloved brothers." Only after the Pope's visit in 2000 to the Holy Land did these numbers see a downward trend to 26 percent.[48]

In November 1980, the Pope stated, with reference to the Declaration on the Relationship of the Church with Judaism (April 1980): "Whoever meets Jesus Christ, meets Judaism. . . . I would like to make these words mine, too." He also added, "it is not just a question of correcting a false religious view of the Jewish people, which, in the course of history, was one of the causes that contributed to misunderstanding and persecution, but above all of the dialogue between the two religions. . . ."[49] On the subject of "continuing religious dialogue between Judaism and the Catholic Church" Pope John Paul II highlighted this issue during an audience of the delegation of the Simon Wiesenthal Center of Los Angeles, which was held shortly after the ceremony marking the fortieth anniversary of the Warsaw Ghetto uprising.[50]

One remedy for lingering problems in Catholic–Jewish relations was suggested by the Pope, when on various occasions he argued for the need to create a special curriculum for Catholic schools. He also reminded Poles of the church's efforts toward improving awareness and education about Jewish history, antisemitism, and the Holocaust, as described in "Guidelines and Suggestions for Implementing the Conciliar Declaration *Nostra Aetate,* No. 4" (1974) as well as "Notes on the Correct Presentation of the Jews and Judaism in Catholic Preaching and Teaching" (1985).[51]

Beyond the Pope's occasional remarks, the Vatican has published materials on the need for greater awareness of the lessons of Jewish suffering. In *Notes* (25), the Vatican stated that it is necessary "to fathom the depths of the extermination of many millions of Jews during World

War II and with respect to the wounds thereby inflicted on the consciousness of the Jewish people, theological reflection is also needed" (October
28, 1985). In September 1997, the Vatican published a three-hundred-page
textbook for religion and catechesis teachers, containing guidelines that
included the obligation to combat antisemitism.[52] According to Father
Prof. Chrostowski, a former co-president of the Polish Council of Christians and Jews, thousands of copies of these textbooks were translated
and shipped to Poland. Documents developed and published by the Vatican in June 1985 were written to help eliminate "negative and inaccurate
presentations of Jews and Judaism in the context of the Catholic faith."
They were also aimed at promoting respect, appreciation, and love for one
another.[53] However, despite these words of the Pope and his pledge from
1985 that not only in Catholic schools but also in churches and catechesis
curricula should be developed, in fact very little or nothing has been done
to integrate teachings about antisemitism and the Holocaust in the official curriculum. In a meeting with representatives of the Jewish community in Warsaw in 1991, the Pope recalled the words of the Polish bishops,
who in a pastoral letter of November 30, 1990 stated: "The same land was
a common homeland for Poles and Jews for ages; the mutual loss of life,
a sea of terrible suffering and of the wrongs endured should not divide,
but unite us. The places of execution, and in many cases, the common
graves, call for this unity."[54]

The Pope's efforts to indoctrinate the young with vital information
about the Holocaust and Polish antisemitism is perhaps another one of
the Pontiff's important legacies. Recognizing that the young are best suited
to break the chains of historical antisemitism in Poland, the Vatican paid
particular attention to this segment of society. But is there any proof that
this effort has succeeded?

Unfortunately, research to date does not indicate that there has been
much success here. Two recent polls highlight a troubling trend of xenophobia and antisemitism. In 2008 a Kraków-based sociologist found
that over the ten-year period from 1998 to 2008, the number of Poles who
believed that contemporary Jews are responsible for killing Jesus Christ
nearly doubled, from 8.5 percent in 1998 to 15 percent in 2008. The continued presence of this classic antisemitic myth is more troubling in light
of the fact that the respondents were high school students. Additionally,
when we look to other forms of prejudice, we note that xenophobia toward

other races and communities is quite apparent in contemporary Polish society.[55] This is even more troubling, and difficult to understand, given the fact that the teaching of classes of Catholicism, including the lessons of Pope John Paul II, has been part of the Polish school program (without regard to educational level and the status of a school) since 1990.

The second area of the church's influence is found in the words and activities of other church officials. Despite the Pope's outspoken and brave comments on antisemitism, on the Holocaust, and about Catholic–Jewish dialogue, why, then, has the church not undertaken aggressive activities to clearly and emphatically condemn the sin of antisemitism? "Couldn't the church in Poland, which has a well-trained staff of professionals," as Father Stanisław Musial stated, "afford to develop a pastoral letter or longer clerical admonition on the subject: 'What is the sin of anti-Semitism?' Who else can assume the Church's role in this? We must recall that it is not only Hitler who killed Jews . . . but Jews were also killed through the sin of antisemitism in previous centuries, in physical violence committed by Christians. . . ."[56] This question is of special importance in a country dominated by one religion, where the number of Catholics is determined to be at about 95.8 percent.[57] Also, the church with its priests and hierarchy is considered the highest authority in the country, especially in small towns and villages.

Although we do not fully know what type of information about Judaism and Jews has been conveyed by the Catholic clergy in their parishes, it can still be assumed that the knowledge of the clergy, and perhaps the anti-Jewish prejudices conveyed by some of them, can explain the continued high level of anti-Jewish prejudices. Due to lack of information on this subject, it is virtually impossible to answer precisely the question of whether the Church contributes to the enhancement of antisemitism and to what extent, particularly in small, provincial towns and in the countryside, where the degree of negative stereotypes against Jews is the highest.

A troubling aspect of church attitudes concerns continuing antisemitic statements expressed by church officials, particularly in the light of the teachings of John Paul II. At the beginning of 2010, the public was appalled by statements made by Bishop Tadeusz Pieronek, who said in an interview with the Italian Catholic journal, *Pontifex Roma,* that the "Shoah, or extermination of the Jews, is a 'Jewish invention' and that memory of the Holocaust has been 'used as a propaganda weapon to achieve often unjustifiable benefits.'" In the same interview, the bishop stated that "the Jews have a good press, due to enormous financial power and unconditional support of the U.S., and it fosters this kind of arrogance, which I personally consider to be unbearable."[58] After a public outcry, he said that his words were misunderstood and misinterpreted. Others in the church were confused by these blatant antisemitic rantings, including Dominican friar Father Tomasz Dostatni, who said, "I know that such views are represented by some people of the Polish Church, but not the Bishop Pieronek. I do not know what's going on with the bishop."[59]

Despite these and other antisemitic statements, some progress by church officialdom has been made. In 1986, the church in Poland began a post-Second Vatican discussion. The first steps toward reconciliation and dialogue with Judaism were made with the appointment by the Episcopal Conference of the Subcommittee for Dialogue with Judaism, led by Muszyński. The subcommittee was initiated after the controversial discussion over the Carmelite convent at the vicinity of Auschwitz. In the fall of 1987, the subcommittee was converted into a full committee, after a visit from John Paul II to Poland and successful meetings with members of the Jewish community in Warsaw. Questions have been raised about whether any significant results occurred. Father Prof. Chrostowski, associated with the committee from its inception, felt that "many bishops and priests did not understand the need and importance of dialogue between religions. They stood behind the opinion that Poland has no Jews, and thus that such a thing like a 'Jewish' problem does not exist. But what about the roots of Christianity?" as Chrostowski put it, "and better understanding of ourselves?"[60] Just a few years later, however, Chrostowski's attitude toward Christian–Jewish dialogue changed significantly, and people (particularly clergy) involved in discussions with Jews were severely criticized. As Chrostowski put it: "Across the path of the well-understood development of Christian–Jewish relations, the Catholic side has been represented by people who want to ingratiate the Jews, while ignoring the basic principles of a dialogue. They say what the Jews want and love to hear, and not what should be said to them."[61]

Not less important than the document *Nostra aetate* and the teachings of the Pope were events at the threshold of the second millennium. On this occasion, the Pope addressed the flock of the Church and asked for repentance and reflection over the sins committed by Catholics against others. At ceremonies marking the Jubilee Year of 2000 in Warsaw, Polish bishops apologized for the sin of antisemitism. Unfortunately, however, these words were not necessarily followed by other church leaders. Controversial statements were made by the late Fr. Jankowski, who in a June 1995 sermon had said that "Poland can no longer tolerate people in power who do not say whether they come from Moscow or from Israel." After this infamous sermon, Jankowski continued his vicious antisemitic rhetoric. He not only compared the Star of David to the swastika and hammer and sickle, but also was quoted as saying that the Jews and their greed "were responsible for the rise of communism and for the outbreak of the Second World War."[62] Four years later, after parliamentary elections, Jankowski announced amid another sermon that there was no place for Jews in the new government.

While not new, this disturbing trend of church-based antisemitism is troubling for another reason. There is often little official reaction from the Church when a senior member expresses this form of hate speech; this was evident in the reactions to both Chrostowski's and Jankowski's statements. While after his first address Jankowski was mildly reprimanded, his second occasion to voice antisemitic comments drew a one-year suspension of pastoral duties (including a ban on public speeches and sermons). However, it was later determined that this decision was not based on his hate speech but on his involvement in politics.[63]

The third and final area of church-affiliated antisemitism relates to the infamous Polish radio station, Radio Maryja, created and led from its inception in 1991 by Fr. Tadeusz Rydzyk. Officially, the owner of Radio Maryja is the Warsaw Province of the Redemptorists, and only its superior has the ability to influence its activity. Nevertheless, the station is considered the most antisemitic media outlet in Poland and is often represented in foreign media as "the voice of the Catholic Church in Poland." According to a 2008 report by the U.S. State Department, "conservative Catholic" Radio Maryja "attracts more than 10 percent of adults in Poland" and is also "one of Europe's most blatantly anti-Semitic media venues. . . . In July 2007, Father Rydzyk was recorded making a number of anti-Semitic slurs."[64]

The market share for Radio Maryja is quite limited: analysis of the research media market for the period August 2003 to January 2004 shows that its audience did not exceed 2.7 percent of listeners during this period, and this number has decreased in recent years to 2.1 percent.[65] Yet the impact of its message is significant. Research conducted by Krzemiński points out two important characteristics of the station's power. First, it is generally not the broadcasts themselves that elicit antisemitic and xenophobic comments but rather the audience calling in to the studio to express hateful viewpoints. Antisemitic comments are not transmitted directly by that station. What is most disturbing, and that gives a basis to its controversial role, is that the programs do not respond to the antisemitic statements by its audience, but rather respond with comments such as "it is better not to talk directly about the Jews, because the enemies of the radio always take advantage of it."[66] It is apparent that the emotional connections between the station and its listeners became even more important than the broadcasts themselves. Krzemiński calls this relationship an "aluzyjnym porozumieniem" (an "allusive agreement") which is frequently apparent during the Radio Maryja programs.[67] The shows also explore the supposedly negative stance of Jews toward the Polish people. Such topics usually occur during discussions about publications, like those by Gross, and usually conclude that thousands of Jews who survived the Holocaust owe their lives to Polish Catholic patriots, who risked their own lives and the lives of their families. Not only do we find this line of thinking on Radio Maryja; the topic is brought up frequently in Polish public discourse. No less interesting is the question of how to interpret the suffering of Poles and Jews during the war, a topic that is an inseparable part of the public debate on Polish–Jewish relations broadcasted by Radio Maryja. The message is that with the question of victimhood, the suffering of Poles and Jews is either equated or the two nations are categorized as one: "the Holocaust can be extended to the Polish nation, because in the end, Jews and Poles constituted one society and for centuries lived in these lands. . . . the extermination of the Jews in the first place was above all a plan, the devil's plan, to exterminate the Jewish population entirely."[68] It can be concluded that the problem of antisemitism, even though present, does not play a prominent role and is not directly discussed on Radio Maryja. Rather, defending the good name of the Poles is an important theme, a moral duty of every Pole. Such a scheme is imprinted in the Christian values that have become an integral part of the Polish nation. National Catholicism is an indestructible part of national identity in Poland; moreover, faith is connected not only with service to God but also to society. Such an attitude inevitably leads to various forms of nationalism, xenophobia, and antisemitism. Even though the radio programs do not directly approach the question of antisemitism, the studies clearly show the existence of a link between hostility toward Jews and listening to Radio Maryja.[69]

Unfortunately, few if any Church officials publicly condemn either the actions of the radio station or the subsequent negative comments from the listening public. As Krzemiński states, "there was little reaction strongly and openly condemning these stereotypical accusations and criticizing the radio's hostile and antisemitic listeners."[70] An equally interesting view on this issue was presented by Dominican Friar Rev. Paweł Gużyński, who in one of the most popular TV shows (public affairs programs) in Poland, confirmed Krzemiński's research results by evoking the memory of his late mother, who, as he stated, "never had xenophobic tendencies," but after she started listening to Radio Maryja, "When I was coming back home, detoxification from the antisemitic and xenophobic threads would take one and a half days. . . ."[71] In April 2007, Father Rydzyk while lecturing in the Higher School of Social and Media Culture established by him in Toruń, where the radio station is based, called Jedwabne a Jewish provocation that aimed to steal from Poland billions of dollars of restitution.

Apart from Radio Maryja, Father Rydzyk has successfully created other media outlets such as a daily newspaper *Nasz Dziennik* and the TV station TV Trwam. The TV station and the daily newspaper air Catholic ideas, but neither is considered a Catholic venue. Because Father Rydzyk does not have an affiliation with the Church per se, he could easily prevent the imprint of the Church hierarchy and the Episcopate on the content of material presented in the broadcasts. The Church has stayed aloof from the controversies surrounding Fr. Rydzyk and his "Media Empire." Similarly Father Kafka, Superior of the Redemptorists, is unwilling to comment on antisemitic statements appearing in Fr. Rydzyk's media. Kafka has even gone on record noting that the previously mentioned scandal associated with Rydzyk's hate speech should be considered an act of "provocation and media manipulation."[72]

Although the Church doesn't have a direct impact on Radio Maryja and its broadcast, the silence of the Church cannot be explained, particularly in the face of viciously antisemitic statements broadcasted by the radio station and its listeners. Perhaps the real truth is that the Church may have made some strides towards reconciliation with its own history and tortured relationship with the Jews of its country, but the Polish Church is ultimately unwilling to fully denounce antisemitism. The Church's silence and unwillingness to criticize its senior leadership in the face of hateful language or to denounce those listeners to Radio Maryja who speak ill of Jews, or remain reticent to construct vigorous curriculum for students, remains a consistent theme.

The major Polish problem is perhaps not antisemitism itself, but rather too much tolerance or even denial of its presence. This was best explained by Adam Michnik, editor in chief of *Gazeta Wyborcza*, the largest Polish liberal daily newspaper, who stated that "the problem is not that someone gives an antisemitic speech, because it happens everywhere and Poland is not an exception, but the problem is that serious people listen to these speeches and tolerate them and keep silence, and that antisemitism is not a sufficient reason to be excluded 'from a good society.'"[73]

Today we rarely encounter antisemitism in the political realm. Since the fall of communism and the rapid move toward democracy, none of the political parties has made antisemitism a part of its political manifestos. Even conservative nationalists have kept their statements about Jews in check; this is not a winning issue for them. Rather, holding a doctrine connected to the national Catholic traditions built on the foundation of a prewar democratic ideology is a more populist theme. At its extreme form, Radio Maryja accentuates this ideology.

It is true that the state of knowledge and awareness among Polish people has improved in recent years. But to combat the problem of antisemitism in Poland effectively, it must be first defined and acknowledged. If, in fact, we are dealing with a large number of people who deny the existence of antisemitism, or who downplay the problem, particularly among people who have influential decision-making powers—both secular and religious—then this goal will never be achieved.

The role of the church in this process is immense and irreplaceable. Many church officials and great authorities such as the Pope John Paul II invariably remind Poles about the sin of antisemitism. Thus, this grassroots process should begin at the stage of training in seminaries. Then future generations might have a chance to receive education free of myths, which in turn will allow for a fair and objective evaluation of history and will over time change Polish attitudes to Jewish history and antisemitic prejudices. Cardinal Stanisław Dziwisz, Pope John Paul II's former secretary and now archbishop of Kraków, acknowledged that "with shame we recognize that, despite the teachings of recent popes on the proper relationship of Catholics and Jews, not all among us have been able to overcome the harmful stereotypes. Where there is contempt for others, there is no Christianity."[74]

The cardinal repeatedly recalled the words of John Paul II, who did not hesitate to call antisemitism a sin. In 2000 during his historic visit to the Holy Land, Pope John Paul II said at a meeting with the president of Israel, "We must work for a new era of reconciliation and peace between Jews and Christians to come. Through my visit I make a pledge that the Catholic Church will do everything possible to make this vision not merely a dream but a reality."[75] One can only hope that the Pope's vision will indeed become reality in the future.

NOTES

1. Alina Cała, a leading Polish scholar, presented an analysis of antisemitism in Poland and Europe in her recent book *Żyd—wróg odwieczny? Anysemityzm w Polsce I jego źródła* (Warsaw: Nisza, 2012).

2. This question was analyzed by Alina Cała in her book *Wizerunek Żyda w polskiej kulturze ludowej* (Warsaw: Oficyna Naukowa, 2005; several editions; the English translation of the book is *The Image of the Jew in Polish Folk Culture* [Jerusalem: Magnes Press, Hebrew University, 1995]).

3. Romulad Jakub Weksler-Waszkinel, *Antysemityzm bez Żydów, Miesięcznik Znak* no. 643 (December 2008).

4. Cała, *Wizerunek Żyda w Polskiej Kulturze Ludowej*, pp. 188–89.

5. For many visiting Poland today, one of the manifestations of antisemitism are little statuettes of a Jew with a coin available in souvenir stores across the country. However, the popularity of these statuettes can only be explained by a belief that they are kept for good luck.

6. As an aside, anti-Jewish riots and pogroms that occurred after the Second World War in Poland were a direct consequence of the belief in blood libel. This applies to both events of August 1945 in Kraków and the infamous Kielce pogrom in July 1946. Likewise, the anti-Jewish riots in Rzeszów were prompted by a rumor about the unresolved death of a girl allegedly killed by a rabbi.

7. Ireneusz Krzemiński, *Postawy antysemickie*. In *Przeciw antysemityzmowi 1936–2009*, ed. Adam Michnik (Kraków: Universitas, 2010), p. 855.

8. National Democracy or Endecja—its name formed from the initials of a right-wing party active in Poland during the interwar period ("en-de")—was founded by Roman Dmowski. Its members and supporters, known as Endeks, often held anti-semitic views.

9. Stefan Bratkowski, "Nowy antysemityzm polski," in Adam Michnik, ed., *Przeciw antysemityzmowi 1936–2009*, p. 5.

10. Ibid., p. 8.

11. Czesław Miłosz, *Żydzi—lata dwudzieste*, in Adam Michnik, ed., *Przeciw antysemityzmowi 1936–2009*, p. 45.

12. In various publications, the number cited of Jews who left Poland after the "March '68" antisemitic campaign is 20,000. However, this theory has never been supported by primary source material. Dariusz Stola, *Kraj bez wyjścia? Migracje z Polski 1949–1989* (Warsaw: IPN, ISP PAN 2010), p. 221.

13. Stanisław Krajewski, *Poland and the Jews: Reflections of a Polish Polish Jew* (Kraków: Austeria Publishing House, 2005), pp. 37–38.

14. Declaration adopted at the meeting of dignitaries of the Catholic Church and Jewish leaders in Geneva on February 22, 1987. The question of the controversies over the Carmelite convent at Auschwitz has been described by many historians and religious and community leaders. See, e.g., Władysław Bartoszewski, *The Convent at Auschwitz* (New York: George Braziller, 1990); *Memory Offended: The Auschwitz Convent Controversy*, ed. Carol Rittner and John K. Roth (New York: Praeger Publishers, 1991).

15. Helena Datner-Śpiewak, "Struktura i wyznaczniki postaw antysemickich," in *Czy Polacy są antysemitami? Wyniki badania sondażowego*, ed. Ireneusz Krzemiński (Warsaw: Oficyna Naukowa, 1996), pp. 32–33.

16. *Antysemityzm w Polsce i na Ukrainie, raport z badań*, ed. Ireneusz Krzemiński (Warsaw: Scholar, 2004), pp. 108–134.

17. Krzemiński, *Postawy antysemickie*, p. 865.

18. Ibid., p. 869.

19. Antoni Sułek, "Zwykli Polacy patrzą na Żydów, czyli co myślimy o mniejszościach," *Gazeta Wyborcza* (January 18, 2010), and the American Jewish Committee report found at http://www.ajc.org/site/apps/nl/content3.asp?c=ijITI2PHKoG&b=846741&ct=1025513.

20. Krzemiński, *Postawy antysemickie*, pp. 869–70.

21. In the 1990 presidential elections, when antisemitic propaganda was widespread, openly antisemitic and racist candidate Bolesław Tejkowski gained support of 67,000 people in the primaries, out of almost 30 million people eligible for voting. Tejkowski lost the primary presidential election.

22. While the number of those considered *modern antisemites* has increased, the surveys indicate that the number of those subscribing to *traditional antisemitism* has not changed (in 1992, the total was 11.5 percent, compared with 11.6 percent in 2002).

23. Andrzej Żbikowski, "Źródła wiedzy Polaków o Żydach. Socjalizacja postaw," in *Czy Polacy są antysemitami?*, p. 65.

24. Ibid., p. 81.

25. "Biedny Chrześcijanin patrzy na Jedwabne: Adam Boniecki i Michał Okoński rozmawiają z Arcybiskupem Henrykiem Muszyńskim," *Tygodnik Powszechny* (March 25, 2001).

26. Konstanty Gebert, *Living in the Land of Ashes* (Kraków and Budapest: Austeria Publishing House, 2008), p. 85.

27. On July 10, 1941 in the town of Jedwabne in northeastern Poland, hundreds of Jews (the exact number of those killed has never been established) were murdered by a group of local ethnic Poles. Though the crime was committed with the consent of the Germans, the massacre was executed by neighbors whom the victims knew very well. The atrocities described by Jan Tomasz Gross in *Neighbors* triggered an important debate in Poland about memory that was eliminated from the public discourse (including intellectual circles) for decades after the war.

28. Alvin Rosenfeld, *Facing Jedwabne (International Perspectives)*, American Jewish Committee 2002, p. 17, http://www.ajc.org/site/apps/nlnet/content3.aspx?c=ijITI2PHKoG &b=846743&ct=1093355

29. *Kościół, Żydzi, Polska. Z księdzem profesorem Waldemarem Chrostowskim rozmawiają: Grzegorz Górny i Rafał Tichy*, ed. Grzegorz Górny (Warsaw: Fronda, 2009), p. 105.

30. The distinguished Polish historian Tomasz Szarota said that the facts revealed in *Neighbors* "are so shattering that they force even me, a historian who has read much and written a good deal about various instances of disgraceful behavior by Poles under German occupation, to come to completely new conclusions. . . . We did not realize that Poles were also perpetrators of the Holocaust. In Jedwabne, they were. . . . Gross has forced us to change our views on the subject of the attitudes of the Poles during the Second World War, and that is an unquestionable service." Quoted in Rosenfeld, website.

31. Ibid.

32. "We wonder whether Jews should not acknowledge that they have a burden of responsibility in regard to Poles, in particular for the period of close cooperation with the Bolsheviks, for complicity in deportations to Siberia, for sending Poles to jails, for the degradation of many of their fellow citizens, etc. The fact that Poles also took part in these repressions does not exclude the fact that the leading role was played by officers of the UB [Security Police] of Jewish descent. This terror lasted until 1956 and a great number of Poles to this day remain buried under nameless head-stones. These victims also need to be considered, as long as we are speaking about Jews victimized by Poles." Cardinal Józef Glemp, May 15, 2001, in Antony Polonsky and Joanna Michlic, eds., *The Neighbors Respond: The Controversy over the Jedwabne Massacre in Poland* (Princeton, N.J.: Princeton University Press 2004), p. 147.

33. Rosenfeld, p. 10.

34. Henryk Muszyński, in *The Neighbors Respond*, pp. 155–56.

35. Quoted by Michał Bilewicz, "Efekt wrażliwości. Rabunek i ludobójstwo," *Miesięcznik Znak* no. 670 (March 2011), pp. 16–17.

36. "Bohaterstwo, przyzwolenie, współudział" (interview by Tomasz Machała with Prof. Michał Głowiński), *Wprost* no. 1457 (2/2011), pp. 18–21.

37. Tomasz Nałęcz, "Niepotrzebny szum wokół książki Grossa," *Gazeta Wyborcza* (January 5, 2011).

38. "Gdzie prawda, gdzie fałsz" (interview by Rafał Kalukin with Henryk Woźniakowski, chief editor of *Znak*), *Wprost* no. 1464 (September 2011), pp. 14–17.

39. "Biedni Polacy na Żniwach" (review of *Golden Harvest* by Marcin Zaremba), *Gazeta Wyborcza* (January 14, 2011).

40. Ireneusz Krzemiński, "Polacy i Ukraińcy o swych narodach i o cierpieniu w czasie wojny i o Zagładzie Żydów," in Krzemiński, ed., *Antysemityzm w Polsce i na Ukrainie, raport z badań*, p. 120.

41. Sułek.

42. Żbikowski, p. 95.

43. Homily at Auschwitz, June 7, 1979, in E. J. Fisher and L. Klenicki, eds., *Spiritual Pilgrimage: Texts on Jews and Judaism, 1979–1995: Pope John Paul II* (New York: Crossroad, 1995), p. 6.

44. Address to the International Catholic–Jewish Liaison Committee on the Twentieth Anniversary of *Nostra Aetate* (October 28, 1985), in *Spiritual Pilgrimage*, p. 56.

45. American Jewish Committee, February 15, 1985.

46. Historic Visit to the Synagogue in Rome, April 13, 1986, in *Spiritual Pilgrimage*, p. 63.

47. Ibid., p. 63.

48. Sułek.

49. Address to the Jewish Community—West Germany, November 17, 1980, in *Spiritual Pilgrimage*, p. 13.

50. Address on the Fortieth Anniversary of the Warsaw Ghetto Uprising, April 13 and 25, 1983, in *Spiritual Pilgrimage*, pp. 27–28.

51. Address to the Jewish Community June 9, 1991, p. 152.

52. "*Wskazówki dla Katechetów*," *Gazeta Wyborcza* (September 19, 1997).

53. Ibid.

54. Address to the Jewish Community in Warsaw, June 9, 1991, in *Spiritual Pilgrimage*, pp. 150–53.

55. Jerzy Sadecki, "Młodzi Polacy są dziś bardziej tolerancyjni" *Gazeta Wyborcza* (April 16, 2009).

56. Stanisław Musiał, "Czarne jest czarne," *Tygodnik Powszechny* (November 16, 1997). An English translation of this article appears in *Żydownik Powszechny* supplement to *Tygodnik Powszechny*, for its 65th anniversary. *Essays in Polish–Jewish Relations* (December 14, 2010).

57. *Główny Urząd Statystyczny: Wyznania religijne, Stowarzyszenia Narodowościowe i Etniczne w Polsce 2006–2008* (Warsaw, 2010), p. 17.

58. Katarzyna Wiśniewska, "Co bp Pieronek powiedział o Żydach," *Gazeta Wyborcza* (January 26, 2010).

59. Ibid.

60. Waldemar Chrostowski, *Rozmowy o Dialogu* (Warsaw: Oficyna Wydawnicza "Vocatio," 1996), p. 23.

61. "Myśl jest bronią," *Nasz Dziennik* (December 19–20), 2009.

62. Andrzej Korboński, "Kościół Katolicki w Polsce wobec antysemitzymu: Grzechy błędów i straconych szans," in B. Oppenheim, ed., *Rachunek Sumienia. Kościół Katolicki wobec antysemityzmu 1989–1999* (Kraków: Wydawnictwo WAM, 1999), pp. 44–45.

63. Ibid.

64. http://www.state.gov/documents/organization/102301.pdf.

65. http://www.pmedia.pl/showludzie.php?wid=3257. According to the CBOS (Center for Public Opinion Research) poll, 8 percent of the self-identified listeners listen to Radio Maryja several times a week, 3 percent once a month, and 4 percent less than once a month. A total of 85 percent never listen to this radio station, while 3 percent of respondents watch TV Trwam at least several times a week, 3 percent once a month, and 2 percent less than twice a month. A total of 92 percent never watch TV Trwam, according to a CBOS poll conducted between May and July, 2008.

66. Ireneusz Krzemiński, ed., *Czego uczy Radio Maria: socjologia treści i recepcji rozgłośni* (Warsaw: Wydanictwo Akademickie i Profesjonalne, 2009), p. 45.

67. Ibid.

68. A statement by one of the guests invited to Radio Maryja, ibid. p. 78.

69. Ibid., p. 19

70. Ibid., pp. 20–27.

71. Tomasz Terlikowski, "Nie słyszałem kazania realnie politycznego," *Gazeta Wyborcza* (December 21, 2010).

72. "Oświadczenie Przełożonego Prowincji Warszawskiej Redemptorystów," *Nasz Dziennik* no. 170 (2883) (July 23, 2007), p. 1.

73. "Wystąpienie Adama Michnika redaktora naczelnego *Gazety Wyborczej*," in *Rachunek Sumienia*, pp. 69–71.

74. Address of Cardinal Stanislaw Dziwisz at the conference commemorating the death of Rev. Stanisław Musiał, March 6, 2009, Jesuit University of Philosophy and Education, Kraków; "Antysemityzm jest grzechem," *Gazeta Wyborcza* (March 30, 2009).

75. Cardinal Stanisław Dziwisz recalled the words of the Pope in his address at the conference mentioned above.

10 Antisemitism among Young European Muslims

Gunther Jikeli

Muslims in Europe

MUSLIMS ARE the largest religious minority in the European Union, and Islam is the fastest growing religion. Estimations suggest that there are between 13 and 20 million European Muslims; approximately 70 percent live in Germany, France, and the United Kingdom. But relative numbers are low; Muslims form approximately 5 percent of the population in Germany, 6–9 percent in France, and 3 percent in the UK. The proportions are significantly higher in many urban areas. Europe's Muslim population is diverse in many aspects: religiously, culturally, ethnically, and economically. Most Muslims in Europe are immigrants or descendants of immigrants from former colonies or countries with special historical ties to the respective European country in which they now reside. The first substantial wave of Muslim immigrants to Europe started after the Second World War in the 1950s with the continent's growing economy and the need for manpower. With the economic crisis of the early 1970s, legislation made immigration difficult, and migration then consisted largely of people arriving to reunite with their families. A third wave included those who arrived in the 1980s and 1990s as refugees rather than as economic migrants. Political persecutions and civil wars were the major reasons that asylum seekers from Turkey, the former Yugoslavia, North Africa, Somalia, and the Middle East moved to European countries.

The history of migration to Europe thus has a variety of facets and has resulted in a diverse landscape of Muslim communities in each European country. The majority of Muslims in Germany are Turkish immigrants or their descendants; around one-quarter of them are ethnic Kurds; the second largest group comes from the former Yugoslavia. Alevis, adherents of a particularly liberal branch of Islam, form 13–25 percent of the Muslim population in Germany. Most Muslims in France—around 80 percent of them—are immigrants or their descendants from former colonies in the Maghreb, mostly Arabs but also many Berber. Other ethnicities in France include people from Turkey, Sub-Saharan Africa, and the Middle East. Most Muslims in the UK are immigrants or their descendants from former colonies in South Asia, today's Pakistan, Bangladesh, and India. This is important to note as Muslims still maintain strong ties to their countries of origin through family and culture, and also in the structure of Muslim organizations.

Many prominent Muslim organizations in Europe are also influenced by Islamist tendencies; their long-term goal is to establish a Muslim society under Shariʾa law—even though they generally renounce violence and aim to achieve their goals through education and political influence. The Muslim Brotherhood is the most influential Islamist organization and is directly or indirectly linked to a number of prominent Muslim organizations in Europe.[1] However, Islam, far from being a homogeneous religion, is interpreted differently by religious groups and individuals across Europe. Muslim organizations only represent a marginal part of the Muslim population. Official membership in these organizations is low, only a minority regularly worship at mosques, and surveys show that few Muslims in Europe feel that they are represented by any Muslim association.[2]

Today, the majority of European Muslims fit into long-standing and integral parts of the fabric of their cities, regions, and countries. Surveys show that the majority of Muslims strongly identify both with their country of residence and with Islam, even though religion is more important to Muslims than to the general European population.[3] Publicly discussed tensions and issues such as terrorism plots by young European Muslims, public approval of the Shariʾa, clashes in reaction to cartoons mocking the prophet Muhammad, public discussions about Muslim women wearing a veil or about outlawing the burkha, forced marriages, and "honor killings" mostly concern a minority of Muslims and do not lead to a general alienation of Muslims from mainstream society. However, Muslim communities face a number of socioeconomic challenges. Unemployment rates are particularly high among Muslims and the average level of formal work qualifications is relatively low. Housing conditions are also poorer than average. Discrimination adds to the socioeconomic disadvantage of Muslims. In addition to racism and xenophobia, Muslims increasingly face problems stemming from negative stereotypes of Islam and Muslims.[4]

Muslim Antisemitism as a Factor in European Antisemitism

Antisemitism among Muslims has become one of the major factors in a number of Western European countries in the twenty-first century.[5] It has added weight to antisemitism from the far Right, the Left, and mainstream society.[6] Antisemitism among European Muslims and Muslim organizations is visible in anti-Israel demonstrations, which in some incidents have led to veritable antisemitic riots, such as in Oslo at the beginning of 2009.[7]

Public debates have taken place with regard to cases of violent assaults on Jews perpetrated by youths of Muslim background, most infamously the murder of three children and a teacher in Toulouse, France, in 2012[8] and the murder of Ilan Halimi in France in 2006 by a group of mostly Muslim youths calling themselves the "gang des barbares,"[9] but also concerning relatively less violent incidents, such as the violent attack on a rabbi and his six-year-old daughter in Berlin in August 2012[10] and an attack on Jewish dancers at a local festival in Hanover, Germany in 2010.[11] Antisemitic attitudes among young people with Muslim background have also been discussed in the context of schools and education in Germany[12] and France.[13] Debates in Britain on antisemitism among Muslims have revolved instead around antisemitism in Islamist organizations or the curricula of Islamic schools. Other incidents in which Muslims or people of Arab origin were identified as perpetrators have triggered only short media reports.[14] But particular examples from smaller cities show that antisemitic attacks from Muslims have had a dramatic impact on the Jewish community.[15]

Systematic data on (ethnic) backgrounds of perpetrators of antisemitic acts are only available for Britain and France to some extent. Based on the annual reports on antisemitic incidents in these countries, it can be estimated that more than 30 percent of perpetrators of violent antisemitic incidents in those two countries are Muslim.[16] Data provided by the German Federal Office for the Protection of the Constitution, Germany's domestic agency, indicate that the percentage of right-wing perpetrators of antisemitic attacks is particularly high there and that the percentage of Muslim perpetrators is lower in Germany than in France and the UK.[17] However, it is noteworthy that even though the percentage of Muslim perpetrators is disproportionally high for violent antisemitic attacks, it is disproportionally low for some other forms of antisemitism, such as threats.[18]

The significantly high percentage of Muslim perpetrators of antisemitic attacks is rarely publicly acknowledged by politicians and human rights groups, and scholars are only beginning to investigate the issue seriously. Werner Bergmann and Juliane Wetzel were the first to point out the specific phenomenon of antisemitism among young European Muslims; they base their comments on comprehensive empirical data that had been gathered by agencies from all European countries in 2002 on behalf of the European Monitoring Center for Racism and Xenophobia (EUMC, now FRA). In their report they noted: "Physical attacks on Jews and the desecration and destruction of synagogues were acts mainly committed by young Muslim perpetrators mostly of an Arab descent in the monitoring period."[19] But the report was not released by the EUMC, an omission that caused a public debate. It has been argued that it was not released because it points out significant Muslim involvement in European antisemitism. Scholars are also reluctant to point to this fact. One of the reasons is the discrimination faced by Muslims. It is feared that naming the problem contributes to their further stigmatization, and some writers and politicians have indeed employed the information in this way.[20]

Islamist Organizations in Europe

Antisemitism is part and parcel of Islamist and Pan-Arabist ideology, but the influence of such thinking on European Muslims is difficult to assess.[21] Both movements emerged in the first half of the twentieth century and adhere to antisemitic interpretations of the world.[22] Surveys show that negative views of Jews are shared by more than 90 percent of the people in countries with Muslim majorities,[23] and it has been pointed out that these anti-Jewish attitudes are often embedded in negative views of the Western world in general.[24] Major Muslim organizations in Europe are affiliated with or linked to global Islamist movements such as the Muslim Brotherhood. For example, the second-largest Muslim organization in Germany, Milli Görüş, is considered a nonviolent Islamist organization ideologically close to the Muslim Brotherhood.[25] In France, the majority of Muslim organizations of the Conseil Français du Culte Musulman—created as a representative body for Muslims in France—have strong ties to Islamist organizations.[26] The Muslim Council of Britain (MCB) is linked to the international Islamist organizations Muslim Brotherhood and Jamaat-I-Islami.[27] On a European level, the most prominent Muslim organization is the European Council of Fatwa, headed by Yusuf al-Qaradawi one of the main ideologues of the Muslim Brotherhood. Antisemitic publications and statements by these and other Islamist organizations have been reported and ties to other openly antisemitic organizations have been revealed. Milli Görüş in Germany, for instance, has not severed its links to the antisemitic pro-Hamas organization Internationale Humanitare Hilfsorganisation e.V. (IHH e.V),[28] even after the latter was outlawed in Germany. Book fairs in mosques associated with Milli Görüş have displayed blatant antisemitic literature.[29] Similarly, the orthodox Sunni Union des Organizations Islamiques de France (UOIF) supports the pro-Hamas Committee for Charity and Assistance to Palestinians (CBSP).[30] The leading Deobandi[31] figure in the UK, Abu Yusuf Riyadhul Haq, is known for his open antisemitism.[32] Also, the Muslim Association of Britain became prominent when its pro-Palestinian rally equated Israel and Nazi Germany.[33] The British All-Party Parliamentary Inquiry into Antisemitism of 2006 gave examples of overtly antisemitic statements of Islamists and Islamist organizations, namely Hizb ut-Tahir, Al-Muhajiroun, and Muslim Public Affairs Committee (MPACUK). The inquiry also mentioned the availability of antisemitic propaganda such as *Mein Kampf* and the *Protocols of the Elders of Zion* in venues such as Arabic bookshops in London.[34] An investigation in the UK of available literature in mosques, Islamic schools, and Islamic cultural centers found that some of Britain's mainstream Islamic institutions give cause for concern. The literature available in a number of British mosques contains hatred against Jews and antisemitic conspiracy theories, including positive references to the *Protocols*.[35] Islamist literature inciting hatred can also be found in a number of public libraries without any critical comment.[36] Another study on Muslim schools published in 2009 revealed that some of the estimated 166 full-time Muslim schools in Britain teach the rejection of Western values and hatred of Jews.[37] However, as outlined earlier, Islamist organizations are hardly representative of the Muslim population in Europe despite their prominence and influence in many European mosques.

The influence of Islam on negative views of Jews has also been discussed.[38] From a sociological point of view, Islam does not exist as a unitary category. There are as many different interpretations of Islam as there are Muslims. Therefore, there is no "Islam as such," and if anti-Jewish attitudes are justified with Islamic sources, then they are interpretations for which individuals are to be made responsible rather than "Islam"; it follows, then, that linking Islam or Muslims in an essentializing way with antisemitism is wrong.[39] However, some Islamic scripture, including parts of the Qur'an and the Hadith, convey derogatory images of Jews or suggest enmity between Muslims and Jews; these passages have been used to justify hostility toward Jews. Furthermore, historically, Jews have often been discriminated against under Islamic rule.[40] Adding to that, a number of publications in the past decade have revealed links and cooperation between leading Muslims and National Socialism and the adoption of antisemitic ideology from the Nazis.[41] But again, these are acts of individuals and particular organizations. Their precise impact on European Muslims remains unclear.[42]

Surveys: Antisemitic Attitudes among Muslims

Surveys suggest that antisemitic attitudes are stronger and are held more frequently among Muslims in Europe than among non-Muslims. However, these surveys have to be interpreted with caution because their focus is not only on antisemitism. The surveys also often include just one item as a measure of antisemitic attitudes. For example, in 2006, the Pew Global Attitudes Project asked Muslims and non-Muslims in a number of countries if they have a "favorable or unfavorable opinion of Jews." In the UK, 47 percent of Muslims and 7 percent of the general population stated that they have an unfavorable opinion of Jews. In France, 13 percent of the general population and 28 percent of Muslims had an unfavorable opinion of Jews. Lastly, in Germany, the figures were 22 percent of the general population and 44 percent of Muslims. The contrast is even greater when "very unfavorable" opinions are compared.[43] In Germany, Katrin Brettfeld and Peter Wetzels included one item on antisemitism in a questionnaire completed by 2,683 students, including 500 Muslims, from Cologne, Hamburg, and Augsburg. It showed that 15.7 percent of

Muslims of migrant background, 7.4 percent of non-Muslims of migrant background, and 5.4 percent of non-Muslims without any background of migration strongly believed that "people of Jewish faith are arrogant and greedy."[44] Another study was published by Jürgen Mansel and Viktoria Spaiser. In 2010, they surveyed 2,404 students with different ethnic backgrounds in Bielefeld, Cologne, Berlin, and Frankfurt. About one-third were Muslim. Antisemitic attitudes related to Israel, religious antisemitism, classic antisemitism, and equations between Israel and the Nazis were significantly higher among Muslim students, and Arab students in particular, than among other students.[45] The researchers also found differences regarding the ethnic background; 24.9 percent of the students with Turkish-Muslim background and 40.4 percent of those with Arab background agreed "completely" with the statement "Jews have too much influence in the world." The percentage among those without a migrant background was only 3 percent. Some justified antisemitic views with their religion: 15.9 percent of Muslim students with Turkish background and 25.7 percent of those with Arab background agreed without reservation with the statement "in my religion it is the Jews who drive the world to disaster."[46]

A survey published in 1997 asked youths of Turkish background in Germany if they thought that Zionism threatened Islam; 33.2 percent said yes.[47] A study from Denmark revealed that a number of antisemitic stereotypes were significantly more common among people with Turkish, Pakistani, Somali, Palestinian, and ex-Yugoslavian backgrounds than among ethnic Danes. The study also shows that anti-Jewish attitudes were more widespread among Muslim immigrants than among Christian immigrants.[48] In Britain, the polling institute Populus interviewed 500 Muslims about their views of Jews in December 2005 but did not compare this to the general population. However, in this survey, 53 percent agreed with the allegation that "Jews have too much influence over foreign policy," 46 percent said that "Jews are in league with the Freemasons to control the media and politics," and 37 percent disclosed that "Jews are legitimate targets as part of the ongoing struggle for justice in the Middle East."[49] A comprehensive survey in Sweden was first published in 2004 on attitudes among pupils; 10,600 students aged 14 to 18 on average completed the questionnaire. Muslims showed the highest percentage of strong antisemitism, with 8.3 percent compared to 3.7 percent among Christians, but those who considered themselves nonreligious followed closely with 7.6 percent. The survey also revealed significant differences between male and female respondents; 12.9 percent of Muslim boys were found to be "intolerant" of Jews, but only 4.8 percent of Muslim girls had that attitude.[50] This has not been confirmed in other studies. Sylvia Brouard and Vincent Tiberj, two French researchers, analyzed data from a representative poll in 2005 on antisemitism among French citizens from African and Turkish immigration in comparison to the general electorate. They pointed out that French citizens of African and Turkish origin show significantly higher levels of antisemitism than the general electorate; 33 percent of those of African or Turkish origin showed such attitudes in a number of items versus 18 percent of the general population. However, antisemitic attitudes recede with time spent in France; results from the second generation born in France show figures even below those of the general population (17 percent). Interestingly, the studies demonstrate that antisemitism among this population is only weakly related to conservative attitudes, ethnocentrism, and authoritarianism but that it correlates strongly with the level of Islamic practice.[51] According to Tiberj, the social jealousy hypothesis, education, and even negative attitudes toward Israel cannot be explanatory factors as respective correlations are relatively weak. In fact, the level of hostility toward Israel is similar among people of African and Turkish origin and the general population in France.[52]

Scholarly Debates on European Muslim Antisemitism—Acknowledgment and Denial

Robert Wistrich has noted that Muslim antisemitism is one of several factors contributing to antisemitism in Europe today. He suggests that Islamists have spread the "Palestinian war against the Jews" from the Middle East to the European Union, which is "perceived as dar al-Kufr, the land of impiety. This is the soil on which fundamentalist paranoia can best flourish."[53] Klaus Holz, on the other hand, believes that experiences of social, racist, and, religious exclusion are major factors for antisemitism among Muslims.[54] John Bunzl and Brian Klug even deny the antisemitic dimension of Muslim hostility toward Jews today. They see attacks against Jewish individuals and property from "alienated Moroccan and Algerian youths in the banlieues of Paris" as "an ethno-religious conflict between two communities with opposed identifications: roughly, French

Muslims with Palestinian Arabs versus French Jews with Israeli Jews."[55] For the French context, however, Michel Wieviorka's study disproves the thesis that antisemitism among young Muslims is basically a reflection of an ethnic conflict between Jews and Muslims. Wieviorka even dedicated a chapter to the issue with the telling title "Un antisémitisme (presque) sans Juifs" (Antisemitism [almost] without Jews").[56] Klug has further interpreted anti-Jewish attacks by "young Muslim immigrants" as "political outrage, not bigotry" and, explicitly, as not antisemitic. He suggests that these attacks are motivated by anti-Zionism and believes "it is closer to the truth to say that anti-Zionism today takes the form of anti-Semitism rather than the other way round."[57] Attempts to rationalize expressions of antisemitism often lead to denial of their antisemitic ideology. Another example is given by Paul Silverstein. He sees attacks against Jews by North African immigrants and their children in France as part of a reaction to the violence they experience from the French state, "directed back at the state and those (including Jews) who seem to represent it."[58] Elsewhere, he explains hostility against Jews as the result of an identification with Palestinians because of perceived similar circumstances of colonial oppression, together with the perception that Jews are privileged over Muslims in Europe and thus "iconic of all which is intolerable in their own lives."[59] Similarly, Matti Bunzl believes that Muslims attack Jews because they see Jews as part of a European hegemony that marginalizes them and that also accounts for the suffering of Palestinians. He characterizes "Muslim violence against Europe's Jews as the extension of an anti-colonial struggle."[60] Pierre-André Taguieff, by contrast, clearly points out the ideological dimension of resurgent antisemitism and sees anti-Zionism and hatred of Israel as a crucial part of it. He insists that "the new Judeophobia which can be observed in the post-Nazi period appears to be centered on a mythical 'anti-Zionism' which treats 'Zionism' like the incarnation of the absolute evil."[61]

A comprehensive analysis of antisemitism among "disenfranchised youths" in France—mainly Muslims of North African origin—was conducted by Michel Wieviorka.[62] The researchers observed antisemitic attitudes that were voiced openly, in public. They note that antisemitic discourse is widespread and the use of the words *Juif* and *Feuj* as insults are taken for granted in some social circles. In keeping with similar results found in a study by Didier Lapeyronnie,[63] Wieviorka and his colleagues observed that the use of antisemitic language among youths puts pressure on individuals to use this very language and to adopt its larger patterns of discourse.[64] My own research on antisemitism and language use confirms this situation in Germany as well.[65] Wieviorka and his team identified two recurrent images of Jews. On the one hand, Jews in France are seen as privileged and successful, often envied, and contrasted to the underprivileged situation of Muslims. On the other hand, globally, Jews are seen as agents of Israeli and American hegemony, a view based on the "oppression of the Palestinians" in particular and "the" Arabs or Muslims in general. It is part of a Manichean vision of the world: the Jew is all powerful and an incarnation of evil, and the Muslim is oppressed and good. This vision, the researchers stated, justifies violence from the latter against the former, as an answer to the humiliation in the banlieues, amplified by TV images of Israeli tanks shooting young Palestinians armed with stones.

A Comparative Study in Germany, France, and the UK: Methods and Analytical Strategy

Why do some young Muslims say they dislike Jews? What images of Jews do they hold? And what are the sources of these images? The remainder of this chapter examines antisemitism among young European Muslims, analyzing a qualitative study based on face-to-face interviews with more than one hundred young male Muslims of different educational backgrounds in Berlin, Paris, and London.[66]

Interviewees were most often approached outdoors[67] in the neighborhoods of Tower Hamlets and Finsbury Park in London, Belleville and Barbes in Paris, and Kreuzberg and Neukölln in Berlin. These districts are traditionally inhabited by immigrants, in the last decades mainly from countries with Muslim majorities. They contain diverse immigrant communities of Muslim cultural and religious backgrounds and corresponding immigrant organizations.

The interviewees were asked if they were willing to give their opinions about their neighborhoods, discrimination, and general political views.[68] They were told that the interviews were for an academic study of young people's views in Germany, France, and Britain. The interviews started off by soliciting views on the interviewees' life in the neighborhood, their occupations and interests, and their experiences of discrimination and possible conflicts in the neighborhood between ethnic or religious communities. The interviewers only directed the conversation and tried to ensure that participants gave some biographical data and commented on perceived discrimination, the Iraq War, the terror attacks of September 11, 2001, and the Middle East conflict. At the end of the interview participants were asked, if they had not already talked about it earlier, if they could befriend or marry a Jew, what they thought of the belief that Jews are rich, and what they thought of equating the sufferings of Jews under the Nazis and the sufferings of Palestinians under the Israelis.

The interview was discontinued if the individual did not fall into the subject group: fourteen through twenty-seven years old, male, and self-identifying as Muslim.[69] Most of the interviews were conducted with one participant at a time. However, by-standing friends were allowed to participate, which led at times to interviews with two or more respondents. Altogether, 117 young male youths in Paris (40), London (40), and Berlin (37) who considered themselves Muslim were interviewed from 2005 to 2007.

The interviews were analyzed from the outset and additional data were collected until a saturation point was reached with regard to evolving patterns of both antisemitic arguments and perceptions of discrimination—that is, until respective arguments were only repeated in new interviews.[70] The initially targeted size of the sample was extended from 60 interviewees to 117 to achieve, in constant comparative analysis, a saturation of patterns of argumentation and an equal distribution of interviewees among the three cities. The analytical strategy is based on a five-stage method of qualitative content analysis:[71] open initial coding of (18) interviews, development of a coding guide, coding of all interviews, production of case overviews of all interviewees, and in-depth single-case analysis.

I use Helen Fein's definition of antisemitism from 1987 and also the "Working Definition of Antisemitism" as guidelines. Fein proposed "to define antisemitism as a persisting latent structure of hostile beliefs towards *Jews as a collectivity* manifested in *individuals* as attitudes, and in *culture* as myth, ideology, folklore and imagery, and in *actions*—social or legal discrimination, political mobilisation against Jews, and collective or state violence—which results in and/or is designed to distance, displace, or destroy Jews as Jews."[72] The Working Definition of Antisemitism was formulated in 2005 by the EUMC, today the European Union Agency for

Fundamental Rights (FRA), with the assistance of a number of organizations. It fits Fein's definition and provides a number of examples, including distinctions between criticism of Israel and antisemitism with reference to Israel. The full Working Definition is included in the appendix to this article.

The objective in qualitative studies is not representativeness but generalizability. In which other contexts and to what other groups do findings apply? This study shows how young male Muslims, randomly approached in areas with a high percentage of Muslim population in Berlin, Paris, and London explain their views to a stranger in face-to-face interviews. The three cities in three different countries and also the different ethnic backgrounds represent significant changes in context. The repetition of patterns of argumentation and similarities among respondents' views within the three cities and across the countries strongly indicate a generalizability beyond the sample of individuals. The fact that the interviewees' ethnic backgrounds largely represent the respective contribution of ethnic backgrounds of Muslims in each of these countries (i.e., mostly Turkish in Germany, mostly Maghrebian in France, and mostly Asian in Great Britain) further enhances the generalizability of the qualitative results for young male Muslims in each of the three countries.

Antisemitic Views

The central question of the study was: what do young European Muslims think of Jews, and what kinds of arguments do they use to support enmity against Jews? Most antisemitic arguments among respondents are fragmented and multifaceted. Although only a small minority expressed "coherent" antisemitic views, those who have only fragmented antisemitic views can also pose a direct threat to Jews. Some interviewees, from all three countries, voiced threats against Jews during the interviews or knew of peers who had been involved in attacks against Jews. Generally, anti-Jewish attitudes are voiced openly by young Muslims, not in coded forms. The majority of interviewees showed antisemitic resentments in at least one way or another according to the Working Definition of Antisemitism and Fein's definition of antisemitism.

What do young Muslims say about why they do not like Jews? Four distinctive patterns of antisemitic argumentation emerged.

1) Attitudes of "Classical" Modern Antisemitism

A number of "classical" antisemitic tropes were voiced, most prominently conspiracy theories and stereotypes associating Jews with money, including characterizations of Jews as rich, stingy, treacherous, and clannish by nature. The tropes characterize Jews as one undifferentiated entity with a common (sinister) "Jewish interest." The widely used terms by interviewees citing "Jewish influence" and "Jewish companies" capture this notion. Jews are portrayed as being behind companies, governments, or the media on a local, national, but above all a global level and in association with the United States. Tropes of "classical" modern antisemitism enhance a negative and potentially threatening image of "the Jews." Nirmal from London, of Asian origin, gave an example:

> Well, obviously if you can see that Jewish are the rich ones around nowadays. They are the one who control everything . . . even Britain because if you see Sainsbury's, Tesco, Iceland, it all belongs to them. They are the rich ones. They're the ones who're controlling the country and the world right now. (Nirmal from London, 18 years old)

The tropes of "Jews rule the world," "rich Jews," and "Jewish control of businesses" are often intermingled. Nirmal combines these three tropes. He does not distinguish between economic and political power. Wealth is equated with power and influence. He cited major supermarket chains in the UK, which also have shops in his area, as evidence for his assumption of control by rich Jews, saying that these companies are owned by "the Jews." Real or imagined rich Jews and Jewish business leaders are seen as evidence for widespread "Jewish control." Nirmal is one of about half of the interviewees who relate Jews to money and he does so in a very explicit way, following a long-standing stereotype in European and other countries. An ADL survey from 2009 revealed that nearly 40 percent of all respondents in seven European countries believed that "Jews have too much power in the business world." This percentage, however, was much lower in the UK (15 percent).[73] Nirmal might have picked this idea up from general society, but he also might have read such allegations on flyers from Islamist organizations who portray these and other companies as "Jewish" and pro-Israeli and advocate for a boycott of these companies.[74] It is not unlikely that he heard such rumors among peers.

2) Negative Views of Jews with Reference to Israel

The interviews show that antisemitic attitudes with reference to Israel are based on a conflation of Jews with Israelis and on a Manichean view of the Middle East conflict. Negative views of Israel can serve as justification for general enmity toward Jews, including German, French, and British Jews. These justifications of hostility can be limited to a brief reference to the Middle East conflict such as "because of Palestine" or "because of the wars with Jews"; others give more specific content by mentioning that Jews allegedly kill children or that "they" have taken away allegedly Palestinian, Arab, or Muslim land. The latter form the main argument to delegitimize the State of Israel. Housni from Paris, of Maghrebian background, for example, stated:

> It doesn't exist, Israel, normally. It mustn't exist. They gave them a small piece of land—hop—they started to take more and more. Now it has become theirs. (Housni from Paris, 19 years old)

This example illustrates that the topos of "Jews have taken Palestinian land" is used to portray Israel as having been built on other people's land. The legitimacy of the existence of the State of Israel is questioned altogether.

The topos "Jews kill children" adds to the portrayal of an evil, demonized State of Israel. If Israelis and Jews are conflated, this is taken as evidence for the evilness of Jews, a topic that stirs up emotions. Memduh, a Turkish participant from Berlin, used this topos as evidence for his argument that "the Jews" started the conflict in the Middle East and that they are to blame:

> The Jews are just starting it. They kill small Muslim children, they do everything, they rape small children, women, even grannies. (Memduh from Berlin, 17 years old)

Memduh added the accusation of perverse rape to the topos and stressed that the children killed are Muslim, possibly because he wanted to show his identification with the Palestinians and to portray Muslims as victims. These strong images allow him to delineate his dualistic views of the Middle East conflict in a few words. "They [the Jews] are killing children" can be used as a metaphor for the whole conflict. The topos of killing children was employed by almost a quarter of interviewees, more often as "Jews kill children" than "Israelis kill children." What is more, all those who used "Israelis kill children" as a topos conflate Jews and Israelis in other contexts. The topos is used as an implicit or explicit allegation against Jews, not only against the State of Israel, the Israeli army, or the government. And, indeed, some participants used it as a direct and justifying argument for hating Jews in their neighborhood. The intensity of hostility against Jews justified by the Middle East conflict is related to the identification with "the Palestinians," either via an Arab or Muslim identity, or both. Not all interviewees identify with Palestinians, but most respondents of Arab background do. Arab identity is an important additional factor that can enhance hostility against European Jews, using justifications related to the Israeli–Palestinian conflict, which is often interpreted as a conflict between Arabs and Israel/the Jews.

At some point during their interviews, the majority of interviewees conflated Israelis and Jews living in Germany, France, or Britain. Some explicitly said that they do not see any differences. Israelis[75] are described as "the Jews," and generalizations are drawn from Israel to all Jews. European Jews are related to Israel. Jews are, for most interviewees, a unitary, organic category. Conflating Jews and Israelis is not necessarily an expression of antisemitism, but in combination with negative attitudes toward Israel, such generalizations enhance negative views of Jews.

About half of the interviewees showed hostile attitudes toward Israel, to different degrees, many in rather unambiguously antisemitic forms. However, it should be noted that for the other half, who did not show such hostile views, Israel and the Middle East conflict is not an important issue and their identification with "the Palestinians" is low.

3) Negative Views of Jews with Reference to Religious or Ethnic Identity

The interviews clearly show that some Muslims relate their negative views of Jews to their ethnic or religious identity or to their perception of Islam. The assumption of a general enmity between Muslims and Jews or between the individual ethnic community and Jews is widespread and voiced approvingly in statements such as "Muslims and Jews are enemies" or "the Arabs dislike Jews."

"Really, we, the Arabs, um, the Muslims and the Jews, we don't understand each other," said Azhar, seventeen years old, from Paris, of Maghrebian origin, adopting the perception of a general enmity toward Jews.

But he is not quite sure if he relates it to his Arab or Muslim identity. Religious and ethnic identities can get blurred. When interviewees speak about "us" with reference to their community it is often not clear (for themselves) if they mean their religious or their ethnic community.

Justifications for hostility toward Jews with reference to Islam, Muslim identity, or ethnic background are sometimes linked to other "classical" stereotypes, such as that of rich and influential Jews, or to resentments over the Middle East conflict, but they cannot be reduced to how Muslims may see the Middle East conflict. There are distinct references to religious or ethnic identity. A number of statements even directly contradict the thesis that hostile attitudes toward Jews among Muslims are rooted largely or solely in the Israeli–Palestinian conflict. Ümit, from Berlin of Turkish origin, expressed this view in the most straightforward way:

> INTERVIEWER: And then you'd rather say that because of the [Middle East] conflict you also have a problem with Israelis?
>
> ÜMIT: No, not because of them. As a Muslim you have problems, not with Israelis, [but] with Jews. . . . Because they have been condemned by God. (Ümit from Berlin, 25 years old)

Ümit believes that Muslim identity necessarily leads to enmity toward Jews, and he explicitly rejects arguments that hostility to Jews is based on the Middle East conflict. Such generalizing and essentializing assumptions of enmity as in his statement deny different views from individuals within the community and different interpretations of Islam. Muslims are portrayed as unified in their attitudes toward Jews.[76] Participants often cannot explain this enmity, but they somehow relate it to Islamic history, the Qur²an, the Middle East conflict, or in the wars in Afghanistan and Iraq. Some root their notions of Jewish enmity in apocalyptic visions and conspiracy theories. Agantuk stated:

> Do you know why Jew people get all their equipments? Because Bush is giving them equipments to get rid of all the Muslim countries. They don't know they got army coming up. Muslim people's army is building up. . . . In our religion, it's written on the Qur'an and it says there's a holy war coming now. They wanna kill all the Muslim people, they're doing it in the TV. But after that the big barriers are gonna open, and they're going [to] come in. They're going to take, wipe out England. (Agantuk from London, 23 years old)

This interviewee combined his assumption of a war between Muslims and Jews with the accusation that, in cooperation with Jews, President Bush wants to kill all Muslims. The perception of a general war between Muslims and Jews, in this case aimed to "wipe out" England, is rooted in the view of a preordained war of religions at the approaching end of times. Others argue that there is mutual hatred, that Jews do not like Muslims or the individual ethnic community, or that Jews are perpetually at war with Muslims or Arabs. Negative views of Jews are then presented as a reaction.

However, it is important to note that it is particular perceptions of Islam and Muslim identity that are relevant for such forms of antisemitism. As in all purported rationales for Jew-hatred, these notions are chimerical[77] and not the actual reason for antisemitic attitudes.

4) Negative Views of Jews without Rationalization

Antisemitic views of "the Jews" cannot be justified; they are always irrational. But some participants do not even attempt to offer arguments or justifications for their hostility. They feel no need to justify or to explain negative views of Jews and hold Jews responsible for allegedly negative deeds or characteristics. Hence, we find views like this one:

> Jewish people are Jewish, that's why we don't like them. (Ganesh, London, 16 years old)

Jewishness—being Jewish in itself—is considered reason enough to despise Jews. Some participants "naturally" accept hatred against Jews and endorse its irrationality. They insist on it even if contradictions become obvious. Some openly hate Jews for being Jews. Or, they adopt negative views of Jews and consider their feelings to be "common sense" and normal. Some respondents gave evidence in declarations, such as the one above, that confirm that negative views of Jews are simply the norm within their social environment.

Such inherently negative views of Jews without any rationalization find expression in a peculiar use of language. Participants accept the idea that in French and German the very term *Jew* carries negative connotations.[78] The term *Jew* can be used generally as a substitute for negative words of attribution. Sabri from Paris, for example, reported a familiar use of the term in relation to stinginess—without any direct relation to actual Jews. Almost all interviewees from France and Germany know the use of the term *Jude* in German or *Juif* or *Feuj* in French as an insult, and many admitted using it themselves in this sense. Halil, of Turkish origin, revealed negative attitudes toward Jews in general and indirectly threatened "Jews who are Jews" when asked if he could imagine having a Jewish friend:

> INTERVIEWER: Would you oppose having a Jewish friend . . . ?
>
> HALIL: Well, . . . yes . . . how can I say, if he's all right, if he's not such a Jew . . . then I wouldn't do anything. (Halil from Berlin, 17 years old)

Halil's inner conflict stems from his general valuation of friendship, which is positive, and his negative rejection of Jews as Jews. The dislike of any group of people for their collective identity itself, not for particular alleged traits or characteristics attached to it, does not stand up to reason and so a resulting contradictory statement is not surprising. Nevertheless, the belief that it is Jewish identity itself that is detestable seems to have a highly aggressive potential: it should be noted that "justifying" hostility to Jews simply because they are Jews is combined by some other participants with explicit calls for extermination of all Jews. And, indeed, the call for extermination is the rationale within this irrationality of hatred of Jews because they are Jews. Consider Bashir's words, particularly his last sentence in the following excerpt:

> BASHIR: [I] would . . . say, . . . that the damned Jews should be burnt. . . . Maybe there are Jews who are kind or so, I don't know.
>
> INTERVIEWER: And those who are kind, should they be burnt, too?
>
> BASHIR: Yes.
>
> INTERVIEWER: Why?
>
> BASHIR: Because they are Jews nevertheless. Jews are, a Jew is a Jew anyway. (Bashir from Berlin, 15 years old)

Such views obviously defy rational arguments and indicate that expressions of antisemitism have nothing to do with Jews as such but are rooted in chimerical assumptions about Jews. From this perspective, justifications for antisemitism are merely attempts to express antisemitic resentments in more plausible ways.

Differences in Negative Views of Jews among Muslims in Berlin, Paris, and London

Differences in attitudes toward Jews among young Muslims living in the three countries were surprisingly small. However, some antisemitic views are shaped differently among interviewees from the three countries. Respondents from Germany, for example, voiced the antisemitic trope of Jews controlling the media rather allusively, saying that Jews manipulate the media to conceal Israel's atrocities. In France, respondents often said that Jews are dominant on French television; the interviewees highlighted the names of Jewish actors and TV presenters. Respondents in the United Kingdom see Jewish influence in the media more in U.S. television channels such as Fox News, Fox TV, and CNN and in the film industry. Surprisingly, despite different national contexts and languages, there are only minor differences between the pejorative use of the term *Jew* in German and French. The term is, however, hardly used or known by interviewees from Britain.

A trope used almost exclusively by some participants from France was the portrayal of Jews as exploitative. Some respondents from France also see the French Jewish community as unjustly having more success than people in their own community. There is envy of the local Jewish community among participants from France, possibly related to the fact that the local Jewish community is more visible for them than for their counterparts in Germany and Britain and that they might share Maghreb origins with many French Jews.

Conspiracy theories focusing on Freemasonry and also the perception of a "war against Muslims" led by Jews were more frequent among participants in London than in Paris or Berlin. Quantitative conclusions of this study must be considered with caution, but it is striking that participants from London often used religious arguments in support of negative views of Jews. More often than interviewees from Paris or Berlin, they also held to the assumption that most large companies are owned by Jews and support Israel in the war against "the Palestinians." The direct influence of Islamist organizations is also stronger among participants from Britain than from the other countries.

In Germany, some participants exhibited views of Jews that are often interpreted as exemplifying secondary antisemitism, motivated by a rejection of German guilt. This is hardly the motive for young people in Germany of migrant background. However, participants complained about allegedly high compensation payments to Israel or used the argument that Jews should be better people than others because of the Holocaust but had failed to be so in Israel. The findings are indicative that specific antisemitic discourses from mainstream society are also adopted by those who do not share the motives for these specific tropes (but share antisemitic feelings nevertheless).

Positive Examples

A few interviewees clearly rejected antisemitic attitudes, and at least some of them should be considered as anti-antisemites.[79] The majority of those who were particularly outspoken in their rejection of antisemitism did so despite their awareness of antisemitism among their friends, parents, ethnic or religious community, or the media. Their stance proves that antisemitic attitudes are not necessarily adopted from an environment in which negative attitudes of Jews are the norm; individuals have the choice of adopting such views. Consequently, people should be held responsible for their views. The motives to reject antisemitism are probably as diverse as the sources and tropes of antisemitism. Nevertheless, an in-depth analysis of interviews with participants who reject antisemitism hints at a number of motivations. At least for Nabil from Berlin, who is of Palestinian origin, the conviction that everybody is equal and nobody should be discriminated against for his or her background seems to be a motive to speak out against antisemitism expressed by his parents and classmates. Jamil's motivation to reject negative assumptions of his parents such as "Jews and Muslims are at war with each other" is rooted in an individualism that prevents him from unquestionably adopting such views. He has also been influenced by a close cousin who questions misogynistic aspects of Muslim societies. Another motivation can be explained with Boualem's views: living illegally in London, he is longing for a simple and normal life and wishes the same for everybody. Ideologies of hatred are not helpful for him but potentially signify more trouble. Raoul, also from London, associates negative views of Jews with old-fashioned views. He has observed that anti-Jewish assumptions are made too easily by some members of his (Bengali) community, whom he perceives as old-fashioned and simplistic. His and also Samed's notion of Islam allows them to openly criticize certain notions of the religion that endorse hatred against others. But Samed's motive to reject hostility against "the Jews" and to argue against assumptions of a general enmity between Muslims and Jews lies, rather, in the fact that he is in love with a Jewish girl in Paris, and such perceptions by friends and family stand in the way of their relationship.

Factors of Influence

The formation of attitudes is a multidimensional process,[80] even more so for complex attitudes such as antisemitic views. In addition to a number of factors of influence, antisemitic attitudes are related to worldviews and to individual psychological processes and mechanisms.[81] The interviews provide only limited data on the latter. However, interviewees referred directly to anti-Jewish views by friends, family, perceptions of religious and ethnic identities, conversations in mosques, diverse media such as television, Internet sources, music, books, newspapers, and, in some cases, school as sources for their antisemitic beliefs.

Being exposed to antisemitic remarks by friends, relatives, antisemitic media, or propaganda certainly enhances antisemitic beliefs but does also not necessarily lead to antisemitic attitudes, as proved by some interviewees who reject antisemitic views despite these factors. Adopting or questioning antisemitic stereotypes and ways of thinking is ultimately a choice made by individuals.

Friends, Peers, and Relatives

Adolescents and young adults are generally strongly influenced in their opinions by peers.[82] Most participants are no exception to this rule and many referred unquestioningly to the antisemitic views of their friends and classmates. What is more, some reported social pressure from their peer group to participate in antisemitic discourse. In some such groups, anti-Jewish attitudes are widespread, and negative views of Jews appear as "common sense" even if Jews are not a constant theme. Antisemitism can be reflected in every-day language, such as with the pejorative use of the term *Jew* in German and French. Particularly worrying are reports of antisemitic behavior by friends or peers, especially if they remained unsanctioned and if participants did not condemn these actions. These add to a normalization of antisemitism and violence against Jews.

Interviewees also mentioned the antisemitic views of their parents and other members of their family. They know that negative views of Jews are not uncommon in their social circles, religious or ethnic communities, or in wider society. Only exceptionally, these views are dismissed as unacceptable or antisemitic; an antisemitic attitude becomes a tenable position.

School

Interviewees also know of anti-Jewish attitudes and behavior from fellow students in school or university. Naresh from London is convinced that a Jewish student in his school would be verbally and physically bullied for no reason but for being Jewish; Bilal from Paris reported that a fellow student hit a Jewish staff member (which he justified). Many participants from Paris and Berlin are accustomed to hearing antisemitic language, including the use of the term *Jew* as an insult from fellow students.

In some cases, interviewees quoted their teachers as a source of antisemitic stereotypes; many had derived the theme of "Jewish influence" from that source. Neoy from London, for example, insisted that it was his history teacher who told him and the whole class in a lesson about the Gulf War that Jews own the media and are very influential people. Others referred to their teachers expressing biased views of the Israeli–Palestinian conflict. Holocaust education in school is also deficient, not only in the sense that participants do not know much about the Holocaust but also because some endorse skewed notions. Aban learned in school that six million Jews were murdered. But he is not convinced of the veracity of this vast number and asked, "How do you still have so many Jews around?" (Aban from London, 26 years old). He believes it would have been impossible for the Hitler to "deal with six million Jews. And then the rest of the world. He can't." Both arguments point to serious deficits of knowledge, an issue that schools could have addressed. For instance, Jewish communities in Europe today cannot be compared to those that existed before the Holocaust, despite the presence today of vibrant communities in some countries. Aban's perception of the history of the Holocaust as focusing solely on the deeds of Hitler is obviously without foundation. However, references to biased assumptions from teachers were exceptional, and other examples show positive influences of teachers and their teaching methods. Moreover, some biased perceptions are explicitly opposed to teachings in school: some are suspicious of Holocaust education in school, suspecting that its motive is to gain support for the State of Israel.[83]

Media

European Muslims follow the media of both their country of origin and their country of residence. Surveys show that Muslims who were born in the country tend to use domestic media more often than those who came at a later stage in their lives.[84] A large majority of interviewees predominantly rely on domestic media—the influence of foreign media is rather indirect and involves parents watching foreign TV or reading newspapers from elsewhere. TV is one of the most important sources quoted as validating antisemitic beliefs about the Israeli–Palestinian conflict and also for supporting stereotypes of rich Jews and Jews running big companies; conspiracy theories appear on television as well. Both foreign and domestic TV were quoted as sources of antisemitic beliefs. However, some of the younger generation face language barriers: young Europeans of Arab background, for example, often hardly understand the Modern Standard Arabic spoken on Arab news channels. Nevertheless, young people watch the images, which are sometimes pointed out to them by their parents. The references made by interviewees give evidence that foreign TV channels, and in particular Arab ones,[85] incite hatred against Jews.

Pictures and programs of German, French, and British TV were also quoted as sources of antisemitic beliefs and conspiracy theories. The picture of the allegedly dying boy Muhammad al-Dura, whose death was wrongly attributed to Israeli soldiers, was shown in the media worldwide in 2000[86] and was referred to by a number of interviewees as an example of the cruelty of Jews killing children.

The Internet was also cited as a source of antisemitic views on the Israeli–Palestinian conflict and as a source of a number of conspiracy theories. For example, Debesh stated that "Big companies, . . . you know Volvo? . . . is owned by Jewish. . . . We got that through the Internet. . . . We did some research" (Debesh from London, 15 years old).

Religious Identity

Muslim identity is a salient part of personal and communal identification for most participants. Many felt a sense of belonging to the global community of Muslims. Research on social identity has shown that "by identifying oneself as a group member, one effectively replaces aspects of individuality and unshared attitudes and behaviors with an 'ingroup prototype' that prescribes shared beliefs, attitudes, and behaviors appropriate to that particular categorization."[87] Therefore, the widespread perception of Muslims and Jews being enemies influences individual perceptions about Jews. The belief goes beyond the adoption of attitudes from friends and family members and can become part of the collective identity. Interviewees used both this generalizing assumption about Muslims and Jews being enemies and specific arguments allegedly rooted in Islam and Islamic history as justifications for their own enmity toward Jews.

Interestingly, the belief that Muslims and Jews are enemies is not necessarily more common among people who practice Islam than among others. A study on Muslims in Germany by Brettfeld and Wetzels found that antisemitism is not only related to the level of religiosity but also to belief patterns. Those with "fundamental" beliefs are more likely to accept antisemitic stereotypes than those with "orthodox-religious" beliefs.[88] Therefore, the content of religious perception is crucial. Another study on prejudices against Muslims and Jews among Danes of Christian background shows similar results for Christians.[89]

Ethnic Identities

It has been pointed out that attitudes toward Jews can vary between different ethnic identities due to historical developments and narratives that are popular within a particular ethnic group.[90] Varying conceptions of Jews among people with different Muslim ethnic identities can be observed on two levels. First, ethnic identity and discourses in the country of origin can be cited directly in arguments for negative views of Jews. These arguments differ to some degree among different ethnicities, and antisemitic attitudes can be enforced by certain ethnic collective identities. Particularly Arab but also such other ethnic identities as Algerian, Egyptian, Pakistani, Bangladeshi, and Maghrebian are seen by some as necessarily correlated to negative views of Jews. Such associations are then adopted as part of the identity of individuals. What makes Arab identity more salient than other ethnic identities on this issue is identification with "the Palestinians" as Arabs. This adds another dimension to the (often-made) religious identification with "the Palestinians" as Muslims. However, this situation only becomes salient if Israelis and Jews are conflated and if the individual holds a Manichean view of the Middle East conflict. Unfortunately, both are more than often the case. It has been argued that anti-Zionism and antisemitism are part and parcel of Arab nationalism.[91] Does this ideology of Arab nationalism influence young Europeans of Arab background in their perceptions about their own identities? Does it determine their attitudes toward Jews? Many participants with Arab backgrounds hold negative views of Jews as part of their Arab identity, while others reject such views. However, the existence of animosity is often an underlying assumption, uttered in passing: "In any case, *nous*, the Arabs, we never get along with them [the Jews]," said one of the participants of Algerian origin (Hafid from Paris, 17 years old). Interviewees used two main rationales for justifying enmity to Jews with Arab identity. They either argued that it is a reaction to the hatred Jews have for Arabs, or they claimed that the Middle East conflict explains why "the Arabs" allegedly dislike Jews. Participants who have Asian, Turkish, or black African background seem to be generally less interested in the Middle East conflict than those of Arab background. Statements such as "Turks dislike Jews" or "Bengalis and Jews hate each other" do occur, but they are relatively rare. Some participants referred to discourses on Jews in their (or their parents') country of origin and have adopted such views. Some respondents of Maghrebian background, for example, referred to the exodus of Jews from these countries and have adopted the perception that Maghrebian Jews prefer to associate with Israel. Other tropes that are voiced in public discourses of the country of origin, such as accusing politicians of being Dönme (crypto-Jews) in Turkey,[92] are not familiar to participants in Europe. In many of the European Muslims' "home" countries, antisemitism and the denial and minimizing of the Holocaust are particularly widespread within the mainstream. The Holocaust is often portrayed in an antisemitic way as a tool used by Israel; conspiracy theories about alleged Nazi–Zionist collaboration are widespread, and Israel is equated with Nazi Germany.[93] The Pew Global Attitudes Project found in 2008 that "While European views towards Jews have become more negative, the deepest anti-Jewish sentiments exist outside of Europe, especially in predominantly Muslim nations. The percentage of Turks, Egyptians, Jordanians, Lebanese and Pakistanis with favorable opinions of Jews is in the single digits."[94] However, while 76 percent in Turkey and Pakistan held unfavorable views of Jews, the numbers in the Arab countries figured in this survey ranged above 95 percent.

We can observe differences between ethnic backgrounds on a quantitative level. That is, interviewees of some ethnic backgrounds, particularly Arab, voice antisemitic attitudes more often and more openly than others. Particular ethnic identities that are opposed to the mainstream collective identity in the country of origin, such as Kurdish or Berber, can be helpful in opposing the antisemitic views of the mainstream. Adherence to some Muslim communities, particularly Alevis, a liberal current of Islam, also correlates with more positive views of Jews.

Islamist Organizations and Mosques

A number of Islamist organizations in Germany, France, and Britain advance antisemitic themes and often cite the Israeli–Palestinian conflict for dissemination of hatred of Jews. Some of these organizations are influential in the participants' local mosques. Interviewees reported that the Israeli–Palestinian conflict is a constant theme of discourses in mosques and among Muslims gathering around mosques, who often have strong anti-Israeli or anti-Jewish tendencies. Stories of Islamic history or of Muhammed's life, which are often told in mosques and madrasas, can also influence conceptions about Jews. Omar and Housni, for example, recalled a story about how a spider web prevented Muhammed from being killed by detractors, and they assumed the detractors were Jews.[95] Other indirect influences on some participants are teachings of a Manichean sort, which posit perceptions of Islam and "true Muslims," on the one hand, and non-Muslims, on the other, and facilitate anti-Jewish attitudes. Such views are taught in some European Islamic institutions.[96] Participants are familiar with radical Islamist organizations such as Hamas, Hizbullah, Muhajiroun, and YMO (Young Muslim Organization). A few interviewees from London mentioned Hizb ut-Tahir as an influential Islamist organization and agree with some of their policies. "They're saying they want an Islamic state in the Muslim world, which I also agree with," said Manoj, and added, "Hizb ut-Tahir is big in this country" (Manoj from London, 26 years old). Hussein referred directly to the organization's attitude on Zionism to support his own attitude. He declared: "Perhaps you can have a link to Hizb ut-Tahrir . . . : they're kind of, the way like we're thinking about Zionists" (Hussein from London, 27 years old). Interviewees from London also quoted leaflets from Muslim organizations urging boycotts against allegedly pro-Israel companies to validate their belief that Jews are rich and run all the large companies. They also believe these companies give financial support to the Israeli army. Some even praised radical Islamist organizations such as Hamas and Hizbullah because they fight Israel and Jews effectively. One participant said about Hamas: "Finally a really good party, that is taking up something against the Jews. That is doing something for their country, not like the PLO . . ." (Suleiman from Berlin, 15 years old). Even though Hamas is active in Europe and disseminates propaganda material,[97] Hamas and also Hizbullah are generally known from mainstream media for their fight against Israel. These and other Islamist organizations use the Israeli–Palestinian conflict for propaganda purposes and often raise money for charity for "the Palestinians." Hence, Islamist organizations are often known for helping Palestine. Azhar gave evidence that these collections are frequent: "Here in the area there are only Arab bakeries, that means, you go there and there is a little jar, where you can read 'for Palestine, help for Palestine" (Azhar from Paris, 17 years old).

The Influence of the Level of Formal Education

Interviewees have very different levels of formal education, ranging from early school leavers to university graduates. Expressions of antisemitic attitudes change with the level of education. Those with a higher level of formal education tend to show antipathy toward Jews in more socially acceptable ways. They use insinuations and make negative allegations about Jews and about Jewish influence in the finance sector and media. They also promote conspiracy theories and the demonization of Israel. However, these people are less prone to offer open approval of violence against Jews or use expressions of hatred. This correlation matches findings on antisemitic attitudes in the general society.[98]

Influences of Experiences and Perceptions of Discrimination

What are the links between experiences or perceptions of discrimination and antisemitic attitudes? European Muslims do face discrimination and many interviewees feel this to be true. They find it mostly outside their own neighborhoods, and it is expressed often through hostile looks, insults, threats, and even physical attacks. Participants talk of certain prejudices, such as stereotyping Arabs as thieves, blacks as aggressive, and Muslims as terrorists. The perception of otherness varies in the three countries. Generally, interviewees in Berlin feel that there is discrimination against *Ausländer* or "foreigners," based on skin color (and hair color). They often perceive themselves as foreigners despite having German nationality. In Paris, the impression is that discrimination is focused foremost on Arabs and blacks, based on skin color, Arab names, and stigmatized areas of residence. In London, many think that discrimination is based on skin color, too, but others believe that it is currently the anti-Muslim prejudices which prevail. Major differences also exist between the three countries in respondents' identifications with the respective national identity. In Germany, interviewees generally accept and internalize their non-acceptance as Germans, despite some of them having a German passport. They demand to be accepted as "foreigners" or "Turks" or "Arabs" within Germany. In France, by contrast, most interviewees consider themselves French even though many have the feeling that they are not accepted as such. In Britain, the non-acceptance as British seems to be less of an issue than in France, although some voiced concerns about either direct or institutional non-acceptance and discrimination against them as members of ethnic or religious minorities. Most respondents from Britain identified Britishness as an important dimension of their identity, often in combination with their ethnic background and in self-descriptions such as "British-Asian."

What is the relationship between perceptions of discrimination and exclusion and antisemitic attitudes?

A number of participants showed that despite having suffered from discrimination they do not believe in antisemitic stereotypes, and many of those who do not feel discriminated against showed blatant forms of hatred against Jews. The same is true for those with a precarious status of residence in opposition to those who are citizens of the country of residence: both groups contain people with and without antisemitic views. If there is a statistical correlation between discrimination and antisemitism, it is not striking within the sample. Looking into possible correlations between antisemitic attitudes and feelings of exclusion—taking the perception of otherness and the self-identification with the nationality as indicators—also shows no connection. The perception of otherness and self-identification with the respective nationality is very different in each of the countries, while antisemitic attitudes are very similar.

Focusing only on statistical correlations, however, may be misleading because the relations between discrimination and antisemitism are too complex to be described as a simple correlation and certainly cannot be called a straightforward relation of cause and effect. Some perceptions of discrimination even include antisemitic views. A number of participants who perceive the Muslim community as being threatened and denigrated in the context of an alleged war against Muslims believe that this threat is led or supported by "the Jews." Jews are imagined as being the driving force behind U.S. military action in Afghanistan and Iraq, fighting a war against "the Muslims" in Palestine, or denigrating Muslims through their influence in the media. These negative views often go hand-in-hand with perceptions of a global war between Muslims and non-Muslims. In this Manichean worldview, Jews are identified as enemies of "the Muslims." Similarly, the rhetoric of victimhood competition can contain antisemitic arguments.[99] A statistical correlation of these perceptions would therefore merely confirm that antisemitic interpretations of discrimination and Manichean perceptions of wars between Muslims and non-Muslims are indeed related to antisemitic attitudes.

Conclusions

Most antisemitic views embraced by young European Muslims are fragmented and multifaceted. They can neither be reduced solely to hatred of Israel nor to references to Islam or Muslim identity. They are not a result of discrimination. The majority of interviewees displayed antisemitic resentments in at least one way or another. Negative attitudes toward Jews were often openly exhibited, at times aggressively, including calls for violence against Jews. Negative views of Jews have even become the norm in some social circles.

Interviewees gave evidence of influence for the genesis or acceptance of antisemitic views, such as friends' and family members' anti-Jewish views, perceptions of religious and ethnic identities, conversations in and around mosques, and diverse media. But none of these identified factors necessarily leads to the development of antisemitic attitudes. Frequent exposure to antisemitic remarks, media, or propaganda certainly enhances negative views of Jews, but such exposure also does not necessarily lead to antisemitic attitudes, as proven by interviewees who reject antisemitic views despite these factors. In the end, the adoption of antisemitic stereotypes and ways of thinking is a choice made by individuals, although the social environment is a major factor.

Many forms, and a number of sources, of antisemitic expressions are probably similar to those expressed by youth from other backgrounds in their respective countries. However, direct references to sources in religious and ethnic identity as well as from Islam in support of negative views of Jews represent a specific dimension. In this sense, the use of the term *Muslim antisemitism* is apt and meaningful.

Four main categories of anti-Jewish hostility emerged from the interviews. First is the persistence of "classic" antisemitic attitudes. This category comprises antisemitic conspiracy theories and well-known stereotypes of Jews, such as assumptions that Jews are rich or stingy. The second category promotes negative views of Jews with reference to Israel. A conflation of Jews and Israelis and a Manichean view of the Palestinian–Israeli conflict are frequent preconditions for such views. Certain tropes such as "Jews kill children" clearly stir up emotions and are used to justify hatred of Jews, including Jews in the neighborhood. A third pattern includes negative views of Jews with direct reference to Islam, Muslim identity, or ethnic identity, as all three are often conflated. These views are often voiced in assumptions such as "Muslims hate Jews." Negative associations of Jews made in accordance with the tenets of collective identity or with perceptions of "Islam" make it difficult for respondents to distance themselves from such assumptions. A fourth category of anti-Jewish hostility is devoid of arguments. Some young Muslims express enmity toward Jews as such and do not bother to give any putative arguments for such enmity. They reveal a normalization of negative views of Jews and show the true character of antisemitism: Jews are hated because they are Jews.

Appendix

WORKING DEFINITION OF ANTISEMITISM[100]

The purpose of this document is to provide a practical guide for identifying incidents, collecting data, and supporting the implementation and enforcement of legislation dealing with antisemitism.

Working definition: "Antisemitism is a certain perception of Jews, which may be expressed as hatred toward Jews. Rhetorical and physical manifestations of antisemitism are directed toward Jewish or non-Jewish individuals and/or their property, toward Jewish community institutions and religious facilities."

In addition, such manifestations could also target the State of Israel, conceived as a Jewish collectivity. Antisemitism frequently charges Jews with conspiring to harm humanity, and it is often used to blame Jews for "why things go wrong." It is expressed in speech, writing, visual forms and action, and employs sinister stereotypes and negative character traits.

Contemporary examples of antisemitism in public life, the media, schools, the workplace, and in the religious sphere could, taking into account the overall context, include, but are not limited to:

- Calling for, aiding, or justifying the killing or harming of Jews in the name of a radical ideology or an extremist view of religion.
- Making mendacious, dehumanizing, demonizing, or stereotypical allegations about Jews as such or the power of Jews as collective—such as, especially but not exclusively, the myth about a world Jewish conspiracy or of Jews controlling the media, economy, government, or other societal institutions.
- Accusing Jews as a people of being responsible for real or imagined wrongdoing committed by a single Jewish person or group, or even for acts committed by non-Jews.
- Denying the fact, scope, mechanisms (e.g. gas chambers) or intentionality of the genocide of the Jewish people at the hands of National Socialist Germany and its supporters and accomplices during World War II (the Holocaust).
- Accusing the Jews as a people, or Israel as a state, of inventing or exaggerating the Holocaust.

- Accusing Jewish citizens of being more loyal to Israel, or to the alleged priorities of Jews worldwide, than to the interests of their own nations.

Examples of the ways in which antisemitism manifests itself with regard to the State of Israel taking into account the overall context could include:

- Denying the Jewish people their right to self-determination, e.g., by claiming that the existence of a State of Israel is a racist endeavor.
- Applying double standards by requiring of it a behavior not expected or demanded of any other democratic nation.
- Using the symbols and images associated with classic antisemitism (e.g., claims of Jews killing Jesus or blood libel) to characterize Israel or Israelis.
- Drawing comparisons of contemporary Israeli policy to that of the Nazis.
- Holding Jews collectively responsible for actions of the State of Israel.

However, criticism of Israel similar to that leveled against any other country cannot be regarded as antisemitic.

Antisemitic acts are criminal when they are so defined by law (for example, denial of the Holocaust or distribution of antisemitic materials in some countries).

Criminal acts are antisemitic when the targets of attacks, whether they are people or property—such as buildings, schools, places of worship and cemeteries—are selected because they are, or are perceived to be, Jewish or linked to Jews.

Antisemitic discrimination is the denial to Jews of opportunities or services available to others and is illegal in many countries.

NOTES

1. See Barry Rubin, *The Muslim Brotherhood: The Organization and Policies of a Global Islamist Movement* (New York: Palgrave Macmillan, 2010). See also Brigitte Maréchal, *The Muslim Brothers in Europe: Roots and Discourse* (Leiden: Brill, 2008).

2. For Germany, see Bundesamt für Migration und Flüchtlinge, *Muslimisches Leben in Deutschland*, 2009, pp. 173–81. For France, see Samir Amghar, "Les mutations de l'islamisme en France. Portrait de l'UOIF, porte-parole de l'islamisme de minorité,'" *La vie des idees* 22/23 (June 2007). For the UK, see Munira Mirza, Zain Ja²far, and Abi Senthilkumaran, *Living Apart Together: British Muslims and the Paradox of Multiculturalism* (London: Policy Exchange, 2007).

3. Gallup, *The Gallup Coexist Index 2009: A Global Study of Interfaith Relations. With an in-depth analysis of Muslim Integration in France, Germany, and the United Kingdom*, 2009.

4. Renate Göllner and Gerhard Scheit argued that people in post-Nazi societies envy Muslims for today's more successful ideology of Islamism as an ideology of collectivity, compared to the time of fascist Nazism. See Gerhard Scheit and Renate Göllner, "Alpendonaunazis für Ahmadinejad," *Hagalil* (April 16, 2010).

5. Robert S. Wistrich provides an excellent overview with numerous examples. See his *A Lethal Obsession: Anti-Semitism from Antiquity to the Global Jihad* (New York: Random House, 2010). See also Pierre-André Taguieff, *Rising from the Muck: The New Anti-semitism in Europe* (Chicago: Ivan R. Dee, 2004).

6. A recent comparative study of eight European countries reveals that 24.5 percent agree that Jews have too much influence in their country and that 41.2 percent suppose that "Jews try to take advantage of having been victims during the Nazi era." However, there are significant differences among the countries. See Andreas Zick, Beate Küpper, and Hinna Wolf, *European Conditions: Findings of a Study on Group-focused Enmity in Europe* (Institute for Interdisciplinary Research on Conflict and Violence, University of Bielefeld, 2009), http://www.amadeu-antonio-stiftung.de/w/files/pdfs/gfepressrelease_english.pdf.

7. Eirik Eiglad, *The Anti-Jewish Riots in Oslo* (Porsgrunn, Norway: Communalism Press, 2010).

8. On March, 19, 2012 Mohamed Merah opened fire in front of the Ozar Hatorah school in Toulouse. The gunman chased people inside the building and shot at them. He grabbed a seven-year-old girl, shooting her at close range. He then retrieved his moped and drove off. Gabriel (4), Arieh (5), their father and teacher at the school, Jonathan Sandler, and Myriam Monsonégo (7) were killed and a seventeen-year-old student was gravely injured. The perpetrator, who also had killed three unarmed French soldiers some days earlier, filmed his crimes, intending to publish them on the Internet and on Al Jazeera. See "Mohammed Merah and Abdelkader Merah: Shootings in Toulouse, France," *New York Times* (April 4, 2012).

9. The self-named "gang des barbares" abducted Ilan Halimi because he was Jewish. Members of the gang tortured him for three weeks and eventually murdered him in a Parisian suburb. See "Meurtre d'Ilan Halimi: le 'gang des barbares' jugé en appel, sans son leader," *Le Monde* (October 25, 2010).

10. Günther Jikeli, "Der neue alte Antisemitismus Müssen Juden sich wieder verstecken?," *Stern* (September 14, 2012).

11. Johannes Wiedermann, "Angriff auf Tanzgruppe: Der alltägliche Antisemitismus in Hannover-Sahlkamp," *Welt Online* (June 25, 2010).

12. Amadeu Antonio Stiftung, *"Die Juden sind schuld." Antisemitismus in der Einwanderungsgesellschaft am Beispiel muslimisch sozialisierter Milieus. Beispiele, Erfahrungen und Handlungsoptionen aus der pädagogischen und kommunalen Arbeit* (Berlin, 2009).

13. Emmanuel Brenner, *Les territoires perdus de la République: antisémitisme, racisme et sexisme en milieu scolaire* (Paris: Mille et Une Nuits, 2004).

14. See, for example, Christine Schmitt, "Bei Gefahr 0800 880280," *Jüdische Allgemeine* (October 25, 2010); "Un rabbin agressé à la gare du Nord," *Le Monde* (April 21, 2007); Nick Cohen, "Following Mosley's East End Footsteps," *The Observer* (April 17, 2005); Leon Symons, "Teacher 'Sacked for Challenging Antisemitism,'" *The Jewish Chronicle* (February 9, 2010); Léa Khayata, "Battles of Paris: Anti-Semitism in the 19th Arrondissement, a Neighborhood with a Recent History of Violence," *Tablet Magazine* (February 11, 2010).

15. Donald Snyder, "For Jews, Swedish City Is a 'Place to Move Away From,'" *Forward* (July 16, 2010).

16. For France, see Commission nationale consultative des droits de l'homme (CNCDH), *La lutte contre le racisme et la xénophobie: rapport d'activité 2008, 2009*, p. 28, http://www.cncdh.fr/IMG/pdf/rapport_racisme_antisemitisme_et_xenophobie_2008.pdf. For the UK, see the reports issued by the Community Security Trust (CST): http://www.thecst.org.uk/.

17. However, a report on Berlin shows that twelve of thirty-three acts of antisemitic and anti-Israeli violence between 2003 and 2005 were committed by "foreigners" and fifteen by right-wing extremists. Senatsverwaltung für Inneres und Sport, Abteilung Verfassungsschutz, *Antisemitismus im extremistischen Spektrum Berlins* (Berlin, 2006), p. 53.

18. The perpetrators of threats, including inscriptions, often remain unknown but according to figures from the French CNCDH for the year 2009, 13 percent of antisemitic threats in France were related to neo-Nazi ideology and 5 percent were committed by people of Arab or Muslim background. Commission nationale consultative des droits de l'homme (CNCDH), *La lutte contre le racisme, a ntisémitisme et la xénophobie. Année 2009, 2010*, p. 45, http://lesrapp orts.ladocumentationfrancaise.fr/BRP /104000267/0000.pdf. Bergmann and Wetzel observed already in 2003 that different forms of antisemitic actions can be assigned to different groups of perpetrators. Bergmann and Wetzel, *Manifestations of anti-Semitism in the European Union*, pp. 25–26.

19. The study is available online: Bergmann and Wetzel, *Manifestations of anti-Semitism in the European Union*, http://www.cohn-bendit.de/depot/standpunkte /Manifestations%20of%20anti-Semitism%20in%20the%20European%20Union_EN.pdf.

20. Peter Widmann, "Der Feind kommt aus dem Morgenland. Rechtspopulistische "Islamkritiker" um den Publizisten Hans-Peter Raddatz suchen die Opfergemeinschaft mit Juden," ed. Wolfgang Benz, *Jahrbuch für Antisemitismusforschung* (2008), pp. 45–68.

21. Thomas Schmidinger, "Zur Islamisierung des Antisemitismus," in *Jahrbuch 2008* (Vienna: Lit Verlag, 2008), pp. 103–139.

22. Jochen Müller, "Von Antizionismus und Antisemitismus. Stereotypenbildung in der arabischen Öffentlichkeit," in *Anitsemitismus in Europa und in der arabischen Welt.*

Ursachen und Wechselbeziehungen eines komplexen Phänomens, ed. Wolfgang Ansorge (Paderborn: Bonifatius, 2006), pp. 163–82; Wistrich, *A Lethal Obsession;* see also Gilles Kepel, Jean-Pierre Milelli, and Pascale Ghazaleh, *Al Qaeda in Its Own Words* (Cambridge, Mass.: Belknap Press of Harvard University Press, 2008).

23. See the Pew Global Attitudes Project, Little Enthusiasm for Many Muslim Leaders, 2009; The Pew Global Attitudes Project, Muslim-Western Tensions Persist, 2011; see www.pewglobal.org.

24. Thomas L. Friedman, "America vs. The Narrative," *New York Times* (November 29, 2009).

25. This publication by the Ministry of the Interior shows that Milli Görüs is considered an Islamist organization by the German authorities. Bundesministerium des Inneren, Verfassungsschutzbericht 2009, p. 228. Other Islamist organizations are also active in Germany. See also Senatsverwaltung für Inneres und Sport, Abteilung Verfassungsschutz, *Antisemitismus im extremistischen Spektrum Berlins,* 2006, pp. 19–23.

26. Samir Amghar, "Les mutations de l'islamisme en France. Portrait de l'UOIF, porte-parole de l'"islamisme de minorité'," *La vie des idees* 22/23 (June 2007), http://www.laviedesidees.fr/Les-mutations-de-lislamisme-en.html.

27. Martin Bright, *When Progressives Treat with Reactionaries: The British State's Flirtation with Radical Islamism* (London: Policy Exchange, 2006); John Ware, "MCB in the Dock," *Prospec* (December 16, 2006).

28. Sabine am Orde, Pascal Beucker, Wolf Schmidt, and Daniel Wiese, "Islamismus in Deutschland: Die netten Herren von Milli Görüs," *Tageszeitung (taz)* (July 18, 2010). The IHH e.V. in Germany has common roots with the Turkish IHH that was central in the organization of the Gaza Flotilla in 2010.

29. Aycan Demirel, "Kreuzberger Initiative gegen Antisemitismus," *DAVID—Jüdische Kulturzeitschrift,* no. 69 (June 2006), http://davidkultur.at/ausgabe.php?ausg=69&artikel=563.

30. The Stephen Roth Institute for the Study of Antisemitism and Racism, *Country Report: France 2007* (Tel Aviv, 2008), http://www.tau.ac.il/Anti-Semitism/asw2007/france.html.

31. About half of all Islamic places of worship in the United Kingdom are run by Deobandi-affiliated scholars. Deobandi is a revivalist, Islamist movement. See Andrew Norfolk, "Hardline takeover of British Masjid," *The Times* (September 7, 2007).

32. Riyadh ul Haq, Riyadh ul Haq sermon on "Jewish Fundamentalism" in full, in *The Times* (September 6, 2007).

33. Michael Whine, "The Advance of the Muslim Brotherhood in the UK," *Current Trends in Islamist Ideology* 2 (2005), pp. 30–39.

34. All-Party Parliamentary Group against Antisemitism (United Kingdom), "Report of the All-Party Parliamentary Inquiry into Antisemitism"(London: The Stationery Office Limited, 2006), pp. 27–29. See also Wistrich, *A Lethal Obsession,* pp. 397–98.

35. Denis MacEoin, *The Hijacking of British Islam: How Extremist Literature Is Subverting Mosques in the UK* (London: Policy Exchange, 2007).

36. James Brandon and Douglas Murray, *Hate on the State: How British Libraries Encourage Islamic Extremism* (London: Centre for Social Cohesion, 2007).

37. Particularly textbooks of the twenty-four Saudi schools in the UK have been criticized in the past for their messages of hate and antisemitism. See Nina Shea, "This Is a Saudi Textbook (After the Intolerance Was Removed)," *The Washington Post* (March 26, 2010); Denis MacEoin, *Music, Chess and Other Sins: Segregation, Integration, and Muslim Schools in Britain* (London: Civitas, 2009).

38. Andrew Bostom, *The Legacy of Islamic Antisemitism: From Sacred Texts to Solemn History* (Amherst, N.Y.: Prometheus Books, 2008).

39. Hans-Peter Raddatz, for example, generalizes Muslims in an essentialist way. See his *Allah und die Juden. Die islamische Renaissance des Antisemitismus* (Berlin: Wolf Jobst Siedler, 2007).

40. Georges Vajda, "Jews and Muslims according to the Hadith," in Bostom, pp. 235–60.

41. For a debate on the role of Arab Muslims during the Holocaust, see Götz Nordbruch, *Nazism in Syria and Lebanon: The Ambivalence of the German Option, 1933–1945* (London and New York: Routledge, 2009); Robert Satloff, *Among the Righteous: Lost Stories from the Holocaust's Long Reach into Arab Lands*(New York: Public Affairs, 2006); Matthias Küntzel, *Jihad and Jew-hatred: Islamism, Nazism and the Roots of 9/11* (New York: Telos, 2007); Martin Cüppers and Klaus-Michael Mallmann, *Halbmond und Hakenkreuz* (Darmstadt: Wissenschaftliche Buchgesellschaft, 2006). There are also a number of positive examples of Muslims who rescued Jews during the Holocaust, e.g., in Albania; see Norman H. Gershman, *Besa, a Code of Honor: Muslim Albanians Who Rescued Jews during the Holocaust* (Jerusalem: Yad Vashem, 2007).

42. See Günther Jikeli and Joëlle Allouche-Benayoun, eds., *Perceptions of the Holocaust in Europe and Muslim Communities,* Muslims in Global Societies Series 7 (Dordrecht and New York: Springer, 2013).

43. The Pew Global Attitudes Project, *The Great Divide: How Westerners and Muslims View Each Other,* pp. 42–43. The survey was conducted before the Lebanon War in summer 2006.

44. Katrin Brettfeld and Peter Wetzels, *Muslime in Deutschland* (Berlin: Bundesministerium des Inneren, 2007), pp. 274–75.

45. These attitudes were measured with the following items: "Because of the Israeli policies, I increasingly dislike Jews"; "Regarding Israel's policy I do understand if one is against Jews"; "In my religion, the Jews bring mischief to the world"; "Jews have too much influence in the world"; "What the State of Israel is doing with the Palestinians is principally nothing else than what the Nazis in the Third Reich did with the Jews"; "The Jews in all the world feel stronger attached to Israel than to the country where they live."

46. Mansel, Jürgen and Viktoria Spaiser. 2010. Abschlussbericht Forschungsprojekt "Soziale Beziehungen, Konfliktpotentiale und Vorurteile im Kontext von Erfahrungen verweigerter Teilhabe und Anerkennung bei Jugendlichen mit und ohne Migrationshintergrund," http://www.vielfalt-tutgut. de/content/e4458/e8260/Uni_Bielefeld _Abschlussbericht_Forschungsprojekt.pdf and http://www.vielfalt-tutgut.de/content /e4458/e8277/Uni_Bielefeld_Tabellenanhang.pdf.

47. Wilhelm Heitmeyer, Joachim Müller, and Helmut Schröder, *Verlockender Fundamentalismus: türkische Jugendliche in Deutschland* (Frankfurt: Suhrkamp, 1997), pp. 181, 271.

48. Christine Agger, "Jødehad er udbredt blandt indvandrere," in *Kristeligt Dagblad* (November 25, 2009).

49. Populus/Times, Muslims Poll (2005), http://www.populus.co.uk/uploads/Muslim_Poll-Times.pdf.

50. The Living History Forum, *Intolerance: Anti-Semitic, Homophobic, Islamophobic and Xenophobic Tendencies among the Young* (Stockholm: Brottsförebyggande rådet [BRA]: 2005), pp. 40, 152–53, http://www.levandehistoria.se/files/INTOLERANCEENG_0.pdf.

51. Among Frenchmen of African or Turkish origin antisemitism reaches 46 percent of practicing Muslims, 40 percent of "infrequently" observant Muslims, 30 percent among nonpracticing Muslims, and 23 percent among those who have no religion. See Sylvain Brouard and Vincent Tiberj, *Français comme les autres: enquête sur les citoyens d'origine maghrébine, africaine et turque* (Paris: Presses de la fondation nationale des sciences politiques, 2005), p. 104.

52. Vincent Tiberj, "Anti-Semitism in an Ethnically Diverse France: Questioning and Explaining the Specificities of African-, Turkish-, and Maghrebian-French," *Working Paper No. 33, American University of Paris*, (2006), p.12, http://www.aup.fr/pdf/WPSeries/AUP_wp33-Tiberj.pdf; Brouard und Tiberj, Francais comme les autres ?

53. Robert S. Wistrich, *European Anti-Semitism Reinvents Itself* (New York: American Jewish Committee, 2005), p. 8. See also Wistrich, *A Lethal Obsession*. On the theological difficulties of Muslims living in non-Muslim majority countries as in Europe and on perceptions of Islamists of those countries, see Nina Wiedl, "Dawa and the Islamist Revival in the West," *Current Trends in Islamist Ideology* 9 (2009), http://www.currenttrends.org/research/detail/dawa-and-the-islamist-revivalin-the-west.

54. Klaus Holz, *Die Gegenwart des Antisemitismus: Islamistische, demokratische und antizionistische Judenfeindschaft* (Hamburg: Hamburger Edition, 2005), p. 9.

55. Brian Klug, "Anti-Semitism—New or Old?," *The Nation* (April 12, 2004). John Bunzl cites this quote approvingly in his "Spiegelbilder—Wahrnehmung und Interesse im Israel-Palästina-Konflikt" in John Bunzl and Alexandra Senfft, eds., *Zwischen Antisemitismus und Islamophobie. Vorurteile und Projektionen in Europa und Nahost* (Hamburg: VSA Verlag, 2008), p. 141.

56. Michel Wieviorka, *La tentation antisémite: haine des Juifs dans la France d'aujourd'hui* (Paris: Laffont, 2005), pp. 143–58. The book has been translated into English by Kristin Couper Lobel and Anna Declerck, as *The Lure of Anti-Semitism: Hatred of Jews in Present-Day France* (Leiden: Brill, 2007).

57. Brian Klug, "The Myth of the New Anti-Semitism," *The Nation* (January 15, 2004).

58. Paul A. Silverstein, "The Context of Antisemitism and Islamophobia in France," *Patterns of Prejudice* 42, no. 1 (2008), p. 4.

59. Paul A. Silverstein, "Comment on Bunzl," in Matti Bunzl, ed., *Anti-Semitism and Islamophobia: Hatreds Old and New in Europe* (Chicago: Prickly Paradigm Press, 2007), pp. 64–65.

60. Bunzl, *Anti-Semitism and Islamophobia*, pp. 26–27.

61. (My transation.) Pierre-André Taguieff, *Prêcheurs de haine. Traversée de la judéophobie planétaire* (Paris: Mille et une nuit, 2004), p. 185.

62. See note 57.

63. Didier Lapeyronnie, "La Demande D'Antisémitisme. Antisémitisme, racisme et exclusion sociale," *Les études du CRIF* no. 9 (Paris, 2005), 44 pp.

64. Wieviorka, pp. 144–45.

65. Günther Jikeli, "Anti-Semitism in Youth Language: The Pejorative Use of the Terms for 'Jew' in German and French Today," *Conflict & Communication Online* 9, no. 1 (2010), pp. 1–13.

66. Unfortunately, mostly for practical reasons I had to restrict the participants to male interviewees. Young men are easier to contact spontaneously in the streets; they are more present than their female counterparts, and are more willing to give an interview. However, as outlined above, most perpetrators of antisemitic incidents are male (and young). Paul Iganski, Vicky Kielinger, and Susan Paterson, *Hate Crimes against London's Jews: An Analysis of Incidents Recorded by the Metropolitan Police Service 2001–2004* (London: Institute for Jewish Policy Research, 2005).

67. Eight out of 117 interviewees were interviewed individually in a youth club. All other interviews took place outdoors in public places.

68. The role of the interviewer was tested, comparing interviews with a male and a female interviewer of Turkish Muslim background and one female and one male interviewer of German Christian background. There was no significant difference in the openness of the interviewees regarding the main topics. All interviewers established a good level of communication with the interviewees. However, some of the male interviewees made sexual advances toward the female interviewer of German Christian background. The non-Muslim background was helpful for emphasizing the role of an outsider in order to probe the topic in greater detail.

69. Respondents were asked about their age and religious affiliation in the course of the interview, not necessarily in the beginning. Therefore, some interviews were also conducted with people of other ages and religious affiliations. Two interviews are included in the analysis with respondents who were thirteen years old and one with a respondent who was age thirty. Their views do not stand out from the rest of the participants.

70. This approach is used in Grounded Theory. However, the analytical strategy applied is too focused for an orthodox method of Grounded Theory. See Jane C. Hood, "Orthodoxy vs. Power: The Defining Traits of Grounded Theory," in Antony Bryant and Kathy Charmaz, eds., *The SAGE Handbook of Grounded Theory* (Thousand Oaks, Calif.: SAGE Publications, 2010), pp. 151–64.

71. Christiane Schmidt, "The Analysis of Semi-structured Interviews," in Uwe Flick, Ernst von Kardoff, and Ines Steinke, eds., *A Companion to Qualitative Research* (London and Thousand Oaks, Calif.: SAGE Publications, 2004), pp. 253–58. The analytical strategy proposed by Schmidt was adopted for this study and was successfully applied by Walter R. Heinz et. al. on semistructured interviews with young people on work-related issues. See Walter R. Heinz et al., "Vocational Training and Career Develop-

ment in Germany: Results from a Longitudinal Study," in *International Journal of Behavioral Development* 22, no. 1 (1998), pp. 77–101.

72. Italics in original. Helen Fein, "Dimensions of Antisemitism: Attitudes, Collective Accusations, and Actions," in Helen Fein, ed., *The Persisting Question. Sociological Perspectives and Social Contexts of Modern Antisemitism* (Berlin and New York: De Gruyter, 1987), p. 67.

73. http://www.adl.org/PresRele/ASInt_13/5465_13.htm.

74. A current example is the website http://www.inminds.com, which also promotes a flyer naming companies to boycott for alleged "Zionist" connections. Currently, Sainsbury's, Tesco, and Iceland are not part of their list. However, I found such a flyer calling for a boycott of Sainsbury's and other companies distributed in Tower Hamlets in 2007.

75. No interviewee distinguished between different political fractions within Israel. But one interviewee, Jamil, of Palestinian background who explicitly rejected negative views of Jews among peers, distinguished between the Jewish population and "Jewish" politics.

76. Tarek Fatah is probably the most prominent contemporary scholar who writes from a Muslim perspective to dispute the assumption that Muslims and Jews are enemies. See Tarek Fatah, *The Jew Is Not My Enemy: Unveiling the Myths That Fuel Muslim Anti-Semitism* (Toronto: McClelland & Stewart, 2010). See also Bassam Tibi, *Islamism and Islam* (New Haven, Conn.: Yale University Press, 2012).

77. I borrowed this term from Gavin I. Langmuir, "Towards a Definition of Antisemitism," in Fein, pp. 86–127.

78. Jikeli, pp. 1–13.

79. Helen Fein stresses the importance of anti-antisemites, pp. 67–85.

80. William Crano and Radmila Prislin, *Attitudes and Attitude Change* (New York; London: Psychology Press, 2008).

81. Scholars have discussed a number of reasons for the development of antisemitic attitudes, including transmission of stereotypes and beliefs, psychological mechanisms of group dynamics, or unreflected projections. For a discussion of different theories, see Samuel Salzborn, *Antisemitismus als negative Leitidee der Moderne: sozialwissenschaftliche Theorien im Vergleich* (Frankfurt and New York: Campus, 2010).

82. Mitchell Prinstein and Kenneth A. Dodge, *Understanding Peer Influence in Children and Adolescents* (New York: Guilford Press, 2008).

83. For a more detailed analysis of young Muslims' views of the Holocaust, see Günther Jikeli, "Perceptions of the Holocaust Among Young Muslims in Berlin, Paris and London," in Jikeli and Allouche-Benayoun, eds., *Perceptions of the Holocaust in Europe and Muslim Communities.*

84. See Erk Simon and Gerhard Kloppenburg, "Das Fernsehpublikum türkischer Herkunft—Fernsehnutzung, Einstellungen und Programmerwartungen," *Media Perspektiven* no. 3 (2007), pp. 142–52; Brettfeld and Wetzels, pp. 95–98.

85. Interviewees referred to Al Manar, LBC, Al Jazeera, and others. Arab news channels are notorious for their antisemitic programs. For examples and reports, visit http://www.memri.org/antisemitism.html.

86. Pierre-André Taguieff, "L'affaire al-Dura ou le renforcement des stéréotypes antijuifs . . . ," *Le Meilleur des mondes* (September 2008).

87. Henry E. Hale, "Explaining Ethnicity," *Comparative Political Studies* 37, no. 4 (May 1, 2004), p. 470.

88. Brettfeld and Wetzels, pp. 279–80.

89. Frans W. P. van der Slik and Ruben P. Konig, "Orthodox, Humanitarian, and Science-Inspired Belief in Relation to Prejudice against Jews, Muslims, and Ethnic Minorities: The Content of One's Belief Does Matter," *International Journal for the Psychology of Religion* 16, no. 2 (2006): pp. 113–26.

90. Gabriel Fréville, Susanna Harms, and Serhat Karakayali, "'Antisemitismus—ein Problem unter vielen.' Ergebnisse einer Befragung in Jugendclubs und Migrant/innen-organizationen," in Wolfram Stender, Guido Follert, and Mihri Özdogan, eds., *Konstellationen des Antisemitismus Antisemitismusforschung und sozialpädagogische Praxis* (Wiesbaden: VS Verl. für Sozialwiss., 2010), pp. 185–96.

91. Müller, "Von Antizionismus und Antisemitismus."

92. Rıfat N. Bali, *A Scapegoat for All Seasons: The Dönmes or Crypto-Jews of Turkey* (Istanbul: Isis Press, 2008).

93. See Meir Litvak and Esther Webman, *From Empathy to Denial: Arab Responses to the Holocaust* (New York: Columbia University Press, 2009). In a number of Turkish newspapers, Israel is frequently equated with Nazi Germany. It is claimed that the Holocaust has been turned into an industry to act as a cover for all of Israel's alleged atrocities, to an extent uncommon in German, French, and British newspapers. See Rıfat N. Bali, "Present-Day Anti-Semitism in Turkey," *Post-Holocaust and Anti-Semitism* (Institute for Global Jewish Affairs), no. 84 (August 16, 2009), http://jcpa.org/article/present-day-anti-semitism-in-turkey/. See also Jikeli and Allouche-Benayoun, eds., *Perceptions of the Holocaust in Europe and Muslim Communities.*

94. Pew Global Attitudes Project, *Unfavorable Views of Jews and Muslims on the Increase in Europe (Full Report)*, 2008, p. 5, http://pewglobal.org/files/2011/03/Pew-2008-Pew-Global-Attitudes-Report-3-September.pdf. The survey conducted in March/April 2011 produced similar results; see The Pew Global Attitudes Project, "Muslim-Western Tensions Persist," 2001; see http://www.pewglobal.org/2011/07/21/muslim-western-tensionspersist/.

95. A popular story, based on a Hadith about Muhammed's flight to Medinah in 622, known as the Hijrah, says that Muhammed hid in a cave and a spider's freshly woven web misled his detractors, usually described as unbelievers or polytheists and not Jews. However, Omar and Housni may have confused that report with descriptions of fights between Muhammed and Jews or with another popular story in which a Jewish woman tried to poison Mohammed, described in the Sira of Ibn Sa'd. See Georges Vajda, "Jews and Muslims according to the Hadith," in Andrew Bostom, ed. *The Legacy of Islamic Antisemitism*, pp. 235–60.

96. Denis MacEoin, *Music, Chess and Other Sins: Segregation, Integration, and Muslim Schools in Britain* (London: Civitas: Institute for the Study of Civil Society, 2009).

97. Intelligence and Terrorism Information Center, "Britain as a Focus for Hamas' Political, Propaganda and Legal Activities in Europe," February 21, 2010, http://www.terrorism-info.org.il/malam_multimedia/English/eng_n/html/hamas_e097.htm.

98. Dirk Baier, Christian Pfeiffer, Julia Simonson, and Susann Rabold, *Jugendliche in Deutschland als Opfer und Täter von Gewalt* (Hanover: Kriminologisches Forschungsinstitut Niedersachsen, 2009), p. 116; Werner Bergmann and Rainer Erb, "Antisemitismus in der Bundesrepublik Deutschland 1996," in Richard Alba, Peter Schmidt, and Martina Wasmer, eds., *Deutsche und Ausländer: Freunde, Fremde oder Feinde?: empirische Befunde und theoretische Erklärungen* (Wiesbaden: Westdeutscher Verlag, 2000), p. 414.

99. Bernard Henri Lévy, *Ce grand cadavre à la renverse* (Paris: Grasset, 2007). See also Jochen Müller, "Auf den Spuren von Nasser. Nationalismus und Antisemitismus im radikalen Islamismus," in Wolfgang Benz and Juliane Wetzel, eds., *Antisemitismus und radikaler Islamismus* (Essen: Klartext, 2007), pp. 85–101.

100. The Working Definition of Antisemitism was adopted in 2005 by the EUMC, now called the European Union Agency for Fundamental Rights (FRA). It is used by a number of international organizations such as the OSCE. Its translation into more than thirty languages is available online at http://www.european-forum-on-antisemitism .org/working-definition-of-antisemitism/.

11 The Banalization of Hate: Antisemitism in Contemporary Turkey

Rıfat N. Bali

On the Turkish Foreign Ministry homepage there is a section titled "Frequently Asked Questions on Foreign Policy" (*sorularla dış politika*).[1] Of the twenty-one questions proffered, ten—in other words, half—are concerned with the Armenian Genocide. The answers given to these questions reflect a view that rejects the claim of a Turkish-perpetrated genocide against the Armenians, a reality accepted by the international community but rejected as an unjust accusation by the Turkish government. The FAQs and answers that the Foreign Ministry feels obligated to give show that Turkey believes itself to have an "Armenian Genocide problem."[2]

In contrast to this extensive grappling with the Armenian issue, there are no questions on the website along the lines of "Is there antisemitism in Turkey?" This would seem to indicate that neither the international community nor civil society organizations and intellectuals in Turkey have seriously pressured the Turkish government to fight antisemitism. As a result, the issue is not even on the Republic's agenda.

Before delving into the reasons for this situation, it will be advantageous to first briefly recall the roots of antisemitism in Turkey as well as to cite the prevailing ideological streams in which it is widespread. We will then cite certain examples of the recurring themes.

Antisemitism in Turkey: Prevalence and Themes

Popular Themes in the Single-Party Period

Antisemitism in Turkey is not a recent phenomenon; rather, its roots stretch back to the founding years of the Republic and can be seen in a number of themes that have appeared at various periods of its history. The principal reason for antisemitism between the years 1923 and 1945, namely the formative years of the Turkish Republic, was economic disparity between the Jews and Muslim Turks and the failure of the country's Jews to fully assimilate into Turkish society. The Turkish satirical magazines of the time were full of caricatures of "the Jewish merchant": dirty, materialistic, afraid of water, hook-nosed, a black marketeer, an opportunist, and utterly unable to speak Turkish without a comical Jewish accent; in short, a similar figure to the Jewish types encountered in Nazi iconography.[3]

One goal of the Kemalist elites and intelligentsia who established the Turkish Republic was to nationalize the country's economy. Within this nationalization process, the country's Jews, along with the rest of the non-Muslim population, faced discrimination, including exclusion from public service, since the Republic's founding cadres viewed them as "foreigners" to the Turkish body politic and society.[4] For them, the true owners of the country were the "real" Turks, the Muslim population that had shed its blood for the homeland during the Turkish War of Independence. In the view of the Kemalist leadership, non-Muslims had not shed their blood or sacrificed for the country during the war but had instead seen it as an opportunity to increase their wealth. Because of this they believed it essential that trade and industry within the country should pass from the hands of non-Muslim entrepreneurs and businessmen into those of the authentic children of the nation, the Muslim Turks. The 1942 Capital Tax Law, which was imposed against non-Muslim merchants in an arbitrary and discriminatory fashion, thereby opening the way for their elimination, was a product of this mindset.[5]

Popular Themes during the Multiparty Period

After having been run by a single ruling party for the first twenty-three years of its existence, Turkey transitioned in 1946 into a period of multiparty democracy. The antisemitic themes found in the country's media and political arena also changed accordingly. Whereas much of the previous hostility toward Jews had seemed to derive from the dominant Kemalist elites who controlled the national discourse, in the new, more open society, antisemitic expression became more visible within the Islamist and ultranationalist camps. These circles, which during the single-party period had been suppressed and largely silenced by the westernizing and secularizing Kemalist regime, were now reinvigorated and their own particular hostilities toward Jews (among others) were now given much wider circulation through their press organs and other writings.[6] The antisemitic themes and motifs found in their publications very closely echoed those found in both the West and in the rest of the Islamic world.

During the tumultuous 1960s and 1970s, the following themes were frequently encountered:[7] (1) Capitalism and communism are both systems that served Zionism's goal of establishing world domination; (2) the Bolshevik Revolution was carried out and brought to fruition by the Jews;[8] (3) communism is a Jewish ideology since its founding father Karl Marx was a Jew;[9] (4) the Rotary and Lions clubs,[10] as well as the Freemasonic lodges, were all subservient to and served the aims of Zionism; (5) the State of Israel was attempting to realize its goal of creating a "Greater Israel" that stretched "from the Nile to the Euphrates" and had cast its covetous eye on the lands of Anatolia; (6) the Dönmes (Sabbateans, or crypto-Jews) controlled Turkey.

Since the 1980s these themes have seen greater variation.[11] Among the new twists are the following: (1) the U.S. administration is under the control of the Jewish lobby, or, more recently, the "neo-cons," who are seen as largely interchangeable; (2) the Holocaust is a fabrication;[12] (3) the State of Israel behaves toward the Palestinian people the same way that the Nazis behaved toward the Jews; (4) the Jews control the American film industry and generate sympathy for Israel among the general public through a stream of Holocaust-themed films; (5) the State of Israel is constantly referred to as "colonialist," "rogue," and "terrorist"; (6) there is general enthusiasm for Hitler and sympathy for his genocidal intentions and practice; (7) the Kurdish separatist PKK organization is supported by Israel;[13] (8) Israel is attempting to purchase southeastern Anatolia within the framework of Turkey's long-term Southeastern Anatolia Development (GAP) project;[14] (9) the Jews control the American media, a view widely accepted even among the secular mainstream media;[15] (10) the Greater Middle East Project is a plan serving Israel's ambitions.[16]

Constant Themes and Publications

In addition to those mentioned above, a number of antisemitic themes have been constants in Turkish public life for decades. Books advocating these frequently appear on the bestseller lists. One common topic is demonization of the concept of Zionism, to the point that in Turkey the appellation *Zionist* has solely negative connotations. The Turkish translations of *The Protocols of the Elders of Zion,* Adolf Hitler's *Mein Kampf,* and Henry Ford's *The International Jew,* which form the basic texts for antisemites the world over, are perennial bestsellers.[17] For example, the *Protocols* was translated and published, either in book form or as a series of newspaper articles, 102 times between 1923 and 2008. Seventy-two percent of these publications were published by Islamist newspapers and publishing houses, 8 percent by publishers who are both ultranationalists and Islamists, and 20 percent by ultranationalists.[18] If the *Protocols* is extremely popular among Islamists, translations of *Mein Kampf* are popular among ultranationalists. *Mein Kampf* was translated and published thirty times between 1940 and 2000. These translations and publications are directly related to political developments within Turkey. The number and frequency of *Protocols* publication runs almost directly parallel to the growth and ascendance of the Islamist movement, while the increase in the number of translations of *Mein Kampf* has been directly related to internal political turmoil. Most of the translations and publications of the latter work appeared in the 1960s and 1970s, decades during which Turkey went through a sort of low-level civil war between ultranationalists and revolutionary leftist militants. The audience to which these books were addressed included lay people as well as people who sympathized with Islamist or ultranationalist ideologies. At least one entire generation was influenced by the antisemitic ideology contained in these books. Because of such a track record, in the year 2005, when new editions of *Mein Kampf* translations suddenly appeared on the shelves of mainstream book stores, up to 100,000 copies—a huge number for Turkish readership—were sold in a matter of a few months.[19] This brief summary of the antisemitic themes frequently encountered in Turkey represents a general list of fundamental assumptions regarding Jews, Judaism, and Zionism that appear in a great part of the country's Islamic and nationalist press and media.

The Foundation of Antisemitism in Turkey: "Atatürk was a Dönme"

Apart from these themes, a highly significant idea particular to the Islamic current in Turkey is the deeply held belief that Mustafa Kemal Atatürk, the founder of the Turkish Republic, was actually a Dönme.[20] The bulk of the Islamist movement would appear to believe this, but does not dare to declare it openly, since Law No. 5816, the Law on Crimes Committed against Atatürk (adopted July 31, 1951), criminalizes the slandering of his memory. Among others, the definition of *slandering* has included the allegation that Atatürk had Dönme roots[21] and that the underlying reason for Kemal's abolishing of the Caliphate and instituting of a secular order in Turkey derives from the desire of World Jewry—of which the Dönme are seen as one arm—to take revenge on the Ottoman Sultan Abdülhamid II.

According to this belief, which manifests itself as a historical conspiracy theory, the Sultan denied Zionist leader Theodor Herzl's request for the lands of Palestine for the purpose of settling Jewish refugees. In response, Herzl and his Zionist movement would later take their revenge by toppling the Sultan by means of the Dönmes and Zionists, who are claimed to have controlled the revolutionary Committee of Union and Progress (CUP), and exiling him to their stronghold, the Jewish-majority city of Saloniki. Among the circumstantial evidence often proffered for this theory of a Jewish plot is the presence of the Jewish attorney and parliamentary deputy for Saloniki, Emmanuel Carasso (1862–1934), on the delegation sent to inform Abdülhamid of his deposition.[22]

Nor is Herzl's thirst for revenge thought to have stopped here. Rather, the Islamists claim, the alleged Dönme Mustafa Kemal abolished the Caliphate and established a secular order in Turkey as further steps in World Jewry's grand plan to establish a second, or "reserve," Jewish state, the Jewish Republic of Turkey.[23]

Other Figures Representing the "Jewish Connection"

In the popular Islamist parlance, there exist, in addition to Carasso, a number of other Turkish Jewish figures whose presence is considered to be irrefutable proof of the "Jewish connection" behind the secularism imposed on Turkey. First among these figures is the last Ottoman Empire's Chief Rabbi Haim Nahum (1872–1960). Nahum was part of the Turkish delegation who participated in the Lausanne Peace Treaty negotiations between Turkey and the Allies after the victory of the Turkish Kemalist forces, in the capacity of an adviser.[24] Most of the Islamists and Nationalists believe that it was Nahum who convinced Ismet Pasha, the chief of the Turkish delegation, to accept the imposition of secularism in Turkey as well as the abolition of the caliphate. The Islamists believe that there exist "Secret Protocols of Lausanne"—an allusion to the *Protocols of the Elders of Zion*—in which the fatal role and action of Haim Nahum in convincing Ismet Pasha to impose secularism is documented.[25]

Another Islamist claim centers on Moise Kohen, a Turkish Jew and fervent advocate of Kemalism, Turkish nationalism, and the Kemalist regime's policy of "Turkification," which called for all non-Muslims and non-Turkish speakers to abjure their particular ethnoreligious identities and become part of the greater Turkish nation. Kohen himself Turkified his name to Tekin Alp (also Munis Tekinalp) and in 1936 published the treatise *Kemalizm* under this new name.[26] Islamists believe that like Mustafa Kemal and Haim Nahum, Kohen was a "Shariʾa-hating Jew." As evidence, they often cite the title of one of the chapters of *Kemalizm*, "To Hell with the Shariʾa Government" ("Kahrolsun Şeriat Hükûmeti").[27]

The Islamists also hate Turkish nationalism, which is in essence a secular ideology, as they believe that nationalism is incompatible with Islamism, since the latter views all Muslims as one nation (*ümmet*). For this reason they believe that Turkish nationalism with its secular character is dividing the Muslim nation. Again, since Moise Kohen was also an ideologue of nationalism, Islamists believed he had "planted the virus of nationalism" within Turkish society in the hope of destroying the unity of the Islamic nation.

The third Jewish figure is Lazzaro Franco, a supplier of household furniture to the Ottoman court. The Islamists believe, falsely, that Franco made a sizable donation to the nationalist Turkish Hearths Association ("Türk Ocakları") in the 1920s to construct their headquarters in Ankara, in return for which his photograph was hung in the building. The Turkish Hearts Association, established in 1912 and closed in 1931, is considered to have been the center par excellence of Turkish nationalist ideology. The circumstantial evidence of some connection thereby allows the Islamists to view Franco as the Jew who, together with Tekinalp, insinuated the virus of nationalism into the Islamic nation.[28]

The last figure is the Jewish dentist Sami Günzberg, who served successively as dentist to the Ottoman court and as the private dentist of Atatürk. The Islamists believe that he was a key figure who influenced Atatürk.[29]

Pointing to these Jewish personalities, the Islamists claim to have discovered Jewish fingerprints all over the secularist order put in place by

Atatürk. Furthermore, since Mustafa Kemal was generally supported by Jews, a commonly held sentiment has taken shape within the Islamist sector that the principal obstacles to their eventual goal of transforming the current Republic of Turkey into a Turkish Islamic Republic are the Jews and Dönmes who control the country.

Islamists also believe that Law 671, passed on November 28, 1925, which banned the bearing of the traditional fez in favor of the Western hat, was imposed by Atatürk against the will of the Turkish people and benefited only a Jewish businessman, Vitali Hakko, who made a fortune by importing and selling hats.[30]

Antisemitism in Turkey Today

Spreading Hate through Bestsellers

The claim that "the Dönmes control Turkey," which had been popular in the 1960s and 1970s but had fallen into abeyance, has in the past decades reemerged. This last opinion has existed and been widespread—even if not often publicly expressed—within Islamist circles for decades, but has taken on new forms and expressions since the Islamist movement's great electoral growth and the coming to power of the Justice and Development Party (Adalet ve Kalkınma Partisi) in the first years of the last decade. A great number of books have been published that purport to show that all secularist and Kemalist writers, politicians, and intellectuals have been Dönmes. One such book was so popular that it broke sales records in Turkey.[31] The two most significant authors in this vein are the journalist Soner Yalçın and the economics professor Yalçın Küçük. Soner Yalçın is the author of the bestselling titles *Efendi: Beyaz Türklerin Büyük Sırrı* (The Great Secret of the White Turks; 2004) and *Efendi-2: Beyaz Müslümanların Büyük Sırrı* (Efendi 2: The Great Secret of the White Muslims; 2006). He claimed in the first book that the Turkish Republic was in the hands of the secular Dönmes who held key positions in society and the political establishment. In *Efendi 2,* he claimed that most of the key figures and Islamist leaders also had Dönme roots. Yalçın Küçük also made the same claims. Basing his research on the study of name origins, or onomastics, he "revealed" the names of those in the Turkish establishment who were of Dönme origin. Other authors also took part in this frenzy.[32] In the second half of the last decade, countless books and Internet postings appeared accusing the past two chiefs-of-staff of the Turkish Armed Forces—the country's starkest symbols and guardians of the republic's Kemalist secularist order—of being Dönmes.[33]

Another bestselling writer about Dönmes is the journalist and author Ergün Poyraz. At the time of this writing, he is under arrest for his alleged part in the Ergenekon organization, an allegedly clandestine, ultra-nationalist organization intent on carrying out a coup d'etat against the AKP government.[34] Poyraz published a series of books in which he claimed that Prime Minister Recep Tayyip Erdoğan and his wife Emine have Jewish roots, and that in the AKP itself, President Abdurrahman Gül and State Minister Bülent Arınç were actors serving the cause of Zionism.[35] During the investigations surrounding the Ergenekon case, the prosecutor claimed that Poyraz had received payments from JITEM, the Intelligence section of the Turkish gendarmerie, for writing such books.[36]

Antisemitism in the New Media and Film

In the new millennium, antisemitic groups and actors have been able to spread their messages much farther than before by means of new information media. Even the most rudimentary Internet searches turn up dozens of Turkish websites featuring antisemitic and anti-Israel propaganda, to say nothing of Facebook groups and other social media. Nor is Turkish television immune to this trend. The extremely popular Turkish action series *Kurtlar Vadisi* (Valley of the Wolves) consistently portrays Jews in the most negative light, always evil and usually as cruel oppressors. Due to its success, the series has already spun off two different movies, *Valley of the Wolves, Iraq*[37] and *Valley of the Wolves, Palestine*,[38] both of which have continued this trope. The first film featured the American actors Billy Zane and Gary Busey, the latter playing a Jewish doctor who harvested the organs of Iraqi detainees and sent them off to London, New York, and Tel Aviv. *Valley of the Wolves, Palestine* featured two "villainous Jew" characters, Samuel Vanunu and Nedim Malik. The Samuel Vanunu character is a stock market speculator who is protected by the Mossad and is influential enough in manipulating the financial markets to engineer a global financial crisis. The character's name is intended to recall Mordechai Vanunu, the former Israeli nuclear technician who revealed the details of Israel's nuclear weapons program to the British press in 1986. The character Nedim Malik is, in turn, a greedy Turkish Jewish yarn trader and usurer. This character was modeled on the real-life Turkish Jewish businessman Nesim Malki (1952–95), a yarn trader and financial speculator who was murdered in 1995.[39] Soner Yalçın, the author of *Efendi* and *Efendi 2* claiming that the Turkish Republic was controlled by Dönmes, was the concept adviser for both films.

Another TV serial, *Ayrılık: Aşkta ve Savaşta Filistin* (Separation: Palestine in Love and War), was broadcast on Turkish State Television (TRT) at prime time in October 2009. The concept consultant for the serial was Hakan Albayrak, a columnist at the Islamist daily *Yeni Şafak*,who is now an adviser to the Anatolian Agency and was one of the Turkish journalists on board the *Mavi Marmara* in the Gaza flotilla raid of 2010.[40] *Ayrılık* depicted IDF soldiers murdering Arab civilians and newborn children in cold blood.[41]

The predictable result of such an extraordinarily hostile atmosphere has been the increasing demonization not only of the terms *Zionism*, but of *Israel* and *Jew* as well. To test such a claim one only need to look to the reader responses of any online article or editorial in the Turkish press dealing with Israel or Palestine. Another bit of evidence can be found in results of a recent public opinion survey conducted by Turkey's Jewish community. In a September 2009 poll of 1,108 people across Turkey, 42 percent of the respondents expressed an aversion to the idea of having a Jewish neighbor.[42]

The Attitude of the Regime

The traditional stance of successive Turkish regimes has claimed that antisemitism does not exist within Turkey. This "official viewpoint" has been reiterated literally hundreds of times by the country's representatives at the highest levels. First among these has been Prime Minister Erdoğan, who gave the following speech to a group meeting of his (AKP) party in the wake of the Israel Armed Forces' Operation Cast Lead against Gaza in 2009, an event that gave rise to vehement antisemitic reactions within the Islamist community and press:[43] "Antisemitism is a crime against humanity, and I [have been] one of the first ones to say this. We are members of the civilization of love. We can never accept ethnic, religious or sectarian discrimination among our citizens. Regardless of their religion, language, race or confession, we are all first-class citizens, gathered together under this flag."[44]

Erdoğan repeated this message sixteen months later. During the courtesy visit of Turkey's Jewish community's newly elected President Sami Herman to the Turkish prime minister, Erdoğan stated that antisemitism was a crime against humanity. He added that in the platforms where he had shared this opinion he always referred to a Turkish republic free of antisemitism.[45] This official view was most recently expressed by the country's president, Abdullah Gül, in a speech he delivered at the 7th OSCE Summit of the Head of States and Government. There Gül gave the following assessment of antisemitism:

> Recent trends in the rise of xenophobia, Islamophobia, antisemitism, discrimination, and racism, regardless of their motives or alleged justifications, call for urgent attention and joint action. Different perceptions about religion and culture driven by hate invite the risk of divisions and even conflicts among and within our societies. I would encourage all of us gathered here in Astana to take the lead in our respective countries in combating these phenomena actively and speak out against all forms of hate speech. As the current chair of the Council of Europe Committee of Ministers, Turkey will pay particular attention to this topic.[46]

Are These Declarations Sincere?

Should we take seriously the utterances of Prime Minister Erdoğan and President Gül? We must reply very clearly and concisely: Absolutely not.

Neither of these AKP politicians has ever shown any hesitation about including the writers of, among others, the newspaper *Vakit* (subsequently renamed *Yeni Akit*) and *Millî Gazete*[47] among the journalistic entourage that accompanies them on official trips abroad. These newspapers are notorious for their long history of publishing the most coarse and extreme antisemitic propaganda—including Holocaust denial. *Vakit* has also been published in Germany since 2001 with a circulation of 10,000. The difference between the Turkish and German attitude is shown in the fact that in December 2004 the German Ministry of Interior intervened and banned the publication and distribution of the paper because of its continuous dissemination of antisemitic propaganda. By contrast, the Turkish government preferred to stand by and watch the paper freely spread hate.[48] The esteem and validation that Turkish officials have consistently shown to the writers whose paper openly disseminates profound hatred—not just against Jews and Israel, but also toward Christians, gays, and Kemalism as a whole—have been consistently criticized by a columnist of the leading centrist daily *Hürriyet*.[49] None of this appears to have had an effect, however, as neither Erdoğan nor Gül has shown the slightest inclination to make changes in their retinues. In this manner, the Turkish Republic has not just continued, at the highest levels, to maintain the writers of a newspaper that issues a constant stream of primitive, coarse, and widespread hatred, but instead has embraced them.

Another hypocritical behavior displayed by the current regime regards the Holocaust. On the one hand, the regime and official administrative circles in Turkey turn a blind eye to the publication and sale of works by those who deny the reality of the Holocaust. On the other hand, in 2010 representatives from both the Turkish Foreign Ministry and the Istanbul governor's office attended (for the first time since its inception in 2005) the ceremony organized by the Chief Rabbinate of Turkey at Istanbul's Neve Shalom Synagogue in honor of International Holocaust Remembrance Day.[50]

Another Face of Prime Minister Erdoğan

One should not underestimate the role of Prime Minister Erdoğan's inflammatory speeches at times of crisis in the region in "indirectly inciting and encouraging antisemitism in Turkey," as a report by Israel's Ministry of Foreign Affairs states.[51] An early example of such statements occurred on January 28, 2009 at the Davos Summit when Erdoğan, in an angry tone, said to Israel's President Shimon Peres, referring to Operation Cast Lead, "When it comes to murder, you people know very well how to kill."[52] But this angry outburst was not merely a staged show for domestic political consumption as some analysts would later comment, but a genuine demonstration of his anger toward Israel. In fact, there were some advance indications of an oncoming crisis. Twelve days before the Davos incident, Erdoğan made the following statement in regards to Operation Cast Lead:

> There is a world media under the control of Israel. This has to be especially pointed out. As a matter of fact, if their publications were objective then the incident would be seen in a very different light, but nobody raises their voice. Nobody says stop this inhumanity. . . . I'm reading from the Torah. The sixth

of the Ten Commandments says "Thou shalt not kill." In Hebrew it's "Lo Tirtsach." Under which law, which religion, with what conscience can they justify the killing of innocent children?[53]

After the tragic *Mavi Marmara* incident in 2010, Erdoğan uttered a number of antisemitic remarks in various declarations. For example, while criticizing Israel on June 4th of that year, he asserted that "the Israeli government has put Israelis into a difficult position due to its irritating manner of conduct that hurt Israel's image in the world." He added, "I am sure that Israelis are disturbed by a perception equating the Star of Zion to the Nazi Swastika."[54] A few days later, at a speech given at the Turkish-Arab Cooperation Forum, Erdoğan repeated the claim that Israel dominates the world media: "When the word *media* is pronounced, Israel and Israel's administration comes to mind. They have the ability to manipulate it as they wish."[55] The next day Erdoğan returned to the same theme, first stating that "the international press is supported by Israel; the press got their instructions from Israel" and then criticized the Turkish press that was critical of the Turkish government's latest overtures to Iran and its handling of the *Mavi Marmara*: "Please put the Israeli newspapers in front of you and then put some of the well-known Turkish newspapers next to them. Believe me: there is no difference apart from language, because these Turkish newspapers are subcontractors [of Israel]."[56]

In these and numerous other instances, Erdoğan incites sharply negative attitudes toward Israel within Turkey that go well beyond policy differences with the Jewish state. The hostility has a visceral quality about it and, as was seen in the streets of Istanbul in January 2009, following the Gaza War, has the capacity to enflame public opinion in ways that make people in Turkey's Jewish community understandably nervous.

The Attitude of the Press and the Intelligentsia

We have thus far delved only into the state's attitude toward antisemitism in Turkey. That of the press and the country's intellectuals is not very different. Both have tended to take a rather indulgent attitude toward Necmettin Erbakan (1926–2011), a professor of mechanical engineering and the founder of the National View ideology that is the bedrock of much of political Islam in Turkey today,[57] due to his advanced age and sympathetic and fatherly demeanor. He is even referred to as *Hodja*, meaning "wise man" or "teacher." In similar fashion, the country's intelligentsia tends to use the term *Hodja* when addressing Marxist economics professor Yalçın Küçük, who has published numerous books, articles, and newspaper columns and has given countless interviews claiming that the Dönme control Turkey.[58]

Nevertheless, Erbakan and his semiofficial mouthpiece *Millî Gazete* have, since the Turkish Islamist movement first began to enter into the political fray in 1969, engaged in a shameless and ongoing campaign of antisemitic slurs and innuendos, as well as outright accusation. He is thus the person primarily responsible for infecting thousands of Turks with the virus of Jewish hatred.[59]

One of the constant antisemitic themes that Erbakan repeated over the years was his demonization of Zionism and Israel. For Erbakan, Zionism was an evil ideology responsible for the demise of the Ottoman Empire. Israel was an artificial state that should be uprooted and transplanted elsewhere, for example, to South America. For Erbakan, Zionism was also synonymous with imperialism. According to his thinking, Wall Street and the United States were run by international Zionism and Theodor Herzl and, as part of the "Grand Plan" of Zionism, World Jewry had its eyes on Turkish territory, as stated in the Old Testament: "On that day the LORD made a covenant with Abraham and said 'To your descendants I give this land, from the river of Egypt to the great River, the Euphrates'" (Genesis 15:18). In short, International Zionism was the secret, sinister puppet master behind all of Turkey's political and economic problems. Furthermore, international Zionism was the main obstacle preventing Erbakan and his party from governing Turkey.

Nor is such behavior limited to Erbakan and Yalçın Küçük. Mehmed Şevket Eygi[60] has for years filled his editorial columns in *Millî Gazete*, the official organ of the National View movement, with antisemitic propaganda, yet he is accepted within Turkish society as a respected conservative voice. İlber Ortaylı, a well-known Ottoman historian and currently director of the Topkapı Palace Museum, has not hesitated to have himself photographed arm-in-arm with Eygi.[61] Nor is Ortaylı the exception here. Some other examples of members of the intelligentsia who consider Eygi a serious intellectual include the following: Ayşe Arman, a reporter for the mainstream *Hürriyet* newspaper who, after interviewing Eygi, stated that she liked him;[62] Cüneyt Ülsever, a columnist at the same newspaper, who called Eygi "one of the most profound persons of culture that were raised in these lands. . . . I take him seriously when he says something on a given subject, even if it is fantastic";[63] and Melih Aşık, a columnist for the mainstream *Milliyet,* who described Eygi as "the sympathetic writer of the Islamist sector."[64] A reporter for the mainstream daily *Sabah* described him as a "moderate intellectual of the Islamist sector."[65] In addition, Mustafa İsen, a former undersecretary of the Ministry of Culture and currently General Secretary to the president, stated that "a person who was undersecretary at the Ministry of Culture must have good relations with Doğan Hızlan[66] and Mehmet Şevket Eygi in order to understand well Turkey's reality,"[67] essentially giving Eygi the same level of importance and legitimacy as Doğan Hızlan, a respectable literary critic.

Likewise, Abdurrahman Dilipak, the antisemitic conspiracy theorist and editorialist for the daily *Vakit,* is also shown great esteem by Turkish politicians and intellectuals as a defender of human rights and as an advocate for democracy. Dilipak was even nominated to the human rights advisory council that reports directly to the prime minister's office.[68] Some examples of the prestige that Dilipak enjoys within AKP circles are the participation of Prime Minister Erdoğan and his wife Emine at the engagement party for Dilipak's daughter, and the visit of Emine Erdoğan to Dilipak's house as a show of support when he was ordered by the court to pay $110,000 as indemnity for an article he published slandering Admiral Güven Erkaya, the late commander-in-chief of the Turkish Naval Forces and a staunch Kemalist known for his fight against the Islamists.[69] In the article he stated that he did not forgive the admiral for his harsh attitude toward the Islamists.[70] A number of journalists and authors who either in the past or currently publish antisemitic literature—*Vakit* writers first and foremost—are regularly invited to appear on mainstream television programs to express their views.

The Perception of Freedom of Press and Expression in Turkey

The hate speech that *Vakit* has continuously propagated has, several exceptions aside,[71] not drawn any reaction from the Turkish press or the intelligentsia. Quite the contrary: *Vakit* has maintained its right to continue publishing in Turkey, despite challenges from abroad. This has meant in practice that it remains free to propagate antisemitism and hate. Thus, when Germany's Ministry of Internal Affairs decided to close down the German office of the *Anadolu'da Vakit* newspaper because of its anti-semitic propaganda and Holocaust denial, Oktay Ekşi, the editor in chief of the mainstream *Hürriyet* and president of the Turkish Press Council, protested this decision.[72]

The strange understanding of the concept of freedom of press—shown here in the case of Oktay Ekşi—is not an isolated case. In December 2001, when the same newspaper was fined for articles containing hate speech, a writer associated with the Association for Liberal Thinking of Ankara criticized this decision, referring to it as an attempt at "silencing the opposition."[73] Ahmet Taşgetiren, a columnist of the Islamist newspaper *Yeni Şafak*, also added his own criticism.[74]

Further examples are abundant. Hasan Bülent Kahraman, a faculty member of the prestigious Sabancı University of Istanbul and a columnist at the mainstream *Sabah*, mentioned in one of his articles that "I do not share its views but *Vakit* is a respectable newspaper."[75] Metin Yılmaz, editor in chief of the popular daily *Sözcü*, stated in an interview that "*Vakit* was doing a fine job of newspaper reporting."[76] The perception that freedom of press also encompasses the freedom to question the true number of Holocaust victims is also encountered among intellectuals. The first example of such an approach is seen in the case of the French author Roger Garaudy. When Garaudy was convicted of Holocaust denial in France in 1998 under the Gayssot Law[77] for his book *Les Mythes fondateurs de la politique Israélienne*, Gülay Göktürk, a leftist columnist for *Sabah*, criticized this decision as contrary to freedom of expression and suggested that her readers consult the denialist website of the Committee for Open Debate on the Holocaust. The only journalist who condemned this attitude was Kürşat Bumin of *Yeni Şafak*. However, in a subsequent debate Göktürk insisted that freedom of expression should also include freedom for antisemitic ideas.[78] In the same context, a faculty member at the law school of Istanbul's prestigious Galatasaray University described the Gayssot Law as "intellectual terrorism." And Sami Selçuk, president of the Supreme Court of Appeal, criticized the same law as "infringement on freedom of expression in its condemnation of Roger Garaudy."[79]

All these examples show that the antisemitism continuously propagated by *Vakit* and other press organs are in no way drawing negative reaction from the mainstream Turkish media or from leftist and liberal intellectual elites. The latter groups have been generally taking a passive attitude and closing their eyes to this ongoing hate propaganda—except in cases of dealing with the denial of Armenian genocide claims. Here these same intellectuals protest—often vehemently—against those deniers as well as against the Turkish state.

The reasons are as follows. Beginning in the early 1990s, Turkey has gradually been transformed into a more liberal society in which, among others, openly Islamist groups and individuals have been participating in the public debate. As part of the liberalization of this society two traditionally marginalized groups, the Islamist movement and the Kurdish nationalist movements, both began to increase their strength within Turkish society. The illegal Kurdish separatist PKK's ongoing fight with the Turkish armed forces resulted in a growing number of losses on both sides, creating great concern within the Turkish society. As a result, leftist and liberal intellectuals began to debate the needs of a liberal and multicultural society, one in which the free exchange of ideas with all ideological factions, including Islamists and Kurdish nationalists, would occur. These intellectuals complained that the Kemalist establishment was out of touch with the needs of the Turkish society and was oppressing political and cultural streams that might pose a challenge to their rule. Thus started the decade of televised debates where representatives of these alternative streams—Islamists first and foremost, but also Kurdish intellectuals—were regularly invited to debate current affairs with leftist, liberal, and Kemalist intellectuals and journalists. Since the predominant obsession of all ideological factions opposing the old school Kemalists was "to liberate the Turkish society from the yoke of the Kemalist establishment and the Turkish armed forces," a loose "alliance of convenience" was soon established between the leftist and liberal intellectuals and the Islamists. The problem was that the leftist and liberal intellectuals were striving to reshape Turkish society into something more democratic and liberal, where the ironclad secularism of the old guard Kemalists would be softened, and as a result they tended to turn a blind eye to the more vehement and extremist expressions of the Islamists, including their pervasive antisemitism. The result of this process was the legitimization and transformation of once-marginal Islamist journalists into respectable mainstream Islamist intellectuals who were regularly invited to any sort of public debate.

The Attitude of Nongovernmental Organizations

The nongovernmental organizations in Turkey that struggle against violations of human rights and discrimination have up until recently generally been deaf to complaints about hate speech, and of antisemitism in particular.[80] After Hrant Dink (1954–2007), the editor in chief of the Istanbul Armenian daily *Agos,* was assassinated on January 19, 2007 by an ultranationalist youth,[81] these organizations finally began to take action to prevent hate speech, claiming that Dink had been a victim of a hate crime. Nonetheless, these activities have focused on hate speech against Armenians, gays, lesbians, Kurds, and Roma, and no complaint worthy of note has been lodged against antisemitism.[82] One such organization, Say Stop to Racism and Nationalism! (commonly known as "Say Stop," has even awarded İlber Ortaylı, the director of the Topkapı Palace Museum, the dubious honor of Racist of the Year for allegedly having made derogatory utterances against Kurds. As a footnote, the editor in chief of the accusing newspaper later felt compelled to weigh in on his writer's accusation, stating that "racist" was a very serious allegation and that people must be very careful about using it.[83]

In a climate in which antisemitic slurs inundate the Web and the Islamist press, this is a prime example of how such organizations express selective hypersensitivity about hostile speech toward some groups and none at all toward others, namely Jews.[84] Perhaps the only exception to this trend has been the Istanbul Branch of the Turkish Human Rights Association. This organization has in the past occasionally protested against the publication of antisemitic materials.

Why Is There No Acknowledgment of an Antisemitism Problem in Turkey?

The answer to this question depends upon who is being asked. It can be answered from four different vantage points:

a) that of the Turkish State;
b) that of Israel and American Jewish organizations;
c) that of Turkey's nongovernmental organizations and intellectuals;
d) that of the Turkish Jewish Community leadership.

For point a), the Republic of Turkey has declared, with the support of the country's Jewish community leaders, that there is no antisemitism in Turkey, that both the Ottoman Empire and its successor Turkish Republic have throughout their history been a safe refuge for Jews, and that Jews have been treated with tolerance. This statement—that the Jews of Turkey have lived there in peace and toleration—is repeated *ad nauseum* and is employed by successive Turkish regimes as a tactic meant to counter pressures from the international community that Turkey acknowledge the truth of the Armenian genocide. The intent behind these claims is to be able to claim, by using the Jews as a reference, that any country that could behave so tolerantly toward one minority (the Jews) could not possibly have perpetrated a crime against humanity against another one (the Armenians). A recent expression of this was Prime Minister's Erdoğan's January 2009 declaration at an AKP Party meeting that took place during Israel's Cast Lead Operation. At the meeting, Erdoğan criticized Israel's operation and than addressed Israel as follows: "We are talking as the grandchildren of the Ottoman [Empire] who welcomed your ancestors, your grandparents when they were [expelled from Spain]. We have always sided with the victims."[85] This statement spurred an op-ed published by Leyla Navaro, a Jewish psychiatrist from Istanbul, who felt compelled to state her sadness at still being perceived by the Turkish regime as a "guest" in Turkey.[86] This op-ed, in turn, triggered a phone call from President Abdullah Gül to Navaro, asking her to be strong and stating that antisemitism in Turkey was found only among marginal groups and that Prime Minister Erdoğan was also fighting them. The Turkish president did not use this opportunity to offer any comments on Erdoğan's latest statement.[87]

In response to point b), the approach of the State of Israel and American Jewish organizations toward the question of antisemitism in Turkey derives less from honest investigation than from politics. For these parties, the most important thing is to ensure the smooth continuation of relations between Turkey and Israel. As a result, concerns about antisemitism in Turkey are continually forced to take a back seat to international relations. With the worsening of relations between these two countries in recent years, the government of Israel and American organizations have begun to acknowledge the existence of antisemitism in Turkey and to level criticism at Ankara for it. For example, during his visit to Ankara in January 2010, Israeli Defense Minister Ehud Barak said that he did "not see signs of antisemitism in Turkey unlike other countries in the world." Recalling that Turkey had always helped liberate Jews, whether from medieval Spain or from Nazi-occupied Europe during the Second World War, Barak then added that "Jews are accepted here [in Turkey]."[88] Nevertheless, a mere ten days after this was reported in the papers, the Center for Political Research in Israel, which performs in-house intelligence analysis for Israel's Ministry of Foreign Affairs, published a report claiming that Prime Minister Erdoğan "indirectly incites and encourages" the spread of antisemitism through his speeches and other utterances.[89]

In response to point c), nongovernmental organizations that struggle against cases of human rights abuse and discrimination tend to share a left-leaning and/or liberal outlook, a critical stance with reference to the state apparatus, and a belief that the Armenians were indeed the victims of a state-sponsored genocide that the Turkish regime should acknowledge. This approach is the complete opposite of that of Turkey's Jewish community, whose policy has been to collaborate with the Turkish state in public relations and lobbying activities and make constant reference to the latter's tolerance of minorities for the purpose of refuting claims of an Armenian genocide. So long as such a situation exists, it is impossible to lay the foundations for an honest dialogue between Jewish community leadership on the one side and those of the nongovernmental organizations and the intellectuals on the other. Furthermore, the Jewish community has no public figure or intellectual who has been critical of the Kemalist establishment and who could thus establish a solid dialogue with the human rights activists. Because of this state of affairs, the Turkish Jewish community is not seen in the public space, while the Armenians and Greeks are quite visible as victims of the Turkish state's behavior. What is more, for many of the leftist/liberal intellectuals, the Holocaust may have been a tragedy, but it was one that does not concern Turkey. For them, the oppressed and victimized groups that deserve attention are not the Jews of Europe but the victims of more local tragedies, Turkey's Kurdish and Armenian populations. In the end, this same group believes that the State of Israel exploits the charge of antisemitism by immediately labeling all critics and criticisms directed toward it as antisemitic, and by using the Holocaust as a "moral shield" against honest criticism. As a result, these groups' sensitivity toward the phenomenon of antisemitism tends to be quite low.

On point d), until recent years, the Turkish Jewish community's leadership had maintained a policy of publicly denying the existence of antisemitism, while in private complaining about it and asking judicial intervention at the highest government levels in Ankara. The logic behind this strategy was the following. Since the intervention of the Turkish armed forces in Cyprus in 1974, the Turkish Jewish Community leadership has adopted a policy of supporting the Turkish Republic's lobbying activities in the United States in two situations: first against Greek American organizations' activities against Turkey after the 1974 intervention accusing Turkey of human rights infringements, and, second, against Armenian American organizations requesting that Turkey recognize that the mass murder of the Ottoman Armenians in 1915 was a genocide. In the lobbying and counterpropaganda activities of the Turkish Republic, the Turkish Jewish community leadership played a key role in supporting these activities by continuously propagating the message that first the Ottoman Empire and then the Turkish Republic was and has always been a haven of tolerance for its minorities. They offer the existence of a Jewish community in Turkey as its best proof. In these activities, the community leaders always downplayed the existence of antisemitism in Turkey, presenting it as a negligible and extremely marginal phenomenon. In this, it was reinforced by the Quincentennial Foundation, an organization established for commemorating and celebrating the five-hundredth anniversary of the arrival into Ottoman lands of Spanish Jews expelled from Spain in 1492. The logic behind this attitude was that, since the community leadership had adopted the policy of supporting Turkey's lobbying activities, declaring publicly that antisemitism existed in Turkey and asking the Turkish government to take measures to prevent it would be contrary to the role assumed by the community, which was to enhance Turkey's image in the United States and abroad as a land of tolerance for its minorities. The second reason was that publicly complaining about antisemitism in Turkey might not cure the phenomenon—quite the contrary, it would probably make it worse, since it would spur the Islamist press, where this antisemitism is mostly encountered, to increase its rhetoric and attacks against the community. Because of its policy of publicly denying the existence of antisemitism, the Jewish community leadership distanced and insulated itself from the very few human rights activists who were sensitive to antisemitism. Although this policy has gradually shifted in recent years to one of publicly complaining about antisemitism, the fact is that the general perception of the Turkish society and intellectuals (with a very few exceptions) is that Turkey is a land free of antisemitism and that the few instances of so-called antisemitic literature are in fact anti-Zionist writings.

Conclusion

Turkey, which desires to join the European Union, assumes that the conditions for membership consist of little more than reciting certain formulas, conducting certain rituals, and giving lip service to general principles. It believes that all it needs to do to convince the EU countries that it is sensitive to the Holocaust and to antisemitism and that it thus shares the same moral principles as the countries of Europe is to participate in International Holocaust Day ceremonies, have its officials visit Auschwitz, and declare that antisemitism is a crime against humanity. By these actions, Ankara believes that everyone in Europe will be persuaded of Turkey's shared values, and it refuses to acknowledge the truth that EU membership will require a radical change of mindset.

But when a newspaper and its writers harbor and propagate the same sort of Jew-hatred nurtured by the Nazis and finds acceptance, approval, and even honor—not only within state circles, but also among the intellectual elites and the general public, and when the state itself repeatedly shows itself completely insensitive to the problem of antisemitism in its own backyard, it is not likely that anyone will be persuaded that such a change of mind—much less of heart—has taken place. The present situation in Turkey is one in which hatred directed at Jews, suspected Jews, and Jewish institutions is routine, and the memory of the Holocaust is little more than a tool to be exploited when convenient by the Turkish Republic in its attempt at EU membership.

NOTES

1. "Questions," mfa.gov.tr/questions.en.mfa.
2. The mass murder of the Ottoman Armenians in the 1915 deportation is accepted as a de facto genocide by the International Association of Genocide scholars. A letter

to this effect was sent to Prime Minister Erdoğan on June 13, 2005. See: http://www .genocidescholars.org/images/OpenLetterTurkishPMreArmenia6-13-05.pdf. The Turkish Republic refuses to accept that the murder of the Ottoman Armenians was a planned action and argues that there had never been a plan to annihilate the Ottoman Armenian population.

3. On this subject, please refer to the following publications: Hatice Bayraktar, "Türkische Karikaturen über Juden (1933-1945)," pp. 85–108, in *Jahrbuch für Antisemitismusforschung* 13 (Berlin: Metropol Verlag, 2004); Laurent Olivier Mallet, "Dessins satiriques et représentations du 'juif' dans l'entre deux-guerres en Turquie: d'un préjugé à l'autre?" in Bernard Heyberger and Sylvia Naef, *La Multiplication des Images en Pays d'Islam: De l'Estampe à la Télévision (17e-21e siècle)*, pp. 247–66; *Actes du colloque image: fonctions et languages. L'incursion de l'image moderne dans l'Orient musulman et sa périphérie* (Istanbul, Université du Bosphore [Boğaziçi Üniversitesi], March 25–27, 1999) (Würzburg: Orient Institute, 2003); Hatice Bayraktar, *Salamon und Rebeka Judenstereotype in Karikaturen der Türkischen Zeitschriften Akbaba, Karikatür und Milli İnkilap 1933-1945* (Berlin: Klaus Schwarz Verlag, 2006).

4. On this subject, see Ayhan Aktar, "Economic Nationalism in Turkey: The Formative Years, 1912-1925," *Boğaziçi Journal Review of Social, Economic and Administrative Studies* 10, nos. 1–2 (1996), pp. 263–90.

5. On this subject, the following publications are available in English and French: Edward C. Clark, "The Turkish Varlık Vergisi Reconsidered," *Middle Eastern Studies* 8, no. 2 (May 1972), pp. 205–217; Rıfat N. Bali, *The Varlik Vergisi Affair: A Study on Its Legacy—Selected Documents* (Istanbul: The Isis Press, 2005); Faik Ökte, *The Tragedy of the Capital Tax Levy*, trans. Geoffrey Cox (London: Croom Held, 1987); Rıfat N. Bali, *L'affaire impôt sur la fortune (Varlık Vergisi)* (Istanbul: Libra Kitap, 2010); Rıfat N. Bali, *The Wealth Tax (Varlık Vergisi) Affair—Documents from the British National Archives* (Istanbul: Libra Kitap, 2012).

6. There are not many studies analyzing these publications. One exception is Esther Debus, *Sebilürreşad, Eine Verglerchende Untersuchung zur Islamischen Opposition der vor- und nachkemalistischen Ära* (Frankfurt: Peter Lang, 1991).

7. For an analysis of that period, see Jacob M. Landau, "Muslim Turkish Attitudes towards Jews, Zionism and Israel," *Die Welt des Islams* XXVIII (1988), pp. 291–300; Jacob M. Landau, "Al dmuta şel ha antisemiyat be ripublika ha Turkit," *Ninth World Congress of Jewish Studies*, Division B, Vol. II, The History of the Jewish People (The Modern Times) (Jerusalem: World Union of Jewish Studies, 1986), pp. 77–82; Jacob M. Landau, "Tofaot şel antişemiyut be sifrut ve be intonut şel ha Republika ha Turkit," in Abraham Haim, ed., *Society and Community, Proceedings of the Second International Congress for Research of the Sephardi and Oriental Jewish Heritage 1984* (Jerusalem: Misgav Yerushalayim, 1991), pp. 225–36. See also Yunus Emre Kocabaşoğlu's series of articles dealing with antisemitism in Turkey: "Hakkımız Olan Tek Şey Unutmaktır," December 19, 2009; "Allah Aşkına, Nedir bu Antisemitizm, Bilen Var mı?" (December 26, 2009); "Büyüklere Masallar 1: Türkiye'de Antisemitizm Yoktur" (January 2, 2010); "Kırılma Noktası 1: Sol Liberal-İslami İttifak" (January 9, 2010); "Salkım Hanım'ın Taneleri" mi, "Yahudi'nin Adı Yok"mu?" (January 16, 2010); "Bilimin Boy Aynası" (Janu-

ary 23, 2010); "Antisemitizm korkusu, İsrail'in Eleştirilmesine Engel mi?" (January 30, 2010); "Dökme Kurşun Harekatı ve Yahudiler" (February 6, 2010); Kırılma Noktası II: Dökme Kurşun Harekatı" (February 13, 2010); "Mazluma da Zalime de Kimlik Sormamak" (February 20, 2010); "Şahide de Kimlik Sormamak" (February 27, 2010). All of these articles have been published at www.bianet.org.

8. For example, General Netcheolodon, *Rus İhtilali ve Ruslar* (Istanbul: Sebil Yayınları, 1975; 2nd ed., 1996); Hikmet Tanyu, *Tarih Boyunca Yahudiler ve Türkler* (Istanbul:Yağmur Yayınları, 1976), 1, pp. 686–92.

9. Tanyu, pp. 254–355; Mustafa Akgün, *Yahudinin Tahta Kılıcı* (Istanbul: Ra Kitap, 1992), p. 113; Ziya Ugur, *İnkilaplar, İhtilaller ve Siyonizm* (Istanbul: Üçdal Neşriyat, 1968), p. 74.

10. For example, Ali Burak, *Görünmeyen Önderler (Rotary ve Lions Kulüpleri)* (Istanbul: Burak Yayınları, 1989); Enver Baytan, *Bütün Cepheleriyle Cihad* (Istanbul: Mevsim Yayıncılık, 1993), 2, p. 317; Cenkhan Yılmaz, *Rotary ve Rotarienler* (Istanbul: Türk Kültür Yayınevi, 1979), p. 5; İ. H. Pirzade, *Türkiye ve Yahudiler* (İstanbul, Ark Matbaacılık, 1968), pp. 28–34.

11. For a study of the themes, see "Antisemitism in the Turkish Media, Part I," Special Dispatch no. 900, April 28, 2005; "Antisemitism in the Turkish Media: Part II—Turkish Intellectuals against Antisemitism," Special dispatch no. 904 (May 5, 2005); "Antisemitism in the Turkish Media: Part III—Targeting Turkey's Jewish Citizens," Special Dispatch no. 916 (June 6, 2005), *www.memri.org*; also Rıfat N. Bali, "The Image of the Jew in the Rhetoric of Political Islam in Turkey," *Cahiers d'etudes surla Méditerranée orientale et le monde Turco-Iranien* No. 28 (June–December 1999), http://cemoti.revues .org/590.

12. For more information, see Rıfat N. Bali, *Musa'nın Evlatları Cumhuriyet'in Yurttaşları* (Istanbul: İletişim Yayınları, 2001), pp. 377–78.

13. For example, Harun Yahya, *İsrail'in Kürt Kartı* (Istanbul: Vural Yayıncılık, 2000); Eşref Günaydın, *Orta İsrail veya Kürdistan Yahudi Kürtler* (Istanbul: Karakutu Yayıncılık, 2010).

14. For more on this project, see www.gap.gov.tr/English. For publications on this view, see Hasan Taşkın, *İstihbarat Raporlarına Göre İsrail'in GAP Senaryosu* (Istanbul: Truva Yayınları, 2005); Hasan Taşkın, *İsrail'in GAP Senaryosu; Güneydoğu Topraklarında Neler Oluyor* (Istanbul: Ozan Yayınları, 2004).

15. For examples of this view, see Taha Kıvanç, "Birand, kendini kolla," *Yeni Şafak* (November 27, 2010; Taha Kıvanç is the pen name of Fehmi Koru, an influential Islamist journalist); Mehmet Ali Birand, "Her şeyi işte bu resim değiştirdi," *Posta* (November 25, 2010; Mehmet Ali Birand is a well-known anchorman and reporter for the mainstream Doğan Media Group); Aylin Yengin, "Fatih Altaylı ile Teke Tek," *Şalom* (March 9, 2011; Fatih Altaylı is the editor in chief of the mainstream *Habertürk* newspaper); Can Dündar, "ABD'deki Musevi Lobisi," *Milliyet* (April 16, 2002; Can Dündar is a well-known journalist and documentary producer who writes for the mainstream Doğan Media Group); Celal Güzel, "Türkiye-İsrail İlişkileri (1)," *Radikal* (January 14, 2010; Hasan Celal Güzel is a former state minister, cabinet spokesperson, and minister of education, youth and sports [December 1987–March 1989]; he was a columnist for

the mainstream *Radikal* newspaper part of the Doğan Media Group); Bülent Erandaç, "Notları yayınlayan beş gazetenin tipik özelliği," *Takvim* (December 5, 2010); Elif Arat, "Ulusötesi Lobilerin Medya Yetenekleri: ABD'deki İsrail Lobisi Örneği," January 5, 2011, www.bilgesam.org/tr/images/stories/sunular/ulusotesilobiler.ppt; the Wise Men's Center for Strategic Studies (known as "Bilgesam") is a think-tank established by retired ambassadors, retired generals, and professors.

16. For example, Hasan Şafak, *Büyük Ortadoğu Projesi İsrail'in İmparatorluk Planı* (Istanbul: Profil Yayınları, 2006).

17. For a chronology of the Turkish translations of these works, see Rıfat N. Bali, *Musa'nın Evlatları Cumhuriyet'in Yurttaşları*, pp. 325–45.

18. Rıfat N.Bali, "The Protocols of the Elders of Zion in Turkey," in Esther Webman, ed., *The Global Impact of the Protocols of the Elders of Zion A Century-Old Myth* (London and New York: Routledge, 2011).

19. Helena Smith, "Mein Kampf Sales Soar in Turkey," *The Guardian* (March 29, 2005).

20. The term *Dönme* means, among other things, "one who has changed religion" or "a convert." In modern Turkish parlance it is used specially to refer to the followers of Sabbetai Sevi, the seventeenth-century rabbi who declared himself Messiah in 1666 and to their descendants. For more on this subject, see Gerschom Scholem, *Sabbatai Sevi, The Mystical Messiah*, trans. R. J. Zwi Werblowsky (Princeton, N.J.: Princeton University Press, 1999); and Marc David Baer, *The Dönme, Jewish Converts, Muslim Revolutionaries and Secular Turks* (Stanford, Calif.: Stanford University Press, 2010).

21. This law was accepted because in 1951 the Ticanis, an Islamist sect whose leader was Kemal Pilavoğlu, attacked and smashed busts of Atatürk all over Turkey.

22. In fact, most Western scholars who have examined this issue have concluded that neither Ottoman nor foreign Jewry strongly influenced or played a significant role within the Young Turk movement. See Elie Kedourie, "Young Turks, Freemasons and Jews," *Middle Eastern Studies* 7 (1971), pp. 89–104; Jacob M. Landau, "The Young Turks and Zionism: Some Comments," *Jews, Arabs, Turks: Selected Essays* (Jerusalem: Magnes Press, 1993), 169–77; Robert Olson, "The Young Turks and the Jews: A Historiographical Revision," *Turcica* 18 (1986), pp. 219–35.

23. For more on this subject see Rıfat N. Bali, *A Scapegoat for All Seasons: The Dönmes or Crypto-Jews of Turkey* (Istanbul: The Isis Press, 2008); Jacob M. Landau, "The Donmes: Crypto Jews under Turkish Rule," *Jewish Political Studies Review*19, nos. 1–2 (Spring 2007), pp. 108–109.

24. For a biography of Nahoum, see *Haim Nahum, A Sephardic Chief Rabbi in Politics,* edited with an introduction by Esther Benbassa, trans. Miriam Kochan (Tuscaloosa: University of Alabama Press, 1995).

25. For a sample of such articles, see M. Latif Salihoğlu, "Lozan'ın Gizli Mimarı Haim Nahum (I)," *Yeni Asya* (August 25, 2007), and "Lozan'ın Gizli Mimarı Haim Nahum (2)," *Yeni Asya*(August 27, 2007); Kadir Mısıroğlu, *Lozan Zafer mi? Hezimet mi?* (Istanbul: Sebil Yayınevi, 1975), 1, pp. 272–73; Abdurrahman Dilipak, *Cumhuriyete Giden Yol* (Istanbul: Beyan Yayınları, 1991), pp. 330–35; Mehmet Şevket Eygi, "Eyvah! ... Lozan'ın Gizli Protokolleri Tehlikede," *Millî Gazete* (August 23, 2007); Dedektif X Bir, "İşte!" *Büyük*

Doğu No. 2 (October 21, 1949) and No. 3 (October 28, 1949); Necip Fazıl Kısakürek, "Yahudi ve Menderes," in *Başmakalelerim 1* (Istanbul: Büyük Doğu Yayınları), pp. 69–71; Hasan Hüseyin Ceylan, "Halifeliğin kaldırılmasında İsmet İnönü-Yahudi Hahambaşısı Haim Nahum İşbirliği," *Yörünge* (December 23, 1990), pp. 35–36; Mustafa Kaplan"yolumuz Açıldı mı?" *Akit* (April 4, 1996); Mustafa Akgün, *Yahudinin Tahta Kılıcı*, p. 180.

26. For a detailed biography, see Jacob M. Landau, *Tekinalp Turkish Patriot 1883–1961* (Istanbul: Nederlands Historisch Archaelogisch Institute, 1984).

27. Tekin Alp, *Kemalizm* (Istanbul: Cumhuriyet Gazete ve Matbaası, 1936), pp. 94–104.

28. This ridiculous belief was voiced three decades ago by the leading Islamist politician at the time, Necmettin Erbakan. See Necmettin Erbakan, "Anarşi ve Siyonizm," *İstanbul Bayram Gazetesi* (quoted in *Millî Gazete*, August 16, 1980). While it is true that a foreigner made a donation toward the construction of the Turkish Hearths headquarters, the person in question was not Franco nor even Jewish, but an American Christian, Arthur Nash. For further expressions of this belief, see: Abdurrahman Dilipak, "Ergenekon'da yeni dönem!" *Anadolu'da Vakit* (May 15, 2009). Dilipak has repeatedly made this claim; see also Abdurrahman Dilipak, "Diyarbakır'da birkaç yüz Çağlayan'da birkaç bin kişi," *Anadolu'da Vakit* (June 25, 2007); and Abdurrahman Dilipak, "Hablemitoğlu, YÖK, Menemen, vs.," *Anadolu'da Vakit* (December 28, 2002). Türk Ocakları refuted these claims but to no avail. See Mustafa Bayramoğlu, "Yalanın Bekası Olur mu?, Türk Ocakları, Ziya Gökalp ve Gerçekler," *Türk Yurdu* 188 (April 2003), pp. 31–32. Dilipak repeated this claim in another article entitled "Diyarbakır'da birkaç yüz Çağlayan'da birkaç bin kişi," *Anadolu'da Vakit* (June 25, 2007) and this generated an open letter to him entitled "Sayın Abdurrahman Dilipak," dated June 26, 2007, by Prof. Orhan Kavuncu, General Secretary of the Turkish Hearths, at their website http://www.turkyurdu.com.tr, where Kavuncu once again refuted these claims.

29. For his biography, see Rıfat N. Bali, *Sarayın ve Cumhuriyetin Dişçibaşısı: Sami Günzberg* (Istanbul: Kitabevi, 2007).

30. Hasan Karakaya, "Kartel 'görev'ini yapıyor . . . Ya Müslüman?, *Anadolu'da Vakit* (December 14, 2007).

31. On this subject, see Rıfat N. Bali, *A Scapegoat for All Seasons*, pp. 325–58.

32. Mehmet Şevket Eygi, *Yahudi Türkler Yahut Sabetaycılar İki Kimlikli, Gizli, Esrarlı ve Çok Güçlü Bir Cemaat* (Istanbul: Zvi Geyik Yayınları, 2000); Ahmed Safi, *Dönmeler Adeti* (Istanbul: Zvi Geyik Yayınları, 2001); Ahmet Almaz, *Tarihin Esrarengiz Bir Sahifesi Dönmeler ve Dönmelerin Hakikati* (Ankara: Kültür Yayınları, 2002); Süleyman Kocabaş, *Dönmelik ve Dönmeler: Türkiye'de Gizli Tarih 2* Kayseri: Vatan Yayınları, 2003); Hüda Derviş, *Türkiye'de Dönme Yahudi Gerçeği* (Ankara: Ark Kitaplar, 2006); Süleyman Yeşilyurt, *Yahudi Dönmeler ve Mum Söndü Ayinleri* Ankara: Kültür Sanat Yayınları, 2007); Ahmet Almaz, *Shekhina ve Sabetaycıların 400 Yıldır Gizlenen Arşivinden-1* (Istanbul: Postiga Yayınları, 2010).

33. "The AKP and Other Turkish Islamists Attempt to Block Secular General From Top Military Post," Special Dispatch no. 1136 (April 11, 2006), www.memri.org. The two chiefs-of-staff were Yaşar Büyükanıt (August 2006–August 2008) and İlker Başbuğ (August 2008–August 2010).

34. For more on this subject, see Gareth H. Jenkins, *Between Fact and Fantasy: Turkey's Ergenekon İnvestigation* (Washington, D.C.: Silk Road Paper, Central Asia-Caucasus Institute Silk Road Studies Program, August 2009), http://silkroadstudies.org/new/docs /silkroadpapers/0908Ergenekon.pdf "Ergenekon (organization)," en.wikipedia.org/wiki /Ergenekon_(organization).

35. Ergün Poyraz, *Musa'nın Çocukları: Tayyip ve Emine* (Istanbul: Togan Yayınları, 2007); *Musa'nın Mücahiti* (Istanbul: Togan Yayınları, 2007); *Musa'nın Gülü* (Istanbul: Togan Yayınları, 2007); *Musa'nın AKP'si* (Istanbul: Gökbörü, 2007).

36. Mustafa Gürlek, "Books Part of Ergenekon's Psychological War," *Today's Zaman* (March 15, 2011).

37. A number of studies have been published on this subject. See Kameel Ahmady, "Valley of the Wolves": Nationalism, Conflict and the Other in Turkish Film" (2006), http://www.kameelahmady.com/articles/Valley%20of%20the%20Wolves.pdf; Lerna K. Yanık, "Valley of the Wolves Iraq: Anti-Geopolitics Alla Turca," *Middle East Journal of Culture and Communication* 2, no. 1 (2009), pp. 153–70; Mehmet Celil Çelebi, "*Valley of Wolves" as a Nationalist Text* (M.A. thesis, Middle East Technical University, Graduate School of Social Sciences, August 2006); Ahmed Khalid Al-Rawi, "Valley of the Wolves as Representative of the Turkish Popular Attitudes towards Iraq," *International Journal of Contemporary Iraqi Studies* 3, no. 1 (May 2009), pp. 75–84; Ioannis N. Grigoriadis, *Upsurge amidst Political Uncertainty Nationalism in Post-2004 Turkey,* SWP Research Paper, Stiftung Wissenschaft und Politik, RP 11 (October 2006), Berlin; "Valley of the Wolves: Iraq," http://en.wikipedia.org/wiki/Valley_of_the_Wolves:_Iraq.

38. For a coverage of this film, see "A Turkish anti-Israeli film titled *Valley of Wolves: Palestine* portrays the Mavi Marmara incident as a premeditated attack by the IDF on innocent people" (January 24, 2011), the Meir Amit Intelligence and Terrorism Information Center, www.terrorism-info.org.il; Şebnem Arsu, "New Film disrupts Turkey's Holocaust Day," *The New York Times* (January 27, 2011).

39. Rasim Ozan Kütahyalı, "20 ay önce: Ergenekon ve ODA," *Taraf* (February 19, 2011).

40. For more information, see "Hakan Albayrak," http://en.wikipedia.org/wiki/Hakan _Albayrak.

41. "Ayrılık," http://en.wikipedia.org/wiki/Ayrılık; Daniel Pipes, "Ayrılık," "Separation"—Turkey's New anti-Semitic "masterpiece" (November 1, 2009), www.danielpipes .org/comments/163931.

42. "Research on Perception of Different Identites and Jews," http://www.turkyahudileri .com/images/stories/dokumanlar/perception%20of%20different%20identities%20and %20jews%20in%20turkey%202009.pdf.

43. Rıfat N. Bali, "Present-Day Anti-Semitism in Turkey," Special Issue no. 84 (August 16, 2009), The Jerusalem Center for Public Affairs Institute for Global Jewish Affairs, www.jcpa.org.

44. "Başbakan Erdoğan'dan antisemitizm ile ilgili önemli açıklamalar," *Şalom* (January 14, 2009).

45. "Başbakan Erdoğan: "Siz benim referansımsınız," *Şalom* (May 5, 2010).

46. "Gül Reiterates the Needs for Concentrated Efforts against Xenophobia, Islamophobia, Antisemitism, Discrimination and Racism" (October 2, 2010), http://www.tccb.gov.tr/news/397/78211/gul-reiterates-the-need-for-concerted-efforts-against-xenophobia-islamophobia-antisemitism-discrimin.html.

47. Ahmet Hakan, "Milli Gazete yazarı Gül'ün Uçağında," *Hürriyet* (December 13, 2009).

48. "Germany's Ban on Newspaper for anti-Semitism Causes Storm in Turkey" (April 12, 2005), www.jihadwatch.org,/2005/04/germanys-ban-on-newspaper-for-anti-semitism-causes-storm-in-turkey.html; "Turkish paper Portrays Schröder as Nazi" (May 11, 2005), www.dw.de/dw/article/0,,1580623,00.html.

49. Ahmet Hakan, "Gül'e İki Kolay Soru," *Hürriyet* (November 9, 2007); Ahmet Hakan, "Cumhurbaşkanı Gül Vakit'i uçağına aldı," *Hürriyet* (February 7, 2008); Ahmet Hakan, "Milli Gazete Yazarı Gül'ün uçağında," *Hürriyet* (December 13, 2009); Ahmet Hakan, "Vakit yine uçakta," *Hürriyet* (September 6, 2010).

50. "Turkish Officials to Attend Auschwitz Holocaust Ceremonies," *Hürriyet Daily News* (January 28, 2011).

51. Barak Ravid, "Israel Accuses Turkish Prime Minister of Inciting anti-Semitism," *Ha'aretz* (January 26, 2010).

52. "David Ignatius" http://en.wikipedia.org/wiki/David_Ignatius.

53. "Lo tir'tsach (öldürmeyeceksin)," *Hürriyet* (January 17, 2009); "Erdoğan'dan 'İsrail'i BM'den atın' mesajı," *Milliyet* (January 17, 2009).

54. Sedat Ergin, "Can the Symbols of Nazism and Judaism Be Considered Equal?," *Hürriyet* (June 22, 2010).

55. "Dünyada medyayı İsrail yönetiyor," *Milliyet* (June 11, 2010).

56. Sedat Ergin, "Komplo teorilerine yeni katkı: Taşeronlar," *Hürriyet* (June 25, 2010).

57. Binnaz Toprak, "Politicisation of Islam in a Secular State: The National Salvation Party in Turkey," in Said Amir Arjomand, ed., *From Nationalism to Revolutionary Islam*, pp. 119–133; Ahmet Yıldız, "Politico-Religious Discourse of Political Islam in Turkey: The Parties of National Outlook," *The Muslim World* 93, no. 2 (April 2003), pp. 187–209; Ömer Çelik, "Turkey and the Fate of Political Islam," in Morton Abramowitz, ed., *The United States and Turkey Allies in Need* (New York: The Century Foundation Press, 2003), pp. 61–84; Türker Alkan, "The National Salvation Party in Turkey," in Metin Heper and Raphael Israeli, eds., *Islam and Politics in Middle East* (London: Crown Helm, 1984); Jacob M. Landau, *Politics and Islam: The National Salvation Party in Turkey* (Salt Lake City: University of Utah, Middle East Center, 1976).

58. Yalçın Küçük, *İsimlerin İbranileştirilmesi Tekelistan* (Istanbul: Salyangoz Yayınları, 2008); *Şebeke-1 Network* (Istanbul: İthaki Yayınları, 2004).

59. For a study of antisemitism among the followers of Milli Görüş in Germany, see the following: Claudia Dantschke, "Feindbild Juden. Zur Funktionalität der antisemitischen Gemeinschaftsideologie in muslimsch geprägten Milieus," *Konstellationen des Antisemitismus* (2010), Part I, pp. 139–46.

60. Eygi (b. 1933) is a graduate of the prestigious French-language Galatasaray Lycée and also of the political science faculty of Ankara University. Since Octo-

ber 1991 he has had a daily column in *Millî Gazete*. For more information, see www .mehmetsevketeygi.com.

61. Yıldız Ateş, "Önce Büyükşehir Belediyesi Yıkılmalı," *Sabah* (January 8, 2006).

62. Ayşe Arman, "Kadınları Kitaplardan tanıyorum," *Hürriyet* (August 29, 2004).

63. Cüneyt Ülsever, "Mehmet Şevket Eygi," *Hürriyet* (September 1, 2004).

64. Melih Aşık, "Dilek ve temenni," *Milliyet* (March 11, 2008).

65. Şirin Sever, "Azgınlık Müslümana Mahsus Bir Şey Değil ki!" *Sabah Pazar* (May 4, 2008).

66. Doğan Hızlan (b. 1937) is a literary critic and a columnist at the mainstream daily *Hürriyet*.

67. Faruk Bildirici, "Çankaya Sofralarının Mimarı," *Hürriyet Pazar* (November 8, 2009).

68. "İnsan Hakları Danışma Kurulu'na Yeni Atamalar," *Sabah* (November 23, 2004).

69. "Emine Erdoğan, Dilipak ailesinin ziyaret etti," *Taraf* (August 29, 2009).

70. Abdurrahman Dilipak, "Mübarek ABD dostu ABD dostu olmasına," *Yeni Akit* (February 2, 2011).

71. Yıldırım Türker, "Vakit nefret vakti," *Radikal* (May 4, 2009); Mansur Akgün, "Vakit, Antisemitik olmak zorunda mı?" *Referans* (January 4, 2010).

72. "Basın Konseyi Başkanı Oktay Ekşi, Vakit'in Almanya'da Kapatılmasını Kınadı" (February 26, 2005), www.basinkonseyi.org.tr.

73. M. Bahattin Seçilmişoğlu, "Türkiye Artık 'Akit"leşmeli,' www.liberal-dt.org.tr.

74. Ahmet Taşgetiren, "Akit'i susturmak," *Yeni Şafak* (December 3, 2001).

75. Hasan Bülent Kahraman, "Kemalizmle mutsuz olmak," *Sabah* (June 30, 2008).

76. Cemal Subaşı, "Referansı Vakit Gazetesi," *Tempo* (November 2010), pp. 162–68.

77. The Gayssot Law, enacted on July 13, 1990, makes it an offense to question the existence or size of the category of crimes aganist humanity. Source: "Gayssot Act," http:en.wikipedia.org/wiki/gayssot_Act.

78. Rıfat N. Bali, *Musa'nın Evlatları Cumhuriyet'in Yurttaşları* (Istanbul: İletişim Yayınları, 2001), pp. 361–62.

79. Rıfat N. Bali, *Musa'nın Evlatları Cumhuriyet'in Yurttaşları* (Istanbul: İletişim Yayınları, 2001), p. 384.

80. They are Helsinki Citizens Assembly (www.hyd.org.tr); the Human Rights Association (www.ihd.org.tr/english); the Human Rights Foundation of Turkey (www.tihv .org.tr); Say Stop to Racism and Nationalism! (www.durde.org); Association for Social Change (www.sosyaldergisim.org); the International Hrant Dink Foundation's (www .hrantdink.org) media watch and hate speech monitoring project (www.nefretsoylemi .org).

81. For a detailed summary, see "Hrant Dink," http://en.wikipedia/org/wiki/Hrant _Dink.

82. For example, T. Cengiz Algan and F. Levent Şensever, eds., *Ulusal Basında Nefret Suçları: 10 Yıl, 10 Örnek* (Istanbul: Sosyal Değişim Derneği, April 2010); Eser Aygül, Günseli Bayraktutan Sütçü, İlden Dizini, Mutlu Binark, Tuğrul Çomu, *Yeni Medyada Nefret Söylemi* (Istanbul: Kalkedon Yayınları, 2010); www.nefretsoylemi.org,

Reports I,II and III, covering the period April 2009–March 2010. Eser Köker, Ülkü Doğanay, *Irkçı Değilim ama . . .* , *Yazılı Basında Irkçı-Ayrımcı Söylemler* (Ankara: Kapasite Geliştirme Derneği, 2010).

83. Ekrem Dumanlı, "Racism Is a Serious Charge," *Today's Zaman* (February 7, 2011).

84. Orhan Kemal Cengiz, "The Racist of the Year in Turkey," *Today's Zaman* (January 30, 2011).

85. "Osmanlı torunuyuz, mazlum yanındayız," *Hürriyet* (January 7, 2009).

86. Leyla Navaro, "Türkiye'de Yahudi Olmak: 500 Yıllık Yalnızlık," *Radikal* (January 22, 2009).

87. "Cumhurbaşkanından Leyla Navaro'ya 'müsterih olun' telefonu," *Şalom* (January 28, 2009).

88. "Barak Dismisses Antisemitism Charges in Turkey, Says He Understands Erdoğan's Criticism," *Today's Zaman* (January 17, 2010).

89. Barak Ravid, "Israel Accuses Turkish PM of Inciting anti-Semitism," *Ha'aretz* (January 26, 2010), http://www.haaretz.com/print-edition/news/israel-accuses-turkish-pm-of-inciting-antisemitism-1.265790.

12 Antisemitism's Permutations in the Islamic Republic of Iran

Jamsheed K. Choksy

According to the Islamic Republic of Iran's official census in the year 2006, Jews made up 0.02 percent of a nationwide population of 70,049,262, or 14,009 men, women, and children.[1] More impressionistic, and therefore possibly less reliable, estimates placed Iran's Jewish population at between 20,000 to 25,000 individuals in 2010. But when the Islamic Republic released results of its 2011 population census, there were only 8,756 Jews in Iran, or less than 0.012 percent of a total population of 75,149,669.[2] During the mid-1970s, the community's demographic number had hovered around 80,000 individuals. Jews were mainly based in large cities like Hamadan, Shiraz, Isfahan, and Kerman, with roughly 75 percent of them living in the capital city of Tehran, due to urbanization and commercial opportunities under the Pahlavi shahs. Since then, many families have immigrated to the United States, to Israel, and to the European Union in search of religious, economic, and political freedom. They left behind empty Jewish neighborhoods that are being repopulated by Shiʿites and financial assets that have been appropriated by the Iranian state.[3]

Jews, like Christians and Zoroastrians, are one of three groups regarded by Muslims as *ahl al-ketab,* or communities with written scripture, who should be accepted and protected under the Shariʿa or Islamic law, including the Shiʿite version of it. Indeed, Jews, Christians, and Zoroastrians are regarded as *dhemmis* or non-Muslims protected, at least by words of statute and law, under Article 13 (the section on Recognized Religious Minorities) of the 1979 (amended 1989) Constitution of the Islamic Republic of Iran: "Zoroastrian, Jewish, and Christian Iranians are the only recognized religious minorities who, within the limits of the law, are free to perform their religious rites and ceremonies, and to act according to their own scriptures in matters of personal affairs and religious education."[4] Unfortunately, a farce has been made of this constitutional provision.[5]

The first Jews reached Iran when Israelites were resettled among the Medes of northwestern Iran in the eighth century BCE. Formal relations commenced when the Zoroastrian monarch Cyrus the Great conquered Babylonia in 539 BCE and set slaves there free. Despite being well established in Iran long before Islam arrived there, members of the Jewish community are not accepted by Iran's Shiʿite leaders as fully Iranian. So although the community is allotted one seat (of a total of 290) in the *majles,* or legislative assembly, Jews are barred from seeking high public office in the executive, judicial, and legislative branches of government. Additionally, Jews, like their Zoroastrian and Christian counterparts, are subject to persistent socioreligious discrimination. With regard to Jews, however, the situation is even more complex. Religious discrimination for being Jewish becomes coupled within the Islamic Republic of Iran with that nation's leaders' anti-Israel stance, and is equated to being Zionist, hegemonic, and anti-Muslim. Anti-Zionism, antisemitism, internal Iranian politics, and Iran's posturing within the Middle East are conflated in a noxious mix directed against Iranian Jews and their coreligionists worldwide. Consequently, Iran's Jews are treated as a fifth column by the Islamic Republic.

Ironically, whereas the Islamic Republic's founder Ayatollah Ruhollah Khomeini (1902–89) denounced the last shah or king for being pro-Israel and tolerant to Jews, saying "he gave his recognition to a government of nonbelievers—of Jews, at that—thereby affronting Islam," Iran's president, Mahmoud Ahmadinejad, is rumored to have Jewish roots.[6] Ahmadinejad is infamous for his denial of the Holocaust, for propagating the infamous *Protocols of the Elders of Zion* (another notoriously antisemitic theme in Iran), for refusing to recognize the nation-state of Israel, for claiming that the "Zionist regime runs counter to the dignity, independence and interests of all world nations," and for threatening the existence of Israel.[7] Lately, however, to serve his own political interests at home and abroad, Ahmadinejad alleges he does not deny the Holocaust. Rather, he goes around claiming, "I am not an antisemite . . . I am opposed to Zionism, which is based on racist ideas, and which has [caused] wars that terrorized others," even as he asserts that "extinguishing the Zionist nation [of Israel] is a global responsibility."[8]

Despite those denials, Ahmadinejad uses antisemitism to appeal to racists at home and in the Arab street, extending his influence beyond Iran with the latter. His repugnant views notwithstanding, Ahmadinejad's second term of executive office ends in July 2013. Iran's constitution bars a two-term president from serving a third consecutive term, and no previous two-term president has been reelected. So, despite his bellicosity and ability to grab the headlines through antisemitic rants, Ahmadinejad is unlikely to be a long-term foe to Jewish communities in Iran, Israel, and elsewhere—and even his military threats against Israel seem increasingly hollow. Nonetheless the Iranian president's tirades are continued by others in his cabinet, as by Vice President Mohammad Reza Rahimi who has alleged that "Zionists control the world's illegal narcotics trade."[9]

Even more than politicians, the *mollahs* or Shiʿite clergymen, however, have utilized the last three decades to become central in the Iranian sociopolitical fabric and are still fighting to retain their power despite challenges from both within the government and from reformists like the Green Movement.[10] Unlike elected politicians, the ayatollahs and their supreme leader—who wields overall ultimate say over Iran's government—are not transient. Many of them, especially politically active ayatollahs, routinely manipulate religious beliefs, historical traditions, and societal mores to propagate hatred for Jews and Judaism.[11] More than any other group in Iranian society, those *mollahs* remain the main source of antisemitism in Iranian society. As a result, the rise and persistence of antisemitism in modern Iran is a very real danger to Jews, to the State of Israel, and to humanity's ideals and values. It also is detrimental to Iran's own society and politics. The roots, manifestations, and impacts of that virulent racism make it clear that constant vigilance is necessary to prevent the spread of antisemitism within Iran and to counter the harm it causes to Iranian Jews.

Religious Roots

The roots of Iranian antisemitism are to be found, alas, in that hardest-to-change aspect of life—distorted interpretations of and fabrications attributed to religion. Ayatollah Khomeini, who took charge of the newly established Islamic Republic of Iran in 1979, had made his views of the country's non-Muslim communities crystal clear in *resalas,* or religious pronouncements, for many years before he became the first post-revolutionary supreme leader. "Every aspect of a non-Muslim is unclean," Khomeini proclaimed in 1987, for instance.[12] Khomeini even produced a list of impurities that were associated with Jews: "urine, feces, semen, bone, blood, dogs, pigs, non-Muslims, wine, beer, and the sweat of camels that eat unclean food."[13] Iran's second supreme leader, Ayatollah Ali Khamenei, reaffirmed his predecessor's viewpoints, adding that Jews, Zoroastrians, and Christians are *kafers,* or "persons who do not acknowledge the truth [i.e., infidels]."[14] Pronouncements by Khomeini and Khamenei are especially consequential because both are regarded as *marjaᶜ* or sources of emulation by pious Shiᶜites. Following in their footsteps, Ayatollah Ahmed Jannati, secretary of the Shura-ye Negahban, or Guardian Council of Iran's Islamic Constitution which supervises elections and other public duties, publicly claimed in November 2005 that members of those three minority groups were "beasts who roam the earth and engage in corruption."

Influential ayatollahs who have served as mentors to Ahmadinejad and other politicians even blame any and all discontent among Iranians on "Jewish machinations." Mohammad Taqi Mesbah Yazdi, an influential member of the Assembly of Experts that elects the supreme leaders, directly linked the public protests that began in July 2009 to "corrupt centers belonging to Jews and Zionists in the world." In May 2011, Yazdi issued a fatwa or religious injunction approving of martyrdom for the purpose of "uprooting of the Zionist regime and its arrogant supporters."[15] Ahmad Khatami, also a member of the Assembly of Experts and a Friday prayer leader in Tehran, has proclaimed that "Jews should be crushed."[16] Ahmad Khatami is a leading candidate to be the next supreme leader of Iran, and so his antisemitism could have long-lasting and major consequences for Iranian society. Many other ayatollahs routinely make similar hate-filled speeches to rouse hostility toward Jews and Israel among their acolytes.[17]

Even the late Hossein Ali Montazeri (1922–2009), often revered as the "people's Ayatollah," who, once cast aside by the revolutionary elites, was a fierce critic of the theocratic regime, did not differ much from the other *mollahs* in attitudes toward Jews and other religious minorities. Yet, as his own battles with the regime intensified, Montazeri became more open to extending additional rights beyond those of medieval-like *dhemmis* in Iran. However, he did not sway from the fundamentalist Shiʿite perception that "non-Muslims are impure" and that "Judaism was racist from its inception." He merely suggested that "any non-Muslim, even a Jew" could make himself or herself "pure through chaste, Muslim-like, behavior."[18] The same holds for the former *majles* or parliament speaker, presidential candidate, and Green Movement leader Seyyed Mehdi Karroubi, who gained considerable support from Jews and Zoroastrians in the 2009 presidential elections. Karroubi had approved of granting them more civil and criminal rights when he served in the parliament, so he earned their goodwill. But he, too, has never endorsed equality with Shiʿites. Seyyed Mohammad Khatami, Iran's fifth president from 1997 to 2005, while more circumspect, has indirectly denied antisemitism exists in modern Iran and has gone so far as to suggest that "western antisemitism and anti-Jewishness" created Zionism which then became "a tool for the imposition of a whole range of wrong policies and practices."[19] So, there is little theological difference and only a marginal pragmatism among the various Shiʿite views toward Jews. Thus, Montazeri's opinion was characterized by one Iranian Jew as "rubbing salt into our wounds."

Ultimately mere tolerance of differences, especially religious ones, is far from acceptance, as the Jews of Iran point out. They are less perturbed by President Ahmadinejad's hostility, presuming his influence will be gone once his term in office ends, but speak of "fearing the incessant attacks from those who claim to be pious spokesmen of the Prophet Muhammad yet spread hate in the name of religion." An Iranian rabbi pointed out to me in 2003: "Politicians may arouse the masses against us when it suits their political ends, but the *mollahs* have constantly spearheaded our persecution. They drove us out of villages that our ancestors had settled long before Islam arrived in Iran. They misrepresent Islam to the masses who ignorantly follow their lead." Indeed, as the rabbi observed, hate speech permeates sermons by Friday prayer leaders like Mollah Ebrahim Mohajerian at the town of Tabas in central Iran who claims to his Shiʿite congregations that "according to the Quʾran, the Bani-Israel are acolytes of Satan and therefore the worst enemies of humanity and particularly of devout Muslims."[20] Moreover, those Muslim preachers have far more influence in shaping the dispositions of average Shiʿites than do politicians from nonclerical backgrounds like Ahmadinejad (even though the Iranian president's comments get far more airtime in the West due to his official position).

Political Augmentations

Because the modern nation-states of Iran and Israel did not have conflict until the advent of the Islamic Republic in 1979, the rise of political antisemitism and its nexus with religiously based anti-Jewish sentiment may seem unusual but is not. The contemporary conjoining of political antisemitism with religious anti-Jewish ideas in Iran occurred during the past one hundred or so years. Accusations of Jews attempting to control Iran, the Middle East, and the world began to be intertwined with Shiʿite repugnance for *dhemmis* due to the influence of European antisemitism. Particularly, and unfortunately, most influential on Iranian intellectuals of the early to middle twentieth century was Germany's National Socialist movement with its racist tenet calling Jews the incarnation of all that is evil.[21]

Iran had experienced economic hardship during the Qajar dynasty, which ruled Iran from 1794 to 1925, as England and Russia expanded their dominions. Iranians found themselves caught between the colonial superpowers' great game, with treaties and foreign laws enforced upon the country. So, Iranian politicians and intelligentsias turned to another European nation—Germany—in an attempt at counterbalancing colonialism. Germany, in turn, saw Iran as a source of metals and minerals needed for industrialization and militarization. Germans began living and working in Iran as engineers, technicians, financiers, advisers, and scholars. As the British and Russians divided up Iran into spheres of influence by the Anglo-Russian Convention of 1907, helped Qajar elites end the Constitutional Revolution of 1905–11, and strangled Iranians' economic independence, more Iranians than ever before began to view Germany as an ally.[22]

When Reza Shah Pahlavi came to the throne in 1925, despite having done so with British funding and Russian training, he, too, distrusted those nations. Consequently, the shah turned to Nazi Germany for political models and industrial technology, and the Nazis became Iran's largest trading partner. In September 1939, Iran formally declared its neutrality in the Second World War, yet supplied raw materials to Adolf Hitler's regime via the Soviet Union. Then in June 1941, hoping to recover the Caucasus and Turkmenistan, Iran claimed to be neutral when the Nazis invaded Soviet territory. All this intrigue culminated in Soviet forces entering Iran from the northwest and the British army coming in from Iraq and India, whereupon the Iranian army surrendered after three days. Reza Shah, forced to abdicate, was exiled to Mauritius and South Africa by the British Raj and his son Mohammad Reza Shah Pahlavi was placed on the throne. In December 1942, U.S. troops—the Persian Gulf Command—entered Iran to man supply lines to Russia.[23]

Reza Shah had not been impartial toward Iran's Jews. He banned their migration from Iran, even arresting and executing Shemuel Haim, who led the Iranian Zionist Organization.[24] That shah's political philosophy demanded Iranian Jews integrate into the modern state he was attempting to create even at the expense of their ethno-religious identity. His son, Mohammad Reza, flirted with Aryanism as a racist aspect of an ill-fated attempt to link his rule to Iran's ancient imperial past. Reza Shah and Mohammad Reza (while crown prince) saw Germany as a cultural partner in addition to a political ally. Yet once he took the throne, Mohammad Reza relied on his Jewish subjects plus Zoroastrian and Christian ones more than orthodox Muslims to support his increasingly autocratic rule.[25] The second Pahlavi shah correctly presumed that religious minorities would accept the safety he could provide against the *mollahs* in exchange for loyalty to the crown. In so doing, both the monarch and the minorities became the focus of fundamentalist ire.

An even more nefarious influence was active against the Jewish community at that time. Many Iranians who lived during the interwar and war years, including most of the older *mollahs* now in power, had childhood memories of Nazi Germany's ostensible support for Iranian independence. They recalled Nazi radio broadcasts and pamphlets in the Farsi or Persian language claiming that Germans and Iranians were Aryan kin and that Jews were anti-Iranian through an alliance with the British who had exploited Iran. Radio Zeesen, broadcasting from Berlin, linked Qurʾanic *suras,* or chapters, about Prophet Muhammad's clashes with Jewish tribes in Arabia to Shiʿite Iranian struggles against the British and

Russians. The presence of a Zionist Association and even a Zionist Association of Jewish Women were seen by Iran's wartime antisemites as alleged confirmation of Nazi propaganda.[26]

Khomeini, then a Shiʿite cleric in his thirties, listened avidly to this Nazi ranting. He even hosted gatherings of *mollahs* and their sons at Qom, during the late 1930s and early 1940s, to hear Germany's increasingly antisemitic message via radio broadcasts. Due to Shiʿite notions of Jews being unclean, impure, and in conflict with Muslims since Muhammad's time, those *mollahs* could assimilate the Nazi bigotry. In the minds of Khomeini and his cohorts, as evidenced by their later fatwas, events like colonialism, the establishment of the modern State of Israel, and the Westernization of Iranian society under the second Pahlavi shah all seemed part of a Zionist master plan to take over Iran, the rest of the Middle East, and eventually the world with the aim of subjugating Muslims.[27] They came to regard Jews, irrespective of location and political disposition, in an even worse light than the British, Russians, Americans, and pro-Western Iranians whom they hoped to run out of Iran. Their antisemitism was fueled further by the Six Day War of 1967, the Yom Kippur War of 1973, and the imperial Iranian regime's support of Israel during those conflicts.

As activist *mollahs* led by Khomeini fought the last shah, they latched on to his support for Israel during its wars with Arab nations, his adoration of Iran's pre-Islamic past linked to the liberation of Israelites from Babylonia, and his promoting of minorities to positions of authority, to denounce the Pahlavi regime. Not only Iranians who benefited from the Pahlavi monarchy but even individuals and groups who tolerated the crown came to be seen as under the supposedly ever-expanding influence of Judaism and Zionism. Jews were blamed, as well, for having supported Mohammad Reza Pahlavi during the populist uprising led by Prime Minister Mohammad Mosaddeq in August 1953. It was even rumored that they had funded the shah's brief exile in Rome and worked with the U.S. Central Intelligence Agency on Operation Ajax to ensure his return to power.[28]

During the Islamic Revolution itself, antisemites spread gossip that Israeli troops assisted the shah's soldiers and policemen by shooting demonstrators with tanks, helicopter gunships, and sniper fire in Tehran on Black Friday (September 8, 1978). Israel's alleged assistance was said to be remuneration for Mohammad Reza Pahlavi's regime having supplied Israel with petroleum during the Yom Kippur War.[29] It also was alleged that Iranian Jews had personally aided in that massacre, despite their having demonstrated in large numbers against the shah on that and other days of the revolution. Thus, all who opposed the *mollahs*' imposition of *velayat-e faqih* or governance by Muslim jurists were also conveniently tarred as puppets of Jews and Zionists worthy of being ousted and kept suppressed for the good of Iran's Muslims. Jews received numerous threats in person and via telephone calls and graffiti, aimed at forcing them out of Iran. Their homes and stores were burglarized and vandalized. Eventually, the Jewish community's leaders met with Ayatollah Khomeini in November 1979 to plead for protection. They were assured by Khomeini that he felt "Jews are different from Zionists," and that Iran's ayatollahs would instruct Muslim Iranians to "leave Jews alone."[30] Yet, in practice there was little change in the oppression unleashed on Iranian Jews after 1979, for Khomeini never really wavered from his antisemitic behaviors.

Religiopolitical Consequences

Outlining attitudes toward Jews and the Jewish state, to which he believed all Iranians should ascribe, Khomeini had written in 1970: "Islam and the Islamic people met their first saboteur in the Jewish people who are at the source of all anti-Islamic libels and intrigues." Using his pulpit as the best-known ayatollah plus his national role as supreme leader, Khomeini linked Jews and Israel to colonialism and anti-American sentiments by adding after his aforementioned words, "then came those other representatives of Satan, the imperialists, with the intent of destroying Islam and . . . distorting Muslim truths."[31]

In another *resala*, Khomeini expanded the framework of antisemitism by alleging, "We see today the Jews even distort editions of the Qurʾan, especially in the occupied territory, for they are bent on the destruction of Islam and the establishment of a universal Jewish government. So they try to destroy Iran for we protest and oppose them." Claiming that "even in Tehran, propaganda centers have set up to spread Zionism," Khomeini urged his followers, "Is it not our duty to destroy all these hotbeds of danger?"[32] Here Iran's first supreme leader was connecting opposition to Jews and Israel with preservation of both Islam and Iran—and in so doing was widening the Iranian theocratic state's rationalization for antisemitic actions at home and abroad. Khomeini was adept at blurring distinctions between Jews, Judaism, Zionism, Israel, colonialism, imperialism, Westernization, international relations, and other nations' supposedly anti-Muslim politics. So he declared: "It is forbidden for any Muslim nation to have commercial and diplomatic relations with countries which play the role of puppets for the great powers as is the case with Israel. It is the duty of all Muslims to oppose such relations, by every means available. Anyone who deals with Israel, its representatives, and its agents is a traitor."[33]

That particular statement is especially significant as it has been used, over and over again, since 1979 to prosecute Iranian Jews for allegedly serving as agents of Israel and Zionism. A tragic outcome was the execution by firing squad in May 1979 of Habib Elghanian, president of the Tehran Jewish Society. Ebrahim Berukim, a wealthy hotel owner, was killed on charges of espionage and corruption in July 1980. Altogether, at least a dozen Jews were slain by firing squad and hanging during the first few years after the Islamic revolution.[34] Indeed, even the Tehran Jewish Society's participation in the revolution did not safeguard its members once the Islamists gained power. Nor did the activities of the anti-Zionist Organization of Iranian Jewish Intellectuals—which had been founded in March 1978, had accepted the main tenets of the Islamic revolution, and endeavored to build a bridge between *mollahs* and Jews—help mitigate antisemitism.[35] Subsiding of revolutionary fervor in the years since then has not mitigated the danger faced by Iranian Jewry. Eleven of them were convicted by an Iranian court in July 2000 on charges of espionage for Israel, although their death sentences were subsequently commuted to jail time.[36] More recently, in the wake of the Stuxnet computer worm attack on Iran's nuclear facilities in 2010, Iranian officials arrested Muslims and Jews, contending they worked for "Zionists."[37] A Jewish woman (who was a dual citizen of Iran and the United States) and her Armenian husband were hanged after a summary trial in camera at Tehran's notorious Evin Prison for political prisoners in March 2011.[38]

The belief that Jews are fundamentally "traitors" to God (i.e., Allah) and country (i.e., Iran) is summed up in a mocking graffito of Mohammad Reza Shah Pahlavi dripping blood sprayed on the outside wall of the synagogue in the city of Shiraz.[39] Similar images were painted on the exterior wall of Zoroastrian fire temples with words faulting the Zoroastrians' ancestors, namely the Achaemenid or Persian kings, for having "freed Jews from the Babylonian captivity," for having "granted Iranian funds to illegally take over Jerusalem and build the [Second] Temple," and therefore for "permitting Jews to have survived." Members of both religious minorities point to those images as linking them to the ousted imperial dynasty and its allies in the West and the Middle East, especially to Israel. The graffito still endures, and is refreshed periodically by members of the Basij, or paramilitary.

The idea that Jews, Judaism, and especially Israel would not exist if not for the actions of Cyrus, Darius, and the other Persian kings of the sixth and fifth centuries BCE has become relatively widespread among activist Shiʿite clergymen. One of them leveled similar charges against me in Qazvin, upon learning that I was a Zoroastrian born in India, was raised in Sri Lanka, and am teaching in the United States. That *mollah* became irate when I told him that Zoroastrians, many of whose ancestors fled from Iran to India during the Middle Ages to escape religious persecution and forced conversion to Islam, were and still are proud their ancestors played a role in saving the Israelites and preserving Judaism.

The motif of Jerusalem as a Muslim site connected to Prophet Muhammad and his descendants, the twelve Shiʿite imams or religious leaders, and therefore "illegally" occupied by Jews forms part of the antisemitism propagated by fundamentalist *mollahs* in Iran. The theocrats even augment those claims by suggesting that Iranians have to rectify the situation. A mural on the courtyard wall of the Tomb of the Prophet Daniel at Sush (ancient Susa) in southwestern Iran depicts the future capture of the Temple Mount by Iranian and Palestinian forces—complete with an English-language caption in addition to one in Farsi.

The site dates back to pre-Islamic Iran as an important shrine for Jews, who see Daniel not only as a prophet but also as an official of the Persian Empire in the mid-fifth century BCE pivotal in ensuring their community's revival. It was transformed into an Islamic holy place shortly after the Arab conquest of Iran in the seventh century CE, because Daniel is placed by Muslims into the prophet lineage that leads to Muhammad. It was rebuilt into its current sugar-loaf form by Seljuk rulers of the eleventh century.[40] Its use now as not just a Shiʿite center of prayer and meditation, but as a center for imparting militancy, intolerance, and racism pains Iranian Jews, who by and large (but not all, for some ignore the propaganda murals and the Muslim presence) shun going there on pilgrimage.

The prominence of the idea of seizing Jerusalem can be traced back to Ayatollah Khomeini, who urged pilgrims to Mecca in February 1971, Muslims worldwide in September 1979, and Iranians specifically on Nav Roz, or Persian New Year, in March 1980, to

> turn your attention to the liberation of the Islamic land of Palestine from the grasp of Zionism, the enemy of Islam and humanity. Do not hesitate to assist and cooperate with those heroic men who are struggling to liberate Palestine. . . . Israel is casting dissension among Muslims with all the diabolical means at its disposal . . . [so] defend the peoples and countries of Islam against international Zionism . . . against the global plunders of the West headed by Zionism, Israel, and Jews.[41]

Ultimately, according to lectures by Khomeini while exiled at Najaf in Iraq during the 1970s, pious Iranians are expected to emulate Prophet Muhammad's dealings with Jews: "Since the Jews of Bani Qurayza were a troublesome group, causing corruption in Muslim society and damaging Islam and the Islamic polity, the most noble messenger eliminated them."[42]

The antisemitism that pervaded all of Khomeini's religious, political, and social speeches and writings—due to his fundamentalist, militant, and intolerant interpretation of Islam and his conjoining of those sentiments to the activist branch of Shiʿism, which he led to political power—still generates violent outbreaks of antisemitism. Accordingly, in December 2010, Basij recruits at the northwestern locale of Hamadan threatened to demolish the Tomb of Esther and Mordecai.

That holy site forms part of an ancient and modern synagogue complex, for the local Jewish community of about 2,500 persons plus Jewish pilgrims from all over Iran, in the former Median and Achaemenian city's center. The new synagogue, built during the time of the last shah, even had a Star of David incorporated into the roof's infrastructure—this is now kept out of public view with foliage along the property's perimeter.[43] Claiming that Israelis were about to storm the Al-Aqsa Mosque on the Temple Mount in Jerusalem, demonstrators chanted, "We the student Basijis . . . warn Zionist regime leaders . . . we will destroy the tomb of these lowly murderers."[44] Yes, Esther and Mordecai are viewed as murderers by Islamists. *Mollahs* are rewriting the biblical tale of the Book of Esther. They claim that Mordecai and Esther brought about the "massacre of 70,000 Iranians" in pre-Islamic times. Here the Shiʿite clerics can draw on antisemitism that unfortunately sprang up among noted Iranian literati and thinkers of the twentieth century like Sadeq Hedayat and Ali Shariati. Those intellectuals, just like the *mollahs,* were seduced by antisemitism in reaction to British colonialism in the Middle East, the Qajar and Pahlavi dynasties' dependence on the West for survival, the rise of nationalism and Aryanism fueled by ideas coming to Iran from Nazi Germany, and the occupation of Iran by the Allies during the Second World War.[45] Again, as in the case of Daniel, and once more irrespective of the historicity of site and biblical events, a locale most holy to Iran's diminishing Jewish community has become a target—in this case, as retaliation for a fabricated massacre and for Israeli presence in Jerusalem and on the West Bank.

Ayatollah Khamenei, Khomeini's successor to the position of supreme leader, expanded the dangerous rhetoric. In a *khotba,* or sermon, delivered after prayer in September 2009, Khamenei referred to Zionism as a "cancer gnawing on Islamic nations." He was resurrecting a theme from 2001 when he had remarked that "the tumor which is Israel should be excised."[46] In February 2010, Khamenei reiterated that all Muslim nations should follow Iran's example by not diplomatically recognizing Israel and by providing material support for Palestinians. "I am very optimistic about the future of Palestine and believe Israel is on the steep path of decline and deterioration," Khamenei said after a meeting with Ramadan Abdullah, Secretary General of Palestinian Islamic Jihad, adding "God willing, its [Israel's] destruction will be imminent."[47]

Another senior ayatollah and *marjaᶜ,* Nasser Makarem Shirazi, takes pride in dismissing the Holocaust as a "superstition" and a "great lie" used to justify the existence of Israel at the expense of Palestinians' suffering.[48] As a result, Neo-Nazi websites operate in Iran with the permission of that country's Ministry of Culture and Islamic Guidance. Privately funded websites, also operating with permits from that ministry, question the Holocaust's veracity through cartoons and videos.[49] Thus, Ayatollah Jannati, who as previously discussed regards Jews as "beasts," has characterized the theocrat-controlled regime in Tehran as an "Anti-Israeli regime; they are our enemies, and we are theirs. The hostility is not personal; it is a matter of principle . . . the very fundamentals that underlay our revolution and belief." Following in the ideological footsteps of his mentor Khomeini and his leader Khamenei, Jannati declares: "Just like we destroyed the regime of the Shah, we will destroy Israel." Likewise, Mohammad Reza Naghdi, a loyalist of Supreme Leader Khamenei and consequently Brigadier General of the Basij paramilitary since October 2009, who was placed under U.S. Department of Treasury sanctions in February 2011, echoed his racist religious mentor in July 2011 by calling for "eradicating the Zionist regime."[50]

As a result, accusing political opponents or their families "of secretly being Jews" or "of being in the pay of Jews and Israel" is not uncommon in contemporary Iran's ever-tumultuous internal tussles.[51] Indeed, unlike their boss Ahmadinejad, many of the Iranian president's men are not associated with antisemitic remarks and threats—and are hounded by fundamentalist *mollahs* for that reason. Activist *mollahs* accused Ahmadinejad's progressive and secularist chief of staff Esfandiyar Rahim Mashaei of harboring pro-Israeli policies and ousted him from the post of first vice president in July 2009. Mashaei was compelled to declare that his personal, positive views of Jews were different from the regime's disposition toward Israel, although he did not retreat from his remark that "Iran is friends with the Israeli people."[52] Vice president for executive affairs Hamid Baghaei also was accused of having made contact with Israeli officials while visiting other Middle Eastern and Western capitals—he eventually was barred from public office for four years on the grounds of misusing official positions.

Ahmadinejad emerges an anomaly among his close supporters for, unlike them, he seems to relish in the infamy that his racist threats against Israel bring. In part, he is playing to anti-Jewish and anti-Israel sentiments among some Iranians, Arabs, and Europeans. Yet his denial of the Holocaust (including hosting a conference on the topic in Tehran in December 2006), belief that Israel will cease to exist, and support of anti-Israel militants including Hamas and Hizbullah have made him a global pariah. Even his challenge to the *mollahs* over Iran's future, with the president pushing a nonclerical agenda, does not earn Ahmadinejad much goodwill outside his country.[53]

Socioreligious Ramifications

The Jewish community in Iran must ensure that bar mitzvahs, bat mitzvahs, weddings, and funerals are discreet affairs due to the constant negativity from fundamentalist ayatollahs and their followers. Even so, they run the risk of raids by officials from the Ministry of Islamic Culture and Guidance, who are tasked with ensuring adherence to "Islamic standards." Allowing men and women to mingle and consumption of alcohol are two frequent charges against Jews arrested by the Islamic Republic's morals police—even though Jews' right to do so is endorsed by the constitution's reference to customary behaviors.[54] On one occasion, in 1983, more than 2,000 Jewish men, women, and children were detained overnight, without charges being filed, after they attended a Shabbat prayer service at a synagogue in Tehran.[55] This incident in particular provoked much trepidation among parents as to whether their offspring had any viable long-term future within Iranian's theocratically controlled society. The Intelligence Ministry closely monitors Jewish religious associations, and those organizations are routinely denied permission for formal contacts with foreign-based Jewish ones. Periodicals and newsletters such as *Tammuz* and *Ofoq-e Bina,* and websites such as www.iranjewish.com, run by the Tehran Jewish Committee, are closely supervised by *mollahs* to ensure the presence of anti-Israeli content.[56] Moreover, a committee of *mollahs* in Qom has been empowered to "combat activities of members of religious minorities."[57]

Iran's Constitution permits Jews to "act according to their own canon in matters of personal affairs and religious education." Yet, Iran's Education Ministry administers minority schools and imposes a state-approved religious textbook. Many Jewish secondary schools have been nationalized or have had Muslim clerics imposed as teachers. The few surviving private schools typically have Muslim directors. Jewish schools must display portraits of Iran's supreme leaders Khomeini and Khamenei plus Qurʾanic quotations and revolutionary slogans in classrooms and hallways. Students are forced to attend in-school gatherings where *mollahs* and revolutionary guards chant praises to the Shiʿite imams. All university applicants, including Jews, must pass an examination in Islamic theology and even then find themselves disqualified from admission to state-run campuses.[58]

Jews, like Iran's other religious minority groups, experience high unemployment and economic impoverishment because they are not readily hired by the large state sector that includes the oil industry.[59] Minority storeowners must display prominent signs indicating they are *najasa,* or ritually unclean—continuing a practice that dates back five hundred years to the Safavid dynasty and was not prohibited even under the two Pahlavi shahs. Most Jewish shopkeepers circumvent this requirement by placing the sign next to the cash register when they see the religious police nearby.[60] Properties belonging to Jews have steadily been confiscated by the state ostensibly because that wealth, estimated at over U.S. $1 billion, had been ill gotten.[61] However, non-Muslims are not excluded from the compulsory and poorly compensated military service and they report being deployed for especially hazardous assignments. During the Iran–Iraq war, they were routinely transferred to suicide brigades to die, involuntarily, for their country.

Despite their centuries-long loyalty to the Islamic Republic and Iranian society, Jews are not on a par with the majority of Iranians in legal disputes. Any non-Muslim responsible for a Muslim's death faces capital punishment, in accordance with medieval Islamic jurisprudence, under the Islamic Republic's Criminal Code. Conversely, Muslims do not face capital punishment or even long prison sentences for murdering a non-Muslim, though they are fined. The Civil Code stipulates that any Jew who converts to Islam becomes the sole inheritor of his or her family's assets.[62] On the other hand, converts from Islam to Judaism are regarded by the state as apostates who can be put to death. Iran bans Jews and other non-Muslims not only from proselytizing but also from most public religious expressions in the presence of Muslims.

As mentioned, Ahmadinejad's government hosted a conference at Tehran in December 2006 to discuss whether the Holocaust occurred—complete with an international cast of antisemites including former Ku Klux Klan imperial wizard David Duke.[63] Perhaps his own alleged paternal family connections to Iran's Jewish community lead Ahmadinejad to antisemitic actions like the Tehran conference as a way of preempting attacks by fundamentalist *mollahs* for not hailing from a long-established Shiʿite family. Iranian propaganda and international denunciation surrounding that conference made Jews across Iran "uncomfortable, embarrassed, and sad at that time," one leader in Tehran later commented. But worse was to come, for the Iranian Jewish community's representatives were compelled to participate in that presidential-sponsored charade. Like others there, they too had to question whether the Holocaust occurred, denounce Israel and Zionism, and declare they saw non-Iranian Jews as "imperialists" and "oppressors."

An even more widespread form of antisemitism manifests itself through the state-run education system. School textbooks, teacher-training manuals, and even calendars falsely claim that Prophet Muhammad was "poisoned by a Jewess."[64] Medieval Jews also are misleadingly linked to Sunnis as co-conspirators in the deaths of Shiʿa imams via popular literature sold in city and village bazaars. Such misinformation leads to Jews being shunned in the workplace by Muslims and often to their dismissal from employment—not just from positions in the state sector but also from private corporations and even universities. Due to the widespread disinformation, most Jews encounter constant suspicion from fundamentalist Shiʿites as "secret agents for Israel, Zionism, and American imperialists" and hear threats that they will be "eliminated before they can do further harm to Shiʿism."[65]

Most distressingly for Iranian Jews, current Supreme Leader Khamenei, who is likely to remain in office long after other politicians like Ahmadinejad have faded from the national scene, never foregoes an opportunity to talk about the "removal of Jews from Iran." Khamenei is even more vocal than Ahmadinejad about "the destruction of the Zionist regime." Even though the international press does not report much on Khamenei, his words are routinely reproduced in the Iranian press—for instance after his meeting in January 2010 with the Mauritanian President General Mohamed Ould Abdel Aziz, whose country severed diplomatic ties with Israel in 2009 to protest events in Gaza.[66] Khamenei's comments influence events in the social sphere of Iranian life. Such words are regarded by militants in the Basij, the Committee on Public Morals, and other Shiʿite organizations as license to persecute Iranian Jews on a daily basis—from name-calling as Jewish children go to and from school to defiling the kosher meals of office co-workers. Made-up issues are aimed at intensifying Shiʿite fears of Jewish impurity and Zionist imperialism, and Holocaust denial is disseminated in a range of audiovisual materials like comic books, radio, and TV programs, CDs, YouTube broadcasts, and even seemingly academic studies.[67] The range and reach of those prejudicial materials is expanding beyond the Islamic Republic of Iran's borders via the Internet to reach and influence Muslims and others disposed negatively toward Jews, Judaism, and Israel around the globe.

In March 2011, a 75-minute messianic documentary titled "The Reappearance is Very Near" aired on Shia TV (which broadcasts in Persian, Arabic, Urdu, and English). Aimed at Muslims who feel oppressed by Western-oriented leaders, the program was distributed globally via the Internet and CD-ROM. It explicitly links the savior's impending arrival to recent revolts in the Arab world, to Iran's Islamic revolution of 1979, and to Tehran's foreign policy under Khamenei and Ahmadinejad. It calls for overthrow of Arab and Western leaders as precursory steps to the Mahdi's advent. It is replete with antisemitic claims that Jews and Israel are the cause of humanity's suffering and also shows Muslim troops from Iran and its allies training to storm Jerusalem.[68]

The message of hate is frighteningly clear: the demagogues in Tehran want Jews and Israel eliminated either before or after their savior appears. Neither Khamenei nor Ahmadinejad have distanced themselves from the video's central messages, although both claimed through intermediaries to have played no role in its production. *Mollahs* fighting Ahmadinejad for power within Iran's government have publicly blamed the president for its production—although Chief of Staff Mashaei, not known for antisemitic thoughts, has denied any such connection. Nonetheless, the documentary's producer is known to be an admirer of Ahmadinejad.

Persistence and Backlash

As analyzed, the roots of modern antisemitism in Iran stem from a fundamentalist Shiʿite notion that Jews are religiously inferior. That religious idea was combined with and politicized by Nazi German influence during the anticolonial struggle of Iranians against Britain and Russia. Identification of minorities as favored by the ousted pro-Western imperial regime of the Pahlavis compounded Iranian Islamists' dislike for the Jewish community. Finally, the Islamic Republic's opposition to the nation-state of Israel, both as a pan-Islamist issue and as a way for Iran's leaders to spread their influence over the Arab Middle East and other Muslim communities, adds fuel to antisemitism.

Yet, antisemitism has never prevented the Islamic Republic's leaders from turning to Iran's Jewish minority when necessary for political ends. Hence, in September 2009, to shore up Iran's image as a tolerant nation after the violent quashing of pro-democracy protests in the wake of a contested presidential election, Ahmadinejad "summoned the minorities to Iran's aid"—as one Iranian political wag privately commented. Iran's president included minority representatives from the parliament, like

Jewish lawmaker Siamak Moreh-Sedeq, on an official entourage to the United Nations General Assembly. Iran is one "big and unified family" with full legal rights for religious minorities, Ahmadinejad declared at a meeting of the no doubt startled minority parliamentarians, according to official reports. Not only could the parliamentarians be punished if they resisted, but their religious communities would suffer the hard-line regime's reprisals as well. "Communal welfare is important, so absence will not be possible" another Iranian minority religious leader apologetically explained before the New York trip. Although Ahmadinejad's co-opting of the Jewish parliamentarian for the state visit to New York was not antisemitic, all five minority delegates were hostages to Iran's deceptive diplomacy. Indeed, they had specific instructions not to engage in any unauthorized "contacts or interviews" while in the United States.[69] Yet including them in official diplomacy demonstrates both the symbolic and actual valence Jews, Zoroastrians, and Christians still hold in Iranian society. On the world stage, the importance of Iran's Jewry as living descendants and therefore representatives of Judaism from its earliest days is not underestimated even by the antisemites who control Iran.

Despite all their destructive and racist behaviors, Iran's ruling hardliners have not succeeded in convincing a majority of their citizens that Jews and Israel warrant demonization. Many Iranians question the regime's support of antisemitic and anti-Israeli policies and groups, embrace their heritage of tolerance for others, and mince no words that the *mollahs* are deluded when denying the Holocaust.[70] Iran's increasingly secular and politically disenfranchised population, over 60 percent of whom are under the age of forty, views supporting antisemitism, threatening Jews and Israel, and funding terrorism in the Middle East as harming their own society and their nation's international standing.

Iranians are well aware that religious discrimination and persecution in general and antisemitism in particular were not always the religio-political norm in Iran. In the Persian empire of antiquity, Cyrus the Great established a policy of religious tolerance as outlined on the Cyrus Cylinder.[71] That monarch's words of acceptance are sometimes described as the first charter of human rights. Subsequently, the Bible recounts, Darius the Great and Xerxes facilitated the Israelite community's resurgence, including reconstruction of the Temple at Jerusalem as even the mollahs know. It should be noted in this context that most Iranian Shi'ite mollahs belong not to the fundamentalist activist school that Ayatollah Khomeini led to power in 1979 but to a quietist nonpolitical majority.[72] Some of them have recounted to me the pride they feel that a symbol of their ancient non-Muslim (i.e., Zoroastrian) ancestors' socioreligious acceptance still survives in the form of Jerusalem's Western Wall.

Approximately 2,500 years after Cyrus's civility, Jews of Persian origin did not experience the death camps of the Holocaust. In Germany, the Nazis debated the status of Iranian Jews and Adolf Eichmann even wrote a dossier urging that all Iranian Jews should be deported or killed.[73] But they continued to be regarded by both the Pahlavi dynasty and the Nazis as citizens of Iran and so beyond Germany's sinister authority. Iran even became a transit point for approximately 2,000 Jews escaping Europe, including the so-called Polish Children of Tehran.[74] Iran's ties with the nation-state of Israel remained vibrant until the Islamic Revolution. The knowledge and values of that harmonious past remain strong in Iran and so bode hope for the future.[75]

NOTES

I am grateful to Harvard University and Indiana University for funding fieldwork in Iran from the 1980s through the 2000s. Drs. Vera Moreen, Matthias Küntzel, and Abram Shulsky most generously provided suggestions from which this article has greatly benefited.

1. Statistical Center of Iran, http://www.unescap.org/esid/psis/population/popin /profiles/iran/popin1.htm, http://www.unescap.org/esid/psis/population/popin/profiles /iran/popin3.htm, and http://www.iranworld.com/Indicators/isc-t143.asp.

2. See, in addition, http://www.google.com/hostednews/afp/article/ALeqM5gIN7O wL5i1NmV9oPFtKWZVUfsV-A?docId=CNG.9eab663bebd069b5f0a3ec51e79b6e5. ba1; and Becky L. Katz, "As Hanukkah Closes, Menorahs Have Flickered in Surprising Place: Iran," *Christian Science Monitor* (September 9, 2010), http://www.csmonitor .com/World/Middle-East/2010/1209/As-Hanukkah-closes-menorahs-have-flickered -in-surprising-place-Iran. For results of the 2011 census see the website of the Iranian government's Department of Planning and Strategic Supervision at www.amar.org.ir. An English language summary of the 2011 results is available at http://english.alarabiya .net/articles/2012/07/29/229078.html.

3. Orly Rahimiyan, "Jewish Community," in M. Kamrava and M. Dorraj, eds., *Iran Today: An Encyclopedia of Life in the Islamic Republic* (Westport, Conn.: Greenwood Press, 2008), pp. 259, 262, 263; and David Menashri, "Iran/Persia 1925–Present," in N. Stillman et al., *Encyclopedia of Jews in the Islamic World* (Leiden: E. J. Brill, 2010), vol. 5, p. 596. On an earlier migration to the newly established country of Israel in the

1950s and its impact on the Iranian community's population in the 1960s, 1970s, and 1980s, see also Eliz Sanasarian, *Religious Minorities in Iran* (Cambridge: Cambridge University Press, 2000), pp. 47, 48.

4. http://www.iranonline.com/iran/iran-info/government/constitution.html.

5. In general, and for parallels with the treatment of the Zoroastrian minority, see Jamsheed K. Choksy, "Despite Shahs and Mollas: Minority Sociopolitics in Premodern and Modern Iran," *Journal of Asian History* 40, pt. 2 (2006), pp. 162–84.

6. On Khomeini's statements regarding Mohammad Reza Pahlavi, see Hamid Algar, editor and translator, *Islam and Revolution: Writings and Declarations of Imam Khomeini* (Berkeley, Calif.: Mizan Press, 1981), pp. 180, 214. On Ahmadinejad's background, see Jamsheed K. Choksy, "Does Ahmadinejad Have Jewish Roots? True or Not, the Rumors Matter," *Foreign Policy* (October 6, 2009), http://www.foreignpolicy.com/articles/2009/10/05/is_mahmoud_ahmadinejad_jewish?page=full. On Ahmadinejad's antisemitic behaviors, see http://english.farsnews.com/newstext.php?nn=8906301449; and Alia Ibrahim and Joel Greenberg, "At Lebanon Rally, Ahmadinejad Vows, 'Zionists Will Disappear,'" *Washington Post* (October 15, 2010), http://www.washingtonpost.com/wp-dyn/content/article/2010/10/14/AR2010101406561.html?sub=AR.

7. On the Iranian government's involvement in distributing the *Protocols*, see Meir Litvak, "The Islamic Republic of Iran and the Holocaust: Anti-Semitism and Anti-Zionism," *Journal of Israeli History* 25, no. 1 (2006), p. 272. For Ahmadinejad's racist and threatening words see Iran's *Press TV* (August 26, 2011), http://www.presstv.ir/detail/195852.html; and the commentaries by Jeffrey Goldberg, "A Little Ahmadinejad Revisionism for You," *The Atlantic* (January 13, 2011), http://www.theatlantic.com/international/archive/2011/01/a-little-ahmadinejad-revisionism-for-you/69505/; and Sohrab Ahmari and James Kirchick, "We Are All Persian Grammarians Now," *American Interest* (May 30, 2012), http://www.the-american-interest.com/article.cfm?piece=1261.

8. On Ahmadinejad's denials, see Jamsheed K. Choksy, "Ahmadinejad's Nationalist Attack on the Islamic Republic," *World Politics Review* (September 17, 2010), http://www.worldpoliticsreview.com/articles/6517/ahmadinejads-nationalist-attack-on-the-islamic-republic; and also http://www.pbs.org/wgbh/pages/frontline/tehranbureau/2009/10/selected-headlines-57.html. On his continued hostility toward Israel, see http://www.politico.com/news/stories/0910/42502_Page2.html; http://www.irantracker.org/roundup/iran-news-roundup-december-16–17–2010; and Howard Schneider, "Ahmadinejad Speaks of Israel's 'Annihilation,'" *Washington Post* (February 26, 2010), http://www.washingtonpost.com/wp-dyn/content/article/2010/02/25/AR2010022505089.html.

9. On Vice President Rahimi's comments see the reports by Thomas Erdbrink, "Iran's Vice President Makes Anti-Semitic Speech at Forum," *New York Times* (June 26, 2012), http://www.nytimes.com/2012/06/27/world/middleeast/irans-vice-president-rahimi-makes-anti-semitic-speech.html?_r=3; and Meir Javedanfar, "In Iran, Anti-Semitic Outbursts Rise under Ahmadinejad," *Al Monitor* (June 28, 2012), http://www.al-monitor.com/pulse/originals/2012/al-monitor/in-iran-anti-semitic-outbursts-r.html.

10. Jamsheed K. Choksy, "Iran's Leadership Struggle Reveals Secular–Islamist Split," *World Politics Review* (May 22, 2011), http://www.worldpoliticsreview.com/articles/8838/irans-leadership-struggle-reveals-secular-islamist-split.

11. See Litvak, pp. 267, 268.

12. Consult details provided at http://www.vohuman.org/Article/Islamic%20era%20histroy%20of%20Zoroastrians%20of%20Iran.htm.

13. Jean-Marie Xaviere, trans., *Sayings of the Ayatollah Khomeini: Political, Philosophical, Social, and Religious* (New York: Bantam, 1980), p. 48.

14. Noted by Farhang Mehr, "Zoroastrians in Twentieth-Century Iran to Present Times," lecture presented at the Eighth World Zoroastrian Congress, London, June 25, 2005.

15. The entire text of Yazdi's ruling is posted on his website at http://mesbahyazdi.com/english/index.asp?contact-us/afq/contact4.htm. Also, see the analysis at http://www.memri.org/report/en/0/0/0/0/0/0/5328.htm.

16. http://www.iranhumanrights.org/2010/01/mesbah-yazdi-provides-the-philosophical-religious-grounds-for-execution-of-opposition/; and http://www.iranhumanrights.org/2010/01/mesbah-yazdi-provides-the-philosophical-religious-grounds-for-execution-of-opposition/.

17. Litvak, p. 272.

18. Jamsheed K. Choksy, "Montazeri's Limited Tolerance of Non-Muslims," *Huffington Post* (December 21, 2009), http://www.huffingtonpost.com/jamsheed-k-choksy/montazeris-limited-tolera_b_399857.html; and Menashri, "Iran/Persia 1925–Present," p. 598.

19. Litvak, pp. 271–72.

20. See http://www.irantracker.org/roundup/iran-news-round-august-29–2011.

21. Discussed in detail by Matthias Küntzel, "Iranian Antisemitism: Stepchild of German National Socialism," *Israel Journal of Foreign Affairs* 4, pt. 1 (2010), pp. 43–51.

22. In general, see Nikki Keddie, "Iran under the Late Qajars," in P. Avery et al., eds., *Cambridge History of Iran*, vol. 7 (Cambridge: Cambridge University Press, 1991), pp. 174–212.

23. Further details are provided by Gavin R. G. Hambly, "The Pahlavi Autocracy: Riza Shah, 1921–1941," and "The Pahlavi Autocracy: Muhammad Riza Shah, 1941–1979," in *Cambridge History of Iran*, vol. 7, pp. 213–51; and Amin Saikal, "Iran's Foreign Policy, 1921–1979," in *Cambridge History of Iran*, vol. 7, pp. 426–40.

24. Orly R. Rahimiyan, "Judeo-Persian Communities of Iran, vi. The Pahlavi Era (1925–1979)," in E. Yarshater, ed., *Encyclopaedia Iranica* (New York: Columbia University Press, 2009), vol. 15; http://iranica.com/articles/judeo-persian-vi-the-pahlavi-era-1925–1979, provides full references.

25. Additional details and citations are provided by Rahimiyan, "Judeo-Persian Communities of Iran, vi." and Menashri, "Iran/Persia 1925–Present," p. 595.

26. On these organizations, see Avi Davidi, "Zionist Activities in Twentieth-Century Iran," in H. Sarshar, ed., *Esther's Children: A Portrait of Iranian Jews* (Beverly Hills, Calif.: Center for Iranian Jewish Oral History, 2002), pp. 238–58; and more briefly Menashri, "Iran/Persia 1925–Present," p. 595.

27. Also consult David Menashri, "The Pahlavi Monarchy and the Islamic Revolution," in Sarshar, pp. 380–402; and Litvak, pp. 268–71.

28. Briefly noted as well by Menashri, "Iran/Persia 1925–Present," pp. 594, 595–96.

29. Ibid., p. 597.

30. Sanasarian, pp. 110–111.

31. Xaviere, pp. 8–9; and Algar, pp. 27, 127.

32. Xaviere, p. 19. See also Algar, p. 47.

33. Xaviere, p. 21.

34. http://www.time.com/time/magazine/article/0,9171,920359,00.html. Also consult Sanasarian, pp. 112–113; and Rahimiyan, "Jewish Community," pp. 261, 262.

35. See further Algar, p. 314 n. 78; and Rahimiyan, "Jewish Community," p. 262.

36. http://www.telegraph.co.uk/news/worldnews/middleeast/iran/1346256/Iran-spares -lives-of-10-Jewish-spies.html.

37. In addition consult http://www.eweek.com/c/a/Security/Iran-Arrests-Nuclear-Spies -Talks-Cybersecurity-567619/; and http://tehrantimes.com/index_View.asp?code=233096.

38. Reported in testimony before the U.S. Senate Foreign Relations Committee by Assistant Secretary of State Michael Posner and noted at http://www.jta.org/news /article/2011/05/15/3087664/state-iran-executed-jewish-woman-husband.

39. Other slogans and graffiti are discussed by Rahimiyan, "Jewish Community," pp. 260–61.

40. For older images see Amnon Netzer and Parviz Varjavand, "The Prophet Daniel," in Sarshar, pp. 14–18.

41. Algar, pp. 195–96, 276, 286.

42. Ibid., p. 89. See also Litvak, p. 271.

43. Older images and a discussion of the new synagogue's construction are provided by Elias Y. Gabbay, "Esther's Tomb," in Sarshar, pp. 20–29.

44. http://globetribune.info/2010/12/12/iranians-threaten-to-destroy-tomb-of-esther/; http://www.google.com/hostednews/afp/article/ALeqM5gIN7OwL5i1NmV9oPFtKWZVUfsV -A?docId=CNG.9eab6633bebd069b5f0a3ec51e79b6e5.ba1; and http://www.csweurope .org/index.php?option=com_content&view=article&id=117:wiesenthal-centre-to-unesco &catid=42:news-releases-2011&Itemid=59.

45. Rahimiyan, "Jewish Community," p. 265, and "Judeo-Persian Communities of Iran, vi. The Pahlavi Era (1925–1979)." Further details are found in Meir Javendanfar, "Iranian Government Stirs up Antisemitism with Invented Massacre," Guardian (December 27, 2010), http://www.guardian.co.uk/commentisfree/belief/2010/dec/27/iranian -antisemitism-graves-jewish-saints. See also Hamid Dabashi, Theology of Discontent: The Ideological Formation of the Islamic Revolution in Iran (New York: New York University Press, 1993), pp. 67–68; and Litvak, p. 269.

46. Quoted at http://www.timesonline.co.uk/tol/news/world/middle_east/article6841604 .ece; and http://archives.cnn.com/2000/WORLD/meast/12/15/mideast.iran.reut/.

47. Cited at http://tehrantimes.com/index_View.asp?code=213925; and http://www .google.com/hostednews/afp/article/ALeqM5hAJ9NlRXyFhGo6nlof1keJVIaH5g.

48. More details are found at http://www.google.com/hostednews/afp/article /ALeqM5jPoWn9Fge9olBvZu-hJEBVbNBVOQ.

One example is an e-book titled The Holocaust: The Jews' Great Lie, published by the so-called World War II Society (www.wwii.ir) based in Iran, on which see http:// www.memri.org/report/en/0/0/0/0/0/0/5705.htm.

49. http://www.pbs.org/wgbh/pages/frontline/tehranbureau/2010/12/extra-the-nazi
-website-amid-irans-chaste-and-virtuous-internet.html; and http://www.eurojewcong
.org/ejc/news.php?id_article=5598.

50. Consult http://www.memritv.org/clip_transcript/en/1484.htm and http://isna.ir
/ISNA/NewsView.aspx?ID=News-1813669&Lang=P.

51. http://www.irantracker.org/roundup/iran-news-roundup-august-25-26-2010.

52. On the controversy generated in Iranian political circles by Mashaei's comments,
see http://www.ynetnews.com/Ext/Comp/ArticleLayout/CdaArticlePrintPreview
/1,2506,L-3570266,00.html; http://www.ft.com/cms/s/0/f2f0ffb2-85b9-11dd-a1ac
-0000779fd18c.html?nclick_check=1#axzz1IPuV7Cxj; http://www.tehrantimes.com
/Index_view.asp?code=175389; http://www.jpost.com/IranianThreat/News/Article
.aspx?id=40; http://www.tehrantimes.com/index_View.asp?code=214085; and Laura Se-
cor, "An Interview with Ahmadinejad's Chief of Staff," *New Yorker* (May 5, 2010), http://
www.newyorker.com/online/blogs/newsdesk/2010/05/esfandiar-rahim-mashaei.html.

53. Jamsheed K. Choksy, "Iran's Leadership Struggle Reveals Secular–Islamist Split,"
World Politics Review (May 13, 2011), http://www.worldpoliticsreview.com/articles/8838
/irans-leadership-struggle-reveals-secular-islamist-split.

54. Jamsheed K. Choksy and Nina Shea, "Religious Cleansing in Iran," *National Review* (July 22, 2009), http://article.nationalreview.com/?q=NjU2MzQ5NjE4YWMzZjV
iN2NiNmU1NDY3N2Fk ZTM1MDg; contra Rahimiyan, "Jewish Community," p. 264.

55. Also noted by Sanasarian, pp. 110–111.

56. See further Rahimiyan, "Jewish Community," p. 262; and http://www.iranjewish
.com/English.htm.

57. E-mail received from a Jewish community leader in Iran in September 2009.

58. Choksy and Shea, "Religious Cleansing in Iran"; and Choksy, "Despite Shahs and
Mollas," pp. 168–69.

59. See also Menashri, "The Pahlavi Monarchy and the Islamic Revolution," p. 402;
and more generally, Choksy, "Despite Shahs and Mollas," p. 166.

60. Compare Hooshang Ebrami, "The Impure Jew," in Sarshar, pp. 101–102.

61. Rahimiyan, "Jewish Community," p. 262.

62. Choksy and Shea, "Religious Cleansing in Iran"; and Choksy, "Despite Shahs and
Mollas," p. 164.

63. Mike Shuster and Renee Montagne, "Iran Hosts Holocaust Deniers at Tehran Conference," National Public Radio (December 12, 2006), http://www.npr.org
/templates/story/story.php?storyId=6612892. See also http://www.foxnews.com/story
/0,2933,236014,00.html.

64. Sanasarian, p. 111.

65. Like much of the data analyzed in the article, I gathered this information during
fieldwork in Iran.

66. http://www.tehrantimes.com/index_View.asp?code=213101.

67. Discussed in detail with many examples by Menashri, "Iran/Persia 1925–Present," pp. 597–99; and Litvak, pp. 273–80.

68. The documentary is online at http://www.shiatv.net/view_video.php?viewkey=
14974e7fd34f975ced5b&page=&viewtype=&category. See also Jamsheed K. Choksy, "Why

is Iran Championing Messianism to the Arab Masses?" *e-International Relations* (April 19, 2011), http://www.e-ir.info/?p=8348; and David Cook, "Messianism in the Shiite Crescent," *Current Trends in Islamist Ideology* 11 (2011), http://www.currenttrends.org /research/detail/messianism-in-the-shiite-crescent.

69. Jamsheed K. Choksy and Nina Shea, "Iran's Nuclear Crisis: Obama Could Play the Human Rights Card," *Christian Science Monitor* (September 26, 2009), http://www .csmonitor.com/2009/0926/p09s01-coop.html.

70. For example see http://www.projetaladin.org/en/en-1-2.html.

71. James B. Pritchard, ed., *Ancient Near Eastern Texts Relating to the Old Testament*, 3rd ed. (Princeton, N.J.: Princeton University Press, 1969, reprinted 1992, 3rd ed.), pp. 315–316. For an on-line translation see Irving Finkel, "Translation of the Text of the Cyrus Cylinder," British Museum, 2010, http://www.britishmuseum.org/explore /highlights/article_index/c/cyrus_cylinder_-_translation.aspx.

72. Jamsheed K. Choksy, "Iran's Theocracy Implodes," *Real Clear World* (August 4, 2009), http://www.realclearworld.com/articles/2009/08/04/irans_theocracy_implodes .html.

73. I am grateful to Matthias Küntzel for this information.

74. Davidi, p. 246.

75. Jamsheed K. Choksy, "Jewish Relations with Zoroastrians," in *Encyclopedia of Jews in the Islamic World*, vol. 5, pp. 690–94; Jamsheed K. Choksy and Stephen A. Szrom, "Shiism, Nationalism, and the Past Clash in Modern Iran," *Huffington Post* (December 3, 2010), http://www.huffingtonpost.com/jamsheed-k-choksy/shiism-nationalism -and-th_b_791417.html; Abbas Milani, "For Jews, There Have Always Been Two Irans," *New York Times* (November 10, 2005), http://www.nytimes.com/2005/11/10/opinion /10iht-edmilani.html; and "Revealing Errors: Iran, Jews, and the Holocaust," *Iranian. com* (February 23, 2006), http://www.iranian.com/AbbasMilani/2006/February/Black /index.html.

13 The Israeli Scene: Political Criticism and the Politics of Anti-Zionism

Ilan Avisar

ONE OF THE greatest ironies of modern Jewish history is that Zionism was considered to be the remedy to the malaise of antisemitism, and today Israel has become the main focus of contemporary antisemitism. Herzl and Pinsker did not simply envision the establishment of a Jewish state to function as a safe shelter from threats and persecutions. The thrust of Zionist thinking was to eliminate the causes of modern antisemitism by obtaining sovereignty, territorial independence, a return to the ancient homeland, a distinct culture, and normalization of the Jewish historical situation so that Jews would be seen as equal members in the family of nations. In the first three decades of Israel's existence, Western guilt over the tragedy of the Holocaust and the young state's own significant achievements, including inspiring military victories over its many enemies, elicited widespread sympathy and respect. And yet, Israel is today the principal focus of antisemitic sentiments and activities. To complicate the irony of history, Israelis themselves have some role in the perpetuation and incitement of contemporary anti-Zionist antisemitism.

On Holocaust Memorial Day of 2011, the acclaimed filmmaker Claude Lanzmann stated the following in an interview for a daily Israeli newspaper:

> There are Israelis who are anti-Semites. In the beginning, they were anti-Semites when they hated the Jews of the ghettoes. Today they are anti-Semites because you are in the midst of a civil war. . . . As a result, there are Israeli anti-Semites who fan the flames of antisemitism in the world. They are the reason journalists and intellectuals in the West get an oversimplified and one-sided picture of a very complex conflict. . . . The civil war in Israel and the internal hatred in Israel cause some of you to be anti-Semites.[1]

Lanzmann's words appear harsh, but they accurately characterize an intense, ongoing political discourse that can be traced to the beginning of Zionism and, more broadly, Jewish history itself. Accusations of anti-semitism against fellow Jews were not uncommon in the course of the Jews' transition to modernity. It was a dramatic process with extreme dis-putes on tradition, integration, or national self-determination, set against the background of the outburst of new forms of modern antisemitism. Jews have absorbed antisemitic arguments, some consciously, some sub-consciously, in their new discourse about the Jewish future in modernity. When Lanzmann mentions Israeli antagonism toward Jews of the ghet-toes, he refers to the notion of Negation of the Diaspora, an early Zionist position that denounced exilic existence and occasionally adopted anti-semitic rhetoric in stressing the contrast between the allegedly meek and rootless Diaspora Jew and the new Zionist farmer fighters in the land of Israel. Amos Oz echoes this observation by noting that the popular Sa-bra image—soft on the inside and rough on the outside—is the result of Jewish assimilation of antisemitic views.[2]

Lanzmann adds that Israeli antisemitism is also the result of a con-temporary "civil war" and internal hatred within Israel. Actually, Israel was spared the tragedy of civil war that often accompanies the forma-tion of nations. Surely, from the early phases of Zionism, the history of modern Israel has been characterized by multiple views, competing ide-ologies, and fierce disputes. The rhetoric of the ideological debates has been replete with extreme expressions, but only rarely have political di-visions escalated to the point of real violence.

Lanzmann's reference to a contemporary civil war is overstated, itself a symptom of the hyperbolic style of political Jewish debates. As Arthur Hertzberg and Aron Hirt-Manheimer stipulate in their book *Jews: The Es-sence and Character of a People,* being a fractious group with a history of internal strife is one of the core components of Jewish identity.[3] Further-more, the Israeli debate today is not unlike the culture wars of other West-ern societies between the progressive Left and the conservative Right. The main difference is that in the case of Israel, the stakes are much higher, even critical. The alternative views for solving the country's political con-flicts often address the prospects for national survival, and the arguments rest on conflicting moral visions and different views of national identity. Seven decades of independence and 150 years of Zionism have not stifled

Jewish debates over the ideal and character of a Jewish state. The divisive issues of national, religious, universal, or ethnic identities inform much of the contemporary engagement with questions of cultural direction and political goals. In addition, the hyperbolic and offensive style of Israeli political debates springs from a highly dense, abrasive society, living in a hot climate, with intense and intimate social relations. It is also a society living on the edge. Israel faces frequent and explicit threats of extermination and is a modern nation whose collective memory bears searing memories of apocalyptic disasters. The land is replete with relics of a highly dramatic history, including the ancient independent kingdoms of Judah and Israel and the Hasmonean dynasty of Greek and Roman times. Living in the third Jewish commonwealth, the average Israeli can readily cite biblical and Talmudic phrases that epitomize the connection between national destruction and any of the following: political miscalculation, religious corruption, social injustice, or divisive internal conflicts. Israelis are also well familiar with the biblical verse, "Thy destroyers and thy demolishers shall emerge from within thee" (Isaiah 49:17).

Some of the harshest critics of the Jewish state are former Israelis who vilify Israel at any opportunity. Affiliated with artistic circles or academic institutions, they build careers on slandering Israel, often receiving extraordinary media attention for their provocative actions or critical postures against Israel. Here is a typical statement made by a film scholar residing in England. It comes in the form of an open letter to filmmakers Ethan and Joel Coen, who won the prestigious Dan David Prize in 2011, an annual award in the amount of U.S. $1 million granted by Tel Aviv University on its campus:

> Your much-celebrated presence will adorn a colonial settler state still vigorously engaged in the business of dispossessing and driving out the indigenous inhabitants, who are the Palestinians. . . . Your appearance in Israel will unfortunately help camouflage the brutal realities of a powerful and illegal military occupation. However much you believe you can go there simply as artists, your presence will be spun to reassure the Israeli public that their ruthless colonial society is "normal," and to promote Brand Israel abroad.[4]

The critical discourse in Israel ranges from political critique of its policies, to preaching for an end to any Jewish characteristics in the state, to calls for the dissolution of Israel as a nation-state. The critical discourse contains explicit calls to accommodate or meet the demands of Israel's adversaries. Taking the side of the Arabs in the conflict reflects pervasive guilty feelings on the part of some Israeli Jews, or an extreme, even perverse sense of justice, or a Pavlovian identification with "the other" of intellectual postmodernist circles. However, with the exception of the self-hating radicals who favor the end of Israel, Israelis and Jews who voice criticism of Israel are part and parcel of the national scene of continuous, intense political debate in the face of real conflicts and complex possibilities. The historical confrontations with the Arabs have yielded a clash between fundamental survival concerns and strongly held ethical values. For many Israelis and Jews, occupying territories and taking oppressive measures against their Arab populations, justified as they may be by security considerations, are morally unbearable. In particular, many artists and intellectuals mobilized themselves on behalf of ethical concerns, articulating their moral sensitivity in numerous texts of literature, scholarship, theater plays, paintings, films, and other forms of art. Most Israelis share these concerns, as wrestling with the moral dimensions of Jewish nationalism has been a significant part of Zionist history. The inevitable moral cost of national struggles against regional adversaries has led in some cases to the most radical conclusion, namely the negation of Jewish nationalism. Here is a typical statement of an Israeli scholar: "Jewish sovereignty has turned out to be the biggest danger to Jewish cultural and moral existence. . . . We envision a state that will not be a nation-state."[5]

Anti-Zionist argumentation has become a major phenomenon in Israeli intellectual life. As the words above indicate, some intellectuals may object to the very concept of the nation-state in general, and one Israeli historian not long ago published a book about how Zionists invented the Jewish people.[6] There are numerous academic publications aimed at the vilification of Jewish nationalism from the disciplines of humanities and social sciences. Recently, three watchdog organizations claimed that about 10 percent of Israeli academics are anti-Zionist, a claim that was instantly countered with charges of McCarthyism.[7]

Those who are not self-proclaimed anti-Zionists and engage in criticizing Israeli policies are deeply convinced of the absolute rightness of their moral stance and they tend to gloss over the potential dangers implied in undermining the national project. Most Israelis possess a strong sense of power and confidence in their country, these feelings springing from the significant national achievements of their thriving state. The contrary or subversive voices are regarded as evidence of the pluralism of ideas in a democratic society and the vitality of the process of forming a national identity. This empowered Israeli subject position in the new discourse of history accounts for the dismissal of antisemitism as a major threat against Israel. Native-born Israelis have been exempted from actual, personal experiences of antisemitism; for them it is a subject associated with history books and historical events like the Holocaust but has no bearing for the present situation of the Jewish state. This is precisely the perspective of filmmaker Yoav Shamir, who made *Defamation* (2009). This documentary film treats with irony the activities of the ADL and its chair, Holocaust survivor Abe Foxman, implying that the concerns about antisemitic incidents treated by the ADL are not founded in reality. The film also follows the trips of Israeli youth to the death camps in Poland, featuring the didactic voices of educators and survivors who warn against the imaginary dangers of antisemitism in present-day Poland. Finally, Shamir features Norman Finkelstein, whose anti-Zionist obsession appears pathological, but the film allows him to make his argument that the Jewish state exploited the universal guilt over the Holocaust to silence critics of its alleged oppressive policies.

In a personal conversation, Yoav Shamir made the claim that Israel's predicament has no connection with antisemitism but rather with current global politics. Indeed, the denial of antisemitism as a new force in the present is related to a recognition of other forces that operate against Israel. Chief among them is the conflict with Arabs and Muslims, who cannot accept the presence of a non-Islamic independent nation in the Middle East, a position that led to several wars with dire consequences especially for the Arabs of the region. The other is the ideology of anti-Western postcolonialism, which has replaced Marxism as the new quasi-religious faith of progressive intellectuals in the West, perpetuating the argument that Israel's existence must be challenged as a criminal colonial enterprise.

Thus, Israel occupies a central place in the two greatest conflicts of the beginning of the twenty-first century—the culture war between the Right and the Left in Western societies and the "Clash of Civilizations" that pits the Western world against extreme Islamic aspirations. This major critical historical position of the Jewish state reflects the failure of one Zionist goal—solving the problem of antisemitism by achieving a normalized national existence and, thereby, being "like all other nations." Furthermore, the discourse regarding Israel in these two conflicts reveals many of the signs and symptoms of traditional antisemitism. Arab enmity toward Israel is often articulated in the most extreme ways, employing expressions that frequently call for the annihilation of the Jewish state. These expressions are genocidal in their intent and in their graphic images. Years of such indoctrination have led to the demonization of the Jewish state and the Jews, a demonization that has absorbed the paradigms and imagery of Western antisemitism. To cite one example from cinema history, the notorious antisemitic Nazi films *Jew Suss* and the *The Eternal Jew,* thought to be lost and officially banned in most Western democracies, have resurfaced after the Holocaust in screenings in the Arab world.[8] In addition to the rhetorical warfare that exploits the discourse of antisemitism, there have been numerous violent attacks against Jews perpetrated by elements from the Arab and Muslim communities in Western societies. So, although this antagonism may be rooted in real political conflict and actual confrontation over territories, and despite the fact that antisemitism is basically a phenomenon of Christianity and Western culture, today's Arab and Islamic warfare against Israel has become to a large extent an antisemitic campaign.

The postcolonialism of the radical Left has also displayed an obsessive fixation on the Jewish state, employing a critical discourse that demonizes and delegitimizes Israel. The fixation on the Jewish state marks a significant inflection of historical anti-Jewish traditions. Whereas traditional antisemitism posited the Jew as the ultimate "other" of Western Christian society, some of the new expressions of antisemitism spring from the notion that the Jewish state epitomizes Western culture.[9] Jews or the Jewish state are now hated by the radicals of the West because they are regarded as oppressors of the new "other." The privileged status of the Arabs of Palestine as the main victims of the world agenda displays a double standard in relation to other underprivileged communities in the world, and this status derives solely from the fact that they struggle against Jews and against the Jewish state.

The line that separates political preference in the Middle East conflict and outright antisemitism was famously articulated by Natan Sharansky's "3D Test": demonization, delegitimation, and the double standard.[10] Two additional criteria can be offered to Sharansky's criteria. The first is the collective charge, the antisemitic disposition to regard all Jews antago-nistically. This collective charge has its roots in the classic Christian view that blamed all Jews for the killing of Jesus. Today's collective charge is manifested in the genocidal threats and the indiscriminate attacks against all Israeli citizens, in the "civilized" anti-Zionists' call for boycott, divest-ment, and sanctions against all Israelis, and in the extension of the Middle East conflict to attacks on Jewish targets all over the world.

The other critical point that characterizes antisemitic objections to the Jewish state is the obsessive nature of this bigotry. As Melanie Phil-lips observed:

> It eclipses in its enormity all other issues and causes; in their clouded eyes, it has become an evil of truly cosmic dimensions. . . . It defines and dis-torts their whole outlook on the world. They think of it when they are talk-ing about something totally unrelated to the Middle East, such as children's rights. It has truly become a disease of the British mind, a kind of geopo-litical Tourette Syndrome, a pathologically uncontrollable spasm of hatred and lies.[11]

The pathological psychological disposition of antisemitism parallels the demonic dimension of the antisemitic discourse. As a discourse, anti-semitism covers the narratives, images, rhetorical devices, and all the con-tent of arguments and literature included in the history of antisemitism. As a disposition, the reference is to the personal preoccupation and the emotional, existential, or political attitudes toward Jews and Judaism. Anti-semitism as a disposition designates those individuals, movements, or organizations whose emotional, existential, or political attitudes toward Jews and Judaism are dominated by antisemitic sentiments. The new anti-Zionist antisemitic discourse is manifested in vicious and venomous jour-nalistic reports, artistic texts, political speeches, or declarations of inter-national organizations. Obviously, when dealing with the contribution of Jews to antisemitism, the distinction between the discourse and dispo-sition of antisemitism is vital, for Jews may contribute to the discourse of antisemitism, although it will be difficult to define them as antisem-ites, with the possible exception of those who display a pathological self-hatred.

About a century ago, the dramatic debates in the face of modernity raised the question: "Where does constructive self-criticism leave off and Jewish self-hatred begin?"[12] Today, the question is: When does legitimate political criticism of Israel leave off and collaboration with antisemitism begin? When does internal critique of national policies become an active force in the service of Israel's defamers and detractors? When do local political views or actions either enflame antisemitism or collaborate with it?

Israeli cinema provides an intriguing case for examining these questions. A creative art with deep ties to social and political realities, cinema is also a medium with a significant role in the evolution of collective identity and the articulation of national values. The story of Israeli cinema reveals a dramatic engagement with the national narrative, covering the full spectrum from contributions to nation formation to expressions of national negation.

Cinema has been a participant in the Zionist enterprise from its earliest stages. Herzl himself engaged in efforts to produce a film on behalf of the Zionist cause in the beginning of the twentieth century.[13] Throughout the years of Zionist settlement, sporadic productions tried to make their contribution to the nation-building process. Limited resources and ideological passion accounted for mostly crude propaganda during the first decades of the Zionist project. Israeli cinema became a significant cultural and social force around 1960, with a new generation of mostly Israeli-born filmmakers dealing with the pressing issues of their society and country, cultivating technological resources, local talent, and specific Israeli genres and cinematic forms. For two decades, Israeli films were a vibrant feature of Israeli culture, with popular ethnic comedies and the notable works of distinguished artists like Ephraim Kishon, Uri Zohar, Menahem Golan, and Moshe Mizrahi. This period ended abruptly in the late 1970s (in what may be called a cut!). Kishon moved to Central Europe, enjoying immense universal success as the author of satires and comedies. Mizrahi moved to France and in 1978 won the Oscar for making the French film *Madame Rosa*. Golan moved to Hollywood, heading Canon films, a successful production company in the 1980s. Zohar, probably the greatest talent in Israeli cinema, was a militant Tel Aviv bohemian who moved to the religious quarters of Jerusalem for a new life as an Orthodox Jew.

The generation change of Israeli filmmakers was accompanied by significant political changes. The rise of the Likud Party to power in the late 1970s created significant historical change, moving the country from the rule of socialist parties to that of right-wing forces. Most of those associated with the Israeli artistic scene identified with leftist ideologies and they combined political opposition to the ideology and actions of the ruling right-wing coalition with fashionable expressions of doubt and critique of the basic notions of nationalism from the perspectives of multiculturalism and postcolonialism. The critical voices of Israeli filmmakers were ironically facilitated by a special act of government subsidy—the formation in 1979 of the Fund for the Promotion of Israeli Quality Films. Eventually the name of the fund was changed to the Israeli Film Fund. Consequently, and over the past four decades, production of films in Israel has been accomplished thanks to public funding. In the article "National Cinema: A Theoretical Assessment," Ian Jarvie discusses the three main arguments on behalf of support for national cinema. These include the protectionist argument—cultivating a local industry as a thriving financial enterprise of professional workers and technological facilities; the cultural defense argument—usually designed to guard against the domination of Hollywood and American mores; and the nation-building argument.[14] In Israel, ironically, government sponsorship led to films that challenged the country's basic national values, celebrated political subversion, offered historical revisionism, and engaged in ideological iconoclasm.

One of the first films of the new public fund was *Transit* (directed by Daniel Wachsmann, 1979)—the story of a drifting Holocaust survivor who cannot find his place in Israel and aspires to return to his "home" in Berlin; Wachsmann's next film was *Hamsin* (1982)—a political tragedy taking place in the Galilee, set against the Arabs' resistance to a government plan to expropriate their lands. The story focuses on the relationship between a Jewish farmer and his Arab employee. The climax is the murder of the Arab—the Jewish protagonist kills his faithful worker after the Arab has an affair with the farmer's sister. The military and Israel's wars have also become subjects for revision. Judd Neeman, a decorated army doctor from the Six Day War, created *Paratroopers* (1978), an army drama about the harsh training and social pressures in the military's elite units, that ultimately lead to the suicide of a young man. Then, *Wooden Gun* (directed by Ilan Moshenson, 1979) was an antiwar drama featuring children in the first years of the state who engage in brutal war games following the national myths of military victories in the War of Independence.

These films launched a radical wave of political protest cinema. The new themes and attitudes offered the excitement of subversive novelty, with heated public debates pitting concerns with national goals against the advocates of moral and political critiques. The extreme views of some of these films have reached the Israeli Supreme Court. *The Vulture* (directed by Yaki Yosha, 1982) offended many with the story of a corrupt military officer who launches a successful business by constructing memorials for fallen soldiers, memorials with bogus details and false information designed to please the bereaved parents in order to gain their financial resources. A special compromise with the filmmaker averted a court decision. Years later in 2003, the Israeli Court upheld the value of freedom of expression by reversing the decision of the Israeli Board of Film Reviews that banned *Jenin, Jenin* (directed by Mohammed Bakri, 2003) from commercial exhibition.[15]

A typical example of Israeli political protest films is the remarkable *Avanti Popolo* (directed by Raphy Bukai, 1986). It follows two Egyptian soldiers during the Six Day War, who try to reach their homes after the disintegration of their army. One of them is a stage actor, the other is a peasant, a pair that recalls a former ideal type of Zionism—the artist farmer. The roles of the two protagonists are played by Israeli Arabs, and the reversal of familiar national myths takes on another political dimension when it becomes clear that this is also a story of Palestinians, whose genteel demeanor is contrasted with that of the crude and cruel Israeli soldiers. The climactic moment occurs when the thirsty Arabs try to reach a water container. The Israeli soldiers coarsely push them back, and then the Arab actor delivers Shylock's famous speech: "I am a Jew. Hath not a Jew eyes? Hath not a Jew hands, organs. . . ." Filmmaker Bukai stated: "The whole idea of building an Arab Shylock came to me when I read an article on Arik Sharon as Israel's 'Man of the Year'. . . . I was stunned by his inability to perceive the other side, his inability to understand that there are other people who deserve to exist with dignity in this world."[16]

The revision of the Six Day War in *Avanti Popolo* was matched by other revisions of the Zionist paradigms of Israeli culture. The new portrayal of Arabs or Palestinians on the screen was regarded by some as an act of national reckoning or ethical correction. Ella Shohat called it the Return of the Repressed,[17] Nurith Gertz contended that the new images sought to counter "the formless, dehumanized Arab depicted in the

Rightist model,"[18] and Judd Neeman noted that "Whereas early Zionist cinema had portrayed a Jewish protagonist as a pioneer conscious of his or her utopian mission, the 1980s conflict films disrupt this sense of telos . . . These films rewrite the Zionist master narrative, using cinematic images to transform it dramatically."[19] The critical embrace of Israeli scholars and film critics was matched by success in foreign film festivals. The Israeli films that sought to rectify the image of the Arab as the negative "other" of the country's national history and to criticize morally questionable actions were received abroad as confirmations of a serious postcolonial critique of the West, underscoring the image of the Jewish state as a repressive regime acting against an indigenous population under brutal military occupation. Israeli filmmakers often make the claim that such films may indeed contain unpleasant representations of Israel, but they are evidence of Israel's vibrant democracy with its pluralism of voices and the admirable vigor of political criticism. But some European critics have identified a strain of self-hatred in these films, and in some cases the hosts have asked their Israeli guests how they have managed to smuggle their films out of Israel, not realizing that the films were actually made with government funding.[20]

The political protest films were critical and defiant, but their negative approach offered no alternative visions, no new model figures or different value systems that might replace the traditional national ethos. Eventually, the initial flirtation with the Arab "other" of Israeli society escalated to radical visions that sought to undermine the national foundations of the Jewish state, ranging from narratives of nausea, defeat, or hopeless corruption to apocalyptic visions.[21] In his article, "The Empty Tomb in the Postmodern Pyramid: Israeli Cinema in the 1980s and 1990s," Judd Neeman declares: "The apocalyptic mode in contemporary Israeli cinema stems from the Holocaust, Zionist Utopianism's decadence, the death ethos as expressed in both military combat and terrorism, and the endangering of secular life by Jewish as well as Islamic fundamentalism."[22] The political profile of these words becomes evident not only by their provocative evenhandedness, but also by what this statement ignores, namely the present genocidal threats against the Jewish state and the complex impact of the Holocaust on Israelis.

The Holocaust has been a decisive force in shaping Israel's collective memory and national identity. In Israel's collective spirit, the Holocaust is more a trauma than a historical lesson, and its place in Israeli discourse reveals the existential anxiety of a nation facing threats of annihilation. The slogan "Never Again" indicates the fear of the explicit genocidal threats against Israel and the distrust of the bystanders, who may be indifferent to Israel's fate or may join the country's enemies. The slogan is mostly expressed to convey the commitment to never again be helpless as were the victims of Hitler's assault. The 1978 film *Operation Jonathan* on the rescue mission of Israeli hostages, directed by Menahem Golan, is replete with references to the Holocaust. The original event contained unsettling similarities with the horrible past, as the hijackers were led by two Germans, who abused their victims in incidents that recall well-known Holocaust stories, culminating in a separation between Jews and non-Jews in a scene reminiscent of the selections in the camps. The world crisis that developed after the hijacking of an Air France plane to Uganda led to no action by others, so that the commander Yoni Netanyahu reminds his soldiers that their mission is to save Jews because nobody else will do it for them. The ending of the film features celebration over the rescue of the hostages along with the pain triggered by the death of Yoni, a telling mixture of the joyful relief of survival with the searing grief over the loss of human life. Both emotions are displayed as private individual feelings and also as public collective behavior, symptoms of the lingering traumatic presence of the Holocaust in the national life of the Jewish state.

The treatment of the Holocaust by Israeli filmmakers reveals the ideological cycle of the Jewish state. After the Second World War, several films were made by Zionist organizations featuring narratives of Holocaust survivors who find a new life in Israel. The films usually focused on the kibbutz as the ideal setting to offer new life to the traumatized survivors, thanks to its values of a collective lifestyle, working the land, and a heroic defense of settlements in the commitment to the building of a new nation. In the 1980s, Israeli films subverted the national ideology of Israel as the haven and recovery site for Holocaust survivors. In *Transit* the protagonist longs to return to his beloved Berlin: Israel for him is just a transit station. Germany appears as a site of longing in other films such as *Berlin Jerusalem* (directed by Amos Gitai, 1989), *Tel Aviv Berlin* (directed by Tzipi Trope, 1987), *Drifting* (directed by Amos Guttman, 1982), *Silver Platter* (directed by Judd Neeman, 1984), and *Streets of Yesterday* (directed by Judd Neeman, 1989). In *Hide and Seek* (directed by Dan Wolman, 1980), the young Israelis are hard-line nationalists, in contrast with the protagonist's grandfather, who devotes his life to translating great works of German literature. And in *Till the End of Night* (directed by Eitan Green, 1985), the protagonist participates in the violent nightlife of Tel Aviv, in sharp contrast to his father, a dignified Christian German whose poignant death symbolizes the passing of refined cultural values in the face of Middle Eastern brutality. Other films revised the survivors' arrival in Israel, presenting absorption as a painful process, their predicament caused by the condescending attitudes of local Israelis (*The Summer of Aviha*, directed by Eli Cohen, 1989) or the extreme pressures of Zionist ideology. In *A New Land* (directed by Orna Ben Dor, 1994), the brutal attitudes of local officials recall the harsh conditions in the Nazi camps, and at the end of the film, the children who escaped the horrors of Europe and sought a new home in Israel fantasize that they fly to another land.[23]

The Holocaust also plays a role in the discourse about Israel's security, and the topic has been mobilized by local political rivals. The enhancement of existential anxieties by the experience of genocide was countered by claims that the Holocaust has generated national paranoia and irrational political behavior. Voices, usually from the Israeli Left, contend that the appropriation of the Holocaust spurs an immoral militarization of Israeli society, unfounded distrust of the rest of the world, and unjustified demonization of Israel's enemies.[24] In the international scene, the Holocaust has also become a central element in the political discourse of Israel. Supporters of Israel often mention the Holocaust as the critical justification for the Jewish state, whereas Israel's detractors are prone to equate Nazism with Zionism.[25] This equation is an antisemitic charge that seeks to perform the ultimate demonization of the Jewish state by identifying Zionism and Israelis with the ultimate markers of evil in modern times. The Israeli political protest films of the 1980s generally avoided evocation of the Holocaust in the context of the presentation of the Arab–Israeli conflict. But as the Holocaust has become a familiar component of popular culture and a frequent feature in political debates,[26] Israeli filmmakers also resort to elements of the Final Solution and apply them to the Middle East conflict. Amos Gitai's film *Kedma* (2009) includes a long sequence that juxtaposes the arrival of Holocaust survivors with the flight of Arabs during the War of Independence, suggesting the analogy and even historical causality between the deported and displaced Jewish victims and Palestinian refugees. Anti-Zionist filmmaker Eyal Sivan made a scene with an Arab barber whose story is supposed to echo the mesmerizing scene with Abraham Bomba, the barber from Treblinka, in Claude Lanzmann's *Shoah*.[27] In 2010, an Israeli filmmaker wrote a script based on the experiences of his mother and her friend, both survivors of the Holocaust, and after winning funding from the Israel Film Fund, changed the script to tell the story of two Palestinian friends (*Lipstikka*, directed by Jonathan Sagall, 2011).

In addition to narratives and characters, there are numerous examples of Holocaust images being applied by Israeli filmmakers to convey moral judgments of Israel's national behavior. The most familiar icon is the picture of the Jewish child raising his hands in horror when facing the armed Nazi troops after the liquidation of the Warsaw Ghetto.[28] The 1979 film *The Wooden Gun* presents a subtle reference to this famous Holocaust image. Yoni, the film's protagonist, flees the scene where he shot his gang rival with a wooden gun, and reaches the hut of a Holocaust survivor on the beach. Traumatized by her past experiences, the survivor has become the neighborhood madwoman, feared and ridiculed by the local kids. Her hut is lit with candles and filled with photos, a sort of private Holocaust museum. She treats the wounded Yoni, who is touched by her tenderness and compassion. The scene between Yoni and the woman reaches a climax when he examines the picture from the Warsaw Ghetto, and all of a sudden the picture comes alive. As Yoni sees his friend/rival as the Jewish child of the picture, he is filled with tears of guilt and remorse. The Holocaust survivor, who bears the name Palestina, becomes the moral compass for the young boy, whose war games are seen as the result of the questionable military ethos the children absorb from their adult parents.

The picture of the child from the ghetto is also mentioned in the highly successful *Waltz with Bashir* (directed Ari Folman, 2008), a winner of numerous international awards, including the Golden Globe in the category of best foreign film. In contrast with the modest local production of *Wooden Gun*, *Waltz with Bashir* was a relatively high-budget movie, a co-production of Israel, France, and Germany, offering an intriguing formal approach—the employment of distinct animation on the 1982 war in Lebanon. Filmmaker Ari Folman recounts his own story as an infantry soldier during that war, and the narrative follows his efforts in the present to recall a traumatic moment from that war.

The subject of the film, the 1982 Lebanon War, was the first controversial and publicly debated war in Israel's history. The political opposition in Israel launched a campaign against the war, challenging the decision to begin the war, arguing about its goals, and voicing criticism against its conduct and the collateral damage to Lebanese and Palestinian civilians. The war in Lebanon was also the first event for which Israel had been subject to an intensive campaign of demonization by the world media. The confrontation of the mighty Israeli army with the smaller forces of Palestinian terrorist organizations in populated civilian areas allowed for the use of the David vs. Goliath trope, with sympathies granted to the weak side of the Palestinians. The massacre in Sabra and Shatilla by the forces of Lebanese Christians mobilized all those who criticized Israel at home and abroad to blame the government and the IDF for the atrocity. Eventually an inquiry committee appointed by the Israeli government concluded that Israeli commanders bore indirect responsibility for allowing the Christian militias to fight in the Palestinian camps without taking into consideration the possibility that these Lebanese allies would perpetrate atrocities against their Palestinian foes. The subsequent resignation of Defense Minister Ariel Sharon and the suggestion of Israeli complicity in the massacre were celebrated by those who opposed the war, but also aroused concerns that the controversial conclusion would provide ammunition for those who sought to demonize and delegitimize Israel.

This is the background for the journey of the film's protagonist in search of a missing memory, supposedly suppressed by the war trauma. The final moments that describe the killings in Sabra and Shatilla offer narrative closure, both to the unfolding story of the war in Lebanon and to the character's quest for truth and relief from his post-traumatic stress disorder. In the final section, Folman refers to the killings in the camps using the term *genocide*. The protagonist's best friend tells him that his massacre trauma is connected to the fact that his parents survived the Holocaust, adding: "You have been forcibly cast in the role of Nazi." The Israeli journalist who was at the scene claims that the sight of the victims reminded him of the picture of the young boy raising his arms after the liquidation of the Warsaw Ghetto, and the graphic animation supplies visual reinforcement for this statement.

This narrative combination of uncovering the mystery of what had happened in bloody battles with the psychological exploration of a character's lingering trauma has been a frequent and powerful narrative ploy in the genre of war films. The war films that focused on the question "what really happened" usually offer a startling or shocking revelation in the course of the quest for truth—consider the examples of *Apocalypse Now*, *Deer Hunter*, *Flags of Our Fathers*, *Redacted*, *In the Valley of Elah*, or *The Manchurian Candidate*. In the case of *Waltz with Bashir*, the conclusion of the movie rehashes an event that received extraordinary attention and actually became a popular and constant feature in the arsenal of Israel's enemies. The dramatic confirmation of the controversial notion of indirect responsibility culminates the narcissistic story of the film's protagonist, adding pathos and self-pity to the prospect of personal redemption while recycling the charge of Israel's responsibility for war crimes, this time with the added Holocaust analogy.

Waltz with Bashir was initially screened in Israel with little public attention. Then the film won several international awards and was nominated for an Oscar in the category of best foreign film. At this point there began a serious debate in Israel about the film. Its success abroad has been a source of national pride, while the film's artistic achievements were celebrated by a massive chorus of film critics, fellow artists, and prominent pundits.[29] On the other hand, many others felt that an increasingly hostile anti-Israeli world is much less likely to appreciate the pluralism of Israel's democracy or the subtleties of moral critique. Instead, self-flagellation or extreme political criticism may lend fuel to the fire of anti-Israel sentiment and ultimately to the rise of antisemitism.

The story of Israeli cinema in this context is not different from the case of other cultural systems in Israel that engage in vigorous critiques or the deconstruction of the underlying principles of the national culture. Israeli cinema thrives in international settings, generating mixed reactions and posing the question of whether the Israeli films represent Israel or only the minority of those in the radical political opposition. The artistic drama of antiwar vision and sentiments clearly bears political implications, especially in the international context. Members of the local film industry pride themselves on the achievements of Israeli cinema as measured by prizes in international festivals. But note that *Beaufort* (directed by Joseph Cedar, 2007), *Lebanon* (directed by Samual Maoz, 2009), and *Waltz with Bashir*—three recent films on the Lebanon war that won respectable awards—feature stories of disintegration, deep confusion, or atrocities against civilians. Israeli filmmakers prefer to bathe in the glory of the awards ceremonies and to ignore the possible political damage; or they passionately contend that such damages go beyond their intentions. Any sense of responsibility to their own society or nation is dismissed in the name of the freedom to express alternative political visions, or the need for subversive ideologies, or the call of ulterior moral considerations. The Israeli films are not the works of the Far Left post-Zionist factions, which systematically foster the Arab narrative, but they do contribute to embed questionable narratives, insightful images, and, occasionally, the recycling of elements of antisemitic discourse. As noted, Israelis are prone to dismissing the dangers of antisemitism. Those who acknowledge the political damage in the international scene consider this consequence a calculated risk of what they regard as the noble task of issuing warnings against immoral national conduct. But in viewing the general output of Israeli cinema, it is very rare to find inspiring stories that would counter-balance the self-inflicted scars that are the inevitable outcome of a steady stream of unredeeming self-criticism.

In the local scene, there have been several expressions of warning against the erosion of Israel's spirit leading to a national crisis. In 1994, the distinguished novelist Aharon Meged wrote the following under the title "The Israeli Urge to Suicide":

A few hundred of our "society's best," men of the pen and of the spirit—academics, authors, and journalists, and to these one must add artists and photographers and actors as well—have been working determinedly and without respite to preach and prove that our cause is not just: Not only that it has been unjust since the Six Day War . . . but since the beginning of Zionist settlement at the end of the last century.[30]

More than ten years later, liberal journalist Ari Shavit wrote in *Ha'aretz* on the Israeli cultural elites, especially in the media and academia: "[they] have blinded Israel and deprived it of its spirit. . . . Their unending attacks, both direct and indirect, on nationalism, on militarism and on the Zionist narrative have eaten away from the inside at the tree trunk of Israeli existence, and sucked away its life force."[31]

Jews possess a tradition of fierce disputations that is constantly on display in Israel. At the same time, throughout its existence, Israel has displayed strength and achievements in nearly all the major fields of a thriving nation—economic growth, political stability, military might, social services, technological developments, and scientific discoveries. Yet it does not enjoy peace, and its enemies seek to destroy it by resorting to a determined propaganda war of demonization and delegitimation. Not all Israelis are alert to it, but the unfading discourse of antisemitism coupled with the everlasting antisemitic disposition remain major threats. In the face of this hostility, ideological disputes, political divisions, and Jewish factiousness should be careful not to fuel the current mode of anti-Zionist antisemitism.

NOTES

1. Shavit, Ari, "Head to Head / Claude Lanzmann, Is Another Holocaust Possible?" *Ha'aretz* (May 2, 2011).

2. Amos Oz made this statement in the film *Amos Oz: The Nature of Dreams* (directed by Yonathan and Masha Zur, 2009).

3. Arthur Hertzberg and Aron Hirt-Manheimer, *Jews: The Essence and Character of a People* (San Francisco: HarperOne, 1998).

4. Haim Bresheeth, "Coen Brothers: Don't Accept Dan David Prize!" (March 13, 2011), British Committee for the Universities of Palestine (BRICUP), http://www.alternativenews.org/english/index.php/topics/economy-of-the-occupation/3399-coen-brothers-dont-accept-dan-david-prize.

5. Ariella Azoulay and Adi Ophir, "100 Years of Zionism, 50 Years of a Jewish State," *Tikkun* (March–April 1998), pp. 68–71.

6. Shlomo Sand, *The Invention of the Jewish People,* trans. Yael Lotan (London and New York: Verso, 2010).

7. *Ha'aretz* (January 22, 2012). The significant role of Israeli cinema in the national debate is demonstrated by the fact that the charges of McCarthyism were made by political scientist Prof. Neve Gordon of Ben-Gurion University of the Negev, Israeli Film Directors Guild chairman Rani Blair, and the chairman of the Israeli Documentary Filmmakers Forum, Uri Rosenwaks.

8. David S. Hull, *Film in the Third Reich* (Berkeley: University of California Press, 1969), pp. 157–77.

9. See Ilan Gur-Ze'ev, "The Existential Threat and Spiritual Challenge of the New Anti-Semitism," lecture given at the New Anti-Semitism conference, University of Haifa, June 22, 2009 (in Hebrew) http://construct.haifa.ac.il/~ilangz/new_antisemitism_opening.pdf.

10. Natan Sharansky, "Anti-Semitism in 3D," *Jerusalem Post*(February 23, 2004).

11. Melanie Philips, "The Oldest Obsession," *Spectator* (February 21, 2011), http://www.spectator.co.uk/melaniephillips/6719200/the-oldest-obsession.thtml.

12. Lawrence Baron, "Theodor Lessing: Between Jewish Self-Hatred and Zionism," *Leo Baeck Institute Yearbook* 26, no. 1 (1981), pp. 323–40, http://leobaeck.oxfordjournals .org/content/26/1/323.full.pdf.

13. Joseph Halachmi, *No Matter What: Studies in the History of the Jewish Film in Israel* (Jerusalem: Steven Spielberg Jewish Film Archive, 1995), pp. 34–46 (in Hebrew).

14. Ian Jarvie, "National Cinema: A Theoretical Assessment," in Mette Hjort and Scott Mackanzei, eds., *Film and Nation* (London: Routledge, 2000), pp. 75–87.

15. Curiously, this inciting documentary that alleges Israel committed atrocities in the 2002 battle in Jenin was scheduled to be shown in the European channel Arte. Following protests against the hate film, its screening was canceled by the channel.

16. Amir Rotem, "Even When They Die, They Look Better than Us," *Davar* (December 21, 1986) (in Hebrew).

17. Ella Shohat, *Israeli Cinema: East/West and the Politics of Representation* (New York and London: I. B. Tauris, revised edition, 2010).

18. Nurith Gertz, "A World without Boundaries: Israel National Identity in the Eighties as Expressed in Cinema and Literature," *Discours Social / Social Discourse* 4, nos. 3 & 4 (1992), pp. 155–70.

19. Judd Neeman, "The Jar and the Blade: Fertility Myth and Medieval Romance in Israeli Political Films," *Prooftexts* 22, nos. 1–2, Special Issue: The Cinema of Jewish Experience (Winter/Spring 2002), pp. 141–56.

20. Dan Fainaru, "Inside Story," *Sight and Sound* (Spring 1992), p. 15.

21. See Ilan Avisar, "Israeli Cinema and the Ending of Zionism," In Fred Lazin and Greg Mahler, eds., *Israel in the Nineties*(Gainesville: University Press of Florida, 1996), pp. 153–68.

22. Judd Neeman, "The Empty Tomb in the Postmodern Pyramid: Israeli Cinema in the 1980's and the 1990's," in Charles Berlin, ed. *Documenting Israel* (Cambridge, Mass.: Harvard College Library, 1995), pp. 117–51.

23. There is a curious moderation of extreme politics when the films are shown on Israeli television. Some television screenings did not include the radical ending that features the children's fantasy to fly away from Israel to a new land. In a similar vein, the television version of Yaki Yosha's *Summertime Blues* (1984)—about the summer of several youngsters before they join the army—eliminated the original ending that shows the protagonists' images with information on their deaths in service.

24. See Ilan Avisar, "The Holocaust in Israeli Cinema as a Conflict of Survival and Morality," in Miri Talmon and Yaron Peleg, eds., *Identities in Motion* (Austin: University of Texas Press, 2011), pp. 151–68. Another view of the impact of the Holocaust on Israel is seen in Judd Neeman's claim that Israeli films "echo a deeply ingrained recognition that the liquidation of the Diaspora sought by Zionism through immigration of millions of Jews to Palestine, was actually achieved by Nazi Germany through extermination of those same millions," in Judd Neeman, "The Tragic Sense of Zionism: Shadow Cinema and the Holocaust," *Shofar* 24, no. 1 (2005), p. 22. See also Elhanan Yakira, *Post-Zionism, Post Holocaust: Three Essays on Denial, Forgetting, and the Delegitimation of Israel*, trans. Michael Swirsky (Cambridge: Cambridge University Press, 2009).

25. Enemies of the Jewish state often make the claim that the establishment of Israel was made possible by the Nazi genocide. This argument is patently false, for it ignores the Zionist accomplishments in establishing a de facto Jewish state and a vibrant national Hebrew culture in the land of Israel before the Second World War and the Holocaust. The political agenda of this bogus argument is designed to reduce the entire content of Jewish nationalism and its modern achievement—the establishment of Israel—to a mere project of survival or an act of guilt performed by the world community. Furthermore, the causal linkage between the horrors of Auschwitz and the creation of Israel also serves to reduce the singularity and enormity of the Holocaust to an event with redemptive closure—as if the state "given" to the victims compensates for the atrocities of genocide. See David Arnow, "The Holocaust and the Birth of Israel: Reassessing the Causal Relationship," *The Journal of Israeli History* 15, no. 3 (1994), pp. 257–83.

26. See Alvin Rosenfeld, *The End of the Holocaust* (Bloomington: Indiana University Press, 2011).

27. The scene appears in a documentary by Eyal Sivan and Michele Khleifi, *Route 181: Fragments of a Journey in Palestine-Israel* (2004). In July 2011, Eyal Sivan and Haim Beresheeth, along with several Israeli academics, joined the Palestinian call for a BDS campaign against Israel: "POINTS OF UNITY," http://www.bdsmovement.net/call.

28. In the mid-1980s, an Israeli play staged such a scene with an Arab child facing Israeli soldiers. The Israeli review board for films and play decided to ban its public performance, but the Supreme Court reversed this decision, citing the right of freedom of expression.

29. The present Web scene of talkbacks and bloggers conveys voices and popular sentiments that are rarely expressed in the printed media.

30. Quoted in Yoram Hazoni, *The Jewish State: The Struggle for Israel's Soul* (New York: Basic Books, 2000), p. 3. The enduring sentiment of survival anxiety and its connection with the internal political conflict was expressed by Moshe Landau, the president of the Israeli Supreme Court in the 1980s: "I fear for the state's survival. I think that the existence of the Jewish state is in danger. I see great external dangers facing us. But the internal dangers are even bigger: the general feeling of bewilderment, the confusion of concepts, the social disintegration. And the weakness of the national will, the lack of readiness to fight. The illusion that peace will obviate our need to fight and defend ourselves. These things give me no rest. They really keep me awake and are affecting my physical health." Interview in *Ha'aretz* (October 6, 2000).

31. Ari Shavit, "*A Spirit of Absolute Folly,*" was published August 11, 2006 in *Ha'aretz*, http://www.think-israel.org/shavit.apocalypselater.html.

14 The Roots of Antisemitism in the Middle East: New Debates

Matthias Küntzel

"WHEN I WITNESSED the events in Imbaba, I realized [the Jews were behind them]," wrote journalist Safaa Saleh on May 13, 2011 in the Egyptian government newspaper *Al-Gumhouriyya,* following clashes between Copts and Muslims in Cairo's Imbaba district that had claimed twelve lives. "There is no disaster in the world that was not caused by the Jews," declared Saleh, calling in evidence a star witness: "Hitler said, 'I could have exterminated all of the Jews, but I left some of them [alive] so that the world would know why I exterminated them.'"[1]

In the West, such statements would have been met with outrage, but not in Egypt, where positive references to Hitler and the destruction of the Jews have been an accepted part of public discourse for decades. In this respect, at least, the uprising of 2011 that deposed former President Husni Mubarak changed nothing.

Irrational ideologies are harder to defeat than illegitimate rulers. This is certainly true in the case of Egypt, where the ousted Mubarak was condemned as a friend of Israel and the protestors carried placards in which the president's face was covered with Stars of David.[2] The emergence of mass movements for change in the Arab world has not, therefore, removed the need to tackle Arab antisemitism; on the contrary, in a context of heightened political activism and major reorientations, that need has become more pressing than ever. It is, therefore, all the more regrettable that researchers into antisemitism are divided into separate camps. While all agree that in no other part of the world is antisemitism as widespread and commonplace as in the Middle East, the unanimity vanishes when it comes to explaining the causes and context of this antisemitism.

On the one hand, there are those who claim that hostility toward Jews in the Arab world has merely developed in direct response to Zionism and Israeli policies. On the other hand, some insist that Islamists and Nazis introduced and reinforced an antisemitic interpretation of the conflict. The former school emphasizes the differences between Arab antisemitism and its European forerunner, while the latter stresses their similarities. The former asserts that the only way to remove the antisemitism is to resolve the Middle East conflict, the latter that that conflict can only be resolved after the removal of the antisemitism. The disagreement is not about whether a connection between the Palestinian conflict and this antisemitism exists, but about the nature of that connection.

The purpose of this chapter is to describe and comment on the key features of this controversy. However, the reader should be aware that the author is a participant, not a neutral observer, in this debate and this attempt to take stock is also a contribution to it.

The Dominant Paradigm

The conventional explanation for Arab antisemitism links it directly to the Middle East conflict. Prominent scholars such as Yehoshafat Harkabi and Bernard Lewis pioneered this still dominant position some decades ago. "Arab anti-Semitism," wrote Harkabi in 1972, "is not the cause of the conflict but one of its results. . . . If the Arab–Israel conflict was settled, anti-Semitic manifestations would die out."[3] In 1985, Bernard Lewis wrote in the same vein, "For Christian anti-Semites, the Palestine problem is a pretext and an outlet for their hatred; for Muslim anti-Semites, it is the cause."[4]

While advancing this argument, Harkabi and Lewis did not try to downplay or excuse the antisemitism itself. On the contrary, according to Harkabi, it was particularly "vigorous and aggressive," "fervent and vengeful." Since it "regards the Jews as a pathological phenomenon, a cancer in the flesh of humanity, it rejects their right to a future and cherishes the ideal of a world without Jews."[5] Lewis too talked of a "Nazi-type anti-Semitism [that] came to dominate Arab discussions on Zionism and Judaism as well as of the state of Israel."[6]

Today many antisemitism researchers and Islamic Studies and Middle East experts draw a different conclusion from the alleged link between this hostility to Jews and an actual conflict. They argue that while the German form of Jew-hatred derived from irrational delusions, the Arab world is behaving less irrationally since its Jew-hatred is underpinned by a genuine conflict of interests. Let me illustrate the point with an example from the Berlin-based Zentrum für Antisemitismusforschung (ZfA), the largest and most important European institution of its kind.

Berlin Learning Process

Around the turn of the millennium, the ZfA tried to organize a conference on the interface between antisemitism and Muslim anti-Zionism. However, the plan met with criticism from outside the institution. "Many of the invited Middle East specialists objected to the notion that anti-Semitism was the only form of racism in the Arab–Israel conflict, and the invitation was revised to mention anti-Arab racism as well."[7]

Werner Bergmann, the deputy head of the ZfA, stated that his institution had undergone a "learning process" in the run-up to the conference, in which certain "experts on Islam and the Middle East had played a central role." In the course of this process, it had been demonstrated that Arab–Islamic antisemitism could only be "fully" understood if, "rather than starting from antisemitism, one approached it as a consequence of the Palestine conflict." According to Bergmann, "all parties to the conflict should become objects of analysis. This means that, in mirror-image fashion, the negative perceptions of the Palestinian people . . . by . . . the Israeli side must also be taken into consideration."[8]

The keyword here is "mirror-image." While research into anti-Arab racism in Israel may well be a worthwhile undertaking, the "mirror-image" approach neglects the distinction between racism and antisemitism and wrongly assumes that Arab antisemitism "mirrors" Jewish behavior.

So the *first* result of this "learning process" was that the ZfA adopted an equidistant position. The planned conference on the relationship between antisemitism and anti-Zionism turned into an international conference on the topic of "the origins of images of the enemy in the Palestine conflict."[9] The "image of the Arab enemy" and the "image of the Jewish enemy" were assumed to be the same sort of thing, as if Israel "in mirror-image fashion" were advocating the destruction of specific Arab states, or major Israeli political parties had described the Arabs as a "cancer in the flesh of humanity" that had to be destroyed in the interests of humanity.

Secondly, the "learning process" entailed a new and partisan view of the Middle East conflict. For example in 2008 the ZfA published a work of reference entitled *Handbuch des Antisemitismus—Länder und Regionen.* In the entry for "Palestine," the volume summarizes the founding of the State of Israel in this way:

> The foundation of the State of Israel has entered Arab political discourse as the *nakba* ("catastrophe"). The flight and expulsion of 700,000 Palestinian Arabs, who left the land in the course of the fighting and the territorial loss of a large proportion of the former Mandate territory were perceived by the Arab side as the result of the ongoing intrigues of European powers. In the 1950s and 60s the Palestine question moved to the centre of the Pan-Arab ideology as a symbol of imperialist threats.[10]

This standard work mentions neither the UN Partition Resolution of 1947 nor the military assault by several Arab states on the newly established Jewish state. Instead, the author presents this key moment in the Middle East conflict solely as "perceived by the Arab side," an approach which inevitably gives plausibility to the "image of the Jewish enemy."

Replacing facts with narratives in this way is intrinsically problematic. Still more serious, however, is the fact that alternative points of view are ignored; indeed, their very existence is not mentioned. In this instance, therefore, the attempt to compare the "images of the enemy" of antisemites and of Jews "mirror-image fashion" has led to a thoroughly biased and misleading account of the Middle East conflict.

Moreover, *thirdly,* this "learning process" has resulted in efforts to find mitigating circumstances for Arab antisemitism. Thus, the German researcher of Islam, Jochen Müller, insists that, unlike its European precursor, Arab antisemitism "is 'at least' based on a real problem, namely the marginalization of the Palestinians." The same line has been taken by the ZfA's Juliane Wetzel, who argues that, in the case of Arab antisemitism, "the motivation is clearly different from that of the [kind of] antisemitism [which] is not based on any kind of real conflict whatsoever."[11] The implicit conclusion of all this is that, if one wants to combat Arab antisemitism, one must first come to grips with the "real conflict with the Jews": to solve the Middle East conflict.

Just recently, there have been indications of a possible shift within the ZfA. In an essay in the institute's 2009 *Jahrbuch für Antisemitismusforschung,* we read that "Israeli policy is *not* the decisive factor in the more recent evolution of Arab antisemitism. . . . Not only the scale, but also the logic underlying current anti-Jewish propaganda can*not* be fully explained by the Middle East conflict."[12] We shall have to wait to see whether there has indeed been a change of mind. There are, in any case, good reasons for such a change, as we will show in the next section.

New Directions in Research

The paradigm in which Arab antisemitism is only seen as the result of the Middle East conflict is facing a mounting challenge, for a number of reasons.

First, the real course of the Middle East conflict refutes the claim that Israeli policies are the cause and antisemitism the effect. If this were the real causal connection, the Israeli withdrawals from Lebanon (2000) and Gaza (2005) should have led to a decline in antisemitism. As we know, the opposite happened. The Israeli withdrawals reinforced rather than weakened the antisemitic uproar.

Second, researchers have uncovered new material that contradicts the link theory. As Hillel Cohen shows in his pioneering study, *Army of Shadows. Palestinian Collaboration with Zionism, 1917–1948*, only a minority of Palestinians reacted antisemitically to Zionism at that time. "Cooperation and collaboration were prevalent, in a variety of forms, throughout the period and among all classes and sectors. Collaboration was not only common but a central feature of Palestinian society and politics."[13] Clearly, therefore, antisemitism was not the inevitable response to the Middle East conflict, since other responses were more widespread than previously recognized.

Third, after the attacks of September 11, 2001, the texts of Islamic antisemitism were subjected to closer scrutiny. Now for the first time the Charter of Hamas was put under the microscope and the similarity of its discourse with that of Nazi antisemitism recognized. Only then did many scholars start to use the Middle East Media Research Institute's translations as sources. This has led to a decline in the willingness to find mitigating circumstances for Arab antisemitism and has given new urgency to the matter of its origins.

Fourth, and this is the decisive point, the opening up of a new field of research has led to the appearance of a series of books that have begun to tackle the issue of the possible contributions of Nazism and Islamism to the rise of this antisemitism. Prior to September 11, the only book dealing with such matters was Robert Wistrich's *Hitler's Apocalypse: Jews and the Nazi Legacy*, published in 1985, in which he described the "ideological rapprochement between Islamic and National-Socialist antisemitism" and dealt with the "connection between the Nazis' 'Final Solution' and the later attempts to destroy the State of Israel."[14] Since 2001, other scholars too have devoted their attention to these topics. [15]

The year 2002 saw the appearance of my book, *Jihad and Jew-Hatred*, which summarizes the contents of the relevant secondary sources against the background of September 11 and shows how the Nazis succeeded in disseminating a firmly antisemitic interpretation of the Middle East conflict in the Arab world.

Since 2004, scholars have focused on Nazi radio propaganda—between 1939 and 1945 the Nazis broadcast daily radio programs from Berlin to the Islamic world in Arabic, Persian, Turkish, and Hindi. Then American historian Jeffrey Herf made a sensational discovery: he found some several thousand pages of transcripts of these broadcasts. His 2009 study, *Nazi Propaganda for the Arab World*, mines this new material, and shows how the Nazis endeavored to popularize the Jew-hatred found in early Islamic sources and radicalized it by combining it with the patterns of European antisemitism. He also shows how this antisemitism outlived the Shoah, for instance in a letter sent to representatives of the Arab League in July 1946 by Hassan al-Banna, the founder of the Muslim Brotherhood, in honor of Amin El-Husseini, the former Mufti of Jerusalem who subsequently became a friend of Heinrich Himmler. The letter stated, "The Mufti is Palestine and Palestine is the Mufti. . . . Yes, this hero . . . fought Zionism, with the help of Hitler and Germany. Germany and Hitler are gone, but Amin Al-Husseini will continue the struggle. . . . Amin! March on! God is with you! We are behind you!"[16] By this time, Hassan Al-Banna's Muslim Brotherhood had become a leading political force. In 1946 it had more than 500,000 members and could mobilize a further 500,000 for its public rallies in Egypt alone.[17]

In 2006, in their book, *Nazi Palestine: The Plans for the Extermination of the Jews in Palestine*, historians Martin Cüppers and Klaus-Michael Mallmann provided the proof that the Nazis planned to do in the Middle East what they were already doing in Eastern Europe: wipe out the Jews with the help of the local non-Jewish population.

Both historians explicitly challenge the dominant idea that Palestinian antisemitism developed as a reaction to the policies of the Zionists, calling this assumption "a classic case of a reversal of cause and effect."[18]

This was followed by the pioneering study *From Empathy to Denial* by Meir Litvak and Esther Webman, which deals with the scale of Holocaust denial and Holocaust approval in the Arab world. They show that even "[Holocaust] justification was not confined to marginal or radical circles and media, but appeared among mainstream producers of culture, and did not arouse any significant criticism or condemnation in the Arab public discourse."[19]

The research efforts have yielded an impressive amount of new knowledge—knowledge apt to change our view of the history of the Middle East conflict.

First of all, research allows us to give a clearer answer to the question of the roots of Arab antisemitism. At the beginning of the 1930s, there were still several competing approaches to the question of how to view and possibly solve the Palestine conflict—the antisemitic approach that the Mufti of Jerusalem was already following before 1933 was only one of them. Nazi propagandists intervened into this state of uncertainty from the outside. They used the Palestine conflict as a vehicle to disseminate their Jew-hatred as widely as possible, working in alliance with the nascent Islamist movement, which had designated Zionism as its mortal enemy for religious reasons. The suggestive mixture of National Socialist slogans, Koranic verses, and quotations from *The Protocols of the Elders of Zion* that were conveyed to the illiterate masses by Nazi radio broadcasts from 1939 onward began to exert its effect. A significant proportion of the Arab world gradually began to view the Middle East conflict through a lens with two superimposed distorting filters: that of early Islamic Jew-hatred and that of modern antisemitism. To paraphrase Jean-Paul Sartre, it was no longer "experience that created the idea of the Jews." Instead, "prejudice distorted the experience."[20]

Secondly, the new research allows us to take a fresh look at the key turning point in the Middle East conflict: the events of 1947 and 1948. On November 29, 1947, the United Nations came out in support of a two-state solution for Palestine. In response, first Arab guerilla forces and then the armies of Arab states went to war with the aim of preventing the implementation of the UN resolution. It was not the foundation of the Jewish state, as the ZfA's handbook claims, but this war and the defeat of the Arab armies in 1949 that created the mass flight and exclusion of Arabs from Palestine, with all the well-known consequences.

However, if what Hillel Cohen concludes as a result of his research is true, that "there can be little doubt that the mufti's inflexible position and refusal to accept any partition proposal were the major reasons for the outbreak of war in 1948,"[21] and if it is true that the majority of Palestinian Arabs abstained from the struggle, so that the Mufti had to rely on the notoriously antisemitic Muslim Brotherhood for his mass support, then our view of the Middle East conflict has to change. For it could then be taken as proof that the hatred of Jews—systematically disseminated by the Nazis between 1939 and 1945 and whipped up still further by Amin el-Husseini and the Muslim Brotherhood from 1946 to 1948—was the main trigger for this defining moment in the Middle East conflict.

All the above information points to the following conclusions: Arab and Muslim antisemitism is no less dangerous than its European predecessor; Israeli policies are only responsible for this antisemitism in a very roundabout way, and to settle the Middle East conflict one must first of all counter this antisemitism.

Not surprisingly, the new publications triggered a major international debate with, at least in the United States, repercussions beyond the academy. In particular, Paul Berman's latest book, *The Flight of the Intellectuals,* sparked off a discussion about the link between Islamism and Nazism in the pages of influential journals and newspapers such as *Foreign Affairs* and the *Wall Street Journal.*

However, the response of much of the academic Islamic and Middle Eastern studies establishment to this new information has been, to say the least, disappointing. Rather than welcoming the new information and embarking on further research to supplement it, the response in the academic journals and congresses has been icy. Indeed, many of the scholars mentioned above have faced personal attacks of a kind rarely encountered in other academic fields.

What sort of arguments have the opponents of the new research put forward? I shall start with a particular category of objection: the accusation that all the above-mentioned authors are consciously or unconsciously engaging in pro-Israeli propaganda.

An "Anti-Arab Propaganda War"?

The clearest statement of this accusation has come from Gilbert Achcar, professor at the School of Oriental and African Studies (SOAS) in London and author of *The Arabs and the Holocaust,* which has won the accolades of leading lights such as Francis R. Nicosia and Peter Novick and been hailed by many other writers as the best existing, if not the definitive, criticism of the new research.

Although Achcar repudiates Arab antisemitism, his criticism of it is motivated by anti-Zionism. In other words he criticizes antisemitism not because it envisages the murder of Jews and renders the Middle East conflict insoluble, but because " . . . these anti-Semitic ravings . . . in fact help Israel produce anti-Arab propaganda." He describes the research institute MEMRI, which documents these "ravings" as "a function of the Arab–Israeli conflict, acting like a subdepartment of the Israeli propaganda services" and Professor Wistrich, possibly the world's most renowned expert on antisemitism, as "another professional of the anti-Arab propaganda war."[22] Achcar does not criticize MEMRI or Wistrich for mistranslation or misinterpretation, but claims that Israel allegedly benefits from their work. Within this mindset, the propaganda trap can only be avoided by excusing or ignoring Arab antisemitism.

René Wildangel, who worked for many years at the Zentrum für Moderner Orient (Centre of Modern Oriental Studies; ZMO) in Berlin, and serves today as an adviser to the Green Party group in the German parliament, is more restrained. He too, however, is convinced that the new research effort is intended to harm the Arab cause and that "concrete historical-political motives" lie behind the "marked emphasis on the Grand Mufti" and have the aim "of discrediting Arab demands in the Middle East conflict."[23] Wildangel seems to find the question of whether discussion of the Mufti serves to propagate myths or establish the real sequence of events of secondary interest.

Peter Wien, assistant professor of history at the University of Maryland, agrees with Wildangel. In his view, the connection between Nazi antisemitism and the Arab world has "been used to contest the legitimacy of 20th-century Arab political movements across the ideological spectrum."[24] I do not believe this to be the case. Nonetheless, any product of research can, of course, be abused for political ends. This is not, however, a reason for halting research, but for protecting it against academic malpractice and the corrupting effects of political bias.

Wien, however, does not draw such a clear distinction between politics and scholarship. He believes that the question of the relationship between the Nazis and the Arab world, "has become paradigmatic in defining *scholarly and political* approaches to key areas of Middle Eastern history."[25] Here politics and scholarship are mixed up in such a way as to imply that certain topics should be avoided for political reasons, such as the desirability of not looking too closely at the nature of certain Arab political movements.

Götz Nordbruch, assistant professor at the Centre for Contemporary Middle Eastern Studies at the University of Southern Denmark, seems to take a similar view. He, too, traces "the latest surge of scholarly interest in this facet of [the] twentieth century" back to political interests. In his view, "the quest for legitimacy of the respective sides in the Arab–Israeli conflict increasingly involves references to Nazi German history." Does Nordbruch really believe that Herf, Litvak and Webman, Cüppers and Mallmann and others referred to in his review article wrote their works in order to promote specific Israeli or Palestinian political agendas? As evidence, he adduces the distribution by the Israeli Foreign Ministry in the summer of 2009 of a picture showing Amin el-Husseini with Adolf Hitler. This was done, he writes, in order "to discredit Israel's Palestinians opponents in today's conflict."[26] But even if this were true, it remains unclear how the distribution of such a photo might bring serious research about the Mufti into disrepute.

The common denominator of all such statements lies in an imperative that recalls the politicized science of the former Soviet Union: keep away from research areas that might harm "the right side" and be of use to the "wrong side." Jeffrey Herf personally experienced this mechanism at work at a conference held in May 2010 in Tel Aviv on Arab Responses to Fascism and Nazism, 1939–1945: "I have presented abundant evidence of that collaboration . . . I even heard one conference participant say that presenting such evidence, even if true, was politically damaging to the Arab and Palestinian cause and thus, presumably, should not be brought forth."[27] So only facts supportive of the political goal can be accepted as historical truths.

The genocidal antisemitism of Hizbullah and Hamas, however, is a fact that no one can deny. So how do the opponents of the new research effort deal with this kind of antisemitism in the Arab world?

A Respectable Type of Antisemitism?

Let us start with Marc Lynch, a professor of political science and international affairs and director of the Institute for Middle East Studies at George Washington University. In a review of Paul Berman's book, *The Flight of the Intellectuals,* for *Foreign Affairs,* Lynch takes up the issue of an episode involving the preacher Yussuf al-Qaradawi, whose program on Al-Jazeera has made him one of the Muslim Brotherhood's most influential ideologues and a leading authority within Sunni Islam.

In January 2009, Qaradawi explained the Holocaust as a just punishment by God. Berman quotes this in his book: "Throughout history, Allah has imposed upon the [Jews] people who would punish them for their corruption. The last punishment was carried out by Hitler. By means of all the things he did to them . . . he managed to put them in their place." In another television show, Qaradawi called for mass murder: "Oh Allah, take this oppressive, Jewish, Zionist band of people. Oh Allah, do not spare a single one of them. Oh Allah, count their numbers, and kill them, down to the very last one." Berman quotes this too.[28]

Lynch avoids mentioning this aggressive antisemitism in his review. Qaradawi is a moderate Muslim, he writes, adding: "At the same time, he . . . is certainly hostile toward Israel."[29] Here Lynch has managed to interpret Qaradawi's approval of the Holocaust as an expression of a—perhaps in his eyes justified—hostility to Israel.

In the next edition of *Foreign Affairs,* Berman criticized these apologetics. He writes that Lynch "hides behind euphemisms—in this case, his phrase 'hostile toward Israel,' when what he really means is 'Hitlerian.'" However, Lynch was not to be deterred, replying that, in the above-mentioned remarks, "Indeed, Qaradawi has voiced extremely hostile views of Israel."[30]

The defensive reaction displayed here by an American Middle Eastern expert writing in the leading foreign policy publication of the United States speaks volumes. Lynch feigns blindness and twists Qaradawi's unmistakably antisemitic statements to fit his own political concern—the wish to work with the "moderate Islamist" Qaradawi. At the same time, he exposes an "orientalist" approach with his attempt to explain Qaradawi's statement condescendingly. If a Christian leader of the Ku Klux Klan had said what Qaradawi proclaimed to his millions of listeners, Lynch would presumably have taken his words seriously and criticized it as "Hitlerian" antisemitism. The words of a Muslim, on the other hand, seem to carry less weight for Lynch, who denies the Muslim Brotherhood preacher the ability to mean what he says. In so doing, he allows himself to do something he would never do if he were dealing with a Western religious figure: translate a eulogy to Hitler into an expression of "hostility to Israel." In order to sustain this policy of denial, it is no surprise to find Lynch denouncing Berman's thoughts about the possible repercussions of Nazi propaganda as "ludicrous efforts . . . [a] construct . . . [and a] cartoonish tale."[31]

Gilbert Achcar, to whom Lynch refers approvingly in *Foreign Affairs,* takes a different tack. He does not deny the existence of the ugly expressions of Arab antisemitism; instead, he makes Israel responsible for them. He sees in Arab antisemitism only "fantasy-laden expressions . . . of an intense national frustration and oppression for which 'the Jews' of Palestine in their majority, as well as Israel, the 'Jewish state' they founded, must, in fact, be held responsible."[32]

Achcar, therefore, wants to distinguish between a pathological European antisemitism and the frustration-based "expressions" of the Arabs. However, were he to examine the "expressions" more closely, he would soon see that they are violent fantasies directed at the destruction of the Jews or Israel. Such fantasies have nothing to do with real conflicts. Otherwise the response would not be antisemitism, but a justified or unjustified fury over a misguided policy, aimed at changing behavior, not annihilation.

Achcar even manages to find excuses for the dissemination of the *Protocols of the Elders of Zion.* He claims to be able to discern a "qualitative difference" between an "antisemitic and an anti-Zionist reading" of the *Protocols* and deems it "necessary" to distinguish between an unforgivable and forgivable distribution of them.[33]

It is, of course, true that the context of Arab antisemitism is very different from the context of Nazi antisemitism. This makes the similarity between today's slogans, cartoons, and fantasies and those of the Nazis all the more striking. But it is precisely these similarities that Lynch and Achcar do not wish to see. In this avoidance they are joined by the other critics of the new research such as Nordbruch in *Middle East Studies* or Peter Wien and Joel Beinin in the *International Journal of Middle East Studies*.[34] It is this pre-emptive denial, or more precisely aversion of the gaze, that unites this group. This attitude is extended even to the treatment of the extreme form of antisemitism—Holocaust denial.

Holocaust Denial as the "Anti-Zionism of Fools"

To claim that Auschwitz is a myth is to designate the Jews as a universal enemy that has for seventy years been deceiving humanity in pursuit of filthy lucre. Holocaust denial takes antisemitism to new heights and incites the same genocidal hatred that paved the way for the Shoah. One would, therefore, prefer not to believe that some in Western academia have found ways of excusing even this.

The title of Gilbert Achcar's book is *The Arabs and the Holocaust.* However, he does not deal with what Arab Holocaust deniers actually say, but insults those who do so. "I will let others savor the perverse satisfaction of cataloging . . . all the inanities about the Holocaust that have been uttered . . . in the Arab world."[35]

His concern is not with the issue itself, but with promoting the notion that Israel is responsible not only for antisemitism, but also for Holocaust denial. His line of reasoning is this: he claims that Israel has constantly attempted to overcome "crises of legitimacy" through "the political exploitation of the memory of the Holocaust." As evidence, Achcar refers to 1982, when, he argues, Israel's international image suffered severe damage in the wake of the invasion of Lebanon so that it resorted to invoking the Holocaust on a particularly massive scale in order to revive its reputation. It was, according to Achcar, this alleged propaganda offensive that first provoked Holocaust denial in the Arab world: "The denial in the Arab world . . . comes from rage and frustration over the escalation of Israeli violence, along with the increased use of the Holocaust. It began with the invasion of Lebanon in 1982."[36]

It is true that in 1982 Israeli Prime Minister Menachem Begin compared Arafat, at that time based in Beirut, to Hitler. However, this discredited Begin particularly in Israel itself. "Many Israelis thought that Begin's Holocaust obsession led to the unfortunate adventure [the Lebanese war]," wrote Peter Novick, a favorite author of Achcar's.[37] This hardly amounts to an Israeli "propaganda offensive."

Still more ridiculous is Achcar's claim that Arab Holocaust denial started in 1982. The documents presented by Herf show that Holocaust denial was already present in the Nazi's Arabic broadcasts as early as 1943, which raged against "the Jews' cursed lies," "the lies . . . of the Jews who are trying to gain the sympathy of the world through their tears."[38]

In May 1945, a Jerusalem-based newspaper, *Filastin*, took up the theme: "The Jews have grossly overstated the number of their victims in Europe. . . . Their propaganda and their 'haggling' over 'these victims' was a means to establish a Jewish state in Palestine." In September 1945, the Egyptian newspaper *Akbhar al-Yawm* declared: "There was Nazi tyranny, but it did not harm the Jews any more than Germans."[39] Litvak and Webman go on to show that Holocaust denial has remained a part of public discourse in Egypt since that time.

Achcar, however, subordinates reality to his political belief-system. He presents Holocaust denial as the desperate reaction of an oppressed group to the onslaught of an all-powerful Israel. "Are all forms of Holocaust denial the same? Should such denial, when it comes from oppressors, not be distinguished from denial in the mouths of the oppressed, as the racism of ruling whites is distinguished from that of subjugated blacks?"[40] Arab Holocaust denial, he asserts, "is not primarily an expression of antisemitism, as western Holocaust denial certainly is, but an expression of what I call the 'anti-Zionism of fools.'"[41]

The latter phrase recalls the dictum of the German socialist leader August Bebel, who, in 1893, described antisemitism as the "socialism of fools"—a mistake that was perhaps understandable fifty years before the Holocaust, but not seventy years after it! For, with this argument, Achcar gives the Holocaust deniers, as long as they belong to what he considers an "oppressed group," a moral carte blanche: what would otherwise be outrageous becomes acceptable. He also brands the Arabs as stupid people who do not know what they are doing. When Arabs deny the Holocaust, he has stated in an interview, "It has nothing to do with any conviction. It's just a way of people venting their anger, venting their frustration, in the only means that they feel is available to them."[42]

As with Lynch, there is something contemptuous about this. When it comes to Arab antisemites, Achcar permits himself to do what he would never do to a French counterpart: refuse to treat them as human beings responsible for their own words and deeds.

While showing no interest in the concrete expressions of Arab Holocaust denial, he at the same time provides Arab Holocaust deniers with a protective cover. In so doing, he offers a striking example of the connection between poor scholarship and moral failure. As the great historian of the Middle East, Elie Kedourie, once remarked, "Moral integrity and scholarly rigor were always complementary." [43]

Nonetheless, Achcar's book was well received among German Middle East scholars. Alexander Flores, an Islamic studies expert at the University of Bremen, gushed with praise for Achcar's "great book." [44] The Berlin-based ZMO talked of a "pioneering book" and in May 2010 invited the author to a government-sponsored reading. This is an "objective and solid study of major significance," asserted Ulrike Freitag, the ZMO's director. "What today moves many people to doubt the Holocaust or the number of victims is related to Israel's instrumentalization of the latter in the Middle East conflict." [45] She fails to explain, however, what she means by Israel's "instrumentalization" of the Holocaust.

A certain understanding for Arab Holocaust deniers was also displayed by Sonja Hegasy, deputy director of the ZMO, when she stated that "Holocaust denial is also a response to the so-called Holocaust industry."[46]

A still more explicit position was adopted by long-standing ZMO employee René Wildangel in his doctoral thesis: "The more strongly the Holocaust was used to legitimate the Israeli state, the more impossible did it become to accept it [the Holocaust] from the Arab point of view."[47] Let us linger awhile over this remark, behind which lurks a two-fold emotional admission. Firstly it expresses the author's extreme hostility to Israel. If we pursue his line of thought, it would also be "impossible" from "the Arab point of view" to admit the existence of the Second Jewish Temple, since the ancient history of Palestine also belongs to the "legitimating basis" for the existence of Israel. Fact turns into fiction and fiction into fact, according to the needs of the anti-Israeli cause.

Secondly, Wildangel takes up the cudgels for the Arab Holocaust deniers using arguments that, like Achcar's, treat Arabs as if they are unable to take responsibility for their own decisions. They are treated here like puppets that, in the Israeli grip, can only move and think reflexively, making it somehow "impossible" for them to accept the historical fact of the Holocaust. However, the Arab Spring of 2011 has refuted this racist assumption, showing the Arab peoples not to be puppets at all.

Imbada and the Arab Spring

Nobody knows what the future holds for the rebellion-wracked countries of the Arab world. On the one hand, there is the hope that the revolutionary experience will strengthen the self-awareness and sense of responsibility of individuals so that the demand for a Jewish scapegoat recedes. "The antisemite is a person who is afraid," wrote Jean-Paul Sartre. "Afraid of his free will, his instincts, his responsibility—of any change, of the world."[48] The insurgent forces have, at least temporarily, shaken off this fear and opened up a new space for reflection.

On the other hand, powerful actors such as the Iranian regime, Hizbullah, Hamas, and the Egyptian Muslim Brotherhood are eyeing their chance. "The Arab revolutions . . . are the realization of the Koranic verses [which say] that the Arabs will gather together and fight the Jews," writes Egyptian journalist Safaa Saleh in the article quoted in my introduction.[49]

It is precisely at such a time—a time of new beginnings—that it becomes more important than ever to publicly raise the issues of the roots and potential consequences of antisemitism in the Middle East. Many things are happening that inspire curiosity and call for a proper explanation.

Why, for example, in May 2011, did Safaa Salah, of her own free will, decide to praise the Holocaust and Hitler? Why did the Egyptian government newspaper *Al-Gumhouriyya* choose to publish her commentary? And why did its publication fail to meet with any visible criticism?

The opponents of the new research effort continue to stifle that curiosity and discredit the search for explanations. To this end they hurl political buzzwords like hand grenades: "Israeli propaganda war!" "Instrumentalization of the Holocaust!" "Anti-Arab propaganda!" While these slogans have no explanatory value, they seem to achieve their goal: they help a particular group of academics rationalize their own intellectual self-deception, while at the same time marking out the boundaries beyond which researchers should not stray, lest they be denounced as "Israeli propagandists." It is all about protecting a particular worldview against the impact of reality. Jeffrey Herf has defined this worldview in terms of "third worldism," "anti-imperialism," "post-colonialism," "subaltern studies," and "anti-Zionism."[50]

The adherents of this approach include groups of people who, at least in Germany, set the tone in important academic centers, such as the ZMO or ZfA. One might think that such centers, by their very nature, would be inclined to support research into the relationship between National Socialism and Islamism in the Middle East. In fact, they refuse to engage in such research, possibly in order to sustain their one-sided view of the Middle East conflict.

The controversy over the roots of antisemitism in the Middle East is, however, more than just an academic discussion. Our field of research has this much in common with earthquake studies: we strive to minimize the devastation that can be caused by the object of our research. In the Middle East, the danger of catastrophe is especially great. Here, positive references to Hitler are still tolerated. Here, the longing to destroy Israel is rarely questioned and even more rarely opposed.

Irrational ideologies are harder to defeat than illegitimate rulers. Until scholarship ceases to misinterpret this Jew-hatred as the product of Jewish behavior, there is little likelihood of a start being made on the long process of the liberation of the Arab peoples from antisemitism.

Translated from the German by Colin Meade

NOTES

1. Article in the Egyptian government daily Al-Gumhouriyya: "The Jews Are behind the Clashes between Egypt's Muslims and Copts," *MEMRI, Special Dispatch Series*, No. 3844 (May 17, 2011).

2. John Rosenthal, "Democracy or Jew-Hatred? More Evidence of Antisemitism at the Egypt Protests," http://pajamasmedia.com/blog/democracy-or-jew-hatred-more-evidence-of-anti-semitism-at-the-egypt-protests/.

3. Yehoshafat Harkabi, *Arab Attitudes to Israel* (Jerusalem: Keter Publishing House, 1972), p. 298.

4. Bernard Lewis, *Semites and Anti-Semites* (London: Weidenfeld and Nicolson, 1986), p. 259.

5. Harkabi, pp. 299–302.

6. Lewis, p. 240.

7. Joel Beinin, review of Jeffrey Herf, *Nazi Propaganda in the Arab World* and Meir Litvak and Esther Webman, "From Empathy to Denial," *International Journal of Middle East Studies* 42, no. 4 (2012), pp. 689–92.

8. Werner Bergmann, "Zur Entstehung von Feindbildern im Konflikt um Palästina," in Wolfgang Benz, ed., *Jahrbuch für Antisemitismusforschung* 12 (Berlin: Metropol, 2003), pp. 16–17. Bergmann refers to the following people as inspirations behind this learning process: Helga Baumgarten (Bierzeit University), Gudrun Krämer (Freie Universität Berlin), Gerhard Höpp (Zentrum Moderner Orient), John Bunzl (Universität Wien), Kai Hafez (Deutsches Orient Institut Hamburg), and Joel Beinin (Stanford University).

9. Press release issued by the Technischen Universität Berlin, "Die Entstehung von Feindbildern im Konflikt um Palästina" (August 31, 2000), at: http://idw-online.de /pages/de/news?print=1&id=23924.

10. Götz Nordbruch, Palästina, in Wolfgang Benz, ed., *Handbuch des Antisemitismus. Judenfeindschaft in Geschichte und Gegenwart, Band 1: Länder und Regionen* (Munich: K. G. Saur, 2008), p. 261. The relevant passage has been quoted in full.

11. Jochen Müller, "Wessen Geistes Kind? Arabischer Nationalismus, Islamismus und Antisemitismus im Mittleren Osten," *Kommune*, no. 2/3 (2003); Juliane Wetzel, "Judenfeindschaft unter Muslimen in Europa," in Wolfgang Benz, ed., *Islamfeindschaft und ihr Kontext* (Berlin: Metropol, 2009), p. 52.

12. Malte Gebert and Carmen Matussek, "'Selbst wenn sie unser Land verlassen würden. . . .' Die Adaption der Protokolle der Weisen von Zion in der arabischen Welt," in Wolfgang Benz, ed., *Jahrbuch für Antisemitismusforschung* 18 (Berlin: Metropol, 2009), p. 68. Author's emphasis.

13. Hillel Cohen, *Army of Shadows* (Berkeley: University of California Press, 2008), p. 259.

14. Robert Wistrich, *Der antisemitische Wahn* (Munich: Max Huber, 1987), pp. 313,304.

15. **2001** saw the publication in Berlin of *Mufti-Papiere. Briefe, Memoranden, Reden und Aufrufe Amin al-Husainis aus dem Exil, 1940–1945*, ed. Gerhard Höpp (Berlin: Klaus Schwarz Verlag). In **2002** Ca Ira-Verlag (Freiburg) published my *Djihad und Judenhass. Über den neuen antijüdischen Krieg*. In **2004** *Blind für die Geschichte? Arabische Begegnungen mit dem Nationalsozialismus*, ed. Gerhard Höpp, Peter Wien, and René Wildangel, was published in Berlin (Klaus Schwarz Verlag) and *Germans and the Middle East*, ed. Wolfgang G. Schwanitz, was published in Madrid (Ibero-americana). **2006** saw the publication of Klaus-Michael Mallmann and Martin Cüppers's *Halbmond und Hakenkreuz. Das Dritte Reich, die Araber und Palästina* (Darmstadt: Wissenschaftliche Buchgesellschaft), Peter Wien's *Iraq Arab Nationalism: Authoritarian, Totalitarian and Pro-Fascist Inclinations 1932–1941* (London: Routledge) and Jeffrey Herf's study, *The Jewish Enemy: Nazi Propaganda during World War II and the Holocaust*, which also refers to developments in the Middle East. **2007** saw the publication of an English version of Jennie Lebl's study, originally written in Serbo-Croat, *The Mufti of Jerusalem Haj-Amin el-Husseini and National-Socialism* in Belgrade (Cigoja-Verlag); René Wildangel's *Zwischen Achse und Mandatsmacht. Palästina und der Nationalsozialismus* in Berlin (Klaus Schwarz Verlag); a new edition of Klaus Gensicke's 1988 book, *Der Mufti von Jerusalem und die Nationalsozialisten* (Darmstadt: Wissenschaftliche Buchgesellschaft), and the English version of *Djihad und Judenhass: Jihad and Jew-Hatred. Islamism, Nazism and the Roots of 9/11* (Telos Press) in New York. In **2008**

David G. Dalin and John F. Rothmann published *Icon of Evil. Hitler's Mufti and the Rise of Radical Islam*, in New York (Random House). **2009** saw the publication in London of Meir Litvak and Esther Webman's study, *From Empathy to Denial: Arab Responses to the Holocaust* (Hurst & Company) and Götz Nordbruch's *Nazism in Syria and Lebanon: The Ambivalence of the German Option 1933–1945* (Routledge); in New Haven of Jeffrey Herf's *Nazi Propaganda for the Arab World* (Yale University Press); and in New York of Gilbert Achcar's *The Arabs and the Holocaust* (Metropolitan Books, Henry Holt and Company). In **2010**, Mallmann and Cüppers's *Nazi Palestine: The Plans for the Extermination of the Jews in Palestin* (Enigma Books) and Paul Berman's *The Flight of the Intellectuals* (Mellville House) were published in New York.

16. Jeffrey Herf, *Nazi Propaganda for the Arab World*, pp. 243–44.

17. Richard P. Mitchell, *The Society of the Muslim Brothers* (London: Oxford University Press, 1969), p. 328.

18. Klaus-Michael Mallmann and Martin Cüppers, *Halbmond und Hakenkreuz*, p. 256.

19. Litvak and Webman, *From Empathy to Denial*, p. 195.

20. Jean-Paul Sartre, "Betrachtungen zur Judenfrage," in Jean-Paul Sartre, *Drei Essays* (West-Berlin, Ullstein, 1970), p. 111.

21. Cohen, p. 10.

22. Achcar, *The Arabs and the Holocaust*, pp. 182 and 213.

23. René Wildangel, "Auf der Suche nach dem Skandal. Eine Reaktion auf den Themenschwerpunkt 'Nazikollaborateure in der Dritten Welt,'" in: iz3W [Informationszentrum 3. Welt] Nr. 313 (July/August 2009).

24. Peter Wien, "Coming to Terms with the Past: German Academia and Historical Relations between the Arab Lands and Nazi Germany," *International Journal of Middle East Studies* 42, no. 2 (2010), p. 311.

25. Ibid., author's emphasis.

26. Götz Nordbruch, "'Cultural Fusion' of Thought and Ambitions? Memory, Politics and the History of Arab-Nazi German Encounters," *Middle Eastern Studies* 47, no. 1 (January 2011), p. 183.

27. "'Das Bild der Dritten Welt wird sich verändern,' Karl Pfeifer im Gespräch mit Jeffrey Herf," *Jungle World* (July 15, 2010).

28. Berman, *Flight of the Intellectuals*, pp. 78, 92.

29. Marc Lynch, "Veiled Truths: The Rise of Political Islam and the West" *Foreign Affairs* (July/August 2010).

30. Paul Berman, "Islamism, Unveiled. From Berlin to Cairo and Back Again" and Marc Lynch, "Lynch Replies," in: *Foreign Affairs* (September/October 2010).

31. "Lynch Replies."

32. Achcar, *The Arabs and the Holocaust*, p. 256.

33. Ibid., p. 208.

34. Nordbruch, "Cultural Fusion"; Wien, "Coming to Terms"; Beinin, review of Herf.

35. Achcar, *The Arabs and the Holocaust*, p. 181.

36. Ibid., p. 256. See also the interview "Gilbert Achcar, Arab Attitudes to the Holocaust" (May 20, 2010), www.SocialistWorker.org.

37. Peter Novick, *Nach dem Holocaust* (Munich: Deutscher Taschenbuch Verlag, 2003), p. 215.

38. Herf, 2009, p. 177.

39. Litvak and Webman, p. 52.

40. Achcar, *The Arabs and the Holocaust,* p. 276.

41. Gilbert Achcar, "Arabs Have a Complex Relationship with the Holocaust," *The Guardian* (May 12, 2010).

42. "Israel's Propaganda War: Blame the Grand Mufti. Gilbert Achcar Interviewed by George Miller," http://mrzine.monthlyreview.org/2010/achcar120510p.html.

43. Alain Silvera, "Elie Kedourie, politique et moraliste," in Sylvia Kedourie, ed., *Elie Kedourie CBE., FBA 1926–1992: History, Philosophy, Politics* (London: Frank Cass, 1998), p. 101.

44. Alexander Flores, "Die Araber, der Holocaust und die universalistische Moral," *Inamo* 16, no. 62 (Summer 2010).

45. Samir Grees, "Krieg der Narrative" (July 5, 2010), www.Qantara.de.

46. Sonja Hegasy, "Araber und Nazi-Deutschland. Kollaborateure und Widersacher," *Qantara.de* (December 1, 2010). Hegasy here makes distorted use of Litvak and Webman's *From Empathy to Denial.* The reference to Finkelstein is absent from the English text of the article ("The Arabs and Nazi Germany. Collaborators and Antagonists, *Qantara.de* (November 26, 2010).

47. Wildangel, *Zwischen Achse und Mandatsmacht,* p. 403.

48. Sartre, p. 134

49. MEMRI (May 17, 2011).

50. Herf, "Das Bild der Dritten Welt."

15 Anti-Zionist Connections: Communism, Radical Islam, and the Left

Robert S. Wistrich

Mᴏsᴛ ʜɪsᴛᴏʀɪᴀɴs tend to regard the ideologies of communism and radical Islam as mutually incompatible. Certainly, there is little in common at first sight between the *Communist Manifesto* and the Holy Qurʾan. Nor does the Islamist cult of death or martyrdom for Allah seem to have much to do with the secular rationalist worldview that influenced Bolshevism and the Western Left a century ago. But the communists who came to power in Russia in 1917, beginning with Lenin himself, were nonetheless quick to see the tactical benefit to themselves of sparking off a Bolshevik-led jihad against Western imperialism in Asia and the Near East. At the Second Congress of the Communist International held in Baku (1920), its president, Grigorii Zinoviev, aggressively called for "kindling a real holy war against the robbers and oppressors . . . a true people's holy war in the first place against British imperialism."[1] The close to two thousand delegates, representing the "enslaved popular masses of the East" (Persia, Armenia, Turkey, Russia, the Arab lands), were ecstatic. About two-thirds of the delegates were Bolshevik Party members. But they made a point of "respecting the religious feelings of the masses" even while educating them (in Zinoviev's words) "to hate and want to fight against the rich in general—Russian, Jewish, German, French."[2] Zinoviev was not the only Bolshevik internationalist of Jewish origin to play a central role in such incitement to holy war.

No less prominent in this "Red-jihadist" campaign was the Comintern's secretary, Karl Radek—a professional revolutionary already active in the pre-1914 Polish, Russian, and German socialist movements. Radek had been one of the architects of the secret anti-Western alliance between the Soviet Union and military circles in Weimar Germany, which culminated in the 1922 Rapallo Treaty. He also had excellent contacts with Turkish leaders including Enver Pasha, who advocated a "Holy War" against the West to restore their own position and bring down the Versailles Treaty. In Baku, Radek did not hesitate to appeal "to the warlike feelings of the people of the East," to "the memory of Genghis Khan" (!), to "holy war," and even "to the mercy of the great conquering Caliphs of Islam." Radek, the Polish-born "Jewish" Bolshevik, was outdoing even Zinoviev—turning to the toiling Muslim masses to repaint the East in sparkling red colors and to "create a new civilization under the banner of communism."

The Leninist-style jihad did not bear fruit for more than thirty years despite the common fount of seething hatred that the Bolsheviks and their Muslim counterparts shared toward the "materialist West." But it is important to note that no less than fifteen times the "Manifesto of the Congress of the Peoples of the East" would use the term *Holy War* in its calls to mobilization against imperialist Britain. Indeed, jihad became an integral part of the more general appeal to the "revolutionary workers and oppressed peasants" to rise up "against the [Western] plunderers and capitalists."[3] Significant, too, was the injection of an anti-Jewish chord alongside the anti-British tone in early communist propaganda to the Muslim East. Here is a typical example from 1920:

> Peoples of the East! . . . What has Britain done to Palestine? There, at first, acting for the benefit of Anglo-Jewish capitalists, it drove Arabs from the land in order to give the latter to Jewish settlers. Then, trying to appease the discontent of the Arabs, it incited them against the same Jewish settlers.[4]

The Palestine Communist Party (CPP) from the early 1920s followed a very similar political line. Visceral anti-Zionism went hand-in-hand with the calls from Moscow to "Arabize" the party. Compromises with Arab nationalism were not slow in coming. The 1929 anti-Jewish pogroms in Palestine, which had a strong Islamist as well as Arab nationalist coloring, were trivialized by the Comintern and the CPP, which praised the violence as an "anti-imperialist" movement against the British Mandate.[5] The predominantly Arab leadership of the CPP in the 1930s even drove it to denounce the entire Jewish community in Palestine as part of a sinister "Zionist-fascist" colonial project. At the same time, the communists supported the ultranationalist and pan-Islamist leadership of Haj Amin el-Husseini, who headed the Arab revolt against Britain between 1936 and 1939.[6] Amin el-Husseini's undisguised admiration for European fascism (especially his courting of Nazi Germany) was well known to the Palestinian communists, but this did not deter them from supporting his anti-Zionist extremism. CPP leaflets called on Arabs, as the "rightful owners of the country," to rise up against the Jews and the imperialists. Communists even denounced the immigration of German Jews (fleeing the Third Reich) to Palestine. Their main criticism of el-Husseini was that he had been too moderate. It was characteristic of the Palestine Communist Party in the mid-1930s that it called on Arabs to march on Tel Aviv and to use force against the "Nazi" Histadrut (the powerful Jewish trade union organization).[7]

El-Husseini's pan-Islamic agitation, his pan-Arabism mixed with virulent antisemitism, and his subsequent calls for a Holy War of Islam (in alliance with Nazi Germany) against world Jewry did not initially undermine communist enthusiasm for his cause.[8] Only the Jewish section within the CPP still protested at the Stalinist policy of unconditional support for the Arab national movement and for pan-Islamism, both of which explicitly negated any Jewish right to national self-determination.[9] No change in this policy would take place until the German invasion of the Soviet Union in June 1941. Henceforth, in Stalin's eyes, el-Husseini's total mobilization on behalf of Nazi Germany and his use of Islamist appeals on behalf of the Axis Powers against international communism turned him into a dangerous enemy.[10] The Palestine communists dutifully followed suit, bending to Soviet foreign policy needs, which eventually included support for the establishment of Israel in 1948.[11] Stalin, like other Soviet leaders, had long since abandoned his earlier belief that the Muslim masses outside the USSR could be readily "Bolshevized."[12]

However, during the next three decades the Soviet Union would gradually emerge as the chief Great Power patron of the Arab states and of the Palestinian cause. It was, moreover, the main architect of the denunciations of Israel as a racist, Nazi state after 1967; together with the Arab states it also masterminded the notorious UN General Assembly resolution equating Zionism with racism, in November 1975.[13] It was again the USSR that invented the delegitimization strategy of branding Israel as an "Apartheid state," by claiming that ideology was based on the racial "separation" of Jews from non-Jews as well as the systematic oppression of the Arab Palestinians.[14] This strategy paid off handsomely in Africa, in the Arab world, among Muslim states, and within the Non-Aligned bloc. In the 1970s and early 1980s the so-called "progressive camp" in the West, led by orthodox communists and Trotskyists (on this point, at least, they could agree), regularly vilified "Zionism" as a "crime against humanity" and as the ultimate symbol of international illegitimacy. This was a language soon adopted by Arab intellectuals, nationalists, Islamists, and Marxists even in countries like Egypt, which signed a peace treaty with Israel in 1979. The Zionism-is-Racism-is-Nazism amalgam was at the very core of this growing ideological convergence that deliberately stoked the fire of Palestinian anger against Israel in order to serve an anti-Western agenda. The USSR and its allies were certainly not averse to secretly supporting Arab terrorism against Israel and the West—including the jihad to reconquer *all* of Palestine—even as they invaded Afghanistan to subjugate a recalcitrant Muslim land, thereby unwittingly provoking a decade-long struggle of the *mujahideen* against communist oppression. Ironically, by the time the Zionism-is-Racism resolution was finally annulled by the UN in September 1991, the USSR was already on its last legs, radical Islam had emerged greatly strengthened from its victory in Afghanistan (thanks to U.S. support), and antisemitism was experiencing a world-wide resurgence. The end of the Cold War certainly did not lead to any diminution of animosity toward either the Jews or Israel.

A decade later, at the end of August 2001, the UN conference in Durban (South Africa) marked a crucial moment in the reemergence of a new-style antisemitism better adapted to the needs of the twenty-first century. At this ostensibly "anti-racist" gathering Israel was singled out "as a sort of modern-day geopolitical Anti-Christ." A flood of antisemitic slanders mixed with political criticism of Israel, Iranian-inspired conspiracy theories, Trotskyist anti-Zionism, and hecklers chanting "Jew, Jew, Jew" under the banner of Human Rights, filled the streets and characterized some of the sessions at Durban. To quote Canadian Member of Parliament Irwin Cotler:

> Durban became the tipping point for the coalescence of a new, virulent, globalizing anti-Jewishness reminiscent of the atmospherics that pervaded Europe in the 1930s. In its lethal form, this animus finds expression as state-sanctioned genocidal anti-Semitism, such as that embraced by Mahmoud Ahmadinejad's Iran, and its terrorist proxies, Hamas and Hezbollah.[15]

But the emergence of this radicalized Islam as a driving force of antisemitism goes back to the Iranian upheaval of 1979, which clearly brought to the forefront the *totalitarian revolutionary* aspects of political Islam as a comprehensive sociocultural system as well as its genocidal brand of antisemitism. Earlier Sunni Muslim thinkers like Sayyid Abul Ala Maududi (founder in 1941 of Pakistan's Jamaat-I Islami and the spiritual godfather of modern radical Islam) as well as the Egyptian Islamist intellectual Sayyid Qutb had already begun the process of presenting Islamist ideology in an innovative way as a coherent universalist creed. Maududi, in particular, aimed to transform society as a whole through a centralized revolutionary leadership on the Leninist model.[16] He explicitly defined Islam as a universalist jihad for the welfare of mankind, taking the Prophet Muhammad as his charismatic model of a revolutionary leader.[17] For Maududi, the seizure of power by a *vanguard* Islamic party would be essential in order to implement the *world revolution* as envisaged by Islam—which transcended any national boundaries. In order to achieve their aims, the Islamist revolutionary elite would, however, have to mobilize the masses—a lesson that would be thoroughly absorbed by the Ayatollah Khomeini in Iran.

Khomeini's own ideology derived its inspiration not only from Maududi and Qutb but also from the input of the Iranian Islamo-Marxist al-Shariati, the leading theoretician of "Red Shiʿism." The Paris-trained Shariati may well have imbibed his belief in the necessity of purificatory violence against the colonialist West from his reading of Algerian Frantz Fanon's seminal *The Wretched of the Earth* (1961). His own "Islamo-Marxist" version of Shiʿite Islam reinterpreted the Prophet Muhammad and icons of Shiʾism, like Ali and Husain, above all as defenders of the poor exploited masses.[18] "Red Shiʿism," with its gallery of redemptive martyrs, was presented by Shariati as the only answer to the toxic alienation of Western society and Muslim loss of identity in societies like the Shah's Iran.[19] Ali Shariati's Islamo-Marxism unreservedly extolled the blood-sacrifice of the *mujahid*—the fighter-martyr ready to die for the sake of the Revolution. Other theorists of the Islamic revolution in Iran were no less focused on the role of heroic martyrdom. Islam, in their eyes, was *the* quintessential religion of agitation, liberation, blood, and martyrdom.[20] Khomeini, however, added to this revolutionary mix a uniquely intransigent brand of anti-Israel and antisemitic vitriol that lastingly transformed Iran.

The Marxist George Habash (leader of the secular pan-Arab Popular Front for the Liberation of Palestine) no less enthusiastically glorified violent martyrdom, the hijacking of airplanes, the killing of civilians, and the hatred of Israel. Habash did not, for example, shrink from the prospect of a third world war if it would serve the Palestinian cause. A leftist with a Greek-Orthodox Christian background, Habash declared that in today's world, "no one is innocent, no one is neutral. A man is either with the oppressed or he is with the oppressors."[21] Already in 1979 he admitted that his own wing of the PLO drew equally on Soviet and Iranian fundamentalist sources of inspiration. "Many have been surprised," he added, "that we, as Marxists, should be on the side of a religious movement like Khomeini's. But beyond ideology, we have in common anti-imperialist, anti-Zionist and anti-Israeli elements."[22]

In the Arab world such a syncretic approach is not uncommon. The charismatic leader of the Lebanese Shiʿite Hizbullah, Hassan Nasrallah (a dedicated follower of the Ayatollah Khomeini), had already learned in the 1990s how to blend radical Islam and the cult of death with a tinge of popular Marxism and antisemitic hatred of Israel. He, too, embraced Khomeini's polarizing division of the world into "oppressors" and "oppressed," using it as part of Hizbullah's domestic political program. In Hizbullah's vision of a coming apocalyptic battle, the Jews, along with America, are aligned with the "party of Satan" (*Hizbu'shaytan*) against the exploited Third World peoples—with particular emphasis on the oppressed Shiʿite masses. Drawing on the Qurʾan and an idiosyncratic version of Marxist theory, Hizbullah has striven for a "universalist" definition of "the oppressed" as potentially including all social classes and religious denominations.[23] This radical Shiʿite universalism does not, of course, extend to Israel or to the United States. For Nasrallah and other Hizbullah leaders like the late Sheikh Fadlallah, there has never been any real difference between Judaism and Zionism. As for the Holocaust, it never happened or else was hugely exaggerated, while the Zionist conquest of Palestine is still consistently presented as being the perfect example of a global "Jewish" conspiracy.[24]

In the cosmic Manichean drama of Good battling Evil, the "Red" Shiʿites in Iran and Lebanon perceive themselves as being in the vanguard of social justice, sacred rebels against a long history of persecution. Moreover, they alone possess God's perfect revelation.[25] Whatever promotes the revolutionary cause in their world-view is *good;* whatever obstructs it has been and is *bad*—a classic Leninist principle. There can be no middle ground between Truth and Error in the radical millenarian revolutionary struggle to establish God's just order on earth. The ideology of the victorious Islamists in Iran also shared something in common with its Marxist rivals, especially the utopian belief in ultimate human redemption and a perfect society to be established through violent revolution. Indeed, Khomeinism would not have been the same without the often volatile and explosive dialogue between itself and the Iranian communists. There was a sense from the 1950s onward that to win the Iranian youth away from Marxism, Islam would have to adopt its own style of Marxist-Leninist rhetoric and to partially "Marxify" itself. The result, to quote Laurent Murawiec, was to create "an Islamo-Marxist hybrid—a monstrous laboratory experiment that was unleashed on the body of Iran and thence the rest of the world of Islam."[26]

It was also no accident that on arriving in the Iranian capital early in 1979, Yasser Arafat would solemnly declare his kinship with the Ayatollah Khomeini, in homage to a revolutionary on a par with such legendary figures as Lenin, Mao, or Che Guevara:

> The path we have chosen is identical; we are moving forward on the same path; we are fighting the same struggle: the same revolution; our nation is one, we have always lived in the same trenches for the same goal and the same slogan. Our slogan is: we are all Muslims, we are all Islamic revolutionaries, all fighting for the establishment of one body of Islamic believers. We will continue our struggle against Zionism and move towards Palestine alongside the Iranian revolutionaries.[27]

This jihadist credo did not prevent Arafat from receiving the red-carpet treatment in Vienna shortly after, where he was honored by Austrian Social-Democratic Chancellor Bruno Kreisky and the leader of the Socialist International, West Germany's Willy Brandt. For the first time, prominent European socialist leaders publicly legitimized the Palestinian jihad as if it were a purely secular national-liberation movement.

Muslim demonizers of America and the Jews for the past three decades have shared with their leftist allies a common loathing for capitalist modernity as the source of the rootless, globalized society that they inhabit today. Moreover, what Soviet propaganda in the 1970s used to routinely denounce as the "Tel Aviv–Washington axis" has now become

"Nazi Israel" and all-devouring America in the terminology of Muslim-leftist propaganda. The "Zionist Crusaders" have been metamorphosed into the warmongering, rapacious imperialists of the New Age, the cursed agents of neo-liberal globalization. During the Second Lebanon War of 2006, even on the European Social Democratic Left it became increasingly commonplace to hear insidious allegations that the foreign policy of the United States was controlled by Jews. In EU countries from Spain to Sweden, for example, the notion of a Jewish–Zionist–American neo-con conspiracy—widely touted by Islamists—had traversed almost all of the Left by the early twenty-first century.[28] The same was true on other continents.

In Great Britain, the Respect party (founded to oppose the Iraq war of 2003) was one of the clearest examples of a European political formation seeking to amalgamate international socialism and Islamism. It comprised elements of the neo-Trotskyite Socialist Workers Party (SWP), activists from the Muslim Association of Britain (MAB), antiglobalization militants, as well as pacifist protesters against the Anglo-American invasion of Iraq.[29] Intense anti-Zionism (including the explicit negation of Jewish statehood in Israel), fierce opposition to neo-liberal economics, hatred of the United States, and the general antiwar platform were among the core principles of the party, whose left-wing leader George Galloway won an impressive general election victory in the London borough of Tower Hamlets in 2005. The Trotskyists and Islamists in the movement found a common platform in glorifying the "Palestinian resistance" and in branding Israel as a criminal "terrorist state." They combined forces in damning the Jewish State as being worse than Apartheid South Africa and demanding a reinforcement of the Boycott Israeli Goods Campaign. Moreover, Respect also expressed its full support for the Islamist movements of Hamas and Hizbullah—allies of Iran who are totally committed to the destruction of Israel. In July 2006, for example, George Galloway went out of his way in an article for the *Socialist Worker* to openly salute Hizbullah in its battle against Israel:

> I glorify the Hizbollah national resistance movement, and I glorify the leader of Hizbollah, Sheikh Sayyed Hassan Nasrallah.[30]

The establishment of Respect marked a point of crystallization for the Marxist–Islamist axis in Britain, which achieved an impressive mass ex-

pression on 15 February 2003 during one of the largest political demonstrations ever held in postwar London. The Islamists might doubtless
disagree with their Trotskyist and Far Left allies about feminism, homo-
sexuality, religion, secularism, and the more general aims of socialism,
but they clearly did share a common anti-Western, antiglobalist, and anti-
Zionist agenda.[31]

Islamists are not, of course, partisans of the traditional class struggle
of the industrial proletariat. But like the Far Left, they passionately hate
America and often repeat the crudest myths of a "Zionist conspiracy,"
while defaming Israel as a racist state. Unabashed leftists like the former mayor of London, Ken Livingstone, are fully in agreement with this
outlook—even when they claim to be fervent promoters of multiculturalism.[32] "Red Ken," as he came to be known, had no compunction about gratuitously insulting the Jewish journalist, Olivier Feingold, or the Reuben
Brothers—wealthy Jewish property dealers (originally from Iraq) over a
redevelopment plan in East London for the 2012 Olympics. At the same
time, Livingstone twice hosted the notoriously bigoted and racist Sheikh
Youssef al-Qaradawi in London, giving this extremist Muslim preacher
the VIP treatment as a "progressive" religious personality and a leading
"moderate." Yet al-Qaradawi, the spiritual guardian of Egypt's Muslim
Brotherhood, was on record for having publicly defended suicide bombings against Israeli civilians (including the murder of children), for advocating the death sentence for homosexuals, and having denounced wom-
en's emancipation. This did not deter the ex-Trotskyist leftist mayor of
London (2000–2008) from comparing the homophobic, antisemitic, and
misogynistic Sheikh Qaradawi to the saintly Pope John XXIII or falsely
claiming that any allegations against the Muslim cleric were an invention of the Mossad. In January 2009, during the Gaza War, the so-called
"moderate" Qaradawi declared: "Oh Allah, take this oppressive, Jewish
Zionist band of people. Oh Allah, do not spare a single one of them. Oh
Allah, count their numbers, and kill them, down to the very last one."
Later that month, on his Al-Jazeera television program, he added the following chilling comment. "Throughout history, Allah has imposed upon
the Jews people who would punish them for their corruption. The last
punishment was carried out by Hitler. By means of all the things he did to
them—even though they exaggerated the issue—he managed to put them
in their place. This was the divine punishment for them. Allah willing,

the next time will be at the hand of the believers."[33] In answer to charges of antisemitism directed at himself for whitewashing Qaradawi and insulting Jewish Londoners, Livingstone typically replied: "For far too long the accusation of antisemitism has been used against anyone who is critical of the policies of the Israeli government, as I have been."[34] This assertion has become a familiar mantra of the Left to evade the well-founded criticism of its *own bias* against Israel as well as providing a cheap alibi for refusing to confront the issue of Muslim antisemitism.

As part of its political strategy the radical Left generally insinuates that contemporary antisemitism is greatly exaggerated, whether in Europe or the Middle East. Even to raise the issue is often considered by leftists and some liberals, too, as an act of Zionist "intellectual terrorism" primarily designed to silence justified opposition toward Israel. At the same time, there is also a broad silence on the Left about the anti-Jewish attitudes rampant in recent years among more recent Muslim immigrants to the European Union. To the extent that Islamic antisemitism is ever acknowledged as a reality on the Left, it is usually blamed either on Israel or on the pro-Israel Diaspora communities. In France, in particular, the accusation of "communitarianism" has been used as a major stigmatizing device against Jewish support for Israel and as an arm of intellectual intimidation. It is mainly intended to politically delegitimize any coherent communal responses to the threats French Jewry have confronted since 2000. What apparently angers leftist *anti-communitarians* (many of them Jewish themselves) is the strong identification of most French Jews with Israel, though Arab solidarity with the Palestinians almost never raises an eyebrow. Linked to this phenomenon is the Manichean conceptual world of "progressive" antiracism, with its glorification of hybridized identities and cultures. In the eyes of those French or British leftists, for whom multiculturalism and "antiracism" have increasingly become a kind of substitute post-Marxist ideology, Israel is seen as a dangerous anachronism and an intolerable obstacle to their utopian vision of universal brotherhood.[35] This is indeed one of the new idols of our own post-modernist age, and the mere existence of a Jewish state seems guaranteed to provoke the wrath of virtually all "true believers" on the Left.

The Left Party in Germany ("Die Linke"), many of whose leaders and members support Hamas and Hizbullah, fail to confront antisemitism and do not disguise their hatred of Israel, is a striking case in point. Some of its most prominent representatives openly call for a boycott of Israeli products. A Left Party member of the German Bundestag, Inge Hölger, gratuitously and falsely blamed the Israeli government in April 2011 for the deaths of two pro-Palestinian activists who had been murdered by radical Islamists. In places like Duisberg (North Rhine-Westphalia) the Left Party has even become a notorious hotbed of antisemitism, pillorying Israel as a warmongering "rogue State," brazenly denouncing the "moral blackmail of the so-called Holocaust" and equating the swastika with the Star of David.[36]

It is revealing that German Left Party leaders like Oskar Lafontaine, Wolfgang Gehrke, and Christine Buchholz not only regard Hamas and Hizbullah as "anticolonial liberation movements" but willfully turn a blind eye to the calls by such Islamist movements for the destruction of Israel. Like the German antiglobalist Left, they actively support boycotting the Israeli economy and assiduously promote the myth of an Israeli "genocide" against the Palestinians in Gaza.[37] Like their counterparts in France, Britain, Norway, Sweden, Spain, and other West European countries, the German leftists generally refrain from denouncing incomparably worse human rights abuses in Sudan, Iran, the Gulf States, or countries like Syria and Libya by Arab despots determined to stay in power. In their highly selective internationalist worldview, Zionist Israel is a uniquely reactionary "imperialist" state (and the sinister agent of American hegemonism) while the Palestinians—including the genocidal antisemitic Hamas—are eternal "victims" who can do no wrong.

The passions set in motion by uncritical identification with the Palestinians and the spread of global jihad have produced a growing cross-fertilization of ideas, practices, and strategic alliances between leftists and Islamists based on anti-Western and anti-Zionist assumptions. In France, after 2000, nominally "anti-Israel" sentiment soon gave rise to physical attacks on Jewish institutions and denunciations of the leaders of French Jewry. Trotskyist revolutionaries of Jewish origin like the late Daniel Bensaïd did not shrink from blaming this state of affairs on Israel itself and on what he termed the "Zionist" tribalism of Jewish communal leaders. The "pyromaniac firemen" of French Jewry, according to the pro-Palestinian Bensaïd, had fused Judaism and Zionism to the point where any political struggle against the Israeli "occupation" was bound to be seen as antisemitic, even if this was not the case. Not only that, but Muslims in France who violently attacked Jews (a fact that Bensaïd, Dominique Vidal, and many other French leftists invariably downplayed) were themselves presented as lamb-like "victims" of French racism, Israeli Jewish oppression, and the Middle East conflict.[38]

The Swiss-born theologian Tariq Ramadan, grandson of Hassan al-Banna—the founder of the Muslim Brotherhood in Egypt—is an interesting illustration from the Muslim side of the growing symbiosis between Islam and the radical Left in the West. A hero of the disoriented Muslim immigrant youth in France, Ramadan soon became an icon for the Islamo-"progressive" alliance in the West. In September 2003, he launched a sharp verbal attack on a number of internationalist French Jewish intellectuals whom he gratuitously accused of being spineless and slavish "communitarian" lackeys of Prime Minister Ariel Sharon's Israel. The polemical hit list included André Glucksmann, Bernard-Henri Lévy, Alain Finkielkraut, Pierre-André Taguieff (a non-Jew), and Bernard Kouchner (later to become foreign minister), who is half-Jewish. Ramadan warned that these intellectuals were only superficially cosmopolitan and "universalist." None of his barbs was true. Nevertheless, the anti-globalist European Social Forum in November 2003 continued to praise Ramadan as a precious Islamist ally, despite his own "communitarist" insistence that the secular Left must accept *Muslim communal specificity*. Ramadan's frontal assault was not only directed against French Jewish intellectuals. He also blamed the Iraq War on Paul Wolfowitz (a "notorious Zionist"), Richard Perle and other neo-con, "pro-Likud" American Jews. This, too, was welcomed by most of his French anti-globalist friends.[39]

One of the more sinister points of convergence between the Western Left and Islamic radicalism in recent years has been the adoption of conspiracy theories and claims that Israel seeks a "final solution" of the Palestinian question in the Nazi sense of the term. The antisemitic libel that Israel uses "Nazi" methods has indeed been rampant for years among Marxists and Islamists. More recently it has spread to broad swathes of public opinion in the West. The short Gaza War of January 2009 and its fallout in the summer of the following year further escalated this flood of anti-Israel abuse, including mendacious charges of inflicting "genocide." Such pronouncements have been especially common in Hugo Chávez's Venezuela—which offers a textbook example of the fusion of Islamist, anti-Western, and anti-Jewish motifs. Indeed, the American State Department felt compelled not so long ago to list the country as a state sponsor of anti-semitism.

There is no doubt that since Commandante Chávez came to power Venezuela's small but prosperous upper-middle-class Jewish community has been under increasing threat. The August 2006 street demonstrations of *Chavistas* (Chávez supporters) included ominous slogans in Caracas such as "Jews go home," "Jewish murderers," "The U.S. and Israel want to destroy Venezuela." Constant incitement in the government (reflecting Chávez's own aggressive rhetoric) has presented Israel as a "genocidal state" and made many Venezuelan Jews feel unwelcome in their own country.[40] The weekly *Los Papeles de Mandinga,* for example, did not shrink from ferociously attacking the head of the Caracas Jewish community for defending the "Nazi mass murderers" who govern Israel.[41]

The relentlessly anti-American Chávez is primarily responsible for the collapse in relations with the Jewish community. A self-declared socialist (who claims to emulate the nineteenth-century liberator of South America, Simón Bolivar), Chávez's declared aim to forge an axis of anti-American leftist regimes across the continent has already been partially achieved. His eclectic worldview includes a heady mix of communism, left-wing nationalism, and increasingly intimate links with the Islamic Revolution in Iran.[42] The ideological inspiration for Chávez's links with the Arab and Muslim world goes back to the 1990s, when he came under the influence of the Argentinean sociologist Norberto Rafael Ceresole. Ceresole, formerly a left-wing Peronist, was (not accidently) much admired by Hizbullah, with whom he developed strong links. Ceresole typically attributed the deadly antisemitic terrorist bombings in Buenos Aires— at the Israeli Embassy and the Jewish communal center, Amia, in the 1990s—to "Jewish terrorism," even though they were undoubtedly instigated by Iran and carried out by Hizbullah agents.[43] Already twenty years ago, Ceresole had come to see Iran as "the center of resistance to Jewish aggression" and as the only state capable of destroying Israel.[44] Shortly thereafter he began to develop an idiosyncratic synthesis of communism, fascism, and radical Islam. Arriving in Venezuela in 1994, he became a close political adviser of Chávez while continuing to maintain close ties with Islamic terrorists. After a temporary expulsion from Venezuela, he returned in 1998, writing a glorified account of the Chávez revolution.

Ceresole held Zionism and world Jewry responsible for all the major evils of the modern world. He particularly admired French Holocaust deniers like Robert Faurisson and Roger Garaudy. Indeed, the former Communist Garaudy (a convert to Islam, who became a Holocaust denier and a fervent anti-Zionist) was a key role-model in Ceresole's own "unmasking" of the Holocaust as a propaganda tool cynically used by Israel and the Jews. The "Holocaust myth," he insisted, had been ruthlessly exploited by Zionists to blackmail Germany, Europe, and America. Since 1948 it had served to justify the rape of "Arab Palestine" and to promote the "messianic-monotheistic creed" of American-Zionist global domination.[45] Ceresole died in 2003, but his antisemitic demonization of Israel left its mark on Chávez.

The anti-Americanism of Chávez has been no less virulent. On visits to China and the Middle East in the summer of 2006, he continually branded the United States as a satanic, fascist-imperialist empire of evil, and Israel as its terrorist tool. This was naturally grist to the mill of his admiring hosts in Tehran, especially the world's most notorious Holocaust-denier, President Mahmoud Ahmadinejad.[46] Chávez also enjoys iconic status among the Hizbullah fighters and their followers in Lebanon. Hassan Nasrallah, for example, has saluted him as a popular hero to the Muslims of Beirut on a par with the Argentinean Ernesto Che Guevara and Iran's Supreme Guide, Ali Khamanei.[47] This pairing of Guevara and Khamanei is itself revealing. Chávez is seen by both Nasrallah and Ahmadinejad as the central figure in the "heroic resistance" of Latin American socialists to American "banditry." It is no accident that Chávez defends Iran's nuclear program and calls his allies in Tehran "brothers who fight for a just world."[48] Nor is it surprising that he should support to the hilt Colonel Muammar Ghaddafi of Libya, another Islamic radical, who after forty years in power, was still prepared to drown his own people in blood when they asked for elementary human liberties. Anti-Zionism, the "anti-imperialism of fools," is along with anti-Americanism the lowest common denominator of these populist demagogues and dictators. In Venezuela, it produced the expulsion of the Israeli ambassador in 2009 and an exodus of many Venezuelan Jews. This mass migration reduced the number of Jews in Venezuela by approximately one-third during the past decade. Its present estimated size is between 12,000 and 16,000.

The bulk of the Venezuelan press has deliberately envenomed an unfriendly climate with its unrestrained demonization of Israel and its incitement against Jews in the name of an authoritarian populist socialism. Jews are said to have been damned with the mark of Cain "for having destroyed Jesus Christ"; they supposedly invented the myth of their own "chosenness" in order to dispossess the Palestinians; they control the economy and government of the United States; and they are allegedly "conspiring in Venezuela to take over our finances, our industries, commerce, construction, government positions, and politics."[49] Above all, the Nazifying of Israel is deemed essential to the purposes of the new Islamist–Leftist axis. For those Latin Americans who take their inspiration from Chávez, there is no question that Israel is doing to innocent Arabs and Palestinians exactly "what Hitler did to the Jews."[50] Like Ahmadinejad and the Iranian leadership, the Venezuelan ruler obsessively repeats that both America and Israel represent the *satanic* face of fascist imperialism—a force doomed to disappear by the joint decree of God, history, and popular justice.[51] The political influence of this growing Venezuela–Iran alliance in the rest of Latin America should not be underestimated. It has already accelerated the anti-Israel dynamic in the region.[52]

By exploiting Venezuela's oil wealth and drug money, cutting shrewd political deals, and making populist appeals, Chávez has achieved a measure of leadership on an awakening continent, eager to take advantage of what is perceived as the declining power of the United States. His close links with an Iranian regime constantly seeking strategic allies in Latin America relies on an expedient combination of geopolitical need, anti-American popular sentiments, and a relentlessly indoctrinated hatred of Israel. Chávez's turn toward radical Islam, Iran, and Hizbullah as political allies in a long-range war to weaken the United States have undoubtedly helped to shuffle all the cards in the region. As for "Zionism," inside Venezuela it is depicted as a sinister conspiracy to accumulate massive wealth and power, while trying to sabotage the success of Chávez's socialist revolution. The rhetoric of class struggle merges with antisemitism masked as "anti-imperialism." The target is a mythical "Jewish lobby" in the service of Israel.[53] In the eclectic mishmash that forms Chávez's radical ideology, we can find some of the cruder elements of populist nationalism, Marxist class struggle, anti-Americanism, antiglobalism, political Islam, and Christian liberation theology.

For a hard-line synthesis of communism and radical Islam, we might better go to another left-wing Venezuelan, Ilich Ramírez Sánchez (more famously known as Carlos), the mastermind of several terrorist assaults in the 1970s, including the taking of hostages at an OPEC conference in Vienna and the Entebbe hijacking. In November 2001, speaking from a Parisian prison to a local neo-fascist publication, Carlos warmly praised the September 11, 2001 terror attacks in New York for having opened a new era in the struggle for world revolution.[54] He described the jihad to liberate Palestine and the Holy Places (Mecca, Medina, and Jerusalem), as well as to bring down the American "hyper-power," as a *sacred* cause that would demand further sacrifices on the scale of 9/11. Carlos told his interviewers from the far-right review *Résistance* that a process of convergence was taking place between different ideologies: "All those who fight the enemies of humanity, meaning U.S. imperialism, the Zionists, their allies and agents, are my comrades. . . . I converted to Islam in October 1975, and I continue to be a communist. There is no contradiction between submission to God and the ideal of a communist society." Carlos maintained that exactly like the ideologists of Al Qaida he was placing the "liberation of Palestine" at the center of his Islamo–communist struggle. Though the general Palestinian situation, like that of the wider Arab-Muslim world, was disastrous, he still believed in the radiant future promised by radical Islam. Sheikh Osama bin Laden, a model *moujahid* (martyr-fighter), had bravely shown the way forward to all "true jihadists" and revolutionaries by heroically striking the Twin Towers and the heart of American capitalism.[55]

The killing in 2011 of Bin Laden in Pakistan by American Special Forces, ten years after 9/11, does not in itself remove the appeal of Al Qaida's radical jihadist ideology to Muslims around the world. On the contrary, in some ways it will strengthen his status as a myth and martyr to the jihadi movement. His jihadi worldview was not only anti-American but deeply antisemitic in an apocalyptic sense—committed to the struggle against Jewry until the End of Days. The assault against Israel was only one feature of his "Islamo-fascist" vision in which the demise of America and world Jewry were the necessary prologue to the establishment of a future worldwide Caliphate. Hence there is no reason for surprise that the antisemitic Muslim Brotherhood and its Hamas offshoots in Gaza should have hailed Bin Laden as a holy Arab warrior and mourned his demise.

A veteran communist like Carlos had no illusions about the heterogeneous, multifaceted and contradictory nature of the radical Islamist movement of which Bin Laden became the most notorious icon and worldwide symbol after 2001. The Venezuelan revolutionary terrorist admitted that political Islam contained many reactionaries, misogynists, and authoritarian enemies of liberty. But he had no doubt that the Taliban in Afghanistan were defending the "world revolution," just as he believed the global jihad movement to be "the spearhead of the anti-imperialist cause."[56] Indeed, he declared, ever since the "disintegration of the atheist socialist camp" in 1989, it was clear to him that only the jihadists had the faith, heroism, and courage to fight for the liberation of the Middle East and other regions of the globe from foreign occupation.[57] In this context he stressed that there was *no* rupture between his communist commitment in the past and his current embrace of jihadism. The linking thread was the Palestinian cause. This was the real point of confluence between hard-line communism, leftist revolution, and radical Islam.[58]

Carlos once again spelled out his personal credo in 2003:

> I am and remain a professional revolutionary, a soldier, a fighter in the purest Leninist tradition. Without this revolutionary avant-garde of permanently mobilized militants—exclusively devoted to prepare, organize and set the Revolution in motion—the latter will never come about.[59]

He added that he had become a militant communist in 1964 at the age of fourteen. But the turning point for him came in 1970 when he first understood that "the Palestinian cause" had become the "incarnation of the world revolution."[60] Islam had reinforced and purified his Marxist revolutionary convictions, granting them a transcendent dimension. One should also add that radical Islam has given a much shriller edge to the anti-Zionism and antisemitism manifested by many others on the Left, who—unlike Carlos or Roger Garaudy—did not choose to convert to Islam.

Radical Islam, in effect, constitutes the third "totalitarian" wave of the twentieth century, following the demise of National Socialism and Soviet-style communism. As an ideological movement, it contains within itself a number of utopian elements that we could define as "Islamo-fascist" (even Islamo-Nazi) as well as "Islamo-communist." Like its predecessors, the

Islamist grand project ultimately involves world conquest and a war to the death against the West—ideological, cultural, political, and military. The Islamists are certainly no less illiberal, antidemocratic, anti-Western, antisemitic, and wedded to violence than their forerunners. Contemporary forms of totalitarian Islam—born with the founding of the Muslim Brotherhood in 1928—are not only fanatical but are committed to a violent revolution that would "purify" the *umma* from all alien and infidel sources of contamination. It is in this context that we need to see its hatred of Jews and Israel. The most obvious manifestation and a potent cause as well as pretext for Islamist antisemitism remains the "Palestine Question." There can be no doubting the centrality of the myth of Palestine within modern totalitarian Islam. Between 1933 and 1945, this took the form of resolute collaboration with Nazism against the West, the revolt in Palestine and the *farūd* in Baghdad (a bloody pogrom in 1941), as well as identification with the Nazi genocidal ideology toward the Jews. Today, it is the Islamists who set the tone with their hysterical propaganda against the Jews and Israel. The heirs of communism and Nazism often follow admiringly in their wake, fascinated by the violent dynamism of Allah's apostles. All three totalitarian ideologies—in the past as in the present—have operated with broadly similar assumptions about the "Jewish peril."

Like the Nazis and communists before them, the Islamists continue to see an all-powerful and ubiquitous Jewish lobby at work, which allegedly determines not only American policies but the entire global agenda. The Islamists regard Israel and world Jewry (along with the United States) as the embodiment of "satanic" forces bent upon world domination.[61] The Jewish–Zionist conspiracy is perceived as a real existential threat to the body politic of Islam as well as endangering its core religious identity. Radical Islam, communism, and its current leftist offshoots are uncompromising about the *illegitimacy* of Israel's very creation and its presence in the Middle East. They are no less committed to its destruction and/or dismantlement. Beyond that, in their vision of a *permanent struggle* against the "eternal Jew," the Islamists resemble the Nazis more than the communists; but they share with communism the same insistence on an inextricable link between "anti-imperialism," the war against Zion, and bringing about the downfall of the West. In combining all of these highly combustible elements, the Islamists have inexorably transformed themselves into the revolutionary avant-garde of antisemitism in the twenty-first century.

NOTES

1. *Congress of the Peoples of the East, Baku, September 1920* (Stenographic Report, London, 1977), quoted in Laurent Murawiec, *The Mind of Jihad* (Cambridge: Cambridge University Press, 2008), p. 211.

2. Ibid., p. 212.

3. *Congress of the Peoples of the East*, pp. 167–73.

4. Murawiec, p. 215.

5. Stephan Grigat, "Mit dem Mufti gegen den Zionismus—mit Gromyko für Israel. Aus der Frühgeschichte der israelischen und palästinenschen Kommunistischen Partei," *Transversal* 2 (2009), pp. 97–127.

6. See Walter Laqueur, *Communism and Nationalism in the Middle East* (New York: Praeger, 1956).

7. Murawiec, p. 237.

8. On Haj Amin's collaboration with Hitler Germany, see the detailed biography by Klaus Gensicke, *The Mufti of Jerusalem and the Nazis: The Berlin Years* (London: Vallentine Mitchell, 2010).

9. Meir Budeiri, *The Palestine Communist Party, 1919–1948* (London: Ithaca Press, 1979), p. 93.

10. Grigat, pp. 112–114.

11. Ibid., pp. 115–116.

12. Early Bolshevik thinking on the revolutionary possibilities of the Muslim world (including that of Stalin) was much influenced by an Indian radical best known under his alias of M. N. Roy (1887–1954). Roy was, in fact, a Hindu-born Islamophile and a leading strategist of the "Red Jihad." See Murawiec, pp. 207–223. Stalin in the 1920s sought to exploit the anti-British revolutionary potential of pan-Islamism but later cooled toward the project. In the 1930s he would purge and execute many of the Muslim National Communists in the USSR who followed the ideas of Sultan Galiev.

13. Bernard Lewis, "The Anti-Zionist Resolution," *Foreign Affairs* (October 1976), pp. 54–64. See also Robert S. Wistrich, *A Lethal Obsession. Anti-Semitism from Antiquity to the Global Jihad* (New York: Random House, 2010), pp. 469–71.

14. Wistrich, *A Lethal Obsession*, pp. 147–50.

15. Quoted in Jeremy Jones, "Durban Sprawl," *Australia-Israel Review* (October 2006). See also Arch Puddington, "The Wages of Durban," *Commentary* (November 2001), pp. 29–34.

16. Sayed Abul Ala Maududi, *Jihad in Islam* (Lahore: Islamic Publications, 1998–2001) is a seminal work.

17. Ibid., pp. 9–10, 13–14.

18. See Ali Shariati, *Red Shiism* (Houston: Free Islamic Literatures, 1974) and his *Reflections on Humanity: Two Views of Civilization and the Plight of Man* (Houston: Free Islamic Literatures, 1974). Also Frantz Fanon, *Les damnés de la terre* (Paris: F. Maspero 1961), a seminal text on the redemptive role of violence in the "anti-imperialist struggle of national liberation."

19. Shariati, *Red Shiism*, p. 8. Also Farhad Khrosrokhavar, *Les nouveaux martyrs d'Allah* (Paris: Flammarion, 2002), p. 72.

20. Khrosrokhavar, p. 76.

21. Jillian Becker, *The PLO: The Rise and Fall of the Palestinian Liberation Organization* (New York: St. Martin's Press, 1984), p. 106.

22. Ibid.

23. Amal Saad-Ghorayeb, *Hizbu'llah: Politics and Religion* (London: Pluto Press, 2002), pp. 16–30.

24. Ibid., pp. 168–86.

25. Ali Shariati, *Red Shiism*, pp. 7–10.

26. Murawiec, *The Mind of Jihad*, p. 286.

27. Ibid., 318. See also Wistrich, *A Lethal Obsession*, pp. 830–78 on Khomeini.

28. Mathan Ravid, "Prejudice and Demonization in the Swedish Middle East Debate during the 2006 Lebanon War," *Jewish Political Studies Review* 21, nos. 1–2 (Spring 2009), pp. 79–94.

29. Eran Benedek, "Britain's Respect Party: The Leftist-Islamist Alliance and Its Attitude toward Israel," *Jewish Political Studies Review* 19, nos. 3–4 (Fall 2007), pp. 153–63.

30. George Galloway, "Hizbollah Is Right to Fight Zionist Terror," *Socialist Worker* (July 29, 2006), p. 3.

31. Mark Strauss, "Antiglobalism's Jewish Problem," *Foreign Policy* (October 28, 2003), http://www.foreignpolicy.com.

32. Wistrich, *A Lethal Obsession*, pp. 400–403.

33. See Oren Kessler, "A Man for All Seasons," *The Jerusalem Post* (February 20, 2010).

34. See Efraim Sicher, *Multiculturalism, Globalization, and Antisemitism: The British Case* (SICSA [Sassoon International Center for the Study of Antisemitism], the Hebrew University of Jerusalem, 2009), pp. 33–37. See also Robert S. Wistrich, "Cruel Britannia: Antisemitism among the Ruling Elites," *Azure* 21 (Summer 2005), pp. 100–127.

35. Alain Finkielkraut, "Le sionisme face à la religion de l'humanité," in Shmuel Trigano, ed., *Le sionisme face à ses détracteurs* (Paris: Raphaël, 2003), pp. 160–70.

36. Benjamin Weinthal, "German Party Branch Equates Israel with Third Reich," *The Jerusalem Post* (May 1, 2011).

37. Philipp Gessler, *Der neue Antisemitismus* (Freiburg: Herder, 2004), pp. 81–111 and also Martine Kloke, "Israelkritik und Antizionismus in der deatschen Linken," in Monika Schwarz-Friesel, Evyatar Friesel, and Jehuda Reinharz, eds., *Aktueller Antisémitismus—Ein Phänomen der Mitte* (Berlin/New York": De Gruyter, 2010), pp. 73–92.

38. Interview with Daniel Ben-Saïd, "Les responsables juifs sont des pompiers pyromanes," *Marianne* (January 28–February 3, 2002).

39. Wistrich, *A Lethal Obsession*, pp. 310–314. See also Paul Berman, *The Flight of the Intellectuals* (New York: Melville House, 2011), pp. 157–204.

40. Among many examples from the Venezuelan press, see "Cianuro en Gotas," *Los papeles de Mandinga* (September 19–25, 2006) and Basem Tajeldine, "La disociación mental del Pueblo Elegido," *Rebelión* (May 26, 2008)—a nakedly antisemitic article.

41. Wistrich, *A Lethal Obsession*, p. 625.

42. "With Marx, Lenin and Jesus Christ," *The Economist* (January 13, 2007).

43. See Norberto Ceresole, "La Argentina en el espacio geopolítico del terrorismo judio," Radio Islam, http://www.radioislam.net/islam/spanish/sion/terror/cap2.htm and http://www.islam-shia.org/http://www.islam-shia.org/.

44. Norberto Ceresole, "Carta abierta a mis amigos iranies," http://www.vho.org/aaargh/espa/ceres/carta.html (a Holocaust denial website).

45. Norberto Ceresole, *Caudillo, Ejército Pueblo: la Venezuela del Commandante Chávez* (Madrid: Ediciones Al-Andalus, 2000).

46. "Chavez et Ahmadinejad, unis contre les Etats-Unis," *Libération* (July 31, 2006).

47. See "Entrevista a Sayyid Hassan Nasrallah, dirigente máximo de Hezbollah," *Izquierda Punto Info*, http://www.organizacionislam.org.ar/conflib/repor-sayyed.htmhttp://www.organizacionislam.org.ar/conflib/repor-sayyed.htm.

48. See Luis Roniger, *Antisemitism, Real or Imagined? Chávez, Iran, Israel, and the Jews* (Analysis of Current Trends in Antisemitism, No. 33, 2009), published by the Vidal Sassoon International Center for the Study of Antisemitism, the Hebrew University of Jerusalem.

49. See the article by Basem Tajeldine on the "Zionist Menace" in Venezuela, in *Diario Vea* (September 14, 2006). Also Tarek Muci Nasir, "Zionist Jews," *El Diario Caracas* (September 2, 2006).

50. "Venezuelan President Chavez on Al-Jazeera: Israel Uses Methods of Hitler," *MEMRI, Special Dispatch Series, No. 1235* (August 8, 2006).

51. "Venezuelan President Chavez and Iranian President Ahmadinejad on Iranian TV," *MEMRI, Special Dispatch Series, No. 1226* (August 2, 2006).

52. Caroline B. Glick, "Why Latin America Turned," *The Jerusalem Post* (December 10, 2010).

53. Ceresole had initially come from the Left-wing Peronist organization, Montoneros, before adopting Holocaust denial, the theory of the Jewish world conspiracy, and the equation of Israel with Nazism. See Roniger, pp. 19–21.

54. See *Le Monde* (October 26, 2001), p. 35. Also Pierre-André Taguieff, *La nouvelle judéophobie* (Paris: Mille et une nuits, 2002), pp. 71–72.

55. "Entretien avec Ilich Ramírez Sánchez, dit Carlos," *Résistance*, 16 (February–March 2002), p. 3.

56. Yolène Dilas-Rocherieux, "Communisme, révolution, islamisme, le credo de Ilich Ramírez Sánchez," *Le Débat* 128 (January–March 2004), pp. 141–46.

57. Pierre-André Taguieff, *La nouvelle propaganda antijuive* (Paris: Presses universitaires de France, 2010), pp. 522–23.

58. Wistrich, *A Lethal Obsession*, p. 300.

59. http://www.workersliberty.org/node/4902.

60. Ilich Ramírez Sánchez dit Carlos, *L'Islam révolutionnaire,* texts presented by Jean-Michel Vernochet (Monaco: Rocher, 2003), pp. 37–39.

61. Robert Wistrich, "Der alte Antisemitismus in neuem Gewand," in Doron Rabinovici et al., eds., *Neuer Antisemitismus? Eine globale Debatte* (Frankfurt: Suhrkamp, 2004), pp. 250–70. The coauthor with Rabinovici is Nathan Sznajder.

16 Present-day Antisemitism and the Centrality of the Jewish Alibi

Emanuele Ottolenghi

Introduction

SINCE THE BEGINNING of the second Intifada in late September 2000, Europe has experienced a dramatic increase in antisemitic incidents.[1] These phenomena have quickly spilled over to other Western countries as well. Though in each country antisemitism comes with its local peculiarities and its original historical baggage, across boundaries and continents much of this resurgence is clearly correlated with the ebb and flow of Middle East violence.[2] The strongest piece of evidence that something irrational is happening in the way Western societies react to Israel's actions is the unparalleled unleashing of hostility and hatred toward Jews that accompanies events in the region.

The phenomenon is so well documented that there is no need to recite statistics and evidence here.[3] There is also a wealth of literature on the nature of current antisemitism: how it resembles and differs from past manifestations, what causes it, what role debates over Israel's actions fulfill within the context of current antisemitism, and so on.[4] It is not the goal here, therefore, to report on a debate that has been largely and comprehensively covered by others.

This article will focus instead on a particular feature of the current antisemitism that has been less commented on. This is the crucial role played by some Jews themselves, mostly intellectuals or academics, who have responded to the latest assault on the Jewish people by excusing it, justifying it, downplaying it, and in effect joining it.[5] The role of Jewish voices in present-day antisemitism is one of the critical novelties in the current resurgence of anti-Jewish prejudice and one that has so far earned only scant attention in scholarly writings.[6]

Jewish and Israeli intellectuals lending their voices to the demonization of Israel and its supporters cancel out any accusations of antisemitism that could otherwise be leveled against those who support these arguments, since it is assumed that a Jew cannot be an antisemite. Regardless of whether this is the case, in a world where identities matter, a Jewish or Israeli background of critics against Israel provides a powerful alibi to those who support, endorse, and articulate the denial of Israel's right to exist and undermine the democratic right of Diaspora Jews to express support for and attachment to Israel. Israel's detractors readily seize upon such Jewish and Israeli censors of Israel both as evidence of the validity of the most extreme arguments against Israel and as a shield against accusations of antisemitism.

By citing these Jews, their rhetoric, and writings, Israel's detractors can prove that Jews argue against Israel in much the same way as they do. And since Jews are presumed to be immune to antisemitism, it must therefore follow that what Jews say is not antisemitic. Given such company, and such similarity of discourse, Jews can hardly be accused of antisemitism, since they rely on the specifics of such rhetoric in support of their argument, which usually appeals to unspecified "Jewish values." By calling Jewish testimony to their defense, Israel's detractors proceed, then, to label their critics as censors, intent on silencing free speech. Denunciations of antisemitism are thereby neutralized as expressions of McCarthyism, and Jews who shield Israel's detractors from these accusations are exalted as dissidents courageously fighting a Jewish witch-hunt in the name of truth and authentic Jewish values.

This line of reasoning validates a number of further arguments—that Israel's supporters are complicit in the cover up of Israel's crimes;[7] that antisemitism (including the Holocaust and its memory)[8] is exploited by Jewish organizations to silence a genuine debate about Israel;[9] that constant recourse to the accusation of antisemitism is causing a backlash against Jews,[10] since the truth cannot be forever sidelined; that if Jews spoke out critically against Israel, it would advance peace (the implication being that Jewish silence, or acquiescence, is an obstacle to peace),[11] and combat antisemitism;[12] and that those Jews who "break ranks" with the "hegemonic discourse" of the mainstream Jewish establishment are not only courageous, but are also continuing the authentic expression of Judaism, as they follow in the footsteps of the Prophetic tradition of speaking truth unto power.[13]

This rhetoric is a discourse about saving the Jews from themselves. The salvation offered depends on ending Zionism and all its consequences.[14] It is, therefore, for all intents and purposes, a linguistic mandate to destroy the Jewish state, articulated or underwritten by Jews in the name of Jewish values and for the sake of the Jewish people, and an instrument aimed at validating the argument that present-day demonization of Israel and anti-Zionism are devoid of antisemitism. In a world where antisemitism is unacceptable in social and political discourse, Israeli and/or Jewish intellectuals complying with the calls of Israel's detractors and demonizers constitute an alibi for antisemitism.

No people engaged in this kind of rhetoric see themselves as antisemites—they are proud to define themselves as anti-Zionists and vigorously reject the charge that they are antisemitic or "self-hating."[15] This essay will show how their writings and public pronouncements, nevertheless, fulfill the role of a powerful alibi against accusations of antisemitism.

This argument is developed through five steps:

1. What is the process by which Jews embrace the discourse of anti-Zionism? I will rely on Sander Gilman's[16] analysis of Jewish self-hatred and argue that this process is at work with at least some Jewish anti-Zionists.
2. What proof is there that antisemitism and anti-Zionism are coterminous? I will make the case that anti-Zionism, distinct from some criticism of specific Israeli actions, is a form of antisemitism and that therefore those Jews who proclaim their Jewishness through their hatred of Israel are indeed adopting an antisemitic discourse and are therefore self-hating.
3. What is the evidence that Jewish and Israeli intellectuals are indeed offering this kind of discourse? I will show that their discourse stems from a desire to redefine Jewish identity according to an anti-Zionist view of Jewish history.
4. How is anti-Zionist discourse received by Israel's detractors and how is it turned into an alibi for antisemitism? I will show how

Jewish anti-Zionist writings and utterances are used by others as the alibi I described for descriptions of Israel that coincide with old antisemitic tropes.

5. What is the nature of the language of salvation engendered in this dialogue between Jewish anti-Zionists and antisemites? I will demonstrate that it is a dialogue essentially advocating a modern, secular variant of conversion for Jews as an answer to the problem of antisemitism.

Step One: Understanding Self-hatred

The label *self-hating Jew* has accompanied the debate over Jewish support and criticism of Israel ever since the establishment of the State of Israel. In recent years, however, it has been revived, with defenders of Israel sometimes throwing the epithet against anti-Zionist Jews, and their targets responding in similar tone. Before using the label, it is important to understand that it is not just a term of abuse, but the object of considerable scholarship based on an impressive body of historical evidence.

The psychological and discursive component of Jewish self-hatred was addressed chiefly in two studies. The first, published in 1935, is a peculiar pamphlet published by an Italian exiled anarchist, Camillo Berneri, who wrote, in Paris, the book *Le juif antisemite*.[17] The second, more recent and academic study is Sander Gilman's *Jewish Self-Hatred* (1986).

Berneri sought to explain self-hating Jews by documenting the historical recurrence of this phenomenon and then explaining it as a typical act of neophyte zeal and the result of a burning desire to burnish their credentials as new Christians. He mentioned Jewish converts, like Pablo Cristiani, who led the medieval trials against the Talmud, and Alfonso de Valladolid, who wrote ferocious anti-Jewish polemics in the fourteenth century. These converted Jews not only became Catholics but also anti-Jewish, placing their knowledge of Judaism at the service of anti-Jewish causes. The Catholic Church, noted Berneri, used them as proof of the fallacy of the Jewish faith. Were they antisemites? According to Berneri:

The Jewish convert and supporter of the Inquisition should not be considered fundamentally antisemitic. To the contrary, if one accepts that the Inquisition was, in its most profound spiritual manifestation, an act of love (eternal punishment being avoided thanks to the temporary suffering of a painful death) then the converted Jew is, in a certain sense, showing a sense of attachment to his old coreligionists by causing their persecution.[18]

That love should bequeath such violence may appear strange. Yet, Berneri's sarcasm offers an insight: the self-hater wishes to bring his erstwhile coreligionists to embrace the new truth he has found and resents them for failing to see it. This conflicted sentiment of love (I want you to see the truth!) and hate (how can you not see the truth?) informs the relation of the neophyte with his former community but also with the novel group of reference—because it is through the zeal he displays in the pursuit of the new truth that the sincerity of his conversion is proven.

Sander Gilman concurs: there is nothing novel or unique about Jews joining anti-Jewish hostility: To be accepted in society means acquiring the reference group's discourse. This problem did not suddenly appear with the emancipation of the Jews in the eighteenth century. It is a problem inherent in the existence of the Jews in the Diaspora, a problem of exile. . . .[19]

History is rich with precedent in this sense. But while before Jewish emancipation, Jews who joined their own enemies sought to aid and abet the efforts to destroy the Jewish people, since emancipation this phenomenon has become more complex. As discussed below, in section three, it usually manifests itself as an attempt by defectors to redefine Jewishness, rather than convert to Christianity, in a way that makes it acceptable to the reference group.

Gilman explains Jewish self-hatred as a Jewish preoccupation with self-image—a preoccupation shared by other minorities. This preoccupation is made particularly pressing for a minority living in the midst of a community that negatively depicts it and blames it for some, if not all, the social ills.[20] Gilman contends that at some point, the minority's perception of self is conditioned by the way the majority perceives the minority. Jews, in other words, come to see themselves as they are viewed by the majority of people amidst whom they live. The more negative the image of the Jew is, and the more that view negatively affects the existence of the Jew, the more pressure the Jew feels to accept that view as a reflection of the truth.

Eventually, some Jews conclude that the stereotyped view of the Jew is an accurate reflection of reality—and they embrace it. The consequence is an effort to distance oneself from it in order to regain acceptability within mainstream society. This metamorphosis comes with a price. It produces, in Gilman's words, a "fragmentation of identity," or "a double bind" that leaves the Jew, who breaks away from the Jewish people and joins the dominant group by embracing its stereotyping of the Jews, caught in no-man's land.

The outcome of this double bind, according to Gilman, is the constant effort to recreate a positive image of the "Other" that is acceptable to the stereotype and that can be distinguished from the negative stereotype:

> [I]n discovering what the Jew is supposed *not* to be, some sense of the constantly changing definition of the "true" Jew can be evolved. As Jews react to the world by altering their sense of identity, what they wish themselves to be, so they become what the group labeling them as Other has determined them to be. The group labeling the Other is able successfully to elude their stereotype and the reality to which it is supposed to relate, since the Other reacts to the stereotyping as if it were a valid set of prescriptive categories of its identity.[21]

To recap: the antisemite creates a negative image of the Jew. This image has troubling consequences for the Jew's existence: lost opportunities, social ostracism, marginalization, discrimination, a precarious existence, persecution, and, in extreme cases, even annihilation. Eventually, some Jews conclude that antisemites are right in depicting the Jews the way they do. The stereotype becomes a reality—and those Jews who reach this conclusion must also conclude they only have themselves to blame for their suffering. To extricate themselves from this position, they abandon Judaism—or those aspects of Judaism that the dominant stereotype considers negative. By doing so, they hope to gain the respectability and the privileges they were previously denied on account of being Jewish. Having projected upon themselves the negative image of prejudice, they now free themselves from it by dumping it onto other Jews who have not yet undertaken the process of abjuration. They also develop an alternative definition of Jewish identity that is at home with the discourse of the dominant group and that separates them from the "bad" Jews, namely the ones who haven't discarded yet their old identity.

In the current circumstances, the reference group views Israel as the proverbial and perennial villain of the piece at best, and as a modern-day incarnation of a Nazi state or of an Apartheid regime at worst. Given such hostile characterizations, some Jewish intellectuals seek acceptance in the wider circles of Western opinion-formers by ingratiating themselves through the adoption of a language about Israel that is disproportionately and unfairly critical at best, and demonizing at worst. It is my contention that this thought process occurs among many prominent Jewish anti-Zionist intellectuals who accept the demonization of Israel as truth, not prejudice. They therefore discard Israel from modern Jewish identity and proceed to build a new identity that is at home with anti-Israel discourse. Having transformed Jewish identity, they thunder against those Jews who refuse to join them, as the traitors of authentic Judaism—one that is devoid of any connection to the land and the State of Israel.

No doubt, such individuals routinely reject the accusation of self-hatred. As Gilman explains, "One of the most successful ways to distance the alienation produced by self-doubt was negative projection. By creating the image of a Jew existing somewhere in the world who embodied all the negative qualities feared within oneself, one could distance the specter of self-hatred, at least for the moment."[22] Gilman, here, is referring to the "invention of the Eastern Jew" among nineteenth-century assimilating Jews. The good Jew who assimilated into good German society was keen to show himself different from the *Ostjuden* everyone—Jews included!—disliked.

The phenomenon of negative projection is similarly at work today with many anti-Zionist Jews—they view themselves as "good" Jews who have broken away from their Zionist brethren and created an alternative—more authentic!—form of Jewish identity. This version of being Jewish in the world is at peace with the dominant views of society and enables them to loathe the "bad" Jews who have so far failed to see the truth of the evil of Zionism in the world. Having established themselves as real and good Jews, they can also claim that their stance against Israel, often assumed in the name of Jewish values, helps fight antisemitism at the same time, by convincing non-Jews that not all Jews support Israel.

Step Two: Antisemitism and Anti-Zionism

This phenomenon of dissociation from and acceptance of prejudice as reality appears today mostly under the rubric of anti-Zionism. But is anti-Zionism synonymous with antisemitism? Even the most fervent and virulent critics of Israel reject accusations of antisemitism; they argue that their animus is directed at Zionism, not Jews as a whole—and frequently offer a list of prominent people with Jewish names who support their views as evidence that, so to speak, some of their best friends are Jewish![23] More seriously, the argument for separating antisemitism from anti-Zionism goes along these lines:

1. Israel is a betrayal of Judaism and is therefore un-Jewish or anti-Jewish.
2. Growing numbers of Jews have come to the realization that point 1 is correct.
3. Championing the dissolution or demise of Israel is therefore a cause that all Jews should embrace in the name of the authentic values of Judaism—which in this argument frequently coincide with liberal and progressive values.
4. Therefore, anti-Zionism is not antisemitism.

It might be far-fetched to argue that anti-Zionism expresses affection for Judaism as a set of values and for the Jews as a social group; still, there can be little doubt that anti-Zionism is a mainstream opinion in today's Europe, and many people who do not hesitate to call themselves anti-Zionists express outrage at the notion that they therefore are antisemites.

Anti-Zionism is a term that is liberally used these days, and, when applied inaccurately, it may be mistaken to include mere criticism of Israel. It is helpful, therefore, to define what it means. What is it precisely that anti-Zionists oppose? To criticize Israel for specific policies that are deemed to be objectionable is not anti-Zionism. Anti-Zionism is the rejection of Zionism, the foundational basis for the Jewish state. It makes four crucial claims:

(1) Jews are a collective bestowed with the distinct features of a *nation* in the modern, secular sense.
(2) The Diaspora condition—living in exile—is defective, both because of the dangers it entails for a vulnerable minority and because of the impediments it creates in the creation and development of a genuine national culture.
(3) A national project leading to at least national autonomy and at best national sovereignty is therefore desirable.

(4) This project has a worldly goal, namely, the achievement of "extensive social results and continuous social development."[24]

Territoriality is an essential component of Zionism, but it is not the only one. Zionism claims that a nation can fulfill its destiny and display its full potential only within the confines of the nation-state. These conditions, for Jews, require that the scattered communities of the Diaspora "ingather," to use the biblical term, to live within a newly formed Jewish polity.

As an essentially secular national movement, Zionism therefore advocated the creation of an independent society, the revival of the Hebrew language, the growth of a distinctive national culture and national life, and—through the development of an independent Jewish society—the return of the Jewish people to a condition of normalcy; that is, the return of the Jews to history as "a people like all peoples." Accordingly, anti-Zionism goes well beyond criticism of Israeli policies and even disagreement on the whereabouts of the Zionist project—after all, for much of its early history, Zionism included advocates of Jewish nationalism who did not insist on Palestine as the exclusive, non-negotiable locus of Jewish self-determination.

Anti-Zionism fundamentally denies either the right or the desirability of the Jewish people to define themselves as a nation, with all the attendant social and political consequences of nationhood. Anti-Zionism not only opposes the creation and continued existence of a sovereign, independent Jewish state but also rejects the idea that the Jews are a people and, as such, are, at least in principle, entitled to self-determination.[25] Even when it recognizes that Jews may be a distinct collective, it still postulates that it is in the Jews' best interest to remain a Diaspora community, extolling the myth of Jewish powerlessness in history as a moral quality and a trait that Jews would do well to keep rather than compromising it through the pitfalls of statehood.[26]

Anti-Zionism attacks the expression of Jewish identity through identification with Israel by denying that authentic Jewish identity has any linkage to Israel,[27] by denying that Jews are a nation, by denying that as a nation they enjoy the rights of other nations, or by assuming that the implementation of that right will invariably yield an immoral outcome, and only in the last instance by criticizing Israel's actions on their merits.

Israel's conduct, even of the worst kind, is, for anti-Zionists, a symptom of the evil they fight, not its essence.[28] Therefore, anti-Zionists expect Jews to join them in their fight against Zionism, and to do so for their own interest.[29] Inasmuch as some Jews do join them, a Jewish presence in their ranks acts as a shield against accusations of antisemitism and as an alibi for it.[30]

Thus, the crucial ingredient that makes anti-Zionism a cover for antisemitism is the postulate according to which Zionism is a betrayal of Jewish values *and* is inherently evil. Seen in these terms, anti-Zionism is a Jewish moral obligation to save Jews from themselves.[31] For Jewish anti-Zionists, this argument helps them claim that they, and not the Zionists, are the standard-bearers of authentic Judaism. For non-Jewish anti-Zionists, the same argument also works: to claim that Zionism is a betrayal of Judaism offers them and their rhetoric a shield against accusations of antisemitism. Israel is perceived as evil,[32] both for its conduct and for its essence as a nation-state based on an ethno-religious identity that Jews, because of their history and their traditions, should reject. Anti-Zionism explains Israel's policies as a product of its essence as a Jewish state. What follows is not that Israel should act differently: more crucially, it should cease to exist *as a Jewish state*.[33]

Herein, therefore, lies the nexus between anti-Zionism and present-day antisemitism. A significant part of contemporary Jewish communities considers Israel as part of their Jewish identity. Yet, their attachment to Israel is chastised for two reasons—first, because anti-Zionists postulate that Israel should cease to exist *as a Jewish state* because its existence is bad for its neighbors; and second because the manifestation of Jewish sovereignty is described as contrary to authentic Judaism and, therefore, bad for Jews. This double assumption engenders hostility toward those Jews who identify with Israel. It also puts pressure on them to conform to anti-Zionist assumptions. If unheeded, such pressure may have negative consequences for their careers, their self-esteem, and even for their physical well-being.

Step Three: Jewish Confessions

A notable literature has flourished since the Palestinian Intifada began in October 2000: books with such titles as *Prophets' Outcast*,[34] *Wrestling with Zion*,[35] and *The Other Israel*[36] abound, which offer a collection of

Jewish voices ready to "break ranks" and denounce Israel. Some are more honest than others in offering a range of views. Some, like Michael Neumann's *The Case against Israel*[37] or Patrick Cockburn's and Jeoffroy St. Claire's *The Politics of Anti-Semitism*[38] are radical polemics that sometimes dangerously border on antisemitism. Despite the vast differences, many Jewish contributors to their pages have one thing in common: they denounce Israel as evil; they accuse Israel and Zionism of having betrayed Judaism's authentic voice; they embrace a narrative of victimization, where the authors present themselves as victims of a Jewish establishment that tries to silence them; and in describing Israel and its policies, they frequently use vocabulary, imagery, and stereotypes that are uncomfortably close to the old repertoire of classical antisemitism.

Exponents of these views freely roam the world to spread them. They are often hosted in the most influential newspapers and magazines and get their books published by the most prestigious publishing houses. Many of them are tenured academics. These are all signs of how mainstream and influential their views are. Yet, they often cast themselves as dissidents, claiming to be following in the footsteps of Judaism's prophetic tradition. For example, the English website and organization Jews for Justice for Palestinians is peppered with quotations from the Talmud and statements by local religious leaders, who invoke sacred Jewish texts and insist that supporting the Palestinian cause is a *Jewish* moral imperative.[39] Similarly, many other Jewish activists explained their decision to side with the Palestinians in the name of their Jewish identity, clarifying how the outcome of the conflict affected their own self-image as Jews and indicating, therefore, that their primary concern was less the Palestinians and more their understanding of themselves.

As Jerome Segal writes in the introduction to his book, *Creating a Palestinian State*,

> Because the Jews are representative of all human suffering, the story of the Jews is allegorically the story of the Palestinians. And in the end, the encounter of the Jews and the Palestinians is the encounter of each people with itself at another point in time. For the Jews of Israel, the Palestinians of today and especially the Palestinian victims of tomorrow's expulsion are all the Jewish victims of history. And for the Palestinians, the Jews of Israel are what a suffering people becomes when it becomes a state. They are in potential Palestinians of a possible future.[40]

Segal is evoking a theme common to much anti-Zionist commentary: by establishing Israel, the Jewish people lost its role as moral conscience of the world; Israel's establishment has transformed the Jews into aggressors and turned their enemies into the new, quintessential victim; by creating a state, the Jews have become blind to the suffering they themselves endured and are now busy inflicting onto another people. And in this new, cruel course of action, the Jews have become a new paradigm—proof that statehood will transform an abused people into an abusive one and evidence, therefore, that statehood is bad, especially for the Jews.

The call for Jews to break ranks and frame their dissociation from Israel in a discourse that links Jewish authenticity to anti-Zionism and blemishes Israel as a morally bankrupt fraud has been frequently heard in recent years.

The Italian columnist Barbara Spinelli[41] spelled out this charge in late 2001. Today's ultranationalist Israel, she wrote, constitutes nothing less than a "scandal." And it is a scandal, above all, for Jews themselves—since, as everyone knows, Jews are the quintessential victims of modern nationalism (nationalism being, for Spinelli as other like-minded intellectuals, virtually coterminous with Nazism). It follows, then, that Jews everywhere have a special duty to speak out against Israel, to apologize to its victims, and to do so publicly.

"If one thing is missing in Judaism," Spinelli wrote, "this is precisely it: a *mea culpa* vis-à-vis the peoples and individuals who had to pay the price of blood and exile to allow Israel to exist." She called upon world Jewry to undertake such an act of contrition forthwith:

> If the initiative does not come from Jerusalem it should at least begin in the Diaspora, where many Jews experience a double and contradictory loyalty: toward Israel and the state to which they belong and where they vote. A solemn *mea culpa*, proclaimed by Jewish communities in the West, to stand by the West, to protect its ramparts, to invite Israeli leaders to end their illegal occupation, to rebuild a faith not identified anymore in the exaltation of a colonial state and the superiority of a people: all this would be an important beginning, and beneficial as well for the nation of Israel.[42]

No one can accuse Jewish intellectuals of being deaf to these calls. For the most part, those answering them have been not the long-standing, all-out, rabid haters of Israel, who need no excuse and waste no pieties in reviling the Jewish state. Rather, they are of a somewhat different complexion. Not only do they tend to speak more circumspectly, but, with whatever degree of disingenuousness, they cloak their hostility to Jewish nationalism (i.e., Israel) in the mantle of solicitude for, precisely, the good name of Jews and Judaism. Echoing Spinelli's sentiments in a collection of essays meant to deny the existence of a new antisemitism in Europe after 2000, Michael Neumann claimed that "the case for Jewish complicity [in Israel's crimes] seems much stronger than the case for German complicity [in the Holocaust]. If many Jews spoke out, it would have an enormous effect."[43] If they do not, Neumann appeared to suggest, they are worse than those Germans who, under Nazi rule, said nothing against the Final Solution. Neumann's view is echoed by Norman Finkelstein, who in his book *The Israel–Palestine Conflict: Image and Reality,* wrote that "The Germans could point in extenuation to the severity of the penalties for speaking out against the crimes of state. What excuse do *we* have?"[44]

Making sure that they would stand up and "be counted," on August 8, 2002, forty-five Jewish intellectuals signed an open letter in the London *Guardian,* and, in a widely hailed act of public abjuration, repudiated their right of return to the Jewish state on account of its allegedly racist policies.[45] Since the statement's original publication, more than eighty additional individuals from around the world have joined their ranks. Michael Kustow, the initiator of the petition, subsequently explained that what motivated him to act was the "pitiless violence" of his "blood relatives," the Israeli people—the "violence," as he put it, of the "traumatized former victim, clinging to past wounds from generation unto generation." His goal was to save his fellow Jews from themselves.

The publicity attending this and similar initiatives by European Jews, abetted in some cases by their Israeli counterparts, has been extensive. There was tremendous excitement in Europe, in 2002, over the declaration by one hundred Israeli academics that their government was planning an imminent "full-fledged ethnic cleansing" of the Palestinian people (a charge that was not withdrawn when the alleged atrocity failed to occur): "We are deeply worried" explained the signatories "by indications that the 'fog of war' could be exploited by the Israeli government to commit further crimes against the Palestinian people, up to FULL FLEDGED ETHNIC CLEANSING."[46]

As the number of Israeli signatories mounted to a final 187, an additional group of 800 American scholars, including *The Israel Lobby*'s co-author John Mearsheimer, signed a supporting petition in December 2002.[47] Despite the fact that no Palestinians were ethnically cleansed, no soul searching occurred among the solicitous Jewish intellectuals who had initiated the appeal. Instead, they moved to happier pastures, to celebrate the refusal of a few hundred Israeli army reservists to serve in the territories.[48] There was even greater excitement when several European Jewish academics turned up among the instigators of a movement to boycott Israeli academic institutions.[49] When critics of the boycott dared suggest that the boycott may be antisemitic, the disproportionate amount of Jewish supporters of the boycott was always at hand as evidence to the contrary:

> Lurking behind the thinking of even well-meaning opponents of the boycott is that it is in some way anti-Semitic. This ignores the fact that the boycott is of Israeli institutions, not individuals (so it would affect the tiny number of Palestinian academics in Israeli institutions, but not a Jewish Israeli working in the UK or US). Second, it ignores the fact that the British Jewish community is itself intensely divided over Israel, between those who will defend Israel at all costs, and the increasingly vocal critics who insist "not in our name." Even a cursory look at the signatories of the various boycott calls will show the large number of prominent Jewish figures among them. It really isn't good enough to attack the messenger as anti-Semitic or a self-hating Jew rather than deal with the message itself, that Israel's conduct is unacceptable.[50]

Jewish politicians also felt the need to join the choir: British MP's Gerald Kaufman[51] and Oona King[52] and South African minister Ronnie Kasrils all called for the boycott of Israeli commercial products. All three used similar rhetoric: they were duty-bound "as Jews" to denounce Israel. Kasrils, for example, when asked about his opposition to Israel in an interview, said: "As a person who was born Jewish, I am morally obliged to speak out against what is being done by the Zionist State of Israel to the Palestinian people,"[53] thus suggesting that those Jews who failed to speak out against Israel were betraying their moral obligations as Jews. This is a commonplace argument. Shamai Leibowitz, an Israeli former tank commander, explained his support for Israel divestment by saying that "The call for divestment reflects true loyalty both to Israel's peaceful existence and to the highest Jewish values."[54]

Many others have likewise seen it as their specifically Jewish duty to denounce Israel.

To mark Holocaust Memorial Day, in January 2005, Anthony Lippman issued just such a *mea culpa* as Spinelli called for. Lippman is the son of a Holocaust survivor, albeit himself a convert to Christianity and an active member of the Church of England. The somber occasion may have moved Lippman temporarily to reclaim his patrimony and feel entitled to speak on behalf of the Jewish people. Writing in Great Britain's weekly conservative magazine, *The Spectator*, under the title, "How I Became a Jew," he averred that the "little band" of Holocaust survivors in Europe

> [H]as a terrible responsibility—to live well in the name of those who did not live and to discourage the building of walls and bulldozing of villages. Even more than this, they—and all Jews—need to be the voice of conscience that will prevent Israel from adopting the mantle of oppressor, and to reject the label "anti-Semite" for those who speak out against Israel's policies in the occupied territories.[55]

By Hitler's standards, a Jew for sure; by the standards of most Jewish communities, though, Lippman would hardly make it onto the roster. Nevertheless, the example is telling: for what the author had to say no less than for the fact that a mainstream publication such as *The Spectator* sought him out to say it. Apparently for the British conservative weekly, the best way to commemorate the Holocaust is to have a Jewish convert to the Church of England claim to represent the Jewish people, and then proceed to fulfill his task by comparing Israel to Nazism and lecturing the Jewish people on what the right code of conduct vis-à-vis Israel is. This is a call on Jews to abandon the main elements of their religious and ethnic identity, turn Jewish identity into a commitment to universal, secular, post-national humanism, and exercise a duty to denounce nationalism.

Similarly responding to the claims of an awakened Jewish conscience has been Jacqueline Rose, an academic whose admiration for Edward Said is inversely proportional to her knowledge of Zionist history.[56] In her book *The Question of Zion* (2005)—dedicated to Said—Rose undertook to save Judaism itself from the curse of nationalism. "What is it," she asks, "about the coming into being of this nation [Israel] and the [Zionist] movement out of which it was born, that allowed it—and still allows it—to shed the burdens of its own history, and so flagrantly to blind itself?"[57] Zionism, she concluded, has to be seen not as the fulfillment of an age-old Jewish dream but as the out-and-out betrayal of Jewish history and the Jewish heritage, an adoption of all that is, historically and morally, un-Jewish: "[I]n the ascendant today is a vision of the Jewish nation that is, I believe—precisely because it has, as it so fervently desired, made itself master of its own destiny—in danger of destroying itself."[58] To save themselves, Jews must discard Israel from their own collective identity.

Can Judaism be saved? Yes, Rose and others assure us, but only by a thoroughgoing renunciation of Zionism. As anti-Zionist polemicist Michael Neumann writes, referring to Uri Avnery, Noam Chomsky, and other Jewish detractors of Israel, "These vigorous critics of Israeli excesses are all Jewish. Their focus on Israel is no evidence of double standards, but of where they feel their responsibilities lie."[59] For Neumann, as for Rose, these voices are needed more than ever today, during the Jews' "dark night of the soul," as Rose calls it, because, in Neumann's words, "Israel's current policies are themselves a threat to Jews and Israelis everywhere."[60] That's why Jews must speak out against Israel.

And so Jews line up to comply, as if condemning Israel in the public square were a secular surrogate to the *Vidui*, the ritual confession of sins recited on the Day of Atonement. Oxford historian Avi Shlaim, for example, felt such a need to advertise his Jewish virtuousness in the press, despite his near-complete estrangement from Jewish tradition since childhood.[61] In an op-ed in the *International Herald Tribune,* he justified his denunciation of Zionism by appealing to a faith he never felt much connection to: "One of the greatest accolades in Judaism," he instructed his readers, "is to be a *rodef shalom,* a seeker of peace." That's why he sincerely believed that "Israel today is the real enemy of the Jews,"[62] namely for having betrayed the kind of liberal Israel he purports to still support.[63] And indeed, one might even chastise Shlaim for not going as far as other fellow travelers. Haim Bresheeth, an Israeli who now lives in Great Britain, calls Israel "a uniquely brutal society."[64] Canadian pianist Anton Kuerti reacted to the 2008–2009 Israeli Cast Lead operation in Gaza by saying "Israel's behaviour makes me ashamed of being a Jew, and Canada's servile support of the United States' position, that it is all Hamas's fault, makes me ashamed of being a Canadian."[65] The British Jewish intellectual and member of the anti-Zionist group *Jews for Justice for* Palestine, Deborah Maccoby, wrote in the *New Statesman* that "it is incumbent on Jews to speak out against Israel's politicide against the Palestinians. Doing so will help to reduce anti-Semitism."[66] And Eva Kohner, an emeritus professor from London, responded to the launch of Operation Defensive Shield, in April 2002, by saying that "I am a survivor of the Holocaust, but, in the past 18 months, for the first time in my life, I am ashamed of being Jewish" after having described Israel's reaction to a lethal wave of suicide attacks as Nazi tactics.[67]

The language of current antisemitism is deeply indebted to these Jewish voices and, in fact, needs them to make its case. Many Jewish intellectuals eagerly denounce Israel in the most virulent terms and call for its destruction. Their denunciation offers a powerful alibi to antisemites. In a post-Auschwitz world, antisemitism has been a taboo—a red line few dare to openly cross. But prejudices may regain some respectability—especially if the objects of their hatred begin to endorse them and espouse them. Antisemites rely on Jews to conceal their prejudice and make it presentable. As for anti-Israel and anti-Jewish Jews, their rhetoric is coated in a self-image of heroism. They present themselves as proud dissenters, purporting to be "critical Jews" who live and speak within the authentic tradition of the Prophets of Israel. In this light, their role as critics of state powers and dissenting voices in society makes them not rebels but authentic interpreters of Jewish morality and whistle-blowers on a Jewish community that in its support for Israel has allegedly lost its moral compass.

Before this claim is elucidated, we briefly turn to showing how antisemites exploit Jewish anti-Zionist discourse.

Step Four: The Jewish Alibi of Modern Antisemitism

Once reassured that not all Jews embrace Zionism, antisemites solicitously take anti-Zionist Jews and use them both as a stick to beat all other Jews and as a shield to fend off accusations of antisemitism. For example, referring to Jewish support for Israel, British historian and columnist Max Hastings had this to say:

> If Israel persists with its current policies, and Jewish lobbies around the world continue to express solidarity with repression of the Palestinians, then genuine anti-Semitism is bound to increase. Herein lies the lobbyists' recklessness. By insisting that those who denounce the Israeli state's behaviour are enemies of the Jewish people, they seek to impose a grotesque choice. The Israeli government's behaviour to the Palestinians breeds a despair that finds its only outlet in terrorism. No one can ever criticise the Jewish Diaspora for asserting Israel's right to exist. But the most important service the world's Jews

can render to Israel today is to persuade its people that the only plausible result of their government's behaviour is a terrible loneliness in the world.[68]

Hastings's words may appear reasonable to some, but a closer look shows they are anything but undiluted antisemitism. First, Hastings blames antisemitism on Jewish support for repression of the Palestinians. One is hard-pressed to find "Jewish lobbies" expressing such support. Pro-Israel advocacy supports a vast array of policy demands, but continued repression is not one of them. Hastings's first point, then, is the casual demonization of Israel as an oppressor, the equally casual characterization of Jewish organizations as moral accomplices to this oppression, and the cavalier exculpation of antisemitism not as a prejudice but as a consequence of inexcusable Jewish behavior. Hastings commits a second serious mistake: without a single shred of evidence, he claims that Israel's defenders demonize those who criticize Israel's behavior. He thus sets up a straw man that makes his extreme characterizations of Jewish groups sound reasonable. Again, there is little doubt that some critics of Israel wish ill to the Jewish state, and Hastings overlooks this fact in order to justify terrorism—something he does by embracing a Marxist notion of causality that is ill-suited to his otherwise well-proven anti-communist credentials. In short, he blames the Jews for Israel's actions, blames the Jews for the antisemitism that in his view inevitably follows, blames the Jews for being shrill and uncritical in their defense of Israel, and exculpates Palestinian terrorism for being the inevitable consequence of Israel's actions. In sum, the Jews are to blame. Given that to this date Hastings has failed to write any indictment of "Arab Lobbies" in the world and refrained from blaming anti-Muslim sentiment on Muslim actions; given that he singles out pro-Israel supporters for the kind of moral task he excuses others from; and given that he demonizes Israel's actions and downplays their causes, one can safely say that the above quotation is strong evidence of antisemitism.

Two years later, after Israel had completed its withdrawal from Gaza, its people had elected a centrist government committed to a two-state solution while the Palestinian people had elected a Hamas government devoted to Israel's destruction, Hastings wrote:

Younger Europeans, not to mention the rest of the world, are more sceptical about Israel's territorial claims. They are less susceptible to moral arguments about redress for past horrors, which have underpinned Israeli actions for almost 60 years. We may hope that it will never become respectable to be anti-Semitic. However, Israel is discovering that it can no longer frighten non-Jews out of opposing its policies merely by accusing them of anti-Semitism.[69]

Again, Hastings manipulates the evidence of mounting antisemitism to blame Israel for it, adding another twist—the accusation that Israel exploits the memory of the Holocaust as a form of moral blackmail and a shield against criticism.

Another influential European intellectual, former Italian Ambassador to the USSR and *Corriere della Sera* columnist Sergio Romano, suggested that Jews use the Holocaust and antisemitism as tools for political blackmail. He equated frequent outcries about the return of antisemitism to the Spanish Inquisition and said that "there is in the world today a tribunal of antisemitism that apparently sits permanently in session and who can summon anyone to give account of their words and feelings."[70]

Given that of the many reports on European antisemitism—one commissioned by the French Interior Ministry and written by Jean-Christophe Rufin; one written by the U.S. Department of State; one drafted by the European Union Monitoring Center against Racism, Anti-Semitism and Xenophobia (EUMC); and several by the Anti-Defamation League—only the ADL might qualify, at least in Romano's eyes, as an example of a "Jewish inquisition" in charge of "ascertaining the index of anti-Semitism" in Christian societies. One must ask how all other institutions and organizations engaged in monitoring and combating antisemitism belong to this "Jewish inquisition."

An open letter signed by 120 scholars of the Università degli Studi di Bologna, Italy's oldest university, appeared less concerned about a "Jewish Inquisition" but more about the possibility that antisemitism would be, after all, deserved unless Jews clarified their views of Israel. In March 2003, the academics declared:

We always considered the Jewish people as an intelligent, sensitive, strong people, maybe more than others, because it was selected through suffering, persecutions, humiliations throughout the centuries, through pogroms and in the end the Nazi death camps. We had many schoolmates and friends who were Jewish, many professional colleagues whom we esteemed and many students from Israel to whom we imparted our teachings, taking them through their degrees. . . . Many of us visited Israel, Gaza and the West Bank in the framework of cultural missions or EU programs and therefore are directly familiar with the situation there. It is for these reasons that today, in the wake of what is happening in the Israeli-Palestinian territory, we feel compelled to write you because we regrettably feel that our esteem and our affection for you, the Jewish people, is turning into a painful rage for what you are doing to the Palestinian people. And believe us when we say that so many other people outside our university, who hold your people in high esteem, today feel the same way. You must realize that today you are doing to the Palestinians what was done to you for many centuries past.[71]

This accusation has no basis in reality—Palestinian casualties for the entire duration of the Second Intifada (over six years) were below 5,000, of whom around 2,000 were civilians. These numbers, which include combatants and are, at any rate, combat casualties rather than the outcome of systematic persecution and extermination, hardly compare to the figures of centuries of Jewish persecution. Then again, prejudice is not known to rely on reality as a basis for its accusations. This is, then, the essence of this statement—concocting a demonic image of the Jews in order to justify their hatred.

There is more.

The appeal expresses a preference for a Jewish people that are at the mercy of history, not masters of their own destiny. In the simplistic, binary terms employed here such mastery inevitably entails a role inversion (from victim to aggressor) that will naturally trigger antisemitism. In the view of these scholars, Jews are deserving of sympathy as victims. But as they see it, Jewish statehood not only entails the loss of innocence that supposedly characterized Jewish existence before Israel's establishment, but its actions justify anti-Jewish sentiment. For the signatories, Israel's behavior has become an excuse for antisemitism.

The academic petition had been triggered by news of a group of Israeli soldiers who refused to serve in Israel's army on political grounds. The scholars appealed to all Israelis to follow that example and refuse to serve. There were indeed several such initiatives during the Second Intifada: soldiers were followed by air force pilots, then by five high school boys about to enlist. They were the new Jewish heroes of the hour. An Israeli academic was again at hand to extol their heroism.[72] On account of their refusal to join the army, the five youngsters were praised as "patriots" and a "beacon of hope" for Israel. Though by all standards in a war lasting over four years a few hundred reservists refusing to serve on ideological grounds would be a normal occurrence soliciting no romantic narrative of heroism, in this case the objectors joined the traveling circus of Jews hired to condemn Israel in front of approving Western audiences and were met with great fanfare and media hype across the Western world. Another such romantic moment occurred when the London *Guardian* published an op-ed with the headline, "Why I Won't Serve Sharon."[73] The author, an Israeli student doing a degree at Oxford University, gained instant celebrity, though when it transpired that as an Israeli studying abroad he had not been asked to serve since 1998, his boisterous writing retreated to the confines of Ivy League tutorials.

This morbid fascination with Jews denouncing Israel takes many forms. In Great Britain, the birthplace of parliamentary democracy and student debates, the possibility that "Zionism is the real enemy of the Jews" and not, possibly, old-fashioned antisemites, or "Zionism is a danger to the Jewish people" was repeatedly debated in respectable forums—including the Cambridge Student Union and the prestigious debating society, Intelligence Squared. In both cases, the lineup of speakers seconding and rejecting the motion was made up entirely of Jews.[74] London's prestigious Frontline Club, for its part, hosted Avi Shlaim and Shlomo Sand, the author of a book claiming that the Jewish people does not exist,[75] to engage each other in conversation about their respective scholarly contributions. As further indication of how blatantly one-sided this forum was, the event was chaired by Jacqueline Rose.[76] Again, for the delight of the audience, Jewish intellectuals were called upon to argue the evils of Zionism, to undermine the claims of nationhood of the Jewish people, and generally speaking to offer a Jewish stamp of approval for polemics that, if expressed by a non-Jewish voice, might otherwise have been labeled as antisemitic.

There is, throughout the rhetoric of the Good Jew, an underlying assumption: Zionism and its political achievements involved a loss of innocence for the Jewish people.[77] The agents of Zionism are considered to have performed unspeakable crimes at its founding. Having proceeded to forget those events or having hidden them beneath a dense fog, Zionist leaders conjured up a "conspiracy of silence" to conceal the past. Fortunately, a small band of heroic Jewish scholars—Israel's new historians and other post-Zionists among others—have unveiled the evidence and exposed the hidden truth for the world to see. As Laurence Silberstein writes in his sympathetic work on Post-Zionism, "[E]very national memory entails a national forgetting. Behind the events that are narrated in a nation's myth of beginnings are events that are eclipsed or 'forgotten.'"[78] Silberstein's central claim is that events were not only "forgotten" in an unconscious act of collective removal, but that there was a knowing complicity to silence them by the powers-that-be, with the active help of a subservient academic world. Those who expose this "conspiracy of silence" are not just honest scholars, but also, as enablers of change, Good Jews.[79] According to this logic, it follows that what is left for the Jewish people to do is repent and undo the damage done—oppose and ultimately remove Jewish Israel, no less.

As periodic reminders are thus voiced to Jews about the perils of siding with Israel, some Jews respond by protesting their bona fide credentials as Anti-Zionists. Their solicitude is awarded by recognition that there are "good" and "bad" Jews—a convenient distinction that enables the antisemite to hate Jews and pretend to be their champion at the same time!

Step Five: Cleansing Israel of the Original Sin

If, in light of the above, one asks what kind of Jews should emerge as the standard-bearers of Jewish identity, the answer is readily available. Exalting the Jew-as-victim offers the right balance to contempt for the muscular Jew who fights back—the Zionist Jew. In other words, those who extol victimhood as quintessentially Jewish frequently demonize Israel for being at the polar opposite of this model.

Zionism, according to this view, is a perversion of Jewish humanism. The American Jewish theologian Marc H. Ellis, for example, states that "While it is clear that the creation and expansion of Israel has been and is a catastrophe for the Palestinians, the use of power by Jews to displace and denigrate the Palestinians has also been a severe trauma for Jewish history and the contemporary Jewish community."[80] Ellis, in other words, does not only embrace the post-Zionist version of Israel's history as fact, but decries its consequences on "Jewish history" and the "contemporary Jewish community," thus suggesting that the Jewish return to history as an independent nation has had a corrupting influence on the moral character of the Jews.

Zionism abandoned the historic posture of Jewish passivity in the face of persecution and affirmed a Jewish right to self-defense. By doing so, it put Jewish self-preservation above any morality supposedly inherent in victimhood. It did so precisely at the time when intellectual trends in the

Western world were relinquishing or rejecting its ancient warrior culture and seeking to replace it with a more pacific view of "soft power," in which victims appear as the quintessential expression of defiance. Unwittingly then, Zionism found itself on the wrong side of history, as far as Western intellectual trends go. As Anatol Lieven opines:

> For equally valid and legitimate reasons, Western Europe and parts of the liberal intelligentsia of the United States on one hand and the greater part of the world's Jewish population on the other drew opposing conclusions from the catastrophe of Nazism. . . . The Western European elites and many U.S. liberal intellectuals essentially decided that the correct response to Nazism and to the hideous national conflicts which preceded, engendered and accompanied it was to seek to limit, transcend and overcome nationalism.[81]

By its recourse to force to protect its right to self-determination, Israel, a sovereign state, faces the sometimes impossible moral dilemma of those who seek to reconcile the amorality of national interest with Jewish morality. This dilemma is made more acute by Jewish history—given that historically Jews were often the victims of that amorality. But current antisemitism relies on Jews to go beyond the moral questioning of specific actions. Relying on the claims put forward by Israel's post-Zionist scholars (which are deemed to be honest, objective, and impartial), antisemites can prove that Zionism engendered a loss of innocence for the Jewish people. Once the consequences of renewed Jewish sovereignty are depicted in dark terms, they can then be used as evidence that Jewish nationalism is inherently evil—much like all nationalism, only more so because Jews, having been victims of nationalism, should know better. Jewish critics of Zionism do not make support for a Jewish state conditional upon a morally irreproachable conduct—though in practice a Jewish state would fail their test, they could at least be amenable to the idea in utopian terms. They go further, seeking instead moral solace in the redemptive notion of a return to innocence through the abandonment of Zionism and the discarding of its consequences. It is doubtful whether an honest assessment of the historical facts would matter to them. It is also undeniable that their unbearable sense of guilt does not stop at the gates of historical truth and feeds largely on scholarly works that have systematically distorted and fabricated the historical record of Israel's creation and its subsequent existence in order to justify the moral argument against its existence.

This fantasy about a lost, primeval state of innocence for the Jewish people develops its own version of the ideal Jew. He or she has no motherland; is a wandering Marrano and a revolutionary with political loyalties that are liberal or progressive; is fully assimilated and yet conscious of a Jewish past. Today, Jews are more easily integrated into the narrative of the modern Western world as previous victims rather than as members of a sovereign nation in arms. Especially in the current age of general prosperity, multilateral diplomacy, and constitutional orders that proscribe war, to appear in the nationalistic, martial role that Israel assumes is to appear "anachronistic," to use Tony Judt's phrase. The only uncontroversial way to express a proud Jewish identity is through the sensitive embodiment of suffering and victimization from the past, and also through the modern expression of the Prophetic tradition—as a dissident intellectual.[82] These are held forth as the positive Jewish role models, in sharp contrast to the Zionist model, which is chastised for having betrayed both European values and what Europe sees as the authentic Jew.

As will be shown in this last section, anti-Zionist Jews and those who exploit them as an alibi for antisemitism do not merely wish Israel to behave differently; they object to the Jewish identity that Zionism has nurtured among Israel's Jewish citizens and Diaspora Jews alike—one that takes pride in the accomplishments of statehood, that strongly embraces the notion of Jewish peoplehood, and that reaffirms the historical bond between the people and the land.

Jewish intellectuals, again, are at the forefront of this argument. Consider the following examples.

Writing in April 2010 about a family member who perished in the Holocaust, the late historian and intellectual Tony Judt pondered the meaning of being Jewish:

> There is no general-purpose answer to this question: it is always a matter of what it means to be Jewish for me—something quite distinct from what it means for my fellow Jews. To outsiders, such concerns are mysterious. A Protestant who does not believe in the Scriptures, a Catholic who abjures the authority of the Pope in Rome, or a Muslim for whom Muhammad is not the Prophet: these are incoherent categories. But a Jew who rejects the authority of the rabbis is still Jewish (even if only by the rabbis' own matrilineal definition): who is to tell him otherwise?
>
> I reject the authority of the rabbis—all of them (and for this I have rabbinical authority on my side). I participate in no Jewish community life, nor

do I practice Jewish rituals. I don't make a point of socializing with Jews in particular—and for the most part I haven't married them. I am not a "lapsed" Jew, having never conformed to requirements in the first place. I don't "love Israel" (either in the modern sense or in the original generic meaning of loving the Jewish people), and I don't care if the sentiment is reciprocated. But whenever anyone asks me whether or not I am Jewish, I unhesitatingly respond in the affirmative and would be ashamed to do otherwise.[83]

This remarkable statement is not only accurate—a baptized Catholic remains a Catholic for the Roman Church even if he or she rejects Papal authority; and a Muslim who rejects the Qur'an and its Prophet is an apostate, not an infidel. But this is beside the point—what is remarkable in Judt's explanation of his Jewishness is that he rejects all the elements commonly ascribed to Jewish identity, cannot pinpoint the substance of his Jewish identity, and yet he is unable to free himself from it. How can a Jew reject the building block of Jewish identity to which most other Jews (and non-Jews as well) cling to, and yet claim still to be a Jew? The only answer is that he or she must seek to convince other Jews (and non-Jews) that Jewish identity must be redefined.

Of a similar mind was his Cambridge-based Marxist colleague, historian Eric Hobsbawm, who, in his seminal work, *Nations and Nationalism,* stated that "People can identify themselves as Jews even though they share neither religion, language, culture, tradition, historical background, blood-group patterns nor an attitude to the Jewish state."[84] While descriptively this may occasionally be true, it appears that Hobsbawm's statement is prescriptive as well. From denying that Jewish identity has any connection to "religion, language, tradition, historical background" or even "an attitude to the Jewish state" to lamenting the insistence by fellow Jews about clinging onto those elements, the journey is short.

In a *London Review of Books* essay published in 2005, where he deplored both Israel's creation and the Jewish religion because in his view they are both obstacles to full Jewish integration in modern Western societies, Hobsbawm predictably went further:

The paradox of the era since 1945 is that the greatest tragedy in Jewish history has had two utterly different consequences. On the one hand, it has concentrated a substantial minority of the global Jewish population in one nation-state: Israel, which was itself once upon a time a product of Jewish emancipation and of the passion to enter the same world as the rest of humanity.

It has shrunk the diaspora, dramatically so in the Islamic regions. On the other hand, in most parts of the world it has been followed by an era of almost unlimited public acceptance of Jews, by the virtual disappearance of the anti-semitism and discrimination of my youth, and by unparalleled and unprecedented Jewish achievement in the fields of culture, intellect and public affairs. There is no historic precedent for the triumph of the *Aufklärung* in the post-Holocaust diaspora. Nevertheless, there are those who wish to withdraw from it into the old segregation of religious ultra-Orthodoxy and the new segregation of a separate ethnic-genetic state-community. If they were to succeed I do not think it will be good either for the Jews or for the world.[85]

The rejection of a Jewish identity based on anything but the most universal abstract values leads Hobsbawm and others like him to conclude that Israel and Judaism are such burdens to Jews that Jews may as well discard them. With these premises, the journey to writings where Jewish intellectuals actively advocate a radical change in Jewish identity that forever eliminates Israel from its core is a short one.

In an essay published in the Jewish magazine *Tikkun*, Marxist scholar Bertel Ollman recounted how, on his way into the operating room, he realized that, had he not survived the surgery, he would have died a Jew. The prospect was so unsettling that, once healed, he wrote his "Letter of resignation from the Jewish people," in which he did just that: he resigned. The reasons were Zionism, Israel, and the support its policies enjoy from other Jews. Ollman might yet reconsider, but for that to happen, Jews would have to embrace his own version of Jewish identity. Paraphrasing a Lenny Bruce joke, he said,

> Noam Chomsky, Mordechai Vanunu and Edward Said are Jewish. Elie Wiesel is *goyish*. So, too, all "Jewish" neo-cons. Socialism and communism are Jewish. Sharon and Zionism are very *goyish*. And, who knows, if this reading of Judaism were to take hold, I may one day apply for readmission to the Jewish people.[86]

Said was not Jewish, though he was the darling of many anti-Zionist Jewish intellectuals. Vanunu is a convert to Anglicanism and his alienation goes so far that he refuses to speak Hebrew—his mother tongue. The only halakhic Jew of Ollman's trinity is Chomsky, who qualifies more for his anti-Israel venom than for his devotion to his ancestry's traditions. What makes Chomsky, Vanunu, and Said "authentic" Jews, then? For Ollman, it's their adherence to a political orthodoxy: being "Jewish" equals being a certain type of progressive intellectual, who finds no small part of his identity by taking an adversarial stance toward Israel.

Ollman may sound outlandish, but he is not alone. For every Jewish intellectual who rejects any premise for Jewish identity that is not firmly rooted in universal, progressive, liberal values, there is an antisemite who applauds the readiness of Jews to abandon anything that makes their Jewish identity distinctive.

The notion that a retreat to religious and national identity is bad both for the Jews and the world is widespread. Italy's foremost historian, Sergio Romano, celebrated, in his book *Lettera a un Amico ebreo* (A Letter to a Jewish Friend), the image of the intellectual, cosmopolitan, stateless, Marrano Jew who harbored skepticism for Zionism as the expression of authentic Judaism:

> They were not Zionists and were not at all attracted by a country of which they could not share either the political philosophy or the predictable religious narrow-mindedness. They knew that in Israel, had they chosen it as their homeland, they would have to live with the Ashkenazic Jews from the shtetl or with Sephardic Jews from Arab countries—archaic characters in a world they had no familiarity with and for which they felt considerable discomfort.[87]

For Romano, Baruch Spinoza is the archetypal Jew he likes because Spinoza, in his view, was, intellectually, a Marrano. What does Romano mean by the idea of a Marrano Jew?

> They came into the world from Jewish parents or mixed marriages and were conscious of a blood link with the great tribe they were born into. But they could not be fully Jewish. Many . . . were attracted to Christianity for esthetical reasons. Others saw baptism as a way out of the small spiritual Ghetto of Jewish traditions. Yet others put their hopes in the emancipation offered by the liberal State or the socialist revolution. . . . The only thing in common in their intellectual curriculum was probably a certain tendency to transgress, to provoke and to be unpredictable.[88]

This tendency, Romano says, is reflected in a "rejection of any automatic loyalty and the desire to escape the 'totalitarian' pressures exerted on their conscience by the two worlds of which [the Marrano Jew] represents the boundary. Ubiquity was the intellectual condition which they felt most at ease with."[89] It is difficult to comprehend how this idealized image of Jews is nothing more than a prejudice toward real-life Jews who, across the centuries, sought to survive on the basis of a Jewish identity that, despite being flexible and dynamic, nevertheless was grounded in a religious tradition, a language, a cultural heritage, a shared ancestry, and an emotional bond with the Land of Israel.

By making authentic Jewishness conditional upon the breaking of all these links, many intellectuals effectively are only prepared to accept Jews if they conform to the "non-Jewish Jew" described, extolled, and embodied by Isaac Deutscher and many others after him.[90] They are accidental Jews—born Jewish but retaining no meaningful bonds with their origins. To exalt them as positive and authentic representatives of Jewish identity suggests that adherence to all other constituent features of traditional Jewish identity is unnecessary and undesirable and Jews would do well to forego it. As Dennis Praeger and Joseph Telushkin have commented: "These people do not feel rooted in anything Jewish, religious or national; their Jewish identity consists of little more than having been born Jews, and they affirm none of Judaism's components. They remain Jews by virtue of having not converted to another religion."[91]

Sergio Romano and Eric Hobsbawm are not alone among Jews who fit this portrait. The Italian columnist Guido Ceronetti, for example, commented on Mordechai Vanunu's release from prison, in 2004, by exalting him as a novel version of Spinoza, defining him as a "true Jew." For Ceronetti, the essence of being Jewish is to be rootless and without a homeland, to be wandering and spiritually restless, cosmopolitan and devoid of loyalties to a nation or a faith.[92]

A former Irish cabinet minister, Justin Keating, expressed similar, if more strident views. In November 2005, he published a controversial article in the monthly Irish magazine *The Dubliner.* His opening statement was that "I have reached the conclusion that the Zionists have absolutely no right in what they call Israel, that they have built their state not beside but on top of the Palestinian people, and that there can be no peace as long as contemporary Israel retains its present form."

He then went on to say that

> Jews have made an immense contribution to civilization, developing as they were between the great empires of Mesopotamia and the Nile, with both of which they had intimate contact, and by which they wanted to avoid being swallowed. They developed a religion and an ethos based on independence, liberty and democracy to which we all owe a debt. That religion is based on

the twin concepts of Law and Righteousness, which inspired over the millennia extraordinary contributions to culture and morality. All admirable. In Israel/Palestine, where are they now? Zionists have betrayed all of this, and that is a tragedy not just for Jews, but for all of us.[93]

Keating's article triggered an acrimonious controversy. The State of Israel demanded an apology from the serving Irish Prime Minister, who refused to oblige. Writing in the next issue of the magazine, Keating defended his position by adding that

Zionism is a blind alley. Entering it, Zionists abandoned Righteousness and the Rule of Law. The defence of Israel endangers all that is best, most noble and valuable for all mankind in the Jewish tradition. I am anti-Zionist because I am pro-Jewish.[94]

Keating, at least, did not go so far as others—in his view, apparently, Jews are allowed to retain their traditions, but only to practice them in perpetual exile. Still, despite the fact that this type of rhetoric falls short of calling for conversion, some Jewish intellectuals appear to be ahead of the game, as their anti-Zionist language is imbued with the salvific language of Christianity.

If one pays close attention to the discourse about Jewish identity that pits anti-Zionist intellectuals and their Israel-hating supporters against pro-Israel Jews, one discovers that the Jew-as-victim they extol is the idealization of innocence and represents, with his unconditional rejection of violence even when confronting extermination, a primeval moral condition that precedes original sin. In politics, that sin is the use of power and the sometimes impossible moral choices and dilemmas that power demands of governments and states.

The notion that Zionism entailed a loss of innocence, which only its abandonment can ever restore, is central to current antisemitism because it enables those who call for the demise of Israel to claim that such demise will save the Jews—much like baptism or the Inquisition's fire once did. The abrupt descent from heaven has been described, in the acrimonious debate over Israel's new historiographical school and its writings, as an "original sin." As Benny Morris put it:

How one perceives 1948 bears heavily on how one perceives the whole Zionist/Israeli experience. If Israel, the haven of a much-persecuted people, was born pure and innocent, then it is worthy of the grace, material assistance, and political support showered upon it by the West over the past forty years—and worthy of more of the same in years to come. If, on the other hand, Israel was born tarnished, besmirched by original sin, then it was no more deserving of that grace and assistance than were its neighbors.[95]

Morris subsequently attributed this theological term to others, and while his former fellow traveler Avi Shlaim denied that the term had even been used,[96] he quickly ridiculed the notion that Israel's creation might have equally been "an immaculate conception"—another Catholic theological concept closely correlated to the notion of sin.[97] Yet, it was the same Shlaim who, more recently, expanded the vocabulary of Christian salvation by deriding Israel on the grounds that the Jewish state wished to have both "thirty pieces of silver" and "the crown of thorns," a clear reference to Judas and the Jesus of the Passion.[98]

How does Israel restore its supposedly lost innocence? By a process of political and moral rehabilitation that will save Jews from the evils inherent in Zionism. The argument that the Jewish state was born in sin is central to this notion of rehabilitation. The use of terms borrowed from Christian theology leaves little doubt as to what subtext informs this discourse, reflecting as it does a vision of Israel that finds echoes in the very theology from which it borrows its terminology.

Giving up Israel's Jewish nature becomes a means to address the charge of "original sin." If the injustice Israel is charged with is inherent to the project that led to its creation—as the notion of original sin suggests—there is only one remedy for addressing that injustice. Original sin is a distinctive Christian theological concept. According to the *Catholic Encyclopaedia,* "Original sin may be taken to mean: (1) the sin that Adam committed; (2) a consequence of this first sin, the hereditary stain with which we are born on account of our origin or descent from Adam."[99] This same theology traditionally postulated that the only salvation from original sin could be provided by baptism—for Jews, conversion to Christianity. If at the individual level a Jew can be saved from original sin through baptism and conversion, what would be the baptism equivalent for Israel?

Present-day antisemitism does not demand baptism and conversion of Jews as individuals. But it surmises that Israel was born in sin. If its birth was characterized by original sin, only an act equivalent to baptism will save Israel from eternal damnation. Ridding Israel of its Jewish nature provides that equivalent: by ceasing to be Jewish, the state of the Jews

454 | Emanuele Ottolenghi

rather than Jews as individuals will be granted forgiveness and salvation, and will be redeemed from the kind of damnation that a pre-baptism condition would have guaranteed. Washing away the stain of the original sin will restore a primeval condition of innocence that somehow characterized Jews prior to Israel's establishment. It will also free the Jewish spirit from the burden of Jewish power and release the potential for the Jews to act as "prophets" in the world again, by being the voice of conscience for the nations amidst which they dwell.[100] If Zionism entails a loss of innocence, paradise will be won over through conversion to the new dominant ethos of the age, the new baptism for a sinful Israel that needs to be saved from itself.[101]

New historians are not alone in using this highly charged Christological language of salvation. For example, in 2000, Bernard Avishai used the term *atonement* in a review of two books by new historians. He was illustrating what tool Israel should deploy to confront its past and achieve peace. The tool was post-Zionism: "One reads Morris and Shlaim, presumably, to find reasons to encourage Israeli leaders to approach peacemaking with pragmatic humility and even an openness to atonement."[102] In 2005, Avishai doubled down in a *Harper's Magazine* essay entitled "Saving Israel from itself."[103] In thinking the "unthinkable" in the *New York Review of Books,* Tony Judt explained European antisemitism as the result of Ariel Sharon's misguided policies. The Jews, once again, had only themselves to blame for their own misfortunes. He then advocated an end to Zionism to be replaced by a bi-national state—the only way to save the Jews from themselves. For Judt, their suffering would be relieved through a simple act of self-effacement, a veritable spiritual and intellectual *auto da fé* for modern times. As Judt wrote,

> In a world where nations and peoples increasingly intermingle and intermarry at will; where cultural and national impediments to communication have all but collapsed; where more and more of us have multiple elective identities and would feel falsely constrained if we had to answer to just one of them; in such a world Israel is truly an anachronism. And not just an anachronism but a dysfunctional one. In today's "clash of cultures" between open, pluralist democracies and belligerently intolerant, faith-driven ethno-states, Israel actually risks falling into the wrong camp.
>
> To convert Israel from a Jewish state to a binational one would not be easy, though not quite as impossible as it sounds: the process has already be-

gun de facto. But it would cause far less disruption to most Jews and Arabs than its religious and nationalist foes will claim.[104]

Judt was a scholar of nationalism and had no illusions about the viability of its alternatives. In his celebrated book, *A Grand Illusion: An Essay on Europe,* he celebrated the nation-state, "the only remaining, as well as the best-adapted, source of collective and communal identification."[105] As for Europe, he summarily dismissed the European effort to paper over national identities as a pipedream:

> From Spain to Lithuania the transition from past to present is being recalibrated in the name of a "European" idea that is itself a historical and illusory product. . . . But what will not necessarily follow is anything remotely resembling continental political homogeneity and supranational stability.[106]

For Israel alone, Judt chose the opposite standard. There, for reasons that defy reason, he assumes that the "only remaining, as well as best-adapted, source of collective and communal identification" is an "anachronism" and that the best way forward is a "conversion" to a non-existent alternative identity, bi-nationalism. There is nothing logical in singling Israel out the way Judt did—and besides, Judt's use of the term *conversion* is no coincidence. That is what anti-Zionism advocacy is truly about. Convert the Jews.

Conclusion

The process by which the Jewish alibi for current antisemitism is created requires the creation of a dichotomy whereby the negative self-image of the Zionist Jew is contrasted with the righteous alternative of the anti-Zionist Jew who combats Zionism and its manifestations in the name of supposedly authentic Jewish values. Central to this dichotomy is the idea that dispersion and statelessness are the authentic, natural, and desirable condition of Jewish existence in the world. Jewish voices are drafted to defend and actively promote this view, so as to shield its proponents from accusations of antisemitism.

Despite Israel's centrality to Jewish communal identity, Jews are targeted for their attachment to and support for Israel and are asked to relinquish them in exchange for legitimacy. This demand, far from being seen as antisemitic, is vigorously pursued in certain quarters in the name of a liberal vision that rejects nationalism and religion as foundations of a collective identity. Guided by a post-national, secular, and pacifist vision of international politics—a "brotherhood-of-mankind" worldview—those who advocate anti-Zionism pose an intolerable dilemma to most Jews: either discard an important component of their identity or face isolation, harassment, and, in time, possible discrimination. Once again, Jews seem out of step with the dominant ethos of society, and for this they are chastised and under pressure to conform.

If this is antisemitism, it is vastly at variance with past forms of anti-Jewish hatred. Regardless, it still bears many hallmarks of the ancient hatred because of its recourse to old antisemitic stereotypes and tropes, because of its double standards toward the Jews, and because of its effort to force an unbearable choice on the Jews: embrace an identity others have tailored for them or face the consequences.

NOTES

1. In Germany, antisemitic acts increased by 69 percent from 1999 to 2000, and although there was a slight decrease in 2002, between 2000 and 2003 the number of antisemitic violent crimes rose significantly; see EUMC Report, "Manifestations of Antisemitism in the EU 2002–2003: Executive Summary," p. 10. EUMC, Vienna, 2004, http://fra.europa.eu/sites/default/files/fra_uploads/184-AS-Main-report.pdf. In France, of the 313 racist, xenophobic, or antisemitic incidents reported in 2002, a total of 193 were directed at Jews, six times the number in 2001. A striking example of this was the rise in antisemitic acts in the spring of 2002 surrounding increased violence between Israelis and Palestinians, including Israel's Operation Defensive Shield, one of Israel's more aggressive responses to Palestinian terror. In France, the rise was particularly pronounced: in April 2002, at the peak of Israel's Operation Defensive Shield, 118 "physical acts of violence towards Jews, their communities, organizations or property," were reported, while 32 such acts were reported in March, and 12 in May. EUMC, "Manifestations," p. 9.

2. "Manifestations," p. 3: "Although we know—and opinion polls show—that anti-Semitism is permanently present in Europe in a more or less hidden way, many of us have hoped that manifest forms of anti-Semitism will not see any revival in Europe again. At present, Jews are rather well integrated economically, socially and culturally in the Member States of the European Union (EU). But the attacks in New York and Washington on September 11 and the conflict in the Middle East have contributed to an atmosphere in Europe, which gives latent anti-Semitism and hate and incitement a new strength and power of seduction. Even rumours that Israel was responsible for

11 September 2001, for the attacks on the World Trade Centre and the Pentagon, and that Jews bring about a situation in their interest in order to put the blame on somebody else, found a receptive audience in some places. Anti-Semitic conspiracy theories are spreading over the Internet, which provides a cheap vehicle for the distribution of hate." See also, more recently, the European Union Agency for Fundamental Rights, *Anti-Semitism—Summary Overview of the Situation in the European Union 2001–2008* (February 2009), p. 23: "As regards general causes for increases and decreases in anti-Semitic activity, the Agency's Annual Reports have noted that for some countries statistical trends allow us to discern an impact of Middle East political developments on anti-Semitic activity," http://194.30.12.221/fraWebsite/attachments/Antisemitism_Update _2009.pdf. It should be added that even when violent incidents are far rarer, the EUMC documented "extremely nasty anti-Semitic everyday discourse which is relatively widespread amongst the general population." "Manifestations," p. 14.

3. There are many reliable surveys and data analysis documenting this correlation. See, for example, the multiple resources on the Anti-Defamation League International site, http://www.adl.org/main_Anti_Semitism_International/Default.htm. See also resources from the Coordination Forum for Countering Antisemitism, http://antisemitism .org.il/list/4.

4. Among them, see, for example, Pierre-André Taguieff, *La nouvelle judeophobie* (Paris: Mille et une nuits, 2002); Paul Igansky and Barry Kosmin, eds., *The New Anti-semitism? Debating Judeophobia in 21st-Century Britain* (London: Profile Books, 2003); Ron Rosenbaum, ed., *Those Who Forget the Past: The Question of Antisemitism* (New York: Random House, 2004); Bernard Harrison, *The Resurgence of Antisemitism: Jews, Israel and Liberal Opinion* (Lanham, Md.: Rowman & Littlefield, 2006); and Denis MacShane, *Globalising Hatred: The New Antisemitism* (London: Weidenfeld & Nicholson, 2008).

5. It is important to premise this argument by clarifying that I am not referring here to the robust debate about the merits of specific Israeli policies, which occurs daily within the Jewish world. Jews of all religious and political persuasions express a diverse range of views on the matter without their disagreements reflecting bias against Israel or the Jewish people. Here, I refer only to those Jews who cross two lines in their views of Israel: first, they embrace a language of delegitimization, demonization, and double standards—to borrow Natan Sharansky's 3 Ds for the new Antisemitism (Natan Sharansky, "3D test of Anti-Semitism: Demonization, Double Standards, Delegitimization," *Jewish Political Studies Review* 17, nos. 1–2 [Spring 2005], http://www.jcpa.org /phas/phas-sharansky-s05.htm)—and in the process they even adopt traditional anti-semitic tropes. And second, they root their arguments against Israel in some supposed claim of Jewish authenticity.

6. There have only been a handful of scholarly studies of the phenomenon to date. See Emanuele Ottolenghi, "Europe's Good Jews," *Commentary* (December 2005), pp. 42–46; Alvin H. Rosenfeld, "Progressive Jewish Thought and the New Anti-Semitism" (The American Jewish Committee, 2006), http://www.ajc.org/atf/cf/%7B42D75369-D582 -4380-8395-D25925B85EAF%7D/PROGRESSIVE_JEWISH_THOUGHT.PDF; Emanuele Ottolenghi, *Autodafé: L'Europa, gli ebrei e l'antisemitismo* (Torino: Lindau, 2007).

7. See, for example, John Pilger, "Listen to the Heroes of Israel," in *The New Statesman* (February 25, 2010), http://www.newstatesman.com/print/201002250009. Pilger relies on Israel-born Holocaust denier, Gilad Atzmon: "proof of the murderous, racist toll of Zionism has been an epiphany for many people; justice for the Palestinians," wrote the expatriate Israeli musician Gilad Atzmon, is now "at the heart of the battle for a better world." However, his fellow Jews in Western countries, such as Britain and Australia, whose influence is critical, are still mostly silent, still looking away, still accepting, . . . the 'brainwashing and reality distortion.' And yet the responsibility to speak out could not be clearer, and the lessons of history—family history for many—ensure that it renders them culpable should their silence persist." See also Henri Picciotto, "Silence is Complicity," in *Counterpunch* (August 11, 2006), http://www.counterpunch.org /picciotto08112006.html: "Many Jews question Israel's policies, but are afraid to speak out in their congregations or even to their families. But the time has come for Jewish dissidents to challenge the policies of the Israeli government. In the short run these policies kill Arabs, mostly innocent civilians; in the long run, they can result only in disaster for Israelis and Jews worldwide."

8. Alan Hart, *Zionism: The Real Enemy of the Jews* (Kent: World Focus Publishing, 2005), p. v: "There is nothing anybody in publishing, the media in general and politics fears more than being accused of anti-Semitism. Since the obscenity of the Nazi Holocaust, the false charge of anti-Semitism is the blackmail card Zionism has played brilliantly to prevent informed and honest debate about who must do what if there is to be a peaceful resolution of the Palestine problem, which is the prerequisite for averting a clash of civilizations, Judeo-Christian v. Islamic."

9. See James Cohen, "The Accusation of Anti-Semitism as Moral Blackmail," *Human Architecture: Journal of the Sociology of Self-Knowledge* VII, no. 2 (Spring 2009), pp. 23–34.

10. See Jerome Slater, "How Bad Can the Jewish Right-wing Get?" Blog entry for August 5, 2010, http://www.jeromeslater.com/2010/08/how-bad-can-jewish-rightwing-get .html.

11. See Antony Lerman, "Diaspora Jews Find Their Voice," in *The Guardian* (May 20, 2009), http://www.guardian.co.uk/commentisfree/2009/may/20/israel-middleeast.

12. See, for example, Tony Klug, "Are Israeli Policies Entrenching Anti-Semitism Worldwide?" *Tikkun* 25, no. 3 (May/June 2010), http://www.tikkun.org/article.php /may2010klug: "In the more likely, if regrettable, event that the current Israeli government will commit itself to no such thing, what should Jewish diaspora communities do? I believe they would be well advised to take a deep breath and reconsider their habitual reflexive responses, which are in part responsible for the mess we are in. No one would expect them to waver from their uncompromising support for the genuine welfare of the Israeli state and people, and I do not propose this. But, with precisely this welfare in mind, it is beyond time for them to distance themselves from the expansionist policies of the Israeli government, its belligerent approach to problem-solving in the region, and its propensity to infringe Palestinian human rights, periodically on a massive scale. Some Jewish groups and many individual Jews are already doing this, to the consternation of certain voluble self-appointed guardians of the Jewish good.

However, in the main, these dissenting Jews are, I believe, helping to lower the temperature of anti-Jewish feeling."

13. See for example Deborah Maccoby's letter to the editor, *The New Statesman* (July 5, 2004): "I believe it is incumbent on Jews to speak out against Israel's politicide against the Palestinians. Doing so will help to reduce anti-Semitism." See also Allan Levine, "Jews are dishonored by a blind defense of Israel," in *Ha'aretz* (May 20, 2011), http:// www.haaretz.com/print-edition/opinion/jews-are-dishonored-by-a-blind-defense-of -israel-1.362926.

14. See Marc H. Ellis, "On Jewish Particularity and Anti-Semitism: Notes from a Jewish Theology of Liberation," in *Human Architecture: Journal of the Sociology of Self-Knowledge* VII, no. 2 (Spring 2009), pp. 103–122.

15. See, for example, Richard Greener, "The 'Self-Hating Jew' Myth: Debunked," *The Huffington Post* (March 30, 2010), http://www.huffingtonpost.com/richard-greener/the -self-hating-jew-myth_b_518984.html: "The myth of the 'self-hating Jew' is a slander against many American Jews who do not march in lockstep to the Likud drummer"; Julian Kossoff, "Tony Judt, Zionism, and the Self-Hating Jew," *The Daily Telegraph Blogs* (August 12, 2010), http://blogs.telegraph.co.uk/news/juliankossoff/100050311/tony -judt-zionism-and-the-self-hating-jew/; and David Herman, "Today's Cultural Icon: The Self-Hating Jew," *The Jewish Chronicle* (November 2, 2010), http://www.thejc.com /comment-and-debate/comment/40488/todays-cultural-icon-self-hating-jew. For a literary representation of the phenomenon, see Howard Jacobson, *The Finkler Question* (New York: Bloomsbury, 2010); also see Michael Marqusee, *If I Am Not for Myself: Journey of an Anti-Zionist Jew* (London: Verso Books, 2010).

16. Sander Gilman, *Jewish Self-Hatred* (Baltimore: Johns Hopkins University Press, 1986).

17. I rely, here, on the Italian translation of the original French, Camillo Berneri, *L'ebreo antisemita* (Rome: Carucci, 1984).

18. Berneri, p. 34.

19. Gilman, p. 16.

20. Ibid., p. 1.

21. Ibid., p. 12.

22. Ibid., p. 270.

23. Far from being a hyperbole, this is precisely the argument used by Jemima Khan in an op-ed article published in *The Guardian* at the beginning of the Second Intifada: after decrying "to overwhelming Jewish influence in US politics and the media" Khan went on say that "Many of my friends are Jewish, as was my paternal grandfather. The sad part is that I know the majority of them desperately want peace in the Middle East, but that peace can only be achieved once the US acts as an honest broker, and the US media as impartial commentators." See Jemima Khan, "Tell the Truth about Israel" in *The Guardian* (November 1, 2000), http://www.guardian.co.uk/world/2000/nov/01 /comment.israelandthepalestinians.

24. Gideon Shimoni, *The Zionist Ideology* (Hanover, N.H.: Brandeis University Press, 1995), p. 85. See also www.zionism-israel.com: "Zionism is the national revival movement of the Jewish people. It holds that the Jews have the right to self-determination in their own national home, and the right to develop their national culture. Histori-

cally, Zionism strove to create a legally recognized national home for the Jews in their historical homeland. This goal was implemented by the creation of the State of Israel. Today, Zionism supports the existence of the state of Israel and helps to inspire a revival of Jewish national life, culture and language."

25. For a discussion of present-day anti-Zionism, see Ted Lapkin, "The Strange Mythology of Anti-Zionism," *Quadrant* 49 (December 2005), p. 21; for a sample of secular, leftist anti-Zionist organizations, see, for example, the statement of purpose of the International Jewish Anti-Zionist Network, http://www.ijsn.net/about_us/purpose/. For the classical anti-Zionist position espoused by such ultra-Orthodox Jewish groups as Neturei Karta, see Rabbi Aharon Cohen, "Anti-Zionism is not Anti-Semitism," *Against Zionism: Jewish Perspectives* (London: The Islamic Human Rights Commission, 2008), http://www.ihrc.org.uk/file/against_zionism_jewish_perspectives.pdf.

26. For a discussion of Jewish powerlessness in history, see David Biale, *Power and Powerlessness in Jewish History* (New York: Schocken Books, 1986); see Emanuele Ottolenghi, "'Paradise Lost': A Review Article of *The Postzionism Debates,* by Laurence Silberstein," *Israel Studies* 8, no. 3 (Summer 2003), pp. 139–50.

27. As Anthony Julius writes in a two-part essay on anti-Zionism, "The anti-Zionist is not just a Jew like other Jews; his dissent from normative Zionist loyalties makes him a better Jew. He restores Judaism's good name; to be a good Jew one has to be an anti-Zionist." See Anthony Julius, "Jewish Anti-Zionism Unravelled, Part One: the Morality of Vanity" in *Z Word* (March 2008), http://www.z-word.com/uploads/assets/documents/zword_Julius_Z4N6s4qT.pdf.

28. See Uri Davis, "Apartheid Israel and the Political Zionist Claim for National Self-Determination" in *Anti-Zionism: Jewish Perspectives* (London: The Islamic Human Rights Commission, 2008), http://www.ihrc.org.uk/attachments/4801_against_zionism_jewish_perspectives.pdf: "I have been an active participant and a vocal opponent to the idea of a Jewish state arguing that a Jewish state is by definition an apartheid state. You can't have a Jewish state that is not an apartheid state," p. 27.

29. See famed historian Eric Hobsbawm's comments on the establishment of Independent Jewish Voices, a British-based group of Jewish anti-Zionist intellectuals who, from the pages of *The Guardian,* launched a new platform in 2007 to challenge what they called the "pro-Israel Jewish establishment": "It is important for non-Jews to know that there are Jews . . . who do not agree with the apparent consensus within the Jewish community that the only good Jew is one who supports Israel." Quoted in Martin Hodgson, "British Jews Break away from 'Pro-Israeli' Board of Deputies," *The Independent* (February 5, 2007), http://www.independent.co.uk/news/uk/this-britain/british-jews-break-away-from-proisraeli-board-of-deputies-435146.html.

30. See Alexei Sayle, "I've got what it takes to lead the PLO: good Jewish looks," *The Independent* (October 3, 2000), http://www.independent.co.uk/opinion/commentators/ive-got-what-it-takes-to-lead-the-plo-jewish-good-looks-637796.html: "I am Jewish, which should make me immune to the charges of anti-Semitism that fanatical Zionists trot out whenever anybody suggests that Israel's constant use of torture and ethnic cleansing might be a teensy bit racist and wrong. I say 'should,' but of course it won't. The Zionists have thought up a good psychobabble condemnation for those Jews like

myself who think that Israel is merely Serbia with yarmulkes and felafel. They call us 'self-haters,' as if our recognition of injustice is somehow a psychological condition. Well, I say better to hate yourself than an entire other people. And it's bollocks anyway."

31. Explaining her support for Independent Jewish Voices, Susie Orbach was quoted as saying that "As a Jew, I feel a particular duty to oppose the injustice that is done to Palestinians. . . . The Israeli government does not speak for me." Quoted in Martin Hodgson, "British Jews Break away from 'Pro-Israeli' Board of Deputies," *The Independent* (February 5, 2007), http://www.independent.co.uk/news/uk/this-britain/british-jews-break-away-from-proisraeli-board-of-deputies-435146.html.

32. As many surveys taken during the Second Intifada have shown, Europeans variously view Israel as "a threat to world peace" (59 percent said so in late 2003, in a EU-sponsored poll: see *Flash Eurobarometer* 151, European Commission, *Iraq and Peace in the World* [November 2003], p. 80); consider Israel as an oppressive an undemocratic regime akin to Apartheid South Africa (see the Anti-Defamation League surveys on European attitudes toward Jews and Israel from 2002, 2004, and 2005, available at www.adl.org); and in more extreme (but by no means marginal) cases, endorse Israel's comparison to Nazi Germany, as a European-wide survey conducted by the Italian daily *Il Corriere della Sera,* in January 2004, conclusively showed (*Il Corriere della Sera,* January 26, 2004).

33. See, for example, Ahmed Samih Khalidi, "A One-State Solution: A Unitary Arab-Jewish Homeland Could Bring Lasting Peace to the Middle East," *The Guardian* (September 29, 2003). See also Michael Tarazi, "Two People, One State," *The New York Times* (October 4, 2004).

34. Adam Shatz, ed., *Prophets' Outcast: A Century of Dissident Jewish Writing about Zionism and Israel* (New York, Nation Books, 2004).

35. Tony Kushner and Alisa Solomon, eds., *Wrestling with Zion: Progressive Jewish-American Responses to the Israel–Palestinian Conflict* (New York: Grove Press, 2003).

36. Jonathan Shainin and Roane Carey, eds., *The Other Israel: Voices of Refusal and Dissent* (New York: New Press, 2002).

37. Michael Neumann, *The Case against Israel* (Petrolia, Calif.: Counterpunch & AK Press, 2005).

38. Alexander Cockburn and Jeffrey St. Clair, eds., *The Politics of Anti-Semitism* (Petrolia, Calif.: Counterpunch Press, 2003).

39. Jews for Justice for Palestinians, "Mission statement," http://www.jfjfp.org.

40. Jerome Segal, *Creating a Palestinian State* (Chicago: Lawrence Hill Books, 1989), p. 5.

41. Barbara Spinelli is the daughter of Italian anti-Fascist politician Altiero Spinelli and the German Jewish intellectual Ursula Hirschman, the sister of economist Albert O. Hirschman.

42. Barbara Spinelli, "Ebraismo senza 'Mea Culpa,'" *La Stampa* (October 28, 2001), p. 1.

43. Michael Neumann, "What Is Antisemitism," in Cockburn and St. Clair, p. 5.

44. Norman Finkelstein, *The Israel–Palestine Conflict: Image and Reality* (London, Verso Books, 2003), p. 4.

45. Michael Kustow and 44 others, "We Renounce Israel Rights," *The Guardian* (August 8, 2002), http://www.guardian.co.uk/theguardian/2002/aug/08/guardianletters4.

46. The letter was originally published on a website called Professors of Conscience, which was closed after the Iraq war ended and no ethnic cleansing occurred. The text of the open letter is still available at http://www.rumormillnews.com/cgi-bin/archive .cgi?read=23500. See Will Youmans, "Pre-empting Transfer" in *Counterpunch* (October 9, 2002), http://www.counterpunch.org/youmans1009.html.

47. The American petition was similarly removed after the end of the Iraq War, but it can still be viewed at http://www.warwithoutend.co.uk/middle-east-and-asia/2002 /12/23/american-academics-join-israeli-colleagues.php. See also Nigel Parry, "800 American Professors Sign Document Warning of Coming Israeli Ethnic Cleansing," *Electronic Intifada* (December 18, 2002), http://electronicintifada.net/content/800-american -professors-sign-document-warning-coming-israeli-ethnic-cleansing/4286.

48. See Avi Shlaim, "Teenagers Who Stand for Honesty, Decency and Sanity," *The Guardian* (March 22, 2004), http://www.guardian.co.uk/world/2004/mar/22/comment ?INTCMP=SRCH.

49. The original boycott letter, published in *The Guardian* on April 6, 2002, was spearheaded by professors Hilary and Steven Rose and is retrievable here: http://www.guardian .co.uk/world/2002/apr/06/israel.guardianletters. For their rationale, see Hilary and Steven Rose, "The Choice Is to Do Nothing or Begin to Bring about Change," *The Guardian* (July 15, 2002), http://www.guardian.co.uk/world/2002/jul/15/comment.stevenrose; Steven Rose, "If Not Boycott, What?" *The Guardian* (May 24, 2006), http://www.guardian .co.uk/commentisfree/2006/may/24/ifnotboycottwhat.

50. Steven Rose, "Why Pick on Israel? Because Its Actions Are Wrong," *The Independent*, June 4, 2007, http://www.independent.co.uk/opinion/commentators/steven-rose -why-pick-on-israel-because-its-actions-are-wrong-451648.html.

51. Gerald Kaufman, "The Case for Sanctions against Israel," *The Guardian* (July 12, 2004): "That a task is difficult does not mean that it should not be attempted. There is no point in seeking to change Israeli policy by appealing to its government's better nature, since such a nature does not exist. Sanctions and an arms ban must be our objective."

52. "Israel Can Halt This Now," *The Guardian* (June 12, 2003).

53. Gamal Nkrumah, "A Matter of Morality," interview with South African Minister for Water, Ronnie Kasrils, *Al-Ahram Weekly*, English version (February 13–19, 2003), issue no. 625.

54. Shamai K. Leibowitz, "In Defense of Divestment," *Against the Current* 114 (January–February 2005), http://www.solidarity-us.org/node/339. Discussing his personal appearance at a debate to support a divestment resolution in Somerville, in November 2004, Leibowitz wrote that "Dozens of Jews were among the many supporters of the divestment resolution who gathered in the Somerville City Hall on Monday, November 8. I, and several others, spoke in favor of this resolution, saying that it is precisely because we are Jews and because we truly care about Israel that we are asking the City of Somerville to pass this resolution."

55. Anthony Lippman, "How I Became a Jew," *The Spectator* (January 22, 2005).

56. Several reviewers wrote negatively about Rose's book; for a reviewer sympathetic to her politics but unforgiving of her scholarly shortcomings, see Simon Louvish, "How

Words Went to War," *The Independent* (June 10, 2005), http://www.independent.co.uk/arts-entertainment/books/reviews/the-question-of-zion-by-jacqueline-rose-752498.html; see also the exchange between Shalom Lappin and Jacqueline Rose in the online journal *Democratiya* (now moved to *Dissent Magazine*): Shalom Lappin, "The Question of Zion," *Democratiya* 6 (Autumn 2006), pp. 11–36, http://www.dissentmagazine.org/democratiya/article_pdfs/d71appin.pdf; Jacqueline Rose, "The Question of Zion: A Reply to Shalom Lappin," *Democratiya* 7 (Winter 2006), pp. 94–115, http://www.dissentmagazine.org/democratiya/article_pdfs/d7rose.pdf; and Shalom Lappin: "The Question of Zion: A Rejoinder to Rose," *Democratiya* 7 (Winter 2006), pp. 116–37, http://www.dissentmagazine.org/democratiya/article_pdfs/d71appin.pdf.

57. Jacqueline Rose, *The Question of Zion* (Princeton, N.J.: Princeton University Press, 2005), p. xii.

58. Ibid., p. 155.

59. Neumann, *The Case against Israel,* p. 181.

60. Ibid., p. 190.

61. Shlaim confirmed his secular background in an interview with Meron Rapoport, which appeared in Israel's *Ha'aretz* to accompany the release of Shlaim's *Iron Wall* to the Israeli market: "Shlaim describes a home in which Judaism was not an important component of his parents' identity. 'Judaism was ritual,' he says. 'My parents used to attend the synagogue once a year, at home we spoke Judeo-Arabic, we listened to Arabic music.' See Meron Rapoport, "No Peaceful Solution," *Ha'aretz* (August 11, 2005).

62. Avi Shlaim, "Is Zionism Today the Real Enemy of the Jews? Yes," *The International Herald Tribune* (February 4, 2005), p. 6.

63. Although, in other circumstances, Shlaim has more openly expressed shame and regret at Israel's founding. See for example, Avi Shlaim, "The New History and the Nakba," London workshop, November 8, 2003 (courtesy of the author): "I feel doubly guilty towards the Pals. As an Englishman, I am ashamed of my adopted country's astonishing record of duplicity and betrayal going all the way back to the Balfour Declaration. As an Israeli, I am burdened by a heavy sense of guilt for the monumental injustice and never-ending suffering that my people have inflicted on the Pals since the beginning of this conflict over 100 years ago."

64. Haim Bresheeth, "Israel's Apartheid," *Prospect Magazine* (July 28, 2007), http://www.prospectmagazine.co.uk/2007/07/israelsapartheid/.

65. "Israel Makes Pianist Feel 'Ashamed of Being a Jew'" *The Vancouver Province* (January 9, 2009), http://www.canada.com/theprovince/news/story.html?id=2f5a79fb-2f23-49bb-a038-6afb7d78cd45.

66. Deborah Maccoby's letter to the editor, *The New Statesman* July 5, 2004.

67. Eva Kohner, letter to the editor, "Ashamed to Be Jewish," *The Daily Telegraph* (April 4, 2002), http://www.telegraph.co.uk/comment/letters/3574934/Ashamed-to-be-Jewish.html.

68. Max Hastings, "A Grotesque Choice," *The Guardian* (March 11, 2004).

69. Max Hastings, "Israel Can No Longer Rely on the Support of Europe's Jews," *The Guardian* June 20, 2006.

70. Sergio Romano, *Lettera a un amico ebreo* (Milan: TEA, 2004), pp. 16–17.

71. Available at http://www.carta.org/agenzia/palestina/0204031etteraAperta.htm, February 13, 2003.

72. Their actions are referenced in the previously cited article by Avi Shlaim, "Teenagers Who Stand for Honesty, Decency and Sanity."

73. Shlomi Segall, "Why I Won't Serve Sharon," *The Guardian* (July 5, 2002).

74. The Intelligence Squared panel is available here: http://www.intelligencesquared .com/events/zionism-today-is-the-real-enemy-of-the-jews2; the panelists supporting the motion were Amira Hass, Jacqueline Rose, and Avi Shlaim; those opposing it were Shlomo Ben Ami, Raphael Israeli, and Melanie Phillips. The Cambridge Union event had Brian Klug, Daphna Baram, and Richard Kuper second the motion and Jeremy Brier, Daniel Shek, and Ned Temko opposing it; see Ben White, "This House Believes That Zionism Is a Danger to the Jewish People," *Electronic Intifada* (February 20, 2006), http:// electronicintifada.net/content/house-believes-zionism-danger-jewish-people/5875.

75. Shlomo Sand, *The Invention of the Jewish People* (London, Verso Books, 2009).

76. The event can be watched here: http://versouk.wordpress.com/2009/11/13/avi-shlaim -in-conversation-with-shlomo-sand-few-modern-conflicts-are-as-attached-to-history -as-that-of-israel-and-palestine-avi-shlaim-professor-of-int/.

77. See, for example, Ilan Zvi Baron, "A Reluctant Zionist," *Open Democracy* (December 17, 2010): "The innocence of Zionism led to not-so-innocent ethnically determined labour and land policies in Palestine, and ultimately to a civil war, and then the first of (too) many Arab-Israeli wars. Zionists may have been innocent, but Zionism certainly was not," http://www.opendemocracy.net/dr-ilan-zvi-baron/reluctant-zionist.

78. Laurence J. Silberstein, *The Postzionism Debates: Knowledge and Power in Israeli Culture,* (New York: Routledge, 1999), p. 147.

79. See, for example, John Pilger, "Ethnic Cleansing and the Establishment of Israel," *The New Statesman* (June 19, 2002): "In challenging the Zionist version of Israel's past, Ilan Pappe is one of Israel's 'new historians,' a distinguished and courageous critic."

80. Ellis, p. 120.

81. Anatol Lieven, *America Right or Wrong* (London: Harper Collins, 2004), p. 192.

82. Ellis, p. 120.

83. Tony Judt, "Toni," *NYR Blog—The New York Review of Books* (April 19, 2010), http://www.nybooks.com/blogs/nyrblog/2010/apr/19/toni/.

84. Eric Hobsbawm, *Nations and Nationalism since 1780: Programme, Myth, Reality* (Cambridge: Cambridge University Press, 1990), p. 8.

85. Eric Hobsbawm, "Benefits of Diaspora," *The London Review of Books* (October 20, 2005).

86. Bertell Olman, "A letter of resignation from the Jewish people" *Tikkun Magazine,* 20 (1): 10, January/February 2005.

87. Romano, p. 100.

88. Ibid., p. 108.

89. Ibid., p. 110.

90. This is how Isaac Deutscher defines the non-Jewish Jew in his famous essay that goes by the same title: "They had in themselves something of the quintessence of Jewish life and of the Jewish intellect. They were *a priori* exceptional in that as Jews they

dwelt on the borderlines of various civilizations, religions, and national cultures. They were born and brought up on the borderlines of various epochs. Their mind matured where the most diverse cultural influences crossed and fertilized each other. They lived on the margins or in the nooks and crannies of their respective nations. Each of them was in society and yet not in it, of it and yet not of it. It was this that enabled them to rise in thought above their societies, above their nations, above their times and generations and to strike out mentally into wide new horizons and into the future." See Isaac Deutscher, "The non-Jewish Jew," in Adam Shatz, ed., *Prophets Outcast* (New York: Nation Books, 2004), p. 5.

91. Dennis Praeger and Joseph Telushkin, *Why the Jews?* (New York: Touchstone Books, 2003), p. 42.

92. Guido Ceronetti, "Lanterna Rossa," *La Stampa* (April 26, 2004).

93. Justin Keating, "The Zionist State Has No Right to Exist," *The Dubliner* (November 2005), http://www.irishsalem.com/individuals/Politicians%20and%20Others/justin-keating/justinkeating-thezioniststate-nov05.php.

94. "Justin Keating Responds," *The Dubliner* (December 2005). The article is no longer available. *The Dubliner* still provides its own version of the controversy here: http://www.thedubliner.ie/the_dubliner_magazine/2007/04/justin_keating.html.

95. Benny Morris, "The New Historiography: Israel Confronts Its Past," *Tikkun* (November/December 1988), 21a.

96. Avi Shlaim, "The Debate about 1948," in *International Journal of Middle East Studies* 27 (1995), p. 292.

97. Ibid.

98. Avi Shlaim, "The War of the Israeli Historians," lecture delivered at Georgetown University, December 1, 2003 (courtesy of the author). Speaking of his opponents, Shlaim says, "[They] put so much store by Israel's claim to moral rectitude that they cannot face up to the evidence of cynical Israeli double-dealings or brutal dispersal and dispossession of the Palestinians. It is an axiom of their narrative that Israel is the innocent victim. Not content with the thirty pieces of silver, these people insist on retaining for Israel the crown of thorns."

99. http://www.newadvent.org/cathen/11312a.htm#VII.

100. It is worth, here, to quote Marc H. Ellis again, at length: "The inclusion of Palestinians in the Jewish vision of the future, in the deep sense that is is no longer possible to be Jewish without living among, with and in solidarity with Palestinians, is one definitive break point between Progressive Jews and Jews of Conscience. Another break is each group's dating when Jews, the Jewish community and the state of Israel went wrong: Progressive Jews citing the occupation and settler movement after the 1967 War as the turning point, thus a return to the 1967 borders more or less solves the problem with Palestinians and the internal troubles within the Jewish community; Jews of Conscience cite the 1948 War, thus the initial occupation and settlements of what became the state of Israel as the place of wrong that devastated Palestinians and the Jewish witness in the world. Here, in the interaction between Palestinians then and now, the Palestinian voice, in its contested understandings, needs to be heard, absorbed and thought through by Jews of all persuasions and taken to heart as a deep and biding

indictment of Jewish particularity as it has been expressed in the post-Holocaust period. The voice heard, action must be initiated, as it has been on some fronts. This action includes rewriting the narrative of the history of the state of Israel, with its effects on Palestinians, as well as the lifting up of Jewish voices who then and now point to a radically different encounter in Israel/Palestine." Marc H. Ellis, "On Jewish Particularity and Anti-Semitism: Notes from a Jewish Theology of Liberation," p. 120.

101. For more on the parallels between Tony Judt's call for Israel's conversion and Christian antisemitism, see Benjamin Balint, "Future Imperfect: Tony Judt Blushes for the Jewish State," in Edward Alexander and Paul Bogdanor, eds., *The Jewish Divide over Israel* (New Brunswick, N.J.: Transactions Books, 2006), pp. 65–77.

102. Bernard Avishai, "Post-Zionist Israel," *The American Prospect* 11, no. 12 (May 8, 2000), p. 46.

103. Bernard Avishai, "Saving Israel from Itself: A Secular Future for the Jewish State," *Harper's Magazine* (January 2005), http://www.harpers.org/archive/2005/01/0080361.

104. Tony Judt, "Israel, The Alternative," in *The New York Review of Books* 50, no. 16 (October 23, 2003).

105. Tony Judt, *A Grand Illusion? An Essay on Europe* (New York: Hill and Wang, 1996).

106. Tony Judt, "The Past Is Another Country: Myth and Memory in Postwar Europe," in István Deák, Jan T. Gross, and Tony Judt, eds., *The Politics of Retribution in Europe* (Princeton, N.J.: Princeton University Press, 2000), p. 317.

17 Holocaust Denial and the Image of the Jew, or: "They Boycott Auschwitz as an Israeli Product"

Dina Porat

THE IMAGE OF THE Jew depicted by Holocaust deniers since the Second World War raises numerous issues, including these two: (1) can this image change once circumstances themselves change? And (2), if so—is the denial of the Holocaust the deniers' final goal, or is it the perpetuation of a certain, always negative image of the Jew?

Hard-core Holocaust denial, which reached its heyday in the 1980s and the 1990s, created a certain image of the "Jew," as Brian Klug put it when he tried to define the distinction between Jews and a "Jew."[1] He argued that antisemitism "is best defined not by an attitude toward Jews but by a definition of a 'Jew,'" and that antisemitism is "the process of turning Jews into a 'Jew.'" His distinction is equally relevant to both the "Jew" in the singular and "Jews" in the plural, because in both cases the quotation marks turn the Jew/Jews into an idea, a symbol, a stereotype, in which each individual is meant to represent his people at large as a collectivity, and both cease to be recognized as part of reality. The process of turning individuals and a people into "Jew/Jews" is at the heart of the following discussion.

This stereotypical image created by Holocaust deniers derived from older images that developed in the centuries prior to the Holocaust, yet those who advance the very idea of denial take the former images much further, and develop a picture of the most abominable type: for if the story of the Holocaust, as claimed and disseminated by the Jewish people, never in fact happened, then this fiction obviously points to a people with a rare ability to invent unheard-of horror stories, that only a sick mind could produce; a people equipped with outstanding skills of self-organization and mobilization capabilities that help spread these lies through the use of all the public media, which they anyhow control, and thereby convince the world that they are truth incarnated; a powerful egoist people capable of brazen blackmailing in order to secure financial and moral gains.

In every period during the long history of antisemitism, different character traits alleged to belong to Jews were at the forefront of verbal and visual portrayals. The characteristics most fostered in modern times are a Jewish craving for power and the wish to dominate the world. The idea that the grip acquired by Jews over world public opinion through the use of their story of the Holocaust was in fact called by some as "proof" of the authenticity of *The Protocols of the Elders of Zion;* this supposition has actually been raised by Holocaust deniers themselves, such as by Germar Rudolf.[2] However, the myth of Jewish power and world control was shattered by the realities of the Holocaust, whose destructive results became possible precisely because the Jewish people at that time were totally helpless and defenseless. Therefore, if one wants, or rather has the urge, to maintain the myth of Jewish power and world control, which serves as the foundation of the leading antisemitic views and convictions in modern times, one is compelled to deny the Holocaust. Denying, distorting, and especially inverting have been techniques of antisemitism since antiquity, and have aimed at creating images of Jews that are the opposite of what is found in reality. One may say that the essence of antisemitism has always been the discrepancy between such images of the "Jew" and his/her/their real abilities and character traits.[3] This discrepancy reached a peak in the wake of the Holocaust.

Since the year 2000, hard-core denial has somewhat weakened, thanks to a number of events and responses: David Irving's trial; the visits of two Popes—John Paul II and Bendictus XVI—to Yad Vashem; the Stockholm Forum; and International Holocaust Memorial Day established by the United Nations (UN), followed by UNESCO.[4] Instead, and perhaps as a result of this weakening, the last decade has evinced the flourishing of new terms defining attitudes toward the Holocaust and the use of its memory. They include Holocaust trivialization, minimization, and relativization alongside Holocaust skepticism and soft-core denial, as well as terms relating to new types of deniers themselves, such as demi- or semi-deniers, and moderate deniers.

Another notable development of the last decade is the activity of the Task Force for International Cooperation on Holocaust Education, Remembrance, and Research, established in the wake of the Stockholm Forum in 2000 and now numbering thirty-four countries. This organization promotes the launching or enhancing of Holocaust education (the teaching of its history, consequences, and implications) in its member states, by allocating budgets, especially for the training of teachers.

In light of these developments, one might ask if the image of the "Jew," and the Jewish State populated by "Jews" has changed, weakened, or become more moderate. In pursuing answers, one should bear in mind that Holocaust denial has been transferred during the last decade from the far right to the agenda of leftists and Islamists, and thus has moved from the former theoretical sphere to the political one. Perhaps, while becoming in some ways more moderate, Holocaust denial has taken the shape of mainly "denying the meaning and the consequences of the Holocaust rather than necessarily denying the facts of the Holocaust itself."[5]

Denying, distorting, and inverting the Holocaust, its meaning, and its consequences reflect numerous goals, among which the following stand out:

(1) The wish to abolish the martyr status claimed by the Jews and bestow it on another group. Even if church teachings have lost much of their former influence, basic Christian ideas regarding suffering and salvation are deeply embedded in the Western world, first and foremost in its culture—especially in music, figurative art, and drama, dating from the early medieval era in Europe, where the Holocaust occurred. According to these ideas, the life and death of Jesus are proof that he who suffers brings salvation. The Christian duty is to identify with the supreme sufferer, Jesus Christ. Since Jews have foresworn such identification, martyrdom can certainly not be attributed to them, as they rejected the salvation offered by Jesus long ago. Therefore, from a theological point of view, some other group must embody the role of the martyr. Once this group has been politically designated, the theological and the political aspects of martyrdom merge together. During recent decades, caricatures and other illustrations representing Palestinian suffering foreground children nailed to crosses and dripping blood to signify a modern continua-

tion of the crucifixion. Such depictions draw on the history of medieval blood libels and update them to present Israelis as menacing Orthodox Jews. The images resemble those found either in *Der Stürmer* or in Mel Gibson's 2004 film *The Passion of the Christ*.[6]

(2) The second goal, related to the first, is to cancel the notion of the Holocaust's uniqueness. This notion is allegedly fostered by egocentric Jews who constantly claim to be the sole bearers of ultimate victimhood and do not recognize the sufferings of others; moreover, such Jews are said to inflict suffering on "the victims of the victims," as Orientalist Edward Said expressed it.[7] Within this scheme, he who inflicts suffering must become an anti-Christ, equated in the modern world with Nazis, the ultimate symbol of modern evil. The Jews were killed during the Holocaust by Christians, but Christians cannot, a priori, be the anti-Christ, so it is up to the Jews to go on fulfilling that role in this twisted morality play. "If the European memory of the Holocaust recognizes the Jews only as victims, then the moment they cease being victims [such as is the case since the establishment of the State of Israel] they become the guilty party," claims the French Jewish scholar Shmuel Trigano,[8] and their status outside the Holocaust context, without the victim label, is inevitably identified with that of the Nazis. They are either the Chosen People or the cursed one. "The ancient denouncement of the Jew, because of his origin, uniqueness, exclusiveness, his national egoism, his being a closed cast," writes the French Jewish philosopher Alain Finkelkraut, "has been revived due to the trauma caused by Nazism, and is expressed in totally modern ways . . . [but it still] originates in the Gospel of Paul or its recycling."[9]

(3) The second goal leads to the third, which is the wish to cancel, or at least abate, the allegedly greedy Jewish claim for the return of property looted by Nazi Germany during the Second World War. This claim seems now even greedier than before, given the recent world economic crisis (exacerbated by the Bernard Madoff affair). It raises again the old image of the rich parasitic Jew, who owned so much that perhaps the Germans and others who plundered him did not commit such a terrible crime. When historian Gitta Sereni asked Franz Stangl, commander of Treblinka, in his prison cell in Düsseldorf, what in fact the Jews were killed for, his spontaneous answer was "They wanted the Jews' money," as if the question were naïve and out of place.[10] One can easily notice the proximity in time

between the Prague Conference convened in June 2009 in order to deal with the necessity to reclaim looted Jewish property, especially works of art, and the Prague Declaration (issued in June 2008 and ratified by the European Parliament in July 2009) that makes the counterclaim: everyone suffered during the Second World War (and the East European countries later had an additional share of suffering at the hands of the Soviet regime); therefore, every individual and every nation is equally entitled to compensation for and commemoration of their suffering.[11]

The Prague Declaration reflects the current *Zeitgeist*, a post-heroic post-modern atmosphere in which everyone is equally entitled to a narrative of suffering, and therefore to equal rights and compensation for that suffering. In this cultural context, suffering and victimhood, both personal and collective, have become an asset of pride. Being a victim means having a moral status, a claim for being just, virtuous, and politically correct, to quote Alain Finkelkraut, who has said that "the Jews have the good fortune to be the kings of misfortune."[12] Another author calls Jews "the stars of sorrow,"[13] to cite one more example among many. We are witnessing a "competition of victimhood," says Bernard-Henri Lévy, one that has turned society into a compilation of grievances.[14] And if so, needless to say, many groups that claim victimhood status use the term *Holocaust* to describe their plight and will not settle for a milder term or description. "*Dueños del dolor, dueños del mundo,*" was the title of an anti-Jewish article in a Venezuelan newspaper: "They who own the pain own the world."[15] So much so, that Elie Wiesel suggested that Jews stop using the term *Holocaust* altogether and find themselves another word.[16] In the 1993 UN Human Rights conference convened in Vienna, no precise decision could be taken at the closing plenary because some dozens of groups from all over the globe claimed to be victimized, and in the 2001 Durban I UN conference it took a difficult struggle to reverse the demand to rewrite *Holocaust* as *holocausts*.[17]

(4) The fourth wish is inevitable in light of the former ones: to discredit acts of commemoration by the Jewish people that create and perpetuate feelings of guilt, of eternal debt, and of an incriminating memory among their fellow nations, especially the Europeans, by documenting, recording, and publishing Nazi atrocities through every means of communication as well as in museums and monuments. Such acts of commemoration serve as a constant reminder of who took part in the acts of

murder and plundering. In order to undermine the validity of the Jewish commemoration activities, and to get rid of these feelings of guilt, the blame is inverted and an opposite claim is made, namely, that the Jews are a nation whose own cruelty, especially toward children, has been genetically coded since biblical times. The Gospel of Mathew begins with King Herod killing all children under the age of two, and the medieval blood libel, which similarly accuses Jews of child murder, has already been mentioned. These ideas have been vociferously pronounced recently on both sides of the ocean, by the Norwegian author Jostein Gaarder (Judaism is "an archaic and war-like religion"), by the American television commentator Bill Moyers (Israeli violence is a consequence of "genetic encoding"),[18] and also by some political figures.

It is becoming increasingly clear that the Holocaust, which was to have been a source of empathy and compassion for the Jews, more and more enhances a negative image of the "Jew" and of the Jewish State and fosters post-Holocaust antisemitism. The pre-Holocaust image of the Jew as an all-powerful, avaricious manipulator of power was a crucial motive for the mass murder of European Jewry. Nowadays, in the post-Holocaust era the Jew is being portrayed in a no less repulsive way, indicating that the changes in social and political circumstances after the Holocaust have become a new source of antisemitism. Holocaust education has also not yet proved itself to be a barrier against antisemitism, for youngsters, whose ignorance is coupled by naiveté, often raise such questions as these: Why the Jews? Why all the Jews? What's wrong with them? Was their murder really initiated without any logical reason, or other good motive? Six million—how indeed did so many Jews, who do not seem to be at all helpless today, allow this to be done to them?[19]

The second question of this paper concerns the aim of present-day Holocaust deniers. Is it indeed denial in and of itself, in various forms and degrees, that they want to achieve, or is it actually the twisting and inversion of the image of the Jew, so that it might continue to fulfill the task it has always fulfilled: to serve as the dark negative counter-mirror of one's own positive image, regardless of reality?

With respect to contradicting images, it is helpful to examine a number of instances in which they clash. First, let us take a look at the self-image of Jews, on the one hand, and those of deniers and human rights activists, on the other, with regard to legislation and definitions of Holocaust denial and antisemitism.

A number of countries—but, to date, no more than fifteen—have enacted laws and other forms of legislation against Holocaust denial, mostly since the 1990s. Denial could have been included under the umbrella of freedom of speech because the deniers do not resort to physical violence. Rather, deniers express their opinion, so that one may say there is an "absence of a criminal motive" in their activities, as the legal term goes. Yet denial of the Holocaust is punishable outside the United States and Canada, where freedom of speech has gained sanctity, precisely because of the image of the Jew it creates. This image constitutes incitement against a whole group of people, and in a way that might provoke violence against them. Moreover, denial intentionally falsifies the facts by intentionally misusing the documentation, as established in the judges' verdict in Holocaust denier David Irving's trial in London in 2001. In this respect, it might be understood as a form of violence against truth itself or at least as an intentional subversion or corruption of the historical record.

Still, the question of whether historical truth should be assessed in court is seriously debated. French philosopher François Bédarida argues that

> it is not by law that one establishes the validity of a historical work. As much as it is legitimate to prosecute incitement to racial hatred, it seems to me stupid and counter productive to forbid a historical lie. The condemnation of revisionism as a gigantic intellectual swindle by the international scientific community is sufficient . . . on condition that the media refrains from providing too big a platform for the holders of counter-truths.[20]

Since early 2005, a working definition of antisemitism, agreed upon by the twenty-seven EU countries, states clearly that "denying the fact, scope, mechanisms (e.g., gas chambers) or intentionality of the genocide of the Jewish people at the hands of National Socialist Germany and its supporters and accomplices during WWII (the Holocaust), [and that] accusing the Jews as a people, or Israel as a state, of inventing or exaggerating the Holocaust" are considered acts of antisemitism. A more recent working definition of Holocaust denial, reached by the ITF member states in 2010, which draws on the EU definition, also defines denial as a form of antisemitism.[21] Antisemitism is by now punishable by laws and other forms of regulations in some twenty countries.

Opinions such as Bédarida's notwithstanding, such legislation and definitions can be regarded as a notable international achievement. However, some will interpret them as resulting from Jewish behind-the-scenes pressure, as one more manifestation of Jewish power. Thus, this very achievement can be used to confirm, still again, the image of a powerful, self-aggrandizing group that cares exclusively about itself, is steeped in its sorrowful past while ignoring the sufferings of others, and brings to trial and even jail courageous individuals who are out to expose what they consider to be the truth and do not shy away from confronting the powerful and the influential. Deniers present themselves as researchers adhering to a basic principle of historical research: they doubt and scrutinize the written word, namely the documents and the testimonies, and they do not readily accept the conventional and the agreed upon. Their skeptical attitude is presumed to be part and parcel of freedom of speech, the core of democratic society. Today they call themselves revisionists, not deniers, because revisionism of history is a main trend of contemporary historiography. They claim that those who oppose open or free scientific criticism belong to the narrow-minded dark forces that shun enlightenment. Human rights activity now is largely about diversity, about universal values, not particular ones. NGO idealists have turned tolerance into a religion and equal rights almost into a cult. In such a context, Jews find themselves facing an ironic twist: they, who have always hoisted the flag of universalism and universal human rights, are depicted in the post-Holocaust period as fostering a backward particularity that goes against many of the current convictions of people who regard themselves as progressive.

The issue of the definition of antisemitism and the legislation against it and against Holocaust denial brings us to a second meeting point between counter mirror images, that of Jews vis-à-vis the liberal European intellectual left, and not only the radical left. The eminent Yad Vashem scholar Israel Gutman argues that during the 1940s, worldwide public opinion regarded antisemitism as the major underlying cause for the Holocaust. However, in the post-Holocaust period the international community could not internalize the implications of a crime of such colossal scale. Thus, a new definition of antisemitism that was called for after the fall of Nazism, and even the very mentioning of antisemitism, were evaded in postwar declarations, treaties, and in other major texts.[22] A striking example is Eleanor Roosevelt's introduction to the first English edition of Anne Frank's *Diary*. Roosevelt, who took a central part in the formulation of the 1948 Universal Declaration of Human Rights, did not mention the terms *antisemitism, Germans,* or *Nazis.* at all, nor did she mention the fact that Anne was Jewish, a perilous status that forced her to spend two years in hiding![23]

Evading mention of the term *antisemitism,* Gutman continues, makes it possible to ignore it as a cause for the Holocaust, and also to blame others for it, first and foremost the Jews themselves, especially the Zionists. The following step was to equate the Zionists with the Nazis and thus to try to do away with the heavy cloud of guilt that has hovered over Europe since 1945. The Left in particular needs this equation to maintain its own sense of self-righteousness. It is not surprising, then, to note that it was the Soviet Union that first came up with this equation after the war, because the Left in Germany, first and foremost the Communist Party, did not have the stamina, courage, and unity to stop the Nazi Party from coming to power before 1933 and thus did not act to prevent the Holocaust. Moreover, it was the Soviet Union that signed the notorious August 1939 Molotov–Ribbentrop Pact, which paved the way for the bloody war during which it became possible to carry out large-scale murder, and not only of Jews. Millions of Soviet citizens and soldiers perished, and the postwar Soviet leaders, who were reluctant to shoulder the heavy responsibility for the pact and for ignoring the signs of an impending German invasion in June 1941, needed a culprit. Therefore, using as always the old tactic of inversion, it was the Soviet Union, joined by extreme leftists in the West, that first accused the Zionist movement of collaborating with the Nazis.[24] It was also the Soviet Union that mustered its followers among UN members to vote for the infamous 1975 decision, according to which Zionism was equated with racism. The racist ideology, needless to say, was the fundamental tenet of the Nazi party and of its aspirations to reorganize the world accordingly.

By equating Israelis and Jews with the Nazis—the most extreme of the rightist movements—today's Left establishes itself at the opposite pole, the reverse image: its followers are to see themselves as righteous and virtuous, an image the Left cannot do without.[25] Thus cruelty, in the forms of contemporary fascism, colonialism, capitalism, and racism is allegedly the true essence of today's Zionist, leaving little doubt that he, the Zionist, and his brother the Jew, could have cooperated with the Nazis, their parallels, during the Holocaust. Therefore, it is from the Left side of the political map, not only from the Arab-Muslim world, that the call for the abolishment of the State of Israel is heard. And since the abolishment of a state, moreover, one established by the UN and ever since a full member of that body, is in itself a colossal crime, unprecedented so far, an accusation of an equally unheard-of colossal crime is required in order to justify it.[26]

These extreme equations, accusations, and comparisons sometimes exploit specifically designated commemoration dates in the Israeli–Jewish calendar as proof of the alleged Zionism–Holocaust connection, especially when the circumstances that led to choosing these dates are forgotten, unknown, or deliberately disregarded. Indeed, Holocaust Memorial Day is commemorated shortly after Passover (in the Hebrew month of Nissan), and a week later, on the 5th of Iyar, there follows Israel's Independence Day. This sequence of dates could be construed to show that Israel's Independence Day is closely related to Holocaust Memorial Day because the Holocaust has served Zionism in order to build the Jewish State. Unfortunately, every Israeli leader and speaker on Holocaust Memorial Days hails the fact that the now thriving state "was born out of the ashes" and is a sweet revenge on Nazi Germany.

Attributing this sequence of dates to a deliberate decision by Israeli authorities in order to form a link between these two events is a grave historical mistake for a number of reasons. The Warsaw Ghetto uprising started on Passover eve, April 19, 1943, because the German SS command wished to present the destruction of the ghetto as a birthday gift to Hitler, who was born on the 20th of April. This intention was not fulfilled because the uprising went on for a few weeks. After liberation, survivors in displaced persons' camps wanted to institute a Holocaust Memorial Day that would be connected to the heroism of Warsaw Ghetto uprising, and since Passover eve itself was out of the question for religious reasons, another date had to be found. In 1959, after innumerable debates and controversies that lasted almost a decade, the date of the 27th of Nissan was chosen. It comes right after the end of the holiday and is a date on which the fighting in the ghetto was exceptionally successful. In the meantime, the State of Israel was born on the 5th of Iyar, 1948, so that there is actually only an incidental connection between the two dates.

Moreover, the Holocaust did not found the State: modern Zionism established its first settlement in 1860 and, over the years, built a thriving self-governing community. Had there not been a 600,000-strong Yi-shuv (the Zionist Jewish entity that resided in pre-State Israel) the 360,000 survivors would not have found a shelter. And the UN November 1947 partition resolution, voting for the establishment of a Jewish State, came indeed after the Holocaust but not as its direct result. Political considerations, such as the Soviet interest in replacing Britain in the Middle East and in preventing American future influence in the area, were much more instrumental than belated empathy.[27]

Despite such solid historical arguments, the more the Holocaust becomes an integral part of Israel's public life, the more this alleged Holocaust–State connection is proclaimed, without a recognition that it plays into the hands of anti-Israeli Holocaust deniers, such as those in the Iranian high echelons, who keep using their "no Holocaust—no State" mantra. They allege that there would be no justification for the Jewish state if not for the Holocaust, which even Israelis acknowledge as the moral basis for their state. These claims serve as yet further proof that the Holocaust is a politically inspired invention used as an instrument in Jewish-Zionist hands in order to extort national gains.

A third and final meeting point between counter mirror images concerns intergenerational relations and postwar national self-images. Second- and third-generation descendants of Nazi and pro-Nazi perpetrators and collaborators understandably welcome any idea or terms that minimize the Holocaust, because such notions assuage tensions within families and communities. The image of their predecessors is thus transformed from cruel murderers and torturers to respectable law-abiding citizens who had to do their share within the framework of their respective regimes during a terrible war and under circumstances beyond their control.[28]

Postwar national self-images, especially in European countries that were Nazi Germany's allies or under its occupation, are seriously challenged by the history and the memory of the Holocaust. Coming to grips with past realities entails a public acknowledgment, linked to educational efforts on a broad scale, of each country's share in the plight of its local Jewish citizens and in its collaboration with Nazi Germany. Such efforts are difficult, for they pinpoint sectors and individuals as the culprits. Seen in these terms, the memory of the Holocaust can be wrenching. It is an obstacle on the road to national reconciliation, complained the French president François Mitterrand, when survivor Serge Klarsfeld protested against putting a wreath of flowers on Marshall Philippe Petain's grave. It was his duty, said Mitterand, "to try to appease the eternal civil wars between the French."[29] The problem is more acute in Eastern Europe, where leaders and parties that had collaborated with the Germans are hailed as anti-communist heroes in today's post-communist era. They are reburied in state funerals and their newly placed statues sometimes adorn the main squares. No wonder, then, that much of the material that denies or minimizes the Holocaust in Eastern Europe and the extensive part taken by the locals in its various stages is being published by *landsmanschaften* members who immigrated mainly to the Americas. Their wish is to maintain a positive image of their fatherlands, for themselves, for their compatriots, and for posterity. As anti-communists, many of them become right-wingers and supporters of the European Right that has recently been gaining strength, paving its way to power by anti-immigration racist arguments, and by traditional antisemitism that is rejustified once the Holocaust may be presented as a Jewish lie, or at least as a gross exaggeration.[30]

* * *

"How do I know that the Holocaust never occurred? I know it for sure because Pope Pius XII did not do or say anything about it. Had such a terrible crime happened, He, who knows everything, would have been the first to know. Had he known, He, who mercifully follows in the footsteps of the Christ, would have immediately acted against the murder of the innocent by all the means at his disposal."[31] This conviction, so simply and forcefully expressed by a devout Christian Holocaust denier, epitomizes the main thrust of our argument: acknowledging and admitting the realities of the Holocaust shatters one's world view, one's positive self-image, one's general well-being, individually as well as collectively. To face it and to come to grips with the fully detailed picture of the past is a difficult demand, because it requires thorough self-scrutiny of past and present values and of one's course of action. Extreme rightists and leftists, liberal left wingers, Catholics and other Christians, second- and third-generation perpetrators, followers of former collaborators, leaders and educators trying to strengthen national identity—all wish to maintain positive self-images, which are being threatened by the memory of the Holocaust. The simple way to feel at ease with one's past and present is therefore to perpetuate the image of the "Jew" as it has always been seen: negatively. To turn the world upside down by acknowledging the Jews as victims and the rest of the world as perpetrators, collaborators, and bystanders is simply out of the question.

This is why Holocaust denial, whether hard core or in the form of minimization, trivialization, skepticism, and so on, is not the deniers' principal goal. The image of the "Jew" depicted by all sorts of deniers as a figure to be scorned, distrusted, derided, and worse, is not a side effect of the denial but rather its target. It enables the denier, individually and collectively, to live in peace with himself and keep his pre-Holocaust world intact. Therefore, whether the Holocaust is being denied outright or in more subtle or oblique ways, the image of the "Jew" does not change. Neither does the image of the Jewish State endowed with Jewish attributes. If the Holocaust did happen, and the Jewish State was built on account of the suffering of others, then the Jews are much like the Nazis. If it did not happen, and it is all a sick Jewish invention, then antisemitism and anti-Zionism are legitimate. Even if it happened in a milder way, it still has given Jews an excuse for indulging self-centered pretensions of ultimate victimhood.

Holocaust denial in its multifaceted forms is rooted in theological, political, economic, and social realities of the postwar period. The battle for the memory of the Holocaust is a struggle for historical ownership and for the projection of respectable images. It is the axis of a prominent international issue, of which the Middle East is but a part, for it has much deeper layers than seen on the surface. As such, Holocaust denial has a future, as Alain Finkelkraut put it in a deeply pessimistic title, *L'avenir d'une negation—Reflexion sur la question du genocide:*[32] The Future of a Negation, which will involve us for a long time in difficult reflections about the Question of Genocide.

NOTES

The subtitle of this chapter, "They Boycott Auschwitz as an Israeli Product," is quoted from words stated by Alain Finkielkraut, Seventh International Conference on Holocaust Education, held at Yad Vashem, 2012.

1. Brian Klug, "The Collective Jew: Israel and the New Antisemitism," *Patterns of Prejudice* 37, no. 2 (2003), p. 124.

2. Sarah Rembiszewski, *The Final Lie: Holocaust Denial in Germany—A Second Generation Denier as a Test Case* (Tel Aviv: Stephen Roth Institute, Tel Aviv University, 1996), p. 57.

3. Klug, p. 123; see also Dina Porat's expert testimony in the "Michael Adams and Christopher Mayhew against Maariv" case, Supreme Court Judge Yaakov Bazak's verdict, *Maariv* (August 10, 1978).

4. See the UN General Assembly resolution of November 21, 2005, no.60/7, on Holocaust Remembrance.

5. Dave Rich, "Holocaust Denial as an Anti-Zionist and Anti-Imperialist Tool for the European Far Left," in *Post-Holocaust and Anti-Semitism* no. 65 (a Jerusalem Center for Public Affairs online publication; February 1, 2008).

6. Joel Kotek, *Cartoons and Extremism: Israel and Jews in Arab and Western Media* (London and Portland, Ore.: Vallentine Mitchell, 2009).

7. Edward Said, *The Politics of Dispossession* (New York: Pantheon, 1994), p. 121.

8. Shmuel Trigano, "Europe's Distortion of the Meaning of the Shoah Memory and Its Consequences for the Jews and Israel," *Post-Holocaust and Anti-Semitism* 42 (March 1, 2006), p. 5, and "The Political Theology of the Memory: Europe Is Morally Ready for a Second Holocaust," *Kivunim Hadashim*17 (January 2008), p. 87.

9. Alain Finkielkraut, *Au nom de l'Autre, reflextion sur l'antisemitisme qui vient* (Jerusalem: Shalem, 2004), pp. 34–35.

10. Gitta Sereny, *Into that Darkness: From Mercy Killing to Mass Murder, a Study of Franz Stangl, the Commandant of Treblinka* (London: Deutsch, 1974 and 1995), p. 232.

11. The June Prague Declaration on European Conscience and Communism, which turned into the Prague Process, was ratified by the European Parliament on July 2009, a few weeks before the seventieth anniversary of the 23 of August. Yet Prof. Zvi Gitelman claims this is not a European decision. See the chapter in this volume by Gitelman.

12. See Finkielkraut.

13. Heinz Heger, *Les hommes au triangle rose,* preface by Guy Hocquenghem (Paris: Persona, 1981), p. 9.

14. Bernard-Henri Lévy's keynote address at the opening of the World Jewish Congress annual convention, December 17, 2006, Paris. He repeated his three pillars of new antisemitism theory in his *Left in Dark Times: A Stand against the New Barbarism* (New York: Random House, 2008), pp. 155–66.

15. Jose Roberto Duque, "Dueños del dolor, dueños del mundo," *Aporrea* (July 20, 2006).

16. Elie Wiesel, "The Memory of the Holocaust on Israel's 60th Anniversary," lecture at Tel Aviv University on May 20, 2008, recorded but not published.

17. I was a member of the Israeli Foreign Ministry delegation to both Vienna and Durban I.

18. Jostein Gaarder: *Aftenposten* (August 30, 2006); Bill Moyer: Commentary broadcast, January 9, 2009.

19. See Anders Lange, *A Survey on Teachers' Experiences and Perceptions in Relation to Teaching about the Holocaust* (Stockholm: The Living History Forum, 2008).

20. *Le Monde* (May 15, 1992).

21. It was reached during the ITF Haifa plenary in mid-December 2010 by the ITF subcommittee on antisemitism and Holocaust denial.

22. See Israel Gutman, "Denying the Holocaust" (lecture at the Study Circle on Diaspora Jewry in the home of the president of Israel), the Hebrew University, Jerusalem, 1985, pp. 12 and 16. In May 2005, Gutman elaborated on this lecture in the Yad Vashem research seminar, recorded but not published.

23. Anne Frank: *The Diary of a Young Girl* (New York: Doubleday, 1952), introduction by Eleanor Roosevelt.

24. Jim Allen, *Perdition: A Play in Two Acts* (London: Ithaca Press, 1987).

25. See Gil Michaeli, an interview in Paris with Finkielkraut, entitled "The Very Existence of Israel Turned in the Eyes of Many into a Monstrous Phenomenon," *Maariv* (November 24, 2006).

26. Lévy, p. 155.

27. See Dan Michman, "From Holocaust to Resurrection! From Holocaust to Resurrection?" *Iyunim Bitkumat Israel* (Studies in Israeli and Modern Jewish Society) 10 (2000), pp. 234–58. Yehuda Bauer reacted in "Did the Holocaust Bring about the Establishment of the State of Israel?" *Iyunim Bitkumat Israel* 12 (2002), pp. 653–54. And Michman: "A Reaction to a Reaction," *Iyunim Bitkumat Israel* 13 (2003), pp. 393–95.

28. Dan Baron, *Legacy of Silence: Encounters with Children of the Third Reich* (Cambridge, Mass.: Harvard University Press, 1989), with a 2003 edition by the Koerber Foundation, Hamburg.

29. Justice Georges Kiejman quotes Mitterand in *Liberation* (October 22, 1992). Klarsfeld's angry answer, in *Le Nouvel Observateur* (October 25, 1992).

30. Michael Shafir, "Between Denial and 'Comparative Trivialization': Holocaust Negationism in Post–Communist East-Central Europe" (Jerusalem: The Vidal Sassoon International Center for the Study of Antisemitism, 2002).

31. See tape number 9, audio recording of the plenary session, August 1980 Revisionist Convention, Pomona College, Claremont, Calif., Institute for Historical Review, in the TAU Wiener collection, W.5891. It is difficult to assess the identity of the speaker.

32. Alain Finkielkraut, *L'avenir d'une negation: Reflexion sur la question du genocide* (Paris: Edition du Seuil, 1982).

18 Identity Politics, the Pursuit of Social Justice, and the Rise of Campus Antisemitism: A Case Study

Tammi Rossman-Benjamin

Introduction

ON NOVEMBER 6, 1968, students from the Black Student Union and the Third World Liberation Front at San Francisco State College (later San Francisco State University) initiated a five-month strike—the longest campus strike in U.S. history—which set in motion a chain of events that changed the face of American higher education. One of the earliest and most significant results of the strike was that acting college president S. I. Hayakawa agreed to the immediate establishment of the nation's first departments of black and ethnic studies, to be housed in a separate school of ethnic studies. These had been the key demands of the strikers themselves, who believed such programs would revolutionize the "white racist" institution and provide students of color with the necessary tools for combating oppression and pursuing social justice within their respective communities.

The student strike at San Francisco State College (SFSC) reflected the broader social upheaval that was characteristic of the 1960s, and the strikers' demands echoed the *cris de coeur* of radical social activists across the nation.[1] On the heels of the SFSC strike, similar battles were waged by students at the University of California Berkeley, Columbia University, Cornell University, and on many other American campuses. By 1971, students had won black studies programs in more than 500 colleges and universities and were responsible for the introduction of ethnic studies courses into the academic programming in almost 1,300 institutions of higher learning.[2]

The establishment of the nation's first departments of black and ethnic studies marked the first time in the history of the modern American research university that the promotion of group identity and the pursuit of social justice played significant roles in the core mission of an academic discipline. Although these goals are meritorious in many respects, their incorporation into the academic programming of institutions of higher education threatened to replace the university's traditional, universally honored mission of pursuing truth and knowledge in an objective and dispassionate way with the more parochial goals of particularistic advocacy and activism. Among its many profound consequences, did this radical break with long-standing scholarly tradition help to pave the way for the dramatic increase in campus antisemitism that has been witnessed in recent years?[3] This question will be examined where the rupture first occurred: San Francisco State University (SFSU).

Founded in 1899, SFSU is one of the oldest of California's public universities. In 1961, the college was incorporated into the California state college system and quickly became known for its emphasis on educational innovation.[4] In 1965, for example, San Francisco State housed the nation's first student-run experimental college, which in turn would serve as a model for the nation's first department of black studies and the first and only college of ethnic studies.[5] Since the 1990s, however, SFSU has also had the dubious distinction of being known as the nation's most antisemitic campus.[6] This essay will explore how the origin and development of SFSU's Department of Black Studies and College of Ethnic Studies may have contributed to the dramatic rise in antisemitism on that campus decades after their establishment. It will also consider what light this might shed on the phenomenon of antisemitism in higher education today.

The Origin of the Department of Black Studies and the College of Ethnic Studies at SFSU

In the mid-1960s, an ideological split arose between those members of the San Francisco State College Negro Student Association (NSA) who favored integration and those who favored separation.[7] The latter group of students was strongly influenced by the Black Panther Party, a black nationalist organization rooted in the principles of revolutionary socialism, which sought to liberate black people from oppression through an armed struggle against racism, capitalism, imperialism, and sexism.[8]

In 1966, under the leadership of Black Panther member Jimmy Garret, who acknowledged coming to SFSC solely to promote a nationalist agenda and to mobilize black students for revolutionary action, the black nationalist students broke away from the NSA and created the Black Students Union (BSU), the first in the nation. Garret and SFSC graduate student George Murray, who at the time was the Black Panther "Minister of Education," encouraged BSU members to see the college as a profoundly flawed and racist institution and to commit themselves to struggling against it.[9] Out of this struggle grew an awareness that offering courses in black studies could be an important way to advance their nationalist goals. These courses would not only counter the "white value and white attitudinal courses"[10] that were being offered at SFSC, but they would also advocate a radically new paradigm of higher education, one that made the promotion of racial identity and the struggle against racism fundamental goals of the academy.[11]

Capitalizing on SFSC's reputation for being open to educational innovation and affording its students a high degree of participation in college affairs, in the fall of 1967 BSU students initiated the first credit-granting black studies courses in the Experimental College, which were taught on a voluntary or part-time basis by faculty and graduate students. By the end of the 1967–68 academic year, it was taken for granted that a black studies program would be established at the college.[12]

Indeed, the concept of such a program had already been considered by the SFSC administration as early as 1966, and soon after black students put forward the idea of black studies in the Experimental College, administrators began meeting with them about the creation of a black studies department. Over the next two years, university administrators sought to develop a proposal and hire a staff for such a department.[13] In February 1968, at the urging of members of the BSU, SFSC president Robert Smith circumvented normal academic procedure and unilaterally appointed Dr. Nathan Hare as special curriculum supervisor to develop and coordinate a black studies curriculum. Although Hare had recently been fired from Howard University for "his militant pro-black activities," Smith was nevertheless anxious for him to come to SFSC in order to diffuse growing racial tensions, declaring that "this college is going to explode wide open . . . if the blacks do not get what they want soon."[14] In the spring semester of 1968 at least fourteen black studies courses were offered under the joint auspices of several departments.[15]

The BSU's dispute over black studies, which motivated the five-month strike, was therefore not about the establishment of a black studies program, but rather about the delay in its establishment and its scope.[16] In late October 1968, when the BSU announced their intention to initiate a strike the following week, they revealed a list of "non-negotiable" demands, which included the following:[17]

- That there be a department of black studies which will grant a bachelor's degree in black studies; that the black studies department chairman, faculty and staff have the sole power to hire and fire without the interference of the racist administration and the chancellor.
- That all black students who wish to, be admitted in fall 1969.
- That the California State College Trustees not be allowed to dissolve any black programs on or off the San Francisco State College campus.

As a result of a highly successful campaign undertaken by BSU members to build coalitions in support of their demands, particularly among students of color who shared their revolutionary goals, members of the Third World Liberation Front (TWLF), a broad coalition of nonblack, third-world student groups, joined the BSU strike action and offered their own set of complementary demands. These included the following:[18]

- That schools of ethnic studies for the ethnic groups involved in the Third World be set up, with students for each particular organization having the authority and the control of the hiring and retention of any faculty member, director, and administrator, as well as the curricula.
- That in the fall of 1969, all applications of nonwhite students be accepted.

On November 6, 1968, the BSU and TWLF initiated a well-organized insurgency that included massive rallies, clashes with police, and the shutting down of the SFSC campus. The BSU/TWLF strike was the first sustained assault against an institution by its students, who in this case em-

ployed violence unprecedented in the history of American higher education.[19] Although roundly condemned by college administrators and trustees and many local and state officials, the students' strategy ultimately
succeeded. On March 21, 1969, nearly five months after the strike had begun, acting president Hayakawa reached a settlement with striking students, conceding to their major demands. These included the immediate
establishment of a degree-granting department of black studies with jurisdiction over existing black studies courses and the right to hire and fire
professors with the advice and consent of a community review board, as
well as the development of a school of ethnic studies, which would house
black studies and three other departments: La Raza studies, Asian American studies, and Native American studies.[20]

The Ideological Basis of Black Studies and Its Influence at SFSU

In an address to BSU students on the eve of the strike, Stokely Carmichael, "Honorary Prime Minister" of the Black Panther Party, described
a vision of black studies that consisted of turning his movement's radical
philosophy into an academic discipline:

> When you talk about black studies you talk about methodology and ideology,
> not just another subject. Not the same methodology the white man uses, but
> a different methodology to communicate to us. Different ideology means
> an ideology brooding in black nationalism. Not just adding black people to
> white history. That's an insidious subterfuge.[21]

Dr. Nathan Hare, who had been hired by the SFSC president to develop the curriculum for a black studies program, shared Carmichael's
vision and incorporated it into "A Conceptual Proposal for a Department
of Black Studies," which he submitted in April 1968.[22] Hare's proposal
included a scathing critique of liberal arts education, which he claimed
"grew out of the leisure class mentality, where it was prestigious to be
nonproductive and to waste time and effort in useless endeavor. Hence
footnoting minutiae and the like." According to Hare, current standards
of scholarship "evolved to restrict the overflow of recruits . . . into existing professional riches," and resulted in racist policies, which excluded
blacks from "the educational escalator."[23]

To address this problem, Hare proposed a curriculum that he believed would not only instill in black students the values of black nationalism, but would also be both a means and an end to combating racism and the entire white racist system of education. Although he did not ignore the importance of strengthening the black identity of individual students, his ultimate goal was the "collective stimulation"[24] of an entire people. His proposal was essentially a political program for community action, aimed at providing students with an opportunity to gain expertise in the issues afflicting the black community and to develop the tools necessary for ending their oppression.

As a political program, black studies was separatist in nature and aimed exclusively at black students. White students interested in learning about the black experience were directed to courses that would ideally be offered through the "regular curriculum" in conventional departments. In this way, Hare differentiated between black education for blacks, which would be politically motivated and directed, and black education for whites, which would serve a purely academic purpose.[25]

A cadre of black professors who could serve as role models for students was an essential component of the curriculum. Hare warned that the participation of white professors "must be cautious and minimal," and that any white professor who taught in the program "would have to be black in spirit in order to last." However, white professors were encouraged to "increase course offerings on minority groups in the regular curriculum from which white students (and interested Negroes) might benefit."[26]

Community involvement was another key component of the curriculum, both in terms of sending student activists into the black community and welcoming community activists to participate in the development of the black studies program. Although he emphasized intraethnic coalitions, Hare also recognized the need for building interethnic coalitions and the importance of improving and increasing the educational participation of all ethnic groups.

The revolutionary ideology and methodology that formed the basis of the black studies proposal had a significant influence on other ethnic groups at SFSC, who were also seeking to establish academic programs with ethnically relevant courses. As Hare had done in his proposal, the coalition of groups comprising the Third World Liberation Front, in a document with their own proposal for ethnic studies programs, decried the "institutionalized condition of negligence and ignorance by the state's educational systems," linking these to racism and the hatred of nonwhite people.[27] And like the proposed program in black studies, these programs would also be rooted in a political activism that sought to confront "the racism, poverty and misrepresentation imposed on minority peoples by the formally recognized institutions and organizations operating in the State of California."[28]

Echoing the separatist ideology of the black studies program, TWLF students pushed for an autonomous school of ethnic studies, which would be "developed, implemented and controlled by Third World people."[29] The hope was that this would lead to a revolution in higher education, which would effect the dismantling of elitist academic standards and challenge the foundations of knowledge in the academy.[30]

The proposed ethnic studies programs also had a community-centered orientation, not only emphasizing a commitment to community service learning, but also encouraging community oversight and involvement.[31] Finally, although each of the ethnic groups represented in the school would have its own program, the school of ethnic studies was to have a multi-racial focus and promote solidarity among people of color for advancing their common goal of combating racism.

The Legacy of Black Studies and Ethnic Studies at SFSU

Although it has been more than forty years since the establishment of the nation's first department of black studies and school of ethnic studies, SFSU's College of Ethnic Studies still houses the school's original four departments and has remained true to the founding visions of these programs. The college's commitment to fighting for the self-determination of communities of color and against racism and oppression, by training activist students and partnering with the community and with one another, can be seen from the current statement of its mission and purpose:

> The mission of the College of Ethnic Studies is to provide safe academic spaces and resources for all to learn the histories and contexts in which to practice the theories of resistance and liberation in order to eliminate racism and other forms of oppression. . . .

> The College was founded on principles of community-based research and teaching, student leadership and activism, and the self-determination of communities of color. . . . Forty years ago the College of Ethnic Studies emerged from a collective struggle for self-determination and this quest continues to be the organizing principle of the college.
>
> . . . Our commitment to self-determination is reflected in the College's founding curricular emphases on liberatory student-centered pedagogies and community participatory learning that promote creative thinking on solving social problems and disparities in communities of color and indigenous peoples.
>
> . . . The primary aim of the College of Ethnic Studies is to actively implement a vision of social justice focusing on eliminating social inequalities that exist on the basis of race and ethnicity.[32]

In addition, each of the four departments within the College of Ethnic Studies has carried on the community-oriented, activist traditions of their predecessors: the Africana Studies curriculum is designed to serve the needs of the black community by providing students with the skills necessary "to serve as agents of awareness and change in their communities";[33] Latino/Latina Studies (formerly La Raza Studies) offers a degree program "with an emphasis on equity, social justice, and community empowerment";[34] The Department of American Indian Studies affirms the vision of its founders, embracing "a commitment to community participation and service—from the community to campus and from the campus to the community—towards the goal of facilitating American Indian self-determination through education";[35] and Asian American Studies has articulated its commitment to serving the Asian American communities.[36]

In 2007, a new program, which focused on training a cadre of activist students to empower another "community of color," joined these four departments: the Arab and Muslim Ethnicities and Diasporas Initiative (AMED). Like the college itself, AMED proclaimed its commitment to "a justice-centered perspective . . . and strong collaboration between university and non-university communities," with a goal of deepening "a sense of fairness, ethics, and solidarity among and between our communities."[37]

The Origins of AMED

The story of the establishment of the AMED program at SFSU in many ways echoes the story of the establishment of black and ethnic studies at the university in the late 1960s. It, too, begins with a group of politically motivated students eager to advance their group's activist goals at the university.

The General Union of Palestine Students (GUPS) is an international organization whose primary goal is organizing student activists to achieve justice and freedom for the Palestinian people.[38] GUPS is closely affiliated with the Palestine Liberation Organization,[39] whose 1968 charter calls for "armed struggle" to liberate all of Palestine, and denies the religious and historic connection of Jews to the land of Israel.[40] A GUPS chapter was founded at SFSU in 1973, eighteen years before the U.S. State Department removed the PLO from its list of terrorist organizations.

In May 2002, GUPS members were reproved by university president Robert Corrigan for physically and verbally harassing Jewish students at a pro-Israel peace rally held on campus. In a letter addressed to the entire campus, Corrigan wrote that "a small but terribly destructive number of pro-Palestinian demonstrators" had engaged in "intimidating behavior and statements too hate-filled to repeat." Furthermore, Corrigan threatened that if, after campus police had reviewed videotapes of the event, there was evidence that students had violated university rules, these violators might be subjected to disciplinary procedures such as suspension or expulsion.[41]

In response to the president's letter, GUPS members issued their own statement, charging that SFSU administrators had discriminated against them by stereotyping them "as aggressive terrorists . . . anti-Semites and hate mongers," making it difficult for the group to reserve rooms, hold events, and exercise their rights of free speech. They called on fellow students to help them challenge these discriminatory policies by participating in a letter-writing campaign to promote their five demands: an apology from President Corrigan; a retraction of his letter; the dropping of all disciplinary action against GUPS; a requirement that administrators take a sensitivity training course regarding Arab Americans; and *the establishment of an Arab and Muslim studies program* "in order to ensure Academic freedom on our campus and a fair and balanced course offering."[42]

On June 21, 2002, Corrigan announced that as a result of an investigation into the behavior of GUPS students at the May 7th rally, he was putting that organization on probation and cutting off their funding for one year.[43] A week later, GUPS students, together with members of the SFSU Muslim Student Association (MSA) and representatives of the American Arab Anti-Discrimination Committee (ADC-SF), lodged a Title VI[44] complaint against SFSU, President Corrigan, and other top university administrators, with the U.S. Department of Education's Office of Civil Rights (OCR). The complaint, which was filed on behalf of Arab American and Muslim American SFSU students and community members, alleged that the university had engaged in a number of discriminatory and unlawful practices that had created a hostile environment for Arab/Muslim American students and nonstudents. Among the numerous examples of unlawful and discriminatory practices cited was the fact that the university had established a Jewish studies department allegedly in response to tensions on campus, but refused to establish an Arab and Islamic studies department. The plaintiffs suggested that to "alleviate the current hostile environment against Arab-Americans and Muslim Americans generated by recent University actions, the creation of an Arabic and Islamic Studies Department is imperative to educate the campus population about these cultures."[45]

At about the same time, Corrigan established the President's Task Force on Inter-Group Relations, whose initial focus was to be on the effect of Middle East issues on campus life. Its members were chosen from among the campus and local communities, and included representatives from GUPS, the MSA, and the ADC-SF, as well as several prominent members of the Arab and Muslim communities.[46] The final report of the President's Task Force was issued in December 2002. Among its many recommendations was the following:[47]

> The Task Force emphasizes its support for establishing an Arab and Islamic Studies Program to be housed in the College of Ethnic Studies and that this program signal a more global approach for the college. The Task Force also recommends that two full-time faculty members be hired to support such a program, preferably one in Arab American Studies and one in Muslim American Studies.

It is clear that the members of the Task Force were aware of the Title VI complaint filed by GUPS, MSA, and ADC-SF, as their report cites it as a source of information utilized in their deliberations. It is also fair to assume that the federal complaint, which was still being evaluated for possible investigation by the OCR and could have resulted in the loss of the university's federal funding,[48] had influenced the Task Force's final recommendations.

Although an initiative in Middle East and Islamic Studies had already been launched at SFSU in the Colleges of Behavioral and Social Sciences and Humanities in 2002,[49] university administrators chose to follow the Task Force's recommendation to establish a new program in Arab and Islamic studies in the College of Ethnic Studies, and by July 2003 the funding for such a program had been approved.[50] However, it was not until the spring of 2007 that the Initiative in Arab and Muslim Ethnicities and Diasporas was launched, with the intended goal of creating an AMED major and master's degree program.[51]

Not surprisingly, for the last several years GUPS has been closely allied with AMED and the College of Ethnic Studies. Since 2003, the group's faculty adviser has been a member of the college's faculty, and since AMED was launched in 2007, GUPS has partnered with that program in mounting events.

Thus, as the BSU and TWLF students had done almost forty years earlier, the GUPS students were able to successfully rally sympathetic students and community members to pressure the SFSU administration into creating an academic program that would advance their organization's activist goals.

Antisemitism[52] at SFSU

Although SFSU saw a dramatic increase in anti-Jewish hostility after 2001 and was dubbed, as a result, "the nation's most antisemitic campus" by the Hillel Jewish student organization,[53] in the decade prior to that the university was already home to some of the worst incidents of antisemitism in its history.[54]

Antisemitic Activity of the Pan African Student Union

In the 1990s, the primary source of antisemitic rhetoric and behavior at SFSU was the Pan African Student Union (PASU), an organization described by one of its members as the "ideological descendant of the original Black Student Union."[55] The PASU students, like members of African American student organizations on campuses across the country, were strongly influenced by the Nation of Islam (NOI) and adopted the NOI's anti-Jewish ideology, which was expressed as a combination of classical antisemitic and anti-Zionist tropes, often "seamlessly merged" to simultaneously delegitimize Jews and the Jewish state.[56]

In May 1994, a ten-foot mural commissioned by the PASU and African Student Alliance to honor Malcolm X, long-time leader and spokesman of the Nation of Islam, was painted on the student union building. The mural also contained yellow Stars of David mingled with skulls and crossbones, dollar signs, and the words "African Blood." Jewish students charged that the symbols were antisemitic and requested that the offensive parts of the mural be painted over. The artist refused, claiming that the mural wasn't intended to offend Jews but to depict Malcolm X's anti-Israel sentiments. In the following days, as the student senate debated what to do about the mural, its supporters broadcast speeches of Malcolm X in the campus plaza and chanted "Zionism is Racism." In a forceful statement condemning the mural, SFSU president Robert Corrigan wrote:

> Particularly offensive is the prominent use within the mural itself of a yellow Star of David. With all its historical associations with Nazi Germany, such a symbol is shocking and utterly abhorrent. If we were to allow the mural to remain as is, we would be contributing to a hostile campus environment, one which says to students: 'We tolerate intolerance; we are silent in the face of bigotry.'[57]

Corrigan ordered the immediate removal of the mural and the next day it was painted over. However, after some students washed off the paint-over, Corrigan had the mural sandblasted and stationed sixty police in riot gear to defend the sandblasters from student protests.[58]

Six months later, PASU and the All-African People's Revolutionary Party, a group founded by former Black Panther Party leader Stokely Carmichael, brought well-known anti-Zionist activist Ralph Schoenman to speak on campus.[59] Flyers promoting the lecture sported the banner "Zionism is Racism!" and described Schoenman as a Jewish scholar, writer, and human rights activist who would be speaking about "Isreali [sic] brutality and Zionist imperialism throughout Africa, Latin Amer., and Palestine." In smaller letters underneath the description of the talk, the flyer read: "Come and learn why students resisted SFSU administration, CSU police, along with the Zionist powers who defaced the mural of Malcolm X at the end of last semester. Come and find out why the Zionists hide behind the term 'anti-Semitic' when they are condemned by the masses for their evil actions against helpless people."[60]

In May 1995, PASU leader and former student body president Troy Buckner-Nkrumah wrote an op-ed piece in the student newspaper, in which he accused "the Zionists" of controlling Congress and the media and attempting to control black leadership throughout the country "by telling black leaders what to do and who they can associate with." Further, Buckner-Nkrumah wrote the following:[61]

- "I do believe the only good Zionist is a dead Zionist, as I believe the only good Nazi is a dead Nazi, or the only good racist is a dead racist."
- "I support Palestinian groups like Hamas who have not sold out their land and continue to put bullets in settlers."
- "At this time in the struggle the Zionist is a prime enemy of the black struggle for liberation. They co-opt our leaders and mislead our people, degrade our people—especially our women—through their influence and participation in the record, television and film industries. Not to mention the destruction the Zionists have caused throughout Africa, by arming and sustaining oppressive and illegal regimes in hopes to control the gold and diamond reserves, as was done in the apartheid state of South Africa since 1948."

In February 1997, PASU members hung a banner over the same wall on which the Malcolm X mural had been painted, calling for the death of Peru's president and his "Zionist commandos." The sign also bore an Israeli flag with a swastika and an American flag with a dollar sign. Soon after that, PASU students handed out flyers equating Zionism with racism and alleging a Zionist conspiracy at SFSU.[62]

A few weeks later, PASU sponsored a lecture by Khalid Muhammad, former national assistant to Nation of Islam leader Louis Farrakhan, entitled "Who Is Pimping the World?"[63] Although Muhammad viciously attacked whites, Catholics, and gays in his talk,[64] his most bigoted statements were directed at the Jews, including the following:[65]

- "The practice of those freakish Rabbis [circumcision] is that they place their lips on the penis of these young boys and after they have cut the foreskin back, suck the blood from the head of the penis of their own young boys."

- "The Federal Reserve is privately owned and a so-called Jew controls the Federal Reserve. . . . Talking about the National Debt, the Federal Debt, someone should ask, well who the hell do we owe. . . . And who in the world has that much money that we would get in debt with them. . . . Who are the rich power brokers behind the scenes? . . . Why is the Federal Reserve controlled by the so-called Jew?"
- "Our entertainers, our basketball players, our football players, our track stars, our baseball players, our entertainers and athletes are in the palm of the white Zionist Jew's hand."
- "The white man is not only practicing racism and Zionism, and with the prostitution ring, the so-called Jew man with the Jew woman all over the world to make a few dollars, he is also practicing sexism. He's a racist, he's a Zionist, an imperialist. He's a no-good bastard. He's not *a* devil, the white man is *the* Devil."

Gadi Meir, a representative of the San Francisco Jewish Community Relations Council who attended the lecture, reported that for each antisemitic epithet he hurled, Muhammad received thunderous applause from the hundreds of African American students who comprised most of the audience. As Muhammad's talk turned to the perpetration of violence against whites—"It is time for blacks to make revolutionary movies where blacks are killing white folks. . . . Kill them so hard, slice their heads to bits right on the screen. Make it so lively that your popcorn feels it is getting soaked in blood off the screen!"—Meir described feeling physically unsafe and wondering how Jewish students felt at SFSU on a daily basis.[66]

In his State of the University address delivered a few months after the Muhammad event, President Corrigan acknowledged that SFSU was considered "the most anti-Semitic campus in the nation," and he openly wondered why faculty had not protested the talk by Muhammad the previous semester.[67] Corrigan seemed to be implying that the lack of such protest suggested that university faculty, particularly those closest to the PASU students, condoned their behavior.

Although the equation of Zionism with racism and the depiction of Israel as an "imperialist" nation were certainly present in at least some of these instances, they were not the most prevalent antisemitic tropes heard. Rather, Jews were portrayed with more classic antisemitic images as "rich power brokers" and "bloodsuckers" who preyed on the black community. Israel and Zionism were not the primary objects of vilification, but rather "white," "racist" Jews, who used their money and power to exploit and oppress nonwhite people. In this context, the "racist," "imperialist" nature of the Jewish state seemed to be offered only as supporting evidence of this alleged "truth" about Jews as such.

Antisemitic Activity of the General Union of Palestine Students

In the next decade, as the primary source of antisemitic discourse and behavior at SFSU shifted from black students and their supporters to Palestinian students and their supporters, so, too, did the nature of the antisemitism. In large measure, this shift was driven by events outside of the university, especially the UN-sponsored World Conference against Racism, Racial Discrimination, Xenophobia and Related Intolerance (WCAR) held in Durban, South Africa, in September 2001. According to Irwin Cotler, former Minister of Justice and Attorney General of Canada, who attended the conference:

> Durban was the "tipping point" for the emergence of a new wave of anti-Semitism masquerading as anti-racism. . . . A conference dedicated to the promotion of human rights as the new secular religion of our time increasingly singled out Israel as a sort of modern-day geopolitical Anti-Christ.[68]

Written in highly politicized language, the WCAR NGO Durban declaration declared Israel "a racist, apartheid state," accused Israel of "crimes against humanity, including ethnic cleansing [and] acts of genocide," validated terrorist acts against Israel, and called for its elimination as a Jewish state. In addition, the declaration advocated "the launch of an international anti-Israel movement as implemented against South African Apartheid," as well as "a policy of complete and total isolation of Israel as an apartheid state, which means the imposition of mandatory and comprehensive sanctions. . . ."[69] Much of the anti-Israel rhetoric promulgated at the Durban conference, which met the working definition of antisemitism established by the European Monitoring Center on Racism and Xenophobia (EUMC) and adopted by the U.S. State Department,[70] was incorporated by the GUPS students into their campus events after 2001.

In April 2002, GUPS, the MSA, and Associated Students were listed on a flyer circulated on campus advertising a pro-Palestinian event, Genocide in the 21st Century.[71] Invoking medieval antisemitic blood libel, the flyer featured a dead baby on a soup-can label, framed by two Israeli flags and the words "Made in Israel—Palestinian Children Meat—Slaughtered According to Jewish Rites Under American License." After Corrigan wrote letters to the groups describing the flyers as "a particularly repellent example of anti-Semitism . . . hate speech in words and image . . . an offense to the Jewish community . . . [and] to the entire University community and all that we stand for,"[72] they were removed from campus. However, the pro-Palestinian event proceeded as scheduled, with a large audience in attendance.

The following day, as Jewish students were commemorating Holocaust Memorial Day in the campus plaza, a raucous rally sponsored by GUPS and MSA, which drew 500–800 students, was held nearby. The featured speaker of the pro-Palestinian event was Abdul Malik Ali, a black imam and former Nation of Islam member, who had been the first Muslim student body president at SFSU and had graduated from the university with a degree in communications and black studies. A familiar figure on California campuses, Malik Ali is well known for his open support of Hamas and Hizbullah, his frequent equation of Jews and Nazis, and his claims that "the apartheid State of Israel" is carrying out a "holocaust" and a "genocide" against the Palestinian people. In his 2002 talk at SFSU, Malik Ali praised suicide bombings against Israeli targets and said that he would be willing to martyr himself in order to kill Israelis.[73] He was also reported to have said that Israelis should return "to Germany, to Poland to Russia. The Germans should hook y'all up. You should go back to Germany."[74]

The antisemitic harassment of Jewish students rose to unprecedented levels in May 2002, when, at the end of a pro-Israel peace rally sponsored by the SFSU Hillel, GUPS students who had been participating in a counter-demonstration surrounded the Hillel students and threatened them verbally and physically. According to Professor Laurie Zoloth, director of the Jewish studies program at SFSU and an eye-witness to the event:

> As the counter-demonstrators poured into the plaza, screaming at the Jews to "Get out or we will kill you" and "Hitler did not finish the job," I turned to the police and to every administrator I could find and asked them to remove the counter demonstrators from the plaza, to maintain the separation of 100

feet that we had been promised. The police told me that they had been told not to arrest anyone, and that if they did, "it would start a riot." I told them that it already was a riot. . . . The police could do nothing more than surround the Jewish students and community members who were now trapped in a corner of the plaza, grouped under the flags of Israel, while an angry, out of control mob, literally chanting for our deaths, surrounded us. . . . There was no safe way out of the Plaza. We had to be marched back to the Hillel House under armed S.F. police guard, and we had to have a police guard remain outside Hillel.[75]

Not long after, a number of Jews at SFSU wrote letters and e-mails to university administrators complaining about the antisemitic content of GUPS's university-hosted website. According to an article in the *Northern California Jewish Bulletin*, the GUPS website contained language referring to the "so-called holocaust" and accusing Zionists of controlling all media, as well as graphic images of Israel's destruction. In addition, the GUPS site was linked to the "Muslim directory," which contained articles referring to the Holocaust as "the lie of the century" and claiming "that the all stories about Holocaust created in sake of Zionist-Jews own benefit [sic]." The "Muslim directory" also contained bloody photos of alleged Israeli massacres, charges of Jewish ritual murder in Chicago in 1955, and a section on the Talmud claiming that "Jews believe gentiles to be non-human, on par with beasts and have free reign to rob, cheat and kill non-Jews or marry Jewish toddlers." The "Muslim directory" was also linked to the Hamas webpage and an online copy of the fraudulent antisemitic text *The Protocols of the Elders of Zion*.[76]

The GUPS-initiated incidents that took place from April to June 2002 marked the beginning of a new era of antisemitism at SFSU. Whereas for the PASU students Jews represented one of several "white, racist" targets of their activism, Jews were in fact the primary target of GUPS student activism. Moreover, challenging the Jewish state and its supporters was understood to be the organization's primary mission. In addition, as the agency of the antisemitic events on campus moved from African American to pro-Palestinian students, other differences became apparent: the focus of the animus shifted from Jews in America to Jews in Israel; the antisemitic tropes employed to describe Jews escalated from terms like "blood suckers" to much more demonic images like "baby killers"; and the threats of physical violence against Jews, including Jewish students at SFSU, increased sharply.

In response to the antisemitic incidents during this two-month period, Corrigan announced that he was taking a number of steps to address the problem, including putting the GUPS students on probation for a year, shutting down their website, and establishing a campus-community task force to investigate "inter-group campus tensions" and suggest ways for improving the campus climate.[77] While these measures proved effective in the short term, they failed to anticipate the ways in which the GUPS students would be able to advance their assault on the Jewish state and its supporters through other avenues, which, ironically, Corrigan himself had helped to open for them.

A week after the president's announcement, an anonymous student posted a statement online in defense of the GUPS students, with a request for "professors, organizations, prominent community members, people from trade unions, or individuals" to sign. Although it is unclear how many signatories were ultimately garnered, the statement itself is significant in three respects, each of which can shed light on the factors that contributed to the rise in antisemitism at SFSU in the coming years, as well as the forms that such antisemitism was to take:[78]

First, the statement reframed the GUPS students' antisemitic behavior and presented it as a legitimate form of protest against oppression:

> All forms of protest and dissent against the policies of the United States and Israel which condemn the Palestinian people to lives of oppression and desperation should continue without reprisal from the university administration.

Second, it linked the students' behavior to the university's own activist traditions of challenging oppression and fighting injustice, which were begun with the establishment of the SFSU Ethnic Studies program:

> This goes against the tradition of free speech, diversity, and opposition to injustice that has been part of San Francisco State University's activist history since the achievement of the first Ethnic Studies program in the nation through a grassroots political campaign.

Finally, the statement called for the divestment of SFSU from the State of Israel. In so doing, it linked for the first time the GUPS students' struggle against the "brutal, racist policies of the Israeli government" with an international campaign to economically harm the Jewish state, launched earlier that year.[79]

GUPS's Collaboration with AMED and the College of Ethnic Studies

Under the sponsorship of a faculty member at the College of Ethnic Studies,[80] GUPS mounted or participated in dozens of pro-Palestinian, anti-Israel events on campus from 2003 on. A few of these are worth noting, because they highlight the collaboration of GUPS with the College of Ethnic Studies and AMED. They also underscore the importance of these alliances for advancing GUPS's political agenda.

In July 2006, GUPS hosted and ran a student session at the Fourth International Al-Awda Convention, held at SFSU.[81] Al-Awda, the Palestine Right to Return Coalition, is an organization that opposes Israel's right to exist as a Jewish state, promotes resistance against it "by any means necessary,"[82] has been associated with groups on the U.S. State Department's list of terrorist organizations,[83]and is at the forefront of the campaign calling for boycott, divestment, and sanctions against Israel (BDS).[84] According to organizers, one of the conference's major themes was the "political and material isolation of the Genocidal Zionist State of Israel." A substantial portion of the conference was devoted to discussing the promotion of anti-Israel boycott and divestment campaigns.

Three individuals involved with the conference had—or would soon come to have—special significance for the GUPS students:

- Dr. Jess Ghannam, the co-founder of Al-Awda and a member of the conference's host committee, was at that time an adjunct faculty member in the College of Ethnic Studies at SFSU, president of the San Francisco chapter of ADC-SF, and a member of the National Council of Arab Americans, an organization that would provide substantial support for the GUPS students.[85] Ghannam had also been on Corrigan's task force, whose recommendations led to the establishment of the AMED program. In 2009, he would cofound the U.S. Campaign for the Academic and Cultural Boycott of Israel (USACBI).
- Dr. Rabab Abdulhadi, a keynote speaker at the conference, was at that time director of the Center for Arab and American Studies at the University of Michigan, Dearborn, but in a few months she would begin her new job as director and senior scholar of the AMED program at SFSU. Abdulhadi would also sit on the advisory board of USACBI.

• Michel Shehadeh, another featured speaker at the conference, had been the Western Regional Director of the Arab-American Anti-Defamation Committee (ADC) when GUPS, the MSA, and ADC-SF had filed their complaint with the OCR. At the time of the conference, Shehadeh was under investigation by the U.S. government on charges of abetting terrorist groups. It was not until 2007, after beginning work as a research associate in the AMED program, that he would be cleared of those charges.[86] Shehadeh, too, would sit on the USACBI advisory board.

During the same week that the Al-Awda conference was taking place, the SFSU student senate met to discuss whether to approve the design for a mural commissioned by the GUPS students, which was to honor the life of the late Columbia University professor Edward Said. The discussion focused on several symbols of political resistance and hostility toward Israel contained in the proposed design, especially the image of a cartoon-like character named Handala, a well-known symbol of Palestinian resistance to Israeli occupation, who held in his left hand a large key with the Arabic term *return* written on it, and in his right hand a sword-like object. During the public comments portion of the meeting, a man identifying himself as a recent SFSU Jewish alumnus stated that he was offended by what he understood this image to symbolize: the Palestinian Right of Return and the eventual destruction of Israel as a Jewish state. The assistant director of the local Hillel also expressed her opinion that Handala represented the destruction of Israel and that such a representation had no place on a public campus. She stated that she had received many e-mails from students who were upset by the mural and asked that the Handala image be removed. Despite these concerns, the student senate approved the mural by a vote of six to two.[87]

However, in October 2006, Corrigan rejected the proposed mural on the grounds that it was "conflict centered," represented a "culture of violence," and showed "hatred towards Jews." He would agree to the mural only if the offending images were removed.[88] The GUPS students launched a petition in opposition to Corrigan's decision, claiming that the mural "stands proudly" in the tradition of SFSU's College of Ethnic Studies, which has "pioneered the study and representation of oppressed people around the world," and that Corrigan's denial of the mural was a rejection of "leaders who fought against injustice and for the rights of oppressed minorities." Furthermore, the students claimed that it was "unjust and undemocratic" to demand that certain images be removed from the mural, which are "legitimate cultural and historical icons of the Palestinian experience."[89] A GUPS student who had been involved in the mural project commented that he believed Corrigan was "afraid of the Palestinian mural . . . because by being Palestinian you're controversial by nature . . . because by simply being Palestinian we debunk the myth that there was no Palestinian people, which takes away every justification for Israel's existence."[90]

Ultimately, the GUPS students agreed to remove the offending images, and in November 2007 the mural took its place next to three other murals on the student center building, including the one depicting Malcolm X, which had caused a similar controversy a dozen years before. On the day of the mural's inauguration, GUPS hosted a number of celebratory events, which were co-sponsored by AMED and the College of Ethnic Studies, as well as several student and community-based organizations, some of them known for their virulent anti-Israel activities. Included in a special brochure[91] created for the inauguration was a congratulatory message from the director of the AMED program, Dr. Rabab Abdulhadi, who wrote:

> It is not an accident that San Francisco State University today becomes the home of the first Palestinian cultural mural on any university campus. This is where students struck 40 years ago to demand that their teachers do not erase the legacies of their ancestors and their historical experiences; where teachers insist on the relevance of our pedagogy to our communities; and where compromises on questions of justice are not tolerated.
>
> It is not an accident that a broadest coalition united around a deep sense of justice came together to make this mural a reality. This was a partnership par excellence between diasporic and indigenous communities and an academic institution conscious of its role and shouldering the responsibility of its mission.

Toward the end of the brochure was a full-page tribute to Naji Al-Ali, the Palestinian artist who had created Handala, with a drawing of Al-Ali's cartoon character, complete with key and sword.

In 2009, the collaboration between GUPS, AMED, and the College of Ethnic Studies rose to a new level, which was most clearly evidenced in two GUPS-organized events. In March of that year, in the wake of the war in Gaza, GUPS students mounted an all-day event, "Palestine

Teach-In: Communities of Color Speak Out!," which was co-sponsored by AMED and Associated Students Performing Arts and Lectures.[92] As advertised, the event consisted of the screening of several films portraying Palestinian suffering and alleged Israeli brutality, followed by a lengthy panel discussion moderated by AMED director Abdulhadi. The ethnically diverse panelists were all activists representing community-based organizations that fight for social justice and have been involved in efforts to harm the Jewish state, including through advocating anti-Israel BDS campaigns.[93] Abdulhadi herself, in addition to having helped establish the U.S. Campaign for the Academic and Cultural Boycott of Israel in 2009, was signatory to a statement on Gaza put out by the California Scholars for Academic Freedom. The statement decried "Israeli war crimes and violations of human rights," and its signatories committed themselves to "participate in campaigns aimed at exerting pressure on international authorities and the governments of Israel and the U.S."[94]

In November 2009, GUPS presented a talk and panel discussion entitled BDS: A Quest for Justice, Human Rights and Peace. According to an on-line announcement, the event was organized "in celebration of the second anniversary of the Edward Said Cultural Mural at SFSU and looking forward to our next steps of positive social change and justice."[95] AMED and the College of Ethnic Studies were listed as co-sponsors of the event, along with eighteen other student and community-based organizations, most of them affiliated with the BDS movement.[96]

The keynote speaker of the event was Omar Barghouti, co-founder of the Palestinian Campaign for the Academic and Cultural Boycott of Israel and an outspoken advocate for the elimination of the Jewish state, which he has argued will be the ultimate outcome of a successful BDS campaign.[97] In his talk, Barghouti compared Israel to Apartheid South Africa and discussed the importance of implementing boycott and divestment campaigns against the Jewish state, saying: "our South African moment has arrived." AMED director Rabab Abdulhadi also spoke at the event, focusing her talk on creating a successful movement for a "free Palestine" and urging Palestinians who live in the United States to use their influence to change American political views on Israel.[98] Dr. Kenneth Monteiro, dean of the College of Ethnic Studies, provided the welcoming address for the event.

Since 2007, the collaboration of GUPS, the College of Ethnic Studies, and AMED has had significant consequences for all three of these organizations. For the GUPS students, the support of the College of Ethnic Studies in general, and AMED in particular, has served to strongly link their own political goals with the mission of the college and its programs. In addition, the fact that academic units support and participate in these events and clearly condone their content has conferred respectability and academic legitimacy on both GUPS and the antisemitic content of its events, including the promotion of activities intended to harm Jews or the Jewish state. Conversely, the GUPS students and their struggle for "justice and freedom for the Palestinian people" have provided the College of Ethnic Studies with the "student leadership and activism" described in the college's mission statement, and they have served to justify the very existence of the AMED program.

The College of Ethnic Studies and the Assault on the Jewish State

The extent to which the political activism of the GUPS students, including its antisemitic aspects, has been embraced by the College of Ethnic Studies and incorporated into its academic programming can be appreciated by considering a major academic conference mounted by the college in October 2009, in honor of the fortieth anniversary of its establishment. Entitled "Ethnic Studies 40 Years Later: Race, Resistance, Relevance,"[99] a central theme of the conference was "what became possible as a result of the strike and the creation of the College of Ethnic Studies."[100] The conference consisted of dozens of symposia and talks, many focusing on the college's role in promoting student activism and the struggle for racial and social justice in communities of color. In several panels, Israel and the Jews were topics of discussion. In all of these cases they were cast in an extremely negative, at times even antisemitic light. Four of these panels are discussed below.

In a symposium entitled "Mapping Arab Diasporas: Justice Centered Activism,"[101] which was chaired by AMED director Rabab Abdulhadi, each of the three panelists had been involved in efforts to undermine the Jewish state: Lila Sharif, a graduate student in Ethnic Studies at University of California San Diego, was active in Al-Awda and the Palestine Youth Network, an organization that strives to foster among Palestinian youth activism for the liberation of "historic Palestine," an area that would include present-day Israel, and embraces BDS campaigns as a means for achieving that end.[102] Loubna Qutami, AMED's first masters' student and a former leader of GUPS during her undergraduate years at SFSU, was a founder of the Palestine Youth Network; and Dr. Ibrahim Aoude, chair of Ethnic Studies at the University of Hawaii, was an endorser of the U.S. Campaign for the Academic and Cultural Boycott of Israel. Among the topics discussed by the panel was the importance of developing strategies for empowering Palestinian youth to participate in the liberation of "historic Palestine." During the talks and subsequent discussion, Israel was accused of genocide, ethnic cleansing, and theft of Palestinian land, and the "Zionist lobby media" was charged with unwarranted attacks on Palestinian political activists.

Four Jewish academics well known for their anti-Zionist views and anti-Israel activism[103] participated in a symposium entitled "Jews, the Middle East Conflict, and Ethnic Studies in the Age of Obama,"[104] which focused on "the fraught relationship of Jews to the Middle East conflict and Ethnic Studies."[105] In his introductory remarks, Dr. Hilton Obenzinger, professor of writing at Stanford University and moderator of the symposium, said that a question of fundamental concern to the panel was how scholars working in areas of Jewish concern could "free themselves from the constraints of rigid pro-Israel frameworks . . . and present alternatives outside of the Zionist consensus that still dominates the country and chokes Jewish studies." Obenzinger himself used the opportunity to condemn Israel's theft of Palestinian land, as well as its "colonial settlement," "Apartheid wall," and "fascist" leadership. UC Berkeley rhetoric professor Judith Butler argued that from its inception, the Jewish state had violated the "sacred principles of social justice" and was therefore illegitimate and should be replaced with a bi-national secular state. Alex Lubin, chair of American Studies at the University of New Mexico, concurred with Butler about the desirability of eliminating Israel as a Jewish nation-state and criticized President Obama for mimicking "the imperial practices of his predecessors" and being complicit with "the most violent policies of the Israeli state" by calling on Palestinians to recognize Israel as a Jewish state. In his talk, Joel Beinin, Stanford University professor of history and Jewish studies, launched a broadside attack on official Jewish organizations of the Bay Area, accusing them of using "McCarthyite tactics" and "slander" to try to suppress the screening of a documentary film about the death of pro-Palestinian activist Rachel Corrie. Beinin also suggested that these organizations and the American Jews who support them "have a loyalty to Israel that supersedes their commitment to freedom of speech and freedom of artistic expression."

The panel "Hidden Jewish Narratives and Identities: Histories and Visions of Jewish Anti-Zionists"[106] was put together by the International Jewish anti-Zionist Network (IJAN) in order to share that organization's "liberation politics, organizing and vision."[107] According to Sara Kershnar, IJAN co-founder and panel moderator, panelists hoped "to explore resistance to Zionism by people who identify as Jewish, and the relevance of that to the Palestine Solidarity Movement specifically, but to anti-colonial, anti-racist liberation struggles more broadly." Kershnar placed these goals squarely within "the tradition of the anti-racist and anti-colonial history of ethnic studies." Comparing Zionism to white supremacy in the United States and Apartheid in South Africa, Kershnar described anti-Zionism as "part of a broader liberatory politic . . . anti-racist, anti-imperialist, in solidarity with class struggle, against the role that Israel plays in global capitalism." She noted that Jews play a strategic role in the struggle against Zionism, "in terms of delegitimizing charges of antisemitism . . . delegitimizing the premise that all Jews are Zionists." According to IJAN activist Kinneret Israel, "Zionism expresses exclusionary and inclusionary racism . . . in the ideals of purification that are made evident through processes of extermination and elimination . . . oppression and exploitation." Israel described the work of IJAN activists "to support movements for Palestinian sovereignty and self-determination, through protest and support of BDS, to create anti-Zionist discourse, and to extricate Jewish identity from Zionism." Mich Levy, IJAN co-founder, distinguished between "critiques of Israeli policy," which have the aim of sustaining the Jewish state, and "critiques of Zionism," which are aimed at a dismantling of the Jewish state. Levy asserted that IJAN's ideology was firmly rooted in the second kind of critique.

Finally, perhaps the most egregious example of anti-Jewish animus came from a panelist in a symposium entitled "Islamophobia in Systems of Knowledge."[108] The speech was delivered by SFSU alumnus Imam Abdul Malik Ali, who had given hundreds of fiery, antisemitic speeches around the country, including to GUPS students at SFSU. (Ironically, Malik Ali was introduced as a "well-known motivational speaker on California college campuses.") According to Malik Ali, Islamophobia is primarily a Jewish creation:

> There is an Islamic revival in the world today that the Americans and the Zionist Jews are very concerned about. . . . What the Western powers understood—the United States and the Apartheid State of Israel—was that Islam was making a move, and if Islam makes a move, we are in trouble, because as you may have noticed, everyone's afraid of Zionist Jews. Politicians are afraid of them, everyone's afraid of them. And every time they come up against us, they always lose. You pick up on that? Hezbollah whooped their butts! Hamas whooped their butts! We are, like, undefeated against Zionist Jews, and they know it, and they know that we're the only ones who aren't afraid of them. And so what they're trying to do is to get the people to hate us as much as possible. And so with their influence in the media, their influence in other areas, the Zionist Jew is really breaking this thing down to the point where everyone will begin to hate us.

Drawing on his experiences as an undergraduate at SFSU, Malik Ali ended his talk by offering the following advice to SFSU students in the audience:

> If you are a radical or revolutionary or progressive, San Francisco State is home court. This is a Zionist-free zone! And that is why the Zionists have to hide behind the Republican Party. The Zionists cannot come out on this campus and say, "We're Zionists!" They can't do it! It's *a **Zionist-free campus**!* . . . We've had Muslim student body presidents here. I was the first one! Do you know we had [Shar³ia compliant] emergency loans, interest free? Interest-free emergency loans—we took over the student government—you have to know this history! I was the first Muslim student body president . . . and this troublemaker to my left [fellow panelist Hatem Bazian] was the third. And we understood: This is San Francisco State! Bring 'em out into the open, because they're like a night flower. There are certain flowers that blossom at night, but when the sun comes out they go back in—that's the Zionist Jew. That's the Zionist Jew! At the nighttime they come out, but once the sunshine comes out, once the light is put on them, they scatter. But bring 'em out into the open! This is *a **Zionist-free zone***, this is ***our home court***, and we'll make sure we ***keep*** it our home court.

While there were no overt calls to violence against Jews or the Jewish state at the conference, as there had been at earlier GUPS events, several panelists used language that blatantly demonized and delegitimized the Jewish state and its supporters, clearly meeting the criteria for antisemitic discourse established by the EUMC's working definition of antisemitism.[109] Moreover, because the conference was fully organized and funded by the College of Ethnic Studies, these instances of antisemitic discourse bore the clear imprimatur of the university, thereby affording them academic legitimacy and enhancing their ability to flourish at SFSU, and, in their many permutations, on other campuses as well.

Understanding the Factors that Allow Antisemitism to Flourish at SFSU

The preceding analysis suggests that while many factors have contributed to the dramatic rise in antisemitism at SFSU over the last two decades, in one way or another, these can all be traced back to a single event in March 1969: Acting President S. I. Hayakawa's decision to accede to the demands of militant students of color for the establishment of departments of black and ethnic studies, to be housed in a separate school of ethnic studies. That decision was instrumental in creating the conditions that would allow campus antisemitism to flourish decades after it was adopted:

- Hayakawa's capitulation to the students' demands, which involved contravening the college's own policies and procedures for establishing new academic programs, demonstrated the vulnerability of the university to the kinds of pressure that the students and their supporters had applied, including physical violence and shutting down the university. More than thirty years later, the GUPS students would take a page from the BSU/TWLF students' playbook. By means of escalating threats of physical violence—in this case against Jews—and filing a federal complaint that could have seriously affected the university's funding and reputation, GUPS students successfully pressured administrators into creating an academic program in Arab and Muslim studies within the College of Ethnic Studies. The AMED program and the college went on to organize and sponsor events with antisemitic content.
- By allowing the establishment of departments whose missions included the promotion of racial/ethnic identity and the pursuit of social justice—rather than the promotion of reason and the pursuit of knowledge—Hayakawa unwittingly facilitated a radical transformation of his university and its time-honored traditions of

scholarship. The eschewal of objective scholarship in favor of political advocacy and activism undoubtedly helped to create a politically charged climate at the university, at least within the College of Ethnic Studies. Moreover, the coupling of political passions with an ideology of victimhood, which was an essential component of the original conceptions of both black and ethnic studies, fomented political hatreds that targeted groups identified as "oppressors." Initially it was "whites" who were targeted by the political animus of the College's programs. In time, it would also be "the Jews."

• The academic freedom policy covering all California State University campuses affirms the 1940 Association of American University Professors' Statement on Academic Freedom and Tenure, which takes as its bedrock assumption that institutions of higher education depend upon "the free search for truth and its free exposition."[110] Although the politically directed missions of the proposed departments violated this crucial tenet of academic integrity and responsibility, Hayakawa's acceptance of their inclusion within the academy nevertheless ensured that these programs and their faculty would be protected by the privilege of academic freedom. This has made these programs relatively impervious to criticism from either inside or outside the university, including to complaints about antisemitism.

• The fact that all of the ethnic studies programs were housed in a separate school, as the TWLF strikers had demanded, undoubtedly served to exacerbate feelings of victimhood and hostility toward those outside of the school, as well as to promote feelings of solidarity among the ethnic groups within it. Once Palestinians were embraced as an "oppressed people of color" within the College of Ethnic Studies, the GUPS students benefited greatly from the interethnic solidarity among students and faculty at the college, gaining many staunch allies in the fight against their "oppressors." It is not surprising that six of the seven SFSU faculty members who endorsed the U.S. Campaign for the Academic and Cultural Boycott of Israel were affiliated with the College of Ethnic Studies, and that two of the college's faculty were on the USACBI advisory board.

• The BSU/TWLF strike revealed the extraordinary power of activist students to effect institutional change. Indeed, the school of ethnic studies and the programs it housed owed their very existence to the dedicated campaigns of the BSU/TWLF students, who were rewarded for their efforts by having their activist goals incorporated into the core missions of the programs they had demanded. Moreover, after these programs were established, the school's faculty continued to work closely with students and student groups, who were essential for carrying out the activist mission of each program, and who could transport the political passions found at the College of Ethnic Studies to the campus square. In the same way, the GUPS students, whose efforts led to the establishment of AMED, were able to ensure that their political goals—the struggle for justice and freedom for the Palestinian people, with its concomitant targeting of the Jewish state and its supporters—were adopted by that program. With AMED and the College of Ethnic Studies promoting the same political goals as the GUPS students, they were able to be even more effective in advancing their pro-Palestinian, anti-Israel agenda in the campus square.

• The students of color who initiated the strike were given material and moral support from organizations and individuals within their communities who shared their activist goals. For example, the BSU members who demanded the establishment of a department of black studies received considerable support from the Black Panther Party and individuals affiliated with other black nationalist groups. Similarly, the GUPS students received significant help from community groups such as the Arab-American Anti-Discrimination Committee and the National Council of Arab Americans, without whose help the AMED program might not have been established. In addition, from their inception the programs within the school of ethnic studies maintained close relationships with their respective communities, not only by exporting programming and student interns into them, but also by affording politically motivated individuals and organizations from those communities unprecedented access to the university. In the 1990s, representatives from antisemitic organizations such as the

Nation of Islam and the All-African People's Revolutionary Party were warmly welcomed by black student groups, and were implicitly condoned by faculty. Ten years later, with the approval of a faculty sponsor from the College of Ethnic Studies and the co-sponsorship of AMED and the College, the GUPS students partnered with numerous community organizations known for their antisemitic animus, such as Al-Awda and the International Solidarity Movement. Indeed, the college itself invited antisemitic speakers from several community organizations to participate in its 2009 conference, including Al-Awda, the Palestine Youth Network, and the International Jewish Anti-Zionist Network. IJAN was even permitted to organize an entire panel at the conference.

Conclusions

WHEREAS, the student organizers and members of the 1968 student strike and the Third World Liberation Front at SF State engaged in courageous acts which led to the founding of Ethnic Studies Departments not just in San Francisco, but across the United States and internationally as well; and . . .

WHEREAS, San Francisco State Students in 1968 played a vital role in the fruition of these programs that today inspire hundreds and thousands of students across the world to unite in the struggle for social justice [and] liberation . . .

THEREFORE BE IT RESOLVED, that I, Gavin Newsom, Mayor of the City and County of San Francisco, do hereby proclaim October 30, 2008 as . . . SF STATE '68 STUDENT STRIKE DAY in San Francisco!

—PROCLAMATION OF SAN FRANCISCO MAYOR GAVIN NEWSOM ON THE OCCASION OF THE 40TH ANNIVERSARY OF THE BSU/TWLF STUDENT STRIKE[111]

It is widely acknowledged that the BSU/TWLF strike ushered in a new era in higher education. It was the catalyst not only for the burgeoning number of black and ethnic studies programs established nationwide in its wake, but also for the introduction and flourishing of other disciplines based largely on identity politics and the pursuit of social justice. According to one study, by the beginning of the twenty-first century more than two-thirds of a large sample of institutions of higher education had programs or departments that emphasized the politics of identity and social activism.[112] The glorification of the role that the strike played in fostering these programs, as evidenced by the proclamation of the mayor of San Francisco on the occasion of the fortieth anniversary of the strike, is a testament to how universally accepted these programs have become and how positively they are viewed.

At the same time, however, many American college campuses have played host to the "new, virulent, globalizing anti-Jewishness"[113] unleashed into the world at the UN-sponsored Durban conference in 2001 and have exhibited dramatic increases in campus antisemitism, often camouflaged as anti-Israelism or anti-Zionism.[114] The case of SFSU raises the possibility that programs whose core mission includes the promotion of group identity and the pursuit of social justice may be linked to expressions of political animosities in general and antisemitism in particular. Although the College of Ethnic Studies is the only one of its kind in the nation, anecdotal evidence may point to a relationship between academic programs at other universities similar to the ones housed at the college, and manifestations of hostility toward Jews and the Jewish state. For example:

- In March 2008, the University of Hawaii's departments of ethnic studies, American studies, Hawaiian studies, women's studies, and two other departments with faculty members affiliated with these programs sponsored a ten-day symposium entitled "Who Are the Palestinians? Remembering the Nakba." The symposium consisted of virulently anti-Israel events, including several lectures by the founders of Al-Awda and a workshop on "Divestment and Boycott" presented by a University of Hawaii professor of ethnic studies.[115]

- In May 2010, several academic units at University of California San Diego—including African American Studies, Ethnic Studies, Critical Gender Studies, and Chicano/a-Latino/a Arts and Humanities—co-sponsored the UCSD Muslim Student Association's week-long event, "Justice in Palestine Week 2010: End the Apartheid." The MSA event featured eight speakers, most of them well-known for their anti-Zionist and antisemitic rhetoric, such as Norman Finkelstein and Hatem Bazian. The week's activities were also endorsed by numerous student groups, including the Black Student Union and Movimiento Estudiantil Chicano(a) de Aztlan.[116]

- In March 2011, the Department of Ethnic Studies at the University of California Riverside hosted a major academic conference entitled "Critical Ethnic Studies and the Future of Genocide: Settler Colonialism/Heteropatriarchy/White Supremacy." The conference featured at least four sessions singling out the Jewish state for opprobrium, such as "Israeli Occupation as Racist Nation Building."[117] Fourteen of the eighteen university faculty who spoke in these sessions had openly endorsed anti-Israel boycott and divestment campaigns.[118]

Looking back at this picture, one sees its many sides. Clearly, the African American experience and the experience of America's other ethnic minorities are worthy of academic study. However, a firm distinction can be made between university programs whose core mission is the production of serious academic scholarship in these areas and those whose primary goal is political or social action for the advancement of the minorities in question. The crucial differences between these two kinds of programs can be seen in a 1999 study contrasting the African American studies departments at Temple University and Harvard University.[119] Similar to the black studies program at SFSU, Temple's department of African American Studies adopted an Afrocentric approach, which eschews the scholarly methodology of traditional disciplines in favor of an approach that is "liberating," advocates social change, and actively engages in community improvement.[120] Under the chairmanship of Henry Louis Gates, Harvard's Department of African and African American Studies took a very difference course from Temple's program. Highly critical of the large number of black studies programs that foregrounded Afrocentricism, which he deemed a form of "ethnic cheerleading" and "intellectually bogus,"[121] Gates sought to establish at Harvard an academically rigorous program that utilized traditional methodologies in the humanities and social sciences and maintained strict boundaries between scholarship and activism.

What the case of black and ethnic studies at SFSU and the other examples cited above suggest is that academic programs that promote ethnic identity and the pursuit of social justice as a central part of their core mission may contribute to the creation of campus climates favorable to the political targeting of those who are deemed "oppressors." In the case history presented here, Jews have been targeted time and again as "oppressors" of choice. Further research is needed to determine if they have been singled out in this negative way at other universities as well. If so, it will also be imperative to assess the extent to which anti-Jewish sentiment on North American campuses can be traced to such programs as those studied in this paper.

The existence of a possible relationship between anti-Jewish animus and academic programs that promote the identity of supposedly oppressed groups and that pursue social justice is cause for deep concern, not only because of its implications for higher education, but also for society at large. In this regard, French philosopher Julien Benda offers a cautionary tale. In 1927, Benda published a small book, *La trahison des clercs (The Treason of the Intellectuals),* in which he accused the French and German intellectuals of his day of abandoning their scholarly mission of pursuing truth and reason in order to become activists for the basest nationalist and racist ideologies. According to Benda, academic life had degenerated to "the intellectual organization of political hatreds," chief among them antisemitism,[122] and he predicted that this betrayal of European intellectuals would propel humanity to "the greatest and most perfect war ever seen in the world."[123] Benda would live to see how prescient he was, and, as a Jew, he would experience first-hand what the "political hatreds" of the learned would mean for his people.

NOTES

1. Readers interested in the sociohistoric background of the SFSC strike would benefit by consulting one or more of the following volumes about the 1960s: Alexander Bloom and Wini Breines, *"Takin' it to the streets": A Sixties Reader* (New York: Oxford University Press, 1995); Edward P. Morgan, *The 60's Experience* (Philadelphia: Temple University Press, 1991); David Burner, *Making Peace with the 60's* (Princeton, N.J.: Princeton University Press, 1996).

2. Bob Wing, "'Educate to Liberate!': Multiculturalism and the Struggle for Ethnic Studies," *ColorLines News for Action* (May 15, 1999), http://colorlines.com/archives /1999/05/educate_to_liberate_multiculturalism_and_the_struggle_for_ethnic_studies .html.

3. Antisemitism has been a long-standing component of university life in America. Expressed for many years in the severely restricted admission and hiring of Jews, campus antisemitism declined in the aftermath of the Holocaust but has shown a recent resurgence, with numerous campuses becoming sites of overt hostility to Jews, Judaism,

and the Jewish State. For a recent review of contemporary campus antisemitism and its historical antecedents, see Eunice G. Pollack, ed., *Antisemitism on the Campus: Past & Present* (Boston: Academic Studies Press, 2011).

4. Fabio Rojas, *From Black Power to Black Studies* (Baltimore: The Johns Hopkins University Press, 2007), 48.

5. Ibid., pp. 58–64.

6. Anthony Chu, "Jewish Studies Gets SF State's First Endowed Chair," *GoldenGater* (September 16, 1997). See SFSU President Corrigan's statement: "San Francisco State is considered the most anti-Semitic campus in the nation," http://www.journalism.sfsu .edu/www/pubs/gater/fa1197/sept16/Endowed.html.

7. http://userwww.sfsu.edu/~afrs/history.html.

8. Jessica Christina Harris, "Revolutionary Black Nationalism: The Black Panther Party," *The Journal of Negro History* 85, no. 3 (Summer 2000), pp. 163–64.

9. Rojas, pp. 51–53.

10. http://userwww.sfsu.edu/~afrs/history.html.

11. Angela Rose Ryan, "Education for the People: The Third World Student Movement at San Francisco State College and City College of New York" (Ph.D. dissertation, The Ohio State University, 2010), p. 63.

12. John H. Bunzel, "Black Studies at San Francisco State," *The Public Interest* 13 (Fall 1968), pp. 22–38.

13. Rojas, p. 71.

14. Bunzel, p. 22.

15. William H. Orrick, Jr., *Shut it Down!: A College in Crisis* (Washington, D.C.: U.S. Government Printing Office, 1969), p. 122.

16. Rojas, p. 72.

17. Orrick, p. 151.

18. Ibid.

19. Ibid., pp. 1–2.

20. http://userwww.sfsu.edu/~afrs/history.html.

21. Ryan, pp. 218–19.

22. Nathan Hare, "A Conceptual Proposal for a Department of Black Studies" (April 29, 1968), found in Orrick, pp. 159–67.

23. Orrick, pp. 160–62. Hare emphasizes his point by writing that it is ludicrous that "the black historian, in adhering to the tradition of 'footnoting,' is placed in the unenviable position of having to footnote white slavemaster historians or historians published by a slaveholding society in order to document his work on the slavery era."

24. Ibid., p. 159.

25. Ibid., p. 161

26. Ibid., p. 163.

27. "Third World Liberation Front: School of Ethnic Area Studies [pg. 1]," TWLF Folder, SF State Strike Special Collections. https://diva.sfsu.edu/bundles/187979.

28. Ibid., p. 2.

29. Ibid.

30. Ryan, p. 228.

31. Ibid., p. 263.

32. http://www.sfsu.edu/~ethnicst/home3.html.

33. http://userwww.sfsu.edu/~afrs/.

34. http://www.sfsu.edu/bulletin/programs/ltns.htm.

35. http://www.sfsu.edu/~ais/.

36. http://www.sfsu.edu/~aas/#.

37. http://www.sfsu.edu/~ethnicst/depts2.html.

38. Raja Abdulhaq, "Rebuilding a General Union of Palestinian Students," *The Electronic Intifada* (December 1, 2008), http://electronicintifada.net/v2/article9981.shtml.

39. Mark A. Tessler, *A History of the Israeli–Palestinian Conflict* (Bloomington: Indiana University Press, 1994), pp. 432–33.

40. http://avalon.law.yale.edu/20th_century/plocov.asp.

41. http://www.sfsu.edu/~news/response/values.htm.

42. http://www.iacenter.org/Palestine/palest_gups.htm.

43. http://www.sfsu.edu/~news/response/133.htm.

44. Title VI of the 1964 Civil Rights Act requires that federally funded public and private universities ensure that their programs and activities are free from discrimination based on "race, color or national origin," or risk losing their federal funding.

45. "GUPS, MSA, and ADC-SF's Complaint Regarding Discriminatory and Other Unlawful Practices at San Francisco State University Directed against the Arab/Muslim-American Community," submitted June 26, 2002 to the U.S. Department of Education Office for Civil Rights, San Francisco Office.

46. http://www.sfsu.edu/~news/response/prelimreport.htm#2.

47. http://www.sfsu.edu/~ohr/noindex/finalreport.html.

48. It was not until January 30, 2004 that the U.S. Department of Education Office of Civil Rights notified the plaintiffs that, after a lengthy evaluation, OCR would not be investigating their complaint.

49. http://bss.sfsu.edu/MEIS/about.html.

50. In a letter to Tomas Almaguer, dean of the College of Ethnic Studies, dated July 23, 2003, John M. Gemello, SFSU provost and vice president for academic affairs, authorized a full-time tenure-track position for a senior scholar in Arab and Muslim Studies: Muslim American Communities in the United States, with an appointment date of Fall 2004.

51. http://zawaya.org/site/downloads/winter2007.pdf, p. 4.

52. For the purposes of this paper, *antisemitism* is defined according to the working definition of the European Monitoring Centre on Racism and Xenophobia (EUMC), which has been adopted by the U.S. Department of State. The EUMC definition includes manifestations of antisemitism that "target the state of Israel, conceived as a Jewish collectivity," http://www.state.gov/g/drl/rls/102406.htm#defining.

53. Gary A. Tobin, Aryeh K. Weinberg, and Jenna Ferber, *The Uncivil University: Intolerance on College Campuses, Revised Edition* (New York: Lexington Books, 2009), p. xx.

54. Lori Eppstein, "SFSU women's Confab to Boost Jewish Profile," *Jewish Bulletin* (March 27, 1998), http://www.jweekly.com/article/full/7882/sfsu-women-s-confab-to-boost-jewish-profile/.

55. http://theblacklistpub.ning.com/profiles/blogs/book-review-we-will-return-in.

56. Eunice G. Pollack, "African Americans and the Legitimization of Antisemitism on the Campus," in Pollack, *Antisemitism on the Campus*, p. 217.

57. http://www.adl.org/sih/SIH-black_student_groups.asp.

58. "Removal of Malcolm X Mural Is Ordered," *The New York Times* (May 25, 1994), http://www.nytimes.com/1994/05/25/us/removal-of-malcolm-x-mural-is-ordered.html; "Art, Politics Unite in Malcolm X Mural," *San Francisco Chronicle* (May 17, 1996), http://www.sfgate.com/cgi-bin/article.cgi?f=/e/a/1996/05/17/NEWS6378.dtl.

59. In his book, *The Hidden History of Zionism*, (London: Pluto Press, 1989), Ralph Schoenman paints Israel as a monster nation and argues for its elimination.

60. http://www.adl.org/sih/sih-print.asp.

61. Troy Buckner-Nkrumah, "Buckner-Nkrumah Tells His Side of the Story," *Golden-Gater* (May 4, 1995), http://www.journalism.sfsu.edu/www/pubs/gater/spring95/may4/buck.htm.

62. Natalie Weinstein, "Anti-Semitic Banner Flies Briefly at S.F. State Plaza," *Jewish Bulletin* (May 2, 1997), http://www.jweekly.com/article/full/5648/anti-semitic-banner-flies-briefly-at-s-f-state-plaza/.

63. http://www.sfgate.com/cgi-bin/article.cgi?f=/e/a/1997/05/22/NEWS16113.dtl.

64. http://www.adl.org/PresRele/ASUS_12/3005_12.asp.

65. http://www.jewishvirtuallibrary.org/jsource/anti-semitism/Khalid.html.

66. Gadi Meir, "Nation of Islam's Key Official Foments Rancor and Rage," *Jewish Bulletin* (May 30, 1997), http://www.jweekly.com/article/full/5842/nation-of-islam-s-key-official-foments-rancor-and-rage/.

67. Anthony Chu, "Jewish Studies Gets SF State's First Endowed Chair," *Golden-Gater* (September 16, 1997), http://www.journalism.sfsu.edu/www/pubs/gater/fa1197/sept16/Endowed.html.

68. Irwin Cotler, "The Disgrace of Durban—Five Years Later," *National Post* (September 12, 2006), http://www.canada.com/nationalpost/news/issuesideas/story.html?id=b7ca427f-6cba-437f-bc8e-aa34162ee251&k=30597&p=1.

69. http://www.eyeontheun.org/view.asp?l=15&p=67.

70. http://www.state.gov/g/drl/rls/102406.htm#defining.

71. http://www.sfsu.edu/~news/response/summary.htm.

72. http://www.sfsu.edu/~news/response/nohate.htm.

73. http://www.investigativeproject.org/227/abdul-malik-ali-at-sf-state-part-i; http://www.investigativeproject.org/237/abdul-malik-ali-at-sf-state-part-ii.

74. Joe Eskenazi, "Size, Vitriol of Anti-Zionist Rally Surprises SFSU Jews," *Jewish Bulletin* (April 12, 2002), http://www.jweekly.com/article/full/17591/size-vitriol-of-anti-zionist-rally-surprises-sfsu-jews/.

75. Dr. Laurie Zoloth, "Fear and Loathing at San Francisco State," in Ron Rosenbaum, ed., *Those Who Forget the Past* (New York: Random House, 2004), 260.

76. Joe Eskenazi, "SFSU Yanks Pro-Palestinian Web Site Denying the Holocaust," *Jewish Bulletin* (June 21, 2002), http://www.jweekly.com/article/full/18015/sfsu-yanks-pro-palestinian-web-site-denying-the-holocaust/.

77. http://www.sfsu.edu/~news/response/133.htm.

78. http://www.indybay.org/newsitems/2002/05/17/1280471.php?show_comments=1.

79. David H. Gellis, "Faculty Urge Divestment from Israel," *The Harvard Crimson* (May 6, 2002), http://www.thecrimson.com/article/2002/5/6/faculty-urge-divestment-from-israel-a/.

80. Matthew Shenoda, a lecturer in ethnic studies whose areas of expertise include "ethnic/Arab american community activism," has been the GUPS faculty adviser since 2003. He has also endorsed the U.S. Campaign for the Academic and Cultural Boycott of Israel.

81. http://www.al-awda.org/sf-conv4.html.

82. http://www.adl.org/israel/anti_israel/al_awda/default.asp.

83. http://www.adl.org/israel/anti_israel/al_awda/support_terrorism.asp.

84. http://www.adl.org/israel/anti_israel/al_awda/ideology.asp.

85. Will Youmans, "First Campus Mural Honoring Edward Said," *The Arab American News* (April 15–21, 2006).

86. http://www.sfsu.edu/~ethnicst/downloads/ETHS%20eNewsletter%20Fall%202007.pdf, p. 2.

87. Minutes of the Student Center Governing Board, July 13, 2006, www.sfsustudentcenter.com/pdfs/scgbmin_2006_0713.pdf.

88. Will Youmans, "Palestinian Mural in San Francisco at Center of Battle," *The Arab American News* (February 17–23, 2007).

89. http://www.petitiononline.com/mural/.

90. These comments were made by one of the panelists of the symposium "Murals at SF State-Counter Hegemonic Narratives of Art, Politics and Survival," which was part of Ethnic Studies 40 Years Later: Race, Resistance, Relevance, a conference organized by the College for Ethnic Studies at SFSU, October 7–10, 2009, https://diva.sfsu.edu/bundles/189536.

91. www.oweis.com/mural-inauguration-program.pdf.

92. http://www.sfsu.edu/~amed/archives/gazateachin.pdf.

93. Fahd Ahmed, an AMED research fellow, represented DRUM-Desis Rising Up & Moving, an organization that advocates for South Asian immigrants and has supported boycotts of Israel; Noura Erekat, a Palestinian who has been a leader in USACBI, represented the National Lawyers Guild, a leading organization in the BDS campaign; Gerald Lenoir, who himself has publicly advocated boycotting Israel, represented the Black Alliance for Just Immigration, an organization that also support BDS; Nancy Hernandez, representing the June Jordan School of Equity, has given talks advocating BDS.

94. http://www.huffingtonpost.com/mark-levine/statement-on-gaza-from-ca_b_155021.html.

95. http://www.us4arabs.com/component/option,com_jcalpro/Itemid,26/extmode,view/extid,4783/.

96. The following sixteen co-sponsoring organizations have publicly supported anti-Israel BDS effort: US Campaign for the Academic and Cultural Boycott of Israel, General Union of Palestinian Students, Al-Awda, National Council of Arab Americans, ANSWER, International Solidarity Movement, Jewish Voice for Peace, Middle East

Children's Alliance, International Jewish Anti-Zionist Network, San Jose Justice for Palestinians, Arab Resource and Organizing Center, American Friends Service Committee, Bay Area Campaign to End Israeli Apartheid, Students for Justice in Palestine UCB, US Palestinian Communities Network, and Palestinian Youth Network.

97. Omar Barghouti, "Self determination, Ethical De-colonization and Equality," *Z-Net* (July 29, 2009), http://www.zcommunications.org/re-imagining-palestine-by-omar-barghouti.

98. Theresa Seiger, "Palestinian Mural Celebrates 2nd Birthday," *Golden Gate XPress* (November 11, 2009), http://xpress.sfsu.edu/archives/life/013924.html.

99. Conference program for Ethnic Studies 40 Years Later: Race, Resistance, Relevance, http://www.sfsu.edu/~ethnicst/downloads/SFSU_40th_Conference_Program_Ed4_ONLINE.pdf.

100. Ibid., 15.

101. https://diva.sfsu.edu/collections/coes/bundles/189315.

102. See http://www.pal-youth.org/index.php?month=1609&page_id=1. The Palestinian Youth Network was one of several organizations that participated in the boycott of Israeli ships at the Port of Oakland in June 2010.

103. The panelists included UC Berkeley Professor Judith Butler, who had signed a University of California divestment from Israel petition and endorsed USACBI; Dr. Joel Beinin, professor of history at Stanford University and former president of the Middle East Studies Association, who has been on the advisory board of the U.S. Campaign to End the Israeli Occupation, an organization that supports BDS efforts; Dr. Alex Lubin, chair of the department of American studies at the University of New Mexico, who has endorsed the USACBI; and Dr. Hilton Obenzinger, associate director of writing at Stanford University, who has been active in divestment campaigns on his own campus and with the Presbyterian Church.

104. https://diva.sfsu.edu/bundles/189313.

105. Conference program, p. 20.

106. https://diva.sfsu.edu/bundles/189533.

107. Conference program, p. 24.

108. https://diva.sfsu.edu/bundles/189511.

109. These included denying the Jewish people their right to self-determination, applying double standards of the Jewish State, and accusing Jewish Americans of dual loyalty.

110. http://www.aaup.org/AAUP/pubsres/policydocs/contents/1940statement.htm.

111. http://www.sfsu.edu/~ethnicst/downloads/40th StrikeConf Final Program2.pdf.

112. Lori A. Turk-Bicakci, "The Development of Social Movement Programs and Departments in Higher Education: Women's and Ethnic Studies from 1975 to 2000" (Ph.D. dissertation, University of California Riverside, September 2007), p. 10.

113. Cotler, "The Disgrace of Durban."

114. U.S. Commission on Civil Rights, *Campus Anti-Semitism: Briefing Report* (Washington, D.C., July 2006), p. 3.

115. http://www.endtheoccupation.org/calendar.php?id=4814. See also: http://hawaiiandpalestine.googlepages.com/panels.

116. See entry for 05.10.2010: http://livetherevival.com/2010/05/01/msa-ucsd-justice-in-palestine-week-2010/.

117. See: http://cesa.ucr.edu/.

118. Fourteen of the speakers in the anti-Israel sessions had been endorsers of either the U.S. Campaign for the Academic and Cultural Boycott of Israel (http://usacbi.wordpress.com/endorsers/) or the Divestment Petition of the Students Against Israeli Apartheid (http://usacbi.wordpress.com/2011/03/15/students-against-israeli-apartheid-at-the-university-of-toronto-and-york-university-launch-campus-divestment-campaign/).

119. Mario L. Small, "Departmental Conditions and the Emergence of New Disciplines: Two Cases in the Legitimation of African-American Studies," *Theory and Society* 28, no. 5 (October 1999), pp. 659–707.

120. Ibid., p. 664.

121. Ibid., p. 691.

122. Julien Benda, with an introduction by Roger Kimball, *The Treason of the Intellectuals* (New Brunswick, N.J.: Transaction Publishers, 2006), p. 27.

123. Ibid., p. 183.

19 The End of the Holocaust and the Beginnings of a New Antisemitism

Alvin H. Rosenfeld

The lie of the six million murdered Jews is not taken seriously by anyone.
—GAMAL ABDUL NASSER[1]

Oh, Allah, do not spare a single one of them.
Oh, Allah, count their numbers, and kill them,
down to the very last one.
—YUSUF AL-QARADAWI[2]

To LIVE AT A time of heightened antisemitism is to live with an old anxiety, no less troubling for being familiar: *How bad is it likely to get?*

Our measure of the bad at its worst has a name that sits heavily in our psyches and ominously in our moral vocabulary: *Auschwitz*. To those moved by its memory, no dread surpasses the dread of that place. To others, Auschwitz, for all of its terrifying associations, is now part of the past and not a major source of present-day concerns. Knowledge of the Holocaust, it is widely believed, nullifies any prospect of its return. Broadly disseminated through virtually every medium of Western culture for decades, such knowledge stands as warning and admonition and constructs what is taken to be a formidable barricade against any recurrence. In this view, whatever anxieties may accompany an awareness of today's hostility to Jews should not be exaggerated into fears of the gruesome past being reenacted. As one often hears, the problems and worries that beset us today do not resemble those of the 1930s and will not plunge us back into such a fearsome time.

The debate about history repeating itself is not one I wish to enter here. Suffice it to say, as every contribution to this book demonstrates, we are once again witnessing a resurgence of hostility to Jews and, especially, to the Jewish state. How aggressive this new antisemitism is likely to get and, ultimately, how destructive it will be if it proceeds unchecked are open questions. Precisely because no certain answers are available, these questions evoke a sense of unease about what may lie ahead. At its most pronounced, this unease converts the resolute power of *"Never Again!"* to its unnerving opposite—*"Ever Again!"*—and revives fears of the catastrophic past finding its way into the future, perhaps imminently so.

Long considered unthinkable, new versions of that past are now being imagined by a range of scholars and writers. Consider the following short list of titles culled from a growing corpus of writings about newly emergent strains of antisemitism. In 2002, Ron Rosenbaum, the author of well-regarded books on Hitler and Shakespeare, wrote "Second Holocaust," an essay prompted by a vision of the destruction of the State of Israel set forth in Philip Roth's *Operation Shylock* (1993). Rosenbaum's essay was followed by Michael Chabon's novel, *The Yiddish Policemen's Union* (2007), which, in its opening pages, posits the destruction of Israel in a lost war in 1948. Also in 2007, the Israeli historian Benny Morris published his chilling essay, "The Second Holocaust Will Not Be Like the First," likewise projecting a catastrophic end to the Jewish State. Daniel Gordis's book, *Saving Israel* (2009), includes a chapter ominously entitled "The Next Six Million." That same year saw the publication of Aaron Klein's *The Late Great State of Israel,* whose title within this context needs no commentary. In 2010, the Italian writer Giulio Meotti published *A New Shoah,* in which he refers to the Holocaust in its opening and closing lines and demonstrates that Israel's most impassioned enemies are inspired by the desire to emulate the Nazi slaughter. As if to confirm this gloomy view, in April 2010, *Haʾaretz* ran an interview with Robert Wistrich under the title "The Holocaust Can Happen Again, Warns Top Antisemitism Scholar." Books and essays with similarly dire prognostications have been produced in recent years by Matthias Küntzel, Nat Hentoff, Hillel Halkin, Richard Rubenstein, Robert Wistrich, David Paterson, Howard Rotberg, Fiamma Nirenstein, and numerous others. Generically diverse, these works are linked by the anxious question posed earlier—*How bad is it likely to get?*—and offer answers that point to growing concerns about what may be in the offing. Two of these books, Küntzel's *Jihad and Jew-Hatred* and Rubenstein's *Jihad and Genocide,* name the sources of this apprehension explicitly in their titles and go on to clarify its historical and ideological contexts, arguing persuasively that antisemitism is at the core of the modern jihadist movements. In his latest book, *How the End Begins,* Ron Rosenbaum follows the likely course of this destructive antisemitism to its fearsome end-point. Here is Rosenbaum musing on the nightmare-in-the-making: "The second Holocaust. It's a phrase we may have to begin thinking about. A possibility we may have to contemplate. A reality we may have to witness."[3]

In more muted versions, this terrifying prospect has appeared intermittently over the years, but in the past decade or so, it has come to the fore more overtly and persistently. Its emergence coincides with a notable increase in Holocaust denial, distortion, and manipulation on a broad range of intellectual, cultural, and political fronts. These developments have the effect of neutralizing or eroding the moral dimensions of a historically grounded awareness of Nazi crimes against Jews. Such awareness, it has long been assumed, would impede the release of aggressive antisemitic passions. To a degree, that has happened, at least within enlightened segments of the Western world; and yet, a post-Holocaust antisemitism is today a fact of public life, increasingly so and on a global scale. Its causes are numerous, but one of them is linked to ongoing efforts to appropriate, denigrate, diminish, or otherwise deny the history and memory of the Shoah, which evokes anxious concerns about the coming of a new, or "second," Shoah. The very notion of "firstness" and "secondness" in this context should be shocking—*is* shocking—and yet, in the perception of a growing number of writers, the projection of a "new" or "next" Holocaust is becoming a familiar, preoccupying theme.

"Second Holocaust" thinking, while increasingly prominent today, goes back many years.[4] Primo Levi registers it in summary fashion in the "Conclusion" to his last book, *The Drowned and the Saved:* "It happened, therefore it can happen again: this is the core of what we have to say."[5] Levi devoted the last forty years of his life to examining and transmitting the radical nature of his experiences in Auschwitz and hoped that a receptive public would be alert to the potential for future violence on a mass scale and guard against it. What he had seen and undergone was severe, and its consequences had to be heeded. For all of his efforts, though, Levi came to believe he had failed. The despondency that marked his last years was at least partly owing to his sense that his work didn't matter, that it was marginal to the concerns of the younger generations, who preferred to remain oblivious to his warnings that what had happened "can happen again." His gloominess no doubt was attributable to a number of factors, but prominent among these was a sense of futility about the fate of Holocaust memory, which he felt was being compromised and distorted, rendered extraneous and inconsequential. One finds similarly downcast sentiments in the writings of Jean Améry, Imre Kertész, Elie Wiesel, and numerous other survivor-writers of the Holocaust. All seem convinced that, despite their best efforts, the public at large either was not interested in learning about the Holocaust as it really was or were being exposed to versions of it that were historically unsound and, consequently, morally skewed.

If there were grounds for their dejection at the time they wrote, matters have since become a good deal worse. An array of trends has accumulated in recent years to facilitate the kind of forgetting that so troubled Levi and numerous others. Manfred Gerstenfeld has compiled an extensive sample of these inimical developments in *The Abuse of Holocaust Memory: Distortions and Responses* (2009).[6] His analysis of this material reveals that the memory of the Holocaust is today beset by cultural pressures and ideological priorities that challenge its place as a pivotal event in modern history. There are those who deny the Holocaust ever happened, minimize its magnitude and consequences, appropriate and instrumentalize the power inherent in its words and images, or invert, distort, deflect, and trivialize its meanings. Others are more positive, even idealistic, in their wish to recall this history and apply what they take to be its "lessons" to contemporary social problems, but their efforts to universalize the Holocaust sometimes result in an overlooking or dilution of its distinctive features. Still others, exhibiting signs of Holocaust fatigue and Holocaust resentment, have simply had enough of talk about the Jews and their sorrows and want no more of it. And then there are those who employ Holocaust references polemically, and often obscenely, in a bitter, ongoing ideological and political struggle against the State of Israel (they have their counterparts in certain defenders of Israel who also invoke the Holocaust irresponsibly). Taken together, these ways of treating the catastrophe visited upon the Jews have the effect of radically altering the representational shapes and moral weight of Holocaust memory. They lend credence to the notion that something like "the end of the Holocaust" is beginning to come into view.

These developments inevitably weaken the force of the moral and ethical imperatives that should arise from any serious confrontation with the Holocaust, making it easier for popular strains of antisemitism to emerge. If, until now, restraints on antisemitism in the Western world have been linked to the memory of the destruction of the Jews and tend to weaken as that memory attenuates, today we are witnessing something like a memory fadeout or encroaching amnesia. As a consequence of the distortion and denial of Holocaust memory, "die Schonzeit ist vorbei," as the German phrase puts it, and attacks on Jews, through word and deed, are, once again, a familiar, if deplorable, reality in many European countries.

Within Arab countries and Ahmadinejad's Iran, efforts to restrain antisemitism are not much in evidence. On the contrary, the center of gravity for Jew-hatred at its most virulent lies within these countries, where older forms of anti-Jewish prejudice now coalesce with an intense, even obsessive opposition to the State of Israel and its supporters. And so, fervent accusations against conniving, conspiratorial, rapacious, treacherous Jews are commonplace. As Gilbert Achcar writes, "Anti-semitism, in both its traditional and Islamicized variants as well as its Holocaust denying corollary, has grown spectacularly in Arab political statements and Arab media."[7]

To fill out this picture, one needs to note the Jew-hatred regularly served up in Islamic religious preachments. As but one example among many that could be cited, consider the following excerpt from a sermon by the Egyptian cleric Muhammad Hussein Yaqub that aired on Al-Rahma TV on January 17, 2009:

> If the Jews left Palestine to us, would we start loving them? Of course not. We will never love them. Absolutely not. . . . They are enemies not because they occupied Palestine. They would have been enemies even if they had not occupied a thing. . . . You must believe that we will fight, defeat, and annihilate them, until not a single Jew remains on the face of the earth. It is not me who says so. The Prophet said: "Judgment Day will not come until you fight the Jews and kill them. The Jews will hide behind stones and trees, and the stones and trees will call: O Muslim, O servant of Allah, there is a Jew behind me, come and kill him. . . . As for you Jews, the curse of Allah upon

you, whose ancestors were apes and pigs. You Jews have sown hatred in our hearts, and we have bequeathed it to our children and grandchildren. You will not survive as long as a single one of us remains."[8]

Citing these words, the Canadian author Tarek Fatah argues that "Islamist hatred of the Jew has little to do with the state of Israel or a supposed love for Palestine. If tomorrow Ahmadinejad was able to fulfill his threat to wipe Israel from the face of the earth, hatred of the Jew would continue unabated." Fatah goes on to say that such racist doctrines are widespread and have "slowly corrupted the attitudes of generations of Muslims," among whom "Jew-hatred [is now] the norm, not the exception."[9]

Thanks to the invaluable work of the media watchdog organization MEMRI and to recent publications by several notable scholars, we now know more than we previously did about the sources of this hatred, including Nazi racist ideology, which penetrated the Middle East in the 1940s and has since proliferated there.[10] To understand its contemporary resonance, especially with reference to the genocide of the Jews, we owe a major debt to Meir Litvak and Esther Webman, who have researched how the Holocaust is treated in Arab and Iranian discourse more thoroughly than anyone else to date. They show in their copiously documented, clarifying study how Arab responses have ranged from justification of Nazi crimes, to denial of these same crimes, to the projection of Nazi words and deeds onto Israeli Jews, who are accused of being latter-day Nazis themselves and of subjecting the Palestinian Arabs to a fate that rivals, if not surpasses, the fate of the Jews during the Third Reich. Within this spectrum of responses, denial has been the most constant and pervasive, finding advocates across the political map. Gamal Abdul Nasser, Anwar Sadat, and Mahmoud Abbas are only a few of the people in positions of political leadership who embraced Holocaust denial at some point in their lives. In general, as Litvak and Webman show, the actual history of the Holocaust has been of little interest within the Arab world. By contrast, Holocaust denial has long been standard fare, largely because it serves a recognizably utilitarian purpose:

The prevalent view in the Arab world has been that Zionism—lacking any moral or historical justification—is based on a series of unfounded historical myths and outright distortions. Arab deniers, therefore, view the Holocaust as one of the major myths that Zionism invented ... [to garner] support [for] the establishment of the State of Israel. . . . Hence, the premise behind Holocaust denial is that refutation of the "lie" would totally undermine Israel's international status and legitimacy.[11]

Curiously, nullification of Holocaust memory has coexisted with its opposite—a gleeful recognition of Jewish suffering and the glorification of the man who, above all others, was responsible for it. Even while they deny it ever took place, Arab writers hail the Nazi slaughter of the Jews as a model to be emulated by Arabs themselves. Writing in the Cairo newspaper *Al-Akhbar,* Egyptian journalist Fatima Abdullah Mahmoud dismisses the Holocaust as a "lie and a fraud" and then declares, "But I personally complain to Hitler, even saying to him from the bottom of my heart, 'If only you had done it brother, if only it had really happened, so that the world could sigh in relief without their evil and sin.'"[12] Like Mahmoud, other Arab writers use a familiar, even tender, form of address in evoking the name of the Nazi mass murderer, paying respect to "Hitler, of blessed memory" and beseeching God to "have mercy on the great Hitler, may he rest in peace."[13] In 1953, Anwar Sadat, who was to go on to become president of Egypt, wrote a tribute to Hitler, addressing the Nazi *Führer* as "My dear Hitler" and went on to declare, "I congratulate you from the bottom of my heart. Even if you appear to have been defeated, in reality you are the victor. . . . We will not be surprised if you appear again in Germany or if a new Hitler rises up in your wake."[14]

To grasp the peculiar psychology that encourages the adoration of Hitler, one needs to recognize how a deep sense of humiliation suffered by the Arabs at the hands of the despised Jews mingles with fantasies of emerging as triumphant victors over these same Jews. To beat the Jews, however, evidently requires nurturing a still deeper level of hatred for them. And what better instructor for cultivating such depravity than Hitler? Hence, the many adulatory references to the Nazi leader in Arab sermons, speeches, and writings about the Jews.

Listen to the Palestinian politician Anwar al-Khatib: "A people who does not know how to hate will not know how to win. . . . God have mercy on Hitler . . . each time we wish to hate the Jews and detest them, there is no better option than to turn to his book *Mein Kampf* to enhance our knowledge of that accursed people and light the fire of enmity in our hearts."[15]

As is well known, *Mein Kampf* has been popular in the Arab world for decades. The same is true for *The Protocols of the Elders of Zion* and other antisemitic texts. To be schooled in these books is to develop an especially murderous form of hatred, one that surpasses what most normal people are capable of imagining. An inspired, malevolent passion, it is emphatically goal-oriented; and the goal—far from hidden, it is overtly, proudly stated—is genocidal. To witness it articulated as plainly as possible, one can do no better than to watch an eerie MEMRI videotape of Egyptian cleric, Amin Al-Ansari, who in January 2009, the day before International Holocaust Remembrance Day, went on one of his country's religious television stations to show graphic footage of the torture and murder of Jews in Nazi camps. Far from being a Holocaust denier, Al-Ansari is a Holocaust exhibitionist and seems to relish displaying graphics of the most gruesome anti-Jewish atrocities. To watch the grotesque pictures he serves up is almost unbearable. And yet, in a calm and steady voice, Al-Ansari directs his viewer's gaze to the horrific scenes unfolding on screen and declares, devoutly, "This is what we hope will happen [to the Jews], but, Allah willing, [next time] at the hands of the Muslims."[16]

Philip Roth captures the goal of these annihilationist fantasies in *Operation Shylock,* when one of his characters, speaking from Israel, reflects on what he suspects is in store for the Jews: "A second Holocaust is *not* going to occur on the continent of Europe *because* it was the site of the first. But a second Holocaust could happen here all too easily, and, if the conflict between Arab and Jew escalates much longer, it will—*it must.* The destruction of Israel in a nuclear exchange is a possibility much less farfetched today than was the Holocaust itself fifty years ago."[17] To which Roth's narrator adds: "Exterminating a Jewish nation would cause Islam to lose not a single night's sleep, except for the great night of celebration."[18]

To prepare for the partying, an especially potent form of antisemitism has been developing in the Middle East, which simultaneously denies the Holocaust and expresses a longing to reenact it. No public figure exemplifies such anti-Jewish animus as passionately and consistently as Iran's Mahmoud Ahmadinejad, who regularly excoriates the Jewish State and calls for its end. Ahmadinejad mocks the sufferings of the Jews during the Nazi years, as he did in his infamous Holocaust cartoon contest (February 6, 2006), and also casts doubt on the veracity of such sufferings, as he tried to do in his sordid Holocaust deniers' conference (December 12,

2006). At the same time, Ahmadinejad's repeated public denunciations of Israel and prophecies of the country's imminent demise have strategically positioned him as the leading advocate of the next Holocaust. Versatile in the spewing of hatred, the president of Iran fulfills the double role of both a Holocaust denier and a Holocaust promoter. Matthias Küntzel, one of his most perceptive critics, sums up Ahmadinejad's thinking with exacting precision: Ahmadinejad "denies the Holocaust" not so much "to revise the past" as "to shape the future: to prepare the way for the next Holocaust. . . . Auschwitz is delegitimized in order to legitimize the elimination of Israel. . . . Israel must vanish."[19]

Virtually all observers of contemporary Jew-hatred agree: A "Second Holocaust," should it come to pass, will find its epicenter in Israel. Once again singled out for genocide, the Jews, according to this apocalyptic vision, are to be murdered en masse, this time in their own country. While the instruments used to destroy them will vary from those of the Nazi period, the goal is fully and recognizably Hitlerian. Here is the Israeli historian Benny Morris' projection of Ahmadinejad's catastrophe-in-the-making:

> The second Holocaust will be quite different. One bright morning, in five or ten years' time, perhaps during a regional crisis, perhaps out of the blue, a day or a year or five years after Iran's acquisition of the Bomb, the mullahs in Qom will convene in secret session, under a portrait of the steely-eyed Ayatollah Khomeini, and give President Ahmadinejad, by then in his second or third term, the go ahead. The orders will go out and the Shihab III and IV missiles will take off for Tel Aviv, Beersheba, Haifa, and Jerusalem, and probably some military sites, including Israel's half dozen air and (reported) nuclear missile bases. Some of the Shihabs will be nuclear-tipped, perhaps even with multiple warheads. Others will be dupes, packed merely with biological or chemical agents, or old newspapers, to draw off or confuse Israel's anti-missile batteries and Home Guard units.
>
> With a country the size and shape of Israel (an elongated 8,000 square miles), probably four or five hits will suffice: No more Israel. A million or more Israelis, in the greater Tel Aviv, Haifa and Jerusalem areas, will die immediately. Millions will be seriously irradiated. Israel has about seven million inhabitants. No Iranian will see or touch an Israeli. It will be quite impersonal.[20]

The post-Auschwitz future was not supposed to turn out this way. Based on the assumption that the memory of the dead would serve to protect the living, educational, cultural, and religious programs on the Holocaust of every conceivable kind have been devised as a shield against future genocides. To a degree, they may have been effective. And yet, with the progressive dilution, distortion, and denial of the historical record of Nazi crimes against the Jews, and with the rise of a new antisemitism, the hope that Holocaust memory might stand as a bulwark against the return of Jew-hatred now seems to rest on shaky foundations. Antisemitism has become resurgent over the past decade, and on a global scale. Moreover, repeated evocations of the Holocaust, instead of acting to retard hostility to Jews, have been used as incitement against them.

Holocaust memory, it turns out, far from being always preventative, is evidently capable of provoking new forms of anti-Jewish animosity, which, at their most extreme, summon up the Nazi death camps as a useful, desirable precedent. Hence, Imre Kértesz's observation that "the anti-Semite of our age no longer loathes Jews; he wants Auschwitz."[21] And hence, as well, the projections of a "next Holocaust" or "Second Holocaust" found in the writings of a growing list of contemporary authors.

No one has described the dynamic that defines this new and potentially genocidal strain of antisemitism more clearly than Kértesz:

"The expression has been so often repeated that it has become almost a cliché: it is necessary to preserve memory of the Holocaust so that it can never again come to pass. But since Auschwitz, nothing has happened that makes a new Auschwitz impossible. On the contrary. Before Auschwitz, Auschwitz was unimaginable. That is no longer so today. Because Auschwitz in fact occurred, it has now been established in our imaginations as a firm possibility. What we are able to imagine, especially because it once was, can be again.[22]

A possibility is not necessarily an inevitability, of course, and a "second Holocaust," while imaginable, does not have to come to pass. Nevertheless, the prospect should not be disregarded, for the language of mass murder is once again being broadly disseminated, with appeals to kill the Jews, "kill them, down to the very last one," now very much in the air.[23] Those who hear in these murderous preachments the preparatory rhetoric of a "Second Holocaust" may be hearing correctly. If, at the same time, one is attentive to widespread denials of the "first" Holocaust, then the dynamic developing here is ominous. In Matthias Küntzel's precise and chilling formulation, "Every denial of the Holocaust contains an appeal to repeat it."[24]

Consider the following. When the former Iranian president Hashemi Rafsanjani boasted, in December 2001, that "the use of even one nuclear bomb inside Israel will destroy everything," the centrifuges in his country's nuclear plants were far fewer and had not yet begun to spin so rapidly. Today they are working overtime. So is the murderous imagination of the current Iranian president, Mahmoud Ahmadinejad, who never tires of pronouncing death sentences on the State of Israel: "The Zionist regime will be wiped out, and humanity will be liberated."[25] He means it. So evidently do his many followers, who ardently declaim "Death to the Jews!" whenever Ahmadinejad speaks about Israel at public rallies. How many millions of others share these murderous sentiments is unknown, but the will to annihilate the Jews seems stronger today than at any time since the end of the Second World War. Moreover, far from being kept as a hidden desire, these genocidal fantasies are openly and exuberantly proclaimed by the would-be perpetrators, and without any shame attaching to them. The aim, proudly, even piously stated and restated, is to liberate the world by destroying the Jews.

Few people took Hitler at his word when he voiced precisely such sentiments three generations ago. The result was Auschwitz—a warning from the past and, to some, a coveted possibility for the future.

What, then, can one do about such threats? At the very least, they need to be acknowledged *as* threats. When asked by *Ha'aretz* journalist Ari Shavit whether he believed another Holocaust was possible, the French filmmaker Claude Lanzmann replied that he did not think so, but then added, "Perhaps a nuclear bomb could cause that." He followed up with some advice for his Israeli interviewer: "Be cautious. Take care. Open your eyes."[26]

Heeding Lanzmann's advice, I close with some reflections on contemporary antisemitism by Philip Spencer, a professor at Great Britain's Kingston University:

> If today, even after the Holocaust, perhaps especially even after the Holocaust, people say they hate Jews and they hate them enough to want to kill them, we need to take them seriously. They very probably mean what they say and they may very well do what they mean. And the reason for this, in

the Nazi case and I suggest now too, is that antisemitism is not a means to another end; it is not a cover for something else; it is not to be understood as a response to this or that difficulty, to unemployment, to exploitation, or even, let me say it, to occupation. . . . It was and is a hatred of Jews, . . . a murderous hatred, one that led . . . to the slaughter of millions. If it was once, mistakenly, not taken seriously, we would be wise not to make this mistake again."[27]

NOTES

1. Nasser's words, taken from a speech of May 1, 1964, are quoted in Matthias Küntzel, *Jihad and Jew-Hatred: Islamism, Nazism, and the Roots of 9/11* (New York: Telos Press, 2007), p. 71.

2. The words of al-Qaradawi are quoted in Paul Berman, *The Flight of the Intellectuals* (Brooklyn, N.Y.: Melville House, 2010), p. 92.

3. Ron Rosenbaum, "'Second Holocaust,' Roth's Invention, Isn't Novelistic," ed. Ron Rosenbaum, *Those Who Forget the Past: The Question of Anti-Semitism* (New York: Random House, 2004), p. 170.

4. Israel is a special case, for given the many Holocaust survivors within its borders, memories of the Shoah come to the fore whenever the country's enemies threaten it with wars of mass destruction. At such times, it is common for the language of a "new Holocaust" to emerge in the media as well as in conversation.

5. Primo Levi, *The Drowned and the Saved*, trans. Raymond Rosenthal (New York: Summit Books, 1988), p. 199.

6. Manfred Gerstenfeld, *The Abuse of Holocaust Memory: Distortions and Responses* (Jerusalem: Jerusalem Center for Public Affairs, 2009).

7. Gilbert Achcar, *The Arabs and the Holocaust: The Arab-Israeli War of Narratives*, trans. G. M. Goshgarian (New York: Metropolitan Books, 2009), p. 248.

8. Tarek Fatah, *The Jew Is Not My Enemy: Unveiling the Myths that Fuel Muslim Anti-Semitism* (Toronto: McClelland & Stewart, 2010), p. xxi.

9. Ibid., xx, xxiii.

10. Jeffrey Herf, Matthias Küntzel, Andrew Bostom, Raphael Israeli, Meir Litvak, Esther Webman, Robert Wistrich, Klaus-Michael Mallmann, and Martin Cüppers.

11. Meir Litvak and Esther Webman, *From Empathy to Denial: Arab Responses to the Holocaust* (New York: Columbia University Press, 2009), pp. 157, 159.

12. *MEMRI, Report number 375* (May 3, 2002), cited in *Jihad and Jew-Hatred*, p. 61.

13. Ibid., p. 211.

14. Küntzel, *Jihad and Jew-Hatred*, p. 70.

15. Litvak and Webman, p. 194.

16. *MEMRI, Special Dispatch 2215* (January 27, 2009).

17. Philip Roth, *Operation Shylock* (New York: Simon & Schuster, 1993), p. 43.

18. Ibid., p. 45.

19. Matthias Küntzel, "Iran's Obsession with the Jews," *The Weekly Standard* (February 19, 2007). For the diffusion of Nazi ideology within parts of the Muslim world, see also, by the same author, "Iranian Antisemitism: Stepchild of German National Socialism," *Israel Journal of Foreign Affairs* IV, no. 1 (2010) and *Die Deutschen und der Iran* (Berlin: WJS Verlag, 2010); and Jeffrey Herf, *Nazi Propaganda for the Arab World* (New Haven, Conn.: Yale University Press, 2009).

20. Benny Morris, "The Second Holocaust Will Not Be Like the First," originally published in German, in *Die Welt* (January 6, 2007), available in English translation on numerous websites, including http://groups.yahoo.com/group/eejh/message/63915.

21. Imre Kértesz, "The Holocaust as Culture," *Szombat* (August 1998), p. 8.

22. Imre Kértesz, "Über den neuen europäischen Antisemitismus," http://print.perlentaucher.de/artikel/3312.html; the translation is mine.

23. Yusuf al-Qaradawi, cited in Paul Berman, p. 92.

24. Matthias Küntzel, "Iran's Obsession with the Jews."

25. Ibid.

26. Ari Shavit, "Head to Head / Claude Lanzmann, Is Another Holocaust Possible?" *Ha'aretz* (February 25, 2011).

27. Philip Spencer, "Anti-Semitism and the Holocaust," Talk to the UCU Meeting (January 27, 2010), www.EngageOnline.org.uk.

List of Contributors

Ilan Avisar is Associate Professor in the Department of Film and Television at Tel Aviv University and the author of several books and numerous articles, including *Screening the Holocaust: Cinema's Images of the Unimaginable* (1998), *Visions of Israel* (1997; 2002), and *The Israeli Scene: Language, Cinema, Discourse* (2005). In 2010, he was appointed the chair of the Second Authority for Television and Radio, the public authority that regulates commercial broadcasts in Israel.

Alejandro Baer is Associate Professor of Sociology and Director of the Center for Holocaust and Genocide Studies at the University of Minnesota. His research expertise includes social memory studies, antisemitism, and the sociology of modern Judaism. He is the author of *Holocausto. Recuerdo y representación* (2006), *El testimonio audiovisual* (2005), and co-editor of *España y Holocausto* (2007).

Rıfat N. Bali is an independent scholar and an associate researcher with the Alberto Benveniste Center for Sephardic Studies and the Sociocultural History of the Jews (École Pratique des Hautes Études/CNRS/Université Paris-Sorbonne). His fields of expertise include the history of Turkish Jews in the Republic of Turkey and antisemitism and conspiracy theories in Turkey. He is the author of numerous books and articles on the history of Turkish Jewry, such as *Model Citizens of the State: The Jews of Turkey during the Multi-Party Period* (2008) and *An Overview of the Turkish Press through the Reports of American Diplomats (1925–1962)* (2011). His publications are found at http://www.rifatbali.com.

Paul Bogdanor is an independent researcher based in the United Kingdom. Co-editor with Edward Alexander of *The Jewish Divide over Israel: Accusers and Defenders* (2006), he is currently working on a book about the Kasztner affair and the Holocaust in Hungary.

Bruno Chaouat is Associate Professor of French at the University of Minnesota. He has published numerous articles on modern and contemporary French literature and on current debates related to the memory of the Holocaust, the Middle East conflict, and the new antisemitism. In his latest book, he traces an intellectual history of twenty years of French thought and literature from the end of the Cold War to the present.

Jamsheed K. Choksy is Professor of Iranian Studies, Adjunct Professor of Religious Studies, and Affiliated Faculty Member of the Islamic Studies Program at Indiana University. He is a consulting editor of the *Encyclopedia Iranica* (Columbia University) and author of *Evil, Good, and Gender: Facets of the Feminine in Zoroastrian Religious History* (2002); *Conflict and Cooperation: Zoroastrian Subalterns and Muslim Elites in Medieval Iranian Society* (1997); and *Purity and Pollution in Zoroastrianism: Triumph over Evil* (1989).

Eirik Eiglad is an independent scholar, located in Telemark, Norway. A writer, editor, translator, and long-time activist in the Scandinavian ecology movement, Eiglad is author of *The Anti-Jewish Riots in Oslo* (2010), *A Question of Power* (2012), editor of Murray Bookchin, *Social Ecology and Communalism* (2007), and currently at work on a project titled *Why Social Ecology?*

Zvi Gitelman is Professor of Political Science and Preston R. Tisch Professor of Judaic Studies at the University of Michigan. He is the author of many books and articles, including *A Century of Ambivalence: The Jews of Russia and the Soviet Union since 1881* (IU Press, 2001) and *Jewish Identities in Post–Communist Russia and Ukraine: An Uncertain Ethnicity* (2012).

Bernard Harrison is a philosopher and literary critic who has written widely on Jewish questions. His most recent books are *Inconvenient Fictions: Literature and the Limits of Theory* (1991); *Word and World: Practice and the Foundations of Language* (2004); and *The Resurgence of Antisemitism: Jews, Israel and Liberal Opinion* (2006). He holds emeritus chairs at the University of Utah and the University of Sussex (UK).

Gunther Jikeli is affiliated with the Groupe Sociétés, Religions, Laïcités (CNRS, Paris) and the International Institute for Education and Research on Antisemitism. He was an adviser on combating antisemitism from April 2011 to March 2012. He is author of *Antisemitismus und Diskriminierungswahrnehmungen junger Muslime in Europa* (2012) and co-editor of *"European Muslims' Perceptions of the Holocaust"* (2012).

Matthias Küntzel is a political scientist in Hamburg, Germany, and an external research associate at the Vidal Sassoon International Center for the Study of Antisemitism at the Hebrew University of Jerusalem. He is also vice chair of the German chapter of Scholars for Peace in the Middle East. He is the author of *Jihad and Jew-Hatred: Islamism, Nazism and the Roots of 9/11* (2007), which won the Gold Award for Religion at the Twelfth Annual Independent Publisher Book Awards in Los Angeles. His most recent books are *Die Deutschen und der Iran: Geschichte und Gegenwart einer verhängnisvollen Freundschaft* (2009) and *Deutschland, Iran und die Bombe* (2012).

Emanuele Ottolenghi is a Senior Fellow at the Foundation for Defense of Democracies, in Washington, D.C. Born in Bologna, Italy, he is the author of *Autodafé: Europe, Israel and the Jews* (2007); *The Iranian Bomb* (2008); *Under a Mushroom Cloud* (2009); *Iran: The Looming Crisis* (2010); and *The Pasdaran: Inside Iran's Islamic Revolutionary Guards Corps* (2011). Ottolenghi writes a monthly column for *Standpoint Magazine* and has published in *The New York Times, The Guardian, The Weekly Standard, The Middle East Quarterly,* and *Commentary Magazine.*

Szilvia Peremiczky is Director of the Hungarian Jewish Museum and Senior Lecturer at the National Rabbinical Seminary and Jewish Studies University, and also guest lectures at the Eötvös Lóránd University of Arts and Sciences (ELTE) in Budapest. A historian of literature and a student of antisemitism, her doctoral dissertation addressed the role of Jerusalem in Jewish literature, a substantially expanded and revised version of which has just been published in Budapest as *Jeruzsálem a zsidó irodalomban* (2012).

Dina Porat, Professor of Jewish History at Tel Aviv University, is head of the Kantor Center for the study of Contemporary European Jewry, which includes the Moshe Kantor Database and the Alfred P. Slaner Chair for the Study of Contemporary Antisemitism and Racism. She is also Chief Historian at Yad Vashem. Porat has written and edited many books and articles on antisemitism and the Holocaust, including the winner of the 2010 National Jewish Book Award, *The Fall of a Sparrow: The Life and Times of Abba Kovner* (2009). She has served as an expert on Israeli Foreign Ministry delegations to UN world conferences and as the academic adviser of the Task Force for International Cooperation on Holocaust Education, Remembrance, and Research.

Alvin H. Rosenfeld is the Irving M. Glazer Chair in Jewish Studies at Indiana University and Director of the Institute for the Study of Contemporary Antisemitism. The author of numerous publications on Jewish writers and Holocaust literature, his most recent books are *The Writer Uprooted: Contemporary Jewish Exile Literature* (IU Press, 2009) and *The End of the Holocaust* (IU Press, 2011). He held a five-year presidential appointment on the United States Holocaust Memorial Council (2002–2007) and presently serves on the U.S. Holocaust Memorial Museum's Executive Committee. He is chair of the Academic Committee of the Museum's Center for Advanced Holocaust Studies.

Tammi Rossman-Benjamin is a lecturer in Hebrew and Jewish Studies at the University of California Santa Cruz and co-founder of the Investigative Taskforce on Campus Antisemitism. She has written many articles about academic anti-Zionism and antisemitism and lectures widely on these developments.

Anna Sommer Schneider received her Ph.D. at the Department of Jewish Studies of the Jagiellonian University, Kraków. Her forthcoming book, which will be published in Poland in 2013, is titled *Saving the Remnant of Polish Jewry: The Activities of the American Jewish Joint Distribution Committee in Poland, 1945–1989*.

Robert S. Wistrich is Neuberger Professor of Modern Jewish History and Director of the Vidal Sassoon International Center for the Study of Antisemitism at the Hebrew University of Jerusalem. Among his many publications, he is author of three prize-winning books, *Antisemitism: The Longest Hatred* (1991), *The Jews of Vienna in the Age of Franz Joseph* (2006), and *A Lethal Obsession: Anti-Semitism from Antiquity to the Global Jihad* (2010). He has also written, edited, or co-directed several well-received television documentary films, including *The Longest Hatred*. Wistrich is editor in chief of *Antisemitism International,* of the ACTA series of research studies, and the *Posen Papers in Contemporary Antisemitism.*

Elhanan Yakira was born and educated in Israel and holds a Ph.D. in philosophy from the Sorbonne. Professor in the department of philosophy of the Hebrew University of Jerusalem, he specializes in early modern philosophy, phenomenology, twentieth-century French philosophy, and political philosophy. Among other books, he is the author of *Post-Zionism, Post-Holocaust: Three Essays on Denial, Forgetting and the Delegitimation of Israel* (2009).

Index

Page numbers followed by a (*t*) refer to tables.